Save up to 35% on your total fuel bill.

Learn how HybriDrive® can electrify your vehicle accessories and save you even more.

Become pat of the world's largest series hybrid fleet.

Ask us to estimate what HybriDrive® series can save you at:

www.hybridrive.co/SAVE

MORE SAVINGS.
MORE ELECTRIC.
MORE PERFORMANCE.

HybriDrive®
PROPULSION SYSTEMS

BAE SYSTEMS

The Little Red Book

2012

Passenger Transport Directory

Editor: Ian Barlex
Design: Debbie Walker

Riverdene Business Park, Molesey Road, Hersham, Surrey KT12 4RG
Tel: 01932 266600 Fax: 01932 266601

TRADE SECTION

Additional entry to the manufacturers and suppliers section:

BAE SYSTEMS

BAE SYSTEMS
HybriDrive® Propulsion Systems
Marconi Way, Rochester, Kent
ME1 2XX
Tel: 01634 20 4578
Web site: www.hybridrive.com
Models: HybriDrive® Series – The world's most successful series hybrid electric propulsion system for transit bus

OPERATOR SECTIONS

Page 84

FIRSTGROUP PLC
• **Regional Director Scotland**
delete Mark Savelli, replace with Neil Barker (from Dec 2011)
• **Overseas Interests**
the group has sold its operation in Germany

Page 85

NATIONAL EXPRESS GROUP PLC
European Development Director:
delete Neil Barker
(moves to FirstGroup from Dec 2011)

Page 88

VEOLIA TRANSPORT UK LTD
Delete references to Paul James Coaches, Leicestershire. Delete depots at Birmingham, Coalville, Heanor and Melton Mowbray

Page 91 (Bristol)
Additional Operator:

CT PLUS CIC
UNITS 7/8, BARTON HILL TRADING ESTATE,
BARTON HILL, BRISTOL BS5 9RD
Tel: 0117 941 3713
Fax: 0117 955 1368
E-mail: bristol@hctgroup.org
Web site: www.ctplusbristol.org

Senior Man: Donna Dixon
Fleet: 12 articulated bus
Chassis: Mercedes
Bodies: Mercedes
Ops incl: Bristol Park & Ride

Page 126 (Greater Manchester)

SOUTH LANCS TRAVEL
Business acquired by D&G Bus
(see Cheshire)
Man Dir: D Reeves

Page 141 (Leicestershire)

ROBERTS TOURS LTD
The Fleet and Chassis lines were omitted from the text:
Fleet: 39 - 20 double-deck bus, 10 single-deck coach, 2 double-deck coach, 1 open-top bus, 3 midibus, 2 midicoach, 1 minibus.
Chassis: 1 LDV, 1 Leyland, 20 MCW, 2 Mercedes, 3 Optare, 12 Volvo.

Operations: add Leicester Park & Ride

VEOLIA TRANSPORT
(ENGLAND) PLC
Business sold to Centrebus and Roberts Tours Ltd

WEST END TRAVEL/RUTLAND TRAVEL
Business sold to Centrebus

Page 202 (City of Glasgow)

FIRST GLASGOW
Regional Man Dir: delete Mark Savelli, replace with Neil Barker (from Dec 2011)

Page 217 (Gwynedd)

SILVER STAR COACH HOLIDAYS LTD
Ceased trading in October 2011

Page 223 (Northern Ireland)

AIRPORTER
Change of address:
1 BAY ROAD, CULMORE ROAD,
LONDONDERRY BT48 7SH

CONTENTS

KEY TO SYMBOLS IN SECTIONS 4 AND 5

♿	Vehicle suitable for disabled
🔧	Seat belt-fitted Vehicle
R24	24 hour recovery service
T	Toilet-drop facilities available
🍴	Coach(es) with galley facilities
🔧	Replacement vehicle available
R	Recovery service available
❄	Air-conditioned vehicle(s)
🚌	Vintage Coach(s) available
🚌	Open top vehicle(s)
🚻	Coaches with toilet facilities
🌿	Hybrid Buses

The Little Red Book

2012

Passenger Transport Directory

74th Annual Edition

Britain's longest established passenger transport directory

ISBN   978 0711 036 604

Published by

**Printed by Ian Allan Printing Ltd,
Riverdene Business Park, Hersham,
Surrey KT12 4RG.**

**Visit the Ian Allan Publishing web site:
www.ianallanpublishing.com**

ADVERTISING IN LRB

For information regarding advertising in the next edition, contact:

Graham Middleton

Tel: 01780 484632

Fax: 01780 763388

E-mail: graham.middleton@ianallanpublishing.co.uk

LIST OF ABBREVIATIONS

ACCT =	Accountant
ADMIN =	Administrative
ASST =	Assistant
CEO =	Chief Executive Officer
CH =	Chief
CHMN =	Chairman
CO =	Company
COMM MAN =	Commercial Manager
CONT =	Controller
DEP =	Deputy
DIR =	Director
ENG =	Engineer
EXEC =	Executive
FIN =	Financial
GEN MAN =	General Manager
H&S =	Health & Safety
HR =	Human Relations
INSP =	Inspector
JNT =	Joint
MAN =	Manager
MAN DIR =	Managing Director
MKTG =	Marketing
OFF =	Officer
OP =	Operating
OPS =	Operations
PLAN =	Planning
PRES =	President
PRIN =	Principal
PROP =	Proprietor(s)
PTNRS =	Partner(s)
REG OFF =	Registered Office
SEC =	Secretary
SUPT =	Superintendent
SVCE =	Service
TRAF MAN =	Traffic Manager
TRAF SUPT =	Traffic Superintendent
TRAN MAN =	Transport Manager

ACKNOWLEDGEMENTS

I would like to acknowledge the help and support of Paul Appleton and his team at Ian Allan – especially Debbie Walker and Margaret Hayes – for their hard work and support in producing this edition. And a particular mention for Graham Middleton and Bethany Griffin, who have worked very hard to liaise with the advertisers.

I must also thank those readers and contributors who have taken the trouble to get in touch to highlight changes and amendments through the year; if you notice something that needs changing, please do not hesitate to contact me via the Stamford office.

Thanks too to Keith Shayshutt and Barry LeJeune, who have kindly allowed us to use some of their photographs, to Mike Heath for proof-reading, and to operators who have helped with logos and illustrations.

And finally, many thanks to all of our advertisers for their support, without which this directory would be difficult to sustain. Please give them your support and tell them you saw their advertisement in LRB. In particular, I would like to thank the Transport Benevolent Fund, main sponsor for this year's edition.

HOW LRB ENTRIES ARE COMPILED

As always, our principal source of data has been the thousands of questionnaires we send out to operators, manufacturers, suppliers and other organisations. We have again made significant changes to the circulation list to try to reflect the many changes that have been happening, to omit ceased businesses, etc. Where we have not received responses, we have tried to use other publicly available sources to ensure the entries are as accurate as possible.

New entrants to the bus and coach market need not wait for LRB to make contact. If you are active in the industry, and would like to appear in the next edition of LRB (free of charge), please write to the editor of LRB at Ian Allan Publishing Ltd, Foundry Road, Stamford, Lincolnshire PE9 2PP, requesting to receive a form for the next edition.

LRB is used by a substantial number of bus and coach operators, as well as by national and local government, trade organisations, tendering authorities, group travel organisers, hotels and leisure attractions.

Welcome to the 2012 edition of the Little Red Book, now in its 74th year as the leading industry directory.

The difficulties in industry and the wider economy have brought about a huge volume of change during the year since I wrote this page for LRB 2011. Reflecting this, we have again had to make a very large number of amendments and updates, as well as introducing many new entries in all sections of the book. It is important that we stay on top of all of this change if the directory is to remain current and useful to its subscribers. Please bear with us in that there will no doubt be further changes during the period it takes, after I write this, for the book to be printed, bound and distributed. We have provided a Stop Press section for changes that we capture at the last minute; and for developments subsequent to the book going to press, you can update your LRB on a monthly basis by taking our sister publication **Buses** magazine, which will continue to have a section in each month's edition to notify updates and changes to LRB.

There are a few enhancements to note in relation to the book this year. Firstly, we have moved the tram systems into a dedicated section – section 5 – rather than have them buried in the counties with the bus and coach operators; and we have taken the opportunity to expand that new section with a second set of entries for the major bus rapid transit systems in use and imminent around the country. BRT is seeing a higher profile, not least with the recent opening of the Cambridgeshire system, and we felt that such a section would be useful and would add to the completeness of the book.

Secondly, given the rate of removal of operators from the directory, due to closure, disposal of the business, or for other reasons; we thought it would be helpful rather than just

to delete the entries, to leave the headings for one edition after closure, and to note that they are no longer trading, or have passed to new owners.

Thirdly, in Section 4 (Operators), we have introduced a new symbol to denote those operators (an increasing number) who are operating hybrid vehicles; those readers with entries in the book will have seen this on their questionnaires earlier this year.

We remain very grateful to the large number of suppliers, authorities, organisations and operators who have taken the trouble to update and return their entries via our questionnaires. We have again been overwhelmed with the quantity returned this year. We have maintained the approach of sending out separate questionnaires for trade suppliers and for organisations and authorities; thus providing more space, allowing for greater detail and supporting notes on the part of the latter, and this has generated a greater level of returns. The usual reminder of course – if there is no change to your entry, please don't worry about re-writing it all.

A simple statement to the effect that there is no change will be fine, but please remember to make sure to tell us who you are!

Once again the industry finds itself facing a multitude of challenges. The results of the Government's spending review are still working their way through the system, but the omens for supported bus services and network coverage are not good, judging by the announcements from many counties regarding future transport funding. Reduced levels of reimbursement for concessionary travel are also having wide reaching effects on the businesses of many

operators listed in this book, and the impending reduction in BSOG looms. A year on from a reference in this column last year, we are still for the moment no wiser on the outcome of the Competition Commission investigation into the industry, but we should hear soon. It is reasonable to assume that these factors will all affect the content of this directory next year.

Further changes have again taken place as part of the normal commercial process; the sale of Arriva to German interests has completed; as has the merger between Transdev and Veolia. As an outcome of the latter transaction, we welcome a new entrant to the ranks of the major operators – RATP. A further substantial transaction, and change to the majors section, has seen the sale of the East London Bus Group to Stagecoach.

Yet despite the difficulties, this industry continues to innovate; to provide a high level of quality; and to achieve strong marks for customer satisfaction. That is a tribute to the people, listed in this book, who run its component businesses, whether they are manufacturers; trade or service suppliers; operators; or their partners in the authorities. We will continue to seek to play our part by capturing the changes and providing an accurate industry reference point.

Ian Barlex, Editor

SECTION 1

Trade Directory

- **Vehicle suppliers and dealers**

- **A-Z listing of suppliers and manufacturers**

- **Bus & Coach industry service providers**

VEHICLE SUPPLIERS & DEALERS

Manufacturers and suppliers of full-size bus and coach chassis and integrals, bus rapid transit vehicles and light rail vehicles

ALEXANDER DENNIS LTD
91 Glasgow Road, Falkirk FK1 4JB
Tel: 01324 621672
Fax: 01324 632469
E-mail: enquiries@alexander-dennis.co.uk
Web site: www.alexander-dennis.com
Range: hybrid single-deck bus; rear-engined low-floor single-deck bus; chassis for rear-engined low-floor midibus; mid-engined coach; rear-engined coach; hybrid double-deck bus; rear-engined low-floor double-deck bus (two- or three-axle); low-floor school bus.

ARRIVA BUS & COACH
Lodge Garage, Whitehall Road West, Gomersal, Cleckheaton, West Yorkshire BD19 4BJ
Tel: 01274 681144
Fax: 01274 651198
E-mail: whiter@arriva.co.uk
Web site: www.arrivabusandcoach.co.uk

AUTOSAN UK
UK Supplier: Blue Ribbon Coach Sales
23 Brook Road, Bomere Heath, Shrewsbury, Shropshire SY4 3PU
Tel/Fax: 01939 290512
E-mail: paul.busman@btopenworld.com
Web sites: www.blueribboncoachsales.com, www.autosancoachsales.com
Range: High-floor school bus, single-deck bus, single-deck coach

AYATS
UK Supplier: Blue Ribbon Coach Sales
23 Brook Road, Bomere Heath, Shrewsbury, Shropshire SY4 3PU
Tel/Fax: 01939 290512
E-mail: paul.busman@btopenworld.com
Web site: www.blueribboncoachsales.com
Ireland supplier: Bartons Transport
Straffan Road, Maynooth, Co Kildare
Tel: 00 353 1 628 6026
Fax: 00 353 1 628 6722
E-mail: info@bartons-transport.ie
Models: Rear-engined integral single and double-deck coach range - up to 15m

BMC PLC
BMC House, Ibstock Road, Coventry CV6 6JR
Tel: 02476 363003
Fax: 02476 365835
E-mail: enquiries@bmcplc.com
Web site: www.bmcplc.com
Models: integral front-engined school bus, integral front-engined midicoach, integral rear-engined 11m low-floor single-deck bus

IRISBUS (UK) LTD
Iveco House, Station Road, Watford WD17 1SR
Tel: 01923 259660
Fax: 01923 259623
E-mail: info@irisbus.co.uk
Web site: www.irisbus.co.uk
Models: midibus, low-floor midibus, minibuses, guided bus system, low-floor rear-engined single-deck bus, rear-engined single-deck coach.

KING LONG UK LTD
Bedworth Road, Coventry CV6 6BP
Tel: 02476 363004
Fax: 02476 365835
E-mail: enquiries@kinglonguk.com
Web site: www.kinglonguk.com
Models: 9m and 12m single-deck coach, 12m low floor single-deck city bus

MAN
UK Suppliers:
MAN Bus & Coach Frankland Road, Blagrove, Swindon SN5 8YU
Tel: 01793 448000
E-mail: bus.sales@man.co.uk
coach.sales@man.co.uk
Web site: www.manbusandcoach.co.uk
MAN Coach Sales Ashburton Road West, Trafford Park, Manchester M17 1QX
Tel: 0161 848 8331
Web site: www.manbusandcoachsales.co.uk
Ireland supplier:
Brian Noone Ltd Straffan Road, Maynooth, Co Kildare
Tel: 00 353 1 628 6311
Fax: 00 353 1 628 5404
E-mail: reception@noone.ie
Web site: www.noone.ie
Models: single-deck low-floor midibus, single-deck low-floor city bus, single-deck school bus, rear-engined coach

MERCEDES-BENZ
UK Supplier:
Evobus (UK) Ltd Cross Point Business Park, Ashcroft Way, Coventry CV2 2TU
Tel: 024 7662 6000
Web site: www.evobus.com
Models: rear-engined coach, rear-engined integral low-floor single-deck bus, rear-engined integral low-floor single-deck articulated bus

MOSELEY (PCV) LTD
Elmsall Way, Dale Lane, South Elmsall, Pontefract, West Yorkshire WF9 2XS
Tel: 01977 609000
Fax: 01977 609900
E-mail: sales@moseleycoachsales.co.uk
Web site: www.moseleycoachsales.co.uk

MOSELEY DISTRIBUTORS LTD
Rydenmains, Condorrat Road, Glenmavis, Airdrie ML6 0PP
Tel: 01236 750501
Fax: 01236 750504
E-mail: enquiries@moseleydistributors.co.uk
Web site: www.moseleydistributors.co.uk

NEOPLAN
UK Supplier:
MAN Bus & Coach Frankland Road, Blagrove, Swindon SN5 8YU
Tel: 01793 448000
E-mail: coach.sales@man.co.uk
Web site: www.manbusandcoach.co.uk
Models: single-deck and double-deck rear-engine integral coaches

OPTARE PLC (Blackburn)
Lower Philips Road, Whitebirk Industrial Estate, Blackburn BB1 5UD
Tel: 0845 838 9901
Fax: 0845 838 9902
E-mail: info@optare.com
Web site: www.optare.com
Models: Optare Olympus, double-deck low-floor bus. Distribution for Optare Toro luxury midicoach and Optare Soroco luxury minicoach.

OPTARE PLC (Leeds)
Manston Lane, Leeds LS15 8SU
Tel: 0113 264 5182
Fax: 0113 260 6635
E-mail: info@optare.com
Web site: www.optare.com
Models: Optare Tempo, rear-engined integral low-floor single-deck city bus. Optare Versa, Optare Solo, Optare Solo SR, Optare Solo EV, rear-engined integral low-floor single-deck midibus.

PLAXTON
Plaxton Park, Cayton Low Road, Eastfield, Scarborough, North Yorkshire YO11 3BY
Tel: 01723 581500
Fax: 01723 581479
E-mail: sales@plaxtonlimited.co.uk
Web site: www.plaxtonlimited.co.uk
Range: coaches, buses, midicoach and midibus bodies
(Part of Alexander Dennis)

SANTANDER ASSET FINANCE
Taylor Road, Trafford Park, Manchester M41 7JQ
Tel: 0161 747 5698
Fax: 0161 275 4501
E-mail: steve.moult@hansar.co.uk
Web site: www.buses247.co.uk

SCANIA (GB) LTD
Delaware Drive, Tongwell, Milton Keynes MK15 8HB
Tel: 01908 210210
Fax: 01908 215040
E-mail: info@scania.co.uk
Web site: www.scania.com
Range: rear-engined low-floor single-deck and double-deck bus chassis, integral low-floor single-deck bus, integral low-floor double-deck bus, rear-engined coach.

SETRA
UK Supplier: Evobus (UK) Ltd Cross Point Business Park, Ashcroft Way, Coventry CV2 2TU
Tel: 02476 626000
Web site: www.evobus.com, www.setra.de
Models: rear-engined integral coaches.

SOLBUS (UK) LTD
16 Browning Avenue, Kettering, Northamptonshire NN16 8NP
Tel: 01536 482049
Fax: 01536 482342
E-mail: phill@solbus-uk.com
Web site: www.solbus-uk.com

TESLA VEHICLES LIMITED
22 Larbre Crescent, Whickham,
Newcastle upon Tyne NE16 5YG
Tel: 0191 488 6258
Fax: 0191 488 9158
E-mail: info@teslavehicles.com
Web site: www.teslavehicles.com

TEMSA EUROPE
Lodge Garage, Whitehall Road West,
Gomersal, Cleckheaton, West Yorkshire
BD19 4BJ
Tel: 01274 681144
Fax: 01274 651198
E-mail: info@temsa.com
Web site: www.temsa.com

VAN HOOL
Bernard Van Hoolstraat 58, Lier-Koningshooikt,
BE2500, Belgium
Tel: 00 32 3 420 20 20
Fax: 00 32 3 482 30 68
E-mail: sales.bc.uk@vanhool.be
Web site: www.vanhool.be
Models: integral coaches

VDL BOVA
Web site: www.vdlbova.nl
UK Supplier:
Moseley (PCV) Ltd
Elmsall Way, Dale Lane, South Elmsall,
Pontefract WF9 2XS
Tel: 01977 609000
Fax: 01977 609900
E-mail: sales@moseleycoachsales.co.uk
Web site: www.moseleycoachsales.co.uk
Moseley in the South Ltd
Summerfield Avenue, Chelston Business Park,
Wellington TA21 9JF
Tel: 01823 653000
Fax: 01823 663502
E-mail: enquiries@moseleysouth.co.uk
Web site: www.moseleysouth.co.uk
Models: Lexio, Magiq, Futura single-deck luxury
coach; Synergy double-deck coach

VDL BUS INTERNATIONAL
UK Supplier: Arriva Bus & Coach
Lodge Garage, Whitehall Road West, Gomersal,
Cleckheaton, West Yorkshire BD19 4BJ
Tel: 01274 681144
Fax: 01274 651198
E-mail: busandcoachsales@arriva.co.uk
Web site: www.arrivabusandcoach.co.uk
Models: rear-engined low-floor single-deck bus,
rear-engined low-floor double-deck bus, rear-
engined coach, rear-engined three-axle single- or
double-deck coach.

VOLVO BUS
Wedgnock Lane, Warwick CV34 5YA
Tel: 01926 401777
Fax: 01926 407407
Web site: www.volvo.com
Models: rear-engined low-floor single-deck bus,
rear-engined low-floor articulated single-deck bus,
mid-engined coach, rear-engined integral coach,
rear-engined low-floor double-deck bus.
Volvo Bus & Coach Sales Centre
Siskin Parkway East, Middlemarch Business Park,
Coventry CV3 4PE
Tel: 02476 210250
Fax: 02476 210258
Web site: www.volvo.com
Range: New & Pre-owned buses and coaches.

WRIGHTBUS LIMITED
Galgorm Industrial Estate, Fenaghy Road,
Ballymena, Northern Ireland BT42 1PY
Tel: 028 2564 1212
Fax: 028 2564 9703
E-mail: info@wright-bus.com
Web site: www.wright-bus.com

BUS RAPID TRANSIT VEHICLES

IRISBUS (UK) LTD
Iveco House, Station Road, Watford WD17 1SR
Tel: 01923 259660 **Fax:** 01923 259623
E-mail: info@irisbus.co.uk
Web site: www.irisbus.co.uk
Models: guided bus system

MINITRAM SYSTEMS LTD
12 Waterloo Park Estate, Bidford on Avon
B50 4JH
Tel: 07770 931274
E-mail: martinp@tdi.uk.com
Web site: www.minitram.com
Models: Rubber tyre-guided/unguided/rail 7.8m
vehicle

VOLVO BUS
Wedgnock Lane, Warwick CV34 5YA
Tel: 01926 401777
Fax: 01926 407407
Web site: www.volvo.com
Models: rear-engined low-floor single-deck bus,
rear-engined low-floor articulated single-deck bus,
rear-engined low-floor double-deck bus (chassis
can be equipped with guide wheels for operation
on guideways).

WRIGHTBUS LIMITED
Galgorm Industrial Estate, Fenaghy Road,
Ballymena, Northern Ireland BT42 1PY
Tel: 028 2564 1212
Fax: 028 2564 9703
E-mail: info@wright-bus.com
Web site: www.wright-bus.com
Models: StreetCar rapid transit vehicle (further
models - see bodybuilders section).

LIGHT RAIL VEHICLES

ALSTOM TRANSPORT
Worldwide headquarters: 48 rue Albert
Dhalenne, F-93482 Saint-Ouen Cedex, France
Tel: 00 33 1 41 66 90 00
Fax: 00 33 1 41 66 96 66
Web site: www.transport.alstom.com
Models: rail vehicles including light rail
vehicles, traction equipment, infrastructure and
maintenance services.

BOMBARDIER TRANSPORTATION
Management Office: 1101 Parent Street,
Saint-Bruno, Quebec J3V 6E6, Canada
Tel: 00 1 450 441 2020
Fax: 00 1 450 441 1515
Web site: www.bombardier.com

**BOMBARDIER TRANSPORTATION
METROS**
Litchurch Lane, Derby DE24 8AD
Tel: 01332 344666
Fax: 01332 266271
Web site: www.bombardier.com/en/
transportation

Models: light rail vehicles, trams, guided or
unguided bi-mode rubber tyred electric vehicle.

MINITRAM SYSTEMS LTD
12 Waterloo Park Estate, Bidford on Avon
B50 4JH
Tel: 07770 931274
E-mail: martyinp@tdi.uk.com
Web site: www.minitram.com
Models: Rubber tyre-guided/unguided/rail 7.8m
vehicle

PARRY PEOPLE MOVERS LTD
Overend Road, Cradley Heath, Dudley
B64 7DD
Tel: 01384 569553
Fax: 01384 637753
E-mail: jpmparry@aol.com
Web site: www.parrypeoplemovers.com
Models: Ultra light rail vehicles and trams

TRAM POWER LTD
99 Stanley Road, Bootle, Liverpool L20 7DA
Web site: www.trampower.co.uk/CityClass.html
Models: Articulated lightweight low-cost tram

BODYBUILDERS (LARGE VEHICLES)

ALEXANDER DENNIS LTD
91 Glasgow Road, Falkirk FK1 4JB
Tel: 01324 621 672
Fax: 01324 632 269
E-mail: enquiries@alexander-dennis.com
Web site: www.alexander-dennis.com

BEULAS
UK Supplier: Base Ltd 57 Clydesdale Place,
Moss Side Industrial Estate, Leyland PR26 7QS
Tel: 01772 425355
Fax: 01772 425348
Web site: www.basecoachsales.co.uk

CAETANO (UK) LTD
Mill Lane, Heather, Coalville LE67 2QE
Tel: 01530 263333
Fax: 01530 263379
E-mail: office@caetano.co.uk
Web site: www.caetano.co.uk
Models: single-deck coach

EXPRESS COACH REPAIRS LTD
Outgang Lane, Pickering, North Yorkshire
YO18 7JA
Tel: 01751 475 215
E-mail: info@expresscoachrepairs.co.uk
Web site: www.expresscoachrepairs.co.uk

FAST EUROPE NV
Hellegatstraat 10, 2590 Berlaar (Lier), Belgium
Tel: 00 32 3613 2222
Fax: 00 32 3613 2220
E-mail: info@fast-europe.eu
Web site: www.fast-europe.eu
UK Supplier:
Moseley (PCV) Ltd Elmsall Way, Dale Lane,
South Elmsall, Pontefract WF9 2XS
Tel: 01977 609000
Fax: 01977 609900
E-mail: sales@moseleycoachsales.co.uk
Web site: www.moseleycoachsales.co.uk

IRIZAR UK
Portland House, Claylands Avenue, Worksop
S81 7BQ

Tel: 01909 500514
Web site: www.irizar.com

KING LONG UK LTD
Bedworth Road, Coventry CV6 6BP
Tel: 02476 363004
Fax: 02476 365835
E-mail: enquiries@kinglonguk.com
Web site: www.kinglonguk.com
Models: 9m and 12m single-deck coach, 12m low floor single-deck city bus

LAWTON SERVICES LTD
Knutsford Road, Church Lawton, Stoke-on-Trent ST7 3DN
Tel: 01270 882056
Fax: 01270 883014
E-mail: andrea@lawtonservices.co.uk
Web site: www.lawtonservices.co.uk

LEICESTER CARRIAGE BUILDERS
Marlow Road, Leicester LE3 2BQ
Tel: 0116 282 4270
Fax: 0116 263 0554
E-mail: rick.johnson@midlandsco-op.com
Web site: www.leicestercarriagebuilders.co.uk

MARCOPOLO
UK Supplier: Base Ltd 57 Clydesdale Place, Moss Side Industrial Estate, Leyland PR26 7QS
Tel: 01772 425355
Fax: 01772 425748
Web site: www.basecoachsales.co.uk

MCV BUS AND COACH LTD
Sterling Place, Elean Business Park, Sutton, Ely CB6 2QE
Tel: 01353 773000
Fax: 01353 773001
E-mail: marketing@mcv-eg.com
Web site: www.mcv-eg.com

MOSELEY (PCV) LTD
Elmsall Way, Dale Lane, South Elmsall, Pontefract, West Yorkshire WF9 2XS
Tel: 01977 609000
Fax: 01977 609900
E-mail: sales@moseleycoachsales.co.uk
Web site: www.moseleycoachsales.co.uk

NEOPLAN
UK Supplier: MAN Bus & Coach UK
Frankland Road, Blagrove, Swindon SN5 8YU
Tel: 01793 448000
E-mail: coach.sales@man.co.uk
Web site: www.manbusandcoach.co.uk
Models: single-deck coach, also integral coach.

NOGE
UK Supplier: MAN Bus & Coach UK
Frankland Road, Blagrove Swindon SN5 8YU
Tel: 01793 448000
E-mail: coach.sales@man.co.uk
Web site: www.manbusandcoach.co.uk
Ireland supplier: Brian Noone Straffan Road, Maynooth, Co Kildare
Tel: 00 353 1 628 6311
Fax: 00 353 1 628 5404
E-mail: reception@noone.ie
Web site: www.noone.ie
Models: two-axle and three-axle integral coach bodies.

OPTARE PLC (Blackburn)
Lower Philips Road, Whitebirk Industrial Estate,

Blackburn BB1 5UD
Tel: 0845 838 9901
Fax: 0845 838 9902
E-mail: info@optare.com
Web site: www.optare.com
Models: Optare Olympus, double-deck low-floor bus; also distribution for Optare Toro luxury midicoach and Optare Soroco luxury minicoach.

OPTARE PLC (Leeds)
Manston Lane, Leeds LS15 8SU
Tel: 0113 264 5182
Fax: 0113 260 6635
E-mail: info@optare.com
Web site: www.optare.com
Models: Optare Tempo, rear-engined integral low-floor single-deck city bus. Optare Versa, Optare Solo, Optare Solo SR, Optare Solo EV, rear-engined integral low-floor single-deck midibus.

PLAXTON
Plaxton Park, Cayton Low Road, Eastfield, Scarborough, North Yorkshire YO11 3BY
Tel: 01723 581500
Fax: 01723 581479
E-mail: sales@plaxtonlimited.co.uk
Web site: www.plaxtonlimited.co.uk
Range: coaches, buses, midicoach and midibus bodies
(Part of Alexander Dennis)

SUNSUNDEGUI
UK Importer: Volvo Bus & Coach Sales Centre
Siskin Parkway East, Middlemarch Business Park, Coventry CV3 4PE
Tel: 02476 210250
Fax: 02476 210258
Web site: www.volvo.com
UK Service: Tramontana Chapelknowe Road, Carfin, Motherwell ML1 5LE
Tel: 01698 861790
Fax: 01698 860778
E-mail: wdt90@tiscali.co.uk
Web site: www.brittnet.net/tramontanacoach

TESLA VEHICLES LIMITED
22 Larbre Crescent, Whickham, Newcastle upon Tyne NE16 5YG
Tel: 0191 488 6258
Fax: 0191 488 9158
E-mail: info@teslavehicles.com
Web site: www.teslavehicles.com

UNVI BUS & COACH
13 Poulton Street, Kirkham, Preston, Lancashire PR4 2AA
Tel: 01772 635820
Fax: 01772 634336
Web site: www.unvibusandcoach.co.uk
Range: single-deck coach, midicoach, minicoach

VAN HOOL
Bernard Van Hoolstraat 58, Lier-Koningshooikt, 2500, Belgium
Tel: 00 32 3 420 20 20
Fax: 00 32 3 482 30 68
E-mail: sales.bc.uk@vanhool.be
Web site: www.vanhool.be
Models: coach bodies

VDL BERKHOF
UK Supplier: Arriva Bus & Coach
Lodge Garage, Whitehall Road West, Gomersal,

Cleckheaton BD19 4BJ
Tel: 01274 681144
Fax: 01274 651198
E-mail: busandcoachsales@arriva.co.uk
Web site: www.arrivabusandcoach.co.uk
Models: rear-engined three-axle or two-axle single-deck coach.

VDL JONCKHEERE
UK Importer: Volvo Bus & Coach Sales Centre
Siskin Parkway East, Middlemarch Business Park, Coventry CV3 4PE
Tel: 02476 210250
Fax: 02476 210258
Web site: www.volvo.com
UK Service: Tramontana Chapelknowe Road, Carfin, Motherwell ML1 5LE
Tel: 01698 861790
Fax: 01698 860778
E-mail: wdt90@tiscali.co.uk
Web site: www.brittnet.net/tramontanacoach

VOLVO BUS
Wedgnock Lane, Warwick CV34 5YA
Tel: 01926 401777
Fax: 01926 407407
Web site: www.volvo.com
Models: rear-engined low-floor single-deck bus, rear-engined low-floor articulated single-deck bus, mid-engined coach, rear-engined integral coach, rear-engined low-floor double-deck bus.
Volvo Bus & Coach Sales Centre
Siskin Parkway East, Middlemarch Business Park, Coventry CV3 4PE
Tel: 02476 210250
Fax: 02476 210258
Web site: www.volvo.com
Range: New & Pre-owned buses and coaches.

WRIGHTBUS LIMITED
Galgorm Industrial Estate, Fenaghy Road, Ballymena, Northern Ireland BT42 1PY
Tel: 028 2564 1212
Fax: 028 2564 9703
E-mail: info@wright-bus.com
Web site: www.wright-bus.com
Models: double-deck low-floor bus body, single-deck low-floor articulated bus body, FTR advanced bus rapid transit vehicle, single-deck low-floor bus, single-deck low-entry coach, single-deck low-floor midibus.

CHASSIS AND INTEGRAL VEHICLES (SMALL VEHICLES - UNDER 9M)

ALEXANDER DENNIS LTD
91 Glasgow Road, Falkirk FK1 4JB
Tel: 01324 621 672
Fax: 01324 632 269
E-mail: enquiries@alexander-dennis.com
Web: www.alexander-dennis.com

AVID VEHICLES LTD
Unit 2U, Admiral Business Park, Nelson Industrial Estate, Cramlington NE23 1WG
Tel: 01670 706100
E-mail: info@avidvehicles.com
Web site: www.avidvehicles.com

BLUEBIRD VEHICLES LTD
Unit 7, Plaxton Park, Cayton Low Road, Scarborough, North Yorkshire YO11 3BQ
Tel: 01723 860800
Fax: 01723 585235

E-mail: info@bluebirdvehicles.com
Web site: www.bluebirdvehicles.com

FORD MOTOR COMPANY
Ford Motor Co Ltd, Eagle Way,
Brentwood CM14 9HE
Tel: 08458 411111
Web site: www.ford.co.uk
Models: Transit, complete minibus or chassis-cowl.

IRISBUS (UK) LTD
Iveco House, Station Road, Watford WD17 1SR
Tel: 01923 259660
Fax: 01923 259623
E-mail: info@irisbus.co.uk
Web site: www.irisbus.co.uk

JOHN BRADSHAW LTD
New Lane, Stibbington, Peterborough
PE8 6LW
Tel: 01780 782621
Fax: 01780 783694
Web site: www.john-bradshaw.co.uk
Models: Electric minibus/taxi

KING LONG UK LTD
Bedworth Road, Coventry CV6 6BP
Tel: 02476 363004
Fax: 02476 365835
E-mail: enquiries@kinglonguk.com
Web site: www.kinglonguk.com
Models: 9m and 12m single-deck coach,
12m low floor single-deck city bus

LEICESTER CARRIAGE BUILDERS
Marlow Road, Leicester LE3 2BQ
Tel: 0116 282 4270
Fax: 0116 263 0554
E-mail: rick.johnson@midlandsco-op.com
Web site: www.leicestercarriagebuilders.co.uk

MERCEDES-BENZ
UK Supplier:
Evobus (UK) Ltd Cross Point Business Park,
Ashcroft Way, Coventry CV2 2TU
Tel: 02476 626000
Web site: www.evobus.co.uk
Models: Complete low-floor minibus or chassis cowl

MINITRAM SYSTEMS LTD
12 Waterloo Park Estate, Bidford on Avon
B50 4JH
Tel: 07770 931274
E-mail: martinp@tdi.uk.com
Web site: www.minitram.com
Models: Rubber tyre-guided/unguided/rail 7.8m vehicle

MISTRAL BUS & COACH PLC
Booths Hall, Chelford Road, Knutsford,
Cheshire WA16 8QZ
Tel: 01565 621 881
Fax: 01565 621 882
E-mail: sales@mistral-group.com
Web site: www.mistral-group.com

MOSELEY (PCV) LTD
Elmsall Way, Dale Lane, South Elmsall, Pontefract,
West Yorkshire WF9 2XS
Tel: 01977 609000
Fax: 01977 609900
E-mail: sales@moseleycoachsales.co.uk
Web site: www.moseleycoachsales.co.uk

MOSELEY DISTRIBUTORS LTD
Rydenmains, Condorrat Road, Glenmavis,
Airdrie ML6 0PP
Tel: 01236 750501
Fax: 01236 750504
E-mail: enquiries@moseleydistributors.co.uk
Web site: www.moseleydistributors.co.uk

NU-TRACK LTD
Steeple Industrial Estate, Antrim,
Northern Ireland BT41 1AB
Tel: 028 9446 9550
Fax: 028 9146 5430
E-mail: enquiries@nu-track.co.uk
Web site: www.nu-track.co.uk

OPTARE PLC (Leeds)
Manston Lane, Leeds LS15 8SU
Tel: 0113 264 5182
Fax: 0113 260 6635
E-mail: info@optare.com
Web site: www.optare.com
Models: Optare Tempo, rear-engined integral
low-floor single-deck city bus. Optare Versa,
Optare Solo, Optare Solo SR, Optare Solo
EV, rear-engined integral low-floor single-deck
midibus.

RENAULT UK LTD
Rivers Office Park, Denham Way,
Maple Cross, Rickmansworth WD3 9YS
Tel: 08000 723372
Web site: www.renault.co.uk
Models: Complete minibus or chassis-cowl;
electric vehicle.

SANTANDER ASSET FINANCE
Taylor Road, Trafford Park, Manchester
M41 7JQ
Tel: 0161 747 5698
Fax: 0161 275 4501
E-mail: steve.moult@hansar.co.uk
Web site: www.buses247.co.uk

TESLA VEHICLES LIMITED
22 Larbre Crescent, Whickham,
Newcastle upon Tyne NE16 5YG
Tel: 0191 488 6258
Fax: 0191 488 9158
E-mail: info@teslavehicles.com
Web site: www.teslavehicles.com

TOYOTA (GB) PLC
PO Box 814, Portsmouth PO6 9AY
Tel: 08447 016202
Web site: www.toyota.co.uk
UK suppliers:
AD Coach Sales **Tel:** 01884 860767;
Holloway Commercials **Tel:** 01902 636661;
Caetano (UK) Ltd **Tel:** 01530 263333
Models: Optimo midicoach, chassis cowl

VAUXHALL MOTORS LTD
Griffin House, Osborne Road, Luton
LU1 3YT
Tel: 01582 721122
Fax: 01582 427400
Vauxhall Mobility: 0800 731 5267
Web site: www.vauxhall.co.uk
Models: Complete minibus or chassis-cowl.
**VOLKSWAGEN COMMERCIAL
VEHICLES**
Yeomans Drive, Blakelands, Milton Keynes
MK14 5AN
Tel: 0800 717131

Web site: www.volkswagen-vans.co.uk
Models: Complete minibus or chassis-cowl.

**BODYBUILDERS (SMALL VEHICLES),
MINIBUS CONVERSIONS**

ADVANCED VEHICLE BUILDERS
Upper Mantle Close,
Clay Cross S45 9NU
Tel: 01246 250022
Fax: 01246 250016
E-mail: info@minibus.co.uk
Web site: www.minibus.co.uk

ALEXANDER DENNIS LTD
91 Glasgow Road, Falkirk FK1 4JB
Tel: 01324 621 672 **Fax:** 01324 632 269
E-mail: enquiries@alexander-dennis.com
Web site: www.alexander-dennis.com

AVID VEHICLES LTD
Unit 8, Arcot Court, Nelson Road,
Nelson Park, Cramlington NE23 1BB
Tel: 01670 707 040
Fax: 01670 715 230
E-mail: sales@avidvehicles.com
Web site: www.avidvehicles.com

BLUEBIRD VEHICLES LTD
Unit 7, Plaxton Park, Cayton Low Road,
Scarborough,
North Yorkshire YO11 3BQ
Tel: 01723 860800
Fax: 01723 585235
E-mail: info@bluebirdvehicles.com
Web site: www.bluebirdvehicles.com

BURNT TREE VEHICLE SOLUTIONS
Burnt Tree House, Knights Way,
Battlefield Enterprise Park,
Harlescott Lane, Shrewsbury SY1 3JE
Tel: 01743 457600
Fax: 01743 457648
E-mail: webenquiry@burnt-tree.co.uk
Web site: www.burnt-tree.co.uk

CHASSIS DEVELOPMENTS
Grovebury Road, Leighton Buzzard
LU7 8SL
Tel: 01525 374151
Fax: 01525 370127
E-mail: sales@chassisdevelopments.com
Web site: www.chassisdevelopments.co.uk

CONCEPT COACHCRAFT
Far Cromwell Road, Bredbury,
Stockport SK6 2SE
Tel: 0161 406 9322
Fax: 0161 406 9588
E-mail: sales@conceptcoachcraft.com
Web site: www.conceptcoachcraft.com

COURTSIDE CONVERSIONS LTD
1 Woodward Road, Howden Industrial Estate,
Tiverton EX16 5HW
Tel: 01884 256048
Fax: 01884 256087
E-mail: courtsidesales@aol.com
Web site: www.courtsideconversions.co.uk

**CVI (COMMERCIAL VEHICLE
INNOVATION)**
Moorfoot View, Bilston, Edinburgh EH25 9SL
Tel: 0844 412 8383
Web site: www.john-clark.co.uk

EVM LTD
Comagh Business Park, Kilbeggan,
Co Westmeath, Republic of Ireland
Tel: 00 353 5793 32699
Fax: 00 353 5793 32691
E-mail: info@evm.ie
Web site: www.evm.ie

EXCEL CONVERSIONS LTD
Excel House, Durham Lane, Armthorpe,
Doncaster DN3 3FE
Tel: 01302 835388
Fax: 01302 835389
E-mail: sales@excelconversions.co.uk
Web site: www.excelconversions.co.uk

EXPRESS COACH REPAIRS LTD
Outgang Lane, Pickering, North Yorkshire
YO18 7JA
Tel: 01751 475 215
E-mail: info@expresscoachrepairs.co.uk
Web site: www.expresscoachrepairs.co.uk

GM COACHWORK LTD
Teign Valley, Trusham, Newton Abbot, Devon
TQ13 0NX
Tel: 01626 853050
Fax: 01626 855066
E-mail: sales@gmcoachwork.co.uk
Web site: www.gmcoachwork.co.uk

INDCAR SA
Poligono Industrial Torres Pujals,
E-17401 Arbucies (Girona), Spain
Web site: www.indcar.com
UK Supplier:
Base Ltd 57 Clydesdale Place, Moss Side
Industrial Estate, Leyland PR26 7QS
Tel: 01772 425355
Fax: 01772 425748
Web site: www.basecoachsales.co.uk

JDC - JOHN DENNIS COACHBUILDERS
25 Westfield Road, Guildford GU1 1RR
Tel: 01483 506678
Fax: 01483 579488
Web site: www.johndennisfire.co.uk

JUBILEE AUTOMOTIVE GROUP
Woden Road South, Wednesbury
WS10 0NQ
Tel: 0800 634 8407
Fax: 0121 502 2258
Web site: www.jubileeauto.net

LAWTON SERVICES LTD
Knutsford Road, Church Lawton, Stoke-on-Trent
ST7 3DN
Tel: 01270 882056
Fax: 01270 883014
E-mail: andrea@lawtonservices.co.uk
Web site: www.lawtonservices.co.uk

LEICESTER CARRIAGE BUILDERS
Marlow Road, Leicester LE3 2BQ
Tel: 0116 282 4270
Fax: 0116 263 0554
E-mail: rick.johnson@midlandsco-op.com
Web site: www.leicestercarriagebuilders.co.uk

MCV BUS AND COACH LTD
Sterling Place, Elean Business Park, Sutton,
Ely CB6 2QE
Tel: 01353 773000
Fax: 01353 773001

E-mail: marketing@mcv-eg.com
Web site: www.mcv-eg.com

MELLOR COACHCRAFT
Miall Street, Rochdale OL11 1HY
Tel: 01706 860610
Fax: 01706 860402
E-mail: mcsales@woodall-nicholson.co.uk
Web site: www.mellor-coachcraft.co.uk

MINIBUS OPTIONS
Bingswood Industrial Estate, Whaley Bridge,
High Peak SK23 7LY
Tel: 01663 735355
E-mail: info@minibusoptions.co.uk
Web site: www.minibusoptions.co.uk

MOSELEY (PCV) LTD
Elmsall Way, Dale Lane, South Elmsall, Pontefract,
West Yorkshire WF9 2XS
Tel: 01977 609000
Fax: 01977 609900
E-mail: sales@moseleycoachsales.co.uk
Web site: www.moseleycoachsales.co.uk

NU-TRACK LTD
Steeple Industrial Estate, Antrim, Northern Ireland
BT41 1AB
Tel: 028 9446 9550
Fax: 028 9446 5430
E-mail: enquiries@nu-track.co.uk
Web site: www.nu-track.co.uk

OPTARE PLC (Leeds)
Manston Lane, Leeds LS15 8SU
Tel: 0113 264 5182
Fax: 0113 260 6635
E-mail: info@optare.com
Web site: www.optare.com

PLAXTON LIMITED
Plaxton Park, Cayton Low Road, Eastfield,
Scarborough, North Yorkshire YO11 3BY
Tel: 01723 581500
Fax: 01723 581479
E-mail: sales@plaxtonlimited.co.uk
Web site: www.plaxtonlimited.co.uk
Range: coaches; midicoach and midibus bodies.
(Part of Alexander Dennis)

PVS MANUFACTURING LTD
40 Killycanavan Road, Ardboe, Dungannon,
Northern Ireland BT71 5BP
Tel: 028 8673 6969
Fax: 028 8673 7178
E-mail: mail@pvsltd.com
Web site: www.conversionspecialists.com

SITCAR
Via Copernico 41, 41041 Casinalbo di Formigine,
Modena, Italy
Tel: 00 39 059 577 0911
Fax: 00 39 059 573361
UK Supplier: Moseley (PCV) Ltd
Elmsall Way, Dale Lane, South Elmsall, Pontefract
WF9 2XS
Tel: 01977 609000
Fax: 01977 609900
E-mail: sales@moseleycoachsales.co.uk
Web site: www.moseleycoachsales.co.uk

STANFORD COACH WORKS
Mobility House, Stanhope Industrial Park,
Wharf Road, Stanford-le-Hope SS17 0EH
Tel: 01375 676088

Fax: 01375 677999
E-mail: sales@stanfordcoachworks.co.uk
Web site: www.stanfordcoachworks.co.uk
Range: mini- and midibuses, mini- and
midicoaches

TESLA VEHICLES LIMITED
22 Larbre Crescent, Whickham, Newcastle upon
Tyne NE16 5YG
Tel: 0191 488 6258
Fax: 0191 488 9158
E-mail: info@teslavehicles.com
Web site: www.teslavehicles.com

UNVI BUS & COACH
13 Poulton Street, Kirkham, Preston, Lancashire
PR4 2AA
Tel: 01772 635820
Fax: 01772 634336
Web site: www.unvibusandcoach.co.uk
Range: single-deck coach, midicoach, minicoach

WILKER GROUP
Frederick Street, Clara, Co Offaly, Republic of
Ireland
Tel: 00 353 5793 31252
E-mail: info@wilkergroup.com
Web site: www.wilkergroup.com
UK subsidiary
Sandy Lane, Ettiley Heath, Sandbach CW11 3NG
Tel: 01270 765999
E-mail: info.uk@wilkergroup.com
Range: low-floor mini- and midibuses, mini- and
midicoaches

DEALERS

AD COACH SALES
Newbridge Coach Depot, Witheridge EX16 8PY
Tel: 01884 860767
Fax: 01884 860711
E-mail: enquiries@adcoachsales.co.uk
Web site: www.adcoachsales.co.uk

ALEXANDER DENNIS LTD
91 Glasgow Road, Falkirk FK1 4JB
Tel: 01324 621 672
Fax: 01324 632 269
E-mail: enquiries@alexander-dennis.com
Web site: www.alexander-dennis.com

ALLIED VEHICLES LTD
230 Balmore Road, Glasgow G22 6LJ
Tel: 0800 916 3096
E-mail: info@alliedvehicles.co.uk
Web site: www.alliedvehiclesltd.com

ARRIVA BUS AND COACH
Lodge Garage, Whitehall Road West, Gomersal,
Cleckheaton, West Yorkshire BD19 4BJ
Tel: 01274 681144
Fax: 01274 651198
E-mail: whiter@arriva.co.uk
Web site: www.arrivabusandcoach.co.uk

B.A.S.E. LTD
57 Clydesdale Place, Moss Side Industrial Estate,
Leyland PR26 7QS
Tel: 01772 425355
Fax: 01772 425748
Web site: www.basecoachsales.co.uk

BLYTHSWOOD MOTORS LTD
Westway Park, Porterfield Road,
Renfrew PA4 8DY

Tel: 0141 221 3165
Fax: 0141 221 3172
E-mail: blythswoodmotors@aol.com
Web site: www.blythswoodmotors.co.uk

BOB VALE COACH SALES LTD
Eastfield House, Amesbury Road, Thruxton,
Andover, Hampshire SP11 8ED
Tel: 01264 773000
Fax: 01264 774833
E-mail: bobvalecoachsales@btconnect.com
Web site: www.bobvalecoachsales.com

BRISTOL BUS & COACH SALES
6/7 Freestone Road, St Philips, Bristol
BS2 0QN
Tel: 0117 971 0251
Fax: 0117 972 3121
E-mail: simon.munden@bristolbusandcoach.
co.uk
Web site: www.bristolbusandcoach.co.uk

BRITISH BUS SALES – MIKE NASH
PO Box 534, Dorking, Surrey
RH5 5XB
Tel: 07836 656692
E-mail: nashionalbus1@btconnect.com
Web site: www.britishbussales.co.uk

CAETANO (UK) LTD
Mill Lane, Heather, Coalville LE67 2QE
Tel: 01530 263333
Fax: 01530 263379
E-mail: enquiries@caetano.co.uk
Web site: www.caetano.co.uk
Models: single-deck coach, single-deck low-floor
midibus.

CONNAUGHT PSV
8 Mosham Close, Blaxton, Doncaster
DN9 3BB
Tel: 01302 770863
Fax: 01302 771666
E-mail: steve@connaughtpsv.co.uk
Web site: www.connaughtpsv.co.uk

DAWSONRENTALS BUS
AND COACH LTD
Delaware Drive, Tongwell, Milton Keynes
MK15 8JH
Tel: 01908 218111
Fax: 01908 610156
E-mail: info@dawsongroup.co.uk
Web site: www.dawsongroup.co.uk

ENSIGN BUS CO LTD
Juliette Close, Purfleet Industrial Park,
Purfleet RM15 4YF
Tel: 01708 865656
Fax: 01708 864340
E-mail: sales@ensignbus.com
Web site: www.ensignbus.com

EVOBUS (UK) LTD
Cross Point Business Park, Ashcroft Way,
Coventry CV2 2TU
Tel: 02476 626000 **Fax:** 02476 626034
Web site: www.evobus.com

DAVID FISHWICK VEHICLE SALES
North Valley, Byron Road, Colne, Lancashire
BB8 0RF
Tel: 0800 294 9474
E-mail: matthew@davidfishwick.net
Web site: www.davidfishwick.net

FLEET AUCTION GROUP
Brindley Road, Stephenson Industrial Estate,
Coalville, Leicestershire LE67 3HG
Tel: 01530 833535
Fax: 01530 813425
E-mail: info@fleetauctiongroup.com
Web site: www.fleetauctiongroup.com

FURROWS COMMERCIAL VEHICLES
Haybridge Road, Hadley, Telford TF1 2FF
Tel: 01952 641433
Fax: 01952 640178
Web site: www.furrowscommercials.co.uk

GM COACHWORK LTD
Teign Valley, Trusham, Newton Abbot TQ13 0NX
Tel: 01626 853050
Fax: 01626 855066
E-mail: sales@gmcoachwork.co.uk
Web site: www.gmcoachwork.co.uk

IAN GORDON COMMERCIALS
Schawkirk Garage, Stair, Ayrshire KA5 5JA
Tel: 01292 591764
Fax: 01292 591484
E-mail: mail@iangordoncommercials.com
Web site: www.iangordoncommercials.com

THOMAS HARDIE COMMERCIALS LTD
Newstet Road, Knowsley Industrial Park,
Liverpool L33 7TJ
Tel: 0151 549 3000
E-mail: info@thardie.co.uk

HEATONS MOTOR CO
53 Bickershaw Lane, Abram, Wigan
WN2 5PL
Tel: 01942 864222
E-mail: info@heatonsmotorco.co.uk
Web site: www.heatonsmotorco.co.uk

B & D HOLT
Cuthbert Street, Bolton BL3 3SD
Tel: 01204 650999
Fax: 01204 665300
E-mail: sales@bdholt.co.uk
Web site: www.bdholt.co.uk

IRISH COMMERCIALS (SALES)
Naas, Co Kildare, Republic of Ireland
Tel: 00 353 45 879881
Fax: 00 353 45 875462
E-mail: info@irishcomms.ie
Web site: www.irishcomms.ie

KING LONG UK LTD
Bedworth Road, Coventry CV6 6BP
Tel: 02476 363004
Fax: 02476 365835
E-mail: enquiries@kinglonguk.com
Web site: www.kinglonguk.com

LVD
Leinster Vehicle Distributors Ltd, Bridge Garage,
Urlingford, Co Kilkenny, Republic of Ireland
Tel: 00 353 56 88 31189
E-mail: sales@lvd.ie
Web site: www.coach-sales.net

THE LONDON BUS EXPORT CO
PO Box 12, Chepstow NP16 5UZ
Tel: 01291 689741
Fax: 01291 689361
E-mail: lonbusco@globalnet.co.uk
Web site: www.bus.uk.com

LOUGHSHORE AUTOS LTD
26 Killycanavan Road, Ardboe,
Dungannon BT71 5BP
Tel: 028 8673 7325
Fax: 028 8673 5882
E-mail: male@loughshoreautosltd.com
Web site: www.loughshoreautosltd.com

MASS SPECIAL ENGINEERING LTD
Anston, Sheffield S25 4SD
Tel: 01909 550480
Fax: 01909 550486

NIGEL McCREE COACH SALES
8 Tamworth Close, Shepshed,
Loughborough, Leicestershire
LE12 9NE
Tel: 01509 502695
E-mail: nigel@nigelmccree.com
Web site: www.nigelmccree.com

MINIS TO MIDIS LTD
135 Nutwell Lane, Doncaster DN3 3JR
Tel: 01302 833203
Fax: 01302 831756
E-mail: sales@ministomidis.com
Web site: www.ministomidis.com

MISTRAL BUS & COACH PLC
Booths Hall, Chelford Road, Knutsford,
Cheshire WA16 8QZ
Tel: 01565 621881
Fax: 01565 621882
E-mail: sales@mistral-group.com
Web site: www.mistral-group.com

MOSELEY (PCV) LTD
Elmsall Way, Dale Lane, South Elmsall, Pontefract,
West Yorkshire WF9 2XS
Tel: 01977 609900
Fax: 01977 609900
E-mail: sales@moseleycoachsales.co.uk
Web site: www.moseleycoachsales.co.uk

MOSELEY IN THE SOUTH LTD
Summerfield Avenue, Chelston Business Park,
Wellington TA21 9JF
Tel: 01823 653000
Fax: 01823 663502
E-mail: enquiries@moseleysouth.co.uk
Web site: www.moseleysouth.co.uk

MOSELEY DISTRIBUTORS LTD
Rydenmains, Condorrat Road, Glenmavis,
Airdrie ML6 0PP
Tel: 01236 750501
Fax: 01236 750504
E-mail: enquiries@moseleydistributors.co.uk
Web site: www.moseleydistributors.co.uk

NEXT BUS LTD
Vincients Road, Bumpers Farm Industrial Estate,
Chippenham, Wiltshire SN14 6QA
Tel: 01249 462462
Fax: 01249 448844
E-mail: sales@next-bus.co.uk
Web site: www.next-bus.co.uk

BRIAN NOONE
Straffan Road, Maynooth, Co Kildare,
Republic of Ireland
Tel: 00 353 1 628 6311
Fax: 00 353 1 628 5404
E-mail: reception@noone.ie
Web site: www.noone.ie

OPTARE PLC (Leeds)
Manston Lane, Leeds LS15 8SU
Tel: 0113 264 5182
Fax: 0113 260 6635
E-mail: info@optare.com
Web site: www.optare.com

OWENS OF OSWESTRY BMC
Unit 3, Four Crosses Business Park, Llanymynech
SY22 6ST
Tel: 01691 652126
Fax: 01691 831142
E-mail: sales@owens-bmc.co.uk
Web site: www.owens-bmc.co.uk

PEMBRIDGE VEHICLE MANAGEMENT
Pembridge House, Park Business Centre, Plough
Road, Goytre, Penperlleni, Usk, Monmouthshire
NP4 0AL
Tel: 01633 485858
Fax: 0845 409 1342
E-mail: sales@minibussales.co.uk
Web site: www.minibussales.co.uk

H W PICKRELL
Holt Place, Gardiners Lane North, Crays Hill,
Billericay CM11 2XE
Tel: 01268 521033
Fax: 01268 284951
E-mail: sales@hwpickrell.co.uk
Web site: www.hwpickrell.co.uk

PLAXTON COACH SALES CENTRE
Ryton Road, Anston, Sheffield S25 4DL
Tel: 01909 551166
Fax: 01909 567994
E-mail: coachsales@plaxtonlimited.co.uk
Web site: www.plaxtonlimited.co.uk
(Part of Alexander Dennis)

SANTANDER ASSET FINANCE
Taylor Road, Trafford Park, Manchester M41 7JQ
Tel: 0161 747 5698
Fax: 0161 275 4501
E-mail: steve.moult@hansar.co.uk
Web site: www.buses247.co.uk

SOUTHDOWN PSV LTD
Silverwood, Snow Hill, Copthorne, West Sussex
RH10 3EN
Tel: 01342 711840
Fax: 01342 719617
E-mail: bussales@southdownpsv.co.uk
Web site: www.southdownpsv.co.uk

STAFFORD BUS CENTRE
Unit 27, Moorfields Industrial Estate, Cotes Heath
ST21 6QY
Tel: 01782 791774
Fax: 01782 791721
E-mail: mail@staffordbuscentre.com
Web site: www.staffordbuscentre.com

STEPHENSONS OF ESSEX
Riverside Industrial Estate, South Street, Rochford
SS4 1BS
Tel: 01702 541511
Fax. 01702 549461
E-mail: sales@stephensonsofessex.com
Web site: www.stephensonsofessex.com

TAYLOR COACH SALES
102 Beck Road, Isleham, Ely CB7 5QP
Tel (mobile): 07850 241848
Tel: 01638 780010

Fax: 01638 780011
E-mail: taylorcoach@live.co.uk
Web site: www.taylorcoachsales.co.uk

TOYOTA (GB) PLC
PO Box 814, Portsmouth PO6 9AY
Tel: 08447 016202
Web site: www.toyota.co.uk
UK suppliers:
AD Coach Sales Tel: 01884 860767;
Holloway Commercials Tel: 01902 636661;
Caetano (UK) Ltd Tel: 01530 263333

TRAMONTANA
Chapelknowe Road, Carfin, Motherwell ML1 5LE
Tel: 01698 861790
Fax: 01698 860778
E-mail: wdt90@tiscali.co.uk
Web site: www.brittnet.net/tramontanacoach

UK BUS DISMANTLERS LTD
Streamhall Garage Estate, Linton Trading Estate,
Bromyard, Herefordshire HR7 4QT
Tel: 01885 488448
Fax: 01885 482127
Web site: www.ukbusdismantlers.co.uk

USED COACH SALES
The Red House, Underbridge Lane, Higher
Walton, Warrington WA4 5QR
Tel: 01925 210202
Web site: www.usedcoachsales.co.uk

VENTURA BUS + COACH SALES
Unit 39, Hobbs Industrial Estate, Newchapel,
Lingfield RH7 6HN
Tel: 01342 835206
Fax: 01342 835813
E-mail: info@venturasales.co.uk
Web site: www.venturasales.co.uk

VOLVO BUS & COACH SALES CENTRE
Siskin Parkway East, Middlemarch Business Park,
Coventry CV3 4PE
Tel: 02476 210250
Fax: 02476 210258
Web site: www.volvo.com
Range: New & Pre-owned buses and coaches.

WACTON COACH SALES & SERVICES
Linton Trading Estate, Bromyard, Herefordshire
HR7 4QL
Tel: 01885 482782
Fax: 01885 482127

WEALDEN PSV LTD
The Bus Garage, 64 Whetsted Road, Five Oak
Green, Tonbridge, Kent TN12 6RT
Tel: 01892 833830
Fax: 01892 836977
E-mail: info@wealdenpsv.co.uk
Web site: www.wealdenpsv.co.uk

WE SELL ANY COACH.COM LTD
23 Brook Road, Bomere Geath, Shrewsbury,
Shropshire SY4 3PU
Tel: 01939 290502
E-mail: paul.busman@btopenworld.com
Web site: www.wesellanycoach.com

TREVOR WIGLEY & SONS BUS LTD
Passenger Vehicle Dismantling/Spares
Works: Boulder Bridge Lane, off Shaw Lane,
Barnsley S71 3HJ
Correspondence: 148 Royston Road,

Cudworth, Barnsley S72 8BN
Tel: 01226 713636
Fax: 01226 700199
E-mail: wigleys@btconnect.com
Web site: www.twigley.com

DREW WILSON COACH SALES
Castlehill Yard, Airdrie Road, Carluke, Lanarkshire
ML8 5EP
Tel: 0141 248 5524
E-mail: enquiries@drewwilson.co.uk
Web site: www.drewwilson.co.uk

YORKSHIRE BUS & COACH SALES
254A West Ella Road, West Ella, Hull HU10 7SF
Tel: 01482 653302
Fax: 01482 653302

A-Z LISTING OF BUS, COACH & TRAM SUPPLIERS

LIST OF CATEGORIES

- Air Conditioning/Ventilation
- Audio/Video Systems
- Badges – Drivers/Conductors
- Batteries
- Bicycle carriers
- Body/Electrical Repairs & Refurbishing
- Brakes and Brake Linings
- Bus Stops/Shelters
  - – see Shelters/Street Furniture
- Cash Handling Equipment
- Chassis Lubricating Systems
- Clutches
- Cooling Systems
- Destination Indicator Equipment
- Door Operating Gear
- Drinks Dispensing Equipment
- Driving Axles and Gears
- Electrical Equipment
- Electronic Control
- Emission Control Devices
- Engineering
- Engines
- Engine Oil Drain Valves
- Exhaust Systems
- Fans & Drive Belts
- Fare Boxes
- Fire Extinguishers
- First Aid Equipment
- Floor Coverings
- Fuel, Fuel Management & Lubricants
- Garage Equipment
- Gearboxes
- Hand Driers (In Coaches)
- Hand Rails
- Headrest Covers & Curtains
- Heating & Ventilation Systems
- Hub Odometers
- In-Coach Catering Equipment
- Information Displays
  - – see Passenger Information Systems
- Labels, Nameplates & Decals
- Lifting Equipment

- Lifts/Ramps (Passenger)
- Lighting & Lighting Design
- Mirrors/Mirror Arms
- Oil Management Systems
- Painting & Signwriting
- Parts Suppliers
- Passenger Information Systems
- Pneumatic Valves/Cylinders
- Rapid Transit/Priority Equipment
- Repairs/Refurbishment
  - – see Body/Electrical Repairs
- Retarders & Speed Control Systems
- Reversing Safety Systems
- Roller Blinds – Passenger & Driver
- Roof Lining Fabrics
- Seat Belts/Restraint Systems
- Seats/Seat Cushions & Seat Frames
- Shelters/Street Furniture
- Shock Absorbers/Suspension
- Steering
- Surveillance Systems
- Suspension
- Tachographs
- Tachograph Calibrators
- Tachograph Chart Analysis Service
- Tickets, Ticket Machines,
  Ticket Systems & Technology
- Timetable Display Frames
- Toilet Equipment
- Transmission Overhaul
- Tree Guards
- Tyres
- Uniforms
- Upholstery
- Vacuum Systems
- Vehicle Recovery
- Vehicle Washing & Washers
- Wheels, Wheeltrims & Covers
- Windows and Windscreens

INDUSTRY SERVICE PROVIDERS

- Accident Investigation
- Accountancy & Audit
- Advisory Services
- Artwork
- Breakdown & Recovery Services
- Cleaning Services
- Coach Driver Agencies
- Coach Hire Brokers/Vehicle Rental
- Coach Interchange & Parking Facilities
- Computer Systems/Software
- Consultants
- Delivery & Collection Services
- Driver Supply
- Driver Training
- Exhibition/Event Organisers
- Ferry Operators
- Finance and Leasing
- Graphic Design
- Health & Safety
- Insurance
- Legal & Operations Advisers
- Livery Design
- Maps for the Bus Industry
- Marketing Services
- Mechanical Investigation
- On-Bus Advertising
- Passenger Representation
- Printing and Publishing
- Promotional Material
- Publications – Magazines & Books
- Quality Management Systems
- Recruitment
- Reference Books
- Timetable Production
- Tour Wholesalers
- Training Services
- Vehicle Certification
- Vehicle Rental
  - – see Coach Hire Brokers/
- Web Design

Air Conditioning/Ventilation

AIRCONCO
Units 10 (Head Office), 6 (Part Centre),
Middleton Trade Park, Oldham Road, Middleton,
Manchester M24 1QZ
Tel: 0845 402 4014
Fax: 0845 402 4041
E-mail: mail@airconco.carriersutrak.co.uk
Web site: www.airconco.ltd.uk

AMA LTD
Unit 17, Springmill Industrial Estate, Avening Road,
Nailsworth GL6 0BH
Tel: 01453 832884
Fax: 01453 832040
E-mail: info@ama.ac
Web site: www.ama-airconditioning.co.uk

ARRIVA BUS AND COACH
Lodge Garage, Whitehall Road West, Gomersal,
Cleckheaton, West Yorkshire BD19 4BJ
Tel: 01274 681144
Fax: 01274 651198
E-mail: whiter@arriva.co.uk
Web site: www.arrivabusandcoach.co.uk

BRT BEARINGS LTD
21-24 Regal Road, Wisbech, Cambridgeshire
PE13 2RQ
Tel: 01945 464097
Fax: 01945 464523
E-mail: brt.sales@brt-bearings.com
Web site: www.brt-bearings.com

CARRIER SUTRAK
Suite Unit 6, The IO Centre, Barn Way,
Northampton NN5 7UW
Tel: 01604 581468
Fax: 01604 758132
E-mail: info.suetrak@carrier.utc.com
Web site: www.carrieraircon.co.uk

CLAYTON HEATERS LTD
Hunter Terrace, Fletchworth Gate, Burnsall Road,
Coventry CV5 6SP
Tel: 02476 691916
Fax: 02476 691969
E-mail: admin@claytoncc.co.uk
Web Site: www.claytoncc.co.uk

DIRECT PARTS LTD
Unit 1, Churnet Court, Churnetside Business
Park, Harrison Way, Cheddleton ST13 7EF
Tel: 01538 361777
Fax: 01538 369100
E-mail: sales@direct-group.co.uk
Web site: www.direct-group.co.uk

EBERSPACHER (UK) LTD
Headlands Business Park, Salisbury Road,
Ringwood BH24 3PB
Tel: 01425 480151 **Fax:** 01425 480152
E-mail: enquiries@eberspacher.com
Web site: www.eberspacher.com

HISPACOLD
See: Clayton Heaters above
Web Site: www.hispacold.es

M A C LTD
34A Waterroyd Lane, Mirfield, West Yorkshire
WF14 9SG
Tel: 01924 491252
Fax: 01924 480170

E-mail: info@mac-aircon.com
Web site: www.mac-aircon.com

OPTARE PARTS DIVISION (Leeds)
Manston Lane, Leeds LS15 8SU
Tel: 0113 264 5182
Fax: 0113 260 6635
E-mail: parts@optare.com
Web site: www.optare.com

OPTARE PRODUCT SUPPORT LONDON
Unit 9, Eurocourt, Olivers Close, West Thurrock
RM20 3EE
Tel: 01708 896860
Fax: 01708 869920
E-mail: london.service@optare.com

OPTARE PRODUCT SUPPORT ROTHERHAM
Denby Way, Hellaby, Rotherham S66 8HR
Tel: 01709 535100
Fax: 01709 535102
E-mail: rotherham.service@optare.com

PLAXTON SERVICE
Ryton Road, Anston, Sheffield S25 4DL
Tel: 01909 551155
Fax: 01909 550050
E-mail: service@plaxtonlimited.co.uk
Web site: www.plaxtonaftercare.co.uk

SCANIA
Scania Bus & Coach (UK) Ltd, Claylands Avenue,
Worksop S81 7DJ
Tel: 01909 500822
Fax: 01909 500165
Web Site: www.scania.co.uk

WEBASTO PRODUCT UK LTD
Webasto House, White Rose Way, Doncaster
Carr, South Yorkshire DN4 5JH
Tel: 01302 322232
Fax: 01302 322231
E-mail: info@webastouk.com
Web site: www.webasto.co.uk

Audio/Video Systems

AUTOSOUND LTD
4 Lister Street, Dudley Hill, Bradford BD4 9PQ
Tel: 01274 688990
Fax: 01274 651318
E-mail: keith.ellis@autosound.co.uk
Web site: www.autosound.co.uk

AVT SYSTEMS LTD
Unit 3 & 4, Tything Road East, Alcester,
Warwickshire B49 6ES
Tel: 01789 400357
Fax: 01789 400359
E-mail: enquiries@avtsystems.co.uk
Web site: www.avtsystems.co.uk

CONCEPT COACHCRAFT LTD
Far Cromwell Road, Stockport,
Cheshire SK6 2SE
Tel: 0161 406 9322
Fax: 0161 406 9588
E-mail: sales@conceptcoachcraft.com
Web site: www.conceptcoachcraft.com

EXPRESS COACH REPAIRS LTD
Outgang Lane, Pickering YO18 7JA
Tel: 01751 475215
Fax: 01751 475215
E-mail: info@expresscoachrepairs.co.uk
Web site: www.expresscoachrepairs.co.uk

FCAV & CO
Brooklyn House, Coleford Road, Bream,
Gloucestershire GL15 6EU
Tel: 07900 572382
Fax: 01594 564556
E-mail: info@fcav.co.uk
Web site: www.fcav.co.uk

INIT - INNOVATIONS IN TRANSPORTATION LTD
49 Stoney Street, The Lace Market,
Nottingham NG1 1LX
Tel: 0870 890 4648
Fax: 0115 989 5463
E-mail: sales@init.co.uk
Web site: www.init.co.uk

KCP CAR & COMMERCIAL LTD
Unit 15, Hillside Business Park, Kempson Way,
Bury St Edmunds, Suffolk IP32 7EA
Tel: 01284 750777
Fax: 01284 750773
E-mail: info@kcpcarandcommercial.co.uk
Web site: www.kcpcarandcommercial.co.uk

LAWTON SERVICES LTD
Knutsford Road, Church Lawton,
Stoke-on-Trent ST7 3DN
Tel: 01270 882056
Fax: 01270 883014
E-mail: andrea@lawtonservices.co.uk
Web site: www.lawtonservices.co.uk

OPTARE PARTS DIVISION (Leeds)
Manston Lane, Leeds LS15 8SU
Tel: 0113 264 5182
Fax: 0113 260 6635
E-mail: parts@optare.com
Web site: www.optare.com

PLAXTON SERVICE
Ryton Road, Anston, Sheffield S25 4DL
Tel: 01909 551155
Fax: 01909 550050
E-mail: service@plaxtonlimited.co.uk
Web site: www.plaxtonaftercare.co.uk

PSV PRODUCTS
The Red House, Underbridge Lane, Higher
Walton, Warrington WA4 5QR
Tel: 01925 210220
Fax: 01925 601534
E-mail: info@psvproducts.com
Web site: www.psvproducts.com

Badges - Drivers/Conductors

GSM GRAPHIC ARTS LTD
Castlegarth Works, Thirsk, YO7 1PS
Tel: 01845 522184
Fax: 01845 522206
E-mail: gsmgraphicarts@gsmgroup.co.uk
Web Site: www.gsmgraphicarts.co.uk

MARK TERRILL PSV BADGES
5 De Grey Close, Lewes BN7 2JR
Tel: 01273 474816
Fax: 01273 474816
Mobile: 07770 666159

Batteries

ARRIVA BUS AND COACH
Lodge Garage, Whitehall Road West, Gomersal,
Cleckheaton, West Yorkshire BD19 4BJ
Tel: 01274 681144
Fax: 01274 651198
E-mail: whiter@arriva.co.uk
Web site: www.arrivabusandcoach.co.uk

BANNER BATTERIES GB LTD
Units 5-8, Canal View Business Park, Wheelhouse
Road, Rugeley, Staffordshire WS15 1UY
Tel: 01889 571100
Fax: 01889 577342
E-mail: alec.morgan@bannerbatteries.com
Web site: www.bannerbatteries.com

BRITISH BUS SALES – MIKE NASH
PO Box 534, Dorking, Surrey RH5 5XB
Tel: 07836 656692
E-mail: nashionalbus1@btconnect.com
Web site: www.britishbussales.co.uk

CUMMINS UK
Rutherford Drive, Park Farm South,
Wellingborough NN8 6AN
Tel: 01933 334200
Fax: 01933 334198
E-mail: cduksales@cummins.com
Web site: www.cummins-uk.com

EXPRESS COACH REPAIRS LTD
Outgang Lane, Pickering YO18 7JA
Tel: 01751 475215
Fax: 01751 475215
E-mail: info@expresscoachrepairs.co.uk
Web site: www.expresscoachrepairs.co.uk

THOMAS HARDIE COMMERCIALS LTD
Newstet Road, Knowsley Industrial Park,
Liverpool L33 7TJ
Tel: 0151 549 3000
E-mail: info@thardie.co.uk

JOHNSON CONTROLS BATTERIES LTD (VARTA and OPTIMA BATTERIES)
3rd Floor, Aston House, 62-68 Oak End Way,
Gerrards Cross, Buckinghamshire SL9 8BR
Tel: 01753 480610
Fax: 01753 480611
E-mail: vb-uk-enquiries@jci.com
Web sites: www.varta-automotive.com
www.optimabatteries.com

KCP CAR & COMMERCIAL LTD
Unit 15, Hillside Business Park, Kempson Way,
Bury St Edmunds, Suffolk IP32 7EA
Tel: 01284 750777
Fax: 01284 750773
E-mail: info@kcpcarandcommercial.co.uk
Web site: www.kcpcarandcommercial.co.uk

MASS SPECIAL ENGINEERING LTD
Houghton Road, North Anston
S25 4JJ
Tel: 01909 550480
Fax: 01909 550486

OPTARE PARTS DIVISION (Leeds)
Manston Lane, Leeds LS15 8SU
Tel: 0113 264 5182
Fax: 0113 260 6635
E-mail: parts@optare.com
Web site: www.optare.com

OPTARE PRODUCT SUPPORT LONDON
Unit 9, Eurocourt, Olivers Close,
West Thurrock RM20 3EE
Tel: 01708 896860
Fax: 01708 869920
E-mail: london.service@optare.com

OPTARE PRODUCT SUPPORT ROTHERHAM
Denby Way, Hellaby, Rotherham
S66 8HR
Tel: 01709 535100
Fax: 01709 535102
E-mail: rotherham.service@optare.com

Bicycle Carriers

PLAXTON SERVICE
Ryton Road, Anston, Sheffield S25 4DL
Tel: 01909 551155
Fax: 01909 550050
E-mail: service@plaxtonlimited.co.uk
Web site: www.plaxtonaftercare.co.uk

Body/Electrical Repairs & Refurbishing

AD COACH SALES
Newbridge Coach Depot, Witheridge
EX16 8PY
Tel: 01884 860787
Fax: 01884 860711
E-mail: enquiries@adcoachsales.co.uk
Web site: www.adcoachsales.co.uk

AK CARPETS LTD
Unit 15, Deanfield Court, Link 59 Business Park,
Clitheroe, Lancashire BB7 1QS
Tel: 01200 444145
Fax: 01200 444180
E-mail: info@akcarpets.com
Web site: www.akcarpets.com

ARRIVA BUS AND COACH
Lodge Garage, Whitehall Road West,
Gomersal, Cleckheaton, West Yorkshire
BD19 4BJ
Tel: 01274 681144
Fax: 01274 651198
E-mail: whiter@arriva.co.uk
Web Site: www.arrivabusandcoach.co.uk

BULWARK BUS & COACH ENGINEERING LTD
Unit 5, Bulwark Business Park, Bulwark,
Chepstow NP16 6QZ
Tel: 01291 622326
Fax: 01291 622726
E-mail: bulwarkbusandcoach@tiscali.co.uk
Web site: www.bulwarkbusandcoach.co.uk

CARLYLE BUS & COACH LTD
Carlyle Business Park, Great Bridge Street,
Swan Village, West Bromwich B70 0X4
Tel: 0121 524 1200
Fax: 0121 524 1201
E-mail: admin@carlyleplc.co.uk
Web Site: www.carlyleplc.co.uk

CHANNEL COMMERCIALS PLC
Unit 6, Cobbs Wood Industrial Estate,
Brunswick Road, Ashford TN23 1EH
Tel: 01233 629272
Fax: 01233 636322
E-mail: info@ccplc.co.uk
Web site: www.channelcommercials.co.uk

COBUS COACH REPAIRS
Lancaster Road, Carnaby Industrial Estate,
Brdilington, East Yorkshire
YO15 3QY
Tel: 01262 603829
Fax: 01262 606738
E-mail: cobusuk@btconnect.com
Web site: www.cobuscoachrepairs.co.uk

CREST COACH CONVERSIONS
Unit 5, Holmeroyd Road, Bentley Moor Lane,
Carcroft, Doncaster DN6 7BH
Tel: 01302 723723
Fax: 01302 724724

CROWN COACHBUILDERS LTD
32 Flemington Industrial Park, Flemington,
Motherwell ML1 1SN
Tel: 01698 276087
Fax: 01698 262676
E-mail: davidgreer@hotmail.com
Web site: www.crowncoachbuilders.co.uk

EASTGATE COACH TRIMMERS
3 Thornton Road Industrial Estate, Pickering
YO18 7HZ
Tel/Fax: 01751 472229
E-mail: info@eastgate-coachtrimmers.co.uk
Web site: eastgate-coachtrimmers.co.uk

EXPRESS COACH REPAIRS LTD
Outgang Lane, Pickering YO18 7JA
Tel: 01751 475215
Fax: 01751 475215
E-mail: info@expresscoachrepairs.co.uk
Web site: www.expresscoachrepairs.co.uk

HANTS & DORSET TRIM LTD
Canada Road, West Wellow, Hampshire
SO51 6DE.
Tel: 02380 644200
Fax: 02380 647802
E-mail: dclack@hdtrim.co.uk
Web site: www.hantsanddorsettrim.co.uk

HAPPICH UK LTD
Unit 30, Fort Industrial Park, Fort Parkway,
Castle Bromwich B35 7AR
Tel: 0121 747 4400
Fax: 0121 747 4977
E-mail: sales@happich.co.uk
Web site: www.happich.com

THOMAS HARDIE COMMERCIALS LTD
Newstet Road, Knowsley Industrial Park,
Liverpool L33 7TJ
Tel: 0151 549 3000
E-mail: info@thardie.co.uk

INVERTEC LTD
Whelford Road, Fairford GL7 4DT
Tel: 01285 713550
Fax: 01285 713548
Mobile: 07802 793828
E-mail: ian@invertec.co.uk
Web site: www.invertec.co.uk

LAWTON SERVICES LTD
Knutsford Road, Church Lawton,
Stoke-on-Trent ST7 3DN
Tel: 01270 882056
Fax: 01270 883014
E-mail: andrea@lawtonservices.co.uk
Web site: www.lawtonservices.co.uk

LEICESTER CARRIAGE BUILDERS
Marlow Road, Leicester LE3 2BQ
Tel: 0116 282 4270
Fax: 0116 263 0554
E-mail: rick.johnson@midlandsco-op.com
Web site: www.leicestercarriagebuilders.co.uk

MARTYN INDUSTRIALS LTD
5 Brunel Way, Durranhill, Harraby, Carlisle
CA1 3NQ
Tel: 01228 544000
Fax: 01228 544001
E-mail: enquiries@martyn-industrials.co.uk
Web site: www.martyn-industrials.com

Total Tool Solutions Limited
Newhaven Business Park
Lowergate
Milnsbridge
Huddersfield
HD3 4HS
T: 01484 642211
F: 01484 461002
E: sales@ttsuk.com
W: www.ttsuk.com

MASS SPECIAL ENGINEERING LTD
Houghton Road, North Anston S25 4JJ
Tel: 01909 550480.
Fax: 01909 550486

MCV BUS & COACH LTD
Sterling Place, Elean Business Park, Sutton,
Cambridge CB6 2QE
Tel: 01353 773000
Fax: 01353 773001
E-mail: vernon.edwards@mcv-uk.com

MELLOR COACHCRAFT
Miall Street, Rochdale OL11 1HY
Tel: 01706 860610 **Fax:** 01706 860042
E-mail: mcsales@woodhall-nicholson.co.uk
Web site: www.mellor-coachcraft.co.uk

MOSELEY (PCV) LTD
Elmsall Way, Dale Lane, South Elmsall, Pontefract,
West Yorkshire WF9 2XS
Tel: 01977 609000
Fax: 01977 609900
E-mail: sales@moseleycoachsales.co.uk
Web site: www.moseleycoachsales.co.uk

MOSELEY DISTRIBUTORS LTD
Rydenmains, Condorrat Road, Glenmavis, Airdrie
ML6 0PP
Tel: 01236 750501
Fax: 01236 750504
E-mail: enquiries@moseleydistributors.co.uk
Web site: www.moseleydistributors.co.uk

OPTARE PARTS DIVISION (Leeds)
Manston Lane, Leeds LS15 8SU
Tel: 0113 264 5182
Fax: 0113 260 6635
E-mail: parts@optare.com
Web site: www.optare.com

OPTARE PRODUCT SUPPORT LONDON
Unit 9, Eurocourt, Olivers Close, West Thurrock
RM20 3EE
Tel: 01708 896860
Fax: 01708 869920
E-mail: london.service@optare.com

OPTARE PRODUCT SUPPORT ROTHERHAM
Denby Way, Hellaby, Rotherham S66 8HR
Tel: 01709 535100
Fax: 01709 535102
E-mail: rotherham.service@optare.com

PLAXTON SERVICE
Ryton Road, Anston, Sheffield S25 4DL
Tel: 01909 551155
Fax: 01909 550050
E-mail: service@plaxtonlimited.co.uk
Web site: www.plaxtonaftercare.co.uk

RH BODYWORKS
A140 Ipswich Road, Brome, Eye,
Suffolk IP23 8AW
Tel: 01379 870666
Fax: 01379 871140
E-mail: enquiries@rhbodyworks.co.uk
Web site: www.rhbodyworks.co.uk

THORNTON BROTHERS LTD
North Seaton Industrial Estate, Ashington,
Northumberland NE63 0YB
Tel: 01670 854500
Fax: 01670 854015
E-mail: info@thornton-t180.co.uk
Web site: www.thornton-t180.co.uk

TRAMONTANA
Chapelknowe Road, Carfin, Motherwell ML1 5LE
Tel: 01698 861790
Fax: 01698 860778
E-mail: wdt90@tiscali.co.uk
Web site: www.brittnet.net/tramontanacoach

TRUCKALIGN CO LTD
VIP Group, VIP Industrial Park, Anchor & Hope
Lane, London SE7 7RY
Tel: 020 8305 5879
Fax: 020 8858 5663
E-mail: admin@vipgroupltd.co.uk
Web site: www.vipgroup.co.uk

TTS UK
Total Tool Solutions Ltd, Newhaven Business
Park, Lowergate, Milnsbridge,
Huddersfield HD3 4HS
Tel: 01484 642211 **Fax:** 01484 461002
E-mail: sales@ttsuk.com
Web site: www.ttsuk.com

VOLVO BUS AND COACH CENTRE
Parts Sales & Body Repair/Refurbishment
Specialists
Byron Street Extension, Loughborough LE11 5HE
Tel: 01509 217700
Fax: 01509 238770
E-mail (Body Support): dporter@
volvocoachsales.co.uk
Web site: www.volvo.com

WILKINSONS VEHICLE SOLUTIONS
62 Scalby Avenue, Scarborough
YO12 6HP
Tel: 01262 603307
Fax: 01262 608208
E-mail: info@wilkinsonsvehiclesolutions.co.uk
Web site: www.wilkinsonsvehiclesolutions.co.uk

Brakes and Brake Linings

ARRIVA BUS AND COACH
Lodge Garage, Whitehall Road West, Gomersall,
Cleckheaton, West Yorkshire BD19 4BJ
Tel: 01274 681144
Fax: 01274 651198
E-mail: whiter@arriva.co.uk
Web site: www.arrivabusandcoach.co.uk

ARVIN MERITOR
Park Lane, Great Alne, Alcester, Warwickshire
B49 6HS
Tel: 01789 768270
Web site: www.meritor.com

CAPARO AP BRAKING LTD
Brake House, Tachbrook Road, Leamington Spa
CV31 3SF
Tel: 01926 473737
Fax: 01926 473836
E-mail: sales.enquiries@caparoapbraking.com
Web site: www.caparoapbraking.co.uk

CRESCENT FACILITIES LTD
72 Willow Crescent, Chapeltown, Sheffield
S35 1QS
Tel/Fax: 0114 245 1050
E-mail: cfl.chris@btinternet.com

DIRECT PARTS LTD
Unit 1, Churnet Court, Churnetside Business
Park, Harrison Way, Cheddleton ST13 7EF
Tel: 01538 361777
Fax: 01538 369100
E-mail: sales@direct-group.co.uk
Web site: www.direct-group.co.uk

IMEXPART LTD
Links 31, Willowbridge Way, Whitwood,
Castleford WF10 5NP
Tel: 0845 605 0404
Fax: 01977 513412
E-mail: sales@imexpart.com
Web site: www.imexpart.com

IMPERIAL ENGINEERING
Delamare Road, Cheshunt, Hertfordshire
EN8 9UD
Tel: 01992 634255
Fax: 01992 630506
E-mail: orders@imperialengineering.co.uk
Web site: www.imperialengineering.co.uk

KCP CAR & COMMERCIAL LTD
Unit 15, Hillside Business Park, Kempson Way,
Bury St Edmunds, Suffolk IP32 7EA
Tel: 01284 750777
Fax: 01284 750773
E-mail: info@kcpcarandcommercial.co.uk
Web site: www.kcpcarandcommercial.co.uk

KELLETT (UK) LTD
8 Stevenson Way, Sheffield S9 3WZ
Tel: 0114 261 1122
Fax: 0114 261 1199
E-mail: sales@kellett.co.uk

**KNORR-BREMSE SYSTEMS FOR
COMMERCIAL VEHICLES LTD**
Century House, Folly Brook Road, Emerald Park
East, Emersons Green, Bristol BS16 7FE
Tel: 0117 984 6100
Fax: 0117 984 6101
Web site: www.knorr-bremse.co.uk

NUTEXA FRICTIONS LTD
PO Box 11, New Hall Lane, Hoylake, Wirral
CH47 4BP
Tel: 0151 632 5903
Fax: 0151 632 5908
E-mail: sales@nutexafrictions.co.uk
Web Site: www.sergeant.co.uk

OPTARE PARTS DIVISION (Leeds)
Manston Lane, Leeds LS15 8SU
Tel: 0113 264 5182
Fax: 0113 260 6635
E-mail: parts@optare.com
Web site: www.optare.com

**OPTARE PRODUCT SUPPORT
LONDON**
Unit 9, Eurocourt, Olivers Close, West Thurrock
RM20 3EE
Tel: 01708 896860
Fax: 01708 869920
E-mail: london.service@optare.com

**OPTARE PRODUCT SUPPORT
ROTHERHAM**
Denby Way, Hellaby, Rotherham S66 8HR
Tel: 01709 535100
Fax: 01709 535102
E-mail: rotherham.service@optare.com

PARTLINE LTD
Dockfield Road, Shipley BD17 7AZ
Tel: 01274 531531
Fax: 01274 531088
E-mail: sales@partline.co.uk
Web site: www.partline.co.uk

PLAXTON SERVICE
Ryton Road, Anston, Sheffield S25 4DL
Tel: 01909 551155
Fax: 01909 550050
E-mail: service@plaxtonlimited.co.uk
Web site: www.plaxtonaftercare.co.uk

ROADLINK INTERNATIONAL LTD
Strawberry Lane, Willenhall, West Midlands
WV13 3RL
Tel: 01902 636206
Fax: 01902 631515
E-mail: sales@roadlink-international.co.uk
Web site: www.roadlink-international.co.uk

TMD FRICTION UK LTD
PO Box 18, Hunsworth Lane, Cleckheaton, West
Yorkshire BD19 3UJ
Tel: 01274 854000
Fax: 01274 854001
E-mail: info@tmdfriction.com
Web site: www.tmdfriction.com

TTS UK
Total Tool Solutions Ltd, Newhaven Business
Park, Lowergate, Milnsbridge, Huddersfield
HD3 4HS
Tel: 01484 642211 **Fax:** 01484 461002
E-mail: sales@ttsuk.com
Web site: www.ttsuk.com

WABCO AUTOMOTIVE UK
Texas Street, Leeds LS27 0HQ
Tel: 0113 251 2510
Fax: 0113 251 2844
E-mail: info.uk@wabco-auto.com
Web site: www.wabco-auto.com

Cash Handling Equipment

CUMMINS-ALLISON LTD
William H Klotz House, Colonnade Point, Central
Boulevard, Prologis Park, Coventry CV6 4BU
Tel: 024 7633 9810
Fax: 024 7633 9811
E-mail: sales@cummins-allison.co.uk
Web site: www.cumminsallison.co.uk

ETMSS LTD
Austin House, 43 Poole Road, Westbourne,
Bournemouth BH4 9DN
Tel: 0844 800 9299
E-mail: info@etmss.com
Web Site: www.etmss.com

JOHN GROVES TICKET SYSTEMS
Unit 10, North Circular Business Centre,
400 NCR, London NW10 0JG
Tel: 0208 830 1222
Fax: 0208 830 1223
E-Mail: sales@jgts.co.uk
Web site: www.jgts.co.uk

MARK TERRILL TICKET MACHINERY
5 De Grey Close, Lewes BN7 2JR
Tel: 01273 474816
Fax: 01273 474816
E-mail: mark.terrill@ukonline.co.uk

QUICK CHANGE (UK)
Yew Tree Cottage, Newcastle, Monmouthshire,
NP25 5NT
Tel: 01600 750650
Fax: 01600 750650
E-mail: ttservices@tiscali.co.uk
Web Site: www.ticket-machines.co.uk

SCAN COIN LTD
Dutch House, 110 Broadway, Salford Quays
M50 2UW
Tel: 0161 873 0505
Fax: 0161 873 0501
E-mail: sales@scancoin.co.uk
Web site: www.scancoin.co.uk

THOMAS AUTOMATION LTD
No 3, The Ark Business Centre, Meadow Lane
Industrial Estate, Loughborough LE11 1JP
Tel: 01509 267611
Fax: 0700 600 7749
E-mail: sales@thomasa.co.uk
Web site: www.thomasa.co.uk

TICKETER
Chilton House, Charnham Lane, Hungerford,
Berkshire RG17 0EW
Tel: 0844 800 9299
E-mail: sales@ticketer.co.uk
Web site: www.ticketer.co.uk

Chassis Lubricating Systems

ARRIVA BUS AND COACH
Lodge Garage, Whitehall Road West, Gomersal,
Cleckheaton, West Yorkshire BD19 4BJ
Tel: 01274 681144

⬤ SCAN COIN

AUTOMATED CASH DEPOSITING SYSTEM

Fast and accurate processing of bank notes, coins and transport tokens plus dropsafe for depositing of non-cash items.

Safe, secure and easy to use.

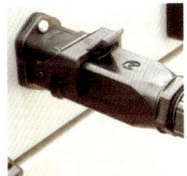
Network capability

Fast coin deposit

High capacity printer

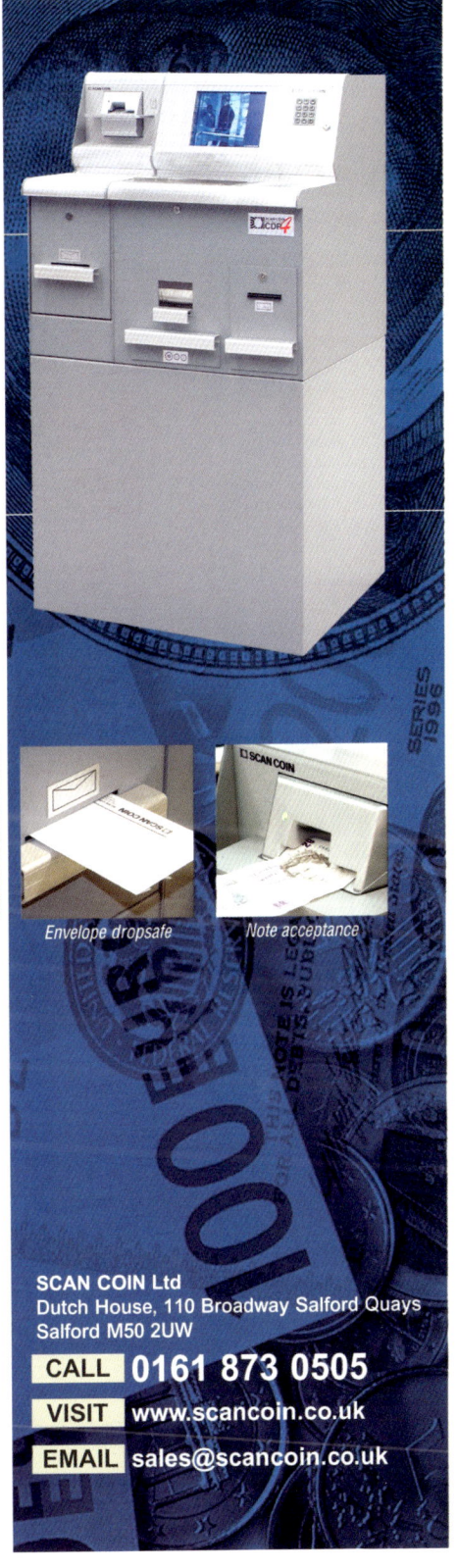
Envelope dropsafe   Note acceptance

- Easy to install, through-the-wall or free-standing
- Front or rear access for changing vaults and for servicing
- Fully customisable user interface
- All totals displayed on-screen
- Multiple coin acceptance and value counting
- Bank notes accepted in any direction
- Vehicle defect reporting
- Exchange rates can be programmed into the system
- Wide range of additional software available

SCAN COIN Ltd
Dutch House, 110 Broadway Salford Quays
Salford M50 2UW

CALL 0161 873 0505
VISIT www.scancoin.co.uk
EMAIL sales@scancoin.co.uk

Fax: 01274 651198
E-mail: whiter@arriva.co.uk
Web site: www.arrivabusandcoach.co.uk

GROENEVELD UK LTD
The Greentec Centre, Gelders Hall Road,
Shepshed, Leicestershire LE12 9NH
Tel: 01509 600033
Fax: 01509 602000
E-mail: info@groeneveld.co.uk
Web site: www.groeneveld.co.uk

PLAXTON SERVICE
Ryton Road, Anston, Sheffield S25 4DL
Tel: 01909 551155
Fax: 01909 550050
E-mail: service@plaxtonlimited.co.uk
Web site: www.plaxtonaftercare.co.uk

Clutches

ARRIVA BUS AND COACH
Lodge Garage, Whitehall Road West, Gomersal,
Cleckheaton, West Yorkshire BD19 4BJ
Tel: 01274 681144
Fax: 01274 651198
E-mail: whiter@arriva.co.uk
Web site: www.arrivabusandcoach.co.uk

CAPARO AP BRAKING LTD
Tachbrook Road, Leamington Spa CV31 3ER.
Tel: 01926 473737
Fax: 01926 473836
E-mail: sales@caparoapbraking.com
Web site: www.caparoapbraking.com

COACH-AID
Unit 2, Brindley Close, Tollgate Industrial Estate,
Stafford ST16 3SU
Tel: 01785 222666
E-mail: workshop@coach-aid.com
Web site: www.coach-aid.com

IMEXPART LTD
Links 31, Willowbridge Way, Whitwood,
Castleford WF10 5NP
Tel: 0845 605 0404 **Fax:** 01977 513412
E-mail: sales@imexpart.com
Web site: www.imexpart.com

KCP CAR & COMMERCIAL LTD
Unit 15, Hillside Business Park, Kempson Way,
Bury St Edmunds, Suffolk IP32 7EA
Tel: 01284 750777
Fax: 01284 750773
E-mail: info@kcpcarandcommercial.co.uk
Web site: www.kcpcarandcommercial.co.uk

KELLETT (UK) LTD
8 Stevenson Way, Sheffield S9 3WZ
Tel: 0114 261 1122
Fax: 0114 261 1199
E-mail: sales@kellett.co.uk

NUTEXA FRICTIONS LTD
PO Box 11, New Hall Lane, Hoylake, Wirral
CH47 4DH
Tel: 0151 632 5903
Fax: 0151 632 5908
E-mail: sales@nutexafrictions.co.uk
Web Site: www.sergeant.co.uk

OPTARE PARTS DIVISION (Leeds)
Manston Lane, Leeds LS15 8SU
Tel: 0113 264 5182

Fax: 0113 260 6635
E-mail: parts@optare.com
Web site: www.optare.com

**OPTARE PRODUCT SUPPORT
LONDON**
Unit 9, Eurocourt, Olivers Close,
West Thurrock RM20 3EE
Tel: 01708 896860
Fax: 01708 869920
E-mail: london.service@optare.com

**OPTARE PRODUCT SUPPORT
ROTHERHAM**
Denby Way, Hellaby, Rotherham S66 8HR
Tel: 01709 535100
Fax: 01709 535102
E-mail: rotherham.service@optare.com

PARTLINE LTD
Dockfield Road, Shipley BD17 7AZ
Tel: 01274 531531
Fax: 01274 531088
E-mail: sales@partline.co.uk
Web site: www.partline.co.uk

PLAXTON SERVICE
Ryton Road, Anston, Sheffield
S25 4DL
Tel: 01909 551155
Fax: 01909 550050
E-mail: service@plaxtonlimited.co.uk
Web site: www.plaxtonaftercare.co.uk

SHAWSON SUPPLY LTD
12 Station Road, Saintfield, County Down,
Northern Ireland BT24 7DU
Tel: 028 9751 0994
Fax: 028 9751 0816
E-mail: info@shawsonsupply.com
Web site: www.shawsonsupply.com

Cooling Systems

ARRIVA BUS AND COACH
Lodge Garage, Whitehall Road West, Gomersal,
Cleckheaton, West Yorkshire BD19 4BJ
Tel: 01274 681144
Fax: 01274 651198
E-mail: whiter@arriva.co.uk
Web site: www.arrivabusandcoach.co.uk

CLAYTON HEATERS LTD
Hunter Terrace, Fletchworth Gate, Burnsall Road,
Coventry CV5 6SP
Tel: 02476 691916
Fax: 02476 691969
E-mail: admin@claytoncc.co.uk
Web Site: www.claytoncc.co.uk

DIRECT PARTS LTD
Unit 1, Churnet Court, Churnetside Business
Park, Harrison Way, Cheddleton ST13 7EF
Tel: 01538 361777
Fax: 01538 369100
E-mail: sales@direct-group.co.uk
Web site: www.direct-group.co.uk

KCP CAR & COMMERCIAL LTD
Unit 15, Hillside Business Park, Kempson Way,
Bury St Edmunds, Suffolk IP32 7EA
Tel: 01284 750777
Fax: 01284 750773
E-mail: info@kcpcarandcommercial.co.uk
Web site: www.kcpcarandcommercial.co.uk

**OPTARE PRODUCT SUPPORT
LONDON**
Unit 9, Eurocourt, Olivers Close, West Thurrock
RM20 3EE
Tel: 01708 896860
Fax: 01708 869920
E-mail: london.service@optare.com

**OPTARE PRODUCT SUPPORT
ROTHERHAM**
Denby Way, Hellaby, Rotherham S66 8HR
Tel: 01709 535100
Fax: 01709 535102
E-mail: rotherham.service@optare.com

PACET MANUFACTURING LTD
Wyebridge House, Cores End Road, Bourne End,
Buckinghamshire SL8 5HH
Tel: 01628 526754
Fax: 01628 810080
E-mail: sales@pacet.co.uk
Web site: www.pacet.co.uk

PARTLINE LTD
Dockfield Road, Shipley BD17 7AZ
Tel: 01274 531531
Fax: 01274 531088
E-mail: sales@partline.co.uk
Web site: www.partline.co.uk

PLAXTON SERVICE
Ryton Road, Anston, Sheffield S25 4DL
Tel: 01909 551155
Fax: 01909 550050
E-mail: service@plaxtonlimited.co.uk
Web site: www.plaxtonaftercare.co.uk

SILFLEX LTD
Coed Cae Lane Industrial Estate, Pontyclun
CF72 9HJ
Tel: 01443 238464 **Fax:** 01443 237781
E-mail: silflex@silflex.com
Web site: www.silflex.com

Destination Indicator Equipment

ARRIVA BUS AND COACH
Lodge Garage, Whitehall Road West, Gomersal,
Cleckheaton, West Yorkshire BD19 4BJ
Tel: 01274 681144
Fax: 01274 651198
E-mail: whiter@arriva.co.uk
Web site: www.arrivabusandcoach.co.uk

HANOVER DISPLAYS LTD
Unit 24, Cliffe Industrial Estate, Lewes BN8 6JL
Tel: 01273 477528
Fax: 01273 407766
E-mail: sales@hanoverdisplays.com
Web site: www.hanoverdisplays.com

INDICATORS INTERNATIONAL LTD
41 Aughrim Road, Magherafelt, Northern Ireland
BT45 6JX
Tel: 028 7963 2591 **Fax:** 028 7963 3927
E-mail: sales@indicators-int.com
Web site: www.indicators-int.com

INVERTEC LTD
Whelford Road, Fairford GL7 4DT
Tel: 01285 713550
Fax: 01285 713548
Mobile: 07802 793828
E-mail: sales@invertec.co.uk
Web site: www.invertec.co.uk

McKENNA BROTHERS LTD
McKenna House, Jubilee Road, Middleton,
Manchester M24 2LX
Tel: 0161 655 3244
Fax: 0161 655 3059
E-mail: info@mckennabrothers.co.uk
Web site: www.mckennabrothers.co.uk

NORBURY BLINDS LTD
41-45 Hanley Street, Newtown, Birmingham
B19 3SP
Tel: 0121 359 4311
Fax: 0121 359 6388
E-mail: info@norbury-blinds.com
Web site: www.norbury-blinds.com

PERCY LANE PRODUCTS LTD
Lichfield Road, Tamworth B79 7TL
Tel: 01827 63821
Fax: 01827 310159
E-mail: sales@percy-lane.com
Web site: www.percy-lane.com

PLAXTON SERVICE
Ryton Road, Anston, Sheffield S25 4DL
Tel: 01909 551155
Fax: 01909 550050
E-mail: service@plaxtonlimited.co.uk
Web site: www.plaxtonaftercare.co.uk

VULTRON INTERNATIONAL LTD
Unit 2 Stadium Way, Elland Road, Leeds
LS11 0EW
Tel: 0113 387 7310
Fax: 0113 387 7317
E-mail: sales@vultron.co.uk
Web site: www.vultron.co.uk

Door Operating Gear

AIR DOOR SERVICES
The Pavilions, Holly Lane Industrial Estate,
Atherstone CV9 2QZ
Tel: 01827 711660
Fax: 01827 713577
E-mail: airdoorservices@aol.com

ARRIVA BUS AND COACH
Lodge Garage, Whitehall Road West, Gomersal,
Cleckheaton, West Yorkshire BD19 4BJ
Tel: 01274 681144
Fax: 01274 651198
E-mail: whiter@arriva.co.uk
Web site: www.arrivabusandcoach.co.uk

CARLYLE BUS & COACH LTD
Carlyle Business Park, Great Bridge Street, Swan
Village, West Bromwich B70 0X4
Tel: 0121 524 1200
Fax: 0121 524 1201
E-mail: admin@carlyleplc.co.uk
Web Site: www.carlyleplc.co.uk

DEANS SYSTEMS (UK) LTD
PO Box 8, Borwick Drive, Grovehill, Beverley
HU17 0HQ
Tel: 01482 868111
Fax: 01482 881890
E-mail: customerservice@deanssystems.com
Web Site: www.doorsystemsgroup.com

EXPRESS COACH REPAIRS LTD
Outgang Lane, Pickering YO18 7JA
Tel: 01751 475215
Fax: 01751 475215

E-mail: info@expresscoachrepairs.co.uk
Web site: www.expresscoachrepairs.co.uk

KCP CAR & COMMERCIAL LTD
Unit 15, Hillside Business Park, Kempson Way,
Bury St Edmunds, Suffolk IP32 7EA
Tel: 01284 750777
Fax: 01284 750773
E-mail: info@kcpcarandcommercial.co.uk
Web site: www.kcpcarandcommercial.co.uk

KELLETT (UK) LTD
8 Stevenson Way, Sheffield S9 3WZ
Tel: 0114 261 1122
Fax: 0114 261 1199
E-mail: sales@kellett.co.uk

KARIVE LIMITED
PO Box 205, Southam, Warwickshire CV47 0ZL
Tel: 03333 446700
Fax: 01926 814898
E-mail: info@karive.co.uk
Web site: www.karive.co.uk

**KNORR-BREMSE SYSTEMS FOR
COMMERCIAL VEHICLES LTD**
Century House, Folly Brook Road, Emerald Park
East, Emersons Green, Bristol BS16 7FE
Tel: 0117 984 6100
Fax: 0117 984 6101
Web site: www.knorr-bremse.co.uk

LAWTON SERVICES LTD
Knutsford Road, Church Lawton, Stoke-on-Trent
ST7 3DN
Tel: 01270 882056
Fax: 01270 883014
E-mail: andrea@lawtonservices.co.uk
Web site: www.lawtonservices.co.uk

OPTARE PARTS DIVISION (Leeds)
Manston Lane, Leeds LS15 8SU
Tel: 0113 264 5182
Fax: 0113 260 6635
E-mail: parts@optare.com
Web site: www.optare.com

**OPTARE PRODUCT SUPPORT
LONDON**
Unit 9, Eurocourt, Olivers Close, West Thurrock
RM20 3EE
Tel: 01708 896860
Fax: 01708 869920
E-mail: london.service@optare.com

**OPTARE PRODUCT SUPPORT
ROTHERHAM**
Denby Way, Hellaby, Rotherham S66 8HR
Tel: 01709 535100
Fax: 01709 535102
E-mail: rotherham.service@optare.com

PARTLINE LTD
Dockfield Road, Shipley BD17 7AZ
Tel: 01274 531531
Fax: 01274 531088
E-mail: sales@partline.co.uk
Web site: www.partline.co.uk

PETERS DOOR SYSTEMS (UK) LTD
Bradbury Drive, Springwood Industrial Estate,
Braintree CM7 2ET
Tel: 01376 555255
Fax: 01376 555292
E-mail: sales@petersdoors.co.uk

PLAXTON PARTS
Ryton Road, Anston, Sheffield S25 4DL
Tel: 0844 822 6224
Fax: 01909 550050
E-mail: parts@plaxtonlimited.co.uk
Web site: www.plaxtonaftercare.co.uk

PLAXTON SERVICE
Ryton Road, Anston, Sheffield S25 4DL
Tel: 01909 551155
Fax: 01909 550050
E-mail: service@plaxtonlimited.co.uk
Web site: www.plaxtonaftercare.co.uk

PNEUMAX LTD
110 Vista Park, Mauretania Road, Nursling,
Southampton SO16 0YS
Tel: 02380 740412
Fax: 02380 739340
E-mail: sales@pneumax.co.uk
Web site: www.pneumax.co.uk

TRANSPORT DOOR SOLUTIONS LTD
43 Broton Drive, Halstead, Essex CO9 1HB
Tel: 01787 473000
Fax: 01787 477040
E-mail: sales@transportdoorsolutions.co.uk
Web site: www.transportdoorsolutions.co.uk

VAPOR-STONE UK LTD
Derwent House, RTC Business Park, London
Road, Derby DE24 8UP
Tel: 01332 228901
Fax: 01332 228909
Web site: www.wabtec.com

WABCO AUTOMOTIVE UK LTD
Texas Street, Morley LS27 0HQ.
Tel: 0113 251 2510
Fax: 0113 251 2844
E-mail: info.uk@wabco-auto.com
Web site: www.wabco-auto.com

Drinks Dispensing Equipment

ARRIVA BUS AND COACH
Lodge Garage, Whitehall Road West, Gomersal,
Cleckheaton, West Yorkshire BD19 4BJ
Tel: 01274 681144
Fax: 01274 651198
E-mail: whiter@arriva.co.uk
Web site: www.arrivabusandcoach.co.uk

BRADTECH LTD
Unit 3, Ladford Covert, Seighford, Stafford
ST18 9QL
Tel: 01785 282800
Fax: 01785 282558
E-mail: sales@bradtech.ltd.uk
Web site: www.bradtech.ltd.uk

DRINKMASTER LTD
Drinkpac House, Plymouth Road, Liskeard
PL14 3PG
Tel: 01579 342082
Fax: 01579 342591
E-mail: info@drinkmaster.co.uk
Web site: www.drinkmaster.co.uk

ELSAN LTD
Bellbrook Park, Uckfield, East Sussex TN22 1QF
Tel: 01825 748200
Fax: 01825 761212
E-mail: sales@elsan.co.uk
Web site: www.elsan.co.uk

EXPRESS COACH REPAIRS LTD
Outgang Lane, Pickering YO18 7JA
Tel: 01751 475215
Fax: 01751 475215
E-mail: info@expresscoachrepairs.co.uk
Web site: www.expresscoachrepairs.co.uk

LAWTON SERVICES LTD
Knutsford Road, Church Lawton, Stoke-on-Trent
ST7 3DN
Tel: 01270 882056
Fax: 01270 883014
E-mail: andrea@lawtonservices.co.uk
Web site: www.lawtonservices.co.uk

PLAXTON PARTS
Ryton Road, Anston, Sheffield S25 4DL
Tel: 0844 822 6224
Fax: 01909 550050
E-mail: parts@plaxtonlimited.co.uk
Web site: www.plaxtonaftercare.co.uk

PLAXTON SERVICE
Ryton Road, Anston, Sheffield S25 4DL
Tel: 01909 551155
Fax: 01909 550050
E-mail: service@plaxtonlimited.co.uk
Web site: www.plaxtonaftercare.co.uk

PSV PRODUCTS
The Red House, Underbridge Lane,
Higher Walton, Warrington WA4 5QR
Tel: 01925 210220
Fax: 01925 601534
E-mail: info@psvproducts.com
Web site: www.psvproducts.com

SHADES TECHNICS LTD
Units E3 & E4, Rd Park, Stephenson Close,
Hoddesdon, Hertfordshire EN11 0BW
Tel: 01992 476830
Fax: 01992 476831
E-mail: sales@shades-technics.com
Web site: www.shades-technics.com

TRAMONTANA
Chapelknowe Road, Carfin, Motherwell ML1 5LE
Tel: 01698 861790
Fax: 01698 860778
E-mail: wdt90@tiscali.co.uk
Web site: www.brittnet.net/tramontanacoach

Driving Axles & Gears

ALBION AUTOMOTIVE LTD
1187 South Street, Scotstoun, Glasgow
G14 0DT
Tel: 0141 434 2400
Fax: 0141 959 6362
E-mail: sales@albion_auto.co.uk
Web site: www.albion_auto.co.uk

ARRIVA BUS AND COACH
Lodge Garage, Whitehall Road West, Gomersal,
Cleckheaton, West Yorkshire BD19 4BJ
Tel: 01274 681144
Fax: 01274 651198
E-mail: whiter@arriva.co.uk
Web site: www.arrivabusandcoach.co.uk

ARVIN MERITOR
Park Lane, Great Alne, Alcester, Warwickshire
B49 6HS
Tel: 01789 768270
Web site: www.meritor.com

DIRECT PARTS LTD
Unit 1, Churnet Court, Churnetside Business
Park, Harrison Way, Cheddleton ST13 7EF
Tel: 01538 361777
Fax: 01538 369100
E-mail: sales@direct-group.co.uk
Web site: www.direct-group.co.uk

HL SMITH TRANSMISSIONS LTD
Enterprise Business Park, Cross Road, Albrighton,
Wolverhampton WV7 3BJ
Tel: 01902 373011
Fax: 01902 373608
Web site: www.hlsmith.co.uk

KCP CAR & COMMERCIAL LTD
Unit 15, Hillside Business Park, Kempson Way,
Bury St Edmunds, Suffolk IP32 7EA
Tel: 01284 750777
Fax: 01284 750773
E-mail: info@kcpcarandcommercial.co.uk
Web site: www.kcpcarandcommercial.co.uk

LH GROUP SERVICES LTD
Graycar Business Park, Barton under Needwood,
Burton-on-Trent DE13 8EN
Tel: 01283 722600 **Fax:** 01283 722622
E-mail: lh@lh-group.com
Web site: www.lh-group.com

OPTARE PARTS DIVISION (Leeds)
Manston Lane, Leeds LS15 8SU
Tel: 0113 264 5182
Fax: 0113 260 6635
E-mail: parts@optare.com
Web site: www.optare.com

PARTLINE LTD
Dockfield Road, Shipley BD17 7AZ
Tel: 01274 531531
Fax: 01274 531088
E-mail: sales@partline.co.uk
Web site: www.partline.co.uk

PLAXTON SERVICE
Ryton Road, Anston, Sheffield S25 4DL
Tel: 01909 551155
Fax: 01909 550050
E-mail: service@plaxtonlimited.co.uk
Web site: www.plaxtonaftercare.co.uk

TTS UK
Total Tool Solutions Ltd, Newhaven Business
Park, Lowergate, Milnsbridge, Huddersfield
HD3 4HS
Tel: 01484 642211 **Fax:** 01484 461002
E-mail: sales@ttsuk.com
Web site: www.ttsuk.com

ZF POWERTRAIN
Stringes Close, Willenhall WV13 1LE
Tel: 01902 366000
Fax: 01902 366504
E-mail: sales@powertrain.org.uk
Web site: www.powertrain.org.uk

Electrical Equipment

ARRIVA BUS AND COACH
Lodge Garage, Whitehall Road West, Gomersal,
Cleckheaton, West Yorkshire BD19 4BJ
Tel: 01274 681144
Fax: 01274 651198
E-mail: whiter@arriva.co.uk
Web site: www.arrivabusandcoach.co.uk

AUTOSOUND LTD
4 Lister Street, Dudley Hill, Bradford BD4 9PQ
Tel: 01274 688990
Fax: 01274 651318
E-mail: keith.ellis@autosound.co.uk
Web site: www.autosound.co.uk

AVT SYSTEMS LTD
Units 3 & 4 Tything Road East, Alcester,
Warwickshire B49 6ES
Tel: 01789 400357
Fax: 01789 400359
E-mail: enquires@avtsystems.co.uk
Web site: www.avtsystems.co.uk

BRADTECH LTD
Unit 3, Ladford Covert, Seighford, Stafford
ST18 9QL
Tel: 01785 282800
Fax: 01785 282558
E-mail: sales@bradtech.ltd.uk
Web site: www.bradtech.ltd.uk

CAREYBROOK LTD
PO Box 205, Southam, Warwickshire
CV47 0ZL
Tel: 03333 446800
Fax: 01926 814898
E-mail: info@careybrook.co.uk
Web site: www.careybrook.com

CARLYLE BUS & COACH LTD
Carlyle Business Park, Great Bridge Street,
Swan Village, West Bromwich B70 0X4
Tel: 0121 524 1200
Fax: 0121 524 1201
E-mail: admin@carlyleplc.co.uk
Web site: www.carlyleplc.co.uk

CRESCENT FACILITIES LTD
72 Willow Crescent, Chapeltown,
Sheffield S35 1QS
Tel/Fax: 0114 245 1050
E-mail: cfl.chris@btinternet.com

DIRECT PARTS LTD
Unit 1, Churnet Court, Churnetside Business
Park, Harrison Way, Cheddleton ST13 7EF
Tel: 01538 361777
Fax: 01538 369100
E-mail: sales@direct-group.co.uk
Web site: www.direct-group.co.uk

EXPRESS COACH REPAIRS LTD
Outgang Lane, Pickering YO18 7JA
Tel: 01751 475215
Fax: 01751 475215
E-mail: info@expresscoachrepairs.co.uk
Web site: www.expresscoachrepairs.co.uk

INTELLITEC MV LTD
Unit 9, Woodway Court, Thursby Road,
Bromborough, Wirral CH62 3PR
Tel: 0151 482 8171
Fax: 0151 482 8977
E-mail: sales@intellitecmv.co.uk
Web site: www.intellitecmv.co.uk

INVERTEC LTD
Whelford Road, Fairford GL7 4DT
Tel: 01285 713550
Fax: 01285 713548
Mobile: 07802 793828
E-mail: ian@invertec.co.uk
Web site: www.invertec.co.uk

KCP CAR & COMMERCIAL LTD
Unit 15, Hillside Business Park, Kempson Way,
Bury St Edmunds, Suffolk IP32 7EA
Tel: 01284 750777
Fax: 01284 750773
E-mail: info@kcpcarandcommercial.co.uk
Web site: www.kcpcarandcommercial.co.uk

NEALINE WINDSCREEN WIPER PRODUCTS
Unit 1, The Sidings Industrial Estate, Birdingbury
Road, Marton CV23 9RX
Tel: 01926 633256
Fax: 01926 632600

OPTARE PARTS DIVISION (Leeds)
Manston Lane, Leeds LS15 8SU
Tel: 0113 264 5182
Fax: 0113 260 6635
E-mail: parts@optare.com
Web site: www.optare.com

PARTLINE LTD
Dockfield Road, Shipley BD17 7AZ
Tel: 01274 531531 **Fax:** 01274 531088
E-mail: sales@partline.co.uk
Web site: www.partline.co.uk

PLAXTON PARTS
Ryton Road, Anston, Sheffield S25 4DL
Tel: 0844 822 6224
Fax: 01909 550050
E-mail: parts@plaxtonlimited.co.uk
Web site: www.plaxtonaftercare.co.uk

PLAXTON SERVICE
Ryton Road, Anston, Sheffield S25 4DL
Tel: 01909 551155
Fax: 01909 550050
E-mail: service@plaxtonlimited.co.uk
Web site: www.plaxtonaftercare.co.uk

PNEUMAX LTD
110 Vista Park, Mauretania Road, Nursling,
Southampton SO16 0YS
Tel: 02380 740412
Fax: 02380 739340
E-mail: sales@pneumax.co.uk
Web site: www.pneumax.co.uk

PRESTOLITE ELECTRIC
Unit 48, The Metropolitan Park, 12-16 Bristol
Road, Greenford, Middlesex UB6 8UP
Tel: 020 8231 1137
Fax: 020 8575 9575
E-mail: eu_info@prestolite.com
Web site: www.prestolite.com

Electronic Control

ACTIA UK LTD
Unit 81, Mochdre Industrial Estate, Newtown
SY16 4LE
Tel: 01686 611150
Fax: 01686 621068
E-mail: mail@actia.co.uk
Web site: www.actia.co.uk

ARRIVA BUS AND COACH
Lodge Garage, Whitehall Road West, Gomersal,
Cleckheaton, West Yorkshire BD19 4BJ
Tel: 01274 681144
Fax: 01274 651198
E-mail: whiter@arriva.co.uk
Web site: www.arrivabusandcoach.co.uk

CRESCENT FACILITIES LTD
72 Willow Crescent, Chapeltown,
Sheffield S35 1QS
Tel/Fax: 0114 245 1050
E-mail: cfl.chris@btinternet.com
Web site: www.cflparts.com

INTELLITEC MV LTD
Unit 9, Woodway Court, Thursby Road,
Bromborough, Wirral CH62 3PR
Tel: 0151 482 8171
Fax: 0151 482 8977
E-mail: sales@intellitecmv.co.uk
Web site: www.intellitecmv.co.uk

KCP CAR & COMMERCIAL LTD
Unit 15, Hillside Business Park, Kempson Way,
Bury St Edmunds, Suffolk IP32 7EA
Tel: 01284 750777
Fax: 01284 750773
E-mail: info@kcpcarandcommercial.co.uk
Web site: www.kcpcarandcommercial.co.uk

KNORR-BREMSE SYSTEMS FOR COMMERCIAL VEHICLES LTD
Century House, Folly Brook Road, Emerald Park
East, Emersons Green, Bristol BS16 7FE
Tel: 0117 984 6100
Fax: 0117 984 6101
Web site: www.knorr-bremse.co.uk

OPTARE PARTS DIVISION (Leeds)
Manston Lane, Leeds LS15 8SU
Tel: 0113 264 5182
Fax: 0113 260 6635
E-mail: parts@optare.com
Web site: www.optare.com

PLAXTON PARTS
Ryton Road, Anston, Sheffield S25 4DL
Tel: 0844 822 6224 **Fax:** 01909 550050
E-mail: parts@plaxtonlimited.co.uk
Web site: www.plaxtonaftercare.co.uk

PLAXTON SERVICE
Ryton Road, Anston, Sheffield S25 4DL
Tel: 01909 551155
Fax: 01909 550050
E-mail: service@plaxtonlimited.co.uk
Web site: www.plaxtonaftercare.co.uk

WABCO AUTOMOTIVE UK
Texas Street, Morley LS27 0HQ.
Tel: 0113 251 2510
Fax: 0113 251 2844
E-mail: info.uk@wabco-auto.com
Web site: www.wabco-auto.com

Emission Control Devices

ARRIVA BUS AND COACH
Lodge Garage, Whitehall Road West, Gomersal,
Cleckheaton, West Yorkshire BD19 4BJ
Tel: 01274 681144
Fax: 01274 651198
E-mail: whiter@arriva.co.uk
Web site: www.arrivabusandcoach.co.uk

CUMMINS UK
40-44 Rutherford Drive, Park Farm South,
Wellingborough NN8 6AN
Tel: 01933 334200
Fax: 01933 334198
E-mail: cduksales@cummins.com
Web site: www.cummins-uk.com

DINEX EXHAUSTS LTD
14 Chesford Grange, Woolston, Warrington
WA1 3BT
Tel: 01925 849849
Fax: 01925 849850
E-mail: dinex@dinex.co.uk

EMISSION CONTROL LIMITED
Global Works, 1/6 Crescent Mews
(off Crescent Road), London N22 7GG
Tel: 020 8888 4982 **Fax:** 020 8881 1353
E-mail: info@emissioncontroluk.com
Web site: www.emissioncontroluk.com

KCP CAR & COMMERCIAL LTD
Unit 15, Hillside Business Park, Kempson Way,
Bury St Edmunds, Suffolk IP32 7EA
Tel: 01284 750777
Fax: 01284 750773
E-mail: info@kcpcarandcommercial.co.uk
Web site: www.kcpcarandcommercial.co.uk

OPTARE PARTS DIVISION (Leeds)
Manston Lane, Leeds LS15 8SU
Tel: 0113 264 5182 **Fax:** 0113 260 6635
E-mail: parts@optare.com
Web site: www.optare.com

PLAXTON SERVICE
Ryton Road, Anston, Sheffield S25 4DL
Tel: 01909 551155
Fax: 01909 550050
E-mail: service@plaxtonlimited.co.uk
Web site: www.plaxtonaftercare.co.uk

Engineering

ARRIVA BUS AND COACH
Lodge Garage, Whitehall Road West, Gomersal,
Cleckheaton, West Yorkshire BD19 4BJ
Tel: 01274 681144
Fax: 01274 651198
E-mail: whiter@arriva.co.uk
Web site: www.arrivabusandcoach.co.uk

BRITCOM INTERNATIONAL LTD
York Road, Market Weighton, East Yorkshire
YO43 3QX
Tel: 01430 871010 **Fax:** 01430 872492
E-mail: sales@britcom.co.uk
Web site: www.britcom.co.uk

BULWARK BUS & COACH ENGINEERING LTD
Unit 5, Bulwark Business Park, Bulwark, Chepstow
NP16 6QZ
Tel: 01291 622326
Fax: 01291 622726
E-mail: bulwarkbusandcoach@tiscali.co.uk
Web site: www.bulwarkbusandcoach.co.uk

COACH-AID
Unit 2, Brindley Close, Tollgate Industrial Estate,
Stafford ST16 3sU
Tel: 01785 222666
E-mail: workshop@coach-aid.com
Web site: www.coach-aid.com

CUMMINS UK
40-44 Rutherford Drive, Park Farm South,
Wellingborough NN8 6AN
Tel: 01933 334200
Fax: 01933 334198
E-mail: cduksales@cummins.com
Web site: www.cummins-uk.com

DIRECT PARTS LTD
Unit 1, Churnet Court, Churnetside Business
Park, Harrison Way, Cheddleton ST13 7EF
Tel: 01538 361777
Fax: 01538 369100
E-mail: sales@direct-group.co.uk
Web site: www.direct-group.co.uk

FTA VEHICLE INSPECTION SERVICE
Hermes House, St John's Road, Tunbridge Wells
TN4 9UZ
Tel: 01892 526171
Fax: 01892 534989
E-mail: enquiries@fta.co.uk
Web site: www.fta.co.uk

THOMAS HARDIE COMMERCIALS LTD
Newstet Road, Knowsley Industrial Park,
Liverpool L33 7TJ
Tel: 0151 549 3000
E-mail: info@thardie.co.uk

HART BROTHERS (ENGINEERING) LTD
Soho Works, Soho Street, Oldham OL4 2AD
Tel: 0161 737 6791

HILTech DEVELOPMENTS LTD
e-volve Business Centre, Cygnet Way, Rainton
Bridge South Business Park, Houghton le Spring,
Durham DH4 5QY
Tel: 0191 305 5094
Fax: 0191 488 9158
E-mail: executive@hiltechdevelopments.com
Web site: www.hiltechdevelopments.com

IMPERIAL ENGINEERING
Delamare Road, Cheshunt, Hertfordshire
EN8 9UD
Tel: 01992 634255
Fax: 01992 630506
E-mail: orders@imperialengineering.co.uk
Web site: www.imperialengineering.co.uk

JBF SERVICES LTD
Southedge Works, Hipperholme, Halifax HX3 8EF
Tel: 01422 202840
Fax: 01422 206070
E-mail: jbfservices@aol.com

KCP CAR & COMMERCIAL LTD
Unit 15, Hillside Business Park, Kempson Way,
Bury St Edmunds, Suffolk IP32 7EA
Tel: 01284 750777
Fax: 01284 750773
E-mail: info@kcpcarandcommercial.co.uk
Web site: www.kcpcarandcommercial.co.uk

**LEYLAND PRODUCT
DEVELOPMENTS LTD**
Croston Road, Leyland, Preston PR26 6LZ
Tel: 01772 621400
Web site: www.leylandtrucksltd.co.uk

LH GROUP SERVICES LTD
Graycar Business Park, Barton under Needwood,
Burton-on-Trent DE13 8EN
Tel: 01283 722600
Fax: 01283 722622
E-mail: lh@lh-group.com
Web site: www.lh-group.com

MARSHALLS COACHES LLP
Firbank Way, Leighton Buzzard LU7 3BD
Tel: 01525 376077
Fax: 01525 850967

Total Tool Solutions Limited
Newhaven Business Park
Lowergate
Milnsbridge
Huddersfield
HD3 4HS
T: 01484 642211
F: 01484 461002
E: sales@ttsuk.com
W: www.ttsuk.com

E-mail: info@marshalls-coaches.co.uk
Web site: www.marshalls-coaches.co.uk

MASS SPECIAL ENGINEERING LTD
Houghton Road, North Anston, Sheffield S25 4JJ
Tel: 01909 550480
Fax: 01909 550486

OPTARE PARTS DIVISION (Leeds)
Manston Lane, Leeds LS15 8SU
Tel: 0113 264 5182
Fax: 0113 260 6635
E-mail: parts@optare.com
Web site: www.optare.com

**OPTARE PRODUCT SUPPORT
LONDON**
Unit 9, Eurocourt, Olivers Close, West Thurrock
RM20 3EE
Tel: 01708 896860 **Fax:** 01708 869920
E-mail: london.service@optare.com

**OPTARE PRODUCT SUPPORT
ROTHERHAM**
Denby Way, Hellaby, Rotherham S66 8HR
Tel: 01709 535100
Fax: 01709 535102
E-mail: rotherham.service@optare.com

PLAXTON SERVICE
Ryton Road, North Anston, Sheffield S25 4DL
Tel: 01909 551155
Fax: 01909 550050
E-mail: service@plaxtonlimited.co.uk
Web site: www.plaxtonaftercare.co.uk

PNEUMAX LTD
110 Vista Park, Mauretania Road, Nursling,
Southampton SO16 0YS
Tel: 02380 740412 **Fax:** 02380 739340
E-mail: sales@pneumax.co.uk
Web site: www.pneumax.co.uk

QUEENSBRIDGE (PSV) LTD
Milner Way, Longlands Industrial Estate, Ossett
WF5 9JE
Tel: 01924 281871
Fax: 01924 281807
E-mail: enquiries@queensbridgeltd.co.uk
Web site: www.queensbridgeltd.co.uk

**TRANSPORT DESIGN
INTERNATIONAL**
Clifford Mill, Stratford upon Avon CV37 8HW
Tel: 01789 205011
Fax: 05603 133119

E-mail: enquiries@tdi.uk.com
Web site: www.tdi.uk.com

TTS UK
Total Tool Solutions Ltd, Newhaven Business
Park, Lowergate, Milnsbridge, Huddersfield
HD3 4HS
Tel: 01484 642211 **Fax:** 01484 461002
E-mail: sales@ttsuk.com
Web site: www.ttsuk.com

Engines

ARRIVA BUS AND COACH
Lodge Garage, Whitehall Road West, Gomersal,
Cleckheaton, West Yorkshire BD19 4BJ
Tel: 01274 681144
Fax: 01274 651198
E-mail: whiter@arriva.co.uk
Web site: www.arrivabusandcoach.co.uk

CREWE ENGINES
Warmingham Road, Crewe CW1 4PQ
Tel: 01270 526333
Fax: 01270 526433
E-mail: sales@creweengines.co.uk
Web site: www.creweengines.co.uk

CUMMINS UK
40-44 Rutherford Drive, Park Farm South,
Wellingborough NN8 6AN
Tel: 01933 334200
Fax: 01933 334198
E-mail: cduksales@cummins.com
Web site: www.cummins-uk.com

DAF COMPONENTS LTD
Eastern Bypass, Thame OX9 3FB
Tel: 01844 261111
Fax: 01844 217111
Web site: www.daftrucks.com

FUEL THEFT SOLUTIONS LTD
PO Box 2494, Stoke-on-Trent ST7 2WR
Tel: 0845 077 3921
Fax: 0845 077 3922
E-mail: sales@dieseldye.com
Web site: www.dieseldye.com

IMEXPART LTD
Links 31, Willowbridge Way, Whitwood,
Castleford WF10 5NP
Tel: 0845 605 0404
Fax: 01977 513412
E-mail: sales@imexpart.com
Web site: www.imexpart.com

The Little Red Book 2012 - in association with Transport Benevolent Fund

IVECO
Iveco Ford Truck Ltd, Iveco Ford House, Station Road, Watford WD1 1SR
Tel: 01923 246400
Fax: 01923 240574

KCP CAR & COMMERCIAL LTD
Unit 15, Hillside Business Park, Kempson Way, Bury St Edmunds, Suffolk IP32 7EA
Tel: 01284 750777
Fax: 01284 750773
E-mail: info@kcpcarandcommercial.co.uk
Web site: www.kcpcarandcommercial.co.uk

LH GROUP SERVICES LTD
Graycar Business Park, Barton under Needwood, Burton-on-Trent DE13 8EN
Tel: 01283 722600
Fax: 01283 722622
E-mail: lh@lh-group.com
Web site: www.lh-group.com

MAN TRUCK & BUS UK LTD
Frankland Road, Blagrove, Swindon SN5 8YU
Tel: 01793 448000
Fax: 01793 448262
Web site: www.manbusandcoach.co.uk

OPTARE PARTS DIVISION (Leeds)
Manston Lane, Leeds LS15 8SU
Tel: 0113 264 5182
Fax: 0113 260 6635
E-mail: parts@optare.com
Web site: www.optare.com

OPTARE PRODUCT SUPPORT LONDON
Unit 9, Eurocourt, Olivers Close, West Thurrock RM20 3EE
Tel: 01708 896860
Fax: 01708 869920
E-mail: london.service@optare.com

OPTARE PRODUCT SUPPORT ROTHERHAM
Denby Way, Hellaby, Rotherham S66 8HR
Tel: 01709 535100
Fax: 01709 535102
E-mail: rotherham.service@optare.com

PARTLINE LTD
Dockfield Road, Shipley BD17 7AZ
Tel: 01274 531531
Fax: 01274 531088
E-mail: sales@partline.co.uk
Web site: www.partline.co.uk

PERKINS GROUP LTD
Vicarage Farm Road, Peterborough PE1 5TP
Tel: 01733 567474
Fax: 01733 582240
Web site: www.perkins.com

QUEENSBRIDGE (PSV) LTD
Longlands Industrial Estate, Milner Way, Ossett WF5 9JE
Tel: 01924 281871
Fax: 01924 281807
E-mail: craig@queensbridgeltd.co.uk
Web site: www.queensbridgeltd.co.uk

SHAWSON SUPPLY LTD
12 Station Road, Saintfield, County Down, Northern Ireland BT24 7DU
Tel: 028 9751 0994

Fax: 028 9751 0816
E-mail: info@shawsonsupply.com
Web site: www.shawsonsupply.com

CRAIG TILSLEY & SON LTD
Moorfield Industrial Estate, Cotes Heath, Stoke on Trent ST21 6QY
Tel: 01782 791524
Fax: 01782 791316

TTS UK
Total Tool Solutions Ltd, Newhaven Business Park, Lowergate, Milnsbridge, Huddersfield HD3 4HS
Tel: 01484 642211 **Fax:** 01484 461002
E-mail: sales@ttsuk.com
Web site: www.ttsuk.com

WALSH'S ENGINEERING LTD
Barton Moss Road, Eccles, Manchester M30 7RL
Tel: 0161 787 7017
Fax: 0161 787 7038
E-mail: walshs@gardnerdiesel.co.uk
Web site: www.gardnerdiesel.co.uk

WEALDSTONE ENGINEERING
Sanders Lodge Industrial Estate, Rushden NN10 6AZ
Tel: 01933 354600
Fax: 01933 354601
Web site: www.wealdstone.co.uk

Engine Oil Drain Valves

ARRIVA BUS AND COACH
Lodge Garage, Whitehall Road West, Gomersal, Cleckheaton, West Yorkshire BD19 4BJ
Tel: 01274 681144
Fax: 01274 651198
E-mail: whiter@arriva.co.uk
Web site: www.arrivabusandcoach.co.uk

FUMOTO ENGINEERING OF EUROPE LTD
Normandy House, 35 Glategny Esplanade, St Peter Port, Guernsey GY1 2BP
Tel: 01481 716987 **Fax:** 01481 700374
E-mail: sales@fumoto-valve.com

PARTLINE LTD
Dockfield Road, Shipley BD17 7AZ
Tel: 01274 531531
Fax: 01274 531088
E-mail: sales@partline.co.uk
Web site: www.partline.co.uk

WALLMINSTER LTD
Unit 22, Chelsea Wharf, 15 Lots Road, London SW10 0QJ
Tel: 020 7352 2727 **Fax:** 020 7352 3990
E-mail: info@tankcontainers.co.uk
Web site: www.tankcontainers.co.uk

Exhaust Systems

ARRIVA BUS AND COACH
Lodge Garage, Whitehall Road West, Gomersal, Cleckheaton, West Yorkshire BD19 4BJ
Tel: 01274 681144 **Fax:** 01274 651198
E-mail: whiter@arriva.co.uk
Web site: www.arrivabusandcoach.co.uk

ARVIN MERITOR
Park Lane, Great Alne, Alcester, Warwickshire B49 6HS

Tel: 01789 768270
Web site: www.meritor.com

CARLYLE BUS & COACH LTD
Carlyle Business Park, Great Bridge Street, Swan Village, West Bromwich B70 0X4
Tel: 0121 524 1200 **Fax:** 0121 524 1201
E-mail: admin@carlyleplc.co.uk
Web site: www.carlyleplc.co.uk

CRESCENT FACILITIES LTD
72 Willow Crescent, Chapeltown, Sheffield S35 1QS
Tel/Fax: 0114 245 1050
E-mail: cfl.chris@btinternet.com
Web site: www.cflparts.com

DINEX EXHAUSTS LTD
14 Chesford Grange, Woolston, Warrington WA1 3BT
Tel: 01925 849849 **Fax:** 01925 849850
E-mail: dinex@dinex.co.uk

EMINOX LTD
North Warren Road, Gainsborough DN21 2TU
Tel: 01427 810088
Fax: 01427 810061
E-mail: enquiry@eminox.com
Web site: www.eminox.com

Eminox design and manufacture exhaust and emission control systems for commercial vehicles. Our emissions systems are approved for retrofitting to buses and coaches for the London LEZ and E-Zones across Europe.

LEZ freephone: 0808 156 2012
T: 01427 810088
F: 01427 810061
E: enquiry@eminox.com
www.eminox.com

North Warren Road, Gainsborough, Lincolnshire DN21 2TU

IMEXPART LTD
Links 31, Willowbridge Way, Whitwood, Castleford WF10 5NP
Tel: 0845 605 0404
Fax: 01977 513412
E-mail: sales@imexpart.com
Web site: www.imexpart.com

KCP CAR & COMMERCIAL LTD
Unit 15, Hillside Business Park, Kempson Way, Bury St Edmunds, Suffolk IP32 7EA
Tel: 01284 750777
Fax: 01284 750773
E-mail: info@kcpcarandcommercial.co.uk
Web site: www.kcpcarandcommercial.co.uk

OPTARE PARTS DIVISION (Leeds)
Manston Lane, Leeds LS15 8SU
Tel: 0113 264 5182
Fax: 0113 260 6635
E-mail: parts@optare.com
Web site: www.optare.com

OPTARE PRODUCT SUPPORT LONDON
Unit 9, Eurocourt, Olivers Close, West Thurrock
RM20 3EE
Tel: 01708 896860
Fax: 01708 869920
E-mail: london.service@optare.com

OPTARE PRODUCT SUPPORT ROTHERHAM
Denby Way, Hellaby, Rotherham S66 8HR
Tel: 01709 535100
Fax: 01709 535102
E-mail: rotherham.service@optare.com

PARTLINE LTD
Dockfield Road, Shipley BD17 7AZ
Tel: 01274 531531
Fax: 01274 531088
E-mail: sales@partline.co.uk
Web site: www.partline.co.uk

TTS UK
Total Tool Solutions Ltd, Newhaven Business
Park, Lowergate, Milnsbridge, Huddersfield
HD3 4HS
Tel: 01484 642211 **Fax:** 01484 461002
E-mail: sales@ttsuk.com
Web site: www.ttsuk.com

Fans & Drive Belts

ARRIVA BUS AND COACH
Lodge Garage, Whitehall Road West, Gomersal,
Cleckheaton, West Yorkshire BD19 4BJ
Tel: 01274 681144
Fax: 01274 651198
E-mail: whiter@arriva.co.uk
Web site: www.arrivabusandcoach.co.uk

BRT BEARINGS LTD
21-24 Regal Road, Wisbech, Cambridgeshire
PE13 2RQ
Tel: 01945 464097
Fax: 01945 464523
E-mail: brt.sales@brt-bearings.com
Web site: www.brt-bearings.com

CARLYLE BUS & COACH LTD
Carlyle Business Park, Great Bridge Street,
Swan Village, West Bromwich
B70 0X4
Tel: 0121 524 1200
Fax: 0121 524 1201
E-mail: admin@carlyleplc.co.uk
Web site: www.carlyleplc.co.uk

CLAYTON HEATERS LTD
Hunter Terrace, Fletchworth Gate, Burnsall Road,
Coventry CV5 6SP
Tel: 02476 691 916 **Fax:** 02476 691 969
E-mail: admin@claytoncc.co.uk
Web site: www.claytoncc.co.uk

CRESCENT FACILITIES LTD
72 Willow Crescent, Chapeltown, Sheffield
S35 1QS
Tel/Fax: 0114 245 1050
E-mail: cfl.chris@btinternet.com
Web site: www.cflparts.com

CUMMINS UK
40-44 Rutherford Drive, Park Farm South,
Wellingborough NN8 6AN
Tel: 01933 334200

Fax: 01933 334198
E-mail: cduksales@cummins.com
Web site: www.cummins-uk.com

DIRECT PARTS LTD
Unit 1, Churnet Court, Churnetside Business
Park, Harrison Way, Cheddleton
ST13 7EF
Tel: 01538 361777
Fax: 01538 369100
E-mail: sales@direct-group.co.uk
Web site: www.direct-group.co.uk

KCP CAR & COMMERCIAL LTD
Unit 15, Hillside Business Park, Kempson Way,
Bury St Edmunds, Suffolk IP32 7EA
Tel: 01284 750777
Fax: 01284 750773
E-mail: info@kcpcarandcommercial.co.uk
Web site: www.kcpcarandcommercial.co.uk

OPTARE PARTS DIVISION (Leeds)
Manston Lane, Leeds LS15 8SU
Tel: 0113 264 5182
Fax: 0113 260 6635
E-mail: parts@optare.com
Web site: www.optare.com

PACET MANUFACTURING LTD
Wyebridge House, Cores End Road,
Bourne End, Buckinghamshire SL8 5HH
Tel: 01628 526754
Fax: 01628 810080
E-mail: sales@pacet.co.uk
Web site: www.pacet.co.uk

PARTLINE LTD
Dockfield Road, Shipley BD17 7AZ
Tel: 01274 531531
Fax: 01274 531088
E-mail: sales@partline.co.uk
Web site: www.partline.co.uk

QUEENSBRIDGE (PSV) LTD
Longlands Industrial Estate, Milner Way,
Ossett WF5 9JE
Tel: 01924 281871
Fax: 01924 281807
E-mail: craig@queensbridgeltd.co.uk
Web site: www.queensbridgeltd.co.uk

Fare Boxes

CUBIC TRANSPORTATION SYSTEMS LTD
AFC House, Honeycrock Lane, Salfords,
Redhill RH1 5LA
Tel: 01737 782200
Fax: 01737 789759
Web site: www.cubic.com

ETMSS LTD
Austin House, 43 Poole Road, Westbourne,
Bournemouth BH4 9DN
Tel: 0844 800 9299
E-mail: info@etmss.com
Web Site: www.etmss.com

JOHN GROVES TICKET SYSTEMS
Unit 10, North Circular Business Centre,
400 NCR, London NW10 0JG
Tel: 020 8830 1222
Fax: 020 8830 1223
E-mail: sales@jgts.co.uk
Web site: www.jgts.co.uk

MARK TERRILL TICKET MACHINERY
5 De Grey Close, Lewes BN7 2JR
Tel: 01273 474816
Fax: 01273 474816
E-mail: mark.terrill@ukonline.co.uk

TICKETER
Chilton House, Charnham Lane, Hungerford,
Berkshire RG17 0EW
Tel: 0844 800 9299
E-mail: sales@ticketer.co.uk
Web site: www.ticketer.co.uk

Fire Extinguishers

ARRIVA BUS AND COACH
Lodge Garage, Whitehall Road West, Gomersal,
Cleckheaton, West Yorkshire BD19 4BJ
Tel: 01274 681144
Fax: 01274 651198
E-mail: whiter@arriva.co.uk
Web site: www.arrivabusandcoach.co.uk

CARLYLE BUS & COACH LTD
Carlyle Business Park, Great Bridge Street,
Swan Village, West Bromwich B70 0X4
Tel: 0121 524 1200
Fax: 0121 524 1201
E-mail: admin@carlyleplc.co.uk
Web site: www.carlyleplc.co.uk

EXPRESS COACH REPAIRS LTD
Outgang Lane, Pickering YO18 7JA
Tel: 01751 475215
Fax: 01751 475215
E-mail: info@expresscoachrepairs.co.uk
Web site: www.expresscoachrepairs.co.uk

FIREMASTER EXTINGUISHER LTD
Firex House, 174-176 Hither Green Lane, London
SE13 6QB
Tel: 020 8852 8585
Fax: 020 8297 8020
E-mail: info@firemaster.co.uk
Web site: www.firemaster.co.uk

HAPPICH UK LTD
Unit 30/31, Fort Industrial Park, Fort Parkway,
Castle Bromwich B35 7AR
Tel: 0121 747 4400
Fax: 0121 747 4977
E-mail: sales@happich.co.uk
Web site: www.happich.co.uk

KCP CAR & COMMERCIAL LTD
Unit 15, Hillside Business Park, Kempson Way,
Bury St Edmunds, Suffolk IP32 7EA
Tel: 01284 750777
Fax: 01284 750773
E-mail: info@kcpcarandcommercial.co.uk
Web site: www.kcpcarandcommercial.co.uk

KELLETT (UK) LTD
8 Stevenson Way, Sheffield S9 3WZ.
Tel: 0114 261 1122
Fax: 0114 261 1199
E-mail: sales@kellett.co.uk

LAWTON SERVICES LTD
Knutsford Road, Church Lawton, Stoke-on-Trent
ST7 3DN
Tel: 01270 882056
Fax: 01270 883014
E-mail: andrea@lawtonservices.co.uk
Web site: www.lawtonservices.co.uk

PARTLINE LTD
Dockfield Road, Shipley BD17 7AZ
Tel: 01274 531531
Fax: 01274 531088
E-mail: sales@partline.co.uk
Web site: www.partline.co.uk

PLAXTON PARTS
Ryton Road, Anston, Sheffield S25 4DL
Tel: 0844 822 6224
Fax: 01909 550050
E-mail: parts@plaxtonlimited.co.uk
Web site: www.plaxtonaftercare.co.uk

PSV PRODUCTS
The Red House, Underbridge Lane, Higher
Walton, Warrington WA4 5QR
Tel: 01925 210220
Fax: 01925 601534
E-mail: info@psvproducts.com
Web site: www.psvproducts.com

First Aid Equipment

ARRIVA BUS AND COACH
Lodge Garage, Whitehall Road West, Gomersal,
Cleckheaton, West Yorkshire BD19 4BJ
Tel: 01274 681144
Fax: 01274 651198
E-mail: whiter@arriva.co.uk
Web site: www.arrivabusandcoach.co.uk

BRADTECH LTD
Unit 3, Ladford Covert, Seighford, Stafford
ST18 9QL
Tel: 01785 282800
Fax: 01785 282558
E-mail: sales@bradtech.ltd.uk
Web site: www.bradtech.ltd.uk

CARLYLE BUS & COACH LTD
Carlyle Business Park, Great Bridge Street,
Swan Village, West Bromwich B70 0X4
Tel: 0121 524 1200
Fax: 0121 524 1201
E-mail: admin@carlyleplc.co.uk
Web site: www.carlyleplc.co.uk

EXPRESS COACH REPAIRS LTD
Outgang Lane, Pickering YO18 7JA
Tel: 01751 475215
Fax: 01751 475215
E-mail: info@expresscoachrepairs.co.uk
Web site: www.expresscoachrepairs.co.uk

FIREMASTER EXTINGUISHER LTD
Firex House, 174-176 Hither Green Lane,
London SE13 6QB
Tel: 020 8852 8585
Fax: 020 8297 8020
E-mail: info@firemaster.co.uk
Web site: www.firemaster.co.uk

HAPPICH V & I COMPONENTS LTD
Unit 30/31, Fort Industrial Park, Fort Parkway,
Castle Bromwich B35 7AR
Tel: 0121 747 4400
Fax: 0121 747 4977
E-mail: sales@happich.co.uk
Web site: www.happich.co.uk

KCP CAR & COMMERCIAL LTD
Unit 15, Hillside Business Park, Kempson Way,
Bury St Edmunds, Suffolk IP32 7EA
Tel: 01284 750777

Fax: 01284 750773
E-mail: info@kcpcarandcommercial.co.uk
Web site: www.kcpcarandcommercial.co.uk

LAWTON SERVICES LTD
Knutsford Road, Church Lawton, Stoke-on-Trent
ST7 3DN
Tel: 01270 882056
Fax: 01270 883014
E-mail: andrea@lawtonservices.co.uk
Web site: www.lawtonservices.co.uk

PARMA INDUSTRIES
34-36 Carlton Park Industrial Estate,
Saxmundham, Suffolk IP17 2NL
Tel: 01728 745700
Fax: 01728 745718
E-mail: sales@parmagroup.co.uk
Web site: www.parmagroup.co.uk

PARTLINE LTD
Dockfield Road, Shipley BD17 7AZ
Tel: 01274 531531
Fax: 01274 531088
E-mail: sales@partline.co.uk
Web site: www.partline.co.uk

PLAXTON PARTS
Ryton Road, Anston, Sheffield S25 4DL
Tel: 0844 822 6224
Fax: 01909 550050
E-mail: parts@plaxtonlimited.co.uk
Web site: www.plaxtonaftercare.co.uk

PSV PRODUCTS
The Red House, Underbridge Lane, Higher
Walton, Warrington WA4 5QR
Tel: 01925 210220
Fax: 01925 601534
E-mail: info@psvproducts.com
Web site: www.psvproducts.com

Floor Coverings

AK CARPETS LTD
Unit 15, Deanfield Court, Link 59 Business Park,
Clitheroe, Lancashire BB7 1QS
Tel: 01200 444145
Fax: 01200 444180
E-mail: info@akcarpets.com
Web site: www.akcarpets.com

ALTRO TRANSFLOR
Works Road, Letchworth Garden City
SG6 1NW
Tel: 01462 707600
Fax: 01462 480010
E-mail: enquiries@altro.com
Web site: www.altro.co.uk

ARRIVA BUS AND COACH
Lodge Garage, Whitehall Road West, Gomersal,
Cleckheaton, West Yorkshire BD19 4BJ
Tel: 01274 681144
Fax: 01274 651198
E-mail: whiter@arriva.co.uk
Web site: www.arrivabusandcoach.co.uk

AUTOMATE WHEEL COVERS LTD
California Mills, Oxford Road, Gomersal,
Cleckheaton BD19 4HQ
Tel: 01274 862700
Fax: 01274 851989
E-mail: sales@wheelcovers.co.uk
Web site: www.wheeltrimshop.com

AUTOMOTIVE TEXTILE INDUSTRIES
Unit 15 & 16, Priest Court, Springfield Business
Park, Grantham NG31 7BG
Tel: 01476 593050
Fax: 01476 593607
E-mail: sales@autotex.com
Web site: www.autotex.com

CARLYLE BUS & COACH LTD
Carlyle Business Park, Great Bridge Street, Swan
Village, West Bromwich B70 0X4
Tel: 0121 524 1200
Fax: 0121 524 1201
E-mail: admin@carlyleplc.co.uk
Web site: www.carlyleplc.co.uk

CONCEPT COACHCRAFT LTD
Far Cromwell Road, Stockport, Cheshire SK6 2SE
Tel: 0161 406 9322
Fax: 0161 406 9588
E-mail: sales@conceptcoachcraft.com
Web site: www.conceptcoachcraft.com

DUOFLEX LTD
Trimmingham House, 2 Shires Road,
Buckingham Road Industrial Estate, Brackley,
Northamptonshire NN13 7EZ
Tel: 01280 701366
Fax: 01280 704799
E-mail: sales@duoflex.co.uk
Web site: www.duoflex.co.uk

EXPRESS COACH REPAIRS LTD
Outgang Lane, Pickering YO18 7JA
Tel: 01751 475215
Fax: 01751 475215
E-mail: info@expresscoachrepairs.co.uk
Web site: www.expresscoachrepairs.co.uk

LAWTON SERVICES LTD
Knutsford Road, Church Lawton, Stoke-on-Trent
ST7 3DN
Tel: 01270 882056
Fax: 01270 883014
E-mail: andrea@lawtonservices.co.uk
Web site: www.lawtonservices.co.uk

MARTYN INDUSTRIALS LTD
5 Brunel Way, Durranhill, Harraby, Carlisle
CA1 3NQ
Tel: 01228 544000
Fax: 01228 544001
E-mail: enquiries@martyn-industrials.co.uk
Web site: www.martyn-industrials.com

PLAXTON PARTS
Ryton Road, Anston, Sheffield S25 4DL
Tel: 0844 822 6224
Fax: 01909 550050
E-mail: parts@plaxtonlimited.co.uk
Web site: www.plaxtonaftercare.co.uk

SAFETY TREAD
450 Blandford Road, Poole, Dorset BH16 5BN
Tel: 0845 604 2471
Fax: 01202 625597
E-mail: sales@safetytread.co.uk
Web site: www.safetytread.co.uk

TIFLEX LTD
Tiflex House, Liskeard PL14 4NB
Tel: 01579 320808
Fax: 01579 320802
E-mail: marketing@tiflex.co.uk
Web site: www.tiflex.co.uk

Fuel, Fuel Management & Lubricants

ARRIVA BUS AND COACH
Lodge Garage, Whitehall Road West, Gomersal,
Cleckheaton, West Yorkshire BD19 4BJ
Tel: 01274 681144
Fax: 01274 651198
E-mail: whiter@arriva.co.uk
Web site: www.arrivabusandcoach.co.uk

CUMMINS UK
40-44 Rutherford Drive, Park Farm South,
Wellingborough NN8 6AN
Tel: 01933 334200
Fax: 01933 334198
E-mail: cduksales@cummins.com
Web site: www.cummins-uk.com

FUEL THEFT SOLUTIONS LTD
PO Box 2494, Stoke on Trent
ST7 2WR
Tel: 0845 077 3921
Fax: 0845 077 3922
E-mail: sales@dieseldye.com
Web site: www.dieseldye.com

INTERLUBE SYSTEMS LTD
St Modwen Road, Parkway Industrial Estate,
Plymouth PL6 8LH
Tel: 01752 676000
Fax: 01752 676001
E-mail: info@interlubesystems.com
Web site: www.interlubesystems.com

J MURDOCH WIGHT LTD
Systems House, Pentland Industrial Estate,
Loanhead, Midlothian EH20 9QH
Tel: 0131 440 3633
Fax: 0131 440 3637
E-mail: enquiries@jmw-group.co.uk
Web site: www.jmw-group.co.uk

TRISCAN SYSTEMS LTD
Phoenix Park, Blakewater Road, Blackburn,
Lancashire BB1 5SJ
Tel: 0845 225 3100
Fax: 0845 225 3101
E-mail: info@triscansystems.com
Web site: www.triscansystems.com

Garage Equipment

ARRIVA BUS AND COACH
Lodge Garage, Whitehall Road West,
Cleckheaton, West Yorkshire BD19 4BJ
Tel: 01274 681144
Fax: 01274 651198
E-mail: whiter@arriva.co.uk
Web site: www.arrivabusandcoach.co.uk

BUTTS OF BAWTRY GARAGE EQUIPMENT
Station Yard, Station Road, Bawtry, Doncaster
DN10 6QD
Tel: 01302 710868
Fax: 01302 719481
E-mail: info@buttsequipment.com
Web site: www.jhmbuttco.com

TERENCE BARKER TANKS
Phoenix Road, Haverhill, Suffolk CB9 7EA
Tel: 01440 712905
Fax: 01440 715460
E-mail: sales.tbtanks.co.uk
Web site: www.terencebarkertanks.co.uk

T T S UK

Total Tool Solutions Limited
Newhaven Business Park
Lowergate
Milnsbridge
Huddersfield
HD3 4HS
T: 01484 642211
F: 01484 461002
E: sales@ttsuk.com
W: www.ttsuk.com

DIRECT PARTS LTD
Unit 1, Churnet Court, Churnetside Business
Park, Harrison Way, Cheddleton ST13 7EF
Tel: 01538 361777
Fax: 01538 369100
E-mail: sales@direct-group.co.uk
Web site: www.direct-group.co.uk

FUEL THEFT SOLUTIONS LTD
PO Box 2494, Stoke on Trent ST7 2WR
Tel: 0845 077 3921
Fax: 0845 077 3922
E-mail: sales@dieseldye.com
Web site: www.dieseldye.com

GEMCO EQUIPMENT LTD
153-156 Bridge Street, Northampton
NN1 1QG
Tel: 01604 828500
Fax: 01604 633159
E-mail: sales@gemco.co.uk
Web site: www.gemco.co.uk

KCP CAR & COMMERCIAL LTD
Unit 15, Hillside Business Park, Kempson Way,
Bury St Edmunds, Suffolk IP32 7EA
Tel: 01284 750777
Fax: 01284 750773
E-mail: info@kcpcarandcommercial.co.uk
Web site: www.kcpcarandcommercial.co.uk

MAJORLIFT HYDRAULIC EQUIPMENT LTD
Arnold's Field Industrial Estate, Wickwar,
Wotton-under-Edge, Gloucestershire
GL12 8JD
Tel: 01454 299299
Fax: 01454 294003
E-mail: info@majorlift.com
Web site: www.majorlift.com

SOMERS TOTALKARE LTD
Unit 1, Coombs Wharf, Chancel Way, Halesowen,
West Midlands B62 8PP
Tel: 0121 585 2700
Fax: 0121 585 2725
E-mail: sales@stkare.co.uk
Web site: www.stkare.co.uk

STERTIL UK LTD
Unit A, Brackmills Business Park, Caswell Road,
Northampton NN4 7PW
Tel: 08707 700471
Fax: 01604 765181
E-mail: info@stertiluk.com
Web site: www.stertiluk.com

PHIL STOCKFORD GARAGE EQUIPMENT LTD
Unit 7, Badger Way, North Cheshire Trading
Estate, Prenton, Wirral L43 3HQ
Tel: 0151 609 1007
Fax: 0151 609 1008
E-mail: info@vehicle-lifts.co.uk
Web site: www.vehicle-lifts.co.uk

TECALEMIT GARAGE EQUIPMENT CO LTD
Eagle Road, Langage Business Park, Plympton,
Plymouth, Devon PL9 8BN
Tel: 01752 219111
Fax: 01752 219128
E-mail: sales@tecalemit.co.uk
Web site: www.tecalemit.co.uk

TTS UK
Total Tool Solutions Ltd, Newhaven Business
Park, Lowergate, Milnsbridge, Huddersfield
HD3 4HS
Tel: 01484 642211 **Fax:** 01484 461002
E-mail: sales@ttsuk.com
Web site: www.ttsuk.com

VARLEY & GULLIVER LTD
57 Alfred Street, Sparkbrook, Birmingham B12 8JR
Tel: 0121 773 2441
Fax: 0121 766 6875
E-mail: sales@v-and-g.co.uk
Web site: www.v-and-g.co.uk

V L TEST SYSTEMS LTD
3-4 Middle Slade, Buckingham Industrial Park,
Buckingham MK18 1WA
Tel: 01280 822488 **Fax:** 01280 822489
E-mail: sales@vltestuk.com
Web site: www.vltest.com

Gearboxes

ALLISON TRANSMISSION
Millbrook Proving Ground, Millbrook, Bedford
MK45 2JQ
Tel: 01525 408600
Fax: 01525 408610
Web site: www.allisontransmission.com

ARRIVA BUS AND COACH
Lodge Garage, Whitehall Road West, Gomersal,
Cleckheaton, West Yorkshire BD19 4BJ
Tel: 01274 681144
Fax: 01274 651198
E-mail: whiter@arriva.co.uk
Web site: www.arrivabusandcoach.co.uk

The Little Red Book 2012 - in association with Transport Benevolent Fund

DAVID BROWN VEHICLE TRANSMISSIONS LTD
Park Gear Works, Lockwood, Huddersfield
HD4 5DD
Tel: 01484 465500
Fax: 01484 465518
E-mail: uk@davidbrown.com
Web site: www.davidbrown.com

GARDNER PARTS LTD
Centurion Court, Centurion Way, Leyland,
Lancashire PR25 3UQ
Tel: 01772 642460
Fax: 01772 621333
E-mail: sales@gardnerparts.co.uk
Web site: www.gardnerparts.co.uk

HL SMITH TRANSMISSIONS LTD
Enterprise Business Park, Cross Road, Albrighton,
Wolverhampton WV7 3BJ
Tel: 01902 373011 **Fax:** 01902 373608
Web site: www.hlsmith.co.uk

KCP CAR & COMMERCIAL LTD
Unit 15, Hillside Business Park, Kempson Way,
Bury St Edmunds, Suffolk IP32 7EA
Tel: 01284 750777
Fax: 01284 750773
E-mail: info@kcpcarandcommercial.co.uk
Web site: www.kcpcarandcommercial.co.uk

LH GROUP SERVICES LTD
Graycar Business Park, Barton under Needwood,
Burton-on-Trent DE13 8EN
Tel: 01283 722600
Fax: 01283 722622
E-mail: lh@lh-group.com
Web site: www.lh-group.com

MITCHELL POWERSYSTEMS
Mitchell Diesel Ltd, Fulwood Road South,
Sutton-in-Ashfield, Nottinghamshire NG17 2JZ
Tel: 01623 445626
Fax: 01623 443041
E-mail: darren.hill@mitchells.co.uk
Web site: www.mitchells.co.uk

OPTARE PARTS DIVISION (Leeds)
Manston Lane, Leeds LS15 8SU
Tel: 0113 264 5182
Fax: 0113 260 6635
E-mail: parts@optare.com
Web site: www.optare.com

OPTARE PRODUCT SUPPORT LONDON
Unit 9, Eurocourt, Olivers Close, West Thurrock
RM20 3EE
Tel: 01708 896860
Fax: 01708 869920
E-mail: london.service@optare.com

OPTARE PRODUCT SUPPORT ROTHERHAM
Denby Way, Hellaby, Rotherham S66 8HR
Tel: 01709 535100
Fax: 01709 535102
E-mail: rotherham.service@optare.com

PARTLINE LTD
Dockfield Road, Shipley BD17 7AZ
Tel: 01274 531531
Fax: 01274 531088
E-mail: sales@partline.co.uk
Web site: www.partline.co.uk

QUEENSBRIDGE (PSV) LTD
Longlands Industrial Estate, Milner Way,
Ossett WF5 9JE
Tel: 01924 281871
Fax: 01924 281807
E-mail: craig@queensbridgeltd.co.uk
Web site: www.queensbridgeltd.co.uk

SHAWSON SUPPLY LTD
12 Station Road, Saintfield, County Down,
North Ireland BT24 7DU
Tel: 028 9751 0994
Fax: 028 9751 0816
E-mail: info@shawsonsupply.com
Web site: www.shawsonsupply.com

VOITH TURBO LTD
6 Beddington Farm Road, Croydon
CR0 4XB
Tel: 020 8667 0333
Fax: 020 8667 0403
E-mail: Road.UK@voith.com
Web site: www.voithturbo.com

Voith Turbo Ltd.
6 Beddington Farm Road,
Croydon, Surrey, CR0 4XB

Phone 0208 667 0333
Fax 0208 667 0403

Road.UK@voith.com

VOR TRANSMISSIONS LTD
Little London House, St Anne's House,
Willenhall, West Midlands WV13 1DT
Tel: 01902 604141 **Fax:** 01902 603868
E-mail: sales@vor.co.uk
Web site: www.vor.co.uk

TREVOR WIGLEY & SONS BUS LTD
Passenger Vehicle Dismantling/Spares
Works: Boulder Bridge Lane, off Shaw Lane,
Barnsley S71 3HJ
Correspondence: 148 Royston Road,
Cudworth, Barnsley S72 8BN
Tel: 01226 713636 **Fax:** 01226 700199
E-mail: wigleys@btintenet.com
Web site: www.twigley.com

ZF POWERTRAIN
Stringes Close, Willenhall
WV13 1LE
Tel: 01902 366000 **Fax:** 01902 366504
E-mail: sales@powertrain.org.uk
Web site: www.powertrain.org.uk

Hand Driers (in coaches)

BRADTECH LTD
Unit 3, Ladford Covert, Seighford,
Stafford ST18 9QL
Tel: 01785 282800
Fax: 01785 282558
E-mail: sales@bradtech.ltd.uk
Web site: www.bradtech.ltd.uk

CARLYLE BUS & COACH LTD
Carlyle Business Park, Great Bridge Street,
Swan Village, West Bromwich
B70 0X4
Tel: 0121 524 1200
Fax: 0121 524 1201
E-mail: admin@carlyleplc.co.uk
Web site: www.carlyleplc.co.uk

CROWN COACHBUILDERS LTD
32 Flemington Industrial Park, Flemington,
Motherwell ML1 1SN
Tel: 01698 276087
Fax: 01698 262676
E-mail: davidgreer@hotmail.com
Web site: www.crowncoachbuilders.co.uk

DEANS POWERED DOORS
PO Box 8, Borwick Drive, Grovehill, Beverley
HU17 0HQ
Tel: 01482 868111
Fax: 01482 881890
E-mail: info@deans-doors.com

HAPPICH UK LTD
Unit 30/31, Fort Industrial Park, Fort Parkway,
Castle Bromwich B35 7AR
Tel: 0121 747 4400
Fax: 0121 747 4977
E-mail: sales@happich.co.uk
Web site: www.happich.co.uk

JBF SERVICES LTD
Southedge Works, Hipperholme,
Halifax HX3 8EF
Tel: 01422 202840
Fax: 01422 206070
E-mail: jbfservices@aol.com

PLAXTON PARTS
Ryton Road, Anston, Sheffield S25 4DL
Tel: 0833 822 6224
Fax: 01909 550050
E-mail: parts@plaxtonlimited.co.uk
Web site: www.plaxtonaftercare.co.uk

PLAXTON SERVICE
Ryton Road, Anston, Sheffield
S25 4DL
Tel: 01909 551155
Fax: 01909 550050
E-mail: service@plaxtonlimited.co.uk
Web site: www.plaxtonaftercare.co.uk

SHADES TECHNICS LTD
Units E3 & E4, Rd Park, Stephenson Close,
Hoddesdon, Hertfordshire EN11 0BW
Tel: 01992 501683
Fax: 01992 501669
E-mail: sales@shades-technics.com
Web site: www.shades-technics.com

UNWIN SAFETY SYSTEMS
Unwin House, The Horseshoe, Coat Road,
Martock TA12 6EY
Tel: 01935 827740
Fax: 01935 827760
E-mail: sales@unwin-safety.co.uk
Web site: www.unwin-safety.com

Handrails

ABACUS TRANSPORT PRODUCTS LTD
Abacus House, Highlode Industrial Estate, Ramsey,
Huntingdon PE26 2RB
Tel: 01487 710700
Fax: 01487 710626
E-mail: sales@abacus-tp.com
Web site: www.abacus-tp.com

ARRIVA BUS AND COACH
Lodge Garage, Whitehall Road West, Gomersal,
Cleckheaton, West Yorkshire BD19 4BJ
Tel: 01274 681144
Fax: 01274 651198
E-mail: whiter@arriva.co.uk
Web site: www.arrivabusandcoach.co.uk

EXPRESS COACH REPAIRS LTD
Outgang Lane, Pickering YO18 7JA
Tel: 01751 475215
Fax: 01751 475215
E-mail: info@expresscoachrepairs.co.uk
Web site: www.expresscoachrepairs.co.uk

GABRIEL & CO LTD
1 Cornwall Road, Smethwick, West Midlands
B66 2JT
Tel: 0121 555 7615
Fax: 0121 555 1922
E-mail: john.gabriel@gabrielco.com
Web site: www.gabrielco.com

LAWTON SERVICES LTD
Knutsford Road, Church Lawton, Stoke-on-Trent
ST7 3DN
Tel: 01270 882056
Fax: 01270 883014
E-mail: andrea@lawtonservices.co.uk
Web site: www.lawtonservices.co.uk

PARTLINE LTD
Dockfield Road, Shipley BD17 7AZ
Tel: 01274 531531
Fax: 01274 531088
E-mail: sales@partline.co.uk
Web site: www.partline.co.uk

PLAXTON PARTS
Ryton Road, Anston, Sheffield S25 4DL
Tel: 0833 822 6224
Fax: 01909 550050
E-mail: parts@plaxtonlimited.co.uk
Web site: www.plaxtonaftercare.co.uk

PLAXTON SERVICE
Ryton Road, Anston, Sheffield S25 4DL
Tel: 01909 551155
Fax: 01909 550050
E-mail: service@plaxtonlimited.co.uk
Web site: www.plaxtonaftercare.co.uk

Headrest Covers & Curtains

ABACUS TRANSPORT PRODUCTS LTD
Abacus House, Highlode Industrial Estate, Ramsey,
Huntingdon PE26 2RB
Tel: 01487 710700
Fax: 01487 710626
E-mail: sales@abacus-tp.com
Web site: www.abacus-tp.com

ARRIVA BUS AND COACH
Lodge Garage, Whitehall Road West, Gomersal,
Cleckheaton, West Yorkshire BD19 4BJ

Tel: 01274 681144
Fax: 01274 651198
E-mail: whiter@arriva.co.uk
Web site: www.arrivabusandcoach.co.uk

DUOFLEX LTD
Trimmingham House, 2 Shires Road,
Buckingham Road Industrial Estate, Brackley,
Northamptonshire NN13 7EZ
Tel: 01280 701366
Fax: 01280 704799
E-mail: sales@duoflex.co.uk
Web site: www.duoflex.co.uk

EXPRESS COACH REPAIRS LTD
Outgang Lane, Pickering YO18 7JA
Tel: 01751 475215
Fax: 01751 475215
E-mail: info@expresscoachrepairs.co.uk
Web site: www.expresscoachrepairs.co.uk

LAWTON SERVICES LTD
Knutsford Road, Church Lawton, Stoke-on-Trent
ST7 3DN
Tel: 01270 882056
Fax: 01270 883014
E-mail: andrea@lawtonservices.co.uk
Web site: www.lawtonservices.co.uk

**LEISUREWEAR DIRECT LTD, inc.
AHEAD OF THE REST**
4A South Street North, New Whittington,
Chesterfield S43 2AB
Tel: 01246 454447
Fax: 0870 755 9842
E-mail: sales@leisureweardirect.com
Web site: www.leisureweardirect.com

ORVEC INTERNATIONAL LTD
Malmo Road, Sutton Fields, Hull HU7 0YF
Tel: 01482 625333
Fax: 01482 625335
E-mail: service@orvec.com
Web site: www.orvec.com

PLAXTON PARTS
Ryton Road, Anston, Sheffield S25 4DL
Tel: 0833 822 6224
Fax: 01909 550050
E-mail: parts@plaxtonlimited.co.uk
Web site: www.plaxtonaftercare.co.uk

Heating & Ventilation Systems

AIRCONCO LTD
Unit 10, Middleton Trade Park, Oldham Road,
Middleton M24 1QZ
Tel: 0845 402014
Fax: 0845 4024041
E-mail: mail@airconco.carriersutrak.co.uk
Web site: www.airconco.ltd.uk

ARRIVA BUS AND COACH
Lodge Garage, Whitehall Road West, Gomersal,
Cleckheaton, West Yorkshire BD19 4BJ
Tel: 01274 681144 **Fax:** 01274 651198
E-mail: whiter@arriva.co.uk
Web site: www.arrivabusandcoach.co.uk

CAREYBROOK LTD
PO Box 205, Southam, Warwickshire CV47 0ZL
Tel: 03333 446800
Fax: 01926 814898
E-mail: info@careybrook.co.uk
Web site: www.careybrook.com

CARLYLE BUS & COACH LTD
Carlyle Business Park, Great Bridge Street,
Swan Village, West Bromwich B70 0X4
Tel: 0121 524 1200
Fax: 0121 524 1201
E-mail: admin@carlyleplc.co.uk
Web site: carlyleplc.co.uk

CLAYTON HEATERS LTD
Hunter Terrace, Fletchworth Gate, Burnsall Road,
Coventry CV5 6SP
Tel: 02476 691 916
Fax: 02476 691 969
E-mail: admin@claytoncc.co.uk
Web site: www.claytoncc.co.uk

EBERSPACHER (UK) LTD
Headlands Business Park, Salisbury Road,
Ringwood BH24 3PB
Tel: 01425 480151
Fax: 01425 480152
E-mail: enquiries@eberspacher.com
Web site: www.eberspacher.com

HAPPICH UK LTD
Unit 30/31, Fort Industrial Park, Fort Parkway,
Castle Bromwich B35 7AR
Tel: 0121 747 4400
Fax: 0121 747 4977
E-mail: sales@happich.co.uk
Web site: www.happich.co.uk

KELLETT (UK) LTD
8 Stevenson Way, Sheffield S9 3WZ
Tel: 0114 261 1122
Fax: 0114 261 1199
E-mail: sales@kellett.co.uk

**NEALINE WINDSCREEN WIPER
PRODUCTS**
Unit 1, The Sidings Industrial Estate,
Birdingbury Road, Marton CV23 9RX
Tel: 01926 633256
Fax: 01926 632600

OPTARE PARTS DIVISION (Leeds)
Manston Lane, Leeds LS15 8SU
Tel: 0113 264 5182
Fax: 0113 260 6635
E-mail: parts@optare.com
Web site: www.optare.com

PACET MANUFACTURING LTD
Wyebridge House, Cores End Road,
Bourne End, Buckinghamshire SL8 5HH
Tel: 01628 526754
Fax: 01628 810080
E-mail: sales@pacet.co.uk
Web site: www.pacet.co.uk

PIONEER WESTON
ERIKS Industrial Services Ltd, Amber Way,
Halesowen, West Midlands B62 8WG
Tel: 0845 006 6000
Fax: 0121 508 6333
E-mail: enquiries@eriks.co.uk
Web site: www.eriks.co.uk

PLAXTON PARTS
Ryton Road, Anston, Sheffield
S25 4DL
Tel: 0833 822 6224
Fax: 01909 550050
E-mail: parts@plaxtonlimited.co.uk
Web site: www.plaxtonaftercare.co.uk

PLAXTON SERVICE
Ryton Road, Anston, Sheffield S25 4DL
Tel: 01909 551155
Fax: 01909 550050
E-mail: service@plaxtonlimited.co.uk
Web site: www.plaxtonaftercare.co.uk

SHADES TECHNICS LTD
Units E3 & E4, Rd Park, Stephenson Close,
Hoddesdon, Hertfordshire EN11 0BW
Tel: 01992 501683
Fax: 01992 501669
E-mail: sales@shades-technics.com
Web site: www.shades-technics.com

WEBASTO PRODUCT UK LTD
Webasto House, White Rose Way, Doncaster
Carr, South Yorkshire DN4 5JH
Tel: 01302 322232
Fax: 01302 322231
E-mail: info@webastouk.com
Web site: www.webasto.co.uk

ARRIVA BUS AND COACH
Lodge Garage, Whitehall Road West, Gomersal,
Cleckheaton, West Yorkshire BD19 4BJ
Tel: 01274 681144
Fax: 01274 651198
E-mail: whiter@arriva.co.uk
Web site: www.arrivabusandcoach.co.uk

FUMOTO ENGINEERING OF EUROPE LTD
Normandy House, 35 Glategny Esplanade,
St Peter Port, Guernsey GY1 2BP
Tel: 01481 716987
Fax: 01481 700374
E-mail: sales@fumoto-valve.com

KCP CAR & COMMERCIAL LTD
Unit 15, Hillside Business Park, Kempson Way,
Bury St Edmunds, Suffolk IP32 7EA
Tel: 01284 750777
Fax: 01284 750773
E-mail: info@kcpcarandcommercial.co.uk
Web site: www.kcpcarandcommercial.co.uk

PARTLINE LTD
Dockfield Road, Shipley BD17 7AZ
Tel: 01274 531531
Fax: 01274 531088
E-mail: sales@partline.co.uk
Web site: www.partline.co.uk

ROADLINK INTERNATIONAL LTD
Strawberry Lane, Willenhall WV13 3RL
Tel: 01902 636206
Fax: 01902 631515
E-mail: sales@roadlink-international.co.uk
Web site: www.roadlink-international.co.uk

BRADTECH LTD
Unit 3, Ladford Covert, Seighford,
Stafford ST18 9QL
Tel: 01785 282800 **Fax:** 01785 282558
E-mail: sales@bradtech.ltd.uk
Web site: www.bradtech.ltd.uk

EXPRESS COACH REPAIRS LTD
Outgang Lane, Pickering YO18 7JA
Tel: 01751 475215

Fax: 01751 475215
E-mail: info@expresscoachrepairs.co.uk
Web site: www.expresscoachrepairs.co.uk

PLAXTON PARTS
Ryton Road, Anston, Sheffield S25 4DL
Tel: 0833 822 6224
Fax: 01909 550050
E-mail: parts@plaxtonlimited.co.uk
Web site: www.plaxtonaftercare.co.uk

PLAXTON SERVICE
Ryton Road, Anston, Sheffield S25 4DL
Tel: 01909 551155
Fax: 01909 550050
E-mail: service@plaxtonlimited.co.uk
Web site: www.plaxtonaftercare.co.uk

PSV PRODUCTS
The Red House, Underbridge Lane,
Higher Walton, Warrington WA4 5QR
Tel: 01925 210220
Fax: 01925 601534
E-mail: info@psvproducts.com
Web site: www.psvproducts.com

SHADES TECHNICS LTD
Units E3 & E4, Rd Park, Stephenson Close,
Hoddesdon, Hertfordshire EN11 0BW
Tel: 01992 501683
Fax: 01992 501669
E-mail: sales@shades-technics.com
Web site: www.shades-technics.com

TRAMONTANA
Chapelknowe Road, Carfin, Motherwell
ML1 5LE
Tel: 01698 861790
Fax: 01698 860778
E-mail: wdt90@tiscali.co.uk
Web site: www.brittnet.net/tramontanacoach

ARRIVA BUS AND COACH
Lodge Garage, Whitehall Road West,
Gomersal, Cleckheaton, West Yorkshire
BD19 4BJ
Tel: 01274 681144
Fax: 01274 651198
E-mail: whiter@arriva.co.uk
Web site: www.arrivabusandcoach.co.uk

FUEL THEFT SOLUTIONS LTD
PO Box 2494, Stoke on Trent
ST7 2WR
Tel: 0845 077 3921
Fax: 0845 077 3922
E-mail: sales@dieseldye.com
Web site: www.dieseldye.com

McKENNA BROTHERS LTD
McKenna House, Jubilee Road, Middleton,
Manchester M24 2LX
Tel: 0161 655 3244
Fax: 0161 655 3059
E-mail: info@mckennabrothers.co.uk
Web site: www.mckennabrothers.co.uk

PLAXTON PARTS
Ryton Road, Anston, Sheffield S25 4DL
Tel: 0833 822 6224
Fax: 01909 550050
E-mail: parts@plaxtonlimited.co.uk
Web site: www.plaxtonaftercare.co.uk

AUTOLIFT LTD
Swallow House, Shilton Industrial Estate,
Shilton, Coventry CV7 9JY
Tel: 02476 613223
Fax: 02476 619323
E-mail: info@autoliftuk.co.uk
Web site: www.autoliftuk.co.uk

ARRIVA BUS AND COACH
Lodge Garage, Whitehall Road West,
Gomersal, Cleckheaton, West Yorkshire
BD19 4BJ
Tel: 01274 681144
Fax: 01274 651198
E-mail: whiter@arriva.co.uk
Web site: www.arrivabusandcoach.co.uk

AVS STEPS LTD
Unit 1, Mereside Industrial Park, Fenns Bank,
Whitchurch, Shropshire SY13 3PA
Tel: 01948 781000
Fax: 01978 780099
E-mail: sales@avssteps.co.uk
Web site: www.avssteps.co.uk

COMPAK RAMPS LTD
VIP Group, VIP Industrial Park,
Anchor & Hope Lane, London
SE7 7RY
Tel: 020 8305 5879
Fax: 020 8858 5663
E-mail: admin@vipgroupltd.co.uk
Web site: www.vipgroup.co.uk

CROWN COACHBUILDERS LTD
32 Flemington Industrial Park, Flemington,
Motherwell ML1 1SN
Tel: 01698 276087
Fax: 01698 262676
E-mail: davidgreer@hotmail.com
Web site: www.crowncoachbuilders.co.uk

DIRECT PARTS LTD
Unit 1, Churnet Court, Churnetside Business
Park, Harrison Way, Cheddleton ST13 7EF
Tel: 01538 361777
Fax: 01538 369100
E-mail: sales@direct-group.co.uk
Web site: www.direct-group.co.uk

EXPRESS COACH REPAIRS LTD
Outgang Lane, Pickering YO18 7JA
Tel: 01751 475215
Fax: 01751 475215
E-mail: info@expresscoachrepairs.co.uk
Web site: www.expresscoachrepairs.co.uk

PASSENGER LIFT SERVICES
Unit 1C, Pearsall Drive, Oldbury,
West Midlands B69 2RA
Tel: 0121 552 0660
Fax: 0121 552 0200
E-mail: enquiries@pls-access.co.uk
Web site: www.passengerliftservices.co.uk

PLAXTON PARTS
Ryton Road, Anston, Sheffield S25 4DL
Tel: 0833 822 6224
Fax: 01909 550050
E-mail: parts@plaxtonlimited.co.uk
Web site: www.plaxtonaftercare.co.uk

PLAXTON SERVICE
Ryton Road, Anston, Sheffield S25 4DL
Tel: 01909 551155
Fax: 01909 550050
E-mail: service@plaxtonlimited.co.uk
Web site: www.plaxtonaftercare.co.uk

PNEUMAX LTD
110 Vista Park, Mauretania Road, Nursling,
Southampton SO16 0YS
Tel: 02380 740412
Fax: 02380 739340
E-mail: sales@pneumax.co.uk
Web site: www.pneumax.co.uk

RATCLIFF PALFINGER
Bessemer Road, Welwyn Garden City,
Hertfordshire AL7 1ET
Tel: 01707 382880
Fax: 01707 327752
E-mail: info@ratcliffpalfinger.co.uk
Web site: www.ratcliffpalfinger.co.uk

RICON UK LIMITED
Littlemoss Business Park, Littlemoss Road,
Droylsden, Manchester M43 7EF
Tel: 0161 301 6000
Fax: 0161 301 6050
E-mail: riconuk@wabtec.com
Web site: www.riconuk.eu

TRUCKALIGN CO LTD
VIP Group, VIP Industrial Park, Anchor & Hope
Lane, London SE7 7RY
Tel: 020 8305 5879
Fax: 020 8858 5663
E-mail: admin@vipgroupltd.co.uk
Web site: www.vipgroup.co.uk

Lighting & Lighting Design

ARRIVA BUS AND COACH
Lodge Garage, Whitehall Road West, Gomersal,
Cleckheaton, West Yorkshire BD19 4BJ
Tel: 01274 681144
Fax: 01274 651198
E-mail: whiter@arriva.co.uk
Web site: www.arrivabusandcoach.co.uk

AUTOSOUND LTD
4 Lister Street, Dudley Hill, Bradford BD4 9PQ
Tel: 01274 688990
Fax: 01274 651318
E-mail: keith.ellis@autosound.co.uk
Web site: www.autosound.co.uk

BRITAX PMG LTD
Bressingby Industrial Estate, Bridlington,
East Yorkshire YO16 4SJ
Tel: 01262 670161
Fax: 01262 605666
E-mail: enquiries@britax-pmg.com
Web site: www.britax-pmg.com

CARLYLE BUS & COACH LTD
Carlyle Business Park, Great Bridge Street,
Swan Village, West Bromwich B70 0XA
Tel: 0121 524 1200
Fax: 0121 524 1201
E-mail: admin@carlyleplc.co.uk
Web site: www.carlyleplc.co.uk

EXPRESS COACH REPAIRS LTD
Outgang Lane, Pickering YO18 7JA
Tel: 01751 475215

Fax: 01751 475215
E-mail: info@expresscoachrepairs.co.uk
Web site: www.expresscoachrepairs.co.uk

HAPPICH UK LTD
Unit 30/31, Fort Industrial Park, Fort Parkway,
Castle Bromwich B35 7AR
Tel: 0121 747 4400
Fax: 0121 747 4977
E-mail: sales@happich.co.uk
Web site: www.happich.co.uk

INVERTEC LTD
Whelford Road, Fairford GL7 4DT
Tel: 01285 713550
Fax: 01285 713548
Mobile: 07802 793828
E-mail: ian@invertec.co.uk
Web site: www.invertec.co.uk

KCP CAR & COMMERCIAL LTD
Unit 15, Hillside Business Park, Kempson Way,
Bury St Edmunds, Suffolk IP32 7EA
Tel: 01284 750777
Fax: 01284 750773
E-mail: info@kcpcarandcommercial.co.uk
Web site: www.kcpcarandcommercial.co.uk

KELLETT (UK) LTD
8 Stevenson Way, Sheffield S9 3WZ.
Tel: 0114 261 1122.
Fax: 0114 261 1199.
E-mail: sales@kellett.co.uk

OPTARE PARTS DIVISION (Leeds)
Manston Lane, Leeds LS15 8SU
Tel: 0113 264 5182
Fax: 0113 260 6635
E-mail: parts@optare.com
Web site: www.optare.com

PARTLINE LTD
Dockfield Road, Shipley BD17 7AZ
Tel: 01274 531531
Fax: 01274 531088
E-mail: sales@partline.co.uk
Web site: www.partline.co.uk

PLAXTON PARTS
Ryton Road, Anston, Sheffield S25 4DL
Tel: 0833 822 6224
Fax: 01909 550050
E-mail: parts@plaxtonlimited.co.uk
Web site: www.plaxtonaftercare.co.uk

PLAXTON SERVICE
Ryton Road, Anston, Sheffield S25 4DL
Tel: 01909 551155
Fax: 01909 550050
E-mail: service@plaxtonlimited.co.uk
Web site: www.plaxtonaftercare.co.uk

RESCROFT LTD
20 Oxleasow Road, East Moons Moat, Redditch
B98 0RE
Tel: 01527 521300
Fax: 01527 521301
E-mail: info@rescroft.com
Web site: www.rescroft.com

Mirrors/Mirror Arms

ASHTREE GLASS LTD
Brownroyd Street, Bradford BD8 9AF
Tel: 01274 546732

Fax: 01274 548525
E-mail: sales@ashtreeglass.co.uk
Web site: www.ashtreeglass.co.uk

EXPRESS COACH REPAIRS LTD
Outgang Lane, Pickering YO18 7JA
Tel: 01751 475215
Fax: 01751 475215
E-mail: info@expresscoachrepairs.co.uk
Web site: www.expresscoachrepairs.co.uk

LAWTON SERVICES LTD
Knutsford Road, Church Lawton, Stoke-on-Trent
ST7 3DN
Tel: 01270 882056
Fax: 01270 883014
E-mail: andrea@lawtonservices.co.uk
Web site: www.lawtonservices.co.uk

PARMA INDUSTRIES
34-36 Carlton Park Industrial Estate,
Saxmundham, Suffolk IP17 2NL
Tel: 01728 745700
Fax: 01728 745718
E-mail: sales@parmagroup.co.uk
Web site: www.parmagroup.co.uk

PARTLINE LTD
Dockfield Road, Shipley BD17 7AZ
Tel: 01274 531531
Fax: 01274 531088
E-mail: sales@partline.co.uk
Web site: www.partline.co.uk

PLAXTON PARTS
Ryton Road, Anston, Sheffield S25 4DL
Tel: 0833 822 6224
Fax: 01909 550050
E-mail: parts@plaxtonlimited.co.uk
Web site: www.plaxtonaftercare.co.uk

VISION PSV
PSV Works, Primatestown, Ashbourne,
Co Meath, Republic of Ireland
Tel: 00 353 1 835 5538
Fax: 00 353 1 835 5541
E-mail: info@visionpsv.com
Web site: www.visionpsv-online.com

Oil Management Systems

ARRIVA BUS AND COACH
Lodge Garage, Whitehall Road West,
Gomersal, Cleckheaton, West Yorkshire
BD19 4BJ
Tel: 01274 681144
Fax: 01274 651198
E-mail: whiter@arriva.co.uk
Web site: www.arrivabusandcoach.co.uk

FUEL THEFT SOLUTIONS LTD
PO Box 2494, Stoke on Trent
ST7 2WR
Tel: 0845 077 3921
Fax: 0845 077 3922
E-mail: sales@dieseldye.com
Web site: www.dieseldye.com

GROENEVELD UK LTD
The Greentec Centre, Gelders Hall Road,
Shepshed, Leicestershire LE12 9NH
Tel: 01509 600033
Fax: 01509 602000
E-mail: info@groeneveld.co.uk
Web site: www.groeneveld.co.uk

INTERLUBE SYSTEMS LTD
St Modwen Road, Plymouth PL6 8LH
Tel: 01752 676000
Fax: 01752 676001
E-mail: info@interlubesystems.co.uk
Web site: www.interlubesystems.co.uk

MARTYN INDUSTRIALS LTD
5 Brunel Way, Durranhill, Harraby,
Carlisle CA1 3NQ
Tel: 01228 544000
Fax: 01228 544001
E-mail: enquiries@martyn-industrials.co.uk
Web site: www.martyn-industrials.com

STERTIL UK LTD
Unit A, Brackmills Business Park, Caswell Road,
Northampton NN4 7PW
Tel: 08707 700471
Fax: 01604 765181
E-mail: info@stertiluk.com
Web site: www.stertiluk.com

Painting & Signwriting

ARRIVA BUS AND COACH
Lodge Garage, Whitehall Road West, Gomersal,
Cleckheaton, West Yorkshire BD19 4BJ
Tel: 01274 681144
Fax: 01274 651198
E-mail: whiter@arriva.co.uk
Web site: www.arrivabusandcoach.co.uk

BLACKPOOL COACH SERVICES
Burton Road, Blackpool FY4 4NW
Tel/Fax: 01253 698686
Web site: www.blackpoolcoachservices.co.uk

**BULWARK BUS & COACH
ENGINEERING LTD**
Gate 3, Bulwark Industrial Estate, Chepstow
NP16 5QZ
Tel: 01291 622326
Fax: 01291 622726

CHANNEL COMMERCIALS PLC
Unit 6, Cobbs Wood Industrial Estate,
Brunswick Road, Ashford TN23 1EH
Tel: 01233 629272
Fax: 01233 636322
E-mail: info@ccplc.co.uk
Web site: www.channelcommercials.co.uk

EXPRESS COACH REPAIRS LTD
Outgang Lane, Pickering YO18 7JA
Tel: 01751 475215
Fax: 01751 475215
E-mail: info@expresscoachrepairs.co.uk
Web site: www.expresscoachrepairs.co.uk

HANTS & DORSET TRIM LTD
Canada Road, West Wellow, Hampshire
SO51 6DE
Tel: 02380 644200
Fax: 02380 647802
E-mail: dclack@hdtrim.co.uk
Web site: www.hantsanddorsettrim.co.uk

LAWTON SERVICES LTD
Knutsford Road, Church Lawton, Stoke-on-Trent
ST7 3DN
Tel: 01270 882056
Fax: 01270 883014
E-mail: andrea@lawtonservices.co.uk
Web site: www.lawtonservices.co.uk

NORBURY BLINDS LTD
41-45 Hanley Street, Newtown, Birmingham
B19 3SP
Tel: 0121 359 4311
Fax: 0121 359 6388
E-mail: info@norbury-blinds.com
Web site: www.norbury-blinds.com

**OPTARE PRODUCT SUPPORT
LONDON**
Unit 9, Eurocourt, Olivers Close, West Thurrock
RM20 3EE
Tel: 01708 896860
Fax: 01708 869920
E-mail: london.service@optare.com

**OPTARE PRODUCT SUPPORT
ROTHERHAM**
Denby Way, Hellaby, Rotherham S66 8HR
Tel: 01709 535100
Fax: 01709 535102
E-mail: rotherham.service@optare.com

RH BODYWORKS
A140 Ipswich Road, Brome, Eye IP23 8AW
Tel: 01379 870666
Fax: 01379 872106
E-mail: mike.ball@rhbodyworks.co.uk
Web site: www.rhbodyworks.co.uk

VOLVO BUS AND COACH CENTRE
Parts Sales & Body Repair/Refurbishment
Specialists
Byron Street Extension, Loughborough LE11 5HE
Tel: 01509 217700
Fax: 01509 238770
E-mail (Body Support): dporter@
volvocoachsales.co.uk
Web site: www.volvo.com

Parts Suppliers

ABACUS TRANSPORT PRODUCTS LTD
Abacus House, Highlode Industrial Estate,
Ramsey, Huntingdon PE26 2RB
Tel: 01487 710700
Fax: 01487 710626
E-mail: sales@abacus-tp.com
Web site: www.abacus-tp.com

AIR DOOR SERVICES
The Pavillions, Holly Lane Industrial Estate,
Atherstone CV9 2QZ
Tel: 01827 711660
Fax: 01827 713577
E-mail: airdoorservices@aol.com

ARRIVA BUS AND COACH
Lodge Garage, Whitehall Road West, Gomersal,
Cleckheaton, West Yorkshire BD19 4BJ
Tel: 01274 681144
Fax: 01274 651198
E-mail: whiter@arriva.co.uk
Web site: www.arrivabusandcoach.co.uk

ASHTREE GLASS LTD
Brownroyd Street, Bradford BO8 9AF
Tel: 01274 546 732
Fax: 01274 548 525
E-mail: sales@ashtreeglass.co.uk
Web site: www.ashtreeglass.co.uk

M BARNWELL SERVICES LTD
Reginald Road, Smethwick B67 5AS
Tel: 0121 429 8011

Fax: 0121 434 3016
E-mail: sales@barnwell.co.uk
Web site: www.barnwell.co.uk

**BRITISH BUS SALES
– MIKE NASH**
PO Box 534, Dorking, Surrey RH5 5XB
Tel: 07836 656692
E-mail: nashionalbus1@btconnect.com
Web site: www.britishbussales.co.uk

BRT BEARINGS LTD
21-24 Regal Road, Wisbech,
Cambridgeshire PE13 2RQ
Tel: 01945 464 097
Fax: 01945 464 523
E-mail: brt.sales@brt-bearings.com
Web site: www.brt-bearings.com

CARLYLE BUS & COACH LTD
Carlyle Business Park, Great Bridge Street,
Swan Village, West Bromwich B70 0X4
Tel: 0121 524 1200
Fax: 0121 524 1201
E-mail: admin@carlyleplc.co.uk
Web site: www.carlyleplc.co.uk

CLAYTON HEATERS LTD
Hunter Terrace, Fletchworth Gate,
Burnsall Road, Coventry CV5 6SP
Tel: 02476 691 916 **Fax:** 02476 691 969
E-mail: admin@claytoncc.co.uk
Web site: www.claytoncc.co.uk

COACH-AID
Unit 2, Brindley Close, Tollgate Industrial Estate,
Stafford ST16 3SU
Tel: 01785 222666
E-mail: workshop@coach-aid.com
Web site: www.coach-aid.com

CRESCENT FACILITIES LTD
72 Willow Crescent, Chapeltown,
Sheffield S35 1QS
Tel/Fax: 0114 245 1050
E-mail: cfl.chris@btinternet.com
Web site: www.cflparts.com

CREST COACH CONVERSIONS
Unit 5, Holmeroyd Road, Bentley Moor Lane,
Carcroft, Doncaster DN6 7BH
Tel: 01302 723723
Fax: 01302 724724

CREWE ENGINES
Warmingham Road, Crewe CW1 4PQ
Tel: 01270 526333
Fax: 01270 526433
E-mail: sales@creweengines.co.uk
Web site: www.creweengines.co.uk

CUMMINS UK
40-44 Rutherford Drive, Park Farm South,
Wellingborough NN8 6AN
Tel: 01933 334200
Fax: 01933 334198
E-mail: cduksales@cummins.com
Web site: www.cummins-uk.com

DINEX EXHAUSTS LTD
14 Chesford Grange, Woolston, Warrington
WA1 3BT
Tel: 01925 849849
Fax: 01925 849850
E-mail: dinex@dinex.co.uk

DIRECT PARTS LTD
Unit 1, Churnet Court, Churnetside Business
Park, Harrison Way, Cheddleton ST13 7EF
Tel: 01538 361777
Fax: 01538 369100
E-mail: sales@direct-group.co.uk
Web site: www.direct-group.co.uk

ERENTEK LTD
Malt Kiln Lane, Waddington, Lincoln LN5 9RT
Tel: 01522 720065
Fax: 01522 729155
E-mail: sales@erentek.co.uk
Web site: www.erentek.co.uk

EXPRESS COACH REPAIRS LTD
Outgang Lane, Pickering YO18 7JA
Tel: 01751 475215
Fax: 01751 475215
E-mail: info@expresscoachrepairs.co.uk
Web site: www.expresscoachrepairs.co.uk

GARDNER PARTS LTD
Centurion Court, Centurion Way, Leyland,
Lancashire PR25 3UQ
Tel: 01772 642460
Fax: 01772 621333
E-mail: sales@gardnerparts.co.uk
Web site: www.gardnerparts.co.uk

HAPPICH UK LTD
Unit 30/31, Fort Industrial Park, Fort Parkway,
Castle Bromwich B35 7AR
Tel: 0121 747 4400
Fax: 0121 747 4977
E-mail: sales@happich.co.uk
Web site: www.happich.co.uk

HART BROTHERS (ENGINEERING) LTD
Soho Works, Soho Street, Oldham OL4 2AD
Tel: 0161 737 6791

THOMAS HARDIE COMMERCIALS LTD
Newstet Road, Knowsley Industrial Park,
Liverpool L33 7TJ
Tel: 0151 549 3000
E-mail: info@thardie.co.uk

IMEXPART LTD
Links 31, Willowbridge Way, Whitwood,
Castleford WF10 5NP
Tel: 0845 605 0404
Fax: 01977 513412
E-mail: sales@imexpart.com
Web site: www.imexpart.com

IMPERIAL ENGINEERING
Delamare Road, Cheshunt, Hertfordshire
EN8 9UD
Tel: 01992 634255
Fax: 01992 630506
E-mail: orders@imperialengineering.co.uk
Web site: www.imperialengineering.co.uk

KCP CAR & COMMERCIAL LTD
Unit 15, Hillside Business Park, Kempson Way,
Bury St Edmunds, Suffolk IP32 7EA
Tel: 01284 750777
Fax: 01284 750773
E-mail: info@kcpcarandcommercial.co.uk
Web site: www.kcpcarandcommercial.co.uk

KELLETT (UK) LTD
8 Stevenson Way, Sheffield S9 3WZ
Tel: 0114 261 1122

Fax: 0114 261 1199
E-mail: sales@kellett.co.uk

**KNORR-BREMSE SYSTEMS FOR
COMMERCIAL VEHICLES LTD**
Century House, Folly Brook Road, Emerald Park
East, Emersons Green, Bristol BS16 7FE
Tel: 0117 984 6100
Fax: 0117 984 6101
Web site: www.knorr-bremse.co.uk

LAWTON SERVICES LTD
Knutsford Road, Church Lawton, Stoke-on-Trent
ST7 3DN
Tel: 01270 882056
Fax: 01270 883014
E-mail: andrea@lawtonservices.co.uk
Web site: www.lawtonservices.co.uk

LH GROUP SERVICES LTD
Graycar Business Park, Barton under Needwood,
Burton-on-Trent DE13 8EN
Tel: 01283 722600
Fax: 01283 722622
E-mail: lh@lh-group.com
Web site: www.lh-group.com

MOCAP LIMITED
Hortonwood 35, Telford TF1 7YW
Tel: 01952 670247
Fax: 01952 670241
E-mail: sales@mocap.co.uk
Web site: www.mocap.co.uk

MOSELEY (PCV) LTD
Elmsall Way, Dale Lane, South Elmsall, Pontefract,
West Yorkshire WF9 2XS
Tel: 01977 609000 **Fax:** 01977 609900
E-mail: sales@moseleycoachsales.co.uk
Web site: www.moseleycoachsales.co.uk

MOSELEY DISTRIBUTORS LTD
Rydenmains, Condorrat Road, Glenmavis,
Airdrie ML6 0PP
Tel: 01236 750501
Fax: 01236 750504
E-mail: enquiries@moseleydistributors.co.uk
Web site: www.moseleydistributors.co.uk

OPTARE PARTS DIVISION (Leeds)
Manston Lane, Leeds LS15 8SU
Tel: 0113 264 5182
Fax: 0113 260 6635
E-mail: parts@optare.com
Web site: www.optare.com

PARTLINE LTD
Dockfield Road, Shipley BD17 7AZ
Tel: 01274 531531
Fax: 01274 531088
E-mail: sales@partline.co.uk
Web site: www.partline.co.uk

PLAXTON PARTS
Ryton Road, Anston, Sheffield S25 4DL
Tel: 0833 822 6224
Fax: 01909 550050
E-mail: parts@plaxtonlimited.co.uk
Web site: www.plaxtonaftercare.co.uk

PNEUMAX LTD
110 Vista Park, Mauretania Road, Nursling,
Southampton SO16 0YS
Tel: 02380 740412
Fax: 02380 739340

E-mail: sales@pneumax.co.uk
Web site: www.pneumax.co.uk

PSV GLASS
Hillbottom Road, High Wycombe HP12 4HJ
Tel: 01494 533131
Fax: 01494 462675
E-mail: sales@psvglass.co.uk
Web site: www.psvglass.com

Q'STRAINT
73-76 John Wilson Business Park, Whitstable,
Kent CT5 3QU
Tel: 01227 773035
Fax: 01227 770035
E-mail: info@qstraint.co.uk
Web site: www.qstraint.com

QUEENSBRIDGE (PSV) LTD
Longlands Industrial Estate, Milner Way,
Ossett WF5 9JE
Tel: 01924 281871
Fax: 01924 281807
E-mail: craig@queensbridgeltd.co.uk
Web site: www.queensbridgeltd.co.uk

ROADLINK INTERNATIONAL LTD
Strawberry Lane, Willenhall, West Midlands
WV13 3RL
Tel: 01902 636206
Fax: 01902 631515
E-mail: sales@roadlink-international.co.uk
Web site: www.roadlink-international.co.uk

ROUTEMASTER BUSES LTD
Unit 3, Gate Farm, Wettenhall Road, Nantwich,
Cheshire CW5 6AL
Tel: 07832 982436
E-mail: info@routemasterbuses.co.uk
Web site: www.routemasterbuses.co.uk

SHADES TECHNICS LTD
Units E3 & E4, Rd Park, Stephenson Close,
Hoddesdon, Hertfordshire EN11 0BW
Tel: 01992 501683
Fax: 01992 501669
E-mail: sales@shades-technics.com
Web site: www.shades-technics.com

SHAWSON SUPPLY LTD
12 Station Road, Saintfield, County Down,
Northern Ireland BT24 7DU
Tel: 028 9751 0994
Fax: 028 9751 0816
E-mail: info@shawsonsupply.com
Web site: www.shawsonsupply.com

TRAMONTANA
Chapelknowe Road, Carfin, Motherwell ML1 5LE
Tel: 01698 861790
Fax: 01698 860778
E-mail: wdt90@tiscali.co.uk
Web site: www.brittnet.net/tramontanacoach

TTS UK
Total Tool Solutions Ltd, Newhaven Business
Park, Lowergate, Milnsbridge, Huddersfield
HD3 4HS
Tel: 01484 642211 **Fax:** 01484 461002
E-mail: sales@ttsuk.com
Web site: www.ttsuk.com

VOLVO BUS AND COACH CENTRE
Parts Sales & Body Repair/Refurbishment
Specialists

Byron Street Extension, Loughborough LE11 5HE
Tel: 01509 217700
Fax: 01509 238770
E-mail (Parts): csparts@volvocoachsales.co.uk
Web site: www.volvo.com

WABCO AUTOMOTIVE UK LTD
Texas Street, Morley LS27 0HQ
Tel: 0113 251 2510
Fax: 0113 251 2844
E-mail: info.uk@wabco-auto.com
Web site: www.wabco-auto.com

WACTON COACH SALES & SERVICES
Linton Trading Estate, Bromyard HR7 4QL
Tel: 01885 482782
Fax: 01885 482127

WALSH'S ENGINEERING
Barton Moss Road, Eccles, Manchester M30 7RL
Tel: 0161 787 7017
Fax: 0161 787 7038
E-mail: walshs@gardnerdiesel.co.uk
Web site: www.gardnerdiesel.co.uk

TREVOR WIGLEY & SON BUS LTD
Passenger Vehicle Dismantling/Spares
Works: Boulder Bridge Lane, off Shaw Lane,
Barnsley S71 3HJ
Correspondence: 148 Royston Road,
Cudworth, Barnsley S72 8BN
Tel: 01226 713636
Fax: 01226 700199
E-mail: wigleys@btintenet.com
Web site: www.twigley.com

ZF POWERTRAIN
Stringes Close, Willenhall WV13 1LE
Tel: 01902 366000
Fax: 01902 366504
E-mail: sales@powertrain.org.uk
Web site: www.powertrain.org.uk

Passenger Information Systems

ARRIVA BUS AND COACH
Lodge Garage, Whitehall Road West, Gomersal,
Cleckheaton, West Yorkshire BD19 4BJ
Tel: 01274 681144
Fax: 01274 651198
E-mail: whiter@arriva.co.uk
Web site: www.arrivabusandcoach.co.uk

AUTOSOUND LTD
4 Lister Street, Dudley Hill, Bradford BD4 9PQ
Tel: 01274 688990
Fax: 01274 651318
E-mail: keith.ellis@autosound.co.uk
Web site: www.autosound.co.uk

M BISSELL DISPLAY LTD
Unit 15, Beechwood Business Park, Burdock
Close, Hanks Green, Cannock, Staffordshire
WS11 7GB
Tel: 01543 502115
Fax: 01543 502118
E-mail: sales@bisselldisplay.com
Web site: www.bisselldisplay.com

HANOVER DISPLAYS LTD
Unit 24, Cliffe Industrial Estate, Lewes BN8 6JL
Tel: 01273 477528
Fax: 01273 407766
E-mail: hanover@hanoverdisplays.com
Web site: www.hanoverdisplays.com

INIT – INNOVATIONS IN TRANSPORTATION LTD
49 Stoney Street, The Lace Market,
Nottingham NG1 1LX
Tel: 0870 890 4648
Fax: 0115 989 5463
E-mail: sales@init.co.uk
Web site: www.init.co.uk

J MURDOCH WIGHT LTD
Systems House, Pentland Industrial Estate,
Loanhead, Midlothian EH20 9QH
Tel: 0131 440 3633
Fax: 0131 440 3637
E-mail: enquiries@jmw-group.co.uk
Web site: www.jmw-group.co.uk

JOURNEY PLAN LTD
30 Canmore Street, Dunfermline
KY12 7NT
Tel: 01383 731048
Fax: 01383 731788
E-mail: support@journeyplan.co.uk
Web site: www.journeyplan.co.uk

McKENNA BROTHERS LTD
McKenna House, Jubilee Road, Middleton,
Manchester M24 2LX
Tel: 0161 655 3244
Fax: 0161 655 3059
E-mail: info@mckennabrothers.co.uk
Web site: www.mckennabrothers.co.uk

SSL SIMULATION SYSTEMS LTD
Unit 12, Market Industrial Estate, Yatton,
Bristol BS49 4RF
Tel: 01934 838803
Fax: 01934 876202
E-mail: ssl@simulation-systems.co.uk
Web site: www.simulation-systems.co.uk

TRAPEZE GROUP (UK) LTD
The Mill, Staverton, Nr Trowbridge,
Bath BA14 6PH
Tel: 0844 561 6771
Fax: 01225 784222
E-Mail: info@trapezegroup.co.uk
Web site: www.trapezegroup.co.uk

VULTRON INTERNATIONAL LTD
Unit 2, Stadium Way, Elland Road,
Leeds LS11 0EW
Tel: 0113 387 7310
Fax: 0113 387 7317
E-mail: sales@vultron.co.uk
Web site: www.vultron.co.uk

Pneumatic Valves/Cylinders

OPTARE PARTS DIVISION
(Leeds)
Manston Lane, Leeds
LS15 8SU
Tel: 0113 264 5182
Fax: 0113 260 6635
E-mail: parts@optare.com
Web site: www.optare.com

PNEUMAX LTD
110 Vista Park, Mauretania Road, Nursling,
Southampton SO16 0YS
Tel: 02380 740412
Fax: 02380 739340
E-mail: sales@pneumax.co.uk
Web site: www.pneumax.co.uk

Rapid Transit/Priority Equipment

ALSTOM TRANSPORT SA
48 rue Albert Dhalenne, F-93482 Saint-Ouen
Cedex, France
Tel: 00 33 1 41 66 90 00
Fax: 00 33 1 41 66 96 66
Web site: www.transport.alstom.com

BALFOUR BEATTY RAIL LTD
86 Station Road, Redhill, Surrey RH1 1PQ
Tel: 01737 785000
E-mail: info@bbrail.com
Web site: www.bbrail.co.uk

BRECKNELL WILLIS & CO LTD
East Street, Chard TA20 1EP
Tel: 01460 64941
Fax: 01460 66122
E-mail: enquiries@brecknellwillis.com
Web site: www.brecknell-willis.co.uk

PARRY PEOPLE MOVERS LTD
Overend Road, Cradley Heath, Dudley B64 7DD
Tel: 01384 569553
Fax: 01384 637753
E-mail: jpmparry@aol.com
Web site: www.parrypeoplemovers.com

SIEMENS TRAFFIC CONTROLS LTD
Sopers Lane, Poole BH17 7ER
Tel: 01202 782000
Web site: www.siemens.co.uk

SUSTRACO LTD
Ashgrove Road, Redland, Bristol BS6 6LY
Tel: 0117 930 0901
Web site: www.ultralightrail.com

Repairs/Refurbishment -
see Body Repairs, above

Retarders & Speed Control Systems

ARRIVA BUS AND COACH
Lodge Garage, Whitehall Road West, Gomersal,
Cleckheaton, West Yorkshire BD19 4BJ
Tel: 01274 681144
Fax: 01274 651198
E-mail: whiter@arriva.co.uk
Web site: www.arrivabusandcoach.co.uk

CHASSIS DEVELOPMENTS LTD
Grovebury Road, Leighton Buzzard LU7 8SL
Tel: 01525 374151
Fax: 01525 370127
E-mail: sales@chassisdevelopments.com
Web site: www.chassisdevelopments.co.uk

GROENEVELD UK LTD
The Greentec Centre, Gelders Hall Road,
Shepshed, Leicestershire LE12 9NH
Tel: 01509 600033
Fax: 01509 602000
E-mail: info@groeneveld.co.uk
Web site: www.groeneveld.co.uk

NUTEXA FRICTIONS LTD
PO Box 11, New Hall Lane, Hoylake, Wirral
CH47 4DH
Tel: 0151 632 5903
Fax: 0151 632 5908
E-mail: sales@nutexafrictions.co.uk
Web Site: www.sergeant.co.uk

PARTLINE LTD
Dockfield Road, Shipley BD17 7AZ
Tel: 01274 531531
Fax: 01274 531088
E-mail: sales@partline.co.uk
Web site: www.partline.co.uk

TELMA RETARDER LTD
25 Clarke Road, Mount Farm, Milton Keynes
MK1 1LG
Tel: 01908 642822
Fax: 01908 641348
E-mail: telma@telma.co.uk
Web site: www.telma.co.uk

VOITH TURBO LTD
6 Beddington Farm Road, Croydon CR0 4XB
Tel: 020 8667 0333
Fax: 020 8667 0403
E-mail: Road.UK@voith.com
Web site: www.voithturbo.com

WABCO AUTOMOTIVE UK LTD
Texas Street, Morley LS27 0HQ.
Tel: 0113 251 2510.
Fax: 0113 251 2844
E-mail: info.uk@wabco-auto.com
Web site: www.wabco-auto.com

Reversing Safety Systems

ARRIVA BUS AND COACH
Lodge Garage, Whitehall Road West, Gomersal,
Cleckheaton, West Yorkshire BD19 4BJ
Tel: 01274 681144
Fax: 01274 651198
E-mail: whiter@arriva.co.uk
Web site: www.arrivabusandcoach.co.uk

AUTOSOUND LTD
4 Lister Street, Dudley Hill, Bradford BD4 9PQ
Tel: 01274 688990
Fax: 01274 651318
E-mail: keith.ellis@autosound.co.uk
Web site: www.autosound.co.uk

ASHTREE GLASS LTD
Brownroyd Street, Bradford BO8 9AF
Tel: 01274 546 732 **Fax:** 01274 548 525
E-mail: sales@ashtreeglass.co.uk
Web site: www.ashtreeglass.co.uk

AVT SYSTEMS LTD
Unit 3 & 4, Tything Road East, Alcester,
Warwickshire B49 6ES
Tel: 01789 400357
Fax: 01789 400359
E-mail: enquiries@avtsystems.co.uk
Web site: www.avtsystems.co.uk

BRIGADE ELECTRONICS PLC
Brigade House, The Mills, Station Road,
South Darenth DA4 9BD
Tel: 01322 420300
Fax: 01322 420343
E-mail: info@brigade-electronics.co.uk
Web site: www.brigade-electronics.com

CARLYLE BUS & COACH LTD
Carlyle Business Park, Great Bridge Street, Swan
Village, West Bromwich B70 0XA
Tel: 0121 524 1200
Fax: 0121 524 1201
E-mail: admin@carlyleplc.co.uk
Web site: carlyleplc.co.uk

CLAN TOOLS & PLANT LTD
3 Greenhill Avenue, Giffnock, Glasgow G46 6QX
Tel: 0141 638 8040
Fax: 0141 638 8881
E-mail: clantools@btconnect.com
Web site: www.clantools.com

EXPRESS COACH REPAIRS LTD
Outgang Lane, Pickering YO18 7JA
Tel: 01751 475215
Fax: 01751 475215
E-mail: info@expresscoachrepairs.co.uk
Web site: www.expresscoachrepairs.co.uk

GROENEVELD UK LTD
The Greentec Centre, Gelders Hall Road,
Shepshed, Leicestershire LE12 9NH
Tel: 01509 600033
Fax: 01509 602000
E-mail: info@groeneveld.co.uk
Web site: www.groeneveld.co.uk

KCP CAR & COMMERCIAL LTD
Unit 15, Hillside Business Park, Kempson Way,
Bury St Edmunds, Suffolk IP32 7EA
Tel: 01284 750777
Fax: 01284 750773
E-mail: info@kcpcarandcommercial.co.uk
Web site: www.kcpcarandcommercial.co.uk

KELLETT (UK) LTD
8 Stevenson Way, Sheffield S9 3WZ
Tel: 0114 261 1122
Fax: 0114 261 1199
E-mail: sales@kellett.co.uk

PARTLINE LTD
Dockfield Road, Shipley BD17 7AZ
Tel: 01274 531531
Fax: 01274 531088
E-mail: sales@partline.co.uk
Web site: www.partline.co.uk

PLAXTON PARTS
Ryton Road, Anston, Sheffield S25 4DL
Tel: 0833 822 6224
Fax: 01909 550050
E-mail: parts@plaxtonlimited.co.uk
Web site: www.plaxtonaftercare.co.uk

PLAXTON SERVICE
Ryton Road, Anston, Sheffield S25 4DL
Tel: 01909 551155
Fax: 01909 550050
E-mail: service@plaxtonlimited.co.uk
Web site: www.plaxtonaftercare.co.uk

Roller Blinds - Passenger & Driver

ARRIVA BUS AND COACH
Lodge Garage, Whitehall Road West,
Gomersal, Cleckheaton, West Yorkshire
BD19 4BJ
Tel: 01274 681144
Fax: 01274 651198
E-mail: whiter@arriva.co.uk
Web site: www.arrivabusandcoach.co.uk

CARLYLE BUS & COACH LTD
Carlyle Business Park, Great Bridge Street,
Swan Village, West Bromwich B70 0XA
Tel: 0121 524 1200
Fax: 0121 524 1201
E-mail: admin@carlyleplc.co.uk
Web site: carlyleplc.co.uk

HAPPICH UK LTD
Unit 30/31, Fort Industrial Park, Fort Parkway,
Castle Bromwich B35 7AR
Tel: 0121 747 4400
Fax: 0121 747 4977
E-mail: sales@happich.co.uk
Web site: www.happich.co.uk

LAWTON SERVICES LTD
Knutsford Road, Church Lawton, Stoke-on-Trent
ST7 3DN
Tel: 01270 882056
Fax: 01270 883014
E-mail: andrea@lawtonservices.co.uk
Web site: www.lawtonservices.co.uk

PLAXTON PARTS
Ryton Road, Anston, Sheffield S25 4DL
Tel: 0833 822 6224
Fax: 01909 550050
E-mail: parts@plaxtonlimited.co.uk
Web site: www.plaxtonaftercare.co.uk

PLAXTON SERVICE
Ryton Road, Anston, Sheffield S25 4DL
Tel: 01909 551155
Fax: 01909 550050
E-mail: service@plaxtonlimited.co.uk
Web site: www.plaxtonaftercare.co.uk

TEMPLE MANUFACTURING CO LTD
Unit 2, First Avenue, West Denbigh, Bletchley,
Milton Keynes MK1 1DX
Tel: 01908 642233
Fax: 01908 373396
E-mail: iantemple@btconnect.com

WIDNEY UK LTD
Plume Street, Aston, Birmingham B6 7SA
Tel: 0121 327 5500
Fax: 0121 328 2466
E-mail: info@widney.co.uk
Web site: www.widney.co.uk

Roof-Lining Fabrics

AK CARPETS LTD
Unit 15, Deanfield Court, Link 59 Business Park,
Clitheroe, Lancashire BB7 1QS
Tel: 01200 444145
Fax: 01200 444180
E-mail: info@akcarpets.com
Web site: www.akcarpets.com

ARDEE COACH TRIM LTD
Artnalivery, Ardee, Co Louth, Republic of Ireland
Tel: 00 353 41 685 3599
Fax: 00 353 41 685 7016
E-mail: info@ardeecoachtrim.com
Web site: www.ardeecoachtrim.com

ARRIVA BUS AND COACH
Lodge Garage, Whitehall Road West, Gomersal,
Cleckheaton, West Yorkshire BD19 4BJ
Tel: 01274 681144
Fax: 01274 651198
E-mail: whiter@arriva.co.uk
Web site: www.arrivabusandcoach.co.uk

AUTOMATE WHEEL COVERS LTD
California Mills, Oxford Road, Gomersal
BD19 4HQ
Tel: 01274 862700 **Fax:** 01274 851989
E-mail: sales@wheelcovers.com
Web site: www.wheeltrimshop.com

AUTOMOTIVE TEXTILE INDUSTRIES
Unit 15 & 16, Priest Court, Springfield Business Park, Grantham NG31 7BG
Tel: 01476 593050
Fax: 01476 593607
E-mail: sales@autotex.com
Web site: www.autotex.com

DUOFLEX LTD
Trimmingham House, 2 Shires Road, Buckingham Road Industrial Estate, Brackley, Northamptonshire NN13 7EZ
Tel: 01280 701366
Fax: 01280 704799
E-mail: sales@duoflex.co.uk
Web site: www.duoflex.co.uk

EXPRESS COACH REPAIRS LTD
Outgang Lane, Pickering YO18 7JA
Tel: 01751 475215
Fax: 01751 475215
E-mail: info@expresscoachrepairs.co.uk
Web site: www.expresscoachrepairs.co.uk

HAPPICH UK LTD
Unit 30/31, Fort Industrial Park, Fort Parkway, Castle Bromwich B35 7AR
Tel: 0121 747 4400
Fax: 0121 747 4977
E-mail: sales@happich.co.uk
Web site: www.happich.co.uk

MARTYN INDUSTRIALS LTD
5 Brunel Way, Durranhill, Harraby, Carlisle CA1 3NQ
Tel: 01228 544000
Fax: 01228 544001
E-mail: enquiries@martyn-industrials.co.uk
Web site: www.martyn-industrials.com

Seat Belts/Restraint Systems

ABACUS TRANSPORT PRODUCTS LTD
Abacus House, Highlode Industrial Estate, Ramsey, Huntingdon PE26 2RB
Tel: 01487 710700
Fax: 01487 710626
E-mail: sales@abacus-tp.com
Web site: www.abacus-tp.com

AMSAFE COMMERCIAL PRODUCTS LTD (formerly SAFETEX)
Unit 16/17, Bookham Industrial Park, Church Road, Bookham KT23 3EV
Tel: 01372 451272
Fax: 01372 451282
E-mail: sales-acsp@amsafe.com
Web site: www.amsafe.com

ARDEE COACH TRIM LTD
Artnalivery, Ardee, Co Louth, Republic of Ireland
Tel: 00 353 41 685 3599
Fax: 00 353 41 685 7016
E-mail: info@ardeecoachtrim.com
Web site: www.ardeecoachtrim.com

ARRIVA BUS AND COACH
Lodge Garage, Whitehall Road West, Gomersal, Cleckheaton, West Yorkshire BD19 4BJ
Tel: 01274 681144
Fax: 01274 651198
E-mail: whiter@arriva.co.uk
Web site: www.arrivabusandcoach.co.uk

CARLYLE BUS & COACH LTD
Carlyle Business Park, Great Bridge Street, Swan Village, West Bromwich B70 0XA
Tel: 0121 524 1200
Fax: 0121 524 1201
E-mail: admin@carlyleplc.co.uk
Web site: www.carlyleplc.co.uk

EXPRESS COACH REPAIRS LTD
Outgang Lane, Pickering YO18 7JA
Tel: 01751 475215
Fax: 01751 475215
E-mail: info@expresscoachrepairs.co.uk
Web site: www.expresscoachrepairs.co.uk

KCP CAR & COMMERCIAL LTD
Unit 15, Hillside Business Park, Kempson Way, Bury St Edmunds, Suffolk IP32 7EA
Tel: 01284 750777
Fax: 01284 750773
E-mail: info@kcpcarandcommercial.co.uk
Web site: www.kcpcarandcommercial.co.uk

LAWTON SERVICES LTD
Knutsford Road, Church Lawton, Stoke-on-Trent ST7 3DN
Tel: 01270 882056
Fax: 01270 883014
E-mail: andrea@lawtonservices.co.uk
Web site: www.lawtonservices.co.uk

PARTLINE LTD
Dockfield Road, Shipley BD17 7AZ
Tel: 01274 531531
Fax: 01274 531088
E-mail: sales@partline.co.uk
Web site: www.partline.co.uk

PLAXTON PARTS
Ryton Road, Anston, Sheffield S25 4DL
Tel: 0833 822 6224
Fax: 01909 550050
E-mail: parts@plaxtonlimited.co.uk
Web site: www.plaxtonaftercare.co.uk

PLAXTON SERVICE
Ryton Road, Anston, Sheffield S25 4DL
Tel: 01909 551155
Fax: 01909 550050
E-mail: service@plaxtonlimited.co.uk
Web site: www.plaxtonaftercare.co.uk

Q'STRAINT
Units 72-76 John Wilson Business Park, Whitstable, Kent CT5 3QT
Tel: 01227 773 035
Fax: 01227 770 035
E-mail: info@qstraint.co.uk
Web site: www.qstraint.com

RESCROFT LTD
20 Oxleasow Road, East Moons Moat, Redditch B98 0RE
Tel: 01527 521300
Fax: 01527 521301
E-mail: info@rescroft.com
Web site: www.rescroft.com

SECURON (AMERSHAM) LTD
The Hill, Winchmore Hill, Amersham HP7 0NZ
Tel: 01494 434455
Fax: 01494 726499
E-mail: uksp@securon.co.uk
Web site: www.securon.co.uk

TEK SEATING LTD
14 Decimus Park, Kingstanding Way, Tunbridge Wells, Kent TN2 3GP
Tel: 01892 515028
Fax: 01892 529751
E-mail: sales@tekseating.co.uk
Web site: www.tekseating.co.uk

TRAMONTANA
Chapelknowe Road, Carfin, Motherwell ML1 5LE
Tel: 01698 861790
Fax: 01698 860778
E-mail: wdt90@tiscali.co.uk
Web site: www.brittnet.net/tramontanacoach

UNWIN SAFETY SYSTEMS
Unwin House, The Horseshoe, Coat Road, Martock TA12 6EY
Tel: 01935 827740
Fax: 01935 827760
E-mail: sales@unwin-safety.co.uk
Web site: www.unwin-safety.com

Seats/Seat Cushions & Seat Frames

ABACUS TRANSPORT PRODUCTS LTD
Abacus House, Highlode Industrial Estate, Ramsey, Huntingdon PE26 2RB
Tel: 01487 710700
Fax: 01487 710626
E-mail: sales@abacus-tp.com
Web site: www.abacus-tp.com

ARDEE COACH TRIM LTD
Artnalivery, Ardee, Co Louth, Republic of Ireland
Tel: 00 353 41 685 3599
Fax: 00 353 41 685 7016
E-mail: info@ardeecoachtrim.com
Web site: www.ardeecoachtrim.com

ARRIVA BUS AND COACH
Lodge Garage, Whitehall Road West, Gomersal, Cleckheaton, West Yorkshire BD19 4BJ
Tel: 01274 681144
Fax: 01274 651198
E-mail: whiter@arriva.co.uk
Web site: www.arrivabusandcoach.co.uk

BERNSTEIN ENGINEERING LTD
Unit 4, East 41 Garside Way, Stocklake, Aylesbury HP20 1BH
Tel: 01296 395889
Fax: 01296 394939
E-mail: contact@bernsteinengineering.co.uk
Web site: www.bernsteinengineering.co.uk

CARLYLE BUS & COACH LTD
Carlyle Business Park, Great Bridge Street, Swan Village, West Bromwich B70 0XA
Tel: 0121 524 1200
Fax: 0121 524 1201
E-mail: admin@carlyleplc.co.uk
Web site: www.carlyleplc.co.uk

COGENT PASSENGER SEATING LTD
Prydwen Road, Swansea West Industrial Park, Swansea SA5 4HN
Tel: 01792 585444
Fax: 01792 588191
E-mail: enquiries@cogentseating.co.uk
Web site: www.cogentseating.co.uk

CHAPMAN DRIVER SEATING
109-138 Northwood Street, Birmingham B3 1SZ
Tel: 0845 838 2305
Fax: 0845 838 2909
E-mail: sales@chapmandriverseating.com
Web site: www.chapmandriverseating.com

DUOFLEX LTD
Trimmingham House, 2 Shires Road,
Buckingham Road Industrial Estate, Brackley,
Northamptonshire NN13 7EZ
Tel: 01280 701366
Fax: 01280 704799
E-mail: sales@duoflex.co.uk
Web site: www.duoflex.co.uk

EXPRESS COACH REPAIRS LTD
Outgang Lane, Pickering YO18 7JA
Tel: 01751 475215
Fax: 01751 475215
E-mail: info@expresscoachrepairs.co.uk
Web site: www.expresscoachrepairs.co.uk

HAPPICH UK LTD
Unit 30/31, Fort Industrial Park, Fort Parkway,
Castle Bromwich B35 7AR
Tel: 0121 747 4400
Fax: 0121 747 4977
E-mail: sales@happich.co.uk
Web site: www.happich.co.uk

HOLDSWORTH FABRICS LTD
HOPTON MILLS, MIRFIELD, WEST YORKSHIRE
WF1 8HE
Tel: 01484 859061
Fax: 01924 495605
E-mail: info@camirafabrics.co.uk
Web site: www.holdsworthfabrics.com

The Little Red Book 2012 - in association with *tbf* Transport Benevolent Fund

JBF SERVICES LTD
Southedge Works, Hipperholme, Halifax
HX3 8EF
Tel: 01422 202840
Fax: 01422 206070
E-mail: jbfservices@aol.com

KAB SEATING LTD
Round Spinney, Northampton NN3 8RS
Tel: 01604 790500
Fax: 01604 790155
E-mail: infouk@cvgrp.com
Web site: www.kabseating.com

LAWTON SERVICES LTD
Knutsford Road, Church Lawton,
Stoke-on-Trent ST7 3DN
Tel: 01270 882056
Fax: 01270 883014
E-mail: andrea@lawtonservices.co.uk
Web site: www.lawtonservices.co.uk

PHOENIX SEATING LTD
Unit 47, Bay 3, Second Avenue,
Pensnett Estate, Kingswinford
DY6 7UZ
Tel: 01384 296622
Fax: 01384 287831
E-mail: sales@phoenixseating.co.uk
Web site: www.phoenixseating.com

P.L.TRIM LTD
Burton Road, Blackpool FY4 4NW
Tel: 01253 696033
Fax: 01253 696033
E-mail: enquiries@pltrim.co.uk
Web site: www.pltrim.co.uk

PLAXTON PARTS
Ryton Road, Anston, Sheffield
S25 4DL
Tel: 0833 822 6224
Fax: 01909 550050
E-mail: parts@plaxtonlimited.co.uk
Web site: www.plaxtonaftercare.co.uk

PLAXTON SERVICE
Ryton Road, Anston, Sheffield
S25 4DL
Tel: 01909 551155
Fax: 01909 550050
E-mail: service@plaxtonlimited.co.uk
Web site: www.plaxtonaftercare.co.uk

RESCROFT LTD
20 Oxleasow Road, East Moons Moat,
Redditch B98 0RE
Tel: 01527 521300
Fax: 01527 521301
E-mail: info@rescroft.com
Web site: www.rescroft.com

SCANDUS UK
Unit 21, Gainsborough Trading Estate,
Rufford Road, Stourbridge DY9 7ND
Tel: 01384 443409
Fax: 01384 443 932
Web site: www.scandusuk.co.uk

TEK SEATING LTD
14 Decimus Park, Kingstanding Way,
unbridge Wells, Kent TN2 3GP
Tel: 01892 515028 **Fax:** 01892 529751
E-mail: sales@tekseating.co.uk
Web site: www.tekseating.co.uk

Shelters/Street Furniture

BUS SHELTERS LTD
Unit 60, Dyffryn Business Park,
Llantwit Major Road, Llandow, Cardiff CF71 7PY
Tel: 01446 795444
Fax: 01446 793344
E-mail: bus@shelters.co.uk
Web site: www.shelters.co.uk

CARMANAH TECHNOLOGIES GROUP
UK Retailer: Green Solar Solutions Ltd, Brighton
Tel: 0845 604 6606
E-mail: info@greensolarsolutionsuk.com
Web site: www.greensolarsolutionsuk.com

GABRIEL & COMPANY LTD
1 Cornwall Road, Smethwick, West Midlands
B66 2JT
Tel: 0121 555 7615
Fax: 0121 555 1922
E-mail: john.gabriel@gabrielco.com
Web site: www.gabrielco.com

MACEMAIN + AMSTAD
Boyle Road, Willowbrook Industrial Estate,
Corby NN17 5XU
Tel: 01536 401331
Fax: 01536 401298
E-mail: sales@macemainamstad.com
Web site: www.macemainamstad.com

QUEENSBURY SHELTERS
Queensbury House, Fitzherbert Road, Farlington,
Portsmouth PO6 1SE
Tel: 023 9221 0052
Fax: 023 9221 0059
E-mail: shelters@queensbury.org
Web site: www.queensburyshelters.co.uk

TRUEFORM ENGINEERING LTD
Unit 4, Pasadena Trading Estate, Pasadena Close,
Hayes UB3 3NQ
Tel: 020 8561 4959
Fax: 020 8848 1397
E-mail: sales@trueform.co.uk
Web site: www.trueform.co.uk

Shock Absorbers/Suspension

ARRIVA BUS AND COACH
Lodge Garage, Whitehall Road West, Gomersal,
Cleckheaton, West Yorkshire BD19 4BJ
Tel: 01274 681144
Fax: 01274 651198
E-mail: whiter@arriva.co.uk
Web site: www.arrivabusandcoach.co.uk

CRESCENT FACILITIES LTD
72 Willow Crescent, Chapeltown,
Sheffield S35 1QS
Tel/Fax: 0114 245 1050
E-mail: cfl.chris@btinternet.com

DIRECT PARTS LTD
Unit 1, Churnet Court, Churnetside Business
Park, Harrison Way, Cheddleton ST13 7EF
Tel: 01538 361777
Fax: 01538 369100
E-mail: sales@direct-group.co.uk
Web site: www.direct-group.co.uk

ERENTEK LTD
Malt Kiln Lane, Waddington, Lincoln LN5 9RT
Tel: 01522 720065

Fax: 01522 729155
E-mail: sale@erentek.co.uk
Web site: www.erentek.co.uk

GLIDE RITE PRODUCTS
Mill Lane, Passfield, Liphook GU30 7RP
Tel: 01428 751711
Fax: 01428 751766
E-mail: info@glide-rite.com
Web site: www.glide-rite.com

IMEXPART LTD
Links 31, Willowbridge Way, Whitwood,
Castleford WF10 5NP
Tel: 0845 605 0404
Fax: 01977 513412
E-mail: sales@imexpart.com
Web site: www.imexpart.com

KCP CAR & COMMERCIAL LTD
Unit 15, Hillside Business Park, Kempson Way,
Bury St Edmunds, Suffolk IP32 7EA
Tel: 01284 750777
Fax: 01284 750773
E-mail: info@kcpcarandcommercial.co.uk
Web site: www.kcpcarandcommercial.co.uk

KELLETT (UK) LTD
8 Stevenson Way, Sheffield S9 3WZ
Tel: 0114 261 1122 **Fax:** 0114 261 1199
E-mail: sales@kellett.co.uk

OPTARE PARTS DIVISION (Leeds)
Manston Lane, Leeds LS15 8SU
Tel: 0113 264 5182
Fax: 0113 260 6635
E-mail: parts@optare.com
Web site: www.optare.com

PARTLINE LTD
Dockfield Road, Shipley BD17 7AZ
Tel: 01274 531531
Fax: 01274 531088
E-mail: sales@partline.co.uk
Web site: www.partline.co.uk

POLYBUSH
Clywedog Road South, Wrexham Industrial
Estate, Wrexham LL13 9XS
Tel: 01978 664316
Fax: 01978 661190
E-mail: sales@polybush.co.uk
Web site: www.polybush.co.uk

ROADLINK INTERNATIONAL LTD
Strawberry Lane, Willenhall, West Midlands
WV13 3RL
Tel: 01902 636206
Fax: 01902 631515
E-mail: sales@roadlink-international.co.uk
Web site: www.roadlink-international.co.uk

SHAWSON SUPPLY LTD
12 Station Road, Saintfield, County Down,
Northern Ireland BT24 7DU
Tel: 028 9751 0994
Fax: 028 9751 0816
E-mail: info@shawsonsupply.com
Web site: www.shawsonsupply.com

Steering

ARRIVA BUS AND COACH
Lodge Garage, Whitehall Road West, Gomersal,
Cleckheaton, West Yorkshire BD19 4BJ

Tel: 01274 681144
Fax: 01274 651198
E-mail: whiter@arriva.co.uk
Web site: www.arrivabusandcoach.co.uk

CRESCENT FACILITIES LTD
72 Willow Crescent, Chapeltown, Sheffield
S35 1QS
Tel/Fax: 0114 245 1050
E-mail: cfl.chris@btinternet.com

DIRECT PARTS LTD
Unit 1, Churnet Court, Churnetside Business
Park, Harrison Way, Cheddleton ST13 7EF
Tel: 01538 361777
Fax: 01538 369100
E-mail: sales@direct-group.co.uk
Web site: www.direct-group.co.uk

HL SMITH TRANSMISSIONS LTD
Enterprise Business Park, Cross Road, Albrighton,
Wolverhampton WV7 3BJ
Tel: 01902 373011
Fax: 01902 373608
Web site: www.hlsmith.co.uk

IMEXPART LTD
Links 31, Willowbridge Way, Whitwood,
Castleford WF10 5NP
Tel: 0845 605 0404 **Fax:** 01977 513412
E-mail: sales@imexpart.com
Web site: www.imexpart.com

IMPERIAL ENGINEERING
Delamare Road, Cheshunt, Hertfordshire
EN8 9UD
Tel: 01992 634255
Fax: 01992 630506
E-mail: orders@imperialengineering.co.uk
Web site: www.imperialengineering.co.uk

KCP CAR & COMMERCIAL LTD
Unit 15, Hillside Business Park, Kempson Way,
Bury St Edmunds, Suffolk IP32 7EA
Tel: 01284 750777
Fax: 01284 750773
E-mail: info@kcpcarandcommercial.co.uk
Web site: www.kcpcarandcommercial.co.uk

OPTARE PARTS DIVISION (Leeds)
Manston Lane, Leeds LS15 8SU
Tel: 0113 264 5182 **Fax:** 0113 260 6635
E-mail: parts@optare.com
Web site: www.optare.com

OPTARE PRODUCT SUPPORT
LONDON
Unit 9, Eurocourt, Olivers Close, West Thurrock
RM20 3EE
Tel: 01708 896860
Fax: 01708 869920
E-mail: london.service@optare.com

OPTARE PRODUCT SUPPORT
ROTHERHAM
Denby Way, Hellaby, Rotherham S66 8HR
Tel: 01709 535100 **Fax:** 01709 535102
E-mail: rotherham.service@optare.com

PARTLINE LTD
Dockfield Road, Shipley BD17 7AZ
Tel: 01274 531531
Fax: 01274 531088
E-mail: sales@partline.co.uk
Web site: www.partline.co.uk

PSS - STEERING & HYDRAULICS
DIVISION
Folgate Road, North Walsham NR28 0AJ
Tel: 01692 406017
Fax: 01692 406957
E-mail: sales@pss.co.uk
Web site: www.pss.co.uk

ROADLINK INTERNATIONAL LTD
Strawberry Lane, Willenhall, West Midlands
WV13 3RL
Tel: 01902 636206
Fax: 01902 631515
E-mail: sales@roadlink-international.co.uk
Web site: www.roadlink-international.co.uk

SHAWSON SUPPLY LTD
12 Station Road, Saintfield, County Down,
Northern Ireland BT24 7DU
Tel: 028 9751 0994
Fax: 028 9751 0816
E-mail: info@shawssonsupply.com
Web site: www.shawssonsupply.com

ZF POWERTRAIN
Stringes Close, Willenhall WV13 1LE
Tel: 01902 366000
Fax: 01902 366504
E-mail: sales@powertrain.org.uk
Web site: www.powertrain.org.uk

Surveillance Systems

AUTOSOUND LTD
4 Lister Street, Dudley Hill, Bradford BD4 9PQ
Tel: 01274 688990
Fax: 01274 651318
E-mail: keith.ellis@autosound.co.uk
Web site: www.autosound.co.uk

AVT SYSTEMS LTD
Unit 3 & 4, Tything Road East, Alcester,
Warwickshire B49 6ES
Tel: 01789 400357
Fax: 01789 400359
E-mail: enquiries@avtsystems.co.uk
Web site: www.avtsystems.co.uk

BRIGADE ELECTRONICS PLC
Brigade House, The Mills, Station Road, South
Darenth DA4 9BD
Tel: 01322 420300
Fax: 01322 420343
E-mail: info@brigade-electronics.co.uk
Web site: www.brigade-electronics.com

CLANTOOLS & PLANT LTD
3 Greenhill Avenue, Giffnock, Glasgow G46 6QX
Tel: 0141 638 8040
Fax: 0141 638 8881
E-mail: clantools@btconnect.com
Web site: www.clantools.com

CYBERLYNE COMMUNICATIONS LTD
Unit 5, Hatfield Way, South Church Enterprise
Park, Bishop Auckland, Durham DL14 6XF
Tel: 01388 773761
Fax: 01388 773778
E-mail: sales@cyberlyne.co.uk
Web site: www.cyberlyne.co.uk

DIRECT PARTS LTD
Unit 1, Churnet Court, Churnetside Business
Park, Harrison Way, Cheddleton ST13 7EF
Tel: 01538 361777

Fax: 01538 369100
E-mail: sales@direct-group.co.uk
Web site: www.direct-group.co.uk

FUEL THEFT SOLUTIONS LTD
PO Box 2494, Stoke on Trent ST7 2WR
Tel: 0845 077 3921
Fax: 0845 077 3922
E-mail: sales@dieseldye.com
Web site: www.dieseldye.com

GROENEVELD UK LTD
The Greentec Centre, Gelders Hall Road,
Shepshed, Leicestershire LE12 9NH
Tel: 01509 600033
Fax: 01509 602000
E-mail: info@groeneveld.co.uk
Web site: www.groeneveld.co.uk

KELLETT (UK) LTD
8 Stevenson Way, Sheffield S9 3WZ.
Tel: 0114 261 1122
Fax: 0114 261 1199
E-mail: sales@kellett.co.uk

KNORR-BREMSE SYSTEMS FOR
COMMERCIAL VEHICLES LTD
Century House, Folly Brook Road, Emerald Park
East, Emersons Green, Bristol BS16 7FE
Tel: 0117 984 6100
Fax: 0117 984 6101
Web site: www.knorr-bremse.co.uk

PSV PRODUCTS
The Red House, Underbridge Lane, Higher
Walton, Warrington WA4 5QR
Tel: 01925 210220
Fax: 01925 601534
E-mail: info@psvproducts.com
Web site: www.psvproducts.com

SYNECTICS MOBILE SYSTEMS
(formerly LOOK CCTV)
Unit 4, Wyrefields, Poulton-le-Fylde FY6 8JX
Tel: 01253 891222
Fax: 01253 891221
E-mail: enquiries@lookcctv.com
Web site: www.lookcctv.com

WABCO AUTOMOTIVE UK LTD
Texas Street, Morley LS27 0HQ.
Tel: 0113 251 2510
Fax: 0113 251 2844
E-mail: info.uk@wabco-auto.com
Web site: www.wabco-auto.com

Suspension

ARRIVA BUS AND COACH
Lodge Garage, Whitehall Road West, Gomersal,
Cleckheaton, West Yorkshire BD19 4BJ
Tel: 01274 681144
Fax: 01274 651198
E-mail: whiter@arriva.co.uk
Web site: www.arrivabusandcoach.co.uk

CRESCENT FACILITIES LTD
72 Willow Crescent, Chapeltown, Sheffield
S35 1QS
Tel/Fax: 0114 245 1050
E-mail: cfl.chris@btinternet.com

ERENTEK LTD
Malt Kiln Lane, Waddington, Lincoln LN5 9RT
Tel: 01522 720065

Fax: 01522 729155
E-mail: sales@erentek.co.uk
Web site: www.erentek.co.uk

IMEXPART LTD
Links 31, Willowbridge Way, Whitwood,
Castleford WF10 5NP
Tel: 0845 605 0404
Fax: 01977 513412
E-mail: sales@imexpart.com
Web site: www.imexpart.com

PARTLINE LTD
Dockfield Road, Shipley BD17 7AZ
Tel: 01274 531531
Fax: 01274 531088
E-mail: sales@partline.co.uk
Web site: www.partline.co.uk

PLAXTON SERVICE
Ryton Road, Anston, Sheffield S25 4DL
Tel: 01909 551155
Fax: 01909 550050
E-mail: service@plaxtonlimited.co.uk
Web site: www.plaxtonaftercare.co.uk

ROADLINK INTERNATIONAL LTD
Strawberry Lane, Willenhall, West Midlands
WV13 3RL
Tel: 01902 636206
Fax: 01902 631515
E-mail: sales@roadlink-international.co.uk
Web site: www.roadlink-international.co.uk

Tachographs

ARRIVA BUS AND COACH
Lodge Garage, Whitehall Road West, Gomersal,
Cleckheaton, West Yorkshire BD19 4BJ
Tel: 01274 681144
Fax: 01274 651198
E-mail: whiter@arriva.co.uk
Web site: www.arrivabusandcoach.co.uk

CHASSIS DEVELOPMENTS LTD
Grovebury Road, Leighton Buzzard LU7 8SL
Tel: 01525 374151
Fax: 01525 370127
E-mail: sales@chassisdevelopments.com
Web site: www.chassisdevelopment.co.uk

THOMAS HARDIE COMMERCIALS LTD
Newstet Road, Knowsley Industrial Park,
Liverpool L33 7TJ
Tel: 0151 549 3000
E-mail: info@thardie.co.uk

KCP CAR & COMMERCIAL LTD
Unit 15, Hillside Business Park, Kempson Way,
Bury St Edmunds, Suffolk IP32 7EA
Tel: 01284 750777
Fax: 01284 750773
E-mail: info@kcpcarandcommercial.co.uk
Web site: www.kcpcarandcommercial.co.uk

MARSHALLS COACHES LLP
Firbank Way, Leighton Buzzard LU7 3BD
Tel: 01525 376077 **Fax:** 01525 850967
E-mail: info@marshalls-coaches.co.uk
Web site: www.marshalls-coaches.co.uk

**OPTARE PRODUCT SUPPORT
LONDON**
Unit 9, Eurocourt, Olivers Close, West Thurrock
RM20 3EE

Tel: 01708 896860
Fax: 01708 869920
E-mail: london.service@optare.com

**OPTARE PRODUCT SUPPORT
ROTHERHAM**
Denby Way, Hellaby, Rotherham S66 8HR
Tel: 01709 535100
Fax: 01709 535102
E-mail: rotherham.service@optare.com

PARTLINE LTD
Dockfield Road, Shipley BD17 7AZ
Tel: 01274 531531
Fax: 01274 531088
E-mail: sales@partline.co.uk
Web site: www.partline.co.uk

PLAXTON SERVICE
Ryton Road, Anston, Sheffield S25 4DL
Tel: 01909 551155
Fax: 01909 550050
E-mail: service@plaxtonlimited.co.uk
Web site: www.plaxtonaftercare.co.uk

SIEMENS VDO TRADING LTD
36 Gravelly Industrial Park, Birmingham B24 8TA
Tel: 0121 326 1234
Fax: 0121 326 1299
Web site: www.siemens-datatrak.com

**WARD INTERNATIONAL
CONSULTING LTD**
70 Marks Tey Road, Fareham PO16 3UR
Tel: 01329 280280
Fax: 01329 667901
E-mail: info@wardint.co.uk
Web site: www.wardint.co.uk

Tachograph Calibrators

ARRIVA BUS AND COACH
Lodge Garage, Whitehall Road West, Gomersal,
Cleckheaton, West Yorkshire BD19 4BJ
Tel: 01274 681144
Fax: 01274 651198
E-mail: whiter@arriva.co.uk
Web site: www.arrivabusandcoach.co.uk

MARSHALLS COACHES LLP
Firbank Way, Leighton Buzzard LU7 3BD
Tel: 01525 376077
Fax: 01525 850967
E-mail: info@marshalls-coaches.co.uk
Web site: www.marshalls-coaches.co.uk

**OPTARE PRODUCT SUPPORT
LONDON**
Unit 9, Eurocourt, Olivers Close, West Thurrock
RM20 3EE
Tel: 01708 896860
Fax: 01708 869920
E-mail: london.service@optare.com

**OPTARE PRODUCT SUPPORT
ROTHERHAM**
Denby Way, Hellaby, Rotherham S66 8HR
Tel: 01709 535100
Fax: 01709 535102
E-mail: rotherham.service@optare.com

PLAXTON SERVICE
Ryton Road, Anston, Sheffield S25 4DL
Tel: 01909 551155
Fax: 01909 550050

E-mail: service@plaxtonlimited.co.uk
Web site: www.plaxtonaftercare.co.uk

SIEMENS VDO TRADING LTD
36 Gravelly Industrial Park, Birmingham B24 8TA
Tel: 0121 326 1234
Fax: 0121 326 1299
Web site: www.siemens-datatrak.com

Tachograph Chart Analysis Service

IBPTS
43 Cage Lane, Felixstowe, Suffolk OP11 9BJ
Tel: 01394 672344
Fax: 01394 672344
E-mail: enquiries@ibpts.co.uk
Web site: www.ibpts.co.uk

CHASSIS DEVELOPMENTS LTD
Grovebury Road, Leighton Buzzard LU7 8SL
Tel: 01525 374151
Fax: 01525 370127
E-mail: sales@chassisdevelopments.com
Web site: www.chassissdevelopments.co.uk

SIEMENS VDO TRADING LTD
36 Gravelly Industrial Park, Birmingham B24 8TA
Tel: 0121 326 1234
Fax: 0121 326 1299
Web site: www.siemens-datatrak.com

**TRANSPORT & TRAINING
SERVICES LTD**
Warrington Business Park North, Long Lane,
Warrington WA2 8TX
Tel: 01925 243500
Fax: 01925 243000
E-mail: tachographsuk@aol.com
Web site:
www.transporttrainingservices.com

Tickets, Ticket Machines, Ticket Systems and Technology

ACT - APPLIED CARD TECHNOLOGIES
Langley Gate, Kington Langley, Chippenham
SN15 5SE
Tel: 01249 751200
Fax: 01249 751201
E-mail: info@weareact.com
Web site: www.weareact.com

ALMEX UK
Metric House, Westmead Industrial Estate
Westlea, Swindon SN5 7AD
Tel: 01793 647934
Fax: 01793 647802
E-mail: info@almex.co.uk
Web site: www.almex.co.uk

ATOS ORIGIN
4 Triton Square, Regents Place, London
NW1 3HG
Tel: 020 7830 4444
Fax: 020 7830 4445
E-mail: ukwebenquiries@atos.net
Web site: www.uk.atos.net

BEMROSEBOOTH LTD
Stockholm Road, Sutton Fields Industrial Estate,
Hull HU7 0XY
Tel: 01482 826343
Fax: 01482 371386
E-mail: lprecious@bemrosebooth.com
Web site: www.bemrosebooth.com

CANN PRINT
Commercial Centre, Main Road, Kilmarnock
KA3 6LX
Tel: 01563 572440
Fax: 01563 544933
E-mail: info@cannprint.com
Web site: www.cannprint.com

CUBIC TRANSPORTATION SYSTEMS LTD
AFC House, Honeycrock Lane, Salfords,
Redhill RH1 5LA
Tel: 01737 782200
Fax: 01737 789759
Web site: www.cubic.com

DE LA RUE
De La Rue House, Jays Close, Viables, Basingstoke
RG22 4BS
Tel: 01256 605000
Fax: 01256 605004
Web site: www.delarue.com

KEITH EDMONDSON TICKET ROLLS
Garden House, Tittensor Road, Tittensor
Stoke-on-Trent ST12 9HQ
Tel: 01782 372305
Fax: 01782 351136
E-mail: keith@tickettrolls.co.uk
Web site: www.tickettrolls.co.uk

ETMSS LTD
Austin House, 43 Poole Road, Westbourne,
Bournemouth BH4 9DN
Tel: 0844 800 9299
E-mail: info@etmss.com
Web Site: www.etmss.com

JOHN GROVES TICKET SYSTEMS
Unit 10, North Circular Business Centre,
400 NCR, London NW10 0JG
Tel: 020 8830 1222
Fax: 020 8830 1223
E-Mail: sales@jgts.co.uk
Web site: www.jgts.co.uk

IMAGINET
Greyfriars House, Greyfriars Road,
Cardiff CF10 3AL
Tel: 029 2057 4500
Fax: 029 2057 4501
E-mail: sales@imaginet.co.uk
Web site: www.imaginet.co.uk

INIT – INNOVATIONS IN TRANSPORTATION LTD
49 Stoney Street, The Lace Market, Nottingham
NG1 1LX
Tel: 0870 890 4648
Fax: 0115 989 5463
E-mail: sales@init.co.uk
Web site: www.init.co.uk

MARK TERRILL TICKET MACHINERY
5 De Grey Close, Lewes BN7 2JR
Tel: 01273 474816
Fax: 01273 474816
E-mail: mark.terrill@ukonline.co.uk

PAYPOINT PLC
1 The Boulevard, Shire Park, Welwyn Garden City
AL7 1EL
Tel: 01707 60300
E-mail: enquiries@paypoint.co.uk
Web site: www.paypoint.co.uk

SCAN COIN LTD
110 Broadway, Salford Quays M50 2UW
Tel: 0161 873 0505
Fax: 0161 873 0501
E-mail: sales@scancoin.co.uk
Web site: www.scancoin.co.uk

SCHADES LTD
Brittain Drive, Codnor Gate Business Park,
Ripley, Derbyshire DE5 3RZ
Tel: 01773 748721
Fax: 01773 745061
Web site: www.schades.com
E-mail: sales@schades.co.uk

THOMAS AUTOMATION LTD
The Ark Business Centre, Meadow Lane
Industrial Estate, Loughborough
LE11 1JP
Tel: 0845 894 4991
Fax: 0700 600 7749
E-mail: sales@thomasa.co.uk
Web site: www.thomasa.co.uk

TICKETER
Chilton House, Charnham Lane, Hungerford,
Berkshire RG10 0EW
Tel: 0844 800 9299
E-mail: sales@ticketer.co.uk
Web site: www.ticketer.co.uk

TRANSPORT TICKET SERVICES LTD
Yew Tree Cottage, Newcastle, Monmouth
NP25 5NT
Tel/Fax: 01600 750650
E-mail: ttservices@tiscali.co.uk
Web site: www.ticket-machines.co.uk

WAYFARER (PARKEON TRANSIT) LTD
10 Willis Way, Fleets Industrial Estate, Poole,
Dorset BH15 3SS
Tel: 01202 339339
Fax: 01202 339369
E-mail: sales_uk@parkeon.com
Web site: www.parkeon.com

Timetable Display Frames

M BISSELL DISPLAY LTD
Unit 15, Beechwood Business Park,
Burdock Close, Hanks Green, Cannock,
Staffordshire WS11 7GB
Tel: 01543 502115
Fax: 01543 502118
E-mail: sales@bisselldisplay.com
Web site: www.bisselldisplay.com

BROADWATER MOULDINGS LTD
Benacre House, Ellough, Beccles,
Suffolk NR34 7XD
Tel: 01502 719310
Fax: 01502 471942
E-mail: info@broadwater.co.uk
Web site: www.broadwater.co.uk

Toilet Equipment

ARRIVA BUS AND COACH
Lodge Garage, Whitehall Road West,
Gomersal, Cleckheaton, West Yorkshire
BD19 4BJ
Tel: 01274 681144
Fax: 01274 651198
E-mail: whiter@arriva.co.uk
Web site: www.arrivabusandcoach.co.uk

BRADTECH LTD
Unit 3, Ladford Covert, Seighford, Stafford
ST18 9QL
Tel: 01785 282800
Fax: 01785 282558
E-mail: sales@bradtech.ltd.uk
Web site: www.bradtech.ltd.uk

CARLYLE BUS & COACH LTD
Carlyle Business Park, Great Bridge Street,
Swan Village, West Bromwich B70 0XA
Tel: 0121 524 1200
Fax: 0121 524 1201
E-mail: admin@carlyleplc.co.uk
Web site: www.carlyleplc.co.uk

ELSAN LTD
Bellbrook Park, Uckfield, East Sussex TN22 1QF
Tel: 01825 748200
Fax: 01825 761212
E-mail: sales@elsan.co.uk
Web site: www.elsan.co.uk

EXPRESS COACH REPAIRS LTD
Outgang Lane, Pickering YO18 7JA
Tel: 01751 475215
Fax: 01924 475215
E-mail: info@expresscoachrepairs.co.uk
Web site: www.expresscoachrepairs.co.uk

LAWTON SERVICES LTD
Knutsford Road, Church Lawton, Stoke-on-Trent
ST7 3DN
Tel: 01270 882056
Fax: 01270 883014
E-mail: andrea@lawtonservices.co.uk
Web site: www.lawtonservices.co.uk

PLAXTON SERVICE
Ryton Road, Anston, Sheffield S25 4DL
Tel: 01909 551155
Fax: 01909 550050
E-mail: service@plaxtonlimited.co.uk
Web site: www.plaxtonaftercare.co.uk

PSV PRODUCTS
The Red House, Underbridge Lane, Higher
Walton, Warrington WA4 5QR
Tel: 01925 210220
Fax: 01925 601534
E-mail: info@psvproducts.com
Web site: www.psvproducts.com

RATCLIFF PALFINGER
Bessemer Road, Welwyn Garden City,
Hertfordshire AL7 1ET
Tel: 01707 382880
Fax: 01707 327752
E-mail: info@ratcliffpalfinger.co.uk
Web site: www.ratcliffpalfinger.co.uk

SHADES TECHNICS LTD
Units E3 & E4, Rd Park, Stephenson Close,
Hoddesdon, Hertfordshire EN11 0BW
Tel: 01992 501683
Fax: 01992 501669
E-mail: sales@shades-technics.com
Web site: www.shades-technics.com

TRAMONTANA
Chapelknowe Road, Carfin, Motherwell ML1 5LE
Tel: 01698 861790
Fax: 01698 860778
E-mail: wdt90@tiscali.co.uk
Web site: www.brittnet.net/tramontanacoach

Transmission Overhaul

ARRIVA BUS AND COACH
Lodge Garage, Whitehall Road West, Gomersal,
Cleckheaton, West Yorkshire BD19 4BJ
Tel: 01274 681144
Fax: 01274 651198
E-mail: whiter@arriva.co.uk
Web site: www.arrivabusandcoach.co.uk

GARDNER PARTS LTD
Centurion Court, Centurion Way, Leyland,
Lancashire PR25 3UQ
Tel: 01772 642460
Fax: 01772 621333
E-mail: sales@gardnerparts.co.uk
Web site: www.gardnerparts.co.uk

HL SMITH TRANSMISSIONS LTD
Enterprise Business Park, Cross Road, Albrighton,
Wolverhampton WV7 3BJ
Tel: 01902 373011
Fax: 01902 373608
Web site: www.hlsmith.co.uk

LH GROUP SERVICES LTD
Graycar Business Park, Barton under Needwood,
Burton-on-Trent DE13 8EN
Tel: 01283 722600 **Fax:** 01283 722622
E-mail: lh@lh-group.com
Web site: www.lh-group.com

OPTARE PARTS DIVISION (Leeds)
Manston Lane, Leeds LS15 8SU
Tel: 0113 264 5182 **Fax:** 0113 260 6635
E-mail: parts@optare.com
Web site: www.optare.com

OPTARE PRODUCT SUPPORT LONDON
Unit 9, Eurocourt, Olivers Close, West Thurrock
RM20 3EE
Tel: 01708 896860
Fax: 01708 869920
E-mail: london.service@optare.com

OPTARE PRODUCT SUPPORT ROTHERHAM
Denby Way, Hellaby, Rotherham S66 8HR
Tel: 01709 535100
Fax: 01709 535102
E-mail: rotherham.service@optare.com

SHAWSON SUPPLY LTD
12 Station Road, Saintfield, County Down,
Northern Ireland BT24 7DU
Tel: 028 9751 0994
Fax: 028 9751 0816
E-mail: info@shawsonsupply.com
Web site: www.shawsonsupply.com

TTS UK
Total Tool Solutions Ltd, Newhaven Business
Park, Lowergate, Milnsbridge, Huddersfield
HD3 4HS
Tel: 01484 642211 **Fax:** 01484 461002
E-mail: sales@ttsuk.com
Web site: www.ttsuk.com

VOITH TURBO LTD
6 Beddington Farm Road, Croydon CR0 4XB
Tel: 020 8667 0333
Fax: 020 8667 0403
E-mail: Road.UK@voith.com
Web site: www.voithturbo.co.uk

VOR TRANSMISSIONS LTD
Little London House, St Anne's Road, Willenhall
WV13 1DT
Tel: 01902 604141 **Fax:** 01902 603868
E-mail: sales@vor.co.uk
Web site: www.vor.co.uk

ZF ECODRIVE – ECODRIVE TRANSMISSIONS LTD
Unit 35, Devonshire Road, Oakhill 61 Industrial
Estate, Walkden, Manchester M28 3PT
Tel: 01204 701812
Fax: 01204 701516
Web site: www.ecodrive.co.uk

ZF POWERTRAIN
Stringes Close, Willenhall WV13 1LE
Tel: 01902 366000
Fax: 01902 366504
E-mail: sales@powertrain.org.uk
Web site: www.powertrain.org.uk

Tree Guards

ARRIVA BUS AND COACH
Lodge Garage, Whitehall Road West, Gomersal,
Cleckheaton, West Yorkshire BD19 4BJ
Tel: 01274 681144
Fax: 01274 651198
E-mail: whiter@arriva.co.uk
Web site: www.arrivabusandcoach.co.uk

GABRIEL & CO LTD
1 Cornwall Road, Smethwick, West Midlands
B66 2JT
Tel: 0121 555 7615 **Fax:** 0121 555 1922
E-mail: john.gabriel@gabrielco.com
Web site: www.gabrielco.com

PLAXTON SERVICE
Ryton Road, Anston, Sheffield S25 4DL
Tel: 01909 551155
Fax: 01909 550050
E-mail: service@plaxtonlimited.co.uk
Web site: www.plaxtonaftercare.co.uk

Tyres

CONTINENTAL TYRE GROUP LTD
Continental House, 191 High Street,
Yiewsley, West Drayton, Middlesex
UB7 7XW
Tel: 01895 425900
Web site: www.conti-online.com

GOODYEAR UK
TyreFort, 88-98 Wingfoot Way, Erdington,
Birmingham B24 9HY
Tel: 0121 306 6000
Fax: 0121 306 6437
Web site: www.goodyear.eu/uk

HANKOOK TYRE UK LTD
Fawsley Drive, Heartlands Business Park,
Daventry, Northamptonshire
NN11 8UG
Tel: 01327 304100
Fax: 01327 304110
E-mail: sales@hankooktyresuk.co.uk
Web site: www.hankooktire-eu.com/uk

LAWTON SERVICES LTD
Knutsford Road, Church Lawton, Stoke-on-Trent
ST7 3DN
Tel: 01270 882056
Fax: 01270 883014
E-mail: andrea@lawtonservices.co.uk
Web site: www.lawtonservices.co.uk

OPTARE PRODUCT SUPPORT LONDON
Unit 9, Eurocourt, Olivers Close, West Thurrock
RM20 3EE
Tel: 01708 896860 **Fax:** 01708 869920
E-mail: london.service@optare.com

OPTARE PRODUCT SUPPORT ROTHERHAM
Denby Way, Hellaby, Rotherham
S66 8HR
Tel: 01709 535100 **Fax:** 01709 535102
E-mail: rotherham.service@optare.com

SNOWCHAINS EUROPRODUCTS
Wrotham Road, Borough Green,
Kent TN15 8DG
Tel: 01732 884408
Fax: 01732 884564
Web site: www.snowchains.co.uk

Uniforms

ALLEN & DOUGLAS CORPORATE CLOTHING LTD
Compton Park, Wildmere Road, Banbury
OX16 7JT
Tel: 01295 272700 **Fax:** 01295 278972
E-mail: sales@aandd.co.uk
Web site: www.aandd.co.uk

T T S UK
Total Tool Solutions Limited
Newhaven Business Park
Lowergate
Milnsbridge
Huddersfield
HD3 4HS
T: 01484 642211
F: 01484 461002
E: sales@ttsuk.com
W: www.ttsuk.com

**LEISUREWEAR DIRECT LTD, inc.
AHEAD OF THE REST**
4A South Street North, New Whittington,
Chesterfield S43 2AB
Tel: 01246 454447
Fax: 0870 755 9842
E-mail: sales@leisureweardirect.com
Web site: www.leisureweardirect.com

Upholstery

**ABACUS TRANSPORT
PRODUCTS LTD**
Abacus House, Highlode Industrial Estate,
Ramsey, Huntingdon PE26 2RB
Tel: 01487 710700 **Fax:** 01487 710626
E-mail: sales@abacus-tp.com
Web site: www.abacus-tp.com

ARDEE COACH TRIM LTD
Artnalivery, Ardee, Co Louth, Republic of Ireland
Tel: 00 353 41 685 3599
Fax: 00 353 41 685 7016
E-mail: info@ardeecoachtrim.com
Web site: www.ardeecoachtrim.com

**AUTOMOTIVE TEXTILE
INDUSTRIES**
Unit 15 & 16, Priest Court, Springfield Business
Park, Grantham NG31 7BG
Tel: 01476 593050
Fax: 01476 593607
E-mail: sales@autotex.com
Web site: www.autotex.com

BLACKPOOL TRIM SHOPS LTD
Brun Grove, Blackpool FY1 6PG
Tel: 01253 766762
Fax: 01253 798443
E-mail: sales@blackpooltrimshops.co.uk
Web site: www.blackpooltrimshops.co.uk

BRIDGE OF WEIR LEATHER CO LTD
Baltic Works, Bridge of Weir, Paisley PA11 33RH
Tel: 01505 612132
Fax: 01505 614964
E-mail: mail@bowleather.co.uk
Web site: www.bowleather.co.uk

DUOFLEX LTD
Trimmingham House, 2 Shires Road,
Buckingham Road Industrial Estate, Brackley,
Northamptonshire NN13 7EZ
Tel: 01280 701366
Fax: 01280 704799
E-mail: sales@duoflex.co.uk
Web site: www.duoflex.co.uk

EXPRESS COACH REPAIRS LTD
Outgang Lane, Pickering YO18 7JA
Tel: 01751 475215
Fax: 01924 475215
E-mail: info@expresscoachrepairs.co.uk
Web site: www.expresscoachrepairs.co.uk

HOLDSWORTH FABRICS LTD
Hopton Mills, Mirfield, West Yorkshire WF1 8HE
Tel: 01484 859061
Fax: 01924 495605
E-mail: info@camirafabrics.co.uk
Web site: www.holdsworthfabrics.com

LAWTON SERVICES LTD
Knutsford Road, Church Lawton, Stoke-on-Trent
ST7 3DN

Total Tool Solutions Limited
Newhaven Business Park
Lowergate
Milnsbridge
Huddersfield
HD3 4HS
T: 01484 642211
F: 01484 461002
E: sales@ttsuk.com
W: www.ttsuk.com

Tel: 01270 882056
Fax: 01270 883014
E-mail: andrea@lawtonservices.co.uk
Web site: www.lawtonservices.co.uk

MARTYN INDUSTRIALS LTD
5 Brunel Way, Durranhill, Harraby,
Carlisle CA1 3NQ
Tel: 01228 544000
Fax: 01228 544001
E-mail: enquiries@martyn-industrials.co.uk
Web site: www.martyn-industrials.com

P.L. TRIM LTD
Burton Road, Blackpool FY4 4NW
Tel: 01253 696033
Fax: 01253 696033
E-mail: enquiries@pltrim.co.uk
Web site: www.pltrim.co.uk

TTS UK
Total Tool Solutions Ltd, Newhaven Business
Park, Lowergate, Milnsbridge, Huddersfield
HD3 4HS
Tel: 01484 642211
Fax: 01484 461002
E-mail: sales@ttsuk.com
Web site: www.ttsuk.com

WIDNEY UK LTD
Plume Street, Aston, Birmingham B6 7SA
Tel: 0121 327 5500
Fax: 0121 328 2466
E-mail: info@widney.co.uk
Web site: www.widney.co.uk

Vacuum Systems

RESCROFT LTD
20 Oxleasow Road, East Moons Moat,
Redditch B98 0RE
Tel: 01527 521300 **Fax:** 01527 521301
E-mail: info@rescroft.com
Web site: www.rescroft.com

TTS UK
Total Tool Solutions Ltd,
Newhaven Business Park, Lowergate,
Milnsbridge, Huddersfield
HD3 4HS
Tel: 01484 642211
Fax: 01484 461002
E-mail: sales@ttsuk.com
Web site: www.tts.co.uk

Vehicle Washing & Washers

ARRIVA BUS AND COACH
Lodge Garage, Whitehall Road West, Gomersal,
Cleckheaton, West Yorkshire BD19 4BJ
Tel: 01274 681144
Fax: 01274 651198
E-mail: whiter@arriva.co.uk
Web site: www.arrivabusandcoach.co.uk

EXPRESS COACH REPAIRS LTD
Outgang Lane, Pickering YO18 7JA
Tel: 01751 475215
Fax: 01924 475215
E-mail: info@expresscoachrepairs.co.uk
Web site: www.expresscoachrepairs.co.uk

KARCHER (UK) LTD
Karcher House, Beaumont Road, Banbury,
Oxfordshire OX16 1TB
Tel: 01295 752000
Fax: 01295 266436
E-mail: enquiries@karcher.co.uk
Web site: www.karcher.co.uk

MARSHALLS COACHES LLP
Firbank Way, Leighton Buzzard LU7 3BD
Tel: 01525 376077
Fax: 01525 850967
E-mail: info@marshalls-coaches.co.uk
Web site: www.marshalls-coaches.co.uk

**NATIONWIDE CLEANING & SUPPORT
SERVICES LTD**
Suite 149, Airport House, Purley Way,
Croydon CR0 0XZ
Tel: 020 8288 3580
Fax: 020 8288 3581
E-mail: enquiries@nationwidefm.com
Web site: www.nationwidefm.com

SMITH BROS & WEBB LTD
Britannia House, Arden Forest Industrial Estate,
Alcester, Warwickshire B49 6EX
Tel: 01789 400096 **Fax:** 01789 400231
E-mail: sales@sbw-wash.com
Web site: www.sbw-wash.com

SOMERS TOTALKARE LTD
Unit 1, Coombs Wharf, Chancel Way, Halesowen,
West Midlands B62 8PP
Tel: 0121 585 2700 **Fax:** 0121 585 2725
E-mail: sales@stkare.co.uk
Web site: www.stkare.co.uk

 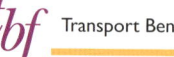

WILCOMATIC LTD
Unit 5 Commerce Park, 19 Commerce Way,
Croydon, Surrey CR0 4YL
Tel: 020 8649 5760
Fax: 020 8686 9571
E-mail: info@wilcomatic.co.uk
Web site: www.wilcomatic.co.uk

Wheels, Wheeltrims & Covers

ABACUS TRANSPORT PRODUCTS LTD
Abacus House, Highlode Industrial Estate,
Ramsey, Huntingdon PE26 2RB
Tel: 01487 710700
Fax: 01487 710626
E-mail: sales@abacus-tp.com
Web site: www.abacus-tp.com

ALCOA WHEEL PRODUCTS EUROPE
Industrieweg 135, 3583 Paal, Belgium
Tel: 00 32 11 458460
Fax: 00 21 11 455630
E-mail: info.wheels@alcoa.com
Web site: www.alcoa.com

ARRIVA BUS AND COACH
Lodge Garage, Whitehall Road West, Gomersal,
Cleckheaton, West Yorkshire BD19 4BJ
Tel: 01274 681144
Fax: 01274 651198
E-mail: whiter@arriva.co.uk
Web site: www.arrivabusandcoach.co.uk

AUTOMATE WHEEL COVERS LTD
California Mills, Oxford Road, Gomersal
BD19 4HQ
Tel: 01274 862700
Fax: 01274 851989
E-mail: sales@wheelcovers.co.uk
Web site: www.euroliners.com

EXPRESS COACH REPAIRS LTD
Outgang Lane, Pickering YO18 7JA
Tel: 01751 475215 **Fax:** 01924 475215
E-mail: info@expresscoachrepairs.co.uk
Web site: www.expresscoachrepairs.co.uk

HATCHER COMPONENTS LTD
Broadwater Road, Framlingham IP13 9LL
Tel: 01728 723675
Fax: 01728 724475
E-mail: info@hatchercomp.co.uk
Web site: www.ilston.net

OPTARE PARTS DIVISION (Leeds)
Manston Lane, Leeds LS15 8SU
Tel: 0113 264 5182
Fax: 0113 260 6635
E-mail: parts@optare.com
Web site: www.optare.com

PARMA INDUSTRIES
34-36 Carlton Park Industrial Estate,
Saxmundham, Suffolk IP17 2NL
Tel: 01728 745700
Fax: 01728 745718
E-mail: sales@parmagroup.co.uk
Web site: www.parmagroup.co.uk

PLAXTON PARTS
Ryton Road, Anston, Sheffield S25 4DL
Tel: 0844 822 6224
Fax: 01909 550050
E-mail: parts@plaxtonlimited.co.uk
Web site: www.plaxtonaftercare.co.uk

Windows and Windscreens

ARRIVA BUS AND COACH
Lodge Garage, Whitehall Road West,
Gomersal, Cleckheaton, West Yorkshire
BD19 4BJ
Tel: 01274 681144
Fax: 01274 651198
E-mail: whiter@arriva.co.uk
Web site: www.arrivabusandcoach.co.uk

AUTOGLASS COACH & BUS SERVICES
1 Priory Business Park, Cardington Road,
Bedford MK44 3US
Tel: 01234 279572
Fax: 01234 279460
Web site: www.autoglass.co.uk

BRITAX PMG LTD
Bressingby Industrial Estate, Bridlington
YO16 4SJ
Tel: 01262 670161
Fax: 01262 605666
E-mail: enquiries@britax-pmg.com
Web site: www.britax-pmg.com

BUS & COACH GLAZING
Ryton Road, Anston, Sheffield S25 4DL
Tel: 0800 220077
Fax: 01909 550050
E-mail: glazing@plaxtonlimited.co.uk
Web site: www.plaxtonaftercare.co.uk

CARLYLE BUS & COACH LTD
Carlyle Business Park, Great Bridge Street,
Swan Village, West Bromwich
B70 0XA
Tel: 0121 524 1200 **Fax:** 0121 524 1201
E-mail: admin@carlyleplc.co.uk
Web site: www.carlyleplc.co.uk

ESPRIT WINDSCREEN SYSTEMS
Unit 44, Winpenny Road, Parkhouse East
Industrial Estate, Newcastle under Lyme,
Staffordshire ST5 7RH
Tel: 01782 565811
Fax: 01782 565766
E-mail: sales@espritws.com
Web site: www.espritws.com

EXPRESS COACH REPAIRS LTD
Outgang Lane, Pickering YO18 7JA
Tel: 01751 475215
Fax: 01924 475215
E-mail: info@expresscoachrepairs.co.uk
Web site: www.expresscoachrepairs.co.uk

B HEPWORTH & CO LTD
4 Merse Road, North Moons Moat,
Redditch B98 9HL
Tel: 01527 61243 **Fax:** 01527 66836
E-mail: bhepworth@b-hepworth.com
Web site: www.b-hepworth.com

JW GLASS LTD
Units 6 & 7, Scropton Road, Hatton DE65 5DT
Tel: 01283 520202
Fax: 01283 520022
E-mail: info@jwglass.co.uk
Web site: www.jwglass.co.uk

LAWTON SERVICES LTD
Knutsford Road, Church Lawton, Stoke-on-Trent
ST7 3DN
Tel: 01270 882056 **Fax:** 01270 883014
E-mail: andrea@lawtonservices.co.uk
Web site: www.lawtonservices.co.uk

NEALINE WINDSCREEN WIPER PRODUCTS
Unit 1, The Sidings Industrial Estate,
Birdingbury Road, Marton CV23 9RX
Tel: 01926 633256 **Fax:** 01926 632600

NUTEXA FRICTIONS LTD
PO Box 11, New Hall Lane, Hoylake,
Wirral CH47 4DH
Tel: 0151 632 5903
Fax: 0151 632 5908
E-mail: sales@nutexafrictions.co.uk
Web Site: www.sergeant.co.uk

OPTARE PARTS DIVISION (Leeds)
Manston Lane, Leeds LS15 8SU
Tel: 0113 264 5182
Fax: 0113 260 6635
E-mail: parts@optare.com
Web site: www.optare.com

OPTARE PRODUCT SUPPORT LONDON
Unit 9, Eurocourt, Olivers Close, West Thurrock
RM20 3EE
Tel: 01708 896860
Fax: 01708 869920
E-mail: london.service@optare.com

OPTARE PRODUCT SUPPORT ROTHERHAM
Denby Way, Hellaby, Rotherham
S66 8HR
Tel: 01709 535100 **Fax:** 01709 535102
E-mail: rotherham.service@optare.com

TTS UK
Total Tool Solutions Limited
Newhaven Business Park
Lowergate
Milnsbridge
Huddersfield
HD3 4HS
T: 01484 642211
F: 01484 461002
E: sales@ttsuk.com
W: www.ttsuk.com

PARTLINE LTD
Dockfield Road, Shipley BD17 7AZ
Tel: 01274 531531
Fax: 01274 531088
E-mail: sales@partline.co.uk
Web site: www.partline.co.uk

PERCY LANE PRODUCTS LTD
Lichfield Road, Tamworth B79 7TL
Tel: 01827 63821
Fax: 01827 310159
E-mail: sales@percy-lane.com
Web site: www.percy-lane.com

PLAXTON PARTS
Ryton Road, Anston, Sheffield S25 4DL
Tel: 01909 550044
Fax: 01909 550050
E-mail: parts@plaxtonlimited.co.uk
Web site: www.plaxtonaftercare.co.uk

PSV GLASS
Hillbottom Road, High Wycombe HP12 4HJ
Tel: 01494 533131
Fax: 01494 462675
E-mail: sales@psvglass.co.uk
Web site: www.psvglass.com

TRAMONTANA
Chapelknowe Road, Carfin, Motherwell ML1 5LE
Tel: 01698 861790 **Fax:** 01698 860778
E-mail: wdt90@tiscali.co.uk
Web site: www.brittnet.net/tramontanacoach

TTS UK
Total Tool Solutions Ltd, Newhaven Business
Park, Lowergate, Milnsbridge, Huddersfield
HD3 4HS
Tel: 01484 642211 **Fax:** 01484 461002
E-mail: sales@ttsuk.com
Web site: www.ttsuk.com

VOLVO BUS AND COACH CENTRE
Parts Sales & Body Repair/Refurbishment
Specialists
Byron Street Extension, Loughborough LE11 5HE
Tel: 01509 217700 **Fax:** 01509 238770
E-mail (Body Support): dporter@
volvocoachsales.co.uk
E-mail (Parts): csparts@volvocoachsales.co.uk
Web site: www.volvo.com

WIDNEY UK LTD
Plume Street, Aston, Birmingham B6 7SA
Tel: 0121 327 5500 **Fax:** 0121 328 2466
E-mail: info@widney.co.uk
Web site: www.widney.co.uk

INDUSTRY SERVICE PROVIDERS

Accident Investigation

PEAK LEGAL SERVICES LTD
41 Longmoor Road, Simmondley, Glossop,
Derbyshire SK13 6NH
Tel/Fax: 01457 855141
Mobile: 07989 092835
E-mail: ford414@btinternet.com

Accountancy & Audit

**BARRONS CHARTERED
ACCOUNTANTS**
Monometer House, Rectory Grove, Leigh on Sea
SS9 2HN

Tel: 01702 481910
Fax: 01702 481911
E-mail: mail@barrons-bds.com
Web site: www.barrons-bds.com

PRE METRO OPERATIONS LTD
Regent House, 56 Hagley Road, Stourbridge, West
Midlands DY8 1QD
Tel: 01384 441325
Fax: 0121 243 9906
E-mail: phil.evans@premetro.co.uk
Web site: www.premetro.co.uk

Advisory Services

AD COACH SALES
Newbridge Coach Depot, Witheridge,
Devon EX16 8PY
Tel: 01884 860787
Fax: 01884 860711
E-mail: enquiries@adcoachsales.co.uk
Web site: www.adcoachsales.co.uk

ADG TRANSPORT TRAINING
Oak Cottage, Royal Oak, Machen, Caerphilly
CF83 8SN
Tel: 01633 441491
Fax: 01633 440591
E-mail: a.dgettins@btinternet.com
Web site: www.adgtransport.co.uk

ANDY IZATT
10 Briton Court, St Thomas's Road, Spalding
PE11 2TS
Tel: 01775 712542
E-mail: andy.izatt@btinternet.com
Web site: andy.izatt.btinternet.co.uk

AUSTIN ANALYTICS
Crown House, 183 High Street, Bottisham,
Cambridge CB25 9BB
Tel: 07730 943415
Fax: 07005 946854
E-mail: john@analytics.co.uk
Web site: www.analytics.co.uk

COLIN BUCHANAN
10 Eastbourne Terrace, London W2 6LG
Tel: 020 7053 1300
Fax: 020 7053 1301
E-mail: london@cbuchanan.co.uk
Web site: www.colinbuchanan.com

CAPOCO DESIGN
Stone Cross House, Chickgrove,
Salisbury SP3 6NA
Tel: 01722 716722
Fax: 01722 716226
E-mail: design@capoco.co.uk
Web site: www.capoco.co.uk

CHADWELL ASSOCIATES LTD
3 Caledonian Close, Ilford, IG3 9QF
Tel: 0208 590 5697
E-mail: ib@chadwellassociates.co.uk

**PETER EDWARDS TRANSPORT
CONSULTANCY LTD**
19 Cardinal Close, Old Rossington, Doncaster
DN11 0XG
Tel: 01302 865658
E-mail: pandcedwards@btinternet.com

ELLIS TRANSPORT SERVICES
61 Bodycoats Road, Chandlers Ford, Hampshire

SO53 2HA
Tel: 023 8027 0447
Fax: 023 8027 6736
E-mail: info@ellistransportservices.co.uk
Web site: www.ellistransportservices.co.uk

GOSKILLS LTD
Concorde House, Trinity Park, Solihull B37 7UQ
Tel: 01216 355520
Fax: 01216 355521
E-mail: info@goskills.org
Web site: www.goskills.org

IBPTS
43 Cage Lane, Felixstowe, Suffolk OP11 9BJ
Tel: 01394 672344
Fax: 01394 672344
E-mail: enquiries@ibpts.co.uk
Web site: www.ibpts.co.uk

**LEYLAND PRODUCT
DEVELOPMENTS LTD**
Aston Way, Leyland, Preston PR26 7TZ
Tel: 01772 435834
E-mail: sales@lpdl.co.uk
Web site: www.lpdl.co.uk

MINIMISE YOUR RISK
11 Chatsworth Park, Telscombe Cliffs,
East Sussex BN10 7DZ
Tel: 01273 580189
Fax: 01273 580189
E-mail: alec@minimiseyourrisk.co.uk
Web site: www.minimiseyourrisk.co.uk

STEPHEN C MORRIS
PO Box 119, Shepperton
TW17 8UX
Tel: 01932 232574
E-mail: buswriter@btinternet.com

MVA
Duke Street, Woking GU21 5DH
Tel: 01483 728051
Fax: 01483 755207
E-mail: info@mvaconsultancy.com
Web site: www.mvaconsultancy.com

PEAK LEGAL SERVICES LTD
41 Longmoor Road, Simmondley, Glossop,
Derbyshire SK13 6NH
Tel/Fax: 01457 855141
Mobile: 07989 092835
E-mail: ford414@btinternet.com

PRE METRO OPERATIONS LTD
Regent House, 56 Hagley Road, Stourbridge,
West Midlands DY8 1QD
Tel: 01384 441325
Fax: 0121 243 9906
E-mail: phil.evans@premetro.co.uk
Web site: www.premetro.co.uk

**PROFESSIONAL TRANSPORT
SERVICES LTD**
12 Silverdale, Stanford-le-Hope,
Essex SS17 8BG
Tel: 01375 675262
E-mail: enquiries@proftranserv.com
Web site: www.proftranserv.co.uk

SALTIRE COMMUNICATIONS
39 Lilyhill Terrace, Edinburgh EH8 7DR
Tel: 0131 652 0205
E-mail: gavin.booth@btconnect.com

TRANSPORT & TRAVEL RESEARCH LTD
Minster House, Minster Pool Walk,
Lichfield, Staffordshire WS13 6QT
Tel: 01543 416416
Fax: 01543 416681
E-mail: enquiries@ttr-ltd.com
Web site: www.ttr-ltd.com

TTS UK
Total Tool Solutions Ltd, Newhaven Business
Park, Lowergate, Milnsbridge, Huddersfield
HD3 4HS
Tel: 01484 642211
Fax: 01484 461002
E-mail: sales@ttsuk.com
Web site: www.ttsuk.com

WARD INTERNATIONAL CONSULTING LTD
70 Marks Tey Road, Fareham PO16 3UR
Tel: 01329 280280
Fax: 01329 667901
E-mail: info@wardint.co.uk
Web site: www.wardint.co.uk

Artwork

BEST IMPRESSIONS
15 Starfield Road, London W12 9SN
Tel: 020 8740 6443
Fax: 020 8740 9134
E-mail: talk2us@best-impressions.co.uk
Web site: www.best-impressions.co.uk

EXPRESS COACH REPAIRS LTD
Outgang Lane, Pickering YO18 7JA
Tel: 01751 475215
Fax: 01751 475215
E-mail: info@expresscoachrepairs.co.uk
Web site: www.expresscoachrepairs.co.uk

FWT
Aztec House, 397-405 Archway Road,
London N6 4EY
Tel: 020 7347 3700
Fax: 020 7347 3701
E-mail: info@fwt.co.uk
Web site: www.fwt.co.uk

GRAPHIC EVOLUTION LTD
Ad House, East Parade, Harrogate HG1 5LT
Tel: 01423 706680
Fax: 01423 502522
E-mail: info@graphic-evolution.co.uk
Web site: www.graphic-evolution.co.uk

TONY GREAVES GRAPHICS
19 Perth Mount, Horsforth, Leeds LS18 5SH
Tel/Fax: 0113 258 4795
E-mail: tony@greavesgraphics.fsnet.co.uk

HATTS GARAGE SERVICES
Foxham, Chippenham SN15 4NB
Tel: 01249 740444
Fax: 01249 740447
E-mail: mike@hattstravel.co.uk
Web site: www.hattsgarageservices.co.uk

MCV BUS & COACH LTD
Sterling Place, Elean Business Park,
Sutton CB6 2QE
Tel: 01353 773000
Fax: 01353 773001
E-mail: vernon.edwards@mcv-uk.com

NEERMAN & PARTNERS
c/o 22 Larbre Crescent, Whickham,
Newcastle-upon-Tyne NE16 5YG
Tel: 0191 488 6258
Fax: 0191 488 9158
E-mail: info@neerman.net
Web site: www.neerman.net

Breakdown & Recovery Services

NB - Operator lists also indicate bus and coach
operators able to provide breakdown and
recovery services.

AD COACH SALES
Newbridge Coach Depot, Witheridge, Devon
EX16 8PY
Tel: 01884 860767
Fax: 01884 860711
E-mail: enquiries@adcoachsales.co.uk
Web site: www.adcoachsales.co.uk

BUZZLINES LTD
Unit G1, Lympne Industrial Park,
Hythe CT21 4LR
Tel: 01303 261870 **Fax:** 01303 230093
E-mail: sales@buzzlines.co.uk
Web site: www.buzzlines.co.uk

CHANNEL COMMERCIALS PLC
Unit 6, Cobbs Wood Industrial Estate,
Brunswick Road, Ashford TN23 1EH
Tel: 01233 629272 **Fax:** 01233 636322
E-mail: info@ccplc.co.uk
Web site: www.channelcommercials.co.uk

COACH-AID
Unit 2, Brindley Close, Tollgate Industrial Estate,
Stafford ST16 3SU
Tel: 01785 222666
E-mail: workshop@coach-aid.com
Web site: www.coach-aid.com

HATTS GARAGE SERVICES
Foxham, Chippenham SN15 4NB
Tel: 01249 740444 **Fax:** 01249 740447
E-mail: mike@hattstravel.co.uk
Web site: www.hattsgarageservices.co.uk

J & K RECOVERY LTD
3 Grovebury Road, Leighton Buzzard,
Bedfordshire LU7 4SQ
Tel: 01525 851011
Fax: 01525 850361
UK Call Centre: 0800 434 6106
Web site: www.lanternrecovery.com

LANTERN RECOVERY SPECIALISTS PLC
Lantern House, 39/41 High Street, Potters Bar
EN6 5AJ
Tel: 0844 247 6090
Fax: 01707 640450
Web site: www.lanternrecovery.com

MARSHALLS COACHES LLP
Firbank Way, Leighton Buzzard, Bedfordshire
LU7 3BD
Tel: 01525 376077 **Fax:** 01525 850967
E-mail: info@marshalls-coaches.co.uk
Web site: www.marshalls-coaches.co.uk

MASS SPECIAL ENGINEERING LTD
Houghton Road, North Anston S25 4JJ.
Tel: 01909 550480
Fax: 01909 550486

OPTARE PRODUCT SUPPORT LONDON
Unit 9, Eurocourt, Olivers Close, West Thurrock
RM20 3EE
Tel: 01708 896860 **Fax:** 01708 869920
E-mail: london.service@optare.com

OPTARE PRODUCT SUPPORT ROTHERHAM
Denby Way, Hellaby, Rotherham S66 8HR
Tel: 01709 535100
Fax: 01709 535102
E-mail: rotherham.service@optare.com

PLAXTON SERVICE
Ryton Road, Anston, Sheffield S25 4DL
Tel: 01909 551155
Fax: 01909 550050
E-mail: service@plaxtonlimited.co.uk
Web site: www.plaxtonaftercare.co.uk

TOURMASTER RECOVERY
Alderlands, James Road, Crowland,
Peterborough PE6 0AA
Tel: 01733 211639
Fax: 01733 211378
E-mail: tourmaster@btconnect.com
Contact: David Dinsey

TRUCKALIGN CO LTD
VIP Group, VIP Industrial Park, Anchor & Hope
Lane, London SE7 7RY
Tel: 020 8305 5879
Fax: 020 8858 5663
E-mail: admin@vipgroupltd.co.uk
Web site: www.vipgroup.co.uk

Cleaning services

EXPRESS COACH REPAIRS LTD
Outgang Lane, Pickering YO18 7JA
Tel: 01751 475215 **Fax:** 01751 475215
E-mail: info@expresscoachrepairs.co.uk
Web site: www.expresscoachrepairs.co.uk

JENNYCHEM
Sort Mill Road, Mid Kent Business Park,
Snodland, Kent ME6 5UA
Tel: 01634 245666 **Fax:** 01634 245777
E-mail: jenny@jennychem.com
Web site: www.jennychem.com

TARA SUPPORT SERVICES LTD
32 Derby Road, Enfield EN3 4AW
Tel: 0845 450 0607
Fax: 0845 450 0608
E-mail: info@tarasupport.co.uk
Web site: www.tarasupport.co.uk

Coach Driver Agencies

COUNTY RECRUITMENT & TRAINING LTD
Harry Harris, 10 Valley Road, River, Dover,
Kent CT17 0QN
Tel: 01304 826220
Fax: 01304 822551
E-mail: harry@pineham98.co.uk
Web site: www.crtweb.co.uk

DRIVER HIRE CANTERBURY
12-17 Upper Bridge Street, Canterbury CT1 2NF
Tel: 01227 479529
Fax: 01227 479531
E-mail: canterbury@driverhire.co.uk
Web site: www.driverhire.co.uk

Coach Hire Brokers/Vehicle Rental

COACH DIRECT LTD
22 South Street, Rochford, Essex SS4 1BQ
Tel: 0843 084 3001
Fax: 0843 084 3002
E-mail: info@coachdirect.co.uk
Web site: www.coachdirect.co.uk

COACHFINDER LTD
Woodbank House, 24 Matley Close, Newton,
Hyde SK14 4UE
Tel: 0161 368 7877
E-mail: enquiries@coachfinder.uk.com
Web site: www.coachfinder.uk.com

DAWSONRENTALS BUS AND COACH LTD
Delaware Drive, Tongwell, Milton Keynes
MK15 8JH
Tel: 01908 218111
Fax: 01908 610156
E-mail: info@dawsongroup.co.uk
Web site: www.dawsongroup.co.uk

HAYWARD TRAVEL (CARDIFF)
2 Murch Crescent, Dinas Powys, Cardiff
CF64 4RF
Tel: 02920 515551
Fax: 02920 515113
E-mail: haytvl@aol.com
Web site: haywardtravel.co.uk

NEXT BUS LTD
The Coach Yard, Vincients Road, Bumpers Farm
Industrial Estate, Chippenham,
Wiltshire SN14 6QA
Tel: 01249 462462
Fax: 01249 448844
E-mail: sales@next-bus.co.uk
Web site: www.next-bus.co.uk

SANTANDER ASSET FINANCE
Taylor Road, Trafford Park, Manchester M41 7JQ
Tel: 0161 747 6016
Fax: 0161 275 4501
E-mail: steve.moult@hansar.co.uk
Web site: www.santanderusedassets.co.uk

YORKSHIRE BUS & COACH SALES
254A West Ella Road, West Ella, Hull HU10 7SF
Tel: 01482 653302
Fax: 01482 653302
E-mail: craig.porteous@virgin.net

Coach Interchange & Parking Facilities

SAMMYS GARAGE
Victoria Coach Station, Arrivals Hall,
3 Eccleston Place, London SW1W 9NF
Tel: 020 7730 8867

TRAVELGREEN COACHES
Canda Lodge, Hampole Bank Lane, Skellow,
Doncaster DN6 8LF
Tel: 01302 722227
Fax: 01302 727999

VICTORIA COACH STATION LTD
164 Buckingham Palace Road,
London SW1W 9TP
Tel: 020 7027 2520
Fax: 020 7027 2511
Web site: www.tfl.gov.uk

Computer Systems/Software

ALMEX UK
Metric House, Westmead Industrial Estate
Westlea, Swindon SN5 7AD
Tel: 01793 647931
Fax: 01793 647932
E-mail: info@almex.co.uk
Web site: www.almex.de

AUTOPRO SOFTWARE
1 Kingsmeadow, Norton Cross, Runcorn
WA7 6PB
Tel: 01928 715962 **Fax:** 01928 714538
E-mail: sales@autoprouk.com
Web site: www.autoprosoftware.co.uk

CIVICA TRANMAN SOLUTIONS
Thornbury Office Park, Midland Way,
Thornbury, Gloucestershire BS35 2BS
Tel: 01454 874002
Fax: 01454 874001
E-mail: tranman@civica.co.uk
Web site: www.civica.co.uk

DISTINCTIVE SYSTEMS LTD
Amy Johnson Way, York YO30 4XT
Tel: 01904 692269 **Fax:** 01904 690810
E-mail: sales@distinctive-systems.com
Web site: www.distinctive-systems.com

OMNIBUS
Hollinwood Business Centre, Albert Street,
Hollinwood, Oldham, Lancashire OL8 3QL
Tel: 0161 683 3100

Fax: 0161 683 3102
Web site: www.omnibus.uk.com

QUARTIX LTD
Chapel Offices, Park Street, Newtown,
Powys SY16 1ZA
Tel: 0870 013 6663
E-mail: enquiries@quartix.net
Web site: www.quartix.net

ROEVILLE COMPUTER SYSTEMS
Station House, East Lane, Stainforth,
Doncaster DN7 5HF
Tel: 01302 841333
Fax: 01302 843966
E-mail: sales@roeville.com
Web site: www.roeville.com

TAGTRONICS LTD
5 Anchor Court, Commercial Road,
Darwen, Blackburn BB3 0DB
Tel: 01254 819200
Fax: 01254 873238
E-mail: howcanwehelp@tagtronics.co.uk
Web site: www.tagtronics.co.uk

TRAPEZE GROUP (UK) LTD
The Mill, Staverton, Trowbridge, Bath
BA14 6PH
Tel: 0844 561 6771
Fax: 01225 784222
E-mail: info@trapezegroup.co.uk
Web site: www.trapezegroup.co.uk

TRAVEL INFORMATION SYSTEMS
Grand Union House, 20 Kentish Town Road,
London NW1 9NX
Tel: 020 7428 1288
Fax: 020 7267 2745
E-mail: enquiries@travelinfosystems.com
Web site: www.travelinfosystems.com

Vix ACIS Ltd
168 Cowley Road, Cambridge
CB4 0DL
Tel: 01223 728700
Fax: 01223 506311
E-mail: enquiries@acis.uk.com
Web site: www.acis.uk.com

Consultants

ADG TRANSPORT TRAINING
Oak Cottage, Royal Oak, Machen,
Caerphilly CF83 8SN
Tel: 01633 441491
Fax: 01633 440591
E-mail: a.dgettins@btinternet.com
Web site: www.adgtransport.co.uk

AUSTIN ANALYTICS
Crown House, 183 High Street,
Bottisham, Cambridge CB25 9BB
Tel: 07730 943415
Fax: 07005 946854
E-mail: john@analytics.co.uk
Web site: www.analytics.co.uk

AUTOPRO SOFTWARE
1 Kingsmeadow, Norton Cross,
Runcorn WA7 6PB
Tel: 01928 715962
Fax: 01928 714538
E-mail: sales@autoprouk.com
Web site: www.autoprosoftware.co.uk

BESTCHART LTD
6A Mays Yard, Down Road, Horndean,
Waterlooville, Hampshire PO8 0YP
Tel: 023 9259 7707
Fax: 023 9259 1700
E-mail: info@bestchart.co.uk
Web site: www.bestchart.co.uk

COLIN BUCHANAN
10 Eastbourne Terrace, London W2 6LG
Tel: 020 7053 1300
Fax: 020 7053 1301
E-mail: london@cbuchanan.co.uk
Web site: www.colinbuchanan.com

CAREYBROOK LTD
PO Box 205, Southam, Warwickshire
CV47 0ZL
Tel: 03333 446800
Fax: 01926 814898
E-mail: info@careybrook.co.uk
Web site: www.careybrook.com

CHADWELL ASSOCIATES LTD
3 Caledonian Close, Ilford IG3 9QF
Tel: 0208 590 5697
E-mail: ib@chadwellassociates.co.uk

CRONER (WOLTERS KLUWER UK LTD)
145 London Road, Kingston upon Thames
KT2 6SR
Tel: 020 8547 3333
Fax: 020 8547 2637
E-mail: info@croner.co.uk
Web site: www.croner.co.uk

DCA DESIGN INTERNATIONAL
19 Church Street, Warwick CV34 4AB
Tel: 01926 499461
Fax: 01926 401134
Web site: www.dca-design.com/transport

PETER EDWARDS TRANSPORT CONSULTANCY LTD
19 Cardinal Close, Old Rossington, Doncaster
DN11 0XG
Tel: 01302 865658
E-mail: pandcedwards@btinternet.com

ELLIS TRANSPORT SERVICES
61 Bodycoats Road, Chandlers Ford,
Hampshire SO53 2HA
Tel: 023 8027 0447
Fax: 023 8027 6736
E-mail: info@ellistransportservices.co.uk
Web site: www.ellistransportservices.co.uk

4 FARTHINGS INTERNATIONAL RECRUITMENT
22 Alexander Close, Twickenham, Middlesex
TW2 5TB
Tel: 020 8898 8813
E-mail: info@4farthings.co.uk
Web site: www.4farthings.co.uk

LEONARD GREEN ASSOCIATES
4 Crawshaw Drive, Reedsholme, Rawtenstall,
Rossendale, Lancashire BB4 8PR
Tel: 01706 218539
E-mail: lgreen22@ntlworld.com

HILTech DEVELOPMENTS LTD
e-volve Business Centre, Cygnet Way, Rainton
Bridge South Business Park, Houghton le Spring,
Durham DH4 5QY
Tel: 0191 305 5094
Fax: 0191 488 9158
E-mail: executive@hiltechdevelopments.com
Web site: www.hiltechdevelopments.com

IBPTS
43 Cage Lane, Felixstowe, Suffolk OP11 9BJ
Tel: 01394 672 344
Fax: 01394 672 344
E-mail: enquiries@ibpts.co.uk
Web site: www.ibpts.co.uk

JACOBS BABTIE GROUP LTD
School Green, Shinfield, Reading RG2 9HL
Tel: 0118 988 1555
Fax: 0118 988 1666
Web site: www.jacobs.com

LEYLAND PRODUCT DEVELOPMENTS LTD
Aston Way, Leyland, Preston PR26 7TZ
Tel: 01772 435834
E-mail: sales@lpdl.co.uk
Web site: www.lpdl.co.uk

MASS SPECIAL ENGINEERING LTD
Houghton Road North Anston, Sheffield S25 4SJ
Tel: 01909 550480.
Fax: 01909 550486.

MINIMISE YOUR RISK
11 Chatsworth Park, Telscombe Cliffs, East Sussex
BN10 7DZ
Tel: 01273 580189
Fax: 01273 580189
E-mail: alec@minimiseyourrisk.co.uk
Web site: www.minimiseyourrisk.co.uk

MOTT MACDONALD
Mott MacDonald House, 8-10 Sydenham Road,
Croydon CR0 2EE
Tel: 020 8774 2000
Fax: 020 8681 5706
E-mail: marketing@mottmac.com
Web site: www.mottmac.com

MYSTERY TRAVELLERS
6A Mays Yard, Down Road, Waterlooville,
Hampshire PO8 0YP
Tel: 023 9259 7707
Fax: 023 9259 1700
E-mail: info@bestchart.co.uk
Web site: www.bestchart.co.uk

NEERMAN & PARTNERS
c/o 22 Larbre Crescent, Whickham,
Newcastle-upon-Tyne NE16 5YG
Tel: 0191 488 6258
Fax: 0191 488 9158
E-mail: info@neerman.net
Web site: www.neerman.net

PARRY PEOPLE MOVERS LTD
Overend Road, Cradley Heath, Dudley B64 7DD
Tel: 01384 569553
Fax: 01384 637753
E-mail: jpmparry@aol.com
Web site: www.parrypeoplemovers.com

PJA LTD
Sterling House, 19/23 High Street, Kidlington,
Oxon OX5 2DH
Tel: 07836 634414
E-mail: info@pj-associates.co.uk
Web site: www.pj-associates.co.uk

PRE METRO OPERATIONS LTD
Regent House, 56 Hagley Road, Stourbridge,
West Midlands DY8 1QD
Tel: 01384 441325
Fax: 0121 243 9906
E-mail: phil.evans@premetro.co.uk
Web site: www.premetro.co.uk

PROFESSIONAL TRANSPORT SERVICES
12 Silverdale, Stanford-le-Hope, Essex
SS17 8BG
Tel: 01375 675262
E-mail: enquiries@proftranserv.com
Web site: www.proftranserv.co.uk

ROBERTSON TRANSPORT CONSULTING LTD
Field House, Braceby, Sleaford, Lincolnshire
NG34 0SZ
Tel: 01529 497354
E-mail: robertson@rtclincs.co.uk

SALTIRE COMMUNICATIONS
39 Lilyhill Terrace, Edinburgh EH8 7DR
Tel: 0131 652 0205
E-mail: gavin.booth@btconnect.com

SPECIALIST TRAINING & CONSULTANCY SERVICES LTD
6 Venture Court, Metcalfe Drive,
Altham Industrial Estate, Accrington BB5 5TU
Tel: 01282 687090
Fax: 01282 687091
E-mail: enquiries@specialisttraining.co.uk
Web site: www.specialisttraining.co.uk

STEER DAVIES GLEAVE
28-32 Upper Ground, London
SE1 9PD
Tel: 020 7910 5000
Fax: 020 7910 5001
E-mail: sdginfo@sdgworld.net
Web site: www.steerdaviesgleave.com

TAS PARTNERSHIP LTD
Guildhall House, 59-61 Guildhall Street,
Preston, Lancashire PR1 3NU
Tel: 01772 204988
Fax: 01722 562070
E-mail: info@taspartnership.co.uk
Web site: www.tas.uk.net

THOMAS KNOWLES - TRANSPORT CONSULTANT
41 Redhills, Eccleshall, Staffordshire
ST21 6JW
Tel: 01785 859414
Fax: 01785 859414
E-mail: thmsknw@aol.com

TRANSPORT CONSULTANCY – R W FAULKS
Penthouse J, Ross Court, Putney Hill,
London SW15 3NY
Tel: 020 8785 1585
E-mail: rexfaulks@aol.com

TRANSPORT DESIGN INTERNATIONAL
Clifford Mill, Stratford upon Avon CV37 8HW
Tel: 01789 205011
Fax: 05603 133119
E-mail: enquiries@tdi.uk.com
Web site: www.tdi.uk.com

TRANSPORT & TRAVEL RESEARCH LTD
Minster House, Minster Pool Walk, Lichfield, Staffordshire WS13 6QT
Tel: 01543 416416
Fax: 01543 416681
E-mail: enquiries@ttr-ltd.com
Web site: www.ttr-ltd.com

TTS UK
Total Tool Solutions Ltd, Newhaven Business Park, Lowergate, Milnsbridge, Huddersfield HD3 4HS
Tel: 01484 642211 **Fax:** 01484 461002
E-mail: sales@ttsuk.com
Web site: www.ttsuk.com

VCA
No1, The Eastgate Office Centre, Eastgate Road, Bristol BS5 6XX
Tel: 0117 951 5151
Fax: 0117 952 4103
E-mail: paul.cooke@vca.gov.uk
Web site: www.vca.gov.uk

WARD INTERNATIONAL CONSULTING LTD
70 Marks Tey Road, Fareham PO14 3UR
Tel: 01329 280280
Fax: 01329 667901
E-mail: info@wardint.co.uk
Web site: www.wardint.co.uk

WEST END TRAVEL & RUTLAND TRAVEL
The Lakeside Bus & Coach Centre, Dixon Drive, Off Leicester Road, Melton Mowbray, Leicestershire LE13 0DA
Tel: 01664 563498
Fax: 01664 568568
E-mail: john.penniston@btconnect.com

Delivery & Collection Services

BUS DELIVERIES (UK) LTD
Omnibus House, 17 Holywell Hill, St Albans, Hertfordshire AL1 1DT
Tel: 01727 752323
E-mail: info@busdelivery.co.uk
Web site: www.busdelivery.co.uk

Driver Supply

WEBB'S
St Peters Farm, Middle Drove, Peterborough PE14 8JJ
Tel: 01945 430123
E-mail: webb-s-cant@fsbdial.co.uk

Driver Training

ADG TRANSPORT CONSULTANCY
Oak Cottage, Royal Oak, Machen, Caerphilly CF83 8SN
Tel: 01633 441491
Fax: 01633 440591
E-mail: a.dgettins@btinternet.com
Web site: www.adgtransport.co.uk

BUZZLINES LTD
Unit G1, Lympne Industrial Park, Hythe CT21 4LR
Tel: 01303 261870
Fax: 01303 230093
Web site: www.buzzlines.co.uk

DATS (DAVE'S ACCIDENT & TRAINING SERVICES)
13 Kingfisher Close, The Willows, Torquay TQ2 7TF
Tel: 07747 686789
E-Mail: davepboulter@btinternet.com
Web site: www.datservices.org

GOSKILLS LTD
Concorde House, Trinity Park, Solihull B37 7UQ
Tel: 01216 355520
Fax: 01216 355521
E-mail: info@goskills.org
Web site: www.goskills.org

HATTS GARAGE SERVICES
Foxham, Chippenham SN15 4NB
Tel: 01249 740444
Fax: 01249 740447
E-mail: mike@hattstravel.co.uk
Web site: www.hattsgarageservices.co.uk

IBPTS
43 Cage Lane, Felixstowe, Suffolk OP11 9BJ
Tel: 01394 672 344
Fax: 01394 672 344
E-mail: enquiries@ibpts.co.uk
Web site: www.ibpts.co.uk

MIDLAND RED COACHES/WHEELS HERITAGE
Postal Office, 23 Broad Street, Brinklow, Warwickshire CV23 0LS
Tel: 02476 633624, 07733 884914
Fax: 02476 354900
E-mail: ashley@wheels.co.uk
Web site: www.wheels.co.uk

MINIMISE YOUR RISK
11 Chatsworth Park, Telscombe Cliffs, East Sussex BN10 7DZ
Tel: 01273 580189 **Fax:** 01273 580189
E-mail: alec@minimiseyourrisk.co.uk
Web site: www.minimiseyourrisk.co.uk

OMNIBUS TRAINING LTD
3 Lombard House, 2 Purley Way, Croydon CR0 3JT
Tel: 020 8006 7259
Fax: 020 8684 7835
E-mail: enquiries@omnibusltd.com
Web site: www.omnibusltd.com

SPECIALIST TRAINING & CONSULTANCY SERVICES LTD
6 Venture Court, Metcalfe Drive, Altham Industrial Estate, Accrington BB5 5TU
Tel: 01282 687090
Fax: 01282 687091
E-mail: enquiries@specialisttraining.co.uk
Web site: www.specialisttraining.co.uk

VOSA
Vehicle & Operator Services Agency, Commercial Projects Unit, Berkeley House, Croydon Street, Bristol BS5 0DA
Tel: 0117 954 3359 **Fax:** 0117 954 3212
E-mail: commercial.training@vosa.gov.uk
Web site: www.vosa.gov.uk

Exhibition/Event Organisers

EXPO MANAGEMENT LTD
Olympus Avenue, Leamington Spa CV34 6BF
Tel: 01926 888123

Fax: 01926 888004
E-mail: info@expom.co.uk
Web site: www.expom.co.uk

MCI EXHIBITIONS LTD
1 Rye Hill Office Park, Birmingham Road, Allesley, Coventry CV5 9AB
Tel: 02476 408020
Fax: 02476 408019
E-mail: gina@motorcycleshow.co.uk
Web site: www.motorcycleshow.co.uk

THE LONDON BUS EXPORT CO
PO Box 12, Chepstow NP16 5UZ
Tel: 01291 689 741
Fax: 01291 689 361
E-mail: lonbusco@globalnet.co.uk
Web site: www.bus.uk.com

UK COACH RALLY
21 The Poynings, Richings Park, Iver, Buckinghamshire SL0 9DS
Tel: 01753 631170
Mobile: 07590 468035
Fax: 01753 655980
E-mail: info@coachdisplays.co.uk
Web site: www.coachdisplays.co.uk

Ferry Operators

BRITTANY FERRIES GROUP TRAVEL
The Brittany Centre, Wharf Road, Portsmouth PO2 8RU
Tel: 0871 244 1456
Fax: 0870 901 3100
E-mail: grouptravel@brittany-ferries.com
Web site: www.brittany-ferries.co.uk/grouptravel

CALEDONIAN MACBRAYNE LTD
Head Office, The Ferry Terminal, Gourock PA19 1QP
Tel: 01475 650100
Web site: www.calmac.co.uk

CONDOR FERRIES LTD
Condor House, New Harbour Road South, Hamworthy, Poole BH15 4AJ
Tel: 01202 207207
Fax: 01202 685184
E-mail: reservations@condorferries.co.uk
Web site: www.condorferries.co.uk

DFDS SEAWAYS
Scandinavia House, Refinery Road, Parkeston CO12 4QG
Tel: 08771 882 0881
Web site: www.dfdsseaways.co.uk

EUROTUNNEL
PO Box 2000, Folkestone CT18 8XY
Tel: 08702 430401
Fax: 01303 288909
Web site: www.eurotunnel.com

IRISH FERRIES LTD
Groups Department, Salt Island, Holyhead LL65 1DR
Tel: 08705 329129
Fax: 01407 760340
Web site: www.irishferries.com

ISLE OF MAN STEAM PACKET COMPANY
Imperial Buildings, Douglas IM1 2BY
Tel: 01624 661661

Fax: 01624 645618
E-mail: resesteam-packet.com
Web site: www.steam-packet.com

NORFOLKLINE
Norfolk House, Eastern Dock, Dover CT16 1JA
Tel: 0870 870 1020
Web site: www.norfolkline.com

NORTHLINK FERRIES LTD
Stromness Ferry Terminal, Ferry Road, Stromness, Orkney KW16 3BH
Tel: 01856 885500
Fax: 01856 851795
E-mail: info@northlinkferries.co.uk
Web site: www.northlinkferries.co.uk

P&O FERRIES
Channel House, Channel View Road, Dover CT17 9TJ
Tel: 08716 641641
Fax: 08707 625325
E-mail: groups@poferries.com
Web site: www.poferries.com

PENTLAND FERRIES
Pier Road, St Margaret's Hope, Orkney KW17 2SW
Tel: 01856 831226
Fax: 01856 831697
Web site: www.pentlandferries.co.uk

RED FUNNEL
Red Funnel Travel Centre, 12 Bugle Street, Southampton SO14 2JY
Tel: 0844 844 9988
Fax: 0844 844 2698
E-mail: post@redfunnel.co.uk
Web site: www.redfunnel.co.uk

SEAFRANCE
Whitfield Court, Honeywood Close, Whitfield, Dover CT16 3PX
Tel: 0871 222 2800
Fax: 0871 282 8549
E-mail: groups@seafrance.fr
Web site: www.seafrance.com

STENA LINE
Station Approach, Holyhead LL65 1DQ
Tel: 08705 20 44 02
E-mail: groups@stenaline.com
Web site: www.stenaline.co.uk/groups

TRANSMANCHE FERRIES
Newhaven Ferry Port, Railway Approach, Newhaven BN9 0DF
Tel: 0800 917 1201
Web site: www.transmancheferries.co.uk
www.ldlines.com

WIGHTLINK ISLE OF WIGHT FERRIES
70 Broad Street, Portsmouth PO1 2LB
Tel: 0870 582 7744
Fax: 023 9285 5257
E-mail: sales@wightlink.co.uk
Web site: www.wightlink.co.uk

AD COACH SALES
Newbridge Coach Depot, Witheridge, Devon EX16 8PY
Tel: 01884 860767
Fax: 01884 860711

E-mail: enquiries@adcoachsales.co.uk
Web site: www.adcoachsales.co.uk

COACH FINANCE DIRECT.COM
Grove Terrace, Langley Moor, County Durham DH7 8JT
Tel: 0845 194 9566
Fax: 0845 456 3442
E-mail: sales@coachfinancedirect.com
Web site: www.coachfinancedirect.com

DAWSONRENTALS BUS AND COACH LTD
Delaware Drive, Tongwell, Milton Keynes MK15 8JH
Tel: 01908 218111
Fax: 01908 218 444
E-mail: contactus@dawsongroup.co.uk
Web site: www.dawsongroup.co.uk

FOREST ASSET FINANCE LTD
Bridge House, 6 Pullman Business Park, Pullman Way, Ringwood, Hampshire BH24 1HD
Tel: 01425 485685
Fax: 01425 473444
E-mail: info@forestassetfinance.co.uk
Web site: www.forestassetfinance.co.uk

LANDMARK FINANCE LTD
Suite 4, Old Grove House, 13 Vine Street, Hazel Grove, Stockport, Cheshire SK7 4JS
Tel: 0161 456 4242
Fax: 0161 483 3733
E-mail: landmarkfinance@btconnect.com
Web site: www.landmarkltd.co.uk

LHE FINANCE LTD
21 Headlands Business Park, Salisbury Road, Ringwood, Hampshire BH24 3PB
Tel: 01425 474070
Fax: 01425 474090
E-mail: sales@lhefinance.co.uk
Web site: www.lhefinance.co.uk

MCV BUS & COACH LTD
Sterling Place, Elean Business Park, Sutton CB6 2QE
Tel: 01353 773000
Fax: 01353 773001
E-mail: vernon.edwards@mcv-uk.com

MISTRAL BUS & COACH PLC
Booths Hall, Chelford Road, Knutsford WA16 8QZ
Tel: 01565 621881
Fax: 01565 621882
E-mail: sales@mistral-group.com
Web site: www.mistral-group.com

NORTON FOLGATE FG PLC
12th Floor, 30 Crown Place, London EC2A 4EB
Tel: 020 7965 4777
E-mail: help@nortonfolgate.co.uk
Web site: www.nortonfolgate.co.uk

SANTANDER ASSET FINANCE
Taylor Road, Trafford Park, Manchester M41 7JQ
Tel: 0161 747 6016
Fax: 0161 275 4501
E-mail: steve.moult@hansar.co.uk
Web site: www.santanderusedassets.co.uk

STOKE PARK FINANCE LTD
The Studio, Kirkhill House, Broom Road East,

Newton Mearns, Glasgow G77 5LL
Tel: 0141 639 1410
Fax: 0141 639 4785
E-mail: stoke-park@btconnect.com
Web site: www.stokeparkfinance.co.uk

VOLVO FINANCIAL SERVICES
Wedgnock Lane, Warwick CV34 5YA
Tel: 01926 498888
Fax: 01926 410278
Web site: www.volvo.com

BEST IMPRESSIONS
15 Starfield Road, London W12 9SN
Tel: 020 8740 6443
Fax: 020 8740 9134
E-mail: talk2us@best-impressions.co.uk
Web site: www.best-impressions.co.uk

BRITISH BUS PUBLISHING LTD
16 St Margaret's Drive, Telford TF1 3PH
Tel: 01952 255669
E-mail: bill@britishbuspublishing.co.uk
Web site: www.britishbuspublishing.co.uk

EXPRESS COACH REPAIRS LTD
Outgang Lane, Pickering YO18 7JA
Tel: 01751 475215
Fax: 01751 475215
E-mail: info@expresscoachrepairs.co.uk
Web site: www.expresscoachrepairs.co.uk

FWT
Aztec House 397-405 Archway Road, London N6 4EY
Tel: 020 7347 3700
Fax: 020 7347 3701
E-mail: sales@fwt.co.uk
Web site: www.fwt.co.uk

GRAPHIC EVOLUTION LTD
Ad House, East Parade, Harrogate HG1 5LT
Tel: 01423 706680
Fax: 01423 502522
E-mail: info@graphic-evolution.co.uk
Web site: www.graphic-evolution.co.uk

HATTS GARAGE SERVICES
Foxham, Chippenham SN15 4NB
Tel: 01249 740444
Fax: 01249 740447
E-mail: mike@hattstravel.co.uk
Web site: www.hattsgarageservices.co.uk

IMAGINET
Greyfriars House, Greyfriars Road, Cardiff CF10 3AL
Tel: 029 2057 4500
Fax: 029 2057 4501
E-mail: sales@imaginet.co.uk
Web site: www.imaginet.co.uk

NEERMAN & PARTNERS
c/o 22 Larbre Crescent, Whickham, Newcastle-upon-Tyne NE16 5YG
Tel: 0191 488 6258
Fax: 0191 488 9158
E-mail: info@neerman.net
Web site: www.neerman.net

PLUM DIGITAL PRINT
Suite 1, Cornerstone House, Stafford Park 13, Telford, Shropshire TF3 3AZ

Tel: 01952 204920
E-mail: steve.rooney@busandcoach.com
Web site: www.busandcoach.com

RH BODYWORKS
A140 Ipswich Road, Brome, Eye IP23 8AW
Tel: 01379 870666
Fax: 01379 871140
E-mail: enquiries@rhbodyworks.co.uk
Web site: www.rhbodyworks.co.uk

Health & Safety

GAUNTLET RISK MANAGEMENT (COVENTRY)
11 Little Church Street, Rugby CV21 3AW
Tel: 07944 092681
Web site: www.gauntletgroup.com/coventry
Contact: Laura Jennings

Insurance

BELMONT INTERNATIONAL LTD
Becket House, Vestry Road, Otford,
Sevenoaks TN14 5EL
Tel: 01732 744700
Fax: 01732 740276
E-mail: phil.white@belmontint.com
Web site: www.belmontint.com

R. L. DAVISON & CO LTD
Bury House, 31 Bury Street, London
EC3A 5AH.
Tel: 020 7816 9876
Fax: 020 7816 9880
E-mail: enquiries@rldavison.co.uk
Web site: www.rldavison.co.uk

ELLIS BATES GROUP
Adam House, Ripon Way, Harrogate,
HG1 2AU
Tel: 01423 522533
Fax: 01423 566303
E-mail: insurance@ellisbatesgroup.com
Web site: www.ellisbatesgroup.com

GAUNTLET RISK MANAGEMENT (COVENTRY)
11 Little Church Street, Rugby CV21 3AW
Tel: 07944 092681
Web site: www.gauntletgroup.com/coventry
Contact: Laura Jennings

P J HAYMAN & CO LTD
Stansted House, Rowlands Castle, Hampshire
PO9 6BR
Tel: 0845 230 0631
Fax: 023 9241 9019
E-mail: info@pjhayman.com
Web site: www.pjhayman.com

OMNI WHITTINGTONS
Arthur Castle House, 33 Creechurch Lane,
London EC3A 5EB
Tel: 020 7743 0900
Fax: 020 7456 1225.
E-mail: stephen.cane@whittingtoninsurance.com
Web site: whittingtoninsurance.com

PEAK LEGAL SERVICES LTD
41 Longmoor Road, Simmondley, Glossop,
Derbyshire SK13 6NH
Tel/Fax: 01457 855141
Mobile: 07989 092835
E-mail: ford414@btinternet.com

RIGTON INSURANCE SERVICES LTD
Chevin House, Otley Road, Guiseley,
Leeds LS20 8BH
Tel: 01943 879539
Fax: 01943 875529
E-mail: enquiries@rigtoninsurance.co.uk
Web site: www.rigtoninsurance.co.uk

TOWERGATE CHAPMAN STEVENS
Towergate House, 22 Wintersells Road, Byfleet,
Surrey KT14 7LF
Tel: 01932 334140
Fax: 01932 351238
E-mail: tcs@towergate.co.uk
Web site:
www.towergatechapmanstevens.co.uk

VOLVO INSURANCE SERVICES
Wedgnock Lane, Warwick CV34 5YA
Tel: 01926 401777
Fax: 01926 407407
Web site: www.volvo.com

WILLIS LTD
51 Lime Street, London EC3M 7DQ
Tel: 020 3124 6000
Fax: 020 3124 6266
Web site: www.willis.com

WRIGHTSURE GROUP
799 London Road, West Thurrock RM20 3LH
Tel: 01708 865533
Fax: 01708 865100
E-mail: info@wrightsure.com
Web site: www.wrightsure.com

Legal & Operations Advisers

BACKHOUSE JONES SOLICITORS
The Printworks, Hey Road, Clitheroe,
Lancashire BB7 9WD
Tel: 01254 828300
Fax: 01254 828301
E-mail: enquiries@backhouse.co.uk
Web site: www.backhousejones.co.uk

BORLAND NINDER DIXON LLP
3 Axe View, Axe Road, Drimpton, Beaminster,
Dorset DT8 3RJ
Tel: 01460 72 769
Fax: 01460 271680
E-mail: chris.borland@tiscali.co.uk

ELLIS TRANSPORT SERVICES
61 Bodycoats Road, Chandlers Ford,
Hampshire SO53 2HA
Tel: 023 8027 0447
Fax: 023 8027 6736
E-mail: info@ellistransportservices.co.uk
Web site: www.ellistransportservices.co.uk

FREIGHT TRANSPORT ASSOCIATION
Hermes House, St John's Road,
Tunbridge Wells TN4 9UZ
Tel: 01892 526171
Fax: 01892 534989
E-mail: enquiries@fta.co.uk
Web site: www.fta.co.uk

IBPTS
43 Cage Lane, Felixstowe, Suffolk OP11 9BJ
Tel: 01394 672 344
Fax: 01394 672 344
E-mail: enquiries@ibpts.co.uk
Web site: www.ibpts.co.uk

PEAK LEGAL SERVICES LTD
41 Longmoor Road, Simmondley, Glossop,
Derbyshire SK13 6NH
Tel/Fax: 01457 855141
Mobile: 07989 092835
E-mail: ford414@btinternet.com

PELLYS LLP SOLICITORS
Sworders Court, North Street, Bishops Stortford,
Hertfordshire CM23 2TN
Tel: 01279 758080
Fax: 01279 467565
E-mail: office@pellys.co.uk
Web site: www.pellys.co.uk

PRE METRO OPERATIONS LTD
Regent House, 56 Hagley Road, Stourbridge,
West Midlands DY8 1QD
Tel: 01384 441325
Fax: 0121 243 9906
E-mail: phil.evans@premetro.co.uk
Web site: www.premetro.co.uk

PROFESSIONAL TRANSPORT SERVICES
12 Silverdale, Stanford-le-Hope, Essex SS17 8BG
Tel: 01375 675262
E-mail: enquiries@proftranserv.com
Web site: www.proftranserv.co.uk

WARD INTERNATIONAL CONSULTING LTD
70 Marks Tey Road, Fareham PO16 3UR
Tel: 01329 280280
Fax: 01329 667901
E-mail: info@wardint.co.uk
Web site: www.wardint.co.uk

WEDLAKE SAINT (PENNINGTONS SOLICITORS LLP)
Abacus House, 33 Gutter Lane, London
EC2V 8AR
Tel: 020 7457 3000
Fax: 020 7457 3240
E-mail: wedlakesaint@penningtons.co.uk
Web site: www.wedlakesaint.co.uk

Livery Design

BEST IMPRESSIONS
15 Starfield Road, London W12 9SN
Tel: 020 8740 6443
Fax: 020 8740 9134
E-mail: talk2us@best-impressions.co.uk
Web site: www.best-impressions.co.uk

CHANNEL COMMERCIALS PLC
Unit 6, Cobbs Wood Industrial Estate,
Brunswick Road, Ashford TN23 1EH
Tel: 01233 629272
Fax: 01233 636322
E-mail: info@ccplc.co.uk
Web site: www.channelcommercials.co.uk

EXPRESS COACH REPAIRS LTD
Outgang Lane, Pickering YO18 7JA
Tel: 01751 475215
Fax: 01751 475215
E-mail: info@expresscoachrepairs.co.uk
Web site: www.expresscoachrepairs.co.uk

GRAPHIC EVOLUTION LTD
Ad House, East Parade, Harrogate HG1 5LT
Tel: 01423 706680
Fax: 01423 502522

E-mail: info@graphic-evolution.co.uk
Web site: www.graphic-evolution.co.uk

TONY GREAVES GRAPHICS
19 Perth Mount, Horsforth,
Leeds LS18 5SH
Tel/Fax: 0113 258 4795
E-mail: tony@greavesgraphics.fsnet.co.uk

HATTS GARAGE SERVICES
Foxham, Chippenham SN15 4NB
Tel: 01249 740444
Fax: 01249 740447
E-mail: mike@hattstravel.co.uk
Web site: www.hattsgarageservices.co.uk

THE LONDON BUS EXPORT CO
PO Box 12, Chepstow NP16 5UZ
Tel: 01291 689741
Fax: 01291 689361
E-mail: lonbusco@globalnet.co.uk
Web site: www.bus.uk.com

McKENNA BROTHERS
McKenna House, Jubilee Road, Middleton,
Manchester M24 2LX
Tel: 0161 655 3244
Fax: 0161 655 3059
E-mail: info@mckennabrothers.co.uk
Web site: www.mckennabrothers.co.uk

NEERMAN & PARTNERS
c/o 22 Larbre Crescent, Whickham,
Newcastle-upon-Tyne NE16 5YG
Tel: 0191 488 6258
Fax: 0191 488 9158
E-mail: info@neerman.net
Web site: www.neerman.net

PB BUS MARKETING SPECIALISTS
2 Trafalgar Close, Chandlers Ford,
Eastleigh, Hampshire SO53 4BW
Tel: 02380 274020
E-mail: enquiries@pbbusmarketing.co.uk
Web site: www.pbbusmarketing.co.uk

Maps for the Bus Industry

BEST IMPRESSIONS
15 Starfield Road, London
W12 9SN
Tel: 020 8740 6443
Fax: 020 8740 9134
E-mail: talk2us@best-impressions.co.uk
Web site: www.best-impressions.co.uk

FWT
Aztec House, 397-405 Archway Road,
London N6 4EY
Tel: 020 7347 3700
Fax: 020 7347 3701
E-mail: sales@fwt.co.uk
Web site: www.fwt.co.uk

TONY GREAVES GRAPHICS
19 Perth Mount, Horsforth, Leeds
LS18 5SH
Tel/Fax: 0113 258 4795
E-mail: tony@greavesgraphics.fsnet.co.uk

PINDAR PLC
31 Edison Road, Aylesbury HP19 8TE
Tel: 01296 390100
Fax: 01296 381233
Web site: www.pindar.com

Marketing Services

ADG TRANSPORT CONSULTANCY
Oak Cottage, Royal Oak, Machen,
Caerphilly CF83 8SN
Tel: 01633 441491
Fax: 01633 440591
E-mail: a.dgettins@btinternet.com
Web site: www.adgtransport.co.uk

IMAGINET
Greyfriars House, Greyfriars Road,
Cardiff CF10 3AL
Tel: 029 2057 4500
Fax: 029 2057 4501
E-mail: sales@imaginet.co.uk
Web site: www.imaginet.co.uk

PB BUS MARKETING SPECIALISTS
2 Trafalgar Close, Chandlers Ford,
Eastleigh, Hampshire SO53 4BW
Tel: 02380 274020
E-mail: enquiries@pbbusmarketing.co.uk
Web site: www.pbbusmarketing.co.uk

Mechanical Investigation

ELLIS TRANSPORT SERVICES
61 Bodycoats Road, Chandlers Ford,
Hampshire SO53 2HA
Tel: 02380 270447
Fax: 02380 276736
E-mail: info@ellistransportservices.co.uk
Web site: www.ellistransportservices.co.uk

**OPTARE PRODUCT SUPPORT
LONDON**
Unit 9, Eurocourt, Olivers Close,
West Thurrock RM20 3EE
Tel: 01708 896860
Fax: 01708 869920
E-mail: london.service@optare.com

**OPTARE PRODUCT SUPPORT
ROTHERHAM**
Denby Way, Hellaby, Rotherham
S66 8HR
Tel: 01709 535100
Fax: 01709 535102
E-mail: rotherham.service@optare.com

PLAXTON SERVICE
Ryton Road, Anston, Sheffield
S25 4DL
Tel: 01909 551155
Fax: 01909 550050
E-mail: service@plaxtonlimited.co.uk
Web site: www.plaxtonaftercare.co.uk

On-Bus Advertising

BEST IMPRESSIONS
15 Starfield Road, London W12 9SN
Tel: 020 8740 6443
Fax: 020 8740 9134
E-mail: talk2us@best-impressions.co.uk
Web site: www.best-impressions.co.uk

CYBERLYNE COMMUNICATIONS LTD
Unit 5, Hatfield Way, South Church Enterprise
Park, Bishop Auckland, Durham DL14 6XF
Tel: 01388 773761
Fax: 01388 773778
E-mail: sales@cyberlyne.co.uk
Web site: www.cyberlyne.co.uk

DECKER MEDIA LTD
Adbus Ltd, Decker House, Lowater Street,
Carlton, Nottingham NG4 1JJ
Tel: 0115 940 2406
Fax: 0115 940 2407
E-mail: sales@deckermedia.co.uk
Web site: www.deckermedia.co.uk

RATCLIFF FERNLEY MEDIA LTD
Evans Business Centre, Hartwith Way,
Harrogate HG3 2XA
Tel: 01423 813470
Fax: 01423 813471
E-mail: enquiries@rfmediauk.com
Web site: www.titanbus.co.uk

Passenger Representation

BUS USERS UK
PO Box 119, Shepperton, Middlesex TW17 8UX
Tel: 01932 232574
E-mail: enquiries@bususers.org
Web site: www.bususers.org

Printing and Publishing

BEMROSEBOOTH LTD
Stockholm Road, Sutton Fields Industrial Estate,
Hull HU7 0XY
Tel: 01482 826343
Fax: 01482 371386
E-mail: lprecious@bemrosebooth.com
Web site: www.bemrosebooth.com

BEST IMPRESSIONS
15 Starfield Road, London W12 9SN
Tel: 020 8740 6443
Fax: 020 8740 9134
E-mail: talk2us@best-impressions.co.uk
Web site: www.best-impressions.co.ukl

THE HENRY BOOTH GROUP
Stockholm Road, Sutton Fields Industrial Estate,
Hull HU7 0XY
Tel: 01482 826343
Fax: 01482 839767
E-mail: mshanley@henrybooth.co.uk
Web site: www.henrybooth.co.uk

BUS & COACH PROFESSIONAL
Suite 1, Cornerstone House, Stafford Park 13,
Telford TF3 3AZ
Tel: 01952 204920
E-mail: steve.rooney@busandcoach.com
Web site: www.busandcoach.com

BUSES WORLDWIDE
37 Oyster Lane, Byfleet, Surrey KT14 7HS
Tel: 01932 352351
E-mail: membership@busesworldwide.org
Web site: www.busesworldwide.org

FWT
Aztec House, 397-405 Archway Road,
London N6 4EY
Tel: 020 7347 3700
Fax: 020 7347 3701
E-mail: sales@fwt.co.uk
Web site: www.fwt.co.uk

GRAPHIC EVOLUTION LTD
Ad House, East Parade, Harrogate HG1 5LT
Tel: 01423 706680 Fax: 01423 502522
E-mail: info@graphic-evolution.co.uk
Web site: www.graphic-evolution.co.uk

TONY GREAVES GRAPHICS
19 Perth Mount, Horsforth, Leeds LS18 5SH
Tel/Fax: 0113 258 4795
E-mail: tony@greavesgraphics.fsnet.co.uk

HB PUBLICATIONS LTD
3 Ingham Grove, Hartlepool TS25 2LH
Tel: 01429 293611
E-mail: sales@hbpub.co.uk
Web site: www.hbpub.co.uk

IAN ALLAN PRINTING LTD
Riverdene Business Park, Molesey Road,
Hersham, Surrey KT12 4RG
Tel: 01932 266600 **Fax:** 01932 266601
E-mail:
jonathan.bingham@ianallanprinting.co.uk
Web site: www.ianallanprinting.co.uk

IMAGE & PRINT GROUP
Unit 9, Oakbank Industrial Estate, Garscube Road,
Glasgow G20 7LU
Tel: 0141 353 1900
Fax: 0141 353 8611
E-mail: alan@imageandprint.co.uk
Web site: www.imageandprint.co.uk

PB BUS MARKETING SPECIALISTS
2 Trafalgar Close, Chandlers Ford, Eastleigh,
Hampshire SO53 4BW
Tel: 02380 274020
E-mail: enquiries@pbbusmarketing.co.uk
Web site: www.pbbusmarketing.co.uk

PINDAR PLC
Pindar House, Thornburgh Road, Eastfield,
Scarborough YO11 3UY
Tel: 01723 581581
Fax: 01723 583086
Web site: www.pindar.com

PLUM DIGITAL PRINT
Suite 1, Cornerstone House, Stafford Park 13,
Telford, Shropshire TF3 3AZ
Tel: 01952 204920
E-mail: steve.rooney@busandcoach.com
Web site: www.busandcoach.com

Promotional Material

BEST IMPRESSIONS
15 Starfield Road, London W12 9SN
Tel: 020 8740 6443
Fax: 020 8740 9134
E-mail: talk2us@best-impressions.co.uk
Web site: www.best-impressions.co.uk

FWT
Aztec House, 397-405 Archway Road,
London N6 4EY
Tel: 020 7347 3700 **Fax:** 020 7347 3701
E-mail: sales@fwt.co.uk
Web site: www.fwt.co.uk

GRAPHIC EVOLUTION LTD
Ad House, East Parade, Harrogate HG1 5LT
Tel: 01423 706680
Fax: 01423 502522
E-mail: info@graphic-evolution.co.uk
Web site: www.graphic-evolution.co.uk

TONY GREAVES GRAPHICS
19 Perth Mount, Horsforth, Leeds LS18 5SH
Tel/Fax: 0113 258 4795
E-mail: tony@greavesgraphics.fsnet.co.uk

IBPTS
43 Cage Lane, Felixstowe, Suffolk OP11 9BJ
Tel: 01394 672 344
Fax: 01394 672 344
E-mail: enquiries@ibpts.co.uk
Web site: www.ibpts.co.uk

IMAGINET
Greyfriars House, Greyfriars Road,
Cardiff CF10 3AL
Tel: 029 2057 4500
Fax: 029 2057 4501
E-mail: sales@imaginet.co.uk
Web site: www.imaginet.co.uk

MARKET ENGINEERING
43-44 North Bar, Banbury OX16 0TH
Tel: 01295 277050
Fax: 01295 277030
E-mail: contact@m-eng.com
Web site: www.marketengineering.co.uk

PB BUS MARKETING SPECIALISTS
2 Trafalgar Close, Chandlers Ford, Eastleigh,
Hampshire SO53 4BW
Tel: 02380 274020
E-mail: enquiries@pbbusmarketing.co.uk
Web site: www.pbbusmarketing.co.uk

PINDAR PLC
Pindar House, Thornburgh Road, Eastfield,
Scarborough YO11 3UY
Tel: 01723 581581
Fax: 01723 583086
Web site: www.pindar.com

PLUM DIGITAL PRINT
Suite 1, Cornerstone House, Stafford Park 13,
Telford, Shropshire TF3 3AZ
Tel: 01952 204 920
E-mail: steve.rooney@busandcoach.com
Web site: www.busandcoach.com

STEPHEN C MORRIS
PO Box 119, Shepperton TW17 8UX
Tel: 01932 232574
E-mail: buswriter@btinternet.com

Publications – Magazines & Books

BRITISH BUS PUBLISHING LTD
16 St Margaret's Drive, Telford TF1 3PH
Tel: 01952 255 669
E-mail: bill@britishbuspublishing.co.uk
Web site: www.britishbuspublishing.co.uk

BUS & COACH BUYER
The Publishing Centre, 1 Woolram Wygate,
Spalding PE11 1NU
Tel: 01775 711777
Fax: 01775 711737
E-mail: bcbsales@busandcoachbuyer.com
Web site: www.busandcoachbuyer.com

BUS & COACH PROFESSIONAL
Suite 1, Cornerstone House, Stafford Park 13,
Telford TF3 3AZ
Tel: 01952 204920
E-mail: steve.rooney@busandcoach.com
Web site: www.busandcoach.com

BUS USER
Bus Users UK, PO Box 2950, Stoke on Trent
ST4 9EW
Tel: 01782 442885

Fax: 01782 442886
E-mail: enquiries@bususers.org
Web site: www.bususers.org

BUSES
Ian Allan Publishing Ltd, Riverdene Business Park,
Molesey Road, Hersham, Surrey KT12 4RG
Tel: 01932 266600
Fax: 01932 266601
Web site: www.busesmag.com

BUSES WORLDWIDE
37 Oyster Lane, Byfleet, Surrey KT14 7HS
Tel: 01932 352351
E-mail: membership@busesworldwide.org
Web site: www.busesworldwide.org

COACH & BUS WEEK
3 The Office Village, Cygnet Park, Hampton,
Peterborough PE7 8FD
Tel: 01733 293240
Fax: 0845 2802927
E-mail: jacqui.grobler@rouncymedia.co.uk
Web site: www.cbwnet.co.uk

CRONER (WOLTERS KLUWER UK LTD)
145 London Road, Kingston upon Thames
KT2 6SR
Tel: 020 8547 3333
Fax: 020 8547 2637
E-mail: info@croner.co.uk
Web site: www.croner.co.uk

JANES URBAN TRANSPORT SYSTEMS
163 Brighton Road, Coulsdon CR5 2YH
Tel: 020 8700 3700
Web site: www.janes.com/www.juts.janes.com

PASSENGER TRANSPORT
Adelaide Wharf, 21 Whiston Road,
London E2 8EX
Tel: 020 7749 6909
E-mail: editorial@passengertransport.co.uk
Web site: www.passengertransport.co.uk

PLUM DIGITAL PRINT
Suite 1, Cornerstone House, Stafford Park 13,
Telford, Shropshire TF3 3AZ
Tel: 01952 204920
E-mail: steve.rooney@busandcoach.com
Web site: www.busandcoach.com

ROUTE ONE
Expo Management Ltd, Unit 4, Minerva Business
Park, Lynch Wood, Peterborough PE2 6FT
Tel: 01733 405730
Fax: 01733 405745
Web site: www.route.one.net

SALTIRE COMMUNICATIONS
39 Lilyhill Terrace, Edinburgh EH8 7DR
Tel: 0131 652 0205
E-mail: gavin.booth@btconnect.com

SOE
22 Greencoat Place, London SW1 1PR
Tel: 02076 301 111
Fax: 02076 306 667
E-mail: soe@soe.org.uk
Web site: www.soe.org.uk

STEPHEN C MORRIS
PO Box 119, Shepperton TW17 8UX
Tel: 01932 232574
E-mail: buswriter@btinternet.com

TRAMWAYS & URBAN TRANSIT
c/o LRTA, PO Box 26, Sawtry PE28 5WY
E-mail: editor@lrta.org
Web site: www.lrta.org

TRANSPORT STATIONERY SERVICES
61 Bodycoats Road, Chandlers Ford, Hampshire
SO53 2HA
Tel: 07041 471008
Fax: 07041 471009

Quality Management Systems

FTA VEHICLE INSPECTION SERVICE
Hermes House, St John's Road, Tunbridge Wells
TN4 9UZ
Tel: 01892 526171
Fax: 01892 534989
E-mail: enquiries@fta.co.uk
Web site: www.fta.co.uk

IBPTS
43 Cage Lane, Felixstowe, Suffolk OP11 9BJ
Tel: 01394 672344
Fax: 01394 672344
E-mail: enquiries@ibpts.co.uk
Web site: www.ibpts.co.uk

MYSTERY TRAVELLERS
6A Mays Yard, Down Road, Waterlooville,
Hampshire PO8 0YP
Tel: 023 9259 7707
Fax: 023 9259 1700
E-mail: info@bestchart.co.uk
Web site: www.bestchart.co.uk

TTS UK
Total Tool Solutions Ltd, Newhaven Business
Park, Lowergate, Milnsbridge, Huddersfield
HD3 4HS
Tel: 01484 642211 **Fax:** 01484 461002
E-mail: sales@ttsuk.com
Web site: www.ttsuk.com

VCA
No1, The Estate Office Centre, Eastgate Road,
Bristol BS5 6XX
Tel: 0117 952 4126
Fax: 0117 952 4104
E-mail: paul.cooke@vca.gov.uk
Web site: www.vca.gov.uk

VOSA COMMERCIAL PROJECTS UNIT
Berkeley House, Croydon Street, Bristol BS5 0DA
Tel: 0117 954 3359
Fax: 0117 954 3496
E-mail: commercial.training@vosa.gov.uk

Recruitment

**COUNTY RECRUITMENT
& TRAINING LTD**
Harry Harris, 10 Valley Road, River, Dover, Kent
CT17 0QN
Tel: 01304 826220 **Fax:** 01304 822551
E-mail: harry@pineham98.co.uk
Web site: www.crtweb.co.uk

**4 FARTHINGS INTERNATIONAL
RECRUITMENT**
22 Alexander Close, Twickenham, Middlesex
TW12 2JW
Tel: 020 8898 8813
E-mail: info@4farthings.co.uk
Web site: www.4farthings.co.uk

Reference Books

BRITISH BUS PUBLISHING LTD
16 St Margaret's Drive, Telford TF1 3PH
Tel: 01952 255669
E-mail: bill@britishbuspublishing.co.uk
Web site: www.britishbuspublishing.co.uk

BUSES WORLDWIDE
37 Oyster Lane, Byfleet, Surrey KT14 7HS
Tel: 01932 352351
E-mail: membership@busesworldwide.org
Web site: www.busesworldwide.org

Timetable Production

BEMROSEBOOTH LTD
Stockholm Road, Sutton Fields Industrial Estate,
Hull HU7 0XY
Tel: 01482 826343
Fax: 01482 371386
E-mail: lprecious@bemrosebooth.com
Web site: www.bemrosebooth.com

BEST IMPRESSIONS
15 Starfield Road, London W12 9SN
Tel: 020 8740 6443
Fax: 020 8740 9134
E-mail: talk2us@best-impressions.co.uk
Web site: www.best-impressions.co.uk

FWT
Aztec House, 397-405 Archway Road, London
N6 4EY
Tel: 020 7347 3700
Fax: 020 7347 3701
E-mail: sales@fwt.co.uk
Web site: www.fwt.co.uk

TONY GREAVES GRAPHICS
19 Perth Mount, Horsforth, Leeds LS18 5SH
Tel/Fax: 0113 258 4795
E-mail: tony@greavesgraphics.fsnet.co.uk

IBPTS
43 Cage Lane, Felixstowe, Suffolk OP11 9BJ
Tel: 01394 672344
Fax: 01394 672344
E-mail: enquiries@ibpts.co.uk
Web site: www.ibpts.co.uk

PB BUS MARKETING SPECIALISTS
2 Trafalgar Close, Chandlers Ford, Eastleigh,
Hampshire SO53 4BW
Tel: 02380 274020
E-mail: enquiries@pbbusmarketing.co.uk
Web site: www.pbbusmarketing.co.uk

PINDAR PLC
Pindar House, Thornburgh Road, Eastfield,
Scarborough YO11 3UY
Tel: 01723 581581
Fax: 01723 583086
Web site: www.pindar.com

PLUM DIGITAL PRINT
Suite 1, Cornerstone House, Stafford Park 13,
Telford, Shropshire TF3 3AZ
Tel: 01952 204920
E-mail: nigel.greenaway@busandcoach.com
Web site: www.plumdigitalprint.co.uk

**PROFESSIONAL TRANSPORT
SERVICES**
12 Silverdale, Stanford-le-Hope, Essex SS17 8BG

Tel: 01375 675262
E-mail: enquiries@proftranserv.com
Web site: www.proftranserv.co.uk

TRAVEL INFORMATION SYSTEMS
Grand Union House, 20 Kentish Town Road,
London NW1 9NX
Tel: 020 7428 1288
Fax: 020 7267 2745
E-mail: enquiries@travelinfosystems.com
Web site: www.travelinfosystems.com

Tour Wholesalers

ACTION TOURS
5 Aston Street, Shifnal, Shropshire TR11 8DW
Tel: 01952 462462
Fax: 01952 462555
E-mail: info@actiontours.co.uk
Web site: www.actionotours.co.uk

ALBATROSS TRAVEL GROUP LTD
Albatross House, 14 New Hythe Lane, Larkfield,
Kent ME20 6AB
Tel: 01732 879191
Fax: 01732 522968
E-mail: sales@albatross-tours.com
Web site: www.albatross-tours.com

CIE TOURS INTERNATIONAL
35 Lower Abbey Street, Dublin 1,
Republic of Ireland
Tel: 00 353 1 703 1888
Fax: 00 353 1 874 5564
E-mail: info@cietours.ie
Web site: www.cietours.com

GREATDAYS TRAVEL GROUP
2 Stamford Park Road, Altrincham WA15 9EN
Tel: 0161 928 9966
Fax: 0161 928 8226
E-mail: sales@greatdays.co.uk
Web site: www.greatdays.co.uk

**INDEPENDENT COACH TRAVEL
(WHOLESALING) LTD**
South Quay Travel and Leisure Ltd, Studios 20/21,
Colman's Wharf, 45 Morris Road, London E14
6PA
Tel: 020 7538 4627
Fax: 020 7538 8239
E-mail: info@ictsqt.co.uk
Web site: www.ictsqt.co.uk

Training Services

ADG TRANSPORT CONSULTANCY
Oak Cottage, Royal Oak, Machen, Caerphilly
CF83 8SN
Tel: 01633 441491
Fax: 01633 440591
E-mail: a.dgettins@btinternet.com
Web site: www.adgtransport.co.uk

BUZZLINES LTD
Unit G1, Lympne Industrial Park, Hythe,
Kent CT21 4LR
Tel: 01303 261870
Fax: 01303 230093
Web site: www.buzzlines.co.uk

**COUNTY RECRUITMENT
& TRAINING LTD**
Harry Harris, 10 Valley Road, River, Dover, Kent
CT17 0QN

Tel: 01304 826220
Fax: 01304 822551
E-mail: harry@pineham98.co.uk
Web site: www.crtweb.co.uk

DATS (DAVE'S ACCIDENT & TRAINING SERVICES)
13 Kingfisher Close, The Willows,
Torquay TQ2 7TF
Tel: 07747 686789
E-Mail: davepboulter@btinternet.com
Web site: www.datservices.org

GOSKILLS
Concorde House, Trinity Park,
Solihull B37 7UQ
Tel: 0121 635 5520
Fax: 0121 635 5521
E-mail: info@goskills.org
Web site: www.goskills.org

IBPTS
43 Cage Lane, Felixstowe, Suffolk OP11 9BJ
Tel: 01394 672344
Fax: 01394 672344
E-mail: enquiries@ibpts.co.uk
Web site: www.ibpts.co.uk

MARKET ENGINEERING
43-44 North Bar, Banbury OX16 0TH
Tel: 01295 277050
Fax: 01295 277030
E-mail: contact@m-eng.com
Web site: www.marketengineering.com

MIDLAND RED COACHES/ WHEELS HERITAGE
Postal Office, 23 Broad Street,
Brinklow, Warwickshire
CV23 0LS
Tel: 02476 633624, 07733 884914
Fax: 02476 354900
E-mail: ashley@wheels.co.uk
Web site: www.wheels.co.uk

MINIMISE YOUR RISK
11 Chatsworth Park, Telscombe Cliffs,
East Sussex BN10 7DZ
Tel: 01273 580189
Fax: 01273 580189
E-mail: alec@minimiseyourrisk.co.uk
Web site: www.minimiseyourrisk.co.uk

OMNIBUS TRAINING LTD
3 Lombard House, 2 Purley Way,
Croydon CR0 3JP
Tel: 020 8006 7259
Fax: 020 8684 7835
E-mail: enquiries@omnibusltd.com
Web site: www.omnibusltd.com

PRE METRO OPERATIONS LTD
Regent House, 56 Hagley Road,
Stourbridge,
West Midlands DY8 1QD
Tel: 01384 441325
Fax: 0121 243 9906
E-mail: phil.evans@premetro.co.uk
Web site: www.premetro.co.uk

PROFESSIONAL TRANSPORT SERVICES
12 Silverdale, Stanford-le-Hope,
Essex SS17 8BG
Tel: 01375 675262
E-mail: enquiries@proftranserv.com
Web site: www.proftranserv.co.uk

SOE
22 Greencoat Place, London
SW1 1PR
Tel: 02076 301 111
Fax: 02076 306 667
E-mail: soe@soe.org.uk
Web site: www.soe.org.uk

SPECIALIST TRAINING & CONSULTANCY SERVICES LTD
6 Venture Court, Metcalfe Drive,
Altham Industrial Estate, Accrington
BB5 5TU
Tel: 01282 687090
Fax: 01282 687091
E-mail: enquiries@specialisttraining.co.uk
Web site: www.specialisttraining.co.uk

TRANSPORT & TRAINING SERVICES LTD
Warrington Business Park, Long Lane,
Warrington WA2 8TX
Tel: 01925 243500
Fax: 01925 243000
E-mail: tachographsuk@aol.com
Web site: www.transporttrainingservices.com

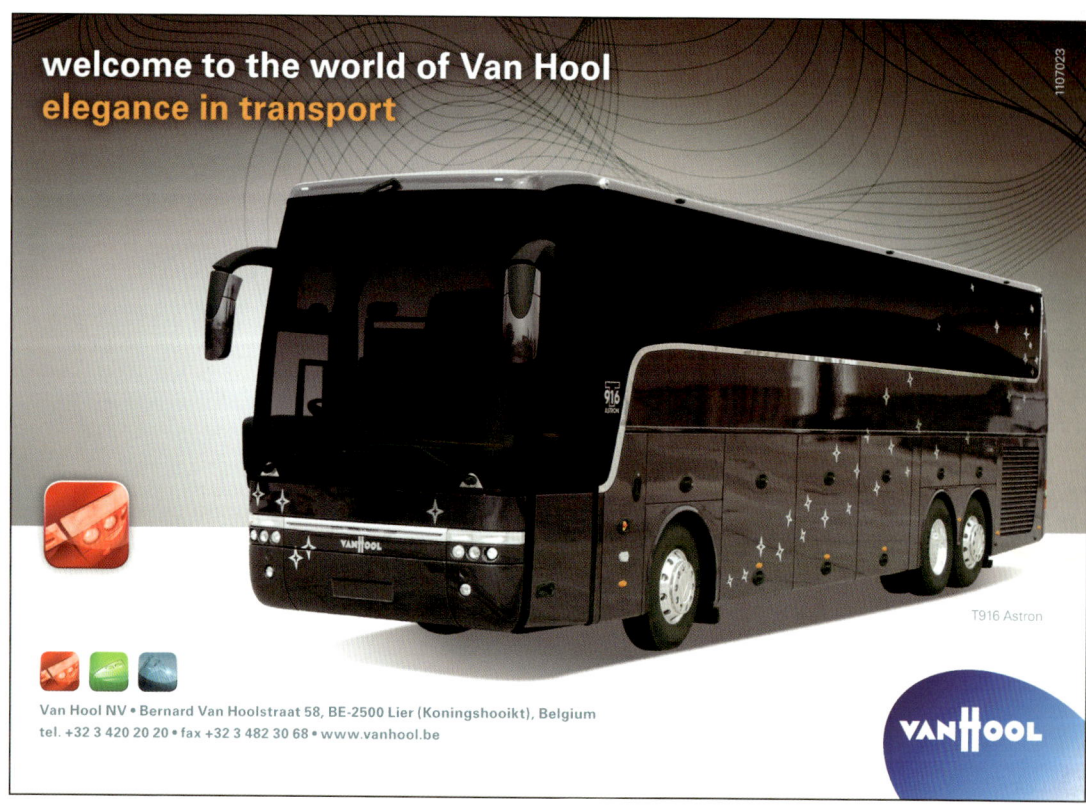

TTS UK

Total Tool Solutions Ltd, Newhaven Business Park, Lowergate, Milnsbridge, Huddersfield HD3 4HS
Tel: 01484 642211 **Fax:** 01484 461002
E-mail: sales@ttsuk.com
Web site: www.ttsuk.com

WEST END TRAVEL & RUTLAND TRAVEL

The Lakeside Bus & Coach Centre, Dixon Drive, Off Leicester Road, Melton Mowbray, Leicestershire LE13 0DA
Tel: 01664 563498
Fax: 01664 568568
E-mail: john.penniston@btconnect.com

PLAXTON SERVICE

Ryton Road, Anston, Sheffield S25 4DL
Tel: 01909 551155
Fax: 01909 550050
E-mail: service@plaxtonlimited.co.uk
Web site: www.plaxtonaftercare.co.uk

VCA

No1, The Estate Office Centre, Eastgate Road, Bristol BS5 6XX
Tel: 0117 952 4126
Fax: 0117 952 4104
E-mail: paul.cooke@vca.gov.uk
Web site: www.vca.gov.uk

IMAGINET

Greyfriars House, Greyfriars Road, Cardiff CF10 3AL
Tel: 029 2057 4500
Fax: 029 2057 4501
E-mail: sales@imaginet.co.uk
Web site: www.imaginet.co.uk

PB BUS MARKETING SPECIALISTS

2 Trafalgar Close, Chandlers Ford, Eastleigh, Hampshire SO53 4BW
Tel: 02380 274020
E-mail: enquiries@pbbusmarketing.co.uk
Web site: www.pbbusmarketing.co.uk

SECTION 2

Tendering & Regulatory Authorities

- **Tendering & Regulatory Authorities etc**

- **ITAs**

- **PTEs**

- **Integrated Transport Regional Authorities**

- **Transport Coordinating Officers**

- **Traffic Commissioners**

- **Office of Fair Trading**

- **Department for Transport**

INTEGRATED TRANSPORT AUTHORITIES

Greater Manchester Combined Authority Transport for Greater Manchester Committee
PO Box 532, Town Hall, Albert Square, Manchester M60 2LA
Tel: 0161 234 4619
Fax: 0161 236 6459
E-mail: tfgmc@manchester.gov.uk
Web site: www.transportforgreatermanchestercommittee.gov.uk
Chair: Cllr A Fender
Vice-Chairs: Cllr R Jones, Cllr Alderd, Cllr D Dickinson.
Clerk: Sir Howard Bernstein

Merseyside ITA
24 Hatton Garden, Liverpool L3 2AN
Tel: 0151 227 5181
Fax: 0151 236 2457
Web site: www.merseytravel.gov.uk
Chair: Cllr Mark Dowd
Clerk: Steve Maddox
Gen Man Mersey Tunnels: John Gillard
Operates with Merseyside PTE (qv) as Merseytravel

South Yorkshire ITA
18 Regent Street, Barnsley S70 2PQ
Tel: 01226 772800
Fax: 01226 772899
Web site: www.southyorks.gov.uk
Chairman: Cllr M Jameson
Vice-Chairman: Cllr Ms D Fox
Clerk/Treasurer: W J Wilkinson

Tyne & Wear ITA
Civic Centre, Barras Bridge, Newcastle upon Tyne NE1 8PD
Tel: 0191 232 8520
Web site: www.twpta.gov.uk
Chairman: Cllr David Wood
Vice-Chair: Cllr J McElroy
Clerk: K G Lavery
Deputy Clerk & Treasurer: D Johnson
Engineer: J Millar
Legal advisor: V A Dodds

West Midlands ITA
Room 120, Centro House, 16 Summer Lane, Birmingham B19 3SD
Tel: 0121 214 7507
Fax: 0121 233 1841
Web site: www.wmpta.org.uk
E-mail for Councillors: tateam@centro.org.uk
E-mail for Committee Team: ptateam@centro.org.uk
Chair: Cllr A Adams
Vice-Chair: Cllr J Hunt
Clerk: Ms S Manzie
Deputy Clerk/Solicitor: C Hinde
Treasurer: Ms A Ridgewell

West Yorkshire ITA
Wellington House, 40-50 Wellington Street, Leeds LS1 2DE
Tel: 0113 251 7218
Fax: 0113 251 7373
Web site: www.wyita.gov.uk
Chair: Cllr James Lewis
Vice-Chair: Cllr Eric Firth
Clerk to the Authority: K T Preston, OBE

PASSENGER TRANSPORT EXECUTIVES

Centro (West Midlands PTE)
Centro House, 16 Summer Lane, Birmingham B19 3SD
Tel: 0121 200 2787
Fax: 0121 214 7010
Web site: www.centro.org.uk
The Executive is responsible to the West Midlands Integrated Transport Authority
Director General: Geoff Inskip
Passenger Services Director: Stephen Rhodes
Strategy & Commissioning Director: Tom Magrath
Corporate Services Director: Steve Chatwin
Finance & Planning Director: James Aspinall
Metro Programme Executive: Paul Griffiths
Head of Marketing and Communications: Conrad Jones
Head of Projects: Stephen Terry-Short

Transport for Greater Manchester
2 Piccadilly Place, Manchester M1 3BG
Tel: 0161 244 1000
Web site: www.tfgm.com
TfGM is responsible to the Transport for Greater Manchester Committee of the Greater Manchester Combined Authority. TfGM is responsible for contracting socially necessary bus services and supporting the local rail service. It also owns the Metrolink light rail system on behalf of the Authority and is responsible for planning for the future of the Metrolink network. TfGM and the Authority are also committed to developing accessible transport, funding Ring and Ride, a fully accessible door to door transport service for people with mobility difficulties. TfGM administers the concessionary fares scheme, which allows participants (pensioners, children and people with disabilities) either free or reduced rate travel. TfGM owns and is responsible for the upkeep of bus stations and on-street infrastructure. It also provides information about public transport through telephone information lines, timetables, general publicity and Travelshops.
Chief Executive: David Leather
Interim Chief Operating Officer: Bob Morris
Finance & Corporate Services Director: Steve Warrener
Bus & Rail Director: Michael Renshaw

Merseyside Integrated Transport Authority and Executive (Merseytravel)
24 Hatton Garden, Liverpool L3 2AN
Tel: 0151 227 5181
Fax: 0151 236 2457
Web site: www.merseytravel.gov.uk
Merseytravel ensures the availability of public transport in Merseyside, including financial support for the Merseyrail rail network and those bus services not provided for by the private sector.
It also promotes public transport by providing bus stations and infrastructure, comprehensive travel tickets and free travel with minimum restrictions for the elderly and those with mobility difficulties. Merseytravel also owns and operates the Mersey ferries and Mersey tunnels.
Chair to ITA: Cllr M Dowd
Chief Executive ITA & Director General PTE: Neil Scales OBE
Clerk to ITA: Steve Maddox

Director of Resources: J R Barclay
Director of Operations: A G Stilwell
Director of Corporate Development: E Chandler
Director of Customer Services: F Rogers

Nexus (Tyne & Wear PTE)
Nexus House, St James Boulevard, Newcastle upon Tyne NE1 4AX
Tel: 0191 203 3333
Fax: 0191 203 3180
Director General: Bernard Garner
Director, Metro: Mick Carbro
Web site: www.nexus.org.uk
Metro: www.twmetro.co.uk
Nexus operates within the policies of the Tyne & Wear Integrated Transport Authority. Nexus owns both the Tyne & Wear Metro system and the Shields Ferry (between North Shields and South Shields). Nexus ensures that bus services not operated commercially are provided where there is evidence of social need; operates a demand-responsive transport system, U-call; and organises the provision of special transport for those who can only use ordinary public transport with difficulty if at all. Nexus administers the Concessionary Travel scheme and provides comprehensive travel information and sales outlets for countywide season tickets, as well as related administrative support for the scheme.
Rolling Stock: 90 light rail cars
Ferries: MFs 'Pride of the Tyne' and 'Shieldsman'

South Yorkshire Passenger Transport Executive
11 Broad Street West, Sheffield S1 2BQ
Tel: 0114 276 7575
Fax: 0114 275 9908
Web site: www.sypte.co.uk
The Executive is responsible to the South Yorkshire Integrated Transport Authority.
Director General: David Brown
Director of Strategy: Ben Still
Director of Customer Experience: David Young

West Yorkshire Passenger Transport Executive (Metro)
Wellington House, 40-50 Wellington Street, Leeds LS1 2DE
Tel: 0113 251 7272
Fax: 0113 251 7333
Web site: www.wymetro.com
WYPTE activities are conducted under the corporate name Metro. Metro is financed and supported by the West Yorkshire Integrated Transport Authority.
Director General: Kieran Preston, OBE
Director of Passenger Services: John Henkel
Director of Development: David Hoggarth

PASSENGER TRANSPORT REGIONAL AUTHORITIES

Strathclyde Partnership for Transport (SPT)
Consort House, 12 West George Street, Glasgow G2 1HN
Tel: 0141 332 6811
Fax: 0141 332 3076
E-mail: enquiry@spt.co.uk
Web site: www.spt.co.uk
Chair: Cllr Jonathan Findlay
Vice Chair: Cllr David Fagan
Chief Executive: Gordon MacLennan

Dep Chief Executive: Valerie Davidson
Asst Chief Executive, Operations:
Eric Stewart
Director, Finance & Human Relations:
Neil Wylie
Director, Projects: Charles Hoskins
Interim Director of Bus Operations:
Bruce Kiloh

Transport for London
Windsor House, 42-50 Victoria Street,
London SW1H 0TL
Tel: 020 7941 4500
Web Site: www.tfl.gov.uk
Chairman: Boris Johnson
Deputy Chairman: Daniel Moylan
Board Members: Peter Anderson, Claudia
Arney, Charles Belcher, Isabel Dedring,
Christopher Garnett, Baroness Tanni Grey-
Thompson, Sir Mike Hodgkinson, Judith Hunt,
Eva Lindholm, Steven Norris, Bob Oddy, Patrick
O'Keeffe, Tony West, Keith Williams, Steve Wright
Transport for London (TfL) took over most of
the functions of London Transport from July 2000.
It is under the control of the Mayor of London
and Greater London Authority. TfL assumed
control of London Underground Ltd in 2003.
Commissioner for Transport:
Peter Hendy, CBE
Managing Director, Finance: Steve Allen
Managing Director, Surface Transport:
Leon Daniels
**Managing Director, London Underground
and London Rail:** Mike Brown
Managing Director, Planning: Michele Dix
**Managing Director, Marketing &
Communications:** Vernon Everitt
General Counsel: Howard Carter
Chief Executive, Crossrail: Rob Holden

TfL subsidiary companies:
London Buses
Palestra, 197 Blackfriars Road, London SE1 8NJ
Tel: 020 7222 5600
Director of Performance: Clare Kavanagh
Director of Operations: Mike Weston
Head of Contracts: Mark O'Donovan
Head of Network Development: John Barry
Victoria Coach Station Ltd
164 Buckingham Palace Road, London SW1W
9TP.
Tel: 020 7027 2520
Fax: 020 7027 2511
London River Services Ltd
Palestra, 197 Blackfriars Road, London SE1 8NJ
Tel: 020 7222 5600
General Manager: Andy Griffiths
London Underground Ltd
55 Broadway, London SW1H 0BD
Tel: 020 7222 5600
Managing Director: Mike Brown

**TfL: London Bus Service Contractors as at
August 2011**
Abellio London Ltd *(see London & Middlesex)*
Arriva London *(see London & Middlesex)*
Arriva Southern Counties *(see Kent)*
Arriva The Shires Ltd *(see Bedfordshire)*
Blue Triangle Ltd *(see Essex, London & Middlesex)*
CT Plus Ltd *(see London & Middlesex)*
Docklands Buses Ltd *(see London & Middlesex)*
First London *(see London & Middlesex)*
London Central Bus Co Ltd *(see London &
Middlesex)*
London General Transport Services Ltd *(see*

London & Middlesex)
London Sovereign *(see London & Middlesex)*
London United Busways Ltd *(see London &
Middlesex)*
Metrobus Ltd *(see West Sussex)*
Metroline Travel Ltd *(see London & Middlesex)*
Quality Line (Epsom Coaches Group) *(see Surrey)*
Stagecoach London *(see London & Middlesex)*
Sullivan Buses *(from Feb 2012) (see
Hertfordshire)*

TRANSPORT CO-ORDINATING OFFICERS

Under the Transport Act 1978 the non-
Metropolitan Counties were given power to
co-ordinate public transport facilities in their
areas. From 1 April 1996 Welsh Counties and
Scottish Regions were replaced by new single-tier
authorities. At the same time and subsequently,
certain English Counties have been replaced by
new single-tier unitary authorities. The major role
is now to secure socially necessary services which
are not provided commercially. Where provided,
the names of most of the responsible officers are
set out below.

ENGLAND

Bath & North East Somerset Council
Guildhall, High Street, Bath BA1 5AW
**Group Manager (Transport & Planning
Policy):** Peter Dawson
Transportation Planning Manager:
Adrian Clarke
Public Transport Team Leader: Andy Strong
Tel: 01225 477000
Fax: 01225 394335
E-mail: transportation@bathnes.gov.uk
Web site: www.bathnes.gov.uk
A Unitary Authority in South West England, and
part of the West of England Partnership.

Bedford Borough Council, Central Bedfordshire Council
Chris Pettifer, Integrated Passenger Transport
Manager, Integrated Passenger Transport Unit,
County Hall, Cauldwell Street,
Bedford MK42 9AP
Tel: 01234 228881
Fax: 01234 228720
Web site: Bedford Borough:
www.bedford.gov.uk
Web site: Central Bedfordshire:
www.centralbedfordshire.gov.uk

Blackburn with Darwen Borough Council
Transport Policy Group, Old Town Hall,
Blackburn BB1 7DY
Tel: 01245 585585
E-mail: transportpolicy@blackburn.gov.uk
Web site: www.blackburn.gov.uk

Blackpool Council
Transportation Division, Layton Depot,
Plymouth Road, Blackpool FY3 7HW
Tel: 01253 476172
Fax: 01253 476198
E-mail: transport.policy@blackpool.gov.uk
Web site: www.blackpool.gov.uk

Bournemouth Borough Council
Mike Holmes, Director of Planning and Transport
Services, Town Hall Annex, St Stephen's Road,
Bournemouth BH2 6EA

Tel: 01202 451199
Fax: 01202 451000
E-mail: highways@bournemouth.gov.uk
Web site: www.bournemouth.gov.uk

Bracknell Forest Borough Council
Transport Group, Time Square, Market Street,
Bracknell RG12 1JD
Tel: 01344 424642
E-mail:
customer.services@bracknell-forest.gov.uk
Web site: www.bracknell-forest.gov.uk

Brighton & Hove City Council
Public Transport Team, King's House,
Grand Avenue, Hove BN3 2LS
Tel: 01273 292480
Web site: www.brighton-hove.gov.uk

Bristol City Council
Public Transport Section, Brunel House,
St George's Road, Bristol BS1 5UY
Tel: 0117 922 4454
Fax: 0117 922 3539
E-mail: public.transport@bristol.gov.uk
Web site: www.bristol.gov.uk

Buckinghamshire County Council
Passenger Transport Contract Manager,
Transport for Buckinghamshire,
10th Floor, County Hall, Walton Street,
Aylesbury HP20 1UY
Tel: 0845 2302882
E-mail: passtrans@buckscc.gov.uk
Web site: www.buckscc.gov.uk

Cambridgeshire County Council
B. E. Jackson, Head of Passenger Transport,
Department of Environment & Transport,
Mailbox ET1015, Shire Hall, Castle Hill,
Cambridge CB3 0AP.
Tel: 01223 717744
Fax: 01223 717789
Web site: www.cambridgeshire.gov.uk

Cheshire East Council, Cheshire West & Chester Council
Integrated Transport Service, Rivacre Business
Centre, Mill Lane, Ellesmere Port CH66 3TL
Tel: 01244 972387
Fax: 01244 603200
Web site: Cheshire East:
www.cheshireeast.gov.uk
Web site: Cheshire West & Chester:
www.cheshirewestandchester.gov.uk

Cornwall Council
Passenger Transport Unit, County Hall,
Truro TR1 3AY
Tel: 01872 322003
Fax: 01872 323844
E-mail: snicholson@cornwall.gov.uk
Web site: www.cornwall.gov.uk

Cumbria County Council
Lonsdale Building, The Courts, Carlisle
CA3 8NA
Tel: 01228 606720
Fax: 01228 606755
E-mail: graham.whiteley@cumbriacc.gov.uk
Web site: www.cumbriacc.gov.uk

Darlington Borough Council
Local Motion Team, Units 8-11, The Beehive,
Lingfield Point, Darlington DL1 1YN

Tel: 0800 4589810
E-mail: dothelocalmotion@darlington.gov.uk
Web site: www.darlington.gov.uk

Derby City Council
Integrated Passenger Transport Unit,
Room C338, Roman House, Friar Gate,
Derby DE1 1XB
Tel: 01332 641744
Fax: 01332 641740
Web site: www.derby.gov.uk

Derbyshire County Council
Public Transport Manager, County Hall,
Matlock DE4 3AG
Tel: 01629 580000
Fax: 01629 585740
E-mail: publictransport@derbyshire.gov.uk
Web site: www.derbyshire.gov.uk

Devon County Council
Bruce Thompson, Transport Co-ordination
Service Manager, County Hall,
Exeter EX2 4QW
Tel: 01392 383244
Fax: 01392 382904
E-mail: bruce.thompson@devon.gov.uk
Web site: www.devon.gov.uk

Dorset County Council
David Dawkins, Integrated Transport Unit
Manager, County Hall, Dorchester
DT1 1XJ
Tel: 01305 224660
Fax: 01305 225166
E-mail: d.dawkins@dorsetcc.gov.uk
Web site: www.dorsetcc.gov.uk

Durham County Council
County Hall, Durham DH1 5UQ
Tel: 0191 383 3435
Fax: 0191 383 4096
Web site: www.durham.gov.uk

East Riding of Yorkshire Council
1st Floor, The Offices, Beverley Depot,
Annie Reed Road, Beverley HU17 0LF
Passenger Services Manager:
David R Boden
Assistant Passenger Services Manager:
Chris Mottershaw
Tel: 01482 395525
Fax: 01482 395090
E-mail: passenger.services@eastriding.gov.uk
Web site: www.eastriding.gov.uk
The Passenger Services Unit is responsible for all
passenger transport (public transport and schools
and SEN transport) in the East Riding.

East Sussex County Council
N Smith, Group Manager (Passenger Transport),
Transport & Environment, County Hall, St Anne's
Crescent, Lewes BN7 1UE.
Tel: 01273 482326
Fax: 01273 474361
E-mail: nick.smith@eastsussexcc.gov.uk
Web site: www.eastsussex.gov.uk

Essex County Council
John Pope, Head of Passenger Transport,
County Hall, Chelmsford CM1 1QH
Tel: 01245 437506
Fax: 01245 496764
E-mail: john.pope@essex.gov.uk
Web site: www.essex.gov.uk

Gloucestershire County Council
Transport Team, Environment Directorate,
Shire Hall, Gloucester GL1 2TH
Tel: 01452 425628
Fax: 01452 425995
E-mail: timetables@gloucestershire.gov.uk
Web site: www.gloucestershire.gov.uk

Halton Borough Council
Transport Co-ordination, Grosvenor House,
Halton Lea, Runcorn WA7 2GW
Tel: 0151 471 7600
Fax: 0151 471 7521
Web site: www.halton.gov.uk

Hampshire County Council
K Wilcox, Head of Passenger Transport,
Hampshire County Council, Environment
Department, The Castle, Winchester
SO23 8UD.
Tel: 01962 846997
Fax: 01962 845855
E-mail: keith.wilcox@hants.gov.uk
Web site: www.hampshire.gov.uk

Hartlepool Borough Council
Ian Jopling, Transport Team Leader, Department of
Neighbourhood Services, Bryan Hanson House,
Hanson Square, Hartlepool TS24 7BT
Tel: 01429 284140
Fax: 01429 860830
E-mail: ian.jopling@hartlepool.gov.uk
Web site: www.hartlepool.gov.uk

Herefordshire Council
James Davies, Public Transport Manager,
Sustainable Communities Directorate,
PO Box 236, Plough Lane, Hereford HR4 0WZ
Tel: 01432 260948
Fax: 01432 383031
E-mail: public.transport@herefordshire.gov.uk
Web site: www.herefordshire.info

Hertfordshire County Council
Passenger Transport Unit, PO Box 99,
Hertford SG13 8TJ
Tel: 01992 556725
E-mail: feedback.ptu@hertscc.gov.uk
Web site: www.intalink.org.uk

Hull City Council
Passenger Transport Services, Kingston House,
Bond Street, Hull HU1 3ER
Tel: 01482 300300
E-mail: passengertransport@hullcc.gov.uk
Web site: www.hullcc.gov.uk

Isle of Wight Council
Martyn Mullins, Public Transport Officer,
Highways & Transport, Enterprise House,
St Cross Business Park, Monks Brook,
Newport PO30 5WB
Tel: 01983 823780
Fax: 01983 823707
E-mail: transport.info@iow.gov.uk
Web site: www.iwight.com

Kent County Council
Commercial Services, Gibson Drive,
Kings Hill, West Malling ME19 4QG
Transport Integration Manager:
Kenneth Cobb
School Transport Manager: Tim Edwards
Local Bus & Information Team Manager:
Steve Pay

Tel: 01622 605481
Fax: 01622 605084
E-mail: transport.integration@kent.gov.uk
Web site: www.kent.gov.uk
Transport Integration plans, procures and
manages Kent County Council's public, school and
client transport. It also works for neighbouring
councils and other organisations in related
transport fields of data management, consultancy
and CRB checks.

Lancashire County Council
Stuart Wrigley, Head of Transport Policy,
PO Box 9, Guild House, Cross Street,
Preston PR1 8RD
Tel: 01772 534660
Fax: 01772 533833
Web site: www.lancashire.gov.uk

Leicester City Council
Transport Development Section,
New Walk Centre, Welford Place,
Leicester LE1 6ZG
Tel: 0116 223 2121
E-mail: transportdevelopment@leicester.gov.uk
Web site: www.leicester.gov.uk

Leicestershire County Council
Tony Kirk, Group Manager (Public Transport),
Department of Highways, Transportation & Waste
Management, County Hall, Glenfield, Leicester
LE3 8RJ
Tel: 0116 265 6270
Fax: 0116 265 7181
E-mail: tkirk@leics.gov.uk
Web site: www.leics.gov.uk

Lincolnshire County Council
A R Cross, Head of Transport Services,
4th Floor, City Hall, Beaumont Fee,
Lincoln LN1 1DN
Tel: 01522 553132
Fax: 01522 568735
Web site: www.lincolnshire.gov.uk

Luton Borough Council
Passenger Transport Unit, Central Depot,
Kingsway, Luton LU4 8AU
Tel: 01582 547219
Fax: 01582 547254
E-mail: ptu@luton.gov.uk
Web site: www.luton.gov.uk

Medway Council
Integrated Transport Team, Gun Wharf,
Dock Road, Chatham ME4 4TR
Tel: 01634 331398
Fax: 01634 331625
E-mail: customer.first@medway.gov.uk
Web site: www.medway.gov.uk

Milton Keynes Council
Passenger Transport Group, Environment
Directorate, Civic Offices, 1 Saxon Gate East,
Milton Keynes MK9 3EJ
Tel: 01908 691691
E-mail: passenger.transport@milton-keynes.
gov.uk
Web site: www.milton-keynes.gov.uk

Norfolk County Council
Tracey Jessop, Head of Passenger Transport,
Department of Planning & Transportation,
County Hall, Martineau Lane, Norwich NR1 2SG
Tel: 01603 223831

Fax: 01603 222144
Web site: www.norfolk.gov.uk

Northamptonshire County Council
Sustainable Transport Manager, Riverside House,
Riverside Way, Bedford Road, Northampton
NN1 5NX
Tel: 01604 236711
Web site: www.northamptonshire.gov.uk

Northumberland County Council
Ian Coe, Transport Support Manager,
County Hall, Morpeth NE61 2EF
Tel: 01670 533986
Fax: 01670 534774
E-mail: ian.coe@northumberland.gov.uk
Web site: www.northumberland.gov.uk

North Lincolnshire Council
Public Transport Team, PO Box 42,
Church Square House, Scunthorpe
DN15 6XQ
Tel: 01724 297460
Fax: 01724 297066
E-mail: public.transport@northlincs.gov.uk
Web site: www.northlincs.gov.uk

North East Lincolnshire Council
Public Transport Section, Municipal Offices,
Town Hall Square, Grimsby DN31 1HU
Tel: 01472 313131
E-mail: transport@nelincs.gov.uk
Web site: www.nelincs.gov.uk

North Somerset Council
Sustainable Travel Team, Somerset House,
Oxford Street, Weston-super-Mare BS23 1TG
Tel: 01934 426426
E-mail: sustainable.travel@n-somerset.gov.uk
Web site: www.n-somerset.gov.uk

North Yorkshire County Council
R Owens, Passenger Transport Officer,
County Hall, Northallerton DL7 8AH
Tel: 01609 780780, Ext 2870
Fax: 01609 779838
Web site: www.northyorks.gov.uk

Nottingham City Council
Public Transport Team, Exchange Buildings North,
Smithy Row, Nottingham NG1 2BS
Tel: 0115 915 5492
E-mail: public.transport@nottinghamcity.gov.uk
Web site: www.nottinghamcity.gov.uk

Nottinghamshire County Council
County Hall, West Bridgford, Nottingham
NG2 7QP
Tel: 0115 982 3823
E-mail: enquiries@nottscc.gov.uk
Web site: www.nottinghamshire.gov.uk

Oxfordshire County Council
R Helling, Public Transport Officer, Environmental
Services, Speedwell House, Speedwell Street,
Oxford OX1 1NE
Tel: 01865 815859
Fax: 01865 815085
E-mail: dick.helling@oxfordshire.gov.uk
Web site: www.oxfordsshire.gov.uk

Peterborough City Council
Accessibility & Travel Group, Midgate House,
Midgate PE1 1TN
Tel: 01733 747474

Fax: 01733 317499
E-mail: buses@peterborough.gov.uk
Web site: www.peterborough.gov.uk

Plymouth City Council
Sustainable Transport Team, Plymouth Transport &
Highways, Department of Development,
Civic Centre, Armada Way, Plymouth PL1 2AA
Tel: 01752 307790
Fax: 01752 305593
E-mail: publictransport@plymouth.gov.uk
Web site: www.plymouth.gov.uk

Borough of Poole
Transportation Services, St John's House,
1 Serpentine Road, Poole BH15 2DX
Tel: 01202 262000
E-mail: transportation@poole.gov.uk
Web site: www.boroughofpoole.com

Portsmouth City Council
Passenger Transport Group, Transport & Street
Management, Guildhall Square, Portsmouth
PO1 2BG
Tel: 023 9282 2251
Web site: www.portsmouth.gov.uk

Reading Borough Council
Mrs P Baxter, Civic Centre, Reading
RG1 7TD
Tel: 0118 939 0813
Web site: www.reading.gov.uk

Redcar & Cleveland Council
Joint Public Transport Group, Belmont House,
Rectory Lane, Guisborough TS14 7FD
Tel: 0845 6126126
E-mail:
public_transport@redcar-cleveland.gov.uk
Web site: www.redcar-cleveland.gov.uk

Rutland County Council
Integrated Transport Team, Catmose,
Oakham LE15 6HP
Tel: 01572 722577
E-mail: enquiries@rutland.gov.uk
Web site: www.rutland.gov.uk

Shropshire County Council
Development Services, Shirehall, Abbey Foregate,
Shrewsbury SY2 6ND
Tel: 0345 678 9006
E-mail: transport@shropshire.gov.uk
Web site: www.shropshire.gov.uk

Slough Borough Council
R Fraser, PO Box 570, Slough SL1 1FA
Tel: 01753 475111
E-mail: enquiries@slough.gov.uk
Web site: www.slough.gov.uk

Somerset County Council
Mark Pedlar, Group Manager, Passenger Transport
Unit, County Hall, The Crescent,
Taunton TA1 4DY
Tel: 01823 358176
Fax: 01823 351356
E-mail: transport@somerset.gov.uk
Web site: www.somerset.gov.uk

Southampton City Council
Passenger Transport Team, Planning &
Sustainability, Floor 1, Castle Way,
Southampton SO14 2PD
Tel: 0800 519 1919

E-mail: public.transport@southampton.gov.uk
Web site: www.southampton.gov.uk

Southend-on-Sea Borough Council
Civic Centre, Victoria Avenue, Southend-on-Sea
SS2 6ER
Tel: 01702 215000
E-mail: council@southend.gov.uk
Web site: www.southend.gov.uk

South Gloucestershire Council
Integrated Transport Unit, PO Box 2081,
Council Offices, Castle Street, Thornbury
BS35 9BP
Tel: 01454 868004
Fax: 01454 864473
E-mail: itu@southglos.gov.uk
Web site: www.southglos.gov.uk

Staffordshire County Council
Charles Soutar, Head of Passenger Transport,
Development Services Department, Riverway,
Stafford ST16 3TJ
Tel: 01785 276735
Fax: 01785 276621
Web site: www.staffordshire.gov.uk

City of Stoke-on-Trent
Passenger Transport Team, Transport Planning
Group, PO Box 630, Civic Centre,
Stoke-on-Trent ST4 1RF
Tel: 01782 234500
Fax: 01782 233243
E-mail: transportation@stoke.gov.uk
Web site: www.stoke.gov.uk

Suffolk County Council
Mitchell Bradshaw, Public Transport Manager,
Environment & Transport Department,
Endeavour House, 8 Russell Road,
Ipswich IP1 2BX
Tel: 01473 265050
Fax: 01473 216884
E-mail: mitchell.bradshaw@et.suffolkcc.gov.uk
Web site: www.suffolk.gov.uk

Surrey County Council
A Teer, Group Manager Passenger Transport,
Room 306, County Hall, Penrhyn Road,
Kingston-on-Thames KT1 2DY
Tel: 020 8541 9371
Fax: 020 8541 9389
E-mail: alan.teer@surreycc.gov.uk
Web site: www.surreycc.gov.uk/passenger_
transport

Swindon Borough Council
Passenger Transport Team, Premier House,
Station Road, Swindon SN1 1TZ
Tel: 01793 466214
E-mail: passengertransport@swindon.gov.uk
Web site: www.swindon.gov.uk

Telford & Wrekin Council
Planning & Transport Department, Darby House,
Lawn Central, Telford TF3 4JA
Tel: 01952 202172
Web site: www.telford.gov.uk

Thurrock Council
Passenger Transport Section, Strategic Planning &
Transportation, Civic Offices, New Road, Grays,
Essex RM17 6SL
Tel: 01375 413882
Fax: 01375 413891

E-mail: passengertransport@thurrock.gov.uk
Web site: www.thurrock.gov.uk

Torbay Council
Strategic Transportation Team, Roebuck House,
Abbey Road, Torquay TQ2 5TF
Tel: 01803 208823
Fax: 01803 208882
E-mail: transportation@torbay.gov.uk
Web site: www.torbay.gov.uk

Warrington Borough Council
Passenger Transport Unit, Palmyra House,
Palmyra Square North, Warrington
WA1 1JN
Tel: 01925 442620
Web site: www.warrington.gov.uk

Warwickshire County Council
K McGovern, Passenger Transport Operations
Manager, Environment & Economy Directorate,
PO Box 43, Shire Hall, Warwick CV34 4SX
Tel: 01926 412930
Fax: 01926 418041
E-mail: passengertransport@warwickshire.
gov.uk
Web site: www.warwickshire.gov.uk

West Berkshire Council
Transport Services Team, Highways & Engineering,
Faraday Road, Newbury RG14 2AF
Tel: 01635 503248
Fax: 01635 519979
E-mail: transport@westberks.gov.uk
Web site: www.westberks.gov.uk

West Sussex County Council
Mark Miller, Group Manager, Transport
Co-ordination, Highways and Transport,
The Grange, Tower Street, Chichester
PO19 1RH
Tel: 01243 777811
E-mail: highwaysandtransporthq@westsussex.
gov.uk
Web site: www.westsussex.gov.uk

Wiltshire Council
Ian White, Head of Service - Passenger Transport,
Passenger Transport Unit, County Hall,
Bythesea Road, Trowbridge BA14 8JN
Tel: 01225 713322
Fax: 01225 713317
E-mail: ian.white@wiltshire.gov.uk
Web site: www.wiltshire.gov.uk

Royal Borough of Windsor & Maidenhead
Passenger Transport Team, Highways &
Engineering, Community Services, Town Hall,
St Ives Road, Maidenhead SL6 1RF
Tel: 01628 796666
Fax: 01628 796774
E-mail: customerservice@rbwm.gov.uk
Web site: www.rbwm.gov.uk

Wokingham Borough Council
Places & Neighbourhoods, PO Box 153,
Wokingham RG40 1WL
Tel: 0118 974 6000
E-mail: transportplanning@wokingham.gov.uk
Web site: www.wokingham.gov.uk

Worcestershire County Council
Passenger Transport Group, PO Box 82,
Pershore Lane, Worcester WR4 0AA
Tel: 01905 768411

Fax: 01905 768438
Web site: www.worcestershire.gov.uk

City of York Council
Transport Planning Unit, 9 St Leonard's Place,
York YO1 7ET
Tel: 01904 551550
Fax: 01904 551340
E-mail: transportplanning@york.gov.uk
Web site: www.york.gov.uk

WALES

Isle of Anglesey County Council
Dewi W Roberts, Principal Officer -
Transportation, Council Offices,
Llangefni, Anglesey LL77 7TW
Tel: 01248 752457
Fax: 01248 757332
E-mail: dwrpl@anglesey.gov.uk
Web site: www.anglesey.gov.uk

Blaenau Gwent County Borough Council
Joint Passenger Transport Unit,
Civic Centre, Ebbw Vale NP3 6XB
Tel: 01495 355444
Fax: 01495 301255
E-mail: info@blaenau-gwent.gov.uk
Web site: www.blaenau-gwent.gov.uk

Bridgend County Borough Council
Passenger Transport Co-ordination Unit,
Communities Directorate, Morien House,
Bennett Street, Bridgend Industrial Estate,
Bridgend CF31 3SH
Tel: 01656 642559
Fax: 01656 642859
E-mail: transportation@bridgend.gov.uk
Web site: www.bridgend.gov.uk

Caerphilly County Borough Council
Huw Morgan, Principal Passenger Transport
Officer, Council Offices, Pontllanfraith,
Blackwood NP12 2YW.
Tel: 01495 235089
Fax: 01495 235045
E-mail: morgash@caerphilly.gov.uk
Web site: www.caerphilly.gov.uk

Cardiff County Council
Traffic & Transportation Service,
County Hall, Atlantic Wharf, Cardiff
CF10 4UW
Tel: 029 2087 2087
E-mail: c2c@cardiff.gov.uk
Web site: www.cardiff.gov.uk

Carmarthenshire County Council
Public Transport Section, Director of Technical
Services, Llansteffan Road, Carmarthen
SA31 3LZ
Tel: 0845 634 0661
E-mail: publictransport@carmarthenshire.gov.uk
Web site: www.carmarthenshire.gov.uk

Ceredigion County Council
Mrs S A Witts, Acting Manager, Corporate
Passenger Transport Unit (CPTU),
Canolfan Rheidol, Rhodfa Padarn,
Llanbadarn Fawr, Aberystwyth
SY23 3UE
Tel: 01970 633555
Fax: 01970 633559
E-mail: cptu@ceredigion.gov.uk
Web site: www.ceredigion.gov.uk

Conwy County Borough Council
Bus Conwy, The Heath, Penmaenmawr Road,
Llanfairfechan LL33 0PF
Tel: 01492 575414
E-mail: bwsconwy@conwy.gov.uk
Web site: www.conwy.gov.uk

Denbighshire County Council
Peter Daniels, Section Manager, Transport
& Infrastructure Department, Caledfryn,
Smithfield Road, Denbigh LL16 3RJ
Tel: 01824 706886
Fax: 01824 706970
E-mail: kerry.smith@denbighshire.gov.uk
Web site: www.denbighshire.gov.uk/travel

Flintshire County Council
Transportation Unit, Directorate of Environment
& Regeneration, County Hall, Mold
CH7 6NF
Tel: 01352 704530
Fax: 01352 704540
Web site: www.flintshire.gov.uk

Gwynedd Council
Public Transport Officer, Council Offices,
Shirehall, Caernarfon LL55 1SH.
Tel: 01286 679541
Fax: 01286 673324
E-mail: bwsgwynedd@gwynedd.gov.uk
Web site: www.gwynedd.gov.uk

Merthyr Tydfil County Borough Council
Martin Haworth, Senior Transport Officer,
Civic Centre, Castle Street, Merthyr Tydfil
CF47 8AN
Tel: 01685 726288
Fax: 01685 387982
E-mail: martin.haworth@merthyr.gov.uk
Web site: www.merthyr.gov.uk

Monmouthshire County Council
Monmouthshire Passenger Transport Unit,
County Hall, Cwmbran
NP44 2XH
Tel: 01633 644777
Fax: 01633 644666
E-mail: passengertransportunit@
monmouthshire.gov.uk
Web site: www.monmouthshire.gov.uk

Neath Port Talbot County Borough Council
S Colinese, Passenger Transport Manager,
The Quays, Brunel Way, Baglan Energy Park,
Neath SA11 2GG
Tel: 01639 686658
Fax: 01639 686107
E-mail: s.colinese@npt.gov.uk
Web site: www.neath-porttalbot.gov.uk

Newport City Council
Transport Team, Telford Street Depot,
Newport NP19 0ES
Tel: 01633 656656
Fax: 01633 244721
Web site: www.newport.gov.uk

Pembrokeshire County Council
M Hubert, Transport and Fleet Manager,
County Hall, Haverfordwest SA61 1TP
Tel: 01437 764551
Fax: 01437 775008
E-mail: hubert.mathias@pembrokeshire.gov.uk
Web site: www.pembrokeshire.gov.uk

Powys County Council
J Forsey, Passenger Transport Manager, Passenger Transport Unit, County Hall, Spa Road East, Llandrindod Wells LD1 5LG
Tel: 0845 607 6060
E-mail: buses@powys.gov.uk
Web site: www.powys.gov.uk

Rhondda Cynon Taf County Borough Council
Integrated Transport Unit, Sardis House, Sardis Road, Pontypridd CF37 1DU
Head of Service – Transportation:
Roger Waters
Integrated Transport Unit Manager:
Charlie Nelson
Principal Transport Officers: Gwyneth Elliott, Caroline Harries, Adrian Morgan
Tel: 01443 494700
Fax: 01443 494875
E-mail:
transportation@rhondda-cynon-taff.gov.uk
Web site: www.rhondda-cynon-taff.gov.uk

City & County of Swansea
Environment Dept – Transportation, Civic Centre, Oystermouth Road, Swansea SA1 3SN
Tel: 01792 637250
Fax: 01792 635270
E-mail: transportation.engineering@swansea.gov.uk
Web site: www.swansea.gov.uk

Torfaen County Borough Council
Torfaen County Borough Council, Civic Centre, Pontypool NP4 6YB
Joint Passenger Transport Unit
(with Blaenau Gwent), Baldwin House, Ebbw Vale NP23 6LD
Tel: 01495 355444
Fax: 01495 301255
Web site: www.torfaen.gov.uk

Vale of Glamorgan Council
C Edwards, Senior Transportation Officer, Passenger Transport Unit, The Dock Offices, Barry Docks, Barry CF63 4RT
Tel: 01446 700111
Fax: 01446 704891
E-mail: cedwards@valeofglamorgan.gov.uk
Web site: www.valeofglamorgan.gov.uk

Wrexham County Borough Council
Transport Co-ordination, Crown Buildings, Chester Street, Wrexham LL13 8BG
Tel: 01978 292000
Fax: 01978 292106
Web site: www.wrexham.gov.uk

SCOTLAND

Councils whose names are marked with an asterisk (*) are the 12 member councils of Strathclyde Partnership for Transport (SPT) (see above), which is responsible for co-ordinating public transport services and infrastructure.

Aberdeen City Council
Ian Mason, Public Transport Unit, St Nicholas House, Broad Street, Aberdeen AB10 1WL
Tel: 01224 523073
Fax: 01224 523764.
E-mail: imason@aberdeencity.gov.uk.
Web site: www.aberdeencity.gov.uk

Aberdeenshire Council
Richard McKenzie, Public Transport Manager, Public Transport Unit, Transportation & Infrastructure, Woodhill House, Westburn Road, Aberdeen AB16 5GB
Tel: 01224 664585
Fax: 01224 662005
E-mail: richard.mckenzie@aberdeenshire.gov.uk
Web site: www.aberdeenshire.gov.uk

Angus Council
Planning & Transport Infrastructure Services, County Buildings, Market Street, Forfar DD8 3LG
Tel: 01307 461774
Fax: 01307 475037
E-mail: plntransport@angus.gov.uk
Web site: www.angus.gov.uk

Argyll and Bute Council*
Facility Services, Integrated Transport, Kilmory, Lochgilphead PA31 8RT
Integrated Transport Manager: Janne Leckie
Public Transport Officer: Douglas Blades
Tel: 01546 604193
Fax: 01546 604291
E-mail: public.transport@argyll-bute.gov.uk
Web site: www.argyll-bute.gov.uk

Clackmannanshire Council
Public Transport Officer, Roads, Traffic & Transportation, Kilncraigs, Greenside Street, Alloa FK10 1EB
Tel: 01259 450000
E-mail: roads@clacks.gov.uk
Web site: www.clacksweb.org.uk

Dundee City Council
Mark Devine, Transport Officer, Planning & Transportation Department, Floor 16, Tayside House, Crichton Street, Dundee DD1 3RB.
Tel: 01382 433831
Fax: 01382 433313
E-mail: mark.devine@dundeecity.gov.uk.
Web site: www.dundeecity.gov.uk

Dumfries & Galloway Council
Douglas Kirkpatrick, Team Leader (Sustainable Travel), Council Offices, English Street, Dumfries DG1 2DD
Tel: 03033 333000
Fax: 01387 260583
E-mail: pe.travel.info@dumgal.gov.uk
Web site: www.dumgal.gov.uk

East Ayrshire Council*
Council Headquarters, London Road, Kilmarnock KA3 7BU
Tel: 01563 576000
Web site: www.east-ayrshire.gov.uk

East Dunbartonshire Council*
Civic Way, Kirkintilloch G66 4TJ
Tel: 0845 045 4510
E-mail: contact.centre@eastdunbarton.gov.uk
Web site: www.eastdunbarton.gov.uk

East Lothian Council
Transport Planning Manager, John Muir House, Haddington EH41 3HA
Tel: 01620 827661
E-mail: policy&projects@eastlothian.gov.uk
Web site: www.eastlothian.gov.uk

East Renfrewshire Council*
Council Headquarters, Eastwood Park, Giffnock G46 6UG
Tel: 0141 577 3425
Web site:
www.eastrenfrewshire.gov.uk

City of Edinburgh Council
Max Thomson, Public Transport Manager, City Development, 1 Cockburn Street, Edinburgh EH1 1BJ
Tel: 0131 469 3631
Fax: 0131 469 3635.
E-mail: max.thomson@edinburgh.gov.uk

Falkirk Council
Stephen Bloomfield, Public Transport Co-ordinator, Development Services, Abbotsfold House, David's Loan, Falkirk FK2 7YZ
Tel: 01324 504723
Fax: 01324 504914
Web site: www.falkirk.gov.uk

Fife Council
Trond Haugen, Transportation Manager - Transportation Services, Fife House, North Street, Glenrothes KY7 5LT
Tel: 01592 413106
Fax: 01592 413061
E-mail: trond.haugen@fife.gov.uk
Web site: www.fifedirect.org.uk

Glasgow City Council*
Land & Environmental Services, Richmond Exchange, 20 Cadogan Street, Glasgow G2 7AD
Tel: 0141 287 9000
Fax: 0141 287 9059
E-mail: land@glasgow.gov.uk
Web site: www.glasgow.gov.uk

The Highland Council
David Summers, Transport Development Officer, Public Transport Dept, Glenurquhart Road, Inverness IV3 5NX
Tel: 01463 702457
Fax: 01463 702606
E-mail: public.transport@highland.gov.uk
Web site: www.highland.gov.uk

Inverclyde Council*
Municipal Buildings, Greenock PA15 1LY
Tel: 01475 717171
Fax: 01475 712181
Web site: www.inverclyde.gov.uk

Midlothian Council
Travel Team - Room 9, Dundas Buildings, 62A Polton Street, Bonnyrigg, Midlothian EH19 3YD
Tel: 0131 561 5443
Fax: 0131 654 2797
E-mail: karl.vanters@midlothian.gov.uk
Web site: www.midlothian.gov.uk

Moray Council
Peter Findlay, Public Transport Manager, Council Office, Academy Street, Elgin IV30 1LL
Tel: 01343 562569
Fax: 01343 545628.
E-mail: transport@moray.gov.uk
Web site: www.moray.gov.uk

North Ayrshire Council*
Cunningham House, Irvine KA12 8EE
Tel: 0845 603 0590
Fax: 01294 324144
Web site: www.north-ayrshire.gov.uk

North Lanarkshire Council*
Civic Centre, Windmillhill Street,
Motherwell ML1 1AB
Tel: 01698 403200
Web site: www.northlanarkshire.gov.uk

Orkney Islands Council
Council Offices, School Place, Kirkwall
KW15 1NY
Tel: 01856 873535
E-mail: transport@orkney.gov.uk
Web site: www.orkney.gov.uk

Perth & Kinross Council
Andrew J Warrington,
Public Transport Manager, The Environment
Service, Pullar House,
35 Kinnoull Street, Perth PH1 5GD
Tel: 01738 476530
Fax: 01738 476510
E-mail: publictransport@pkc.gov.uk
Web site: www.pkc.gov.uk

Renfrewshire Council*
North Building, Renfrewshire House,
Cotton Street, Paisley PA1 1WB
Tel: 0141 842 5000
Web site: www.renfrewshire.gov.uk

Scottish Borders Council
B Young, Transport Policy Manager, Council
Headquarters, Newtown St Boswells,
Melrose TD6 0SA
Tel: 01835 824000
Fax: 01835 823008
Web site: www.scotborders.gov.uk

Shetland Islands Council
Ian Bruce, Service Manager - Transport
Operations, Infrastructure Service Dept.,
Grantfield, Lerwick ZE1 0NT
Tel: 01595 744872
Fax: 01595 744869
E-mail: ian.bruce@sic.shetland.gov.uk
Web site: www.shetland.gov.uk

South Ayrshire Council*
County Buildings, Wellington Square,
Ayr KA7 1DR
Tel: 0845 601 2020
Web site: www.south-ayrshire.gov.uk

South Lanarkshire Council*
Council Offices, Almada Street, Hamilton
ML3 0AA
Tel: 01698 454444
Web site: www.southlanarkshire.gov.uk

Stirling Council
Council Headquarters, Viewforth,
2 Pitt Place, Stirling FK8 2ET
Tel: 0845 277 7000
Web site: www.stirling.gov.uk

West Dunbartonshire Council*
Council Offices, Garshake Road,
Dunbarton, G82 3PU
Tel: 01389 737633
Web site: www.west-dunbarton.gov.uk

Western Isles Council
Western Isles Council (Comhairle nan Eilean
Siar), Sandwick Road, Stornoway, Isle of Lewis
HS1 2BW
Tel: 0845 600 7090
Fax: 01851 705349
E-mail: enquiries@cne-siar.gov.uk
Web site: www.cne-siar.gov.uk

West Lothian Council
Ian Forbes, Public Transport Manager,
County Buildings, Linlithgow EH49 7EZ
Tel: 01506 775282
Fax: 01506 775265
E-mail: ian.forbes@westlothian.gov.uk
Web site: www.westlothian.gov.uk

TRAFFIC COMMISSIONERS

Web site: www.vosa.gov.uk
Acting Senior Traffic Commissioner:
Mrs Beverley Bell

EASTERN TRAFFIC AREA
City House, 126-130 Hills Road,
Cambridge CB2 1NP
Tel: 0300 123 9000
Fax: 01223 309684
Traffic Commissioner: Richard Turfitt
Deputy Traffic Commissioners: Marcia Davis,
Gillian Ekins, Fiona Harrington, Mary Kane, Roger
Seymour.
Area covered: Buckinghamshire,
Cambridgeshire, Essex, Hertfordshire,
Leicestershire, Lincolnshire, Norfolk,
Northamptonshire, Suffolk, Bedford, Central
Bedfordshire, Leicester, Luton, Milton Keynes,
Peterborough, Rutland, Southend-on-Sea,
Thurrock.

NORTH EASTERN TRAFFIC AREA
Hillcrest House, 386 Harehills Lane,
Leeds LS9 6NF
Tel: 0300 123 9000
Fax: 0113 249 8142
Traffic Commissioner: Vacant
Deputy Traffic Commissioners:
Mark Hinchcliffe, Patrick Mulvenna, Liz Perrett.
Area covered: Durham, Northumberland,
Nottinghamshire, North Yorkshire, South
Yorkshire, Tyne & Wear, West Yorkshire,
Darlington, East Riding, Hartlepool, Kingston
upon Hull, Middlesbrough, North Lincolnshire,
North East Lincolnshire, Nottingham, Redcar &
Cleveland, Stockton-on-Tees, York.

NORTH WESTERN TRAFFIC AREA
Suite 4, Stone Cross Place, Stone Cross Lane,
Golborne, Warrington WA3 2SH
Tel: 0300 123 9000
Fax: 01942 728297
Traffic Commissioner: Mrs Beverley Bell
Deputy Traffic Commissioners: Mark
Hinchcliffe, Patrick Mulvenna, Liz Perrett.
Area covered: Cumbria, Derbyshire, Greater
Manchester, Lancashire, Merseyside, Blackburn
with Darwen, Blackpool, Cheshire East, Cheshire
West & Chester, City of Derby, Halton,
Warrington.

SCOTTISH TRAFFIC AREA
Level 6, The Stamp Office, 10 Waterloo Place,
Edinburgh EH1 3EG
Tel: 0300 123 9000

Fax: 0131 229 0682
Traffic Commissioner: Miss Joan Aitken
Deputy Traffic Commissioner: Richard
McFarlane
Area covered: Scotland

SOUTH EASTERN & METROPOLITAN TRAFFIC AREA
Ivy House, 3 Ivy Terrace, Eastbourne BN21 4QT
Tel: 0300 123 9000
Fax: 01323 726679
Traffic Commissioner: Vacant
Deputy Traffic Commissioners: Chris Heaps,
Mary Kane, Jonathan Black.
Area covered: East Sussex, Greater London,
Kent, Surrey, West Sussex, Brighton & Hove,
Medway.

WELSH TRAFFIC AREA
38 George Road, Edgbaston, Birmingham B15 1PL
Tel: 0300 123 9000
Fax: 0121 609 4250
Traffic Commissioner: Nick Jones
Deputy Traffic Commissioners: J Astle,
M Dorrington, T Seculer, C R Seymour.
Area covered: Wales.

WEST MIDLAND TRAFFIC AREA
38 George Road, Edgbaston,
Birmingham B15 1PL
Tel: 0121 123 9000
Fax: 0121 609 4250
Traffic Commissioner: Nick Jones
Deputy Traffic Commissioners: J Astle,
M Dorrington, T Seculer, C R Seymour.
Area covered: Herefordshire, Shropshire,
Staffordshire, Warwickshire, West Midlands,
Worcestershire, Stoke-on-Trent, Telford & Wrekin.

WESTERN TRAFFIC AREA
2 Rivergate, Temple Quay,
Bristol BS1 6EH
Tel: 0300 123 9000
Fax: 0117 929 8352
Traffic Commissioner: Sarah Bell
Deputy Traffic Commissioners: Jonathan
Black, Fiona Harrington, Tim Hayden, Lester
Maddrell.
Administrative Director: Tim Hughes.
Area covered: Cornwall, Devon,
Gloucestershire, Hampshire, Oxfordshire,
Somerset, Wiltshire, Bath & North East Somerset,
Bournemouth, Bracknell Forest, Bristol, Isle
of Wight, North Somerset, Plymouth, Poole,
Portsmouth, Reading, Slough, Southampton, South
Gloucestershire, Swindon, Torbay, West Berkshire,
Windsor & Maidenhead, Wokingham.

OFFICE OF FAIR TRADING

The Office of Fair Trading (OFT) plays a leading
role in promoting and protecting consumer
interests throughout the UK, while ensuring that
businesses are fair and competitive. The tools
to carry out this work are the powers granted
to the OFT under consumer and competition
legislation.
Address: Fleetbank House, 2-6 Salisbury Square,
London EC4Y 8JX
Tel: 020 7211 8000
Fax: 020 7211 8800
Web site: www.oft.gov.uk
E-mail: enquiries@oft.gsi.gov.uk
Enquiries: 08457 22 44 99

Tendering & Regulatory Authorities

DEPARTMENT FOR TRANSPORT

4/24 Great Minster House, 76 Marsham Street,
London SW1P 4DR
Tel: 020 7944 3000
Web site: www.dft.gov.uk

Executive Agencies: (include)
Driving Standards Agency (DSA)
Driver and Vehicle Licensing Agency (DVLA)

Highways Agency (HA)
Chief Executive: Graham Dalton
Tel: 08457 50 40 30
Web Site: www.highways.gov.uk

Vehicle Certification Agency (VCA)
Chief Executive: Paul Markwick
No1, The Estate Office Centre,
Eastgate Road, Bristol BS5 6XX
Tel: 0117 952 4126
Fax: 0117 952 4104
E-mail: paul.cooke@vca.gov.uk
Web site: www.vca.gov.uk

Vehicle and Operator Services Agency (VOSA)
(see also Driver Training,
A-Z Manufacturers section)
Chief Executive: Alistair Peoples
Berkeley House, Croydon Street,
Bristol BS5 0DA
Tel: 0300 123 9000
Fax: 0117 954 3212
E-mail: enquiries@vosa.gov.uk
Web site: www.vosa.gov.uk

Advisory Non-Departmental Bodies: (include)

The Disabled Persons Transport Advisory Committee
2/3 Great Minster House,
76 Marsham Street,
London SW1P 4DR
Tel: 020 7944 8011
Minicom: 020 7944 3277
Fax: 020 7944 6998
E-mail: dptac@dft.gsi.gov.uk
Web site: www.dptac.independent.gov.uk
Chair: Dai Powell OBE
The Disabled Persons Transport Advisory Committee (DPTAC) is a statutory body established under Section 125 of the Transport Act 1985 to advise the Secretary of State for Transport on matters affecting the transport needs of disabled people. Membership is limited to a Chairman plus twenty members, at least half of whom must be disabled.

Mobility and Inclusion Unit
(address as above)
Tel: 020 7944 8021

Minicom: 020 7944 3277
Fax: 020 7944 6102
E-mail: miu@dft.gsi.gov.uk
Web site: www.dptac.gov.uk

Disability Rights Commission
Web site: www.drc-gb.org.uk

Executive Non-departmental Bodies: (include)

Health and Safety Commission
Health and Safety Executive
Tribunals
Traffic Areas

Public Corporations
Civil Aviation Authority
Transport for London

Rail Accident Investigation Branch
The Wharf, Stores Road,
Derby DE21 4BA
Chief Inspector: Carolyn Griffiths
Tel: 01332 253300
Fax: 01332 253301
E-mail: enquiries@raib.gov.uk
Web site: www.raib.gov.uk

RAIB is the independent railway accident investigation organisation for the UK and is listed in LRB because its remit covers street tramways.

NOTES

SECTION 3

Organisations and Societies

- **British Operators Organisations**

- **Institutions**

- **International Associations**

- **Other Organisations**

- **First Aid and Sports Associations**

- **Trade Organisations**

- **Societies**

- **Passenger Transport Museums**

BRITISH OPERATORS' ORGANISATIONS

ALBUM – ASSOCIATION OF LOCAL BUS COMPANY MANAGERS

The Association represents the professional views of the Executive Directors and Senior Managers of those bus companies owned by district council and major independent operators on matters specifically affecting locally-owned bus company management and operations.

Chairperson: Mark Howarth, Western Greyhound Ltd, Western House, St Austell Street, Summercourt, Newquay, Cornwall TR8 5DR
Tel: 01637 871871
Secretary: Thomas W W Knowles, 41 Redhills, Eccleshall, Stafford ST21 6JW
Tel & Fax: 01785 859414
Web site: www.album-bus.co.uk

THE COACH TOURISM COUNCIL

10 Bermondsey Exchange, 179-181 Bermondsey St, London SE1 3UW
Tel: 0870 850 2839
Fax: 020 7407 6880
E-mail: admin@coachtourismcouncil.co.uk
Web site: www.coachtourismcouncil.co.uk, www.findacoachholiday.com
Chairman: Sean Taggart **Chief Executive:** Chris Wales **Administration:** Paul Ovington
The CTC's mission is to promote tourism and travel by coach.

COMMUNITY TRANSPORT ASSOCIATION

Highbank, Halton Street, Hyde SK14 2NY
Tel: 0161 351 1475
Fax: 0161 351 7221
Advice Service Tel: 0845 130 6195
E-mail: infi@ctauk.org
Web site: www.ctauk.org
The community transport sector is vast. There are over 100,000 minibuses serving over 10 million passengers every year being operated for use by voluntary and community groups, schools, colleges and Local Authorities, or to provide door-to-door transport for people who are unable to use other public transport. This door-to-door transport is not limited to minibuses though; there are very many voluntary car schemes throughout the UK where volunteers will use their own cars to provide transport for individuals. Overcoming social exclusion is at the heart of what community transport has always been about. The CTA is committed to helping its members achieve this objective in their area both in terms of the direct support it can offer such as training, developmental support etc. but also by lobbying on behalf of the movement with government and other important agencies.

CONFEDERATION OF PASSENGER TRANSPORT UK

Drury House, 34-43 Russell Street, London WC2B 5HA
Tel: 020 7240 3131
Fax: 020 7240 6565
E-mail: cpt@cpt-uk.org
Web site: www.cpt-uk.org
The Confederation of Passenger Transport UK (CPT) is the trade association representing the UK's bus and coach operators and the light rail sector. CPT has wide responsibilities ranging from representation on government working parties (national, local, EU); establishing operating codes of practice; advising on legal, technical and mechanical standards; management of the Bonded Coach Holiday Scheme, a government recognised consumer travel protection scheme and Coach Marque, an industry quality standard; 24-hour Crisis Control service for members; organisation of industry events and the first point of contact for the media on transport and other related issues.

OFFICERS AND COUNCIL

President: Steve Whiteway
Chairman: Ian Morgan
Chief Executive: Simon Posner
Manager, Chief Executive's Office: Miss Ling Tang
Finance Director: Ray Coyne
Communications Director: John Major
Operations Director: Stephen Smith
Media Relations Manager: Hassard Stacpoole
Director of Membership: Peter Gomersall
Director of Policy Development: Steven Salmon
Director of Coaching: Steven Barber
Deputy Director, Operations: John Burch
Fixed Track Executive: David Walmsley
Coaching Executive: Graham Messenger
Committee Executive: Graham Sutton
Operations & Touring Executive: Alf Scrimgour

Director of Government Relations, Scotland: George Mair
29 Drumsheugh Gardens, Edinburgh EH3 7RN
Tel: 0131 272 2150
Fax: 0131 272 2152

Director of Government Relations, Wales: John Pockett
1 Lewis Terrace, Darren Parc, Pontypridd CF37 2AF
Tel: 01443 485814
Fax: 01443 485816

Director of Government Relations, EU: David Watson
Drury House, 34-43 Russell Street, London WC2B 5HA
Tel: 020 7240 3131
Fax: 020 7240 6565

Regional Managers
East Midlands & Yorkshire: Keith McNally
Tel: 0121 633 7770
E-mail: keithm@cpt-uk.org
London & Home Counties: Karen Tiley
Drury House, 34-43 Russell Street, London WC2B 5HA
Tel: 020 7240 3131
E-mail: karent@cpt-uk.org
Northern: David Holding
Foxwood House, 6 The Dene, Chester Moor, Chester-le-Street DH2 3TB
Tel: 0191 388 7694
E-mail: davidh@cpt-uk.org
North Western: Phillipa Sudlow
210 Crow Lane East, Newton le Willows, Merseyside WA12 9UA
Tel: 01925 229497
E-mail: phillipas@cpt-uk.org
Scotland: Jeremy Tinsley
29 Drumsheugh Gardens, Edinburgh EH3 7RN
Tel: 0131 272 2150
E-mail: jeremyt@cpt-uk.org

Wales: Colin Thomas
Tel: 01633 270800
E-mail: colint@cpt-uk.org
West Midlands: Phil Bateman
3A Broadlane North, Wednesfield, Wolverhampton WV12 5UH
Tel: 07768 145445
E-mail: philb@cpt-uk.org
South West: John Burch
"Avercombe", 28 Belmont Road, Ilfracombe, Devon EX34 8DR
Tel: 07940 929881
E-mail: johnb@cpt-uk.org

GUILD OF BRITISH COACH OPERATORS

PO Box 5657, Southend on Sea, Essex SS1 3WT
Tel: 08456 126225
E-mail: admin@coach-tours.co.uk
Web site: www.coach-tours.co.uk
Chairman: Ian Fraser, The Kings Ferry
Vice Chairman: Matt Clayson, TGM Group
Treasurer: Ian Luckett, Lucketts Travel
Administrator: Richard Delahoy
An association of top quality coach companies dedicated to providing a first class service. Guild members provide luxury coaches throughout Britain, offering comprehensive travel management services. With around 1,000 coaches, a wide geographical spread and a guaranteed commitment to the highest standards, Guild members can meet *all* your travel needs.

PASSENGER TRANSPORT EXECUTIVE GROUP

Wellington House, 40-50 Wellington Street, Leeds LS1 2DE
Tel: 0113 251 7204
Fax: 0113 251 7333
Web site: www.pteg.net
Chair: Geoff Inskip
Director, PTEG Support Unit: Jonathan Bray
PTEG brings together and promotes the interests of the six Passenger Transport Executives (PTEs) in England. Leicester City Council, Nottingham City Council, Strathclyde Partnership for Transport and Transport for London are associate members.

INSTITUTIONS

THE CHARTERED INSTITUTE OF LOGISTICS & TRANSPORT

Logistics & Transport Centre, Earlstrees Court, Earlstrees Road, Corby NN17 4AX
Tel: 01536 740100
Fax: 01536 740101
E-mail: enquiry@ciltuk.org.uk.
Web site: www.ciltuk.org.uk
President: Peter Hendy
Chief Executive: Steve Agg
The Chartered Institute of Logistics and Transport (UK) is the professional body for individuals and organisations involved in all disciplines, modes and aspects of logistics and transport.

The Institute's 22,000 members have privileged access to a range of benefits and services, which support them, professionally and personally, throughout their careers and help connect them with world-wide expertise.

For further information and to join please contact Membership Services, **Tel:** 01536 740104 or visit the CILT(UK) web site above

THE INSTITUTE OF THE MOTOR INDUSTRY

Fanshaws, Brickendon, Hertford SG13 8PQ
Tel: 01992 511521
Fax: 01992 511548
E-mail: imi@motor.org.uk
Web site: www.motor.org.uk
The Institute of the Motor Industry (IMI) is the professional association for individuals working in the retail motor industry and is the leading awarding body of vocational qualifications in the automotive sector. With some 25,000 members and 45,000 registered students at 350 assessment centres, the IMI is focused on improving professional standards through the recognition, qualification and development of individuals. Qualifications offered by the Institute include NVQs/SVQs, technical certificates, vehicle sales awards, Quality Assured Awards and Certificate/Diploma in automotive retail management (ARMS).

The IMI governs the industry's Automotive Technician Accreditation (ATA) initiative, which has more than 4500 nationally-accredited technicians since launching in 2005.

OFFICERS AND VICE PRESIDENTS

Patron: HRH Prince Michael of Kent KCVO FIMI.
President: Garel Rhys CBE FIMI
Honorary Treasurer: Edward Clark FIMI.
Chairman of the Council: Steve Nash FIMI
Chief Executive: Sarah Sillars FIMI
Company Secretary: Alan Tyrer FIMI

THE INSTITUTE OF TRANSPORT ADMINISTRATION

The Old Studio, 25 Greenfield Road, Westoning MK45 5JD
Tel: 01525 634940 **Fax:** 01525 750016
E-mail: info@iota.org.uk
Web site: www.iota.org.uk
Registered Friendly Society: No 53 SA

OFFICERS

President: Wing Cdr Peter Green FInstTA
Deputy President: Alan Whittington FInstTA, FRSA, FIBC
Trustees: Brian Bigwood FInstTA, Christopher Sullivan MInstTA, Geoff Fletcher MInstTA
National Treasurer and Chairman, Finance & General Purposes Committee: Clive Aisbitt FInstTA
Chairman Education, Membership & Training Committee: Eric Davies FInstTA
Chairman External Affairs Committee: Mike Walker FInstTA
Director of the Institute: David J S Dalglish FInstTA, FRSA

THE INSTITUTION OF MECHANICAL ENGINEERS

1 Birdcage Walk, London SW1H 9JJ
Tel: 020 7222 7899
Fax: 020 7222 4557
E-mail: enquiries@imeche.org
Web site: www.imeche.org.uk
Chief Executive: Stephen Tetlow
President: Professor Rod Smith
Engineering Director: Dr Colin Brown C Eng FIMechE
The Institute was founded in 1847, and incorporates as the Automobile Division the former Institution of Automobile Engineers and as the Railway Division the former Institution of Locomotive Engineers.

SOE

22 Greencoat Place, London SW1P 1PR
Tel: 020 7630 1111
Fax: 020 7630 6677
E-mail: soe@soe.org.uk
Web site: www.soe.org.uk
President: Gary Gilby IEng, FSOE, FIPlantE
Chief Executive: Nick Jones FCA
The SOE is the umbrella professional body for those working in road transport and plant engineering. The IRTE is a professional sector within the SOE.

TRL LTD (TRANSPORT RESEARCH LABORATORY)

Crowthorne House, Nine Mile Ride, Wokingham RG40 3GA
Tel: 01344 773131
Fax: 01344 770356
E-mail: enquiries@trl.co.uk
Web site: www.trl.co.uk
Chief Executive: Dr Susan Sharland
Finance Director: Tim Andrews

INTERNATIONAL ASSOCIATIONS

THE INTERNATIONAL ASSOCIATION OF PUBLIC TRANSPORT (UITP)

Offices: Rue Sainte Marie 6, B-1080, Brussels, Belgium
Tel: 00 32 2 673 6100
Fax: 00 32 2 660 1072
E-mail: info@uitp.org
Web site: www.uitp.org
President: Alain Flausch
Secretary General: Hans Rat

INTERNATIONAL ROAD TRANSPORT UNION (IRU)

Founded in 1948 in Geneva, the IRU is an international association of national road transport federations which has consultative status in the United Nations. One of its two Transport Councils is concerned with road passenger transport.
General Secretariat: IRU, Centre International, 3 Rue de Varembe, B.P.44, 1211 Geneva 20, Switzerland
Tel: 00 41 22 918 2700
Fax: 00 41 22 918 2741
E-mail: info@iru.org
Web site: www.iru.org
President: Janusz Lacny
Secretary General: Martin Marmy

WORLD ROAD ASSOCIATION (PIARC)

The Association is an international body with headquarters in Paris, administered by an elected President and other office bearers. Members are recruited from governments, local authorities, technical and industrial groups and private individuals whose interests are centred on roads and road traffic. The association is maintained by subscriptions from its members. International congresses are held every four years.

OFFICE BEARERS

President: Anne-Marie Leclerc (Canada)
Past President: C Jordan (Australia)
Vice President: K Inoue (Japan)
Secretary General: J F Corte (France), PIARC, La Grande Arche, Paroi Nord, Level 5, 92055 La Defense Cedex, France
Tel: 00 33 1 47 96 81 21
Fax: 00 33 1 49 00 02 02

BRITISH NATIONAL COMMITTEE

The British National Committee's role is to ensure adequate representation of British methods and experience on PIARC's international committees and Congresses, to disseminate the findings of those committees and generally look after British interests. The present officers of this committee are:
Patron: Minister for Transport
UK Chairman: Joe Burns
UK Hon Sec/Hon Treasurer: John Smart IHT 119 Britannia Walk, London N1 7JE
Tel: 020 7391 9977
Fax: 020 7387 2808
E-mail: john.smart@iht.org
Web site: www.piarc.org

OTHER ORGANISATIONS

ASSOCIATION OF TRANSPORT CO-ORDINATING OFFICERS (ATCO)

c/o Ian White, Head of Service - Passenger Transport, Wiltshire Council, Passenger Transport Unit, County Hall, Blythesea Road, Trowbridge BA14 8JN
Tel: 01225 713322
Fax: 01225 713317
E-mail: ian.white@wiltshire.gov.uk
Chairman: Bruce Thompson, Devon County Council
Tel: 01392 383244
E-mail: bruce.thompson@devon.gov.uk
Chairman (from November 2011): Tracy Jessop, Norfolk County Council
Tel: 01603 223831
E-mail: tracy.jessop@norfolk.gov.uk
Web site: www.atco.org.uk
ATCO members include senior staff directly concerned with strategic policy development and implementation for securing of passenger transport services for a wide range of public authorities. These include shire counties and unitary councils in England, Wales and Scotland, Passenger Transport Executives, TfL, the Isle of Man, the States of Jersey and Northern Ireland. The Association has been running for 37 years. Through exchanging information and views the Association helps formulate policies and standards and promotes transport initiatives aimed at achieving better passenger transport services for all.

Members give advice to the Department for Transport, Local Government Group, the Welsh Assembly and the Convention of Scottish Local Authorities. ATCO works actively with the Community Transport Association and Passenger Transport Executive Group, Confederation of Passenger Transport, Passenger Focus and Bus Users UK.

BUS USERS UK

PO Box 119, Shepperton, Middlesex TW17 8UX
Tel: 01932 232574
E-mail: enquiries@bususers.org
Web site: www.bususers.org
Bus Users UK was formed in 1985 to bring together national and local organisations with an interest in bus services and concerned individual bus users to seek to give an effective voice to the consumer. It is actively involved in developing constructive dialogue between the users and providers of bus services. It publishes a quarterly newsletter – Bus User.
Life President: Dr Caroline Cahm MBE PhD
Chair: Gillian Merron

General Manager: Stephen Morris
Finance Administrator: Bill Wright
Senior Officer for Wales:
Mrs Margaret Everson
Officer for Wales: Barclay Davies
Welsh Office: PO Box 1045, Cardiff CF11 1JE
Tel: 029 2022 1370
E-mail: wales@bususers.org
Bus User Editor: Gavin Booth
39 Lilyhill Terrace, Edinburgh EH8 7DR
Tel: 0131 652 0205
E-mail: editor@bususers.org

BUSK

18 Windsor Road, Newport NP19 8NS
Tel: 01633 274944
E-mail: buskuk@aol.com
Web site: www.busk-uk.com
Formerly known for its Belt Up School Kids campaign, BUSK is now known through the European Union as an authority on vehicular safety for children and young people.

CAMPAIGN FOR BETTER TRANSPORT

16 Waterside, 44-48 Wharf Road,
London N1 7UX
Tel: 020 7566 6480
Fax: 020 7566 6493
Web site: www.bettertransport.org.uk
E-mail: info@bettertransport.org.uk
The Campaign for Better Transport, formerly Transport 2000, is a campaign and research group that seeks greener, cleaner transport patterns through greater use of public transport, walking and cycling.
President: Michael Palin
Chief Executive: Stephen Joseph OBE

COACH DRIVERS CLUB

Unit 4, Minerva Business Park, Lynch Wood,
Peterborough PE2 6FT
Tel: 01733 405738
Fax: 01733 405745
E-mail: lauren.kirt@coachdriversclub.com
Web site: www.coachdriversclub.com
The Coach Drivers Club is a membership club for coach drivers, coaching and tourism. It offers accident cover, magazine, yearbook, members' website, legal advice.

GOSKILLS

Concorde House, Trinity Park, Solihull B37 7UQ
Tel: 0121 635 5520
Fax: 0121 635 5521
E-mail: info@goskills.org
Web site: goskills.org
Strategic Director of Skills: Vicki Ball
Commercial Director: Jackie O'Brien
Chief Finance Officer: John Kinder
GoSkills is the Sector Skills Council for passenger transport.

LIGHT RAIL TRANSIT ASSOCIATION

C/o 138 Radnor Avenue, Welling, Kent DA16 2BY
E-mail: office@lrta.org
Web site: www.lrta.org
Founded in 1937 to advocate and encourage interest in light rail and modern tramways. Monthly magazine is Tramways & Urban Transit. Membership enquiries to:
Membership Secretary: Roger Morris
E-mail: membership@lrta.org
President: Geoffrey Claydon
Chairman: Geoff Lusher
Deputy Chairman: Andrew Braddock

LOCAL GOVERNMENT ASSOCIATION

Local Government House, Smith Square,
London SW1P 3HZ
Tel: 020 7664 3000
Fax: 020 7664 3030
E-mail: info@local.gov.uk
Web Site: www.lga.gov.uk
The Local Government Association was formed by the merger of the Association of County Councils, the Association of District Councils and the Association of Metropolitan Authorities in 1997. The LGA has just under 500 members, including all shire district councils; metropolitan district councils; county councils; unitary authorities; London authorities; and Welsh authorities. In addition, the LGA represents police authorities, fire authorities and passenger transport authorities. The LGA provides the national voice for local communities in England and Wales; its members represent over 50 million people, employ more than 2 million staff and spend over £65 billion on local services. Amongst the LGA's policy priorities is integrated transport; local authorities lead the way in encouraging the use of public transport and thereby reducing congestion, ill-health and environmental damage through a programme of partnerships between local authorities and other agencies.
President: Lord Richard Best
Chairman: Sir Merrick Cockell (Conservative, Kensington & Chelsea)
Vice-Chairs: Sir Jeremy Beecham (Labour, Newcastle), Baroness Margaret Eaton OBE (Conservative, Bradford), Cllr Richard Kemp (Liberal Democrat, Liverpool)
Chief Executive: Paul Coen

LONDON TRAVELWATCH

6 Middle Street, London
EC1A 7JA
Tel: 020 7505 9000
Fax: 020 7505 9003
E-mail: info@londontravelwatch.org.uk
Web site: www.londontravelwatch.org.uk
Formerly the London Transport Users Committee, London TravelWatch is the independent statutory body set up to represent the interests of the users of all transport for which the Greater London Authority and Transport for London is responsible for operating, providing, procuring and licensing. London TravelWatch is also the Rail Passengers Committee for London.
Chair: Sharon Grant
Chief Executive: Janet Cooke

PASSENGER FOCUS

7th Floor, Piccadilly Gate, Store Street,
Manchester M1 2WD
Tel: 0300 123 2140
Fax: 0161 236 1574
E-mail: info@passengerfocus.org.uk
Web site: www.passengerfocus.org.uk
Passenger Focus is the independent passenger watchdog, set up by the Government to protect the interests of rail passengers and bus passengers in England (outside London).
Chairman: Colin Foxall CBE
Board Members: David Burton, David Leibling, Deryk Mead CBE, Bill Samuel, Barbara Saunders OBE, Stella Mair Thomas, Nigel Walmsley
Bus Advisers: Gavin Booth, Mike Parker
Chief Executive: Anthony Smith
Passenger Team Director: David Sidebottom

ROAD OPERATOR SAFETY COUNCIL (ROSCO)

Osborn House, 20 High Street South, Olney,
Buckinghamshire MK46 5JF
Tel: 01234 714420
E-mail: admin@rosco-uk.org
Web site: www.rosco-uk.org
'ROSCO' has been providing a safe driving award scheme for UK Bus and Coach Operators since 1955. Over 100 companies and 50,000 drivers enter the scheme each year. Awards are presented to drivers who avoid any prosecution for Road Traffic Act offences, and do not have any blameworthy accidents.
Chairman: Peter J S Shipp
Vice Chairman: John E H Miller
Executive Officer: Gill Edmondson

THE ROYAL SOCIETY FOR THE PREVENTION OF ACCIDENTS

28 Calthorpe Road, Edgbaston,
Birmingham B15 1RP
Tel: 0121 248 2000
Fax: 0121 248 2001
E-mail: help@rospa.com
Web site: www.rospa.com
RoSPA promotes safety at work and in the home, at leisure and in schools, on (or near water) and on the roads, through providing information, publicity, training and consultancy.
The Society works with central and local government, the caring services, the police and public and private sector organisations large and small. Some work is funded by grant and sponsorship, but most relies on the support of the Society's membership.
The Society also produces and supplies a comprehensive selection of publications ranging from reference books to low-cost booklets for mass distribution.
Training Offered: Training courses cover practical skills and management training through to professional qualifications in Health and Safety.
President: Lord Jordan of Bournville CBE
Chief Executive: Tom Mullarkey MBE

STATUS

Michael Hughes, Status Manager, Department of Engineering & Technology, Manchester Metropolitan University, Chester Street, Manchester M1 5GD
Tel: 0161 247 6240
Fax: 0161 247 6779
Web site: www.status.org.uk
E-mail: m.p.hughes@mmu.ac.uk
STATUS others members, from all areas of the specialist road transport industry, with engineering development and test services, technical legislative consultancy and a range of general technical information.
It is involved on behalf of its members in contributing to consultation documents, influencing transport related legislation and lobbying government departments and agencies. The organisation can call on a diverse range of personnel to help deal with more difficult problems. A primary benefit is the availability of telephone consultancy on technical or legislative matters.
STATUS plays a prominent role in representing its members' interests on legislative matters and lobbies government agencies on behalf of members.
A monthly newsletter is published, featuring industry related stories.

TRANSPORT BENEVOLENT FUND

22-25 Finsbury Square, London EC2A 1DX
Tel: 08450 100 500
Fax: 0870 831 2882
Web site: www.tbf.org.uk
E-mail: help@tbf.orgo.uk
TBF is a Registered Charity (No 1058032) and was founded in 1923. Membership is open to most staff engaged in the public transport industry. Members pay £1 a week and in return are granted, at the discretion of the Trustees, cash help, convalescence, recuperation, a wide range of complementary medical treatments, legal advice, and medical equipment in times of need. Membership covers the employee and their partner and dependent children. Subject to age and length of membership, free membership may be awarded on leaving the industry. There are payroll deduction facilities in many companies.
Director: Chris Godbold
Senior Trustee: Ray Jordan (President)
Patrons: Sir Wilfrid Newton, CBE (Past Chairman, London Transport), Brian Souter (Stagecoach Group), Lew Adams OBE (BT Police Authority), Sir Moir Lockhead OBE (FirstGroup), Peter Hendy CBE (Transport for London), Robert Crow (RMT), Graham Stevenson (UNITE), Gerry Doherty (TSSA), Keith Norman (ASLEF), David Martin (Arriva), Keith Ludeman (Go-Ahead Group), Roger Bowker CBE (East London Bus Group), Bob Rixham (UNITE), Nigel Stevens (Transdev), John O'Brien (Veolia Transport UK), Ian Coucher (Network Rail) Simon Posner (CPT).

SPORTS ASSOCIATIONS

NATIONAL PASSENGER TRANSPORT SPORTS ASSOCIATION
President: Ian Davies
Vice President: Geoff Lusher
Chairman: Murray Macdonald
Acting Secretary: Geoff Lusher, 86 Heritage Court, Warstone Lane, Jewellery Quarter, Birmingham B18 6HU
Tel: 01384 555507
Fax: 01384 555510
E-mail: geoffandbarbara@sky.com
Web site: www.tran-sport.co.uk
The association organises inter-company sporting activities for the bus, coach, light rail and heavy rail industries. Currently 16 different sports are covered, each with competitions through the year, with trophies provided often by bus sponsors. Corporate membership is provided to large transport undertakings. Further information is available from the address above.

TRADE ORGANISATIONS AND ASSOCIATIONS

BEAMA LTD
The British Electrotechnical & Allied Manufacturers' Association
Founded 1902, Incorporated 1905.
Offices: Westminster Tower, 3 Albert Embankment, London SE1 7SL
Tel: 020 7793 3000
Fax: 020 7793 3003
E-mail: info@beama.org.uk

Web site: www.beama.org.uk
Objectives: By co-operative action to promote the interests of the industrial, electrical and electronic manufacturing industries of Great Britain.
Chief Executive Officer: Dr Howard Porter

FEDERATION OF ENGINE REMANUFACTURERS
18 Livonia Road, Sidmouth, Devon EX10 9JB
Tel: 01935 513232
Fax: 01935 519192
E-mail: enquiries@fer.co.uk
Web Site: www.fer.co.uk.
Director: Brian Ludford

FREIGHT TRANSPORT ASSOCIATION VEHICLE INSPECTION SERVICE
Hermes House, St John's Road, Tunbridge Wells TN4 9UZ
Tel: 01892 526171
Fax: 01892 534989
Web Site: www.fta.co.uk
The Freight Transport Association represents the interests of over 11,000 companies throughout the UK. FTA carries out over 100,000 vehicle inspections each year including many PSVs. The FTA Vehicle Inspection Service supports operators in maintaining their vehicles in a roadworthy condition - both mechanically and legally. Further details are available from Alan Osborne, Head of Vehicle Inspection Services, FTA, Tunbridge Wells (01892 526171).
Publications: Freight (monthly journal), FTA Yearbook.
Chief Executive: Richard Turner.

LOW CARBON VEHICLE PARTNERSHIP
83 Victoria Street, London SW1H 0HW
Tel: 020 3178 7859
Fax: 020 3008 6180
E-mail: secretariat@lowcvp.org.uk
Web site: www.lowcvp.org.uk
The LowCVP is an action and advisory group providing a forum through which partners can work together towards shared goals and take the lead in the transition to a low-carbon future for road transport in the UK.
Bus Working Group Chairman: Bob Bryson (Alexander Dennis)

MIRA LTD
Registered Office: MIRA Ltd, Watling Street, Nuneaton CV10 0TU
Tel: 024 7635 5000
Fax: 024 7635 5355
E-mail: enquiries@mira.co.uk
Web site: www.mira.co.uk
MIRA is an independent product engineering and technology centre and offers skills in innovation, problem-solving and consultancy.
Chairman: Michael Beasley CBE
Chief Executive Officer: Dr George Gillespie
Director of Finance & Company Secretary: C J N Phillipson
Director of Engineering: G. Townsend

SOCIETY OF MOTOR MANUFACTURERS & TRADERS (SMMT)
71 Great Peter Street, London SW1P 2BN
Tel: 020 7235 7000
Fax: 020 7344 1676
E-mail: buscoachweb@smmt.co.uk
Web site: www.smmt.co.uk
Chief Executive: Paul Everitt

THE VEHICLE BUILDERS & REPAIRERS ASSOCIATION LTD
Belmont House, Gildersome, Leeds LS27 7TW
Tel: 0113 253 8333
Fax: 0113 238 0496
E-mail: vbra@vbra.co.uk
Web site: www.vbra.co.uk
The VBRA is the representative organisation for vehicle manufacturers and vehicle/car body repairers. An OFT approved Code of Practice has been drawn up to govern the conduct of members.
Director General: Malcolm Tagg

SOCIETIES

THE ASSOCIATION OF FRIENDS OF THE BRITISH COMMERCIAL VEHICLE MUSEUM TRUST
The Association was formed when The British Commercial Vehicle Museum was opened in 1983. Its aims are to support the full-time staff in matters of publicity, fund raising, maintenance and documentation of exhibits, work in the archives, organising rallies, etc. Facilities for members include a newsletter, free admission to the museum to undertake museum work and socialise with colleagues. New members are always welcome and special rates exist for families, students and senior citizens.
Hon Chairman: H Hatcher
Hon Secretary: A Pritchard
Hon Treasurer: A Pritchard
Members of the Committee: E Simister, D Lewis, J Gardner
Museum Manager: A Buchan
Address: The British Commercial Vehicle Museum, King Street, Leyland, Preston PR25 2LE
Tel: 01772 451011

ASTON MANOR ROAD TRANSPORT MUSEUM
The Old Tram Depot, 208-216 Witton Lane, Aston, Birmingham B6 6QE
Tel: 07768 457911
Web site: www.amrtm.org.uk
Company limited by guarantee. Registered as a charity.
The museum is uniquely housed in a former depot of Birmingham's first-generation tramways. The display of commercial and passenger vehicles reflects the history of construction and operation in the West Midlands, and there are numerous displays of transport artefacts, tickets, notices and photographs. Joining as a Friend of the Museum gives entitlement to free entry and a quarterly newsletter. The museum is open on Saturdays, Sundays and Bank Holidays throughout the year, with a range of special events featuring a free heritage bus service to and from the city centre. The Museum is situated opposite Villa Park and on National Express West Midlands bus services 7 and 11. It is served by both Witton and Aston railway stations.
Further information from:
Chairman: Geoff Lusher, 86 Heritage Court, Warstone Lane, Jewellery Quarter, Birmingham B18 6HU
E-mail: geoffandbarbara@sky.com

BRITISH BUS PRESERVATION GROUP
25 Oldfield Road, Bexleyheath DA7 4DX
Tel: 0844 357 4598
Fax: 07092 131054
E-mail: enquiries@bbpg.co.uk

Web site: www.bbpg.co.uk

The BBPG was formed in 1990 and has been responsible for securing the future of more than 250 historic buses and coaches, many of which were saved at extremely short notice from being broken up. The society has more than 600 members, both individuals and preservation groups. The BBPG caters for all bus enthusiasts, whether or not they own a bus.

Chairman: Glyn Matthews.
Secretary: Mike Lloyd.
Storage: Nick Larkin.

BRITISH TROLLEYBUS SOCIETY

Formed as the Reading Transport Society in 1961, the present title was adopted in 1971, having acquired a number of trolleybuses for preservation from all over Britain. In 1969 it founded the Trolleybus Museum at Sandtoft, near Doncaster, where its vehicles are housed and regularly operate on mains power from the overhead wiring. West Yorkshire Transport Circle merged into the Society in January 1991. Currently membership stands at about 320. Members receive the monthly journal Trolleybus containing news and articles from home and abroad. Additionally members can subscribe to Bus Fare and Wheels, monthly magazines for motorbus operation in the Thames Valley and West Yorkshire areas respectively. Monthly meetings are also held in Reading, London and Bradford.

Secretary: A. J. Barton, 2 Josephine Court, Southcote Road, Reading RG30 2DG
Tel: 0118 958 3974

BUSES WORLDWIDE

37, Oyster Lane, Byfleet, Surrey KT14 7HS
Tel: 01932 352351
E-mail: membership@busesworldwide.org
Web site: www.busesworldwide.org
Buses Worldwide is the publisher of "Buses Worldwide", "Maltese Transport News and British Buses Abroad magazines plus other ad-hoc books. Regular meetings are held in London and Manchester. Overseas visits are arranged for Members.

Chairman: Richard Stedall
Vic-Chairman: Steve Guess
Secretary: Simon Brown
Membership: Stuart Harvey
News Editor: Norman Bartlett

CLASSIC BUS HERITAGE TRUST LTD (INCORPORATING THE ROUTEMASTER HERITAGE TRUST)

The Classic Bus Heritage Trust aims to advance preservation of buses and coaches by fostering the interests of the general public. It is a Registered Charity.

Treasurer & Hon Sec: W. Ackroyd, 8 Twining Road, Ventnor, Isle of Wight PO38 1TX

ESSEX BUS ENTHUSIASTS' GROUP

272 Shoebury Road, Southend-on-Sea, Essex SS1 3TT
E-mail: admin@signal-training.com
Web site: www.essexbus.org.uk
EBEG was formed in 1962, under its previous title, Eastern National Enthusiasts' Group. The present title was adopted in 1987 to reflect more fully the activities of the group. EBEG publishes a monthly illustrated magazine Essex Bus News, holds regular meetings in South and North Essex, and offers publications, photo sales, and coach tours. Annual

subscription of £20 includes 12 issues of Essex Bus News.
Chairman: Chris Stewart
Secretary: Alan Osborne
Membership: Richard Delahoy

GB BUS GROUP

Membership Enquiries: 192 Alvechurch Road, West Heath, Birmingham B31 3PW
Tel: 0121 624 8641
Web site: www.gb-bg.co.uk
Chairman: Tony Allen
Secretary: Hazel Roberts
Treasurer: Frank Gold
The GB Bus Group was formed in 2006 to help attract new enthusiasts to the hobby. It provides a monthly magazine as well as a full range of bus and coach fleet books covering UK and Ireland. The GB Bus Group is a member of the UK Transport Group.

HISTORIC COMMERCIAL VEHICLE SOCIETY

The Society was founded in 1958 and four years later absorbed the Vintage Passenger Vehicle Society and the London Vintage Taxi Club. Its membership of over 4,000 owns more than 6,000 preserved vehicles. Activities include the organisation of rallies, among them the well known London to Brighton and Trans-Pennine runs. The club caters for all commercial vehicles over 20 years old.

OFFICERS
President: Lord Montagu of Beaulieu
Senior Exec Officer and Vice-President: M. Banfield, Iden Grange, Cranbrook Road, Staplehurst TN12 0ET
Tel: 01580 892929
Fax: 01580 893227
E-mail: hcvs2011@gmail.com
Web site: www.hcvs.co.uk

LEYLAND NATIONAL GROUP

E-mail: secretary@leylandnationalgroup.co.uk
Web site: www.leylandnationalgroup.co.uk
The Leyland National Group was formed in 1997 and has members throughout Great Britain and abroad. Although the group does not own any vehicles itself, some of its members are bus owners. There are more than 100 Leyland Nationals from a variety of operators preserved by group members. However, one does not need to own a bus to join the group, as membership is open to anyone with an interest in Leyland Nationals. The group also caters for those interested in the derivatives of the Leyland National; the Leyland-DAB, Leyland B21 and Leyland National bodied rail vehicles. Members receive a colour illustrated quarterly magazine, exclusive access to the members' only area on the group's website as well as other benefits. Please contact the Membership Secretary for more info about the group, the benefits of membership and to receive a membership application form.
Chairman: Alan Fairbrother
Secretary: Dean Lefevre, 2 Forest Cottages, Whatlington, Battle, East Sussex TN33 0NT
E-mail: secretary@leylandnationalgroup.co.uk
Treasurer: Mike Bellinger
Magazine Editor: Mick Berg
Membership Secretary: Tim Wild, 27 Dukeshill Road, Bracknell, RG42 2DU
Tel: 01344 640095
E-mail: membership@leylandnationalgroup.co.uk

LINCOLNSHIRE VINTAGE VEHICLE SOCIETY

Road Transport Museum, Whisby Road, North Hykeham, Lincoln LN6 5TR
Tel: 01522 500566/689497
E-mail: info@lvvs.org.uk
Web site: www.lvvs.org.uk
The LVVS was founded in 1959 by local businessmen with the aim of forming a road transport museum. Charitable status was obtained some time ago, and with a capital grant from its local district council, it has now completed the first stage of its new museum project. Over 60 vehicles dating from the 1920s to the 1980s can be seen in the new exhibition hall with many more in the workshop.
Opening times: November–April Sundays 13.00-16.00. May–October Mon-Fri 12.00-16.00, Sun 10.00-16.00.
Chairman: S Milner
Hon Treasurer: J Child
Secretary: Mrs J Jefford

LONDON OMNIBUS TRACTION SOCIETY (LOTS)

Unit N305, Westminster Business Square, 1-45 Durham Street, Vauxhall, London SE11 5JH
Web site: www.lots.org.uk
Formed in 1964, LOTS is the largest bus enthusiast society in the United Kingdom. A colour Illustrated monthly newsletter is sent to all members. This covers all the current operators in the former London Transport area and includes General and Industry News, Route Developments, Vehicle News for the area, subsequent vehicle movements and service vehicle updates. Meetings are held most months in central London featuring guest speakers, slide and film presentations during the year as well as the annual free bus rides from central London using vehicles of London interest.

Regular LOTS publications include fleet allocations and route working publications as well as the popular annual London Bus and Tram Fleetbook and the London Bus annual review. A quarterly 64 -page glossy magazine, the London Bus Magazine (LBM) has been produced for almost 40 years.

Regular sales lists are produced and sent out to all members. An information service is also available to all members to help answer those historical queries.

The Autumn Transport Spectacular (ATS) is held in London every autumn and is one of London's biggest transport sales.

All enquiries should be directed to the above address.

THE M & D AND EAST KENT BUS CLUB

42 St Albans Hill, Hemel Hempstead HP3 9NG
E-mail: mdekbusclub@gmail.com
Web site: www.mdekbusclub.org.uk
This club was formed in 1952 with the object of bringing together all those interested in road passenger transport in an area covering Kent and East Sussex. Facilities for members include a monthly news booklet (illustrated), information service, tours, meetings, vehicle photograph sales and vehicle preservation. A series of publications is also produced, including illustrated fleet histories.
Hon Chairman: J V Spillett
Hon Sec: P J Evans
Hon Editor: N D King

Hon Treasurer: N D King
Membership Officer: J A Fairley
Photographic Officer: B Weeden
Sales Officer: to be appointed
Tours Officer: D R Cobb
Management Committee: N D King, R A Lewis, J V Spillett, P J Evans, D M Jones. There are Area Organisers in Ashford, Dover, Folkestone, Hastings, North-East Kent, Maidstone and the Medway Towns.

THE NATIONAL TRAMWAY MUSEUM

Crich, Matlock DE4 5DP
Tel: 01773 854321
Fax: 01773 854320
The Society was founded in 1955 to establish and operate a working tramway museum. The Museum is at Crich Tramway Village, Crich, near Matlock, in Derbyshire, and owns over 70 English, Irish, Scottish, Welsh and overseas tramcars. Members receive a copy of the Society's quarterly journal and can participate in the running of the museum.
Patron: HRH The Duke of Gloucester GCVO
Vice-Presidents: G S Hearse, W G S Hyde, G B Claydon, D J H Senior, A W Bond
Chairman: C Heaton
Vice-Chairman: R T Pennyfather
Hon Secretary: I M Dougill
Hon Treasurer: P R Moore
Operations Superintendent: K. B. Hulme

NATIONAL TROLLEYBUS ASSOCIATION

2 St John's Close, Claines, Worcester WR3 7PT
Tel: 01449 740876
Web site: www.trolleybus.co.uk/nta
Formed in 1963, and incorporated in 1968 as The Trolleybus Museum Co Ltd. The vehicles and ancillary equipment collected by the NTA since its inception are now owned by the company, which is limited by guarantee and is a registered charity. Members receive Trolleybus Magazine, a printed and illustrated bi-monthly journal documenting all aspects of trolleybus operation past and present throughout the world.
Chairman: R D Helliar-Symons
Secretary: J H Ward
Treasurer: I G Martin
Membership Secretary: I G Martin
Enquiries: tmbmembsec@hotmail.com

THE OMNIBUS SOCIETY LTD

The Omnibus Society was founded in 1929. Today it is a nationwide organisation with a network of provincial branches, offering a comprehensive range of facilities for those interested in the bus and coach industry. The Society has accumulated a wealth of information on public road transport. Members have the opportunity to receive and exchange data on every aspect of the industry including route developments, operational/traffic matters and fleet changes. Each branch has a full programme of activities and publishes its own Branch Bulletin to give local news of route changes, etc. A scheme exists whereby members subscribe to receive bulletins from branches other than that of which they are a member. A programme of indoor meetings is customary during winter, including film shows, invited speakers and discussions. In the summer months visits to manufacturers and tours to operators are featured. The Society maintains a comprehensive library and archive which may be visited by members and non-members

undertaking research, together with separate photographic and ticket collections.
Address: 100 Sandwell Street, Walsall WS1 3EB
Tel: 01922 629358
E-mail: oslibrary@btconnect.com
Web site: www.omnibussoc.org.

OFFICERS
President (2011): Francois-Xavier Perin
President (2012): Roger French
Vice-Presidents: F P Groves, A W Mills, G Wedlake, T F McLachlan, K W Swallow, Professor John Hibbs, B LeJeune.
Chairman: S C Morris.
Secretary: A. J. Francis, 185 Southlands Road, Bromley BR2 9QZ.
Treasurer: H. L. Barker, 31 High Street, Tarporley CW6 0DP.
Librarian/Archivist: Alan Mills
Editor, Society's Publications: Cyril McIntyre
Members of the Council: K D Barclay, I D Barlex, G A Booth, D M Persson, D Roy, J D Howie and nominations from each branch
Branch Officers:
Midland Branch: G Lusher, 86 Heritage Court, Warstone Lane, Birmingham B18 6HU
South Wales and West Branch:
A J Armstrong, 16 Stanley Grove, Weston-super-Mare BS23 3EB
Northern Branch: Dave Sturrock, 8 Whiteley Grove, Newton Aycliffe DL5 4NH
North Western & Yorkshire Branch:
P. Wilkinson, 10 Bradley Close, Timperley, Altrincham WA15 6SH
Scottish Branch: I. Allan, 10 Miller Avenue, Crossford, Dunfermline KY12 8PY
Essex & South Suffolk Group: J. L. Rugg, 86 Worthing Road, Laindon SS15 6JU
East Midland Group: A. Oxley, 4 Gordon Close, Attenborough, Nottingham NN4 9UF
Herts & Beds Group: R. C. Barton, 5 Viscount Court, Knights Field, Luton LU2 7LD
London Historical Research Group:
D A Ruddom, 57 Bluebridge Road, Brookmans Park, Hatfield AL9 7UW
Provincial Historical Research Group:
A E Jones, 8 Poplar Drive, Church Stretton S76 7BW

THE PSV CIRCLE

Unit 1R, Leroy House, 436 Essex Road, London N1 3QP
E-mail: enquiries@psv-circle.org.uk
Web site: www.psv-circle.org.uk
The aim of the PSV Circle is to be the definitive source of all knowledge on Public Service Vehicles and Operators throughout the United Kingdom. We produce a wide range of Publications including operator fleet histories, chassis lists, body lists, as well as current fleet lists covering Great Britain and Ireland.
HONORARY OFFICERS
Chairman: Mike Still
Secretary: John Skilling
Treasurer: Mike Bissex
Membership Secretary: Steve Fitzgerald
Rally Sales Team & Website Manager:
Paul Young
News Sheet Despatch Manager:
Adrian Clarke

RIBBLE ENTHUSIASTS' CLUB

23 Richmond Road, Hindley Green, Wigan WN2 4ND
Tel: 01942 253497

E-mail: mjyat@msn.com
Founded in 1954 by the late T. B. Collinge for the study of road transport past and present and in particular Ribble Motor Services and associated companies. Meetings are held and a monthly news sheet produced.
Life President: A E Chapman
Life Vice President: M. Shires
Vice President: C Bowles
Committee Chairman: D Bailey MBE
Secretary/Tours: M J Yates, 23 Richmond Road, Hindley Green, Wigan WN2 4ND
Treasurer: R A Harpum, 107 New Road, West Parley, Ferndown, Dorset BH22 8EA
Records: S Blake, 23 Fairfield Road, North Shore, Blackpool FY1 2RA
Sales Dept: Mrs T Ashcroft, 11 Regent Road, Walton le Dale, Preston PR5 4QA
Sales Dept: Assistant: Mrs J Yates, 23 Richmond Road, Hindley Green, Wigan WN2 4ND
Archive: B Ashcroft, 11 Regent Road, Walton Le Dale, Preston PR5 4QA
Editor: R Kenyon, 18 Hatfield Road, Accrington BB5 6DF
Membership Sec: B Downham, 203 Brindle Road, Bamber Bridge, Preston PR5 6YL
Committee Member: D Barrow, 25 Birley Street, Bury, Lancashire BL9 5DT

ROADS AND ROAD TRANSPORT HISTORY ASSOCIATION

E-mail: enquiries@rrtha.org.uk
Web site: www.rrtha.org.uk
Founded in 1992, the association promotes, encourages and co-ordinates the study of the history of roads and road transport, both passenger and freight. It aims to encourage those interested in a particular aspect of transport to understand their chosen subject in the context of developments in other areas and at other periods. It publishes a newsletter four times a year and holds an annual conference each autumn. Membership is open to professional bodies/transport societies, museums and individuals.
President: Professor John Hibbs, OBE
Chairman: Garry Turvey, CBE
Hon. Secretary: P Jaques, 21 The Oaklands, Droitwich, Worcestershire WR9 0QE

ROUTEMASTER ASSOCIATION

31 Pooley Avenue, Egham, Surrey TW20 8AD
Web site: www.routemaster.org.uk
The Routemaster Association was formed over 20 years ago in 1988 and is now believed to be the largest single type bus owners group in the UK, if not the world.
Today, our aims are more valid so than ever before.
- We pool knowledge and operating experience
- We collect and make available technical information
- We look into the past and future developments
- We assist in the procurement and make available spare parts
- We make available information on known Suppliers
- We cater for the historical and preservation interest
- We enable contact with other Routemaster owners

The Routemaster Association exists to help unite Routemaster owners and to assist them in keeping their vehicles running. These days, the remnants of the London fleets are widely distributed across the world, with many now owned by small operators, preservationists or other private owners. Through the economies of scale, together we can commission parts that are now longer available.

Membership is open to all operators and owners of Routemaster type vehicles, as well as to suppliers of parts or services for these vehicles, and also to those with a genuine interest in Routemasters.

All enquiries should be directed to the above address, or via the *contact page* on the website.
President: Colin Curtis OBE
Chairman & Vice President: Andrew Morgan
Secretary: Graham Lunn
E-mail: secretary@routemaster.org.uk
Sales Officer: Rob Duker
Press & Publicity Officer: Dave Paskell

THE SAMUEL LEDGARD SOCIETY
58 Kirklees Drive, Farsley, Pudsey,
West Yorkshire LS28 5TE
Tel: 0113 236 3695
Fax: 0113 259 1125
E-mail: antonyfirewalk@hotmail.com
Web Site: www.samuelledgardsociety.org.uk
The Samuel Ledgard Society was formed in 1998 at the Rose & Crown Inn, Otley, during the second annual reunion of the devotees of this well-known bus company. Reunions are held twice yearly at Armley during April and Otley on or about October 14. A Christmas dinner is also part of the established calendar of events. The quarterly journal of the Society, The Chat, is published in March, June, September and December each year. Founding officers were Barry Rennison, Tony Greaves and Don Bate, all of whom have a wealth of knowledge about the Samuel Ledgard company. Membership is open to all with a subscription of £5 - contact any member of the Committee for details.
Hon President: Mrs Jenny Barton
COMMITTEE
Chairman: Barry Rennison
Vice-Chairman: Tony Edwards
Treasurer: Bryan Whitham
Secretary: Margaret Rennison

SCOTTISH TRAMWAY & TRANSPORT SOCIETY
PO Box 7342, Glasgow G51 4YQ
Tel: 0141 445 3883 **Fax:** 0141 440 2955
E-mail: stts.glasgow@virgin.net
Web site: www.scottishtransport.org
The Society aims to study and preserve the history of all aspects of Scottish transport, and to publish the results..
Chairman: Ian Stewart
Gen Secretary: Hugh McAulay
Hon Treasurer: Alan Ramsay

SOUTH YORKSHIRE TRANSPORT MUSEUM
Waddington Way, Aldwarke, Rotherham S65 3SH
Tel: 0114 255 3010
The Sheffield Bus Museum Trust was formed in 1987 with the purpose of co-ordinating the bus preservation movement in Sheffield and to establish a permanent museum. This was initially achieved at the former Sheffield Tramways Company's Tinsley Tram Depot but in 2007 the Trust moved its collection to new premises at Aldwarke, Rotherham. At the same time the museum was re-branded to the name above.

The majority of the Trust's collection is local and extremely varied, ranging from a 1926 Sheffield tramcar to a 1985 Dennis Domino. In recent years the Museum Trust has benefitted from Heritage Fund Lottery grants. The museum is an educational charity and promotes an ever-expanding schools visits programme. The museum is open to the public on a monthly basis from March to December.
Chairman: M W Greenwood
Membership Secretary: Dr John Willis, 2 Pwll-Y-Waen, Ty'n-Y-Groes, Conwy LL32 8TQ

SOUTHDOWN ENTHUSIASTS' CLUB
Web site: www.southdownenthusiastsclub.org.uk
The Southdown Enthusiasts' Club (founded 1954) covers the major bus operators in East Sussex, West Sussex, Hampshire and East Kent.
Hon Secretary: Norman Simes, 11 High Cross Fields, Crowborough TN6 2SN (send large SAE for membership details)
Hon Sales Officer: David Chalkley, 6 Valebridge Drive, Burgess Hill RH15 0RW (postal sales only)
Hon Photo Circuit Officer: Calvin Churchill, 53 Monks Close, Lancing BN15 9DB

SWINDON VINTAGE OMNIBUS SOCIETY
10 Fraser Close, Nythe, Swindon SN3 3RP
Tel: 01793 526001
E-mail: davenicol@talktalk.net
Web site: www.freewebs.com/svos112168
The Society was formed in 1968. A magazine is published bi-monthly. The Membership Fee for 2011 is £12 adult, £10 senior citizen and £6 child. Two vehicles are owned, both ex Swindon Corporation, a 1960 Daimler CVG6 and a 1975 Bristol RESL.
Secretary: David Nicol
Membership Secretary: Nigel Robinson

THE TRANSPORT MUSEUM SOCIETY OF IRELAND
Howth Castle Demesne, Howth, PO Box 11737, Dublin 13
Tel: 00 353 1 848 0837
E-mail: info@nationaltransportmuseum.org
Web site: www.nationaltransportmuseum.org
A commercial vehicle collection of trams, buses, fire appliances, military vehicles, lorries and horse-drawn vehicles. Open daily (June to August), Sat/Sun/Bank Holidays (Sept-May): Mondays to Fridays 1000-1700, Sat/Sun/Bank Holidays 1400-1700.
Hon Chairman: John Kelleher
Hon Secretary: John Molloy
Hon Admin Assistant to Officers (Contact): William Kelly

THE TRANSPORT MUSEUM, WYTHALL
Birmingham & Midland Motor Omnibus Trust, The Transport Museum, Chapel Lane, Wythall, Worcestershire B47 6JX
Tel: 01564 826471
E-mail: enquiries@wythall.org.uk
Web site: www.wythall.org.uk
The Trust dates back to 1973, taking its present title in 1977, when it became a registered educational charity to establish and develop a regional transport museum.

The museum comprises an exhibition hall, plus two other halls, housing 100 buses, coaches and battery-electric vehicles, mostly operated and/or built in the Midlands. The Museum is also licensed

as a bus operator and some exhibits can be hired for appropriate work.
Trustees: David Taylor (Chairman), Paul Gray (Treasurer), Philip Ireland (Museum Manager), Malcolm Keeley (Collections Manager).

TRAMWAY & LIGHT RAILWAY SOCIETY
Web site: www.tramwayinfo.co.uk
Founded in 1938, the Tramway & Light Railway Society caters for those interested in all aspects of tramways. Members receive Tramfare, a bi-monthly illustrated magazine. There are regular meetings throughout the country. The Society promotes tramway modelling, drawings, castings, and technical details are available to modellers. There are also comprehensive library facilities. For fuller details of the Society and of membership please write to the Membership Secretary.
HONORARY OFFICERS
President: P J Davis.
Vice-Presidents: E R Oakley, G B Claydon, C.B
Chairman: J R Prentice, 216 Brentwood Road, Romford RM1 2RP.
Secretary: G R Tribe, 47 Soulbury Road, Linslade, Leighton Buzzard LU7 7RW.
Membership Secretary: H J Leach, 6 The Woodlands, Brightlingsea CO7 0RY.

THE TRANSPORT TICKET SOCIETY (TTS)
The TTS is for anyone interested in transport tickets, past and present. Facilities include a monthly illustrated journal, regular meetings, ticket exchange pools, monthly ticket distributions, and postal auctions of scarce tickets.
Membership Secretary: Steve Skeavington, 6 Breckbank, Forest Town, Mansfield NG19 0PZ
Web site: www.transport-ticket.org.uk

THE TRANSPORT TRUST
202 Lambeth Road, London SE1 7JW
Tel: 020 7928 6464 **Fax:** 020 7928 6565
E-mail: info@transporttrust.com
Web Site: www.transporttrust.com
Patron: HRH Prince Michael of Kent
The Trust is the national charity for the preservation and restoration of Britain's transport heritage.

PASSENGER TRANSPORT MUSEUMS

This list is in addition to those shown in the main Society section above.

ABBEY PUMPING STATION
Contact address: Corporation Road, Leicester LE4 5PX
Tel: 0116 299 5111 **Fax:** 0116 299 5125
Web site: www.leicester.gov.uk/museums
www.leicestermuseums.ac.uk

AMBERLEY WORKING MUSEUM
Amberley, Arundel BN18 9LT
Tel: 01798 831370 **Fax:** 01798 831831
E-mail: office@amberleymuseum.co.uk
Web site: www.amberleymuseum.co.uk

ASTON MANOR ROAD TRANSPORT MUSEUM
See Societies section

BLACK COUNTRY LIVING MUSEUM TRANSPORT GROUP
Tipton Road, Dudley DY1 4SQ

Tel: 0121 557 9643
Web site: www.bclm.co.uk

BRISTOL ROAD TRANSPORT COLLECTION
E-mail: william.staniforth@virgin.net
Web site: www.bristolbusevents.co.uk

BRITISH COMMERCIAL VEHICLE MUSEUM
King Street, Leyland PR25 2LE
Tel: 01772 451011
Fax: 01772 451015
E-mail: enquiries@bcvm.co.uk
Web site: www.bcvm.co.uk

CASTLE POINT TRANSPORT MUSEUM
105 Point Road, Canvey Island SS8 7TP
Tel: 01268 684272
E-mail:
castlepointtransportmuseum@yahoo.co.uk
Web site:
www.castlepointtransportmuseum.co.uk

CAVAN AND LEITRIM RAILWAY
Narrow Gauge Station, Station Road, Dromod,
Co Leitrim, Ireland
Tel/Fax: 00353 71 9638599
E-mail: info@irish-railway.com
Web site: www.irish-railway.com

COBHAM BUS MUSEUM - THE LONDON BUS PRESERVATION TRUST LTD
Cobham Hall, Brooklands Road, Weybridge,
Surrey, KT13 0QN
E-mail: cobhambusmuseum@aol.com
Web site: www.lbpt.org

COVENTRY TRANSPORT MUSEUM
Millennium Place, Hales Street, Coventry
CV1 1PN
Tel: 024 7623 4270
Fax: 024 7623 4284
E-mail: enquiries@transport-museum.com

DOVER TRANSPORT MUSEUM
Willingdon Road, Port Zone White Cliffs Business
Park, Whitfield, Dover CT16 2HJ
Tel: 01304 822409
E-mail: info@dovertransportmuseum.org.uk
Web site: www.dovertransportmuseum.org.uk
Chairman & General Manager: D Atkins

EAST ANGLIA TRANSPORT MUSEUM
Chapel Road, Carlton Colville, Lowestoft
NR33 8BL
Tel: 01502 518459
Fax: 01502 584658
E-mail: enquiries@eatm.org.uk
Web site: www.eatm.org.uk

GRAMPIAN TRANSPORT MUSEUM
Alford, Aberdeenshire AB33 8AE
Tel: 01975 562292
Fax: 01975 562180
E-mail: info@g-t-m.freeserve.co.uk
Web site: www.gtm.org.uk

IPSWICH TRANSPORT MUSEUM
Old Trolleybus Depot, Cobham Road, Ipswich
IP3 9JD
Tel: 01473 715666
E-mail: enquiries@ipswichtransportmuseum.
co.uk

Web site: www.ipswichtransportmuseum.co.uk
Chairman: Tony King
Vice Chairman: Mark Smith
Secretary: Mike Abbott
Finance: Bernard Simpson
An independent museum, run by volunteers,
devoted to telling the story of transport and
engineering in the Ipswich area. Exhibits range
from horse drawn carriages to an electric tram,
trolleybuses and motor buses.

ISLE OF WIGHT BUS MUSEUM
Contact address: 28 Westmill Road, Newport
PO30 5RG
Tel: 01983 526422
E-mail: nharris.westmill@tiscali.co.uk

KEIGHLEY BUS MUSEUM TRUST LTD
Contact address: 47 Brantfell Drive, Burnley
BB12 8AW
Tel: 01282 413179
E-mail: shmdboard@aol.com
Web site: www.kbmt.org.uk
Secretary: D A Jones CMILT
Keighley Bus Museum houses some 55 historic
buses, coaches, and ancillary vehicles. It also
operates a small selection of historic buses for
hire.

LONDON TRANSPORT MUSEUM
Covent Garden Piazza, London WC2E 7BB.
Tel: 020 7379 6344; recorded information
020 7565 7299
E-mail: resourcedesk@ltmuseum.co.uk
Web site: www.ltmuseum.co.uk

MIDLAND ROAD TRANSPORT GROUP - BUTTERLEY
Contact address: 21 Ash Grove,
Mastin Moor, Chesterfield S43 3AW
Tel: Midland Road Transport Group
- 01246 473619
Tel: Midland Railway 01773 747674, Visitor
Information Line (01773) 570140.

MUSEUM OF TRANSPORT
Kelvin Hall, 1 Bunhouse Road, Glasgow G3 8DP
Tel: 0141 287 2720 (school bookings on
0141 565 4112/3)
Fax: 0141 287 2692

MUSEUM OF TRANSPORT, GREATER MANCHESTER
Boyle Street, Cheetham,
Manchester M8 8UW
Tel: 0161 205 2122 **Fax:** 0161 202 1110
E-mail: email@gmts.co.uk
Web site: www.gmts.co.uk
**Chairman, Greater Manchester Transport
Society:** Dennis Talbot
The museum charts the development of public
transport in Greater Manchester, with exhibits
ranging from a Victorian horse-drawn bus to a full
size prototype Metrolink tram.

NATIONAL MUSEUM OF SCIENCE AND INDUSTRY
Exhibition Road, London SW7 2DD
Tel: 0207 942 4105 or 01793 814466
E-mail: s.evans@nmsi.ac.uk

THE NORTH OF ENGLAND OPEN AIR MUSEUM
Beamish, Durham DH9 0RG
Tel: 0191 370 4000 **Fax:** 0191 370 4001

E-mail: museum@beamish.org.uk
Web site: www.beamish.org.uk

THE NATIONAL TRAMWAY MUSEUM
See Societies Section

NORTH WEST MUSEUM OF ROAD TRANSPORT
The Old Bus Depot, 51 Hall Street, St Helens
WA10 1DU
E-mail: general@hallstreetdepot.info
Web site: www.hallstreetdepot.info

NOTTINGHAM TRANSPORT HERITAGE CENTRE
Contact address: Mere Way, Ruddington,
Nottingham NG11 6NX
Tel: 0115 940 5705
E-mail: geoffrey.clark3@ntworld.com
Web site: www.nthc.co.uk

OXFORD BUS MUSEUM
Station Yard, Long Hanborough,
Witney OX29 8LA
Tel: 01993 883617
Web site: www.oxfordbusmuseum.org.uk
The museum has two exhibition halls tracing the
history of local transport. Restoration can be
viewed from the workshop gallery. The museum is
open throughout the year.

SCOTTISH VINTAGE BUS MUSEUM
M90 Commerce Park, Lathalmond, Dunfermline,
Fife KY12 0SJ
Tel: 01383 623380
Web site: www.busweb.co.uk/svbm

THE TRANSPORT MUSEUM, WYTHALL
Birmingham & Midland Motor
Omnibus Trust
See Societies section

TRANSPORT MUSEUM SOCIETY OF IRELAND
Howth Castle Demesne, Howth,
Dublin 13, Ireland
Tel/Fax: 00 353 1 848 0831
E-mail: info@nationaltransportmuseum.org
Web site: www.nationaltransportmuseum.org

THE TROLLEYBUS MUSEUM AT SANDTOFT
Belton Road, Sandtoft, North Lincolnshire
DN8 5SX
Tel: 01724 711846
E-mail: trolleybusmuseum@sandtoft.org
Web site: www.sandtoft.org
President: J S King
Managing Director: S Harrison
Secretary: C B Lake
Finance Director: F Whitehead
The museum is home to the world's largest
collection of historic trolleybuses, and is open
selected weekends from April to December.

ULSTER FOLK & TRANSPORT MUSEUM
Contact address: Cultra, Holywood,
Belfast BT18 0EU
Tel: 028 9042 8428

WIRRAL TRANSPORT MUSEUM
1 Taylor Street, Birkenhead CH41 1BG
Tel: 0151 647 2128
E-mail: birkenheadtram@tiscali.co.uk
Web site: www.culture24.org.uk

Transport Benevolent Fund

Ian Allan Publishing is pleased that the Transport Benevolent Fund (TBF) has agreed to sponsor the *Little Red Book* for the third year running.

This is a partnership that works. The *Little Red Book* is an invaluable resource for operators throughout the country, while the TBF is an invaluable resource for their staff.

TBF has been around since 1923 and is a registered charity in England and Wales (1058032) and in Scotland (SC040013). It started life as an organization to help public transport workers in London, but opened membership to all public transport workers throughout England, Scotland and Wales in 1996. Since the start of the national recruitment campaign in 2000, membership has climbed from 8,000 to about 35,000, making it by far the fastest growing charity exclusive to this industry. As the TBF Director, Chris Godbold, says 'we must be doing something right'.

Anyone engaged in the industry can join TBF for just £1 a week, normally deducted through the payroll. That cost has not increased since 1994 and there are no plans to increase it in the foreseeable future either. The £1 covers the member, their partner and dependent children and provides help when need, hardship or distress arises. All benefits are awarded

at the discretion of the trustees, all of whom must be working in the industry to serve.

Unlike many organizations which seek facilities to recruit public transport employees into membership, TBF exists only to serve the public transport industry. To quote Chris again, 'TBF has to get it right – the nature of the industry means that word would very soon spread if we didn't!'. Luckily the word that spreads is that TBF does just what it says it does – and often rather more.

There is no age limit on joining TBF, but the person must be engaged in the industry on the day they apply to join. All members are asked to contribute through the government's Gift Aid scheme, as this increases the £1 by 25p thanks to the tax concession. There is no waiting period, as members can apply for help as soon as they have their membership card – even if they have not started paying.

There is no bar on pre-existing conditions, though help may have to be limited initially where a new member has an underlying problem and has delayed joining. All calls are dealt with by real people – TBF does not have a call centre or lists of options for callers. They just speak to someone whose only role is to help them.

The heads of all the main transport groups are patrons

of TBF, as are the leaders of the transport trades unions. Many members qualify for free membership in retirement because of their length of membership, and those whose service is terminated early for medical reasons may get free membership much earlier.

A number of employers now meet the cost of membership for their staff and TBF is always happy to discuss the arrangements. There are eight regionally-based organizers who get to know company managements and workforces.

The main TBF benefits are listed opposite. More information is available from TBF itself. Significant improvements were made to benefits in 2011 and the trustees are constantly looking to see if there are other un-met needs that could be met. To quote Chris for the final time, 'Yes, it really only costs £1 a week and yes, it really does all it says it does. If you're not already a member, it's the one public transport charity you need to join.'

tbf

Transport
Benevolent
Fund

SECTION 4

ARRIVA

ARRIVA PLC

1 Admiral Way, Doxford International
Business Park, Sunderland SR3 3XP
Tel: 0191 520 4000
Fax: 0191 520 4001
E-mail: enquiries@arriva.co.uk
Web site: www.arriva.co.uk

Chief Executive:
David Martin
Finance Director:
Martin Hibbert
Director – Human Resources:
Alison O'Connor
Managing Director – Mainland Europe:
David Evans
Managing Director – UK Trains:
Bob Holland

Arriva UK Bus

487 Dunstable Road, Luton, LU4 8DS
Tel: 01582 587000

Managing Director – UK Bus:
Mike Cooper
**Operations and Commercial
Director – UK Bus:**
Mark Yexley
Engineering Director – UK Bus:
Ian Tarran
**Finance & Business Development
Director – UK Bus:**
Peter Telford
People & Change Director – UK Bus:
Jo Humphries

**Regional Managing Director, Yorkshire,
North East & Scotland:**
Nigel Featham
**Regional Managing Director,
North West & Wales:**
Phil Stone
Regional Managing Director, Midlands:
Bob Hind
**Regional Managing Director, Shires &
Southern Counties:**
Heath Williams

**Operating Regions,
Group Companies,
Principal Depots
(UK Bus):**

• Arriva Scotland West
(see Renfrewshire)
Depots at Inchinnan, Johnstone

• Arriva Yorkshire
(see North Yorkshire, West Yorkshire)
Depots at Castleford, Dewsbury, Heckmondwike,
Selby, Wakefield

• Arriva North East
(see Tyne & Wear)
Depots at Ashington, Belmont, Blyth, Darlington,

Durham, Newcastle, Redcar,
Stockton, Whitby

• Arriva North West
(see Greater Manchester
Merseyside)
Depots at Birkenhead, Bolton,
Bootle, Liverpool Green Lane,
Liverpool Speke, Manchester,
Runcorn, St Helens, Southport,
Winsford, Wythenshawe

• Arriva Buses Wales
(see Conwy)
Depots at Aberystwyth,
Bangor, Chester, Llandudno, Rhyl,
Wrexham

• Arriva Midlands
(see Derbyshire, Leicestershire, Shropshire,
Staffordshire)
Depots at Bridgnorth, Burton-upon-Trent,
Cannock, Derby, Oswestry, Shrewsbury, Stafford,
Stoke on Trent (Wardles), Tamworth, Telford,
Thurmaston, Wigston

• Arriva Shires
(see Bedfordshire, Buckinghamshire, Hertfordshire)
Depots at Aylesbury, Hemel Hempstead, High
Wycombe, Luton, Milton Keynes (MK Metro),
Stevenage, Ware, Watford

• Arriva London
(see London & Middlesex)
Depots at Barking, Battersea, Brixton, Clapton,
Croydon, Edmonton, Enfield, Hackney, Norwood,
Palmers Green, Stamford Hill, Thornton Heath,
Tottenham, Wood Green

• Arriva Southern Counties
(see Essex, Kent, Surrey)
Depots at Cranleigh, Dartford, Gillingham, Grays,
Guildford, Maidstone, Northfleet, Sheerness,
Southend, Tonbridge (New Enterprise), Tunbridge
Wells

• The Original Tour
(see London & Middlesex)
Depots at Rainham, Wandsworth

• T G M Group Ltd
(see Durham, Essex, London & Middlesex, Surrey)
Includes Classic Coaches, Excel Passenger
Logistics, Flight Delay Services, Linkline Coaches,
Network Colchester, Network Harlow OFJ
Connections, Tellings Golden Miller Coaches
Depots at Colchester, Gatwick, Harlesden,
Harlow, Heathrow Airport, Stanley, Stansted
Airport

• Other Operations
(see West Yorkshire)
Huddersfield Bus Company, K-Line Travel,
White Rose Bus Company (jointly owned with
Centrebus)
Depots at Elland, Honley, Huddersfield, Leeds

Overseas Interests:
Arriva has extensive overseas interests in the
Czech Republic (bus), Denmark (bus and rail),
Germany (bus and rail), Hungary (bus), Italy (bus),
Netherlands (bus and rail), Poland (rail), Portugal
(bus), Slovakia (bus), Spain (bus), Sweden (bus
and rail)

UK Rail Franchises:
Arriva Trains Wales, Cross Country

Other Interests:
Arriva Bus & Coach
(see Trade Directory)

FIRSTGROUP PLC

395 King Street, Aberdeen AB24 5RP
Tel: 01224 650100
Fax: 01224 650140
Web Site: www.firstgroup.com

Chairman:
Martin Gilbert
Chief Executive:
Tim O'Toole CBE
Acting Finance Director (from November 2011):
Nick Chevis
Commercial Director:
Sidney Barrie
Managing Director, UK Rail:
Vernon Barker
Non-Executive Directors:
Audrey Baxter, David Begg, Colin Hood, John Sievwright, Martyn Williams

UK Bus

Managing Director UK Bus:
Giles Fearnley
Business Efficiency & Engineering Director:
David Liston
Finance Director:
Graeme Jenkins
Safety Director:
Janet Ault
Regional Managing Director, North:
Dave Alexander
Regional Managing Director, Scotland:
Mark Savelli
Regional Managing Director, South East & Midlands:
Nigel Barrett
Regional Managing Director, London:
Adrian Jones
Regional Managing Director, South West & Wales:
Justin Davies

Operating Regions, Group Companies, Principal Depots (UK Bus):

• **First Aberdeen, First Aberdeen Coaching Unit**
(Includes Grampian Coaches, Kirkpatrick of Deeside, Mairs Coaches)
(see City of Aberdeen)

• **First Scotland East**
(see Stirling)
Depots at Balfron, Bannockburn, Dalkeith, Galashiels, Larbert, Linlithgow, Livingston, Musselburgh, North Berwick

• **First Glasgow**
(see City of Glasgow)
Depots at Blantyre, Cumbernauld, Dumbarton, Glasgow (3), Overtown

• **First West and North Yorkshire**
(see North Yorkshire, West Yorkshire)
Depots at Bradford, Bramley, Halifax, Huddersfield, Leeds, York

• **First South Yorkshire**
(see South Yorkshire)
Depots at Doncaster, Rotherham, Sheffield

• **First Manchester**
(Includes First Cheshire, First Pioneer Bus)
(see Cheshire, Greater Manchester, Merseyside)
Depots at Birkenhead, Bolton, Bury, Chester, Manchester, Oldham, Tameside, Wigan, Wrexham

• **First Midlands**
(Includes First Leicester, First Northampton, First North Staffordshire, First Wyvern)
(see Leicestershire, Northamptonshire, Staffordshire, Worcestershire)
Depots at Hereford, Kidderminster, Leicester, Newcastle-under-Lyme, Northampton, Redditch, Stoke-on-Trent, Worcester

• **First East of England**
(Includes First Eastern Counties, First Essex)
(see Essex, Norfolk, Suffolk)
Depots at Basildon, Braintree, Chelmsford, Clacton, Colchester, Great Yarmouth, Hadleigh, Harwich, Ipswich, Kings Lynn, Lowestoft, Norwich

• **First London**
(see London & Middlesex)
Depots at Alperton, Dagenham, Greenford, Hayes, Leyton, Northumberland Park, Park Royal, Uxbridge, Westbourne Park, Willesden Junction

• **First in Berkshire**
(see Berkshire)
Depots at Bracknell, Slough

• **First Cymru**
(see City & County of Swansea)
Depots at Bridgend, Cardiff, Carmarthen, Haverfordwest, Llanelli, Port Talbot, Swansea

• **First Bristol, Somerset & Avon**
(see Bristol, Somerset)
Depots at Bath, Bridgwater, Bristol (3), Taunton, Weston super Mare

• **First Hampshire & Dorset**
(see Hampshire)
Depots at Bridport, Fareham, Portsmouth, Southampton, Weymouth, Yeovil

• **First Devon & Cornwall**
(see Cornwall, Devon)
Depots at Barnstaple, Camborne, Plymouth

• **Greyhound UK Ltd**
(see Hampshire)

Overseas Interests:
First has a bus operation in the Republic of Ireland - First Aircoach (See Republic of Ireland) and in Germany and the USA

UK Rail Operations:
First Capital Connect, First Great Western, First Trans Pennine Express, First ScotRail, First GB Railfreight, First Hull Trains

The Little Red Book 2012 - in association with Transport Benevolent Fund

Go-Ahead

GO-AHEAD GROUP PLC
6th Floor, 1 Warwick Row, London SW1E 5ER
Tel: 020 7821 3939
Fax: 0191 221 0315
E-mail: enquiries@go-ahead.com
Web Site: www.go-ahead.com

Non-Executive Chairman: Sir Patrick Brown
Group Chief Executive: David Brown
Group Finance Director: Keith Down
Group Company Secretary: Carolyn Sephton
Non-Executive Directors: Andrew Allner,
Katherine Innes Ker, Rupert Pennant-Rea

UK Bus
Managing Director, Bus Development:
Martin Dean

Operating Regions
Group Companies
Principal Depots
(UK Bus):

• **Go North East** *(see Tyne & Wear)*
Depots at Chester le Street, Gateshead,
Hexham, Newcastle, Peterlee, Stanley,
Sunderland, Washington, Winlaton

• **Oxford Bus Company** *(see Oxfordshire)*
Depot at Oxford

• **Thames Travel** *(see Oxfordshire)*
Depot at Wallingford

• **Konectbus Ltd** *(see Norfolk)*
Depot at Dereham

• **Go-Ahead London**
(includes Blue Triangle, Docklands Buses, London
Central, London General)
(see Essex, London & Middlesex)
Depots at Belvedere, Bexleyheath, Camberwell,
Merton, New Cross, Peckham, Putney, Rainham,
Silvertown, Southwark, Stockwell, Sutton,
Waterloo, Wimbledon

• **Metrobus** *(see West Sussex)*
Depots at Crawley, Croydon, Orpington

• **Brighton & Hove Bus & Coach Company**
(see East Sussex)
Depots at Brighton (2), Hove

• **Go South Coast**
(includes Bells Coaches, Bluestar, Damory
Coaches, Kingston Coaches, Levers Coaches,
Marchwood Motorways, Southern Vectis, Tourist
Coaches, Wilts & Dorset)
(see Dorset, Hampshire, Isle of Wight, Wiltshire)
Depots at Blandford, Bournemouth, Eastleigh,
Figheldean, Fovant, Lymington, Newport IOW,
Poole, Ringwood, Salisbury, Swanage, Totton

• **Plymouth Citybus** *(see Devon)*
Depot at Plymouth

Overseas interests:
The group has bus operations in the United
States

UK Rail Franchises:
London Midland, South Eastern, Southern

national express

NATIONAL EXPRESS GROUP PLC
7 Triton Square, London NW1 3HG
Tel: 0845 130130
E-mail: info@nationalexpress.com
Web Site: www.nationalexpressgroup.com

Chairman:
John Devaney
Group Chief Executive:
Dean Finch
Group Finance Director:
Jez Maiden
Deputy Chairman:
Jorge Cosmen
Non-Executive Directors:
Joaquin Ayuso, Miranda Curtis, Sir Andrew Foster,
Chris Muntwyler, Elliott Sander, Tim Score
Company Secretary:
Tony McDonald
Trains Director (UK):
Andrew Chivers
European Development Director:
Neil Barker

Chief Executive, ALSA Group:
Javier Carbajo
Chief Executive Officer, North America:
David Duke

UK Bus and Coach
Interim Managing Director, UK Bus:
Peter Coates
Operations Director, UK Bus & Coach:
Alex Perry
Managing Director, UK Coach:
Andrew Cleaves

Operating Regions
Group Companies
Principal Depots
(UK Bus):

• **Kings Ferry Travel Group**
(see Kent)

• **National Express Coach**
(See West Midlands)

• **National Express Dundee**
(see Dundee City)

• **Midland Metro**
(see Section 5 – Tram Systems)

• **National Express West Midlands**
(See West Midlands)
Depots at Birmingham, Coventry, Dudley, Walsall,
West Bromwich, Wolverhampton

Overseas interests:
National Express has extensive interests in
Spain (ALSA, Continental Auto), Canada (Stock
Transportation) and the USA (Durham School
Services)

UK Rail Franchises:
c2c, National Express East Anglia

Major Groups

STAGECOACH GROUP PLC

10 Dunkeld Road, Perth PH1 5TW
Tel: 01738 442111
Fax: 01738 643648
E-mail: info@stagecoachgroup.com
Web Site: www.stagecoachgroup.com

Non-Executive Chairman:
Sir George Mathewson
Chief Executive:
Sir Brian Souter
Finance Director:
Martin Griffiths
Non-Executive Directors:
Ewan Brown CBE, Ann Gloag OBE, Helen Mahy,
Garry Watts MBE, Phil White CBE,
Will Whitehorn

UK Bus and Coach
Managing Director UK Bus:
Les Warneford
Commercial Manager:
Paul Southgate
Regional Directors:
Robert Andrew, Sam Greer, Bob Montgomery

Operating Regions
Group Companies
Principal Depots
(UK Bus):

• **Stagecoach East Scotland**
(Includes Bluebird Buses, JW Coaches,
Rennies of Dunfermline, Fife Scottish Omnibuses,
Stagecoach Highland,
Stagecoach in Orkney, Stagecoach in Perth,
Strathtay Scottish Omnibuses)
*(see City of Aberdeen, Aberdeenshire, City of Dundee,
Fife, Highland, Orkney, Perth & Kinross)*
Depots at Aberdeen, Arbroath, Aviemore,
Banchory, Blairgowrie, Cowdenbeath, Dundee,
Dunfermline (2), Elgin, Forfar, Fort William,
Glenrothes, Inverness, Kirkwall, Leven (Aberhill),
Perth, Peterhead, Portree, St Andrews, Tain,
Thurso, Wick

• **Stagecoach West Scotland**
(Includes Stagecoach Glasgow, Western Buses)
(see South Ayrshire)
Depots at Ardrossan, Arran, Ayr, Cumnock,
Dumfries, Glasgow, Kilmarnock, Stranraer

• **Scottish Citylink Coaches** (part owned)
(see City of Glasgow)

• **Stagecoach North East**
(Includes Stagecoach Hartlepool, Newcastle,
South Shields, Sunderland, Teesside, Transit)
(see Durham, Tyne & Wear)
Depots at Hartlepool, Newcastle (2), South
Shields, Stockton, Sunderland

• **Stagecoach North West**
(Includes Stagecoach in Cumbria and North
Lancashire, Merseyside and South Lancashire)
(see Cumbria, Lancashire, Merseyside)
Depots at Barrow, Carlisle, Chorley, Kendal,
Lancaster, Liverpool, Preston, Workington

• **Stagecoach Manchester**
(see Greater Manchester)
Depots at Manchester (2), Stockport, Tameside

• **Stagecoach Yorkshire**
(Includes Stagecoach Chesterfield, Stagecoach
Sheffield, Stagecoach Yorkshire)
(see South Yorkshire)
Depots at Barnsley, Chesterfield, Rawmarsh,
Shafton, Sheffield (2)

• **Stagecoach Supertram**
(see Section 5 – Tram Systems)

• **Stagecoach East Midlands**
(Includes Stagecoach East Midlands, Hull,
Lincolnshire)
*(see East Riding, Lincolnshire, North & North East
Lincolnshire, Nottinghamshire)*
Depots at Gainsborough, Grimsby, Hull, Lincoln,
Mansfield, Newark, Scunthorpe, Skegness,
Worksop

• **Stagecoach East**
(Includes Stagecoach in Bedford, Cambridgeshire,
Peterborough, The Fens)
(see Bedfordshire, Cambridgeshire)
Depots at Bedford, Cambridge, Ely, Fenstanton,
Peterborough

• **Stagecoach Oxfordshire**
(see Oxfordshire)
Depots at Banbury, Oxford, Witney

• **Stagecoach Midlands**
(see Northamptonshire, Warwickshire)
Depots at Corby, Kettering, Leamington Spa,
Northampton, Nuneaton, Rugby,
Stratford upon Avon

• **Stagecoach London**
(see London & Middlesex)
Depots at Barking, Bow, Bromley, Catford,
Leyton, Plumstead, Rainham, Romford,
West Ham

• **Stagecoach West**
(Includes Stagecoach Cheltenham, Cotswolds,
Gloucester, Swindon, Wye & Dean)
(see Gloucestershire)
Depots at Cheltenham, Coleford, Gloucester,
Stroud, Swindon

• **Stagecoach South East**
(Includes Stagecoach in East Kent & East Sussex,
Hampshire, Hants & Surrey, Stagecoach South)
(see East Sussex, Hampshire, Kent, West Sussex)
Depots at Aldershot, Andover, Ashford,
Basingstoke, Chichester, Dover, Eastbourne,
Folkestone, Hastings, Herne Bay, Portsmouth,
Thanet, Winchester, Worthing

• **Stagecoach South West**
(Includes Stagecoach Devon, Stagecoach
Somerset)
(see Devon, Somerset)
Depots at Barnstaple, Exeter, Exmouth,
Torquay, Wellington

• **Stagecoach in South Wales**
(see Torfaen)
Depots at Aberdare, Blackwood, Brynmawr,
Caerphilly, Cwmbran, Islwyn, Merthyr, Porth

Coaching
• Megabus; Scottish Citylink Coaches
(jointly owned with Comfort DelGro)

Overseas Interests:
The group has significant bus and coach
operations in North America

Other Interests
National Transport Tokens

UK Rail Franchises:
East Midlands Trains, Island Line, South West
Trains, Virgin West Coast (joint venture)

ABELLIO

2nd Floor, I Ely Place, London EC1N 6RY
Tel: 020 7430 8270
Fax: 020 7430 2239
E-mail: info@abellio.com
Web site: www.abellio.com
Chief Executive: Anton Valk
Chief Operating Officer: Dominic Booth
Chief Financial Officer: Richard Emmerink
Finance Director, UK: Lesley Batty
Non-Executive Director: Ian Brown

Group Companies (UK Bus):
• **Abellio London**
(see London & Middlesex)
Depots at Beddington, Battersea, Walworth
• **Abellio Surrey**
(see Surrey)
Depots at Byfleet, Fulwell, Hayes

Overseas Interests
Abellio has bus and rail interests in Germany
and a bus operation (Probo Bus) in the Czech
Republic
UK Rail Franchises
Merseyrail, Northern Rail
Parent Company
Abellio is part of the NedRail Group

CENTREBUS GROUP

102 Cannock Street, Leicester LE4 9HR
Tel: 0116 246 0030
Fax: 0116 246 7221
E-mail: info@centrebus.com
Web site: www.centrebus.info
Directors: Peter Harvey, Julian Peddle, Keith
Hayward, David Shelley

Group Operations:
• **Bowers Coaches**
(see Derbyshire)
Depot at Chapel-en-le-Frith
To be merged with Dove Holes operations of
Trent Barton (see Wellglade, Derbyshire) as
the jointly owned High Peak Bus Company.
• **Centrebus in Essex, Hertfordshire and
Bedfordshire**
(see Bedfordshire, Essex, Hertfordshire)
Depots at Dunstable, Harlow, Stevenage
• **Centrebus in Leicestershire and
Northamptonshire**
(see Leicestershire, Northamptonshire)
Depots at Corby, Hinckley, Leicester, Melton
Mowbray
• **Centrebus in Lincolnshire (incl Kimes
Buses)**
(see Lincolnshire)
Depots at Folkingham, Grantham
• **Centrebus in West Yorkshire**
(see West Yorkshire)
Includes Huddersfield Bus Company (Jointly
owned with Arriva)
Depots at Elland, Huddersfield
K-Line Travel (Jointly owned with Arriva)
Depot at Huddersfield
White Rose Bus Company
Depot at Leeds

COMFORT DELGRO

Comfort DelGro House, 3rd Floor, 329
Edgware Road, London NW2 6JP
Tel: 020 8218 8888

Fax: 020 8218 8899
Web Site: www.comfortdelgro.com.sg
Chief Executive, UK & Ireland: Jaspal
Singh

Group Companies (UK Bus):
• **Metroline Travel**
(see London & Middlesex)
Depots at Brentford, Cricklewood, Edgware,
Harrow Weald, Holloway, Kings Cross,
Perivale, Potters Bar, West Perivale, Willesden
• **Scottish Citylink Coaches** (part owned)
(see City of Glasgow)
• **Westbus Coach Services**
(see London & Middlesex)

Other Interests:
Citylink (Ireland)
(see Republic of Ireland)
Also Computer Cab and other taxi interests

Overseas Interests:
The group has extensive interests in Australia,
China, Malaysia, Singapore and Vietnam
Parent Company:
Comfort DelGro Corporation

EAST LONDON BUS GROUP

Business sold to Stagecoach during 2011.
See Stagecoach London.

EYMS GROUP LTD

252 Anlaby Road, Hull HU3 2RS
Tel: 01482 327142
Fax: 01482 212040
Web Site: www.eymsgroup.co.uk
Chairman: Peter Shipp
Finance Director: Peter Harrison

Group Companies:
• **East Yorkshire Motor Services**
(including Scarborough & District Motor
Services)
(see East Riding, North Yorkshire)
Depots at Beverley, Bridlington, Driffield,
Elloughton, Hornsea, Hull, Pocklington,
Scarborough, Withernsea
• **Finglands Coachways**
(see Greater Manchester)
Depot at Manchester
• **Whittle Coach & Bus**
(see Shropshire)
Depot at Kidderminster

RATP DEV UK LTD

Busways House, Wellington Road, Twickenham
TW2 5NX
Tel: 020 8400 6667
Fax: 020 8943 2688
E-mail: paul.matthews@ratpdev.com
Web site: www.ratpdev.com
Chief Executive, UK: Paul Matthews

Group Companies (UK):
• **Bath Bus Company**
(see Somerset)
Depot at Bath
• **London United Busways**
(see London & Middlesex)
Depots at Fulwell, Hounslow, Hounslow
Heath, Park Royal, Shepherd's Bush, Stamford
Brook, Tolworth, Twickenham

• **Metrolink**
(see Section 5 – Tram Systems)
• **Yellow Buses (Bournemouth
Transport)**
(see Dorset)
Depot at Bournemouth

Overseas interests:
RATP Dev has bus and rail interests in 12
countries worldwide.

ROTALA PLC

Beacon House, Long Acre, Birmingham B7 5JJ
Tel: 0121 322 2222
Fax: 0121 322 2718
E-Mail: info@rotalaplc.co.uk
Web Site: www.rotalaplc.com
Chairman: John Gunn
Chief Executive: Simon Dunn
Finance Director: Kim Taylor
Non-Executive Directors: Robert Dunn,
Geoffrey Flight

Group Companies:
• **Central Connect**
(see West Midlands)
Depot at Birmingham
• **Diamond Bus**
(See West Midlands, Worcestershire)
Depots at Droitwich, Redditch
• **Flights Hallmark**
(See London & Middlesex, West Midlands, West
Sussex)
Depots at Birmingham, Crawley, Heathrow,
Isleworth
• **Preston Bus**
(see Lancashire)
Depot at Preston
• **Wessex Connect, Bath Connect**
(see Bristol, Somerset)
Depots at Avonmouth, Filton, Keynsham

VEOLIA TRANSDEV UK

3rd Floor, 401 King Street, Hammersmith,
London W6 9NJ
Tel: 020 8600 5650 **Fax:** 020 8600 5651
E-mail: information@transdevplc.co.uk
Web Site: www.transdevplc.co.uk
UK Divisional Director:
Nigel Stevens
Finance Director:
Peter Brogden
**Light Rail & Corporate Services
Director:**
Julia Thomas

**Operating Regions & Group Companies
(UK):**
• **Blazefield Lancashire**
(includes Burnley & Pendle, Lancashire United)
(see Lancashire)
Depots at Blackburn, Burnley
• **Blazefield Yorkshire**
(includes Harrogate & District, Keighley &
District, Transdev York, Yorkshire Coastliner)
(see North Yorkshire, West Yorkshire)
Depots at Harrogate, Keighley, Malton, York
• **London Sovereign**
(see London & Middlesex)
Depots at Edgware, Harrow
• **Nottingham City Transport**
(part owned)
(see Nottinghamshire)

- **Nottingham Express Transit**
(part of operating group) *(see Section 5 – Tram Systems)*

Overseas interests:
Veolia Transdev has extensive bus and rail interests worldwide.

VEOLIA TRANSPORT (UK) LTD

Main group merged with Transdev. Residual UK businesses still operated separately (see county entries as below).

- **Veolia Transport Cymru PLC**
(Formerly Bebb Travel PLC, Long's Coaches, Pullman Coaches, Thomas of Barry)
(see Newport, Rhondda Cynon Taf, City & County of Swansea)

Depots at Abercrave, Cross Gates, Newport
- **Veolia Transport England PLC**
(Formerly Astons Coaches, Paul James Coaches)
(See Leicestershire, Worcestershire)
Depots at Birmingham, Coalville, Heanor, Melton Mowbray, Nottingham, Rotherham, Houghton le Spring

WELLGLADE LTD

Mansfield Road, Heanor, Derbyshire
DE75 7BG
Tel: 01773 536309
Fax: 01773 536310
Chairman: B R King
Deputy Chairman: R I Morgan
Group Finance Director: G Sutton
Director of Investments: K Belfield

Group Companies:
- **Derby Community Transport**
(see Derbyshire)
Depot at Derby
- **Kinchbus** *(see Leicestershire)*
Depot at Loughborough
- **Notts & Derby**
(see Derbyshire)
Depot at Derby
- **TM Travel**
(see South Yorkshire)
Depot at Halfway
- **Trent Barton**
(see Derbyshire)
Depots at Ashfield, Belper, Derby, Dove Holes, Langley Mill, Nottingham
Dove Holes operations are to be merged with Bowers (see Centrebus) as the jointly owned High Peak Bus Company..

♿	Vehicle suitable for disabled	⊿	Seat belt-fitted Vehicle	**R24**	24 hour recovery service
T	Toilet-drop facilities available	**⫲**	Coach(es) with galley facilities	⬛	Replacement vehicle available
R	Recovery service available	❄	Air-conditioned vehicle(s)	▭	Vintage Coach(es) available
▭	Open top vehicle(s)	⋔	Coaches with toilet facilities	⬛	Hybrid Buses

---

BEDFORD, CENTRAL BEDFORDSHIRE, LUTON

AtoB TRAVEL (LUTON) LTD
NEW CITY COACHES
♿⊿❄
UNIT 54, BILTON WAY, LUTON LU1 1UU
Tel: 01582 733333
Fax: 01582 733331
Web site: www.atobexec.com
Fleet: 75 – single-deck coach, minicoach, midicoach
Chassis incl: Ayats, Ford, Iveco, LDV, MAN, Mercedes, Renault, Scania, Volvo.
Bodies incl: Ayats, Ford, Jonckheere, Irizar, LDV, Mercedes, Noge, Plaxton.
Ops incl: school contracts, private hire.
Livery: Silver

ARRIVA THE SHIRES LTD
♿⋔⊿**R**⬛**T**
487 DUNSTABLE ROAD, LUTON LU4 8DS
Tel: 01582 587000/08701 201088
Web site: www.arrivabus.co.uk
Fleet Names: Arriva the Shires & Essex, MK Metro, Green Line, Super Bus.
Regional Man Dir: Heath Williams **Area Man Dir:** Paul Adcock **Comm Dir:** Kevin Hawkins
Fin Dir: Beverley Lawson
Fleet (incl MK Metro): 687 – 125 double-deck bus, 352 single-deck bus, 66 single-deck coach, 144 midibus.
Chassis: 48 Alexander Dennis, 73 DAF, 142 Dennis, 26 Leyland, 30 Mercedes, 88 Optare, 94 Scania, 10 Transbus, 16 Van Hool, 81 VDL, 79 Volvo.
Bodies: 77 Alexander, 48 Alexander Dennis, 27 Caetano, 37 East Lancs, 4 Leyland, 25 Mercedes, 40 Northern Counties, 88 Optare, 152 Plaxton, 2 Scania, 10 Transbus, 2 UVG, 31 Van Hool, 144 Wright.
Ops incl: local bus services, school contracts, excursions & tours, private hire, express.
Liveries: Arriva UK Bus, TfL Red, Green Line,

Green Line/Easybus, National Express, Local Brands.
Ticket System: Wayfarer 3, Prestige.
Fleet excludes Harlow Garage, transferred to TGM Group *(see Essex)*

BARFORDIAN COACHES LTD
❄⋔⫲⊿
500 GOLDINGTON ROAD, BEDFORD
MK41 0DX
Tel: 01234 355440
Fax: 01234 355310
E-mail: info@barfordiancoaches.co.uk
Web site: www.barfordiancoaches.co.uk
Gen Man: Jackie Bullard
Fleet: 19 - 3 double-deck bus, 1 single-deck bus, 10 single-deck coach, 2 double-deck coach, 1 minibus, 3 minicoach.
Ops incl: school contracts, excursions & tours, private hire, continental tours.
Livery: Orange/Yellow
A subsidiary of Souls Coaches Ltd (see Buckinghamshire).

CEDAR COACHES
♿⋔⊿❄
ARKWRIGHT ROAD, BEDFORD
MK42 0LE
Tel: 01234 354054
Fax: 01234 219210
E-mail: nikki@cedarcoaches.co.uk
Web site: www.cedarcoaches.co.uk
Dirs: Nikki Graham, Donna Reid, Kevin Reid
Fleet: 34 - 20 double-deck bus, 6 single-deck coach, 1 double-deck coach, 7 minicoach.
Chassis: Alexander Dennis, Ayats, BMC, Bova, Irisbus, Iveco, King Long, Mercedes, Optare, Scania.
Ops incl: local bus services, school contracts, private hire.
Livery: Red/Yellow

CENTREBUS LTD
♿
UNIT 34, HUMPHRYS ROAD, WOODSIDE INDUSTRIAL ESTATE, DUNSTABLE, LU5 4TP
Tel: 0844 357 6520
E-mail: info@centrebus.com
Web site: www.centrebus.co.uk
Man Dir: Peter Harvey **Ops Dir:** Neil Harris
Fleet (Bedfordshire): 46 – 2 single-deck bus, 44 midibus.
Chassis: 30 Dennis, 1 MAN, 9 Optare, 2 Scania, 4 VDL.
Bodies: 2 Alexander, 4 Caetano, 1 East Lancs, 5 Northern Counties, 9 Optare, 25 Plaxton.
Ops incl: local bus services
Livery: Blue/Orange/White
Ticket system: Wayfarer 3
Part of the Centrebus Group

CHILTERN TRAVEL
⊿⋔❄⬛
THE COACH HOUSE, BARFORD ROAD, BLUNHAM MK44 3NA
Tel: 01767 641400
Fax: 01767 641358
E-mail: chilterntravel@hotmail.com
Web Site: www.chilterntravel.com
Proprietor: Trevor Boorman
Fleet: 18 single-deck coach.
Chassis: 2 Bova, 1 Mercedes, 5 Setra, 10 Volvo.
Bodies: 2 Bova, 10 Jonckheere, 1 Mercedes, 5 Setra.
Ops incl: private hire, continental tours, school contracts.
Livery: White/Blue

EXPRESSLINES LTD
♿⊿❄
FENLAKE ROAD INDUSTRIAL ESTATE, BEDFORD MK42 0HB

Tel: 01234 268704
Fax: 01234 272212
E-mail: info@expresslinesltd.co.uk
Web site: www.expresslinesltd.co.uk
Dirs: Chris Spriggs, Richard Harris
Fleet: 23 - 4 midibus, 5 midicoach, 12 minicoach.
Chassis: 12 Ford Transit, 5 Mercedes, 4 Optare.
Bodies: 8 Optare, 15 Other.
Ops incl: local bus services, school contracts, private hire.
Livery: Red/White/Silver
Ticket System: Wayfarer & Almex

GRANT PALMER PASSENGER SERVICES

UNIT 2, LAWRENCE WAY, DUNSTABLE
LU6 1BD
Tel/Fax: 01582 600844
E-mail: info@grantpalmer.com
Web site: www.grantpalmer.com
Dirs: Grant Palmer, Peter Morgan, Jeff Wilson.
Fleet: 28 - 7 double-deck bus, 4 single-deck bus, 17 midibus.
Chassis: 3 Dennis, 4 Enterprise, 5 Leyland, 1 MAN, 13 Mercedes, 2 Volvo.
Bodies: 5 Alexander, 1 ECW, 2 East Lancs, 3 Marshall, 3 Northern Counties, 13 Plaxton, 1 Roe
Ops incl: local bus services, school contracts, private hire.
Livery: Red/White
Ticket System: Wayfarer 3

HERBERTS TRAVEL

UNIT 5, OLD ROWNEY FARM, SHEFFORD
SG17 5QH
Tel: 01234 382000
Fax: 01234 381117
E-mail: booking@herberts-travel.co.uk
Web site: www.herberts-travel.co.uk
Man Dir: D M Dougall **Ops Dir:** D S Dougall
Fleet Eng: S Myers
Fleet: 21 - 6 double-deck bus, 5 midibus, 4 midicoach, 1 minibus, 5 minicoach.
Chassis: 5 Ford Transit, 5 Leyland, 3 MCW, 4 Mercedes, 2 Optare, 1 Toyota, 1 Volvo.
Bodies: 4 Alexander, 1 Caetano, 2 ECW, 1 Leyland, 1 MCW, 4 Optare, 1 Plaxton, 6 other.
Ops incl: private hire, school contracts, local bus services.
Livery: White.
Ticket system: Wayfarer

LANDMARK COACHES LTD

UNIT 6, ARLESEY BUSINESS PARK,
MILL LANE, ARLESEY SG16 6RF
Tel: 01462 434577
Fax: 01462 835817
Web site: www.landmarkhire.com
Fleet: 24 - 1 double-deck bus, 6 single-deck coach, 2 midicoach, 15 minibus.
Ops incl: school contracts, private hire.
Livery: Red/White

MARSHALLS COACHES

UNIT 4, FIRBANK WAY, LEIGHTON BUZZARD
LU7 4YP
Tel: 01525 376077
Fax: 01525 850967
E-mail: info@marshalls-coaches.co.uk
Web site: www.marshalls-coaches.co.uk

Prop: Glen Marshall
Fleet: 34 - 6 double-deck bus, 24 single-deck coach, 2 double-deck coach, 2 midicoach.
Chassis: 2 Bova, 1 Bristol, 4 Dennis, 1 Iveco, 2 Leyland, 3 MAN, 2 Mercedes, 1 Neoplan, 1 Scania, 17 Volvo.
Bodies: 3 Ayats, 1 Beulas, 2 Bova, 1 Mercedes, 1 Neoplan, 17 Plaxton, 1 Scania, 7 Other..
Ops incl: private hire, school contracts.
Livery: Blue/Multicoloured.

PREMIER CONNECTIONS TRAVEL LTD

THE COACH YARD, EATON GREEN PARK,
EATON GREEN ROAD,
LUTON AIRPORT, LU2 9HD
Tel: 01582 424140
Fax: 01582 727093
E-mail: sales@premier.gb.com
Web site: www.premiercoachhire.co.uk
Ops incl: school contracts, private hire
Livery: Silver/White (coaches), Yellow (school buses)

RED KITE COMMERCIAL SERVICES

UNIT 2, LEYS YARD, DUNSTABLE ROAD,
TILSWORTH, LEIGHTON BUZZARD LU7 9PU
Tel: 01525 211441
Props: D Hoar, R H Savage
Fleet: 17 - 13 double-deck bus, 2 single-deck coach, 2 midibus.
Chassis: Leyland, Optare, Volvo
Ops incl: local bus services, school contracts, excursions and tours, private hire, school contracts.
Livery: Red/Blue

SAFFORD'S COACHES LTD

HIGHBURY FIELDS, ELTISLEY ROAD,
GREAT GRANSDEN, SANDY SG19 3AR
Tel: 01767 677395
Fax: 01767 677742
E-mail: saffordcoaches@btconnect.com
Web site: www.saffordscoaches.co.uk
Dirs: Miss T Gillett, Mrs S I Gillett
Ch Eng: Mr C Chapman.
Fleet: 13 - 1 single-deck bus, 8 single-deck coach, 1 midibus, 1 midicoach, 2 minibus.
Chassis: 1 Bova, 1 Ford Transit, 1 Irisbus, 2 Mercedes, 8 Volvo.
Bodies: 1 Alexander Dennis, 1 Berkhof, 1 Bova, 2 Jonckheere, 1 Mellor, 3 Plaxton, 1 Sitcar, 1 Van Hool, 2 Other.
Ops incl: school contracts, excursions & tours, private hire, continental tours.
Livery: White/Blue/Yellow

SHOREYS TRAVEL

119 CLOPHILL ROAD, MAULDEN MK45 2AE
Tel: 01525 860694
Fax: 01525 861850
E-mail: shoreystravel@talk21.com
Partners: D Shorey, G Shorey
Ch Eng: D Bunker
Fleet: 10 double-deck bus.
Ops incl: school contracts, private hire.
Livery: White/Green
Ticket System: Wayfarer.

STAGECOACH EAST

BEDFORD BUS STATION, ALL HALLOWS,
BEDFORD MK40 1LT
Tel: 01234 220030

Fax: 01234 343534
E-mail: bedford.enquiries@stagecoachbus.com
Web site: www.stagecoachbus.com/bedford
Fleet Name: Stagecoach in Bedfordshire
Regional Man Dir: Robert Andrew
Man Dir: Andy Campbell
Comm Dir: Philip Norwell
Eng Dir: Bob Dennison
Fleet (Bedford): 117 – 24 double-deck bus, 45 single-deck bus, 38 single-deck coach, 10 midibus.
Chassis: 13 Alexander Dennis, 11 Dennis, 10 Optare, 27 Transbus, 56 Volvo.
Bodies: 16 Alexander, 13 Alexander Dennis, 10 Optare, 8 Northern Counties, 43 Plaxton, 27 Transbus.
Ops incl: local bus services, school contracts, private hire, express.
Livery: Stagecoach UK Bus
Ticket System: ERG
Part of Stagecoach East (with Stagecoach in Cambridgeshire)

TATES COACHES

44 HIGH STREET, MARKYATE
AL3 8PA
Tel: 01582 840297
Fax: 01582 840014
E-mail: info@tatescoaches.co.uk
Web site: www.tatescoaches.co.uk
Dirs: A M Tate, A J Tate, S W Tate
Fleet: 9 single-deck coach
Chassis: 1 Bova, 1 DAF, 1 Dennis, 1 EOS, 1 MAN, 2 Mercedes, 2 Scania.
Bodies: 1 Bova, 1 Caetano, 1 Hispano, 2 Irizar, 2 Neoplan, 1 Van Hool, 1 Wadham Stringer.
Ops incl: school contracts, excursions & tours, private hire, continental tours.
Livery: Blue/Cream/Orange

THREE STAR COACHES.COM

UNIT 1, GUARDIAN BUSINESS PARK,
DALLOW ROAD, LUTON LU1 1NA
Tel: 01582 722626
Fax: 01582 484034
E-mail: sales@threestarcoaches.com
Web Site: www.threestarcoaches.com
Man Dir: Colin Dudley,
Ops Man: Kevin Green
Ch Eng: Michael Nallaby
Co Sec: Isabelle Dudley
Fleet: 14 – 1 single-deck bus, 7 single-deck coach, 2 double-deck coach, 4 midicoach.
Chassis: 2 Ayats, 3 Dennis, 6 Mercedes, 1 Optare, 1 Scania, 1 Volvo
Bodies: 2 Ayats, 4 Berkhof, 1 Mercedes, 1 Optare, 4 Plaxton, 2 Other.
Ops incl: school contracts, excursions & tours, private hire.
Livery: Blue

THE VILLAGER MINIBUS (SHARNBROOK) LTD

SHARNBROOK UPPER SCHOOL,
ODELL ROAD, SHARNBROOK
MK44 1JL
Tel: 01234 781920
E-mail: villager.sharn@btconnect.com
Man: Stan Jones
Fleet: 1 minibus
Chassis: 1 Ford Transit
Ops incl: local bus services, private hire

ALDERMASTON COACHES

ALDERMASTON, READING RG7 5PP
Tel: 0118 971 3257
Fax: 0118 971 2722
E-mail: anne@aldermastoncoaches.co.uk
Prop: Philip M Arlott
Fleet: 9 – 5 single-deck coach, 3 midicoach, 1 minibus.
Chassis: 1 LDV, 3 Mercedes, 5 Volvo.
Bodies: 1 Jonckheere, 1 LDV, 3 Plaxton, 1 Sunsundegui, 3 Others.
Ops incl: private hire, school contracts.
Livery: White

APPLE TRAVEL LTD

STOKE WHARF, STOKE ROAD, SLOUGH SL2 5AU
Tel: 01753 821310
Fax: 01753 693912
E-mail: enquiries@appletravelltd.co.uk
Web site: www.appletravelltd.co.uk
Fleet: 12 – 8 single-deck coach, 2 midicoach, 2 minibus.
Ops incl: private hire, school contracts.
Livery: White with Red, Green

BAILEYS COACHES LTD

RED SHUTE HILL, HERMITAGE RG18 9QL
Tel: 01635 203005
Fax: 01635 203006
E-mail: info@baileyscoaches.co.uk
Web site: www.baileys-of-newbury.co.uk
Fleet: 10 – 6 single-deck coach, 3 midicoach, 1 minibus.
Chassis: 2 Irisbus, 1 Iveco, 3 Mercedes, 4 VDL.
Bodies: 6 Beulas, 1 Ferqui, 1 Indcar, 1 Marcopolo, 1 Other.
Livery: Grey/Silver/Maroon

BURGHFIELD MINI COACHES LTD

BURGHFIELD FARM, MILL ROAD, BURGHFIELD, READING RG30 3SS
Tel/Fax: 0118 959 0719
E-mail: burghfield.coaches@virgin.net
Dir: Susan McCouid
Fleet: 33 – 29 minibus, 4 minicoach.
Chassis: Citroen, Ford, Mercedes, Peugeot, Renault, Volkswagen.
Ops incl: local bus services, school contracts, private hire.

COURTNEY

22 IVANHOE ROAD, HOGWOOD INDUSTRIAL ESTATE, FINCHAMPSTEAD, WOKINGHAM RG40 4QQ
Tel: 0118 973 3486
Fax: 0118 932 8796
E-mail: sales@courtneycoaches.com
Web site: www.courtneycoaches.com
Prop: William Courtney-Smith
Dir & Co Sec: Miss Hayley Smith, Mrs Belinda Sheppard
Fleet: 36 – 5 double-deck bus, 30 double-deck bus, 1 minibus.
Chassis: 6 Alexander Dennis, 25 Optare, 1 Renault, 1 Scania, 2 VDL, 1 Volvo.
Bodies: 5 Alexander Dennis, 3 East Lancs, 27 Optare, 1 Other

Ops incl: local bus services, contract hire.
Livery: Orange/White.
Ticket System: Ticketer

D & P COACHES

3 VULCAN CLOSE, SANDHURST GU47 9DD
Tel: 01252 861250 **Fax:** 01252 861234
E-mail: enquiries@dp-coaches.co.uk
Web site: www.dp-coaches.co.uk
Fleet: 8 – 6 single-deck coach, 2 midicoaches.
Chassis: 1 Neoplan, 5 Scania, 2 Toyota.
Bodies: 2 Caetano, 5 Irizar, 1 Neoplan.
Ops incl: private hire, excursions & tours.
Livery: White with Blue

FERNHILL TRAVEL LTD

LONGSHOT LANE, BRACKNELL RG12 1RL
Tel: 01344 621413
Fax: 01344 488669
E-mail: office@fernhill.co.uk
Web site: www.fernhill.co.uk
Ops incl: school contracts, private hire
Livery: Red/White

FIRST IN BERKSHIRE

COLDBOROUGH HOUSE, MARKET STREET, BRACKNELL RG12 1JA
Tel: 01344 782200
Fax: 01344 868332
E-mail: contact.berkshire@firstgroup.com
Web site: www.firstgroup.com
Regional Man Dir: Adrian Jones
Fleet: 108 – 17 double-deck bus, 50 single-deck bus, 14 single-deck coach, 27 midibus.
Chassis: 8 Bluebird, 1 BMC, 34 Dennis, 28 Mercedes, 6 Optare, 21 Scania, 10 Volvo.
Bodies: 13 Alexander Dennis, 8 Bluebird, 1 BMC, 1 Irizar, 6 Marshall, 28 Mercedes, 6 Optare, 21 Plaxton, 17 Wright.
Ops incl: local bus services, school contracts, express.
Livery: FirstGroup UK Bus/Bespoke Products.
Ticket System: Wayfarer 3.

HAYWARDS COACHES

169 NEW GREENHAM PARK, THATCHAM RG19 6HN
Tel: 0118 947 4561
Fax: 01635 821128
E-mail: info@haywardscoaches.co.uk
Web site: www.haywardscoaches.co.uk
Dir: Simon Weaver
Fleet: see Weaveway Travel
Livery: Electric Blue
A subsidiary of Weaveway Travel

HODGE'S COACHES (SANDHURST) LTD

100 YORKTOWN ROAD, SANDHURST GU47 9BH.
Tel: 01252 873131
Fax: 01252 874884
E-mail: enquiries@hodges-coaches.co.uk
Web site: www.hodges-coaches.co.uk
Man Dir: P Hodge **Dirs:** M Hodge, M Hodge
Fleet: 21 – 17 single-deck coach, 3 midicoach, 1 minibus.
Chassis: 1 Ford, 3 MAN, 4 Scania, 3 Toyota, 10 Volvo.

Bodies: 8 Berkhof, 8 Caetano, 3 Fast, 1 Ford, 1 Van Hool.
Ops incl: excursions & tours, private hire, continental tours, school contracts.
Livery: Blue/Gold

HORSEMAN COACHES LTD

2 ACRE ROAD, READING RG2 0SU
Tel: 0118 975 3811
Fax: 0118 975 3515
Recovery: 0118 975 3811
E-mail: privatehire@horsemancoaches.co.uk
Web site: www.horsemancoaches.co.uk
Man Dir: Keith Horseman
Ops Dir: James Horseman **Ch Eng:** Derrick Holton
Sales Man: Trevor Underwood
Fleet: 59 – 50 coach, 9 midicoach.
Chassis: 1 Dennis, 4 Iveco, 9 Toyota, 45 Volvo.
Bodies: 3 Berkhof, 4 Beulas, 9 Caetano, 42 Plaxton, 1 UVG.
Ops incl: local bus services, school contracts, excursions & tours, private hire, continental tours.
Livery: multi-coloured

KINGFISHER MINI COACHES

357 BASINGSTOKE ROAD, READING RG2 0JA
Tel: 0118 931 3454
Fax: 0118 931 1322
Prop: Kevin Pope
E-mail: info@kingfisherminicoaches.co.uk
Web site: www.minicoachhirereading.co.uk
Fleet: 13 – 10 minibus, 3 minicoach
Chassis: 1 Ford Transit, 7 LDV, 5 Mercedes.
Ops incl: private hire, school contracts
Livery: White/Orange

MEMORY LANE VINTAGE OMNIBUS SERVICES

78 LILLIBROOKE CRESCENT, MAIDENHEAD SL6 3XQ
Tel: 01628 825050
Fax: 01628 825851
E-mail: admin@memorylane.co.uk
Web site: www.memorylane.co.uk
Prop: M J Clarke
Fleet: 6 – 3 double-deck bus, 3 single-deck bus
Chassis: 6 AEC.
Bodies: 2 ECW, 3 Park Royal, 1 Willowbrook.
Ops incl: private hire
Livery: Original operators

NEWBURY & DISTRICT LTD

169 NEW GREENHAM PARK, THATCHAM RG19 6HN
Tel: 01635 33855
Fax: 01635 821128
E-mail: info@newburyanddistrict.co.uk
Web site: www.newburyanddistrict.co.uk
Dir: Simon Weaver
Fleet: 14 – 9 double-deck bus, 5 single-deck bus.
Chassis: 9 Alexander Dennis, 2 MAN, 3 Optare.
Bodies: 9 Alexander Dennis, 2 MCV, 3 Optare.
Ops incl: local bus services
Livery: Black, Silver/Black
Ticket System: Wayfarer 3
A subsidiary of Weaveway Travel

READING & WOKINGHAM COACHES

🚌♿🍴❄

33 MURRAY ROAD, WOKINGHAM RG41 2TA
Tel: 0118 979 3983
Fax: 0118 979 4330
Web site: www.readingandwokinghamcoaches.co.uk
Props: Mark Way, Sharon Way.
Fleet: 15 - 9 single-deck coach, 1 double-deck coach, 2 midicoach, 1 minicoach, 2 minibus.
Chassis: 1 Dennis, 1 Irisbus, 1 LDV, 3 Mercedes, 3 Neoplan, 1 Scania, 1 Setra, 1 Toyota, 3 Volvo.
Bodies: Beulas, Caetano, Irizar, Jonckheere, Mercedes, Neoplan, Plaxton, Setra.
Ops incl: excursions & tours, private hire, school contracts, continental tours.
Livery: White

READING HERITAGE TRAVEL

🚌

PO BOX 147, READING RG1 6PP
Tel: 07850 220151
Transport Man: M J Russell
Fleet: 1 double-deck bus.
Chassis: 1 AEC
Bodies: 1 Park Royal
Ops incl: private hire
Livery: Red/Cream
Ticket System: Almex

READING TRANSPORT LTD

♿🖊

GREAT KNOLLYS STREET, READING RG1 7HH
Tel: 0118 959 4000
Fax: 0118 957 5379
Recovery: 0118 958 7625
E-mail: info@reading-transport.co.uk.

Web site: www.reading-buses.co.uk
Fleet Name: Reading Buses, Newbury Buses
Chairman: David Sutton **Ch Exec Off:** James Freeman **Fin Dir:** Greg Chambers **Perf Dir:** Jaqui Gavaghan **HR Dir:** Caroline Anscombe
Fleet: 132 - 92 double-deck bus, 34 single-deck bus, 6 midibus.
Chassis: 31 Alexander Dennis, 12 Optare, 89 Scania.
Bodies: 31 Alexander Dennis, 41 East Lancs/Darwen, 12 Optare, 26 Scania, 22 Wright.
Ops incl: local bus services.
Livery: colour-branded routes
Ticket System: Ticketer

STEWARTS OF MORTIMER (PRIVATE HIRE) LTD

♿🚌🍴❄

JAMES LANE, GRAZELEY GREEN, READING, RG7 1NE
Tel: 0118 983 1231
Fax: 0118 983 1232
E-mail: quotes@somph.co.uk
Web site: www.somph.co.uk
Man Dir: A Cotton
Fleet: 27 - 8 single-deck coach, 6 single-deck bus, 11 midicoach, 2 minibus.
Chassis: Alexander Dennis, Ford, Irisbus, Mercedes, VDL, Volvo.
Bodies: Alexander Dennis, Ford, Mercedes, Plaxton, Unvi.
Ops incl: private hire, contracts.
Livery: Silver

WEAVAWAY TRAVEL

♿🚌🍴❄❄🔧

169 NEW GREENHAM PARK, THATCHAM RG19 6HN

Tel: 01635 820028
Fax: 01635 821128
E-mail: info@weavaway.co.uk
Web site: www.weavaway.co.uk
Dir: Simon Weaver
Fleet: 28 - 16 single-deck coach, 10 double-deck coach, 2 midicoach.
Chassis: 12 Irisbus, 2 Mercedes, 10 Neoplan, 4 Van Hool.
Bodies: 10 Neoplan, 14 Plaxton, 4 Van Hool.
Ops incl: school contracts, private hire.
Liveries: Black, Blue & Black
See also Newbury & District. Incorporating Abingdon Coaches (Oxfordshire], Countywide Top Travel [Hampshire], and Haywards Coaches.

WHITE BUS SERVICES

🚌❄🔧

NORTH STREET GARAGE, WINKFIELD, WINDSOR SL4 4TP
Tel: 01344 882612
Fax: 01344 886403
E-mail: office@whitebus.co.uk
Web site: www.whitebus.co.uk
Man Dir: Doug Jeatt
Fleet: 15 - 7 single-deck bus, 8 single-deck coach.
Chassis: 2 Alexander Dennis, 3 DAF, 6 Dennis, 2 Optare, 2 Volvo.
Ops incl: local bus services, school contracts, private hire.
Livery: White/grey
Ticket System: Wayfarer 3 & Saver

WINDSORIAN COACHES

Name now owned by London Mini Coaches – see London & Middlesex

ABUS LTD

♿🚌

104 WINCHESTER ROAD, BRISLINGTON, BRISTOL BS4 3NL
Tel: 0117 977 6126 **Fax:** 0117 972 3121
E-mail: alan@abus.co.uk
Web site: www.abus.co.uk
Man Dir: Alan Peters
Fleet: 24 - 19 double-deck bus, 1 single-deck bus, 4 midibus
Chassis: 2 Bristol, 12 DAF, 2 Leyland, 4 Optare, 2 Scania, 2 Volvo.
Bodies: 2 Alexander Dennis, 2 ECW, 3 East Lancs, 2 Northern Counties, 15 Optare.
Ops incl: local bus services
Livery: Cream/White/Maroon
Ticket System: Wayfarer 3

AZTEC COACH TRAVEL

♿❄🚌🔧

6/8 EMERY ROAD, BRISLINGTON BS4 5PF
Tel: 0117 977 0314
Fax: 0117 977 4431
E-mail: myrtletree@holding4337.freeserve.co.uk
Web site: www.azteccoaches.co.uk
Man Dir: Iain Fortune **Fleet Eng:** D Harvey
Ops Man: P Rixon.
Fleet: 15 - 13 midicoach, 2 minibus.
Chassis: 1 Freight Rover, 14 Mercedes.
Bodies: 4 Autobus Classique, 2 Optare, 7 Reeve Burgess.
Ops incl: excursions & tours, private hire, continental tours, school contracts.
Livery: White with diagonal red/orange stripes.

BERKELEY COACH & TRAVEL

🚌♿❄🎫

HAM LANE, PAULTON BS39 7PL
Tel & Fax: 01761 413196
E-mail: mail@berkeleycoachandtravel.co.uk
Web Site: www.berkeleycoachandtravel.co.uk
Proprietor: Mr Tim Pow
Fleet: 5 - 4 single-deck coach, 1 minicoach
Chassis: Mercedes, Volvo.
Bodies: Optare, Van Hool.
Ops incl: school contracts, private hire.
Livery: Silver

BLAGDON LIONESS COACHES LTD

See Somerset

BLUE IRIS COACHES

❄🚌🔧❄🎫

25 CLEVEDON ROAD, NAILSEA BS48 1EH
Tel: 01275 851121
Fax: 01275 856522
E-mail: enquiry@blueiris.co.uk
Web site: www.blueiris.co.uk
Dirs: Philip Hatherall, Tony Spiller
Fleet: 17 - 2 single-deck bus, 9 single-deck coach, 6 midicoach.
Chassis: 2 Optare, 9 Scania, 6 Toyota.
Bodies: 1 Berkhof, 6 Caetano, 6 Irizar, 2 Optare, 2 Van Hool.
Ops incl: local bus services, school contracts, private hire, continental tours.
Livery: 2-tone Blue/White.
Ticket System: Wayfarer

PETER CAROL PRESTIGE COACHING

🚌🍴❄❄🔧

BAMFIELD HOUSE, WHITCHURCH BS14 0XD
Tel: 01275 839839
Fax: 01275 835604
E-mail: bookings@petercarol.co.uk
Web site: www.petercarol.co.uk
Gen Man: Peter Collis
Fleet: 9 - 9 single-deck coach.
Chassis: 1 BMC, 2 Bova, 1 MAN, 5 Mercedes.
Bodies: 1 BMC, 2 Bova, 5 Mercedes, 1 other body.
Ops incl: excursions & tours, private hire.

CITISTAR LTD

Ceased trading as an operator since LRB 2011 went to press

EAGLE COACHES

❄🚌❄🔧

FIRECLAY HOUSE, NETHAM ROAD, ST GEORGE BS5 8HU
Tel: 0117 955 7130
Fax: 0117 941 1107
E-mail: sales@eagle-coaches.co.uk
Web site: www.eagle-coaches.co.uk
Partners: A J Ball, J A Ball
Fleet: 23 - 20 single-deck coach, 1 midicoach, 1 minicoach, 1 minibus.
Chassis: 15 DAF, 1 Iveco, 1 LDV, 1 Mercedes, 1 Temsa, 3 VDL, 1 Volvo.
Ops incl: excursions & tours, continental tours.
Livery: Yellow with Red/Orange

EASTVILLE COACHES LTD

15 ASHGROVE ROAD, REDLAND BS6 6NA
Tel: 0117 300 5550
Fax: 0117 300 5551
Man Dir: T Reece.
Fleet: 9 - 4 double-deck bus, 1 double-deck coach, 4 single-deck coach.
Chassis: 1 Bova, 3 Leyland, 5 Volvo.
Bodies: 2 Alexander, 1 Bova, 1 ECW, 1 Northern Counties, 4 Van Hool.
Ops incl: local bus services, school contracts, private hire, continental tours.
Livery: Myosotis Blue/White.

EUROTAXIS LTD

JORROCKS ESTATE, WESTERLEIGH ROAD, WESTERLEIGH BS37 8QH
Tel: 0871 250 5555 **Fax:** 0871 250 4444
Recovery: 0871 250 5555
E-mail: juan@eurotaxis.com
Web site: www.eurotaxis.com
Fleet Name: Eurocoaches.
Dirs: Juan Sanzo, Keith Sanzo, Anne Sanzo, William Sanzo.
Fleet: 75 – 8 double-deck bus, 2 single-deck bus, 20 single-deck coach, 15 midicoach, 10 minibus, 20 minicoach.
Chassis incl: 30 Mercedes, 25 Volvo.
Bodies incl: 2 Mercedes, 6 Setra, 1 Sunsundegui, 10 UVG, 1 Van Hool.
Ops incl: local bus services, school contracts, private hire, excursions & tours, continental tours.
Livery: White with Blue.
Ticket system: Portable.

FIRST BRISTOL, SOMERSET & AVON

ENTERPRISE HOUSE, EASTON ROAD, BRISTOL BS5 0DZ
Tel: 0117 955 8211
Fax: 0117 955 1248
Web site: www.firstgroup.com
Reg Man Dir: Justin Davies **Reg Finance & Planning Dir:** Amelia Price **Service Delivery Dir:** Tony McNiff **Comm & Business Growth Dir:** Marc Reddy **Reg Eng Standards Dir:** Chris Jones
Fleet: 600 – 214 double-deck bus, 336 single-deck bus, 8 single-deck coach, 9 articulated bus, 21 midibus, 12 minibus.
Chassis: 20 Alexander Dennis, 192 Dennis, 12 Mercedes, 21 Optare, 2 Scania, 1 VDL, 352 Volvo.
Ops incl: local bus services, school contracts.
Livery: FirstGroup UK Bus
Ticket System: Wayfarer

GLENVIC OF BRISTOL LTD

THE OLD COLLIERY, STANTON WICK, PENSFORD BS39 4BZ
Tel: 01761 490116
Fax: 0117 907 7032
Dirs: Paul Holvey, Philip Holvey **Ops Man/Co Sec:** Paul Holvey **Eng:** Nick Reed
Fleet: 13 - 4 double-deck bus, 5 single-deck coach, 4 minicoach.
Chassis: 2 LDV, 7 Leyland, 2 Mercedes, 2 Volvo.

GRAHAM'S COACHES OF BRISTOL

7 WYCK BECK ROAD, BRENTRY BS10 7JD
Tel/Fax: 0117 950 9398

E-mail: wyckbeck@yahoo.co.uk
Props: Graham P Smith, Yvonne M E Smith
Fleet: 6 - 3 double-deck bus, 3 single deck coach.
Chassis: 1 DAF, 3 Leyland, 2 Volvo.
Bodies incl: 1 Jonckheere, 2 Van Hool.
Ops incl: private hire, school contracts.
Livery: White/Red/Maroon

ARNOLD LIDDELL COACHES

89 JERSEY AVENUE, BRISLINGTON BS4 4QX.
Tel: 0117 977 2011
Web site: www.arnoldliddellcoaches.com
Prop: Michael Liddell **Gen Man:** Arnold Liddell
Fleet Eng: Robert Liddell
Fleet: 2 - 1 single-deck coach, 1 midicoach.
Chassis: 1 Leyland, 1 Mercedes.
Ops incl: excursions & tours, school contracts.
Livery: Blue/White.

MARTINS SELF DRIVE MINICOACH HIRE

GRINDELL ROAD GARAGE, 1 GRINDELL ROAD, REDFIELD BS5 9PG
Tel: 0117 955 1042
Fax: 0117 939 3383
Fleet: 12 - 12 minibus.
Chassis: 12 Ford Transit.
Ops incl: Self Drive Minicoach Hire.

MIKE'S TRAVEL

50 CASTLE STREET, THORNBURY BS35 1HB
Tel: 01454 281417
E-mail: info@mikestravel.co.uk
Web site: www.mikestravel.co.uk
Fleet: 12 – 8 single-deck coach, 1 single-deck bus, 3 minibus.
Chassis: DAF, Leyland, MAN, Mercedes
Ops incl: local bus services, school contracts, private hire.

NORTH SOMERSET COACHES

UNIT 3A, COATES ESTATE, SOUTHFIELD ROAD, NAILSEA BS48 1JN
Tel/Fax: 01275 859123
E-mail: sales@northsomersetcoaches.co.uk
Web site: www.northsomersetcoaches.co.uk
Prop: David Fricker
Fleet: 10 – 2 double-deck bus, 4 single-deck bus, 3 single–deck coach, 1 midibus, also heritage vehicles.
Chassis: 1 DAF, 4 Dennis, 1 Mercedes, 4 Volvo.
Bodies: 1 Alexander, 1 Berkhof, 2 East Lancs, 1 Ikarus, 5 Plaxton.
Ops incl: local bus services, school contracts, excursions & tours, private hire.
Livery: Red/Cream/Black
Ticket System: Wayfarer Saver

PREMIER TRAVEL LTD

ALBERT CRESCENT, ST PHILIPS, BRISTOL BS2 0SU
Tel: 0117 9300 5550
Fax: 0117 9300 5551
Man Dir: Glenn Bond
Fleet: 5 - 1 double-deck bus, 2 single-deck coach, 1 double-deck coach, 1 minicoach.
Chassis: 1 Bova, 1 DAF, 1 Freight Rover, 1 Leyland, 1 Volvo.
Bodies: 1 Bova, 1 ECW, 2 Van Hool.

Ops incl: school contracts, continental tours, private hire.
Livery: White/Red with blue lettering.

SOUTH GLOUCESTERSHIRE BUS & COACH COMPANY

THE COACH DEPOT, PEGASUS PARK, GYPSY PATCH LANE, PATCHWAY BS34 6QD
Tel: 0117 931 4340
Fax: 0117 979 9400
E-mail: sgbc@btconnect.com
Web site: www.southgloucestershirebus.co.uk
Man Dir: Roger Durbin
Gen Man: Mike Owen
Workshop Man: Mark Wood **Route Man:** Martyn Edney
Fleet: 73 – 11 double-deck bus, 6 single-deck bus, 48 single-deck coach, 8 minibus.
Chassis: 8 DAF, 8 Leyland, 5 Mercedes, 3 Optare, 11 Scania, 36 Volvo.
Bodies: 6 Alexander, 22 Caetano, 1 ECW, 3 East Lancs, 1 Leyland, 1 Northern Counties, 3 Optare, 14 Plaxton, 17 Van Hool, 1 Wadham Stringer, 4 Other.
Ops incl: local bus service, school contracts, excursions & tours, private hire, continental tours, express.
Livery: Blue/White.
Ticket system: Wayfarer 2

SOMERBUS LTD

See Somerset

TURNERS COACHWAYS (BRISTOL) LTD

59 DAYS ROAD, ST PHILIPS BS2 0QS
Tel: 0117 955 5333
Fax: 0117 955 6948
E-mail: admin@turnerscoachways.co.uk
Web site: www.turners-coachways.co.uk
Man Dir: Tony Turner
Private Hire Man: Liz Venn
Traf Man: Tony Harvey
Fleet: 31 - 30 single-deck coach, 1 minicoach.
Chassis: 7 Scania, 2 Setra, 1 Toyota, 20 Volvo.
Bodies: 2 Berkhof, 7 Irizar, 14 Jonckheere, 1 Optare, 2 Plaxton, 2 Setra, 2 Van Hool.
Ops incl: school contracts, private hire
Livery: Silver/Blue

WESSEX CONNECT

PEGASUS PARK, GYPSY PATCH LANE, PATCHWAY BS34 6QD
Tel: 0117 969 8661 **Fax:** 0117 969 8662
E-mail: info@connectbuses.com, bristol@rotala.co.uk
Web site: www.wessexconnect.com
Fleet Names: Wessex Connect, Ulink.
Man Dir: Simon Dunn **Reg Dir:** Russell Barrington-Crowe
Fleet: 138 – 18 double-deck bus, 62 single-deck bus, 52 midibus, 6 minibus.
Chassis: 17 Alexander Dennis, 61 Dennis, 16 Mercedes, 1 Scania, 4 Transbus, 5 VDL, 34 Volvo.
Bodies: 20 Alexander, 5 Alexander Dennis, 2 East Lancs, 6 Koch, 5 MCV, 77 Plaxton, 1 Scania, 4 Transbus, 18 Wright.
Ops incl: local bus services, Bristol Park and Ride.
Part of Flights Hallmark, a subsidiary of Rotala

The Little Red Book 2012 - in association with Transport Benevolent Fund

ARRIVA THE SHIRES LTD
See MK Metro Ltd, also Arriva The Shires Ltd (Bedfordshire)

BRAZIERS MINI COACHES
17 VICARAGE ROAD, WINSLOW, BUCKINGHAM MK18 3BE
Tel: 01296 712201
E-mail: pbrazier@btconnect.com
Web site: www.brazierscoaches.co.uk
Prop: Peter Brazier
Fleet: 2 minicoach.
Chassis/Bodies: 2 LDV.
Ops incl: private hire, school contracts.

CAROUSEL BUSES
THE BUS GARAGE, LANSDALES ROAD, HIGH WYCOMBE HP11 2PB
Tel: 01494 533436
E-mail: enquiries@carouselbuses.com
Web site: www.carouselbuses.com
Man Dir: Steve Burns **Fin Dir:** John Robinson
Ops Man: Noel Clark **Eng Man:** Mick Cook
Fleet: 55 - 25 double-deck bus, 29 single-deck bus, 1 midibus.
Chassis: 2 AEC, 1 DAF, 8 Dennis, 1 Enterprise, 3 Irisbus, 7 Leyland, 10 MAN, 10 MCW, 3 Mercedes, 2 VDL, 8 Volvo.
Bodies: 5 Alexander Dennis, 1 Alexander, 5 East Lancs, 3 Irisbus, 4 Leyland, 5 Marshall, 5 MCV, 10 MCW, 3 Mercedes, 3 Northern Counties, 2 Park Royal, 6 Plaxton.
Ops incl: local bus services, school contracts.
Livery: Red
Ticket system: Wayfarer 3

CLIFF'S COACHES LTD
UNIT 6, BINDERS INDUSTRIAL ESTATE, CRYERS HILL, HIGH WYCOMBE HP15 6LJ
Tel: 01494 714878 **Fax:** 01494 713491
E-mail: info@cliffscoaches.co.uk
Web site: www.cliffscoaches.co.uk
Dirs: C & J D Neighbour
Fleet: 10 - 4 single-deck coach, 2 midicoach, 4 minibus
Ops incl: excursions & tours, private hire
Livery: Blue/White

DRP TRAVEL
1 THE MEADWAY, LOUGHTON, MILTON KEYNES MK5 8AN
Tel: 01908 394141
E-mail: drptravel@talktalk.net
Web site: www.drptravel.co.uk
Man: D R Pinnock
Fleet: 2 minibus
Chassis: 1 Mercedes, 1 Renault.
Ops incl: school contracts, private hire.
Livery: Blue/White

HOWLETTS COACHES
UNIT 2, STATION ROAD INDUSTRIAL ESTATE, WINSLOW MK18 3DZ
Tel: 01296 713201 **Fax:** 01296 715879
E-mail: info@howlettscoaches.co.uk
Web site: www.howlettscoaches.co.uk
Prop: R S Durham
Fleet: 11 - 4 double-deck bus, 1 double-deck coach, 6 single-deck coach.

Chassis: 1 Bedford, 3 DAF, 1 EOS, 2 Leyland, 2 MCW, 1 Neoplan, 1 Temsa.
Ops incl: private hire, continental tours, school contracts.
Livery: Brown/White.

J & L TRAVEL LTD
MOUNT PLEASANT, TAYLORS LANE, ST LEONARDS, TRING HP23 6LU
Tel: 01296 696046
E-mail: info@jlcoaches.com
Web site: www.jlcoaches.com
Fleet: 11 - 4 double-deck bus, 7 single-deck coach.
Ops incl: excursions & tours, private hire, school contracts
Livery: White with Red lettering

LANGSTON & TASKER
23 QUEEN CATHERINE ROAD, STEEPLE CLAYDON MK18 2PZ
Tel/Fax: 01296 730347
Partners: Mrs J Langston, Mrs M A Fenner
Man: J Langston **Ops Man:** A P Price
Fleet: 16 - 11 single-deck coach, 5 midicoach.
Chassis: 3 Dennis, 2 Leyland, 4 Mercedes, 1 Toyota, 6 Volvo.
Bodies: 2 Caetano, 2 Duple, 9 Plaxton, 1 Transbus, 1 Other.
Ops incl: local bus services, school contracts, private hire.
Livery: White/Red
Ticket system: Wayfarer

MAGPIE TRAVEL LTD
BINDERS INDUSTRIAL ESTATE, CRYERS HILL, HIGH WYCOMBE HP15 6LJ
Tel: 01494 715381
Dirs: David Harris, Martin Ash
Co Sec: Amanda Ash
Fleet: 18 - 3 single-deck bus, 6 single-deck coach, 2 midibus, 4 midicoach, 3 minibus.
Ops incl: local bus services, school contracts, private hire.
Livery: White/Black
Ticket System: Almex

MASONS COACHES
LONG MARSTON AIRFIELD, CHEDDINGTON LANE, LONG MARSTON HP23 4QR
Tel: 01296 661604 **Fax:** 01296 660341
E-mail: info@masonsminicoachhire.co.uk
Web site: www.masonsminicoachhire.co.uk
Fleet: 6 - 5 single-deck coach, 1 midicoach.
Ops incl: excursions & tours, private hire, school contracts, continental tours.

MK METRO LTD
52 COLTS HOLM ROAD, OLD WOLVERTON, MILTON KEYNES MK12 5RN
Tel: 01908 223710
Fax: 01908 223737
Web site: www.arrivabus.co.uk
Reg Man Dir: Heath Williams **Area Man Dir:** Paul Adcock **Comm Dir:** Kevin Hawkins
Fin Dir: Beverley Lawson
Fleet (Milton Keynes): 107 - 1 double-deck bus, 49 single-deck bus, 24 single-deck coach, 33 midibus.
Chassis: 9 Alexander Dennis, 8 DAF, 15 Dennis,

1 Leyland, 5 Mercedes, 33 Optare, 26 Scania, 10 VDL.
Bodies: 9 Alexander Dennis, 22 Caetano, 1 Leyland, 33 Optare, 5 Mercedes, 7 Plaxton, 2 Scania, 2 UVG, 8 Van Hool, 18 Wright.
Ops incl: local bus services, school contracts, express.
Liveries: Arriva UK Bus, National Express, Local Brands.
Ticket System: Wayfarer 3
Part of Arriva The Shires (see Bedfordshire)

MOTTS COACHES (AYLESBURY) LTD
GARSIDE WAY, AYLESBURY HP20 1BH
Tel: 01296 398300 **Fax:** 01296 398386
E-mail: info@mottstravel.com
Web site: www.mottstravel.com
Fleet Name: Motts Travel
Man Dir: M R Mott **Ops Dir:** C J Mott **Eng Dir:** I Scutt **Tours Dir:** C Joel **Traf Man:** S Lane
Fleet: 53 - 6 double-deck bus, 4 single-deck bus, 32 single-deck coach, 2 double-deck coach, 2 midibus, 7 midicoach
Chassis: 4 Leyland, 9 Mercedes, 4 Neoplan, 4 Scania, 32 Volvo.
Bodies: 10 Alexander Dennis, 3 Irizar, 12 Jonckheere, 4 Neoplan, 12 Plaxton, 3 Sitcar, 1 Sunsundegui, 2 Unvi, 6 Other.
Ops incl: local bus services, school contracts, excursions & tours, private hire, continental tours.
Livery: White/Yellow/Green.
Ticket System: Wayfarer.

REDLINE BUSES
8 GATEHOUSE WAY, AYLESBURY HP19 8DB
Tel: 01296 426786 **Fax:** 01296 431013
E-mail: kwk@redlinebuses.com
Web site: www.redlinebuses.com
Prop: Khan Wali
Fleet: 43 - 12 double-deck bus, 16 single-deck bus, 7 single-deck coach, 6 midibus, 2 minibus.
Chassis: 3 Alexander Dennis, 12 Dennis, 1 Enterprise, 5 Leyland, 2 Mercedes, 5 Optare, 1 Transbus, 14 Volvo.
Bodies: 10 Alexander, 3 Alexander Dennis, 1 Caetano, 3 Jonckheere, 1 Leyland, 6 Marshall, 2 Northern Counties, 5 Optare, 10 Plaxton, 1 Transbus, 1 Van Hool, 1 Wright.
Ops incl: local bus services, school contracts, private hire.
Livery: Red.
Ticket System: Wayfarer TGX.

RED ROSE TRAVEL
OXFORD ROAD, DINTON, AYLESBURY HP17 8TT
Tel: 01296 747926 **Fax:** 01296 612196
E-mail: admin@redrosetravel.com
Web site: www.redrosetravel.com
Dir: Taj Khan
Fleet: 26 - 1 double-deck bus, 14 single-deck bus, 11 midibus.
Chassis: 6 Alexander Dennis, 6 Dennis, 6 Mercedes, 5 Optare, 3 Volvo.
Bodies: 3 Alexander, 5 Alexander Dennis, 1 Caetano, 2 East Lancs, 5 Optare, 7 Plaxton, 3 UVG.
Ops incl: local bus services, private hire.
Livery: Red/Yellow
Ticket System: Wayfarer 3.

SOULS COACHES LTD

R24 T

2 STILEBROOK ROAD, OLNEY
MK46 5EA
Tel: 01234 711242
Fax: 01234 240130
Recovery: 07739 097775
E-mail: sales@souls-coaches.co.uk
Web site: www.souls-coaches.co.uk
Man Dir: David Soul
Sales Man: Wendy Cheshire
Traf Man: Neil McCormick
Ops Man: Steve Neale
Workshop Man: Drew Blunt
Fleet: 49 - 5 double-deck bus, 2 single-deck bus,
35 single-deck coach, 3 double-deck coach,
3 midicoach, 1 minibus.
Chassis: 1 Alexander Dennis, 10 Dennis, 1 LDV,
1 Leyland, 2 Mercedes, 1 Neoplan, 5 Setra,
3 Toyota, 1 Transbus, 24 Volvo.
Bodies: 1 Alexander, 1 Alexander Dennis,
3 Caetano, 2 East Lancs, 7 Jonckheere, 1 LDV,
2 Mercedes, 1 Neoplan, 1 Optare, 21 Plaxton,
5 Setra, 1 Transbus, 3 Other.
Ops incl: local bus services, school contracts,
excursions & tours, private hire, continental tours.
Livery: Red/Gold
Ticket System: Wayfarer.
Souls also own Barfordian Coaches (see
Bedfordshire) and Nightingales of Beccles Ltd
(see Suffolk)

STAR TRAVEL

19 KINGS ROAD, AYLESBURY
HP21 7RR
Tel: 01296 715786
Fleet: 8 – 6 midibus, 2 minibus.
Chassis: 2 Dennis, 3 Mercedes, 3 Optare.
Ops incl: local bus services.
Liveries: Blue/White, Route Brands.

THREE STAR COACHES.COM

UNIT 1, GUARDIAN BUSINESS PARK,
DALLOW ROAD, LUTON LU1 1NA
Tel: 01582 722626
Fax: 01582 484034
E-mail: sales@threestarcoaches.com
Web Site: www.threestarcoaches.com
Man Dir: Colin Dudley,
Ops Man: Kevin Green
Ch Eng: Michael Nallaby
Co Sec: Isabelle Dudley
Fleet: 14 – 1 single-deck bus, 7 single-deck coach,
2 double-deck coach, 4 midicoach.
Chassis: 2 Ayats, 3 Dennis, 6 Mercedes, 1 Optare,
1 Scania, 1 Volvo.
Bodies: 2 Ayats, 4 Berkhof, 1 Mercedes,
1 Optare, 4 Plaxton, 2 Other.
Ops incl: school contracts, excursions & tours,
private hire.
Livery: Blue

VALE TRAVEL

T

61 FLEET STREET, AYLESBURY
HP20 2PA
Tel: 01296 484348
Fax: 01296 435309
E-mail: vale_travel@yahoo.co.uk
Web site: www.valetravel.org.uk
Prop: Wazir Zaman
Fleet: 17 – 4 single-deck bus, 5 single-deck coach,
6 midibus, 1 midicoach, 1 minibus.
Chassis: 5 Dennis, 1 LDV, 3 Mercedes, 3 Optare,
1 Toyota, 4 Volvo.
Bodies: 2 Alexander, 1 Caetano, 3 East Lancs,
1 Jonckheere, 1 LDV, 1 Northern Counties,
3 Optare, 2 Plaxton, 2 Van Hool, 1 Other.
Ops Inc: local bus services, school contracts,
private hire.
Livery: Multi
Ticket System: Wayfarer

WOOTTENS

THE COACH DEPOT, LYCROME ROAD,
LYE GREEN, CHESHAM HP5 3LG
Tel: 01494 774411
Fax: 01494 784597
E-mail: info@woottens.co.uk
Web sites: www.woottens.co.uk,
www.tigerlinebuses.com
Man Dir: M J Wootten
Dirs: A H Moseley,
R Graham, M Stones, S Beech.
Fleet Names: Woottens (coaches), Tiger Line
(buses)
Fleet: 26 - 3 double-deck bus, 8 single-deck bus,
15 single-deck coach.

Chassis: 12 Leyland, 14 Volvo.
Bodies: 2 Alexander, 1 Berkhof, 1 ECW,
6 East Lancs, 1 Leyland, 14 Plaxton,
1 Willowbrook.
Ops incl: local bus services, excursions and
tours, continental tours, private hire, school
contracts.
Livery: White with coloured swirls.
Ticket System: Wayfarer.
Part of the Bowen Travel Group – see
Staffordshire

Z & S INTERNATIONAL

AYLESBURY BUSINESS CENTRE,
CHAMBERLAIN ROAD, AYLESBURY
HP19 8DY
Tel/Fax: 01296 415468
E-mail: info@zands.co.uk
Web site: www.zands.co.uk
Prop: Umar Zaman
Fleet: 31 - 7 double-deck bus, 1 double-deck
coach, 8 single-deck bus, 5 single-deck coach,
8 midibus, 2 midicoach.
Chassis: 1 Alexander Dennis, 5 Dennis,
6 Leyland, 5 Mercedes, 5 Optare, 2 Scania,
1 VDL, 6 Volvo.
Bodies: 2 Alexander, 1 Alexander Dennis,
2 Jonckheere, 5 Leyland, 5 Marshall, 1
Northern Counties, 6 Optare, 4 Plaxton,
1 Sitcar, 1 Sunsundegui, 3 Van Hool.
Ops incl: local bus services, school contracts,
excursions & tours, private hire.

♿	Vehicle suitable for disabled	🔗	Seat belt-fitted Vehicle
T	Toilet-drop facilities available	🍴	Coach(es) with galley facilities
R	Recovery service available	❄	Air-conditioned vehicle(s)
🚌	Open top vehicle(s)	👥	Coaches with toilet facilities

R24	24 hour recovery service
✎	Replacement vehicle available
🚌	Vintage Coach(es) available
🍃	Hybrid Buses

AARDVARK & FIRST CHOICE COACHES

GOODMANS BUSINESS PARK, THIRD DROVE, FENGATE, PETERBOROUGH PE1 5QR
Tel: 01733 561222 **Fax:** 01733 349268
E-mail: aardvarkcoaches@aol.com
Web site: www.aardvarkcoaches.webeden.co.uk
Ops incl: school contracts, private hire, excursions & tours.
Livery: White.

ANDREWS COACHES

20 CAMBRIDGE ROAD, FOXTON CB22 6SH
Tel: 0844 357 0602
Fax: 0844 357 6992
E-mail: andrewscoaches@aol.com
Web site: www.andrewscoaches.co.uk
Man Dir: F Miller **Dir:** J Miller
Ops Sup: A Miller
Fleet: 7 single-deck coach
Chassis: 4 Dennis, 1 Scania, 2 Volvo.
Bodies: 1 Berkhof, 3 Duple, 1 Jonckheere, 1 Plaxton, 1 Van Hool.
Ops incl: school contracts, excursions & tours, private hire, continental tours.
Livery: White

BURTONS COACHES

Ceased trading since LRB 2011 went to press. Bus operations acquired by Stephensons of Essex (see Essex).

C & G COACHES

HONEYSOME LODGE, HONEYSOME ROAD, CHATTERIS PE16 6SB
Tel: 01354 692200
Fax: 01354 694433
Recovery: 07771 962105
E-mail: info@candgcoaches.co.uk
Web site: www.candgcoaches.co.uk
Partners: Mrs C Day, G Ellwood, R Day
Ops Man: C Smith
Fleet: 24 - 1 double-deck bus, 23 single-deck coach.
Chassis: 3 Bedford, 1 Bova, 2 Leyland, 1 MCW, 1 Neoplan, 11 Scania, 5 Volvo.
Bodies: 2 Berkhof, 1 Bova, 2 Duple, 1 ECW, 8 Irizar, 1 MCW, 1 Neoplan, 8 Plaxton, 1 Van Hool.
Ops incl: school contracts, excursions & tours, private hire, continental tours.
Livery: White/Red/Yellow

COLLINS COACHES

UNIT 4, CAMBRIDGE ROAD INDUSTRIAL ESTATE, MILTON, CAMBRIDGE CB4 6AZ
Tel: 01223 658309
Fax: 01223 424739
E-mail: collinscoaches@btconnect.com
Web site: www.collinscoaches-cambridge.co.uk
Partners: C R Collins, R T Collins
Off Man: Jacky Liptrot
Garage Man: R D Curtis
Fleet: 19 3 single-deck coach, 3 midicoach, 13 minibus.
Chassis: 1 Bedford, 2 Dennis, 5 Ford Transit, 2 Freight Rover, 4 Iveco, 2 LDV.
Ops incl: excursions & tours, school contracts, private hire.
Livery: White/Orange

DECKER BUS

70-72 AARON ROAD INDUSTRIAL ESTATE, WHITTLESEY PE7 2EX
Tel: 01733 351694 **Fax:** 01733 359438
Recovery: 07521 194734
E-mail: anthea@deckerbus.co.uk
Web site: www.deckerbus.co.uk
Prop: Anthea Head
Fleet: 16 – 7 double-deck bus, 3 single-deck bus, 3 single-deck coach, 2 open top bus, 1 minicoach.
Chassis incl: 2 Bova, 1 Dennis, 2 Leyland, 2 Scania, 3 Volvo.
Bodies incl: 2 Bova, 1 Caetano, 1 Ikarus.
Ops incl: school contracts, excursions & tours, private hire, express.
Livery: Various Colours

RON W DEW & SONS LTD

CHATTERIS ROAD, SOMERSHAM PE28 3DN
Tel: 01487 740241 **Fax:** 01487 740341
E-mail: sales@dews-coaches.com
Web site: www.dews-coaches.com
Man Dir: Simon Dew **Ops Dir:** Jim Darr
Maintenance Man: Tom Williams
Fleet incl: double-deck bus, single-deck bus, single-deck coach, midibus, heritage vehicles.
Chassis: Bedford, Iveco, Leyland, Mercedes, Optare, Scania, Setra, Volvo.
Bodies: Alexander, Beulas, Duple, East Lancs, Irizar, Jonckheere, Marshall, Mercedes, Optare, Plaxton, Van Hool.
Ops incl: local bus services, excursions & tours, private hire, continental tours, school contracts.
Livery: Green/Grey.

EMBLINGS COACHES

BRIDGE GARAGE, GUYHIRN, WISBECH PE13 4ED
Tel: 01945 450253 **Fax:** 01945 450770
E-mail: john@emblings.co.uk
Man Dir: John Embling
Fleet incl: double-deck bus, single-deck bus, single-deck coach.
Ops incl: local bus services, school contracts, private hire.

FENN HOLIDAYS

WHITTLESEY ROAD, MARCH PE15 0AG
Tel: 01354 653329
Fax: 01354 650647
E-mail: info@fennholidays.co.uk
Web site: www.fennholidays.co.uk
Man Dir: Peter Fenn **Dir:** Margaret Fenn
Fleet: 3 single-deck coach, 1 minibus.
Chassis: 1 Bova, 1 Mercedes, 2 Van Hool.
Bodies: 1 Bova, 2 Van Hool, 1 Other.
Ops incl: excursions & tours, private hire, continental tours
Livery: Multicoloured
Ticket System: Setright.

FREEDOM TRAVEL COACHES (UK) LTD

UNIT 21, THE DOCK, ELY CB7 4GS
Tel: 01353 614451
E-mail: info@freedomtravelcoaches.co.uk
Web site: www.freedomtravelcoaches.co.uk
Dirs: D R Evans, S P Evans
Ops incl: local bus services, school contracts, private hire.
Livery: White.

GRETTON'S COACHES

ARNWOOD CENTRE, NEWARK ROAD, PETERBOROUGH PE1 5YH
Tel: 01733 311008
Fax: 01733 319859
Prop: Roger Gretton
Fleet: 15 - 12 single-deck coach, 3 midicoach.
Chassis: 1 Bedford, 2 Mercedes, 12 Scania.
Bodies: 10 Plaxton, 5 Van Hool.
Ops incl: school contracts, excursions & tours, private hire.
Livery: Silver/Red/Maroon

GREYS OF ELY

41 COMMON ROAD, WITCHFORD, ELY CB6 2HY
Tel: 01353 662300
Fax: 01353 662412
E-mail: sales@greysofely.co.uk
Web site: www.greysofely.co.uk
Man Dir: R Grey
Ops Man: C Covill
Fleet: 25 – 5 double deck bus, 3 single-deck bus, 13 single-deck coach, 2 midicoach.
Chassis: 3 Alexander Dennis, 1 DAF, 8 Dennis, 3 Leyland, 2 Mercedes, 1 Transbus, 1 Van Hool, 6 Volvo.
Bodies: 1 Alexander, 1 Caetano, 3 Duple, 1 ECW, 3 Jonckheere, 2 Optare, 10 Plaxton, 1 Sunsundegui, 2 Transbus, 1 Van Hool.
Ops incl: school contracts, excursions & tours, private hire.
Liveries: Cream/Green, Silver Grey.

IMPRESSION HOLIDAYS & EXCURSIONS LTD
(formerly PETERBOROUGH TRAVEL CONSULTANTS)

71 LEDBURY ROAD, PETERBOROUGH PE3 9RF
Tel: 01733 267025
Fax: 01733 267025
E-mail: enquiries@impressionholidays.com
Web site: www.impressionholidays.com
Prop: Mrs P C Greeves
Fleet: 3 - 2 single-deck coach, 1 minicoach.
Chassis: 1 Mercedes, 2 Setra.
Ops incl: excursions & tours, school contracts, private hire, continental tours.
Livery: Blue/White/Red

JANS COACHES

23 TOWNSEND, SOHAM CB7 5DD
Tel: 01353 721344
Fax: 01353 721341
E-mail: janscoaches@aol.com
Dirs: Roland Edwards, Janet Edwards, Stuart Edwards
Fleet: 8 - 3 double-deck bus, 3 single-deck coach, 1 double-deck coach, 1 minicoach.
Chassis: 1 Dennis, 1 Iveco, 1 Leyland, 2 MAN, 2 MCW, 1 Neoplan.
Bodies: 1 Berkhof, 1 Indcar, 2 MCW, 3 Neoplan, 1 Northern Counties.
Ops incl: excursions & tours, private hire, continental tours, school contracts.
Livery: White.

Cambridgeshire, City of Peterborough

KIDDLES COACHES LTD

THE OLD SIDINGS, NEEDINGWORTH ROAD,
ST IVES PE27 4NB
Tel: 01480 462330 **Fax:** 01487 462338
E-mail: kiddlescoaches@btconnect.com
Web site: www.kiddlescoaches.com
Dirs: R Willmore, J Willmore.
Ops incl: school contracts, private hire,
continental tours.
Livery: White.

MIL-KEN TRAVEL LTD

11 LYNN ROAD, LITTLEPORT, ELY CB6 1QG
Tel: 01353 860705 **Fax:** 01353 863222
E-mail: milken@btconnect.com
Web-site: www.milkentravel.com
Man Dir: Jason Miller **Ops Man:** Jon Miller
Fleet Eng: Ian Martin
Fleet: 33 - 30 single-deck coach, 1 minibus,
2 minicoach.
Chassis: 1 LDV, 2 Mercedes, 30 Volvo.
Bodies: 2 Jonckheere, 1 LDV, 22 Plaxton,
1 Sitcar, 1 Unvi, 3 Van Hool, 3 Volvo.
Ops incl: school contracts, private hire.
Livery: White with Red, Blue, Yellow.

C G MYALL & SON

CHERRY TREE HOUSE, THE CAUSEWAY,
BASSINGBOURN, ROYSTON SG8 5JA
Tel: 01763 243225
Ops incl: local bus services, school contracts,
private hire.
Livery: White

NEAL'S TRAVEL LTD

102 BECK ROAD, ISLEHAM, ELY CB7 5QP
Tel: 01638 780066 **Fax:** 01638 780011
E-mail: sales@nealstravel.com
Web site: www.nealstravel.com
Dirs: Bridget Paterson, Graham Neal,
Lionel Neal, Nancy Neal
Fleet: 16 – 9 single-deck coach, 1 midibus,
4 midicoach, 2 minibus.
Chassis: 9 Mercedes, 7 Volvo.
Bodies: 2 Autobus, 5 Jonckheere, 2 Mercedes,
1 Plaxton, 2 Sunsundegui, 4 Other.
Ops incl: local bus services, school contracts,
private hire.
Livery: White/Blue, Silver/Blue
Ticket system: Wayfarer

D A PAYNE COACH HIRE

STATION LANE, OFFORD CLUNY,
ST NEOTS PE19 5ZA
Tel: 01480 811777 **Fax:** 01480 811799
E-mail: paul@dapaynecoachehire.co.uk
Web site: www.dapaynecoachhire.co.uk
Partners: Mr David Payne, Mrs Sara Hart,
Mr Paul Hart
Fleet: 11 – 3 double-deck bus, 1 single-deck
bus, 3 single-deck coach, 1 midibus, 1 midicoach,
2 minibus.
Ops incl: school contracts, excursions & tours,
private hire, continental tours.

RICHMOND'S COACHES

THE GARAGE, HIGH STREET, BARLEY,
ROYSTON SG8 8JA
Tel: 01763 848226
Fax: 01763 848105

E-mail: postbox@richmonds-coaches.co.uk
Web site: www.richmonds-coaches.co.uk
Dirs: David Richmond, Michael Richmond,
Andrew Richmond
Sales & Marketing Man: Rick Ellis
Asst Ops Man: Craig Ellis
Ch Eng: Patrick Granville
Exc & Tours Man: Natalie Richmond
Fleet: 25 – 12 single-deck coach, 2 double-deck
coach, 4 midicoach, 5 minibus, 2 minicoach.
Chassis: Bova, DAF, Mercedes, Optare, Van Hool,
VDL, Volvo.
Bodies: Bova, Optare, Plaxton, Sitcar, Van Hool.
Ops incl: local bus services, school contracts,
excursions & tours, private hire, continental tours.
Livery: Cream/Brown
Ticket System: Wayfarer 3

ROBINSON KIMBOLTON

19 THRAPSTON ROAD, KIMBOLTON,
HUNTINGDON PE28 0HW
Tel: 01480 860581 **Fax:** 01480 860801
E-mail: coaches@robinsonkimbolton.co.uk
Web site: www.robinsonkimbolton.co.uk
Man Dir: Charles Robinson
Fleet: 11 - 9 single-deck coach, 2 minibus
Chassis: 2 Mercedes, 1 Scania, 8 Volvo.
Bodies: 2 Mercedes, 9 Van Hool.
Ops incl: school contracts, excursions & tours,
private hire.
Livery: Cream/Red/Brown

SAFFORD'S COACHES LTD

HIGHBURY FIELDS, ELTISLEY ROAD,
GREAT GRANSDEN, SANDY SG19 3AR
Tel: 01767 677395 **Fax:** 01767 677742
E-mail: saffordcoaches@btconnect.com
Web site: www.saffordscoaches.co.uk
Dirs: Miss T Gillett, Mrs S I Gillett
Ch Eng Mr C Chapman.
Fleet: 13 - 1 single-deck bus, 8 single-deck coach,
1 midibus, 1 midicoach, 2 minibus.
Chassis: 1 Bova, 1 Ford Transit, 1 Irisbus,
2 Mercedes, 8 Volvo.
Bodies: 1 Alexander Dennis, 1 Berkhof, 1 Bova,
2 Jonckheere, 1 Mellor, 3 Plaxton, 1 Sitcar,
1 Van Hool, 2 Other.
Ops incl: school contracts, excursions & tours,
private hire, continental tours.
Livery: White/Blue/Yellow

E SHAW & SON

49 HIGH STREET, MAXEY,
PETERBOROUGH PE6 9EF
Tel: 01778 342224
Fax: 01778 380378
E-mail: enquiries@shawscoaches.co.uk
Web site: www.shawscoaches.co.uk
Fleet Name: Shaws of Maxey
Partners: Jane Duffellen, Richard Shaw,
Christopher Shaw
Fleet: 20 - 1 single-deck bus, 16 single-deck
coach, 3 midicoach.
Chassis: 2 Bova, 1 DAF, 1 Dennis,
2 Mercedes, 1 Optare, 1 Toyota,
12 Volvo.
Bodies: 1 Autobus, 1 Berkhof, 1 Beulas, 2 Bova,
4 Jonckheere, 1 Optare, 8 Plaxton, 1 Sitcar,
1 Other.
Ops incl: local bus services, school contracts,
excursions & tours, private hire, continental tours.
Livery: Blue/White

STAGECOACH EAST

100 COWLEY ROAD, CAMBRIDGE CB4 0DN
Tel: 01223 433250 **Fax:** 01223 433275
E-mail:
cambridge.enquiries@stagecoachbus.com
Web site: www.stagecoachbus.com
Fleet Names: Stagecoach in Cambridge,
Stagecoach in the Fens, Stagecoach in
Peterborough
Man Dir: Andy Campbell **Comm Dir:** Philip
Norwell **Eng Dir:** Bob Dennison
Fleet (Cambs): 275 - 149 double-deck bus,
105 single-deck bus, 7 single-deck coach,
8 midibus, 6 open-top bus.
Ops incl: local bus services, park & ride, city
sightseeing, express.
Livery: Stagecoach UK Bus, National Express.
Ticket system: Wayfarer 3
Part of Stagecoach East (with Stagecoach in
Bedford)

SUN FUN INTERNATIONAL

SUN FUN HOUSE, MEADOW DROVE,
EARITH PE28 3SA
Tel: 01487 843333 **Fax:** 01487 843285
E-mail: sales@sunfunholidays.co.uk
Web site: www.sunfuninternational.com
Ops incl: excursions & tours, private hire,
continental tours.

TOWLERS COACHES LTD

CHURCH ROAD, EMNETH, WISBECH
PE14 8AA
Tel: 01945 583645 **Fax:** 01945 583645
E-mail: towlerscoaches@btconnect.com
Dirs: Mark Towler, Wendy Shepherd,
Anton Towler, Joanne Walton
Fleet: 9 - 4 double-deck bus, 5 single-deck coach.
Chassis: 1 Iveco, 4 Leyland, 2 Scania, 2 Volvo.
Bodies incl: 1 Beulas, 2 Berkhof, 4 Northern
Counties, 1 Van Hool.
Ops incl: school contracts, excursions & tours,
private hire.
Livery: White

UPWELL & DISTRICT COACHES

THE COACH DEPOT, SCHOOL ROAD,
UPWELL PE14 9EW
Tel & Fax: 01945 773461
Partners: Caroline Parsons, William Hircock.
Fleet: 2 single-deck coach, 1 midicoach.
Chassis: 1 Alexander Dennis, 1 Mercedes,
1 Scania.
Ops incl: excursions & tours, private hire, school
contracts.
Livery: Red/White/Blue.

VEAZEY COACHES LTD

WINWICK GARAGE, HAMERTON ROAD,
HUNTINGDON PE28 5PX
Tel: 01832 293263 **Fax:** 01832 293142

VICEROY OF ESSEX LTD See Essex

WEBB'S

ST PETER'S FARM, MIDDLE DROVE PE14 8JJ
Tel: 01945 430123
E-mail: webb-s-cant@fsbdial.co.uk
Prop: Barry Webb
Fleet: 3 - 1 midicoach, 1 minicoach, 1 minibus.

WHIPPET COACHES LTD

UNIT 1 & 2, ROWLES WAY, BUCKINGWAY
BUSINESS PARK, SWAVESEY
CB24 4UG
Tel: 01954 230011
Web site: www.go-whippet.co.uk
Dirs: J T Lee, P H Lee, M H Lee.
Fleet: double-deck bus, single-deck bus,
single-deck coach, midibus, minibus.
Chassis: Dennis, Leyland, Scania, Volvo.
Bodies: Alexander, Duple, East Lancs, Leyland,
Northern Counties, Plaxton, Van Hool.
Ops incl: local bus service, school contracts,
excursions & tours, private hire, express.
Livery: Blue/Cream with logo.
Ticket System: Almex Eurofare.

W & M TRAVEL

211 MAIN ROAD, CHURCH END,
PARSON DROVE, WISBECH PE13 4LF
Tel: 01945 700492
Fax: 01945 700964
E-mail: bill@norman.wanadoo.co.uk
Dir: W Norman
Fleet: 6 single-deck coach.
Chassis: 5 Dennis, 1 Scania.
Ops incl: local bus services, school contracts,
excursions & tours, private hire

ANGEL TRAVEL

108 GORSEY LANE, WARRINGTON WA2 7RY
Tel: 07930 526132 **Fax:** 01925 445591
E-mail: angeltravelwarrington@yahoo.co.uk
Web site: www.angeltravelwarrington.com
Dir: Richard Keane
Fleet: 3 minibus.
Chassis: Ford, LDV.
Ops incl: school contracts, private hire,
excursions & tours.
Livery: Blue/White

ANTHONYS TRAVEL

8 CORMORANT DRIVE, RUNCORN WA7 4UD
Tel: 01928 561460 **Fax:** 01928 561460
Emergency: 07920 154240
E-mail: enquiries@anthonystravel.co.uk
Web site: www.anthonys-travel.co.uk
Partners: Richard Bamber, Anthony Bamber,
Anne Bamber **Ops Man:** Jodie Waring
Ch Eng: Stephen Knight
Fleet: 16 – 2 single-deck bus, 10 single-deck
coach, 4 minicoach.
Chassis: 2 LDV, 3 MAN, 9 Mercedes, 2 Scania.
Bodies: 1 Berkhof, 1 Irizar, 2 LDV, 4 Mercedes,
5 Neoplan, 2 Optare, 1 Setra.
Ops incl: local bus services, school contracts,
private hire, excursion & tours.
Livery: multi coloured
Ticket system: Wayfarer

ARRIVA NORTH WEST & WALES

Runcorn, Winsford operations – see Arriva
Manchester (Greater Manchester)
Chester operations – see Arriva Buses Wales
(Conwy)

ARROWEBROOK COACHES LTD

THE OLD COACH YARD, WERVIN ROAD,
CROUGHTON CH2 4DA
Tel: 01244 382444 **Fax:** 01244 379777
Dirs: A G Parsons, P A Parsons
Ops Incl: local bus services, school contracts,
private hire.
Livery: White/Green.

BARRATT'S COACHES LTD

UNIT 15, MILLBANK WAY, SPRINGVALE
INDUSTRIAL ESTATE, ELWORTH CW11 3GQ
Tel: 08450 625096 **Fax:** 08450 627728
E-mail: barrattscoaches@aol.com
Man Dir: Gillian Barratt
Fleet: 12 – 10 single-deck coaches, 1 double-
deck coach, 1 midicoach.
Chassis: 1 Dennis, 1 Mercedes, 1 Neoplan,
Volvo.
Bodies: 1 Alexander Dennis, 1 Jonckheere,
1 Mercedes, 1 Neoplan, 4 Plaxton, 4 Van Hool.
Ops incl: local bus services, school contracts,
excursions & tours, private hire.
Livery: White.

BOSTOCK'S COACHES

SPRAGG STREET GARAGE, CONGLETON
CW12 1QH
Tel: 01260 273108 **Fax:** 01260 276338
E-mail: bostocks@holmeswood.uk.com
Web site: www.holmeswood.uk.com
Dirs: J F Aspinall, M Aspinall, C H Aspinall, D E

Aspinall, M F Aspinall, M J Forshaw
Ops Man: M E Bostock **Tours Man:**
J Bostock-Gibson **Ch Eng:** M Boniface
Fleet: see Holmeswood Coaches
Ops incl: local bus services, excursions & tours,
private hire, continental tours, school contracts.
Livery: Green
(Subsidiary of Holmeswood Coaches, Lancashire)

CARVERS COACHES

UNIT 10, INDIGO BUSINESS PARK, INDIGO
ROAD, ELLESMERE PORT CH65 4AJ
Tel: 0151 355 8888 **Fax:** 0151 356 0220
Web site: www.carverscoaches.co.uk
Prop: M Carver
Fleet: 13 - 4 double-deck bus, 1 double-deck
coach, 8 single-deck coach.
Ops incl: school contracts, private hire
Livery: White/Red

D & G BUS

26 THE MEADOWS, KINGSTONE,
UTTOXETER ST14 8QE
Tel: 01270 252970 **Fax:** 01889 562756
E-mail: info@dgbus.co.uk
Web site: www.dgbus.co.uk
Man Dir: D Reeves
Fleet: 30 – 12 single-deck bus, 18 midibus.
Chassis: 4 DAF, 7 Dennis, 18 Optare, 1 Volvo.
Bodies: 2 East Lancs, 2 Marshall, 18 Optare,
3 Plaxton, 4 Wright.
Ops incl: local bus services, school contracts.
Livery: Cream/Blue
Ticket System: Wayfarer

DOBSON'S BUSES LTD

WINCHAM PARK, CHAPEL STREET,
WINCHAM, NORTHWICH CW9 6DA
Tel/Fax: 01606 350200
Man Dir: Ian Dobson **Ch Eng:** Paul Dobson
Office Man: Richard Dobson
Fleet: 13 - 7 double-deck bus, 1 single-deck bus,
1 single-deck coach, 2 midibus, 2 midicoach.
Chassis: 4 Dennis, 1 Iveco, 4 Leyland, 1 MCW,
3 Mercedes.
Ops incl: school contracts, private hire.
Livery: Red/Cream

FIRST IN CHESTER & THE WIRRAL

669 NEW CHESTER ROAD, ROCK FERRY
CH42 1PZ
Tel: 0151 645 8661
See First Manchester. Includes former Chester
City Transport

JOHN FLANAGAN COACH TRAVEL

See Walkers & Flanagan's Coaches (Cheshire)

GOLDEN GREEN TRAVEL

COWBROOK LANE, GAWSWORTH,
MACCLESFIELD SK11 0JH
Tel: 01298 83583
E-mail: sales@goldengreentravel.co.uk
Web site: www.goldengreentravel.co.uk
Partners: John Worth, Gill Worth,
Derek J Lownds
Fleet: 11 single-deck coaches
Chassis and Bodies: Mercedes
Ops incl: local bus services, school contracts,
excursions & tours, private hire

HALTON BOROUGH TRANSPORT LTD

MOOR LANE, WIDNES WA8 7AF
Tel: 0151 423 3333 **Fax:** 0151 424 2362
E-mail: enquiries@haltontransport.co.uk
Web site: www.haltontransport.co.uk
Fleet Name: Halton Transport
Man Dir: Chris Adams **Eng Man:** Phil Matthews
Traf Man: David Steadman **Fin Man:** Adele
Cookson
Fleet: 63 - 62 single-deck bus, 1 midibus.
Chassis: 20 Alexander Dennis, 36 Dennis,
7 Transbus.
Bodies: 4 Alexander Dennis, 21 East Lancs,
26 Marshall, 12 MCV.
Ops incl: local bus services.
Livery: Red/Cream.
Ticket System: Wayfarer III

HULME HALL COACHES LTD

1 STANLEY ROAD, CHEADLE HULME SK8 6PL
Tel: 0161 486 1187
Fax: 0161 482 8125
E-mail: hulmehallcoaches@talk21.com
Gen Man: Philip Keogh **Traf Man:** Ian Johnson
Fleet Eng: Philip Henshall
Fleet: 15 - 4 double-deck bus, 8 single-deck bus,
3 single-deck coach.
Chassis: 4 Leyland, 11 Volvo.
Bodies: 6 Alexander, 3 ECW, 1 Northern
Counties, 5 Plaxton.
Ops incl: school contracts, private hire.
Livery: Red/Cream
Ticket System: Wayfarer 2

LAMBS

BUXTON STREET, HAZEL GROVE,
STOCKPORT SK7 4BB
Tel: 0161 456 1515 **Fax:** 0161 483 5011
E-mail: lambs139@aol.com
Web site: www.lambscoaches.net
Dirs: Geoffrey Lamb, Graham Lamb,
Mrs Christine Lamb.
Fleet: 6 single-deck coach, 1 midicoach.
Chassis: 3 DAF, 2 Mercedes, 1 Scania, 1 Volvo.
Bodies: 1 Plaxton, 1 Setra, 5 Van Hool.
Ops incl: private hire, school contracts.
Livery: White/Blue

LE-RAD COACHES & LIMOUSINES

R24
328 HYDE ROAD, WOODLEY SK6 1PF
Tel: 0161 430 2032
Recovery: 07703 145500
Prop: Derek & Jean Mycock
E-mail: le.radtravel@yahoo.co.uk
Fleet: 2 - 1 single-deck coach, 1 minicoach.
Chassis: 1 Ford, 1 LDV.
Ops incl: excursions & tours, private hire.

ROY McCARTHY COACHES

THE COACH DEPOT, SNAPE ROAD,
MACCLESFIELD SK10 2NZ
Tel: 01625 425060
Fax: 01625 619853
E-mail: sales@roymccarthycoaches.co.uk
Web site: www.roymccarthycoaches.co.uk
Senior Partner: Andy McCarthy
Fleet: 11 single-deck coach.
Chassis: 2 Alexander Dennis, 1 Bedford, 2
Dennis, 7 Volvo.
Bodies: 1 Berkhof, 10 Plaxton.

Ops incl: school contracts, excursions & tours,
private hire, continental tours.
Livery: Blue/Cream

MARPLE MINI COACHES

5 GROSVENOR ROAD, MARPLE SK6 6PR.
Tel: 0161 881 9111
Owner: G W Cross
Fleet: 2 minicoach
Chassis: Ford Transit, LDV.
Ops incl: school contracts, private hire.
Livery: White/Gold.

MAYNE COACHES LTD

MARSH HOUSE LANE, WARRINGTON
WA1 7ET
Tel: 01925 445588
Fax: 01925 232300
E-mail: coaches@mayne.co.uk
Web site: www.mayne.co.uk
Dirs: S B Mayne **(Chairman & Man Dir)**,
D Mayne **(Co Sec)**, C S Mayne, S L Mayne
Gen Man: R W Vernon **Sales Man:** A J Dykes,
D Williams **Eng Dir:** C F Pannel
Eng Man: E Sutcliffe **Traffic Man:** J Drake
Fleet: 42 - 4 double-deck bus, 38 single-deck
coach.
Chassis: 2 Alexander Dennis, 2 Dennis, 4 Bova,
1 Leyland, 26 Scania, 7 Volvo.
Bodies: 4 Bova, 4 East Lancs, 19 Irizar, 10 Plaxton,
3 Scania, 2 UVG.
Ops incl: local bus services, school contracts,
excursions & tours, private hire.
Livery: Cream/Red

MEREDITHS COACHES LTD

LYDGATE, WELL STREET, MALPAS SK14 8DE
Tel: 01948 860405
Fax: 01948 860162
E-mail: info@meredithscoaches.co.uk
Web site: www.meredithscoaches.co.uk
Dirs: J K Meredith, Mrs M E Meredith,
D J Meredith **Co Sec:** Mrs Kirin Meredith
Ch Eng: C Bellis
Fleet: 18 single-deck coach
Chassis: Leyland, Scania, Volvo.
Bodies: Irizar, Jonckheere, Plaxton.
Ops incl: local bus services, school contracts,
private hire.
Livery: Cream with Red/Yellow

MILLMANS COACHES

STATION YARD, GREEN LANE, PADGATE,
WARRINGTON WA1 4JR
Tel: 01925 822298
Fax: 01925 813181
Prop: Eric Millman
Fleet: 6 single-deck coach
Chassis: 1 DAF, 5 Leyland.
Bodies: 6 Plaxton
Ops incl: local bus services, school contracts,
excursions & tours, private hire.
Livery: Blue/White

MOORE'S COACHES LTD

6 HEREFORD WAY, MIDDLEWICH CW10 9GS
Tel/Fax: 01606 836733
Dirs: Carol Moore, Jose Perez-Garcia.
E-mail: moorestravel@aol.com
Web site: www.moorescoaches.co.uk
Fleet: 3 single-deck coach.

Chassis: 3 Volvo.
Bodies: 1 Berkhof, 1 Jonckheere, 1 Van Hool.
Ops incl: school contracts, private hire.
Livery: White.

SELWYNS TRAVEL SERVICES

R24
CAVENDISH FARM ROAD, WESTON,
RUNCORN WA7 4LU
Tel: 01928 529036
Fax: 01928 591872
Recovery: 01928 572108
E-mail: info@selwyns.co.uk
Web site: www.selwyns.co.uk
Man Dir: Selwyn A Jones **Gen Man:** Alan P
Williamson **Co Sec/Acct:** Richard E Williams
Fleet Eng: Cledwyn Owen
Fleet: 65 - 46 single-deck coach, 9 midicoach,
10 minibus.
Chassis: 26 DAF, 2 MAN, 13 Mercedes, 4 Scania,
6 Tecnobus, 10 VDL, 4 Volvo.
Bodies: 2 Berkhof, 8 Caetano, 6 Pantheon,
11 Plaxton, 34 Van Hool, 4 Other.
Ops incl: local bus services, school contracts,
excursions & tours, private hire, express,
continental tours.
Liveries: White/Blue/Orange/Green, National
Express.
Ticket System: Wayfarer
See also Greater Manchester

SHEARINGS HOLIDAYS

BARLEYCASTLE LANE, APPLETON,
WARRINGTON WA4 4SR
Tel: 01925 214600
Fax: 01925 262606
See Shearings Holidays, Greater Manchester.

SMITHS OF MARPLE

72 CROSS LANE, MARPLE SK6 7PZ
Tel: 0161 427 2825
Fax: 0161 449 7731
Web site: www.smithsofmarple.com
Dirs: Anthony Vernon, Angie Vernon.
Fleet: 12 - 5 double-deck bus, 2 single-deck bus,
3 single-deck coach, 2 midicoach
Ops incl: local bus services, school contracts,
excursions & tours, private hire.
Livery: White/Orange-Rose.
Ticket System: Wayfarer

JIM STONES COACHES

THE JAYS, LIGHT OAKS ROAD, GLAZEBURY,
WARRINGTON WA3 5LH
Tel/Fax: 01925 766465
E-mail: jimstones@ic24.net
Web site: www.jimstonescoaching.com
Partners: J B Stones, Mrs J P Stones
Gen Man: R Dyson **Fleet Eng:** S Mayo
Fleet: 15 single-deck bus.
Chassis: 13 Alexander Dennis, 1 Leyland, 1 Volvo.
Bodies: 13 Alexander Dennis, 1 DAB, 1 Wright
Ops incl: local bus services, school contracts
Livery: Blue/White
Ticket System: Almex, Wayfarer 3, Setright

WALKERS & FLANAGAN'S COACHES

OLD ROAD, ANDERTON, NORTHWICH
CW9 6AG
Tel: 01606 76666
Fax: 01606 781069
E-mail: walkers@holmeswood.uk.com,
flanagans@holmeswood.uk.com

Web site: www.holmeswood.uk.com
Dirs: J F Aspinall, M Aspinall, C H Aspinall, D E
Aspinall, M F Aspinall, M J Forshaw
Ops Man: M E Bostock **Tours Man:**
J Bostock-Gibson **Ch Eng:** M Boniface
Fleet: see Holmeswood Coaches
Ops incl: local bus services, excursions & tours,
private hire, continental tours, school contracts.
Livery: Green
(Subsidiary of Holmeswood Coaches, Lancashire)

WARRINGTON BOROUGH TRANSPORT LTD
🚌R
WILDERSPOOL CAUSEWAY, WARRINGTON
WA4 6PT
Tel: 01925 634296 **Fax:** 01925 418382
E-mail: mail@wbtltd.co.uk
Web site:
www.warringtonboroughtransport.co.uk

Fleet Name: Network Warrington
Chairman: Les Hoyle
Man Dir: David Squire **Fin Dir:** Ann Marie
Slavin **Ops Dir:** Charlie Shannon **Comm Man:**
Phil Pearson **Eng Dir:** Damian Graham
Fleet: 115 - 18 double-deck bus, 12 single-deck
bus, 85 midibus.
Chassis: 6 DAF, 31 Dennis, 4 Leyland, 6 Optare,
26 Volvo, 42 VDL.
Bodies: 15 Alexander, 27 Marshall, 4 MCV, 2
Northern Counties, 6 Optare, 60 Wright.
Ops incl: local bus services, school contracts,
private hire.
Livery: Red/Cream
Ticket System: Wayfarer 3

WARRINGTON COACHWAYS LTD
🚌🚐
ATHLONE ROAD, LONGFORD,
WARRINGTON WA2 8JJ

Tel/Fax: 01925 415299
Fleet Names: Bennett's Travel, Warrington
Coachways
Props: B A Bennett, D B Bennett.
Ops incl: local bus services, school contracts,
private hire.
Livery: White/Blue.

WHITEGATE TRAVEL LTD
🚐
UNIT 38, COSGROVE BUSINESS PARK,
DAISY BANK LANE, ANDERTON
CW9 6AA
Tel: 01606 786833
Dir: K Prince
Fleet: 13 – 2 midibus, 5 midicoach, 6 minibus.
Chassis: 3 LDV, 10 Mercedes.
Ops incl: local bus services, school contracts,
private hire.
Livery: Yellow/White

CORNWALL

A-LINE COACHES
🚐
CHAPEL COTTAGE, ST JOHN,
TORPOINT PL11 3AW
Tel/Fax: 01752 822740
E-mail: alinecoaches@yahoo.com
Web site: www.alinecoaches.co.uk
Prop: J Goddard
Ops incl: local bus services, private hire,
school contracts.

BAKER'S COACHES
THE GARAGE, DULOE, LISKEARD
PL14 4PL
Tel: 01503 262359
Fax: 01503 262422
E-mail: bakersatduloe@aol.com
Web site: www.bakers-coaches.com
Fleet Name: KTM Coaches
Fleet incl: single-deck coach, midicoach,
minibus
Ops incl: school contracts, private hire.

CARADON RIVIERA TOURS
Ceased trading since LRB 2011 went to press.

DAC COACHES LTD
🚐👥🅸🅁R24🔧T
RYLANDS GARAGE, ST ANN'S CHAPEL,
GUNNISLAKE PL18 9HW
Tel: 01822 834571
Fax: 01822 833881
Recovery: 01822 834571
E-mail: dac.coaches@btconnect.com
Web site: www.daccoaches.co.uk
Dirs: Bernard Harding, Nick Smith
Fleet: 16 – 8 single-deck bus, 6 single-deck
coach, 2 midicoach.
Chassis: 3 Iveco, 8 Mercedes, 5 Volvo.
Bodies: 3 Beulas, 1 Caetano, 1 Jonckheere,
2 Mercedes, 8 Plaxton, 1 Van Hool.
Ops incl: local bus services, school contracts,
excursions & tours, private hire, continental
tours.
Livery: White with multicoloured logos.
Ticket System: Almex A90.

DARLEY FORD TRAVEL
🚐👥🅸❄
DARLEY FORD, LISKEARD PL14 5AS
Tel: 01579 362272

Fax: 01579 363425
Web site: www.darleyford.co.uk
Owner: Albert J Deeble
Fleet: 8 – 8 single-deck coaches
Chassis: 2 Scania, 6 Volvo.
Ops incl: private hire, excursions & tours,
continental tours.
Livery: White

FIRST DEVON & CORNWALL LTD
See Devon

GROUP TRAVEL
🚌🚐👥❄
DUNMERE ROAD GARAGE,
DUNMERE ROAD, BODMIN
PL31 2QN
Tel: 01208 77989
Fax: 01208 77989
E-mail: benneymoon@btinternet.com
Web site: www.grouptravelcoachhire.co.uk
Dirs: Dawn Moon, David Benny
Fleet: 21 - 7 single-deck coach, 2 midicoach,
11 minibus, 1 minicoach.
Chassis: 2 Autosan, 1 Bova, 2 Dennis, 1 MAN,
1 Marshall, 10 Mercedes, 1 Optare, 1 Setra,
2 Volvo.
Bodies: 1 Bova, 1 Caetano, 1 Jonckheere,
Marshall, 5 Mellor, 1 Optare, 5 Plaxton, 1
Setra, 1 Van Hool, 4 other.
Ops incl: local bus services, school contracts,
excursions & tours, private hire
Livery: Avalon Signs
Ticket system: Almex A90

HILLS SERVICES LTD
See Devon

HOOKWAYS JENNINGS
Ceased trading since LRB 2011 went to press.

HOPLEYS COACHES LTD
👥🚐
GOVER FARM, GOVER HILL,
MOUNT HAWKE, TRURO
TR4 8BH
Tel: 01872 553786
E-mail: hopleyscoaches@tiscali.co.uk
Web site: www.hopleyscoaches.com
Partners: B Hopley, D R Hopley,
N A Hopley.

Fleet: 16 - 1 double-deck bus, 4 single-deck
bus, 11 single-deck coach.
Ops incl: local bus services, school contracts,
excursions & tours, private hire.
Livery: Red/White/Grey.
Ticket System: Wayfarer 3.

MOUNTS BAY COACHES
🚐👥❄
4 ALEXANDRA ROAD, PENZANCE
TR18 4LY
Tel: 01736 363320
Fax: 01736 366985
E-mail: mountsbaycoaches@btconnect.com
Web site: www.mountsbaycoaches.co.uk
Dir: Jeff Oxenham
Fleet: 9 - 7 single-deck coach, 2 midicoach
Chassis: 2 Toyota, 7 Volvo.
Bodies: 2 Caetano, 7 Van Hool.
Ops incl: school contracts, excursions &
tours, private hire.
Livery: Blue/White

OTS MINIBUS & COACH HIRE
🚐🔧
THE DEPOT, LAMANVA, PENRYN
TR10 9BJ
Tel/Fax: 01326 378100
E-mail: office@otsfalmouth.co.uk
Web site: www.otsfalmouth.co.uk
Dirs: Stephen Moore, Ben Moore
Fleet: 5 - 1 single-deck coach, 1 midicoach,
2 minibus, 1 minicoach.
Chassis: 4 Mercedes, 1 Volvo.
Ops incl: local bus services, school contracts,
private hire.
Livery: White with Blue & Brown
Ticket system: Microfare 3

PENMERE MINIBUS SERVICES
🚌🚐
28 BOSEMEOR ROAD, FALMOUTH
TR11 4PU
Tel: 01326 378100
Web site: www.penmereminibus.co.uk
Man: Ben Moore
Fleet: 6 – 1 single-deck coach, 1 midicoach,
4 minicoach.
Chassis: 4 Mercedes, 1 Optare, 1 Volvo.
Ops incl: school contracts, private hire.
Livery: White.

ROSELYN COACHES LTD

MIDDLEWAY GARAGE, ST BLAZEY ROAD, PAR PL24 2JA
Tel: 01726 813737
Fax: 01726 813739
Recovery: 01726 813737
E-mail: info@roselyncoaches.co.uk
Web site: www.roselyncoaches.co.uk
Dir: Jonathan Ede
Dir: Karen Paramor
Ch Eng: Graham Paramor
Ops Man: John Stoneman
Fleet: 48 - 15 double-deck bus,
32 single-deck coach, 1 open top bus.
Chassis: 1 Bova, 2 DAF, 2 Dennis, 8 Leyland, 3 Scania, 32 Volvo.
Bodies: 10 Alexander Dennis, 1 Bova, 1 Caetano, 5 East Lancs, 1 Jonckheere, 2 Northern Counties, 2 Optare, 12 Plaxton, 12 Van Hool, 2 Wright.
Ops incl: local bus services, school contracts, excursions & tours, private hire, continental tours.
Livery: Green/Gold

SUMMERCOURT TRAVEL LTD

THE OLD COACH GARAGE,
ST AUSTELL STREET, SUMMERCOURT,
NEWQUAY TR8 5DR
Tel: 01726 861108
Fax: 01726 860093
E-mail: rob@summercourttravel.com
Web site: www.summercourttravel.com
Dirs: R D Ryder, S C Ryder, S M Ryder
Fleet: 18 – 3 double-deck bus, 1 single-deck bus, 13 midibus, 1 minibus.
Chassis: 3 Alexander Dennis, 1 LDV, 1 Leyland, 13 Mercedes.
Ops incl: local bus services, school contracts, private hire.
Livery: White

TAVISTOCK COMMUNITY TRANSPORT

GREENLANDS, ST ANN'S CHAPEL,
GUNNISLAKE PL18 9HW
Tel: 01822 833574
E-mail: keithp44@btinternet.com

Fleet Name: Tavistock Country Bus
Chairman: K W Potter **Sec:** A Everitt
Fleet: 1 minibus
Chassis: Iveco
Body: G M Coachwork.
Ops incl: local bus services, private hire.
Livery: Red/White
Ticket System: Wayfarer

TILLEY'S COACHES

THE COACH STATION, WAINHOUSE
CORNER, BUDE EX23 0AZ
Tel: 01840 230244 **Fax:** 01840 230752
Man Dir: Paul Tilley
Fleet: 12 single-deck coaches
Ops incl: school contracts, private hire, excursions & tours
Livery: White/Cream/Maroon.

TRELEY COACH HIRE

ST BURYAN GARAGE, ST BURYAN,
PENZANCE TR19 6DZ
Tel: 01736 810322
Fax: 01736 810708
Dirs: A J Ley, A D Ley
Ops Man: M Smart
Fleet: 4 - 3 single-deck coach, 1 minicoach
Chassis: 3 Alexander Dennis, 1 Mercedes.
Bodies incl: 1 Berkhof, 1 Duple, 1 Wadham Stringer.
Ops incl: school contracts, private hire.
Livery: White/Orange/Red/Yellow

WESTERN GREYHOUND LTD

WESTERN HOUSE, ST AUSTELL STREET,
SUMMERCOURT, NEWQUAY
TR8 5DR
Tel: 01637 871871
Recovery: 07967 833419
E-mail: enquiries@westerngreyhound.com
Web site: www.westerngreyhound.com
Man Dir: Mark Howarth
Dir & Co Sec: Mari Howarth
Dir: Robin Orbell
Fleet: 129 - 20 double-deck bus, 8 single-deck bus, 40 midibus, 54 minibus, 1 open-top bus, 6 heritage.
Chassis: 5 AEC, 8 Alexander Dennis, 2 Bristol, 62 Mercedes, 40 Optare, 12 Volvo.

Bodies: 2 Alexander Dennis, 2 ECW, 14 East Lancs, 8 Mercedes, 40 Optare, 5 Park Royal, 58 Plaxton.
Ops incl: local bus services, school contracts, private hire.
Livery: Green
Ticket System: ERG (electronic)

WHEAL BRITON TRAVEL

MOOR COTTAGE, BLACKWATER,
TRURO TR4 8HH
Tel: 01872 560281
Fax: 01872 560691
Web site: www.whealbritontravel.com
Prop: Stephen J Palmer
Fleet: 22- 20 single-deck coach, 1 midicoach, 1 minibus.
Chassis: 1 LDV, 1 Toyota, 20 Volvo.
Bodies: 1 Caetano, 5 Jonckheere, 14 Plaxton, 2 Van Hool.
Ops incl: school contracts, excursions & tours, private hire, continental tours
Livery: Cream

WILLIAMS TRAVEL

DOLCOATH INDUSTRIAL PARK,
DOLCOATH ROAD, CAMBORNE
TR14 8RA
Tel: 01209 717152
Fax: 01209 612511
E-mail: enquiries@williams-travel.co.uk
Web site: www.williams-travel.co.uk
Prop: Fred Williams
Operations Man: Garry Williams
Workshop Man: Shaun Hoskins
Tours Man: Paula Hoskins
Fleet: 51 – 6 double-deck bus, 2 single-deck bus, 20 single-deck coach, 4 midibus, 5 midicoach, 12 minibus, 2 minicoach.
Chassis: 2 Bova, 3 DAF, 1 Dennis, 5 Ford Transit, 8 Iveco, 2 LDV, 10 Mercedes, 20 Volvo.
Bodies: 2 Bova, 2 Carlyle, 6 ECW, 1 Esker, 2 Ikarus, 1 Jonckheere, 2 LDV, 2 Mellor, 6 Mercedes, 2 Plaxton, 2 Sitcar, 6 Van Hool, 1 Volvo, 1 Wadham Stringer, 15 Other.
Ops incl: local bus services, school contracts, excursions & tours, private hire, continental tours.
Livery: White with Red & Orange.
Ticket System: Wayfarer.

Cornwall

ALBA TRAVEL LTD

BECK BANK, GREAT SALKELD,
PENRITH CA11 9LN
Tel: 01768 870219
Fax: 01768 870819
E-mail: enquiries@albatravelcumbria.co.uk
Web site: www.albatravelcumbria.co.uk
Dir: Alan Holmes
Fleet incl: midibus, midicoach, minibus.
Chassis: Ford, Mercedes, Optare, Volkswagen.
Ops incl: local bus services, excursions & tours,
private hire.
Livery: White with Maroon/Yellow

FRANK ALLISON LTD

MAIN STREET, BROUGH,
KIRKBY STEPHEN CA17 4AY
Tel: 01768 341328
Fax: 01768 341517
Web site: www.grand-prix-services.com
E-mail: julie@grandprixservices.co.uk
Fleet Name: Grand Prix Services
Dir: Frank Allison
Fleet: 11 – 1 single-deck bus,
6 single-deck coach, 1 midicoach, 2 minibus,
1 minicoach.
Chassis: 1 Ford Transit, 1 LDV, 1 Leyland,
2 Mercedes, 6 Volvo.
Bodies: 1 Caetano, 2 Duple, 1 Ford, 1 LDV,
3 Plaxton, 1 Van Hool, 1 Wright, 1 Other.
Ops incl: local bus services, school contracts,
excursions & tours, private hire.
Livery: White
Ticket System: Wayfarer TGX150

APOLLO 8 TRAVEL

KNOTT HALL FARM, LOWGILL,
KENDAL LA8 9DG
Tel: 01539 824086
Fax: 01539 824239
E-mail: info@apollo8travel.co.uk
Web site: www.apollo8travel.co.uk
Ops incl: local bus services, private hire
Livery: White

ROBERT BENSON COACHES LTD

7 MAIN ROAD, SEATON,
WORKINGTON CA14 1ES
Tel: 01900 511245
Web site: www.robertbensonworkington.co.uk
Fleet incl: single-deck coach, midicoach, minibus,
minicoach
Chassis: Mercedes, Volkswagen, Volvo.
Ops incl: private hire, school contracts

D K & N BOWMAN

BURTHWAITE HILL, BURTHWAITE,
WREAY, CARLISLE CA4 0RT
Tel: 01697 473262
Fax: 01697 473262
E-mail: enquiries@bowmans-coaches.co.uk
Web site: www.bowmans-coaches.co.uk
Partners: David K Bowman, Nora Bowman
Manager: Andrew Bowman
Fleet: 8 – 7 single-deck coach, 1 vintage coach.
Chassis: 3 AEC, 1 Dennis, 3 Scania, 1 Volvo.
Bodies: 1 Duple, 1 Jonckheere, 2 Plaxton,
3 Van Hool.
Ops incl: school contracts, excursions and tours,
private hire.
Livery: Royal Ivory/Red

S H BROWNRIGG

ENNERDALE MILL, EGREMONT
CA22 2PN
Tel: 01946 820205
Fax: 01946 821919
E-mail: enquiries@shbrownrigg.co.uk
Web site: www.shbrownrigg.co.uk
Dir: R J Cook **Ops Man:** B Marshall
Senior Officers: Mrs D Marshall, Mrs L Holliday
Fleet: 25 - 14 single-deck coach, 3 midibus,
3 midicoach, 5 minibus.
Chassis: 1 Ford Transit, 2 Leyland, 9 Mercedes,
1 Scania, 1 Volkswagen, 11 Volvo.
Bodies: 16 Plaxton, 1 Van Hool, 8 Other.
Ops incl: school contracts, private hire.
Livery: Purple/White

CALDEW COACHES LTD

6 CALDEW DRIVE, DALSTON,
CARLISLE CA5 7NS
Tel/Fax: 01228 711690
E-mail: caldewcoachesltd@aol.com
Web site: www.caldewcoaches.co.uk
Dirs: Hugh McKerrell, Ann McKerrell, Bill Rogers
Co Sec: Mandy Rogers
Fleet: 14 - 2 single-deck coach, 8 midicoach,
4 minicoach.
Chassis: 1 Bova, 12 Mercedes, 1 Other.
Bodies: 1 Bova, 12 Mercedes, 1 Other.
Ops incl: school contracts, excursions & tours,
private hire.
Livery: Red/White

CARR'S COACHES

CONTROL TOWER, SILLOTH INDUSTRIAL
ESTATE, SILLOTH CA7 4NS
Tel: 01697 331276
Fax: 01697 333823
Web site: www.carrs-coaches.co.uk
Prop: A J Markley
Ch Eng: Paul Allison
Fleet: 7 - 4 single-deck coach, 1 midicoach,
2 minibus.
Chassis: 1 Dennis, 1 Ford Transit, 2 Mercedes,
2 Scania.
Bodies: 1 Berkhof, 2 Irizar, 2 Van Hool,
2 Other.
Ops incl: local bus services, school contracts,
private hire.
Livery: Blue/White.

CLARKSON COACHWAYS LTD

UNIT 2B, ASHBURNER WAY,
WALNEY ROAD INDUSTRIAL ESTATE,
BARROW IN FURNESS LA14 5UZ
Tel: 01229 828022
Fax: 01229 828067
E-mail: info@clarksoncoachways.co.uk
Web site: www.clarksoncoachways.co.uk
Dirs: Susan Clarkson, Neil Clarkson
Fleet: 10 - 5 single-deck coach, 1 open-top bus,
2 midicoach, 1 minibus, 1 minicoach.
Chassis: 3 Dennis, 1 Ford Transit, 1 Irisbus,
1 LDV, 1 Leyland, 2 MAN, 1 Mercedes.
Bodies: 1 Alexander, 2 Berkhof, 1 Beulas,
1 Caetano, 2 Crest, 2 Marcopolo, 1 Optare.
Ops incl: school contracts, excursions & tours,
private hire.
Livery: two-tone Green

COAST TO COAST PACKHORSE LTD

CHESTNUT HOUSE, CROSBY GARRETT,
KIRKBY STEPHEN CA17 4PR
Tel: 01768 371777
Fax: 01768 371777
E-mail: enquiries@c2cpackhorse.co.uk
Web site: www.c2cpackhorse.co.uk
Props: S & L Jones.
Fleet: 2 minibus.
Chassis: 2 Ford Transit.
Ops incl: local bus services, school contracts,
private hire.

CUMBRIA COACHES LTD

ALGA HOUSE, BRUNEL WAY, DURRANHILL
INDUSTRIAL ESTATE, CARLISLE CA1 3NQ
Tel: 01228 404300
Fax: 01228 404309
E-mail: enquiries@cumbriacoaches.co.uk
Web site: www.cumbriacoaches.co.uk
Fleet: 9 single-deck coach.
Chassis: 1 Bova, 1 Dennis, 1 Neoplan, 1 Setra,
5 Volvo.
Bodies: 1 Bova, 1 Neoplan, 2 Plaxton, 1 Setra,
1 UVG, 3 Van Hool.
Ops incl: excursions & tours, private hire,
express, continental tours, school contracts.

JOHN HOBAN TRAVEL LTD

22 KING STREET, WORKINGTON CA14 4DJ
Tel: 01900 603579
Fax: 01900 62741
E-mail: enquiries@johnahoban.co.uk
Web site: www.johnhoban.co.uk
Partners: John Hoban, Allison Hoban
Fleet: 10 - 8 midicoach, 7 minibus.
Chassis: 1 Fiat, 1 Iveco, 11 Mercedes, 2
Volkswagen.
Ops incl: local bus services, school contracts,
private hire.
Livery: White with Blue/Brown

IRVINGS COACH HIRE LTD

JESMOND STREET, CARLISLE CA1 2DE
Tel: 01228 521666
Fax: 01228 515792
Recovery: 07803 833845
E-mail: office@irvings-coaches.co.uk
Web site: www.irvings-coaches.co.uk
Man Dir: R Irving **Dir:** Miss A Irving **Tran Man:**
J K Cartner
Fleet: 11 - 10 single-deck coach, 1 midicoach.
Chassis: 1 Bova, 1 Mercedes, 9 Volvo.
Bodies: 1 Bova, 1 Caetano, 1 Duple, 1
Jonckheere, 3 Plaxton, 4 Van Hool.
Ops incl: excursions & tours, private hire, school
contracts.
Livery: Orange/Black/White.

K & B TRAVEL LTD

33 KING STREET, PENRITH CA11 7AY
Tel: 01768 868600
Fax: 01768 862715
E-mail: mail@kbtravel.co.uk
Web site: www.kbtravel.co.uk
Man Dir: G Lund **Dirs:** B Bainbridge **(Co Sec)**,
T Lund
Fleet: 10 - 6 single-deck coach, 3 midicoach,
1 minibus.

Chassis: 4 Mercedes, 4 Neoplan, 2 Volvo.
Bodies: 4 Neoplan, 1 Plaxton, 2 Van Hool, 3 Other.
Ops incl: excursions & tours, private hire, school contracts, continental tours.
Livery: Blue with Green lettering

LAKES HOTEL & SUPERTOURS
1 HIGH STREET, WINDERMERE LA23 1AF
Tel: 01539 442751
Fax: 01539 446026
E-mail: admin@lakes-supertours.com
Web site: www.lakes-supertours.com
Dirs: R Minford, A Dobson
Fleet: 3 minibus.
Chassis: 2 Renault, 1 Vauxhall.
Ops incl: excursions & tours.
Livery: White/Purple/Gold.

LECKS TRAVEL
HAVERTHWAITE, ULVERSTON LA12 8AB
Tel: 01539 587128 **Fax:** 01539 531225
Ops incl: local bus services, excursions & tours, private hire.

MESSENGERS COACHES LTD
MEALSGATE STATION, WIGTON
CA7 1JP
Tel: 01697 371111
Fax: 01697 371112
E-mail: angie@messengerscoaches.co.uk
Web site: www.messengerscoaches.co.uk
Man Dir: Liam Walker **Dir:** Mrs Angie Walker
Fleet: 10 - 9 single-deck coach, 1 midicoach.
Chassis: 1 Mercedes, 1 Leyland, 8 Volvo.
Bodies: 2 Jonckheere, 4 Plaxton, 4 Van Hool.
Ops incl: school contracts, excursions & tours, private hire, continental tours.
Livery: White/Blue

MOUNTAIN GOAT LTD
VICTORIA STREET, WINDERMERE
LA23 1AD
Tel: 01539 445161
Fax: 01539 445164
E-mail: enquiries@mountain-goat.com
Web site: www.mountain-goat.com
Dirs: Peter Nattrass, Stephen Broughton, Norman Stoller **Fleet Man:** Steve Loveland
Office Man: Sue Todd
Fleet: 15 - 14 minicoach, 1 car.
Chassis: Mercedes, Renault.
Ops incl: local bus services, excursions & tours, private hire, continental tours.
Livery: Green/Red on White

NBM HIRE LTD
CROMWELL ROAD, PENRITH CA11 7JW
Tel: 01768 892727
Fax: 01768 899680
E-mail: sales@nbmtravel.co.uk
Web site: www.nbmtravel.co.uk

Fleet: 12 single-deck coach, 4 midibus, 1 midicoach, 4 minibus.
Chassis: Bova, DAF, Dennis, Iveco, LDV, Mercedes, Optare, Scania, Volvo.
Ops incl: local bus services, excursions & tours, private hire, school contracts
Livery: White/Blue

REAYS COACHES LTD
STRAWBERRY FIELDS, SYKE PARK, WIGTON CA7 9NE
Tel: 01697 349999 **Fax:** 01697 349900
E-mail: info@reays.co.uk
Web site: www.reays.co.uk
Fleet Names: Reays, City Hopper, Village Hopper.
Man Dir: Chris Reay
Dir: Nicola Reay
Ops Man: Chris Bowness
Fleet: 60 - 4 single-deck bus, 19 single-deck coach, 23 midibus, 7 midicoach, 6 minibus, 1 minicoach.
Chassis: 6 Bova, 1 DAF, 14 Enterprise, 4 Iveco, 1 LDV, 18 Mercedes, 1 Van Hool, 4 VDL, 11 Volvo.
Bodies: 8 Alexander, 6 Bova, 2 Jonckheere, 1 LDV, 4 MCV, 2 Mercedes, 31 Plaxton, 2 Van Hool.
Ops incl: local bus services, school contracts, excursions & tours, private hire, continental tours.
Livery: Reays Blue & White Triangles.
Ticket System: Wayfarer

ROBINSONS COACHES
STATION ROAD GARAGE, APPLEBY
CA16 6TX
Tel: 01768 351424
Prop: S E Graham
Fleet: 10 - 1 single-deck bus, 5 single-deck coach, 1 midicoach, 3 minibus.
Chassis: 1 DAF, 2 Dennis, 2 Iveco, 1 LDV, 1 Mercedes, 1 Scania, 1 Volkswagen, 1 Volvo.
Bodies: 1 Alexander Dennis, 1 Beulas, 1 Bova, 1 LDV, 1 Onyx, 1 Plaxton, 2 Van Hool, 1 Wadham Stringer, 1 Other.
Ops incl: local bus services, school contracts, private hire.
Livery: Green/White

KEN ROUTLEDGE TRAVEL
ALLERDALE HOUSE WORKSHOPS, LOW ROAD, BRIGHAM, COCKERMOUTH CA13 0XH
Tel: 01900 822795 **Fax:** 01900 822593
Fleet: 10 - 5 midicoach, 5 minibus.
Chassis: Mercedes
Ops incl: local bus services, private hire.

SIMS TRAVEL
HUNHOLME GARAGE, BOOT, HOLMROOK CA19 1TF
Tel: 01946 723227 **Fax:** 01946 723158
E-mail: info@simstravel.co.uk
Web site: www.simstravel.co.uk

Partners: Andrew Sim, Peter Sim
Fleet: 10 - 6 single-deck coach, 2 midicoach, 2 minibus.
Chassis: 2 Bova, 4 Mercedes, 1 Neoplan, 3 Volvo.
Bodies: 1 Berkhof, 2 Bova, 1 Neoplan, 2 Van Hool, 4 Other.
Ops incl: excursions & tours, private hire, school contracts.
Livery: White/Red/Maroon

STACEY'S COACHES LTD
UNIT 3, MILLRACE ROAD, WILLOWHOLME INDUSTRIAL ESTATE, CARLISLE CA2 3RS
Tel: 01228 511127
Web site: www.staceys-coaches.co.uk
Fleet: 26 – 6 single-deck coach, 7 midicoach, 11 minibus, 2 minicoach.
Chassis: 4 Bova, 7 LDV, 13 Mercedes, 2 Van Hool.
Ops incl: local bus services, excursions & tours, school contracts, private hire
Liveries: White, Silver

STAGECOACH IN CUMBRIA AND NORTH LANCASHIRE
BROADACRE HOUSE, 16-20 LOWTHER STREET, CARLISLE CA3 8DA
Tel: 0871 200 2233 **Fax:** 01772 255757
E-mail:
northwest.enquiries@stagecoachbus.com
Web site: www.stagecoachbus.com
Fleet Names: Stagecoach in Cumbria, Stagecoach in Lancaster.
Man Dir: Nigel Winter **Eng Dir:** Paul W Lee
Comm Man: James Mellor
Fleet: 311 - 103 double-deck bus, 145 single-deck bus, 10 single-deck coach, 53 midibus.
Chassis: 36 Alexander Dennis, 71 Dennis, 11 Leyland, 39 MAN, 56 Optare, 12 Scania, 86 Volvo.
Ops incl: local bus services, school contracts, excursions & tours, private hire, express.
Livery: Stagecoach UK Bus
Ticket System: Wayfarer TGX

TITTERINGTON COACHES LTD
CENTRAL BUILDINGS, CORNMARKET, PENRITH CA11 7HT
Tel: 01768 863594 **Fax:** 01768 892577
E-mail: enquiries@titteringtonholidays.co.uk
Web site: www.titteringtonholidays.co.uk
Fleet Name: Titterington Holidays
Dirs: Ian Titterington, Paul Titterington, Colin Titterington
Fleet: 16 - 15 single-deck coach, 1 minibus.
Chassis: 2 Leyland, 1 MAN, 1 Mercedes, 2 Setra, 1 Volkswagen, 9 Volvo.
Bodies: 5 Jonckheere, 1 Mercedes, 1 Neoplan, 5 Plaxton, 2 Setra, 1 Van Hool, 1 Volkswagen.
Ops incl: excursions & tours, private hire, continental tours, school contracts.
Livery: Mustard/White/Brown

♿ Vehicle suitable for disabled	⬛ Seat belt-fitted Vehicle	R24 24 hour recovery service	
▮ Toilet-drop facilities available	⬛ Coach(es) with galley facilities	◣ Replacement vehicle available	
R Recovery service available	❄ Air-conditioned vehicle(s)	📟 Vintage Coach(es) available	
▭ Open top vehicle(s)	⬛ Coaches with toilet facilities	⬛ Hybrid Buses	

Cumbria

TOWER COACHES

THE GARAGE, BURNFOOT, WIGTON
CA7 9HL
Tel: 01697 349600
Props: M D Sellars, Mrs T Sellars
Ops incl: school contracts, private hire.
Livery: Dark Blue/Grey
Ticket System: Almex A

THE TRAVELLERS CHOICE

See Lancashire

TUER MOTORS LTD

BRIDGE HOUSE, MORLAND, PENRITH
CA10 3AY
Tel: 01931 714224
Fax: 01931 714236
Fleet: 6 - 3 single-deck coach, 1 midicoach,
2 minibus
Chassis: 1 DAF, 1 Ford Transit, 2 Mercedes,
2 Volvo.
Bodies: 1 Ford, 1 Ikarus, 2 Plaxton, 1 Van Hool,
1 Other.
Ops incl: excursions & tours, private hire, school
contracts, continental tours.
Livery: Cream/Red

WOOFS OF SEDBERGH

UNIT 2, BUSK LANE, SEDBERGH LA10 5HF
Tel: 01539 620414
E-mail: office@woofs.f9.co.uk
Web site: www.woofsofsedbergh.co.uk
Prop: G Woof
Fleet: 12 – 3 midibus, 4 midicoach, 5 minibus.
Chassis: 1 Ford Transit, 1 LDV, 10 Mercedes.
Ops incl: local bus services, school contracts,
private hire.

WRIGHT BROS (COACHES) LTD

CENTRAL GARAGE, NENTHEAD,
ALSTON CA9 3NP
Tel: 01434 381200 **Fax:** 01434 382089
E-mail: info@wrightbros.co.uk
Web site: www.wrightscoaches.co.uk
Chmn/Man Dir: J G Wright **Dir:** C I Wright.
Fleet: 13 - 9 single-deck coach, 2 double-deck
coach, 1 midibus, 1 midicoach.
Chassis: 2 Mercedes, 11 Volvo.
Bodies: 3 Jonckheere, 7 Plaxton, 2 Van Hool,
1 Other.
Ops incl: local bus services, school contracts,
private hire, continental tours.
Liveries: Cream/Black/Gold, Yellow (double-deck
sleepers).
Ticket System: Almex.

ANDREW'S OF TIDESWELL LTD

ANCHOR GARAGE, TIDESWELL
SK17 8RB
Tel: 01298 871222
Fax: 01298 872412
E-mail: info@andrews-of-tideswell.co.uk
Web site: www.andrews-of-tideswell.co.uk
Dirs: R B Andrew, P D Andrew
Fleet: 25 - 4 double-deck bus, 15 single-deck
coach, 2 double-deck coach, 1 midicoach,
3 minibus.
Chassis: 1 DAF, 1 Ford Transit, 4 Leyland,
3 Mercedes, 4 Neoplan, 12 Volvo.
Bodies: 2 Crest, 4 East Lancs, 1 Ford, 4 Neoplan,
6 Plaxton, 8 Van Hool.
Ops incl: excursions & tours, private hire,
continental tours, school contracts
Livery: Cream/Ivory/Red flash.

ARRIVA MIDLANDS LTD

852 MELTON ROAD, LEICESTER LE4 8BT
Tel: 0116 264 0400
Fax: 0116 260 5605
E-mail: myattk.midlands@arriva.co.uk
Web site: www.arriva.co.uk
Fleet Name: Arriva serving Derby
Regional Man Dir: R A Hind **Fin Dir:** J Barlow
Ops Dir: A Lloyd **Eng Dir:** M Evans
Area Business Man (Derbyshire): R Godfrey
Fleet: 642 - 133 double-deck bus, 147 single-
deck bus, 5 articulated bus, 218 midibus,
139 minibus.
Chassis: 1 Bova, 115 DAF, 182 Dennis, 4 Leyland,
35 Mercedes, 83 Optare, 49 Scania, 56 VDL,
117 Volvo
Bodies: 57 Alexander Dennis, 1 Caetano,
65 East Lancs, 2 Marshall, 29 Mercedes,
9 Northern Counties, 83 Optare, 131 Plaxton,
42 Scania, 8 UVG, 202 Wright, 13 Other.
Ops incl: local bus services, school contracts,
private hire, express.
Liveries: Arriva, Wardles (Red/White, Red/
Cream).
Ticket System: Wayfarer 150 & 200

BAGNALLS COACHES

THE COACH STOP, GEORGE HOLMES WAY,
SWADLINCOTE DE11 9DF
Tel: 01283 551964
Fax: 01283 552287
E-mail: info@bagnallscoaches.com
Web site: www.bagnallscoaches.com
Dir/Ops Man: John Bagnall
Dir/Clerk: Pat Bagnall **Dir/Ch Eng:** Karl Bagnall
Dir/Clerk: Gavin Bagnall
Fleet: 15 - 1 single-deck bus, 12 single-deck
coach, 2 midicoach.
Chassis: 1 Mercedes, 14 Volvo.
Bodies: 1 East Lancs, 2 Jonckheere, 2 Plaxton,
9 Van Hool, 1 Other.
Ops incl: local bus services, excursions & tours,
private hire, school contracts.
Livery: various

BAKEWELL COACHES

24 MOORHALL ESTATE, BAKEWELL DE45 1FP
Tel: 01629 813995
Prop: A Barks
Fleet: 1 single-deck coach
Chassis: Setra

BOWERS COACHES

ASPINCROFT GARAGE, CHAPEL-EN-LE-FRITH
SK23 0NU
Tel: 01298 812204
Fax: 01298 816103
E-mail: enquiries@bowerscoaches.co.uk
Web site: www.bowersbuses.com
Fleet: 29 - 2 single-deck bus, 3 single-deck coach,
24 midibus.
Chassis: 4 DAF, 7 Mercedes, 14 Optare, 4 Scania.
Bodies: 4 Alexander, 14 Optare, 5 Plaxton,
3 Van Hool, 3 Wright.
Ops incl: local bus services, school contracts,
excursions & tours, private hire, continental tours.
Livery: Red/Yellow/White.
A subsidiary of the Centrebus Group. To be
merged with Trent Barton Dove Holes operation
as High Peak Bus Company in late 2011.

CLOWES COACHES

BARROWMOOR, LONGNOR NEAR
BUXTON SK17 0QP
Tel: 01298 83292
Fax: 01298 83838
E-mail: clowescoach@btconnect.com
Prop: George Clowes
Fleet: 14 – 9 single-deck coach, 4 midibus,
1 minicoach
Bodies: 4 Alexander Dennis, 6 Duple, 2 Irizar,
2 Van Hool.
Ops incl: local bus services, school contracts,
excursions & tours, private hire.
Livery: Cream
Ticket system: Card

COX'S OF BELPER

GOODS ROAD, BELPER DE56 1UU
Tel: 01773 822395
Fax: 01773 821157
E-mail: bernardbembridge@btinternet.com
Web site: www.coxsofbelper.co.uk
Props: Bernard Bembridge, Maureen Bembridge
Fleet: 6 - 3 single-deck coach, 2 midicoach,
1 minicoach.
Chassis: 1 Dennis, 1 Freight Rover, 2 Mercedes,
2 Volvo.
Bodies: 1 Jonckheere, 2 Optare, 1 Plaxton,
1 Van Hool.
Ops incl: school contracts, private hire.
Livery: White/Blue

CRESSWELL'S COACHES (GRESLEY) LTD

3 SHORTHEATH ROAD, MOIRA,
SWADLINCOTE DE12 6AL
Tel: 01283 217229
Fax: 01283 550043
E-mail: sales@cresswellscoaches.com
Web site: www.cresswellscoaches.com
Man Dir: David Cresswell **Ch Eng:** Steve Lloyd
Fleet: 16 - 11 single-deck coach, 3 midibus,
2 minibus.
Chassis: 3 Irisbus, 4 Mercedes, 1 Optare, 8 Volvo.
Bodies: 3 Beulas, 1 Jonckheere, 1 Optare,
6 Plaxton, 1 Van Hool, 1 Volvo, 3 Other.
Ops incl: local bus services, school contracts,
excursions & tours, private hire, continental tours.
Livery: White/Orange
Ticket System: Wayfarer

CRISTAL HIRE COACHES OF SWANWICK
Ceased trading since LRB 2011 went to press

DAWSON'S MINICOACHES
Ceased trading since LRB 2011 went to press

DERBY COMMUNITY TRANSPORT
See Notts & Derby Buses
Part of the Wellglade Group

K & H DOYLE LTD
LYDFORD ROAD, ALFRETON
DE55 7RQ
Tel: 01773 546546   **Fax:** 01773 546547
E-mail: info@doylescoaches.co.uk
Web site: www.doylescoaches.co.uk
Prop: K Doyle
Fleet: 26 – 2 double-deck bus, 6 single-deck bus, 18 midibus.
Chassis: 20 Dennis, 6 Optare.
Bodies: 2 Alexander, 6 Optare, 18 Plaxton.
Ops incl: local bus services, school contracts.
Livery: Green.

TIM DRAPER'S GOLDEN HOLIDAYS
SEVERN SQUARE, ALFRETON
DE55 7BQ
Tel: 01773 830921
Fax: 01773 590034
E-mail: tim.draper@btconnect.com
Web site: www.timdrapers.co.uk
Dirs: Tim Draper, Pam Draper, Claire Draper
Fleet: 7 - 5 single-deck coach, 2 minibus.
Chassis: 1 DAF, 1 Iveco, 1 LDV, 1 MAN, 1 Mercedes, 2 Volvo.
Ops incl: excursions & tours, school contracts, private hire.
Livery: White/Red/Yellow

DUNN MOTOR TRACTION
DELVES ROAD, HEANOR GATE INDUSTRIAL ESTATE, HEANOR DE75 7RJ
Tel: 01773 714013
Fax: 01773 713257
Web site: www.brightsites.org.uk/yourbus
Fleet Name: Your Bus
Man Dir: Scott Dunn **Gen Man:** Stephen Bryce
Fleet: double-deck bus, single-deck bus, single-deck coach, midibus.
Chassis: Dennis, Mercedes, Volvo.
Bodies: Alexander, Caetano, Mercedes, Northern Counties, Plaxton, Wright.
Ops incl: local bus services, school contracts, express.
Liveries: Buses: Magenta; **Coaches:** National Express.

'E' COACHES OF ALFRETON
1 MANOR COURT, RIDDINGS
DE55 4DG
Tel/Fax: 01773 541222
E-mail: info@ecoachesofalfreton.co.uk
Web site: www.ecoachesofalfreton.co.uk
Owner: Kieron Bacon
Fleet: 6 – 1 single-deck coach, 1 midibus, 3 midicoach, 1 minibus.
Chassis: 1 Iveco, 1 Leyland, 4 Mercedes.
Bodies: 1 Beulas, 3 Plaxton, 2 Other.
Ops incl: school contracts, excursions & tours, private hire.
Livery: White/Blue.

FELIX BUS SERVICES LTD
157 STATION ROAD, STANLEY, ILKESTON DE7 6FJ
Tel: 0115 932 5332
Fax: 0115 932 6096
E-mail: office@felixbusandcoach.co.uk
Web site: www.felixbusandcoach.co.uk
Dirs: Geoffrey Middup, Ian Middup, Carole Middup
Fleet: 13 - 8 single-deck bus, 3 single-deck coach, 2 midibus.
Chassis: 2 Irisbus, 2 Optare, 3 Scania, 2 VDL, 4 Volvo.
Bodies: 2 Alexander Dennis, 2 Optare, 6 Plaxton, 3 Wright.
Ops incl: local bus services, school contracts, excursions & tours, private hire, continental tours.
Livery: Red/White
Ticket system: Wayfarer TGX150

FLIGHTS HALLMARK
See West Midlands

GLOVERS COACHES LTD
MOOR FARM ROAD EAST, ASHBOURNE DE6 1HD
Tel/Fax: 01335 300043
E-mail: info@gloverscoaches.co.uk
Web site: www.gloverscoaches.co.uk
Dirs: Stephen Mason, Heather Mason
Fleet: 14 – 2 single-deck bus, 11 single-deck coach, 1 midicoach.
Chassis: 1 Dennis, 1 Mercedes, 12 Volvo.
Bodies: 1 Alexander, 1 Jonckheere, 1 Northern Counties, 11 Plaxton.
Ops incl: local bus services, school contracts, excursions & tours, private hire, continental tours.
Livery: Blue/Cream.
Ticket System: Wayfarer

GOLDEN GREEN LUXURY TRAVEL
See Cheshire

HARPUR'S COACHES
WINCANTON CLOSE, DERBY DE24 8NB
Tel: 01332 757677   **Fax:** 01332 757259
E-mail: harpurscoaches@tiscali.co.uk
Web site: www.harpurscoaches.co.uk
Man Dir: Nick Harpur
Fleet: 22 - 7 double-deck bus, 15 single-deck coach.
Chassis: 3 Leyland, 2 MCW, 17 Volvo.
Bodies: 4 Alexander, 1 East Lancs, 2 MCW, 15 Plaxton.
Ops incl: school contracts, excursions & tours, private hire.
Livery: Cream/Brown

HAWKES TOURS
EAGLE CENTRE MARKET, DERBY DE1 2AZ
Tel: 01332 205400
Fax: 01332 202024
E-mail: david@hawkescoaches.freeserve.co.uk
Web site: www.hawkestours.co.uk
Fleet: 12 – 5 double-deck bus, 7 single-deck coach.
Chassis: 5 MCW, 3 Setra, 4 Volvo.
Bodies: 1 Jonckheere, 5 MCW, 3 Plaxton, 3 Setra.
Ops incl: school contracts, excursions & tours, private hire.
Livery: Blue

HENSHAWS COACHES LTD
57 PYE HILL ROAD, JACKSDALE NG16 5LR
Tel: 01773 607909
Prop: Paul Henshaw
E-mail: paul@henshawscoaches.co.uk
Web site: www.henshawscoaches.co.uk
Fleet: 3 single-deck coach.
Chassis: 1 Bova, 1 Mercedes, 1 Van Hool.
Bodies: 1 Bova, 1 Mercedes, 1 Van Hool.
Ops incl: excursions & tours, private hire, school contracts, continental tours.
Livery: White/Orange

G & J HOLMES (COACHES) LTD
124A MARKET STREET, CLAY CROSS S45 9LY
Tel/Fax: 01246 863232
E-mail: gj.holmes@tiscali.co.uk
Web site: www.gandjholmescoachesltd.co.uk
Fleet Name: Hallmark
Fleet: 11 – 1 single-deck coach, 6 midibus, 4 midicoach.
Chassis: 5 Mercedes, 5 Optare, 1 Volvo.
Bodies: 6 Optare, 5 Plaxton.
Ops incl: local bus services, school contracts, private hire.
Livery: White, or Silver/Blue

HULLEYS OF BASLOW
DERWENT GARAGE, BASLOW, BAKEWELL DE45 1RP
Tel: 01246 582246
Fax: 01246 583161
E-mail: www.hulleys-of-baslow.co.uk
Web site: office2008@hulleys-of-baslow.co.uk
Dirs: Peter Eades (Eng), Richard Eades (Ops)
Fleet: 19 - 13 single-deck bus, 3 single-deck coach, 3 midibus.
Chassis: 1 Alexander Dennis, 1 DAF, 9 Dennis, 4 MAN, 3 Optare, 1 Volvo.
Bodies: 1 Alexander Dennis, 7 MCV, 6 Optare, 4 Plaxton, 1 Wright.
Ops incl: local bus services, school contracts, private hire.
Livery: Buses: Cream/Blue; **Coaches:** White/Blue
Ticket System: Wayfarer 3

JOHNSON BROS TOURS LTD
GREEN ACRES, GREEN LANE, HODTHORPE, WORKSOP S80 4XR
Tel/Recovery: 01909 720337 / 721847
Fax: 01909 722886
E-mail: lee@johnsonstours.co.uk
Web site: www.johnsonstours.co.uk
Dirs: C A Johnson, S Johnson, A Johnson, L Johnson, S Johnson **Ops Man:** S Smallshaw
Fleet: 118 - 70 double-deck bus, 4 single-deck bus, 30 single-deck coach, 4 double-deck coach, 4 midibus, 2 midicoach, 1 minibus, 3 minicoach.
Chassis incl: 2 Alexander Dennis, 1 Ayats, 3 Bova, 30 Bristol, 2 DAF, 2 Ford Transit, 6 Irisbus, 4 Iveco, 4 MAN, 4 Mercedes, 6 Neoplan, 6 Scania, 3 Van Hool, 20 Volvo.
Bodies: 1 Ayats, 6 Beulas, 2 Berkhof, 3 Bova, 2 Caetano, 30 ECW, 5 East Lancs, 6 Irizar, 4 Jonckheere, 6 Neoplan, 30 Northern Counties, 25 Plaxton, 6 Scania, 2 Sunsundegui, 3 Van Hool, 1 Volvo.
Ops incl: local bus services, school contracts, excursions & tours, private hire, express, continental tours.

Livery: Blue Fade with Stars
Ticket System: ITSO
See also Redfern Travel Ltd

LEANDER TRAVEL
Ceased trading

LITTLE TRANSPORT LTD
HALLAM FIELDS ROAD, ILKESTON
DE7 4AZ
Tel/Fax: 0115 932 8581
Recovery: 0115 932 8581
E-mail: enqiries@littlestravel.co.uk
Web site: www.littlestravel.co.uk
Fleet Name: Little's Travel
Dirs: Steve Wells, Paul Wright
Fleet: 27 – 9 double-deck bus, 3 single-deck bus,
13 single-deck coach, 2 midibus.
Chassis: 3 Dennis, 2 Irisbus, 4 Leyland, 2 Optare,
8 Scania, 1 Temsa, 1 VDL, 6 Volvo.
Bodies: 2 Alexander, 2 Beulas, 4 ECW, 3 East
Lancs, 6 Irizar, 1 Marcopolo, 5 Optare, 2 Plaxton,
1 Scania, 1 Temsa.
Ops incl: local bus services, school contracts,
excursions & tours, private hire, continental tours.
Livery: White with pink lettering.
Ticket system: Almex

MACPHERSON COACHES LTD
THE GARAGE, HILL STREET, DONISTHORPE,
SWADLINCOTE DE12 7PL
Tel: 01530 270226   **Fax:** 01530 273669
E-mail: travel@macphersoncoaches.co.uk
Web site: www.macphersoncoaches.co.uk
Man Dir: D C N MacPherson
Traffic Man: R Gadsby
Fleet Eng: C Underwood
Fleet: 14 - 4 double-deck bus, 7 single-deck
coach, 1 midibus, 1 midicoach, 1 minicoach.
Chassis: 1 Dennis, 4 Leyland, 3 Mercedes, 6 Setra.
Bodies: 3 Alexander Dennis, 2 Caetano, 1 East
Lancs, 1 Mercedes, 6 Setra, 1 Other.
Ops incl: local bus services, school contracts,
excursions & tours, private hire, continental tours.
Livery: Red & Cream.
Ticket System: Wayfarer.

NOTTS & DERBY BUSES
MEADOW ROAD, DERBY DE1 2BH
Tel/Fax: 01332 204568
E-mail: sfrost@nottsderby.co.uk
Man Dir: Brian King **Fin Dir:** Graham Sutton
Man: Stuart Frost
Fleet: 61 - 21 double-deck bus, 32 single-deck
bus, 1 single-deck coach, 5 midibus, 1 midicoach,
1 minibus.
Chassis: 1 Alexander Dennis, 1 DAF, 5 Dennis,
10 Leyland, 6 Optare, 27 Volvo, 11 Other.
Bodies: 6 Alexander Dennis, 3 ECW,
19 Northern Counties, 10 Optare, 5 Plaxton,
1 Transbus, 7 Volvo, 10 Other.
Ops incl: local bus services, school contracts,
private hire
Livery: Green/White/Blue
Ticket System: Almex
Incorporating Derby Community Transport
Part of the Wellglade Group

PROTOURS LTD
UNIT 2, RYDER CLOSE, SWADLINCOTE
DE11 9EU

Tel: 01283 217012
Fax: 01283 550685
E-mail: bookings@protours.co.uk
Web Site: www.protours.co.uk
Dept Man: Kevin Ramsdall
Fleet: 12 - 11 single-deck coach, 1 midicoach
Chassis: 1 BMC, 11 Volvo.
Bodies: 10 Berkhof, 1 BMC, 1 Plaxton.
Ops incl: excursions & tours, private hire,
express, continental tours, school contracts
Livery: Blue & White with Yellow.

REDFERN TRAVEL LTD
THE SIDINGS, DEBDALE LANE,
MANSFIELD WOODHOUSE,
MANSFIELD NG19 7FE
Tel/Recovery: 01623 627653
Fax: 01909 625787
E-mail: andy@redferntravelltd.co.uk
Web site: www.johnsonstours.co.uk
Dirs: C A Johnson, S Johnson, A Johnson,
L Johnson, S Johnson
Ops Man: A Moran
Fleet: 118 - 70 double-deck bus, 4 single-deck
bus, 30 single-deck coach, 4 double-deck coach,
4 midibus, 2 midicoach, 1 minibus, 3 minicoach.
Chassis incl: 2 Alexander Dennis, 1 Ayats,
3 Bova, 30 Bristol, 2 DAF, 2 Ford Transit, 6 Irisbus,
4 Iveco, 4 MAN, 4 Mercedes, 6 Neoplan, 6 Scania,
3 Van Hool, 20 Volvo.
Bodies: 1 Ayats, 6 Beulas, 2 Berkhof, 3 Bova,
2 Caetano, 30 ECW, 5 East Lancs, 6 Irizar,
4 Jonckheere, 6 Neoplan, 30 Northern Counties,
25 Plaxton, 6 Scania, 2 Sunsundegui, 3 Van Hool,
1 Volvo.
Ops incl: local bus services, excursions & tours,
private hire, express, continental tours, school
contracts.
Livery: Green Fade/Stars
Ticket System: ITSO
(Subsidiary of Johnson Bros Tours Ltd)

K V & G L SLACK LTD
THE TRAVEL CENTRE, LUMSDALE,
MATLOCK DE4 5LB
Tel: 01629 582826
Fax: 01629 580519
E-mail: enquiries@slackscoaches.co.uk
Web site: www.slackscoaches.co.uk
Man Dir: G L Slack **Ch Eng:** R M Slack
Co Sec: D R Slack
Tran Man: J Gough
Fleet: 22 - 17 single-deck coach, 3 midicoach,
2 minibus.
Chassis: 3 Alexander Dennis, 5 DAF, 3 Dennis,
2 Ford Transit, 2 Irisbus, 2 Iveco, 3 MAN,
3 Mercedes, 2 Neoplan, 1 Scania, 1 Volvo.
Bodies: 5 Beulas, 1 Esker, 1 Jonckheere,
2 Neoplan, 3 Plaxton, 2 Sitcar, 1 Unvi.
Ops incl: excursions & tours, private hire,
continental tours, school contracts.

STAGECOACH YORKSHIRE
UNIT 4, ELDON ARCADE, BARNSLEY S70 4PP.
Tel: 01246 207103 **Fax:** 01246 216540
E-mail:
Chesterfield.enquiries@stagecoachbus.com
Fleet Names incl: Stagecoach in Chesterfield
Web site: www.stagecoachbus.com
Man Dir: Gary Nolan **Eng Dir:** John Taylor
Comm Dir: Dave Skepper
Ops Dir: Richard Kay

Fleet (Chesterfield): 113 - 11 double-deck bus,
79 single-deck bus, 13 single-deck coach,
10 midibus.
Chassis: 43 Dennis, 22 MAN, 24 Optare,
10 Scania, 14 Volvo.
Ops incl: local bus services, express.
Liveries: Stagecoach UK Bus, National Express.
Ticket System: ERG TP5000.

TM TRAVEL LTD
See South Yorkshire

TRENT BARTON
MANSFIELD ROAD, HEANOR DE75 7BG
Tel: 01773 712265
Fax: 01773 536333
E-mail: customer.services@trentbarton.co.uk
Web site: www.trentbarton.co.uk
Chairman: B R King **Deputy Chairman:**
R I Morgan **Man Dir:** J Counsell **Group Fin
Dir:** G Sutton **Comm Dir:** A Hornby
Head of Development: K L Shayshutt
Fleet: 305 - 286 single-deck bus, 19 single-deck
coach.
Chassis: 4 Dennis, 7 Mercedes, 127 Optare,
97 Scania, 67 Volvo.
Bodies: 15 Irizar, 6 Mercedes, 12 Northern
Counties, 127 Optare, 9 Plaxton, 133 Wright.
Ops incl: local bus services.
Livery: Red
Ticket System: Init
Part of the Wellglade Group. Operations at Dove
Holes will be merged with Bowers Coaches in
late 2011 to form High Peak Bus Company, jointly
owned with Centrebus.

WARRINGTON COACHES LTD
ILAM MOOR LANE, ILAM, ASHBOURNE
DE6 2AZ
Tel: 01335 350204
Fax: 01335 350204
E-mail: info@warringtoncoaches.co.uk
Web site: www.warringtoncoaches.co.uk
Dirs: Lynton Boydon, Maureen Boydon, Keith
Warrington.
Fleet: 10 - 4 single-deck coaches, 3 midicoach,
3 minicoach
Chassis: 1 BMC, 4 Dennis, 1 Ford Transit, 2 LDV,
2 Mercedes.
Bodies: 1 BMC, 2 LDV, 1 Marcopolo, 3 Plaxton,
2 Other.
Ops incl: local bus services, school contracts,
excursions & tours, private hire.
Livery: White/Silver with Red/Gold/Black

P J WILDE & D A WARD
121 PARKSIDE, HEAGE, BELPER DE56 2AG
Tel/Fax: 01773 852374
Fleet Name: Albert Wilde Coaches
Dirs: Philip J Wilde, David Ward
Fleet: 5 single-deck coach.
Chassis: 3 DAF, 1 Leyland, 1 MAN.
Bodies: 1 Duple, 1 Jonckheere, 3 Van Hool
Ops incl: excursions & tours, school contracts.

WOODWARD'S COACHES LTD
100 HIGH STREET EAST, GLOSSOP SK13 8QF
See Courtesy Coaches, Greater Manchester

YESTERYEAR MOTOR SERVICES
Ceased trading

A B COACHES LTD

WILLS ROAD, TOTNES INDUSTRIAL ESTATE,
TOTNES TQ9 5XN
Tel: 01803 864161 **Fax:** 01803 864008
E-mail: abcoaches@btconnect.com
Web site: www.abcoaches.co.uk
Man Dir: Martin Chalk **Dirs:** Mrs Rebecca
Chalk, Brian Smith
Fleet: 15 single-deck coach.
Ops incl: school contracts, excursions & tours,
private hire.
Livery: Cream/Red

AXE VALLEY MINI TRAVEL

BUS DEPOT, 26 HARBOUR ROAD,
SEATON EX12 2NA
Tel/Fax: 01297 625959
Fleet Name: AVMT
Prop: Mrs F M Searle
Traf Man: J R Paddon.
Fleet: 12 - 6 double-deck bus, 2 single-deck bus,
4 midibus.
Chassis: 3 Dennis, 4 Leyland, 2 MCW, 3 Optare.
Ops incl: local bus services.
Livery: Maroon/White.
Ticket System: Wayfarer.

AYREVILLE COACHES

Ceased trading since LRB 2011 went to press.

BEACON BUS

DOLTON BEACON GARAGE, DOLTON,
WINKLEIGH EX19 8PS
Tel: 01805 804240
Web site: www.beaconbus.co.uk
Fleet: 55 - 4 single-deck bus, 7 single-deck coach,
12 midibus, 4 midicoach, 28 minibus.
Chassis: BMC, LDV, Mercedes, Scania, Volvo.
Ops incl: local bus services, school contracts,
private hire.
Livery: White

BLAKES COACHES LTD

EAST ANSTEY, TIVERTON EX16 9JJ
Tel: 01398 341160 **Fax:** 01398 341594
E-mail: info@blakescoaches.co.uk
Web site: www.blakescoaches.co.uk
Man Dir: David Blake **Dir:** Janet Blake
Fleet: 9 - 7 single-deck coach, 1 midicoach,
1 minicoach.
Chassis: 1 Ford Transit, 2 MAN, 4 Scania,
1 Toyota, 1 Volvo.
Bodies: 1 Beulas, 1 Caetano, 2 Irizar, 1 Neoplan,
3 Van Hool, 1 Other.
Ops incl: school contracts, excursions & tours,
private hire, continental tours
Livery: Silver/Green/Blue

CARMEL COACHES LTD

STATION ROAD, NORTHLEW,
OKEHAMPTON EX20 3BN
Tel: 01409 221237 **Fax:** 01409 221226
E-mail: info@carmelcoaches.co.uk
Web site: www.carmelcoaches.co.uk
Dirs: Tony Hazell, Michael Hazell,
Carolyn Alderton.
Fleet: 39
Chassis: 9 Bova, 3 DAF, 8 Dennis, 1 Iveco, 1 King

Long, 1 LDV, 9 Mercedes, 1 Optare, 1 Scania,
4 Volvo, 1 Other.
Bodies: 1 Alexander Dennis, 1 Berkhof, 1 Beulas,
9 Bova, 1 Duple, 1 Irizar, 3 Jonckheere, 1 LDV,
1 King Long, 2 Marcopolo, 1 Optare, 14 Plaxton,
1 Sitcar, 1 Sunsundegui, 1 UVG, 1 Van Hool.
Ops incl: local bus services, school contracts,
excursions & tours, private hire.
Livery: White
Ticket System: Almex

CHELSTON LEISURE SERVICES LTD

LONG ROAD, PAIGNTON TQ4 7BL
Tel: 01803 666736
E-mail: info@dialabus.info
Web site: www.dialabus.info
Fleet Names: Dial-A-Bus, Local-Link.
Fleet: 16 - 10 midibus, 6 minibus.
Chassis: 4 Dennis, 1 Iveco, 4 Mercedes, 7 Optare.
Ops incl: local bus services.
Livery: Blue/White.

COUNTRY BUS

KING CHARLES BUSINESS PARK,
OLD NEWTON ROAD, HEATHFIELD,
NEWTON ABBOT TQ12 6UT
Tel: 01626 833664 **Fax:** 01626 835648
E-mail: info@countrybusdevon.co.uk
Web site: www.countrybusdevon.co.uk
Man Dir: Ms A Ellison
Fleet: 38 - double-deck bus, single deck bus,
single-deck coach, midibus, minibus.
Ops incl: local bus services, school contracts,
private hire.
Livery: White with Blue.
Ticket System: Setright.

CRUDGE COACHES LTD

TURBURY FARM, DUNKESWELL,
HONITON EX14 4QN
Tel: 01404 841657 **Fax:** 01404 841668
E-mail: kscrudge@btinternet.com
Dirs: Kevin Crudge, Mrs Susan Crudge
Fleet: 10 - 7 single deck coach, 1 midicoach,
1 minibus, 1 minicoach.
Chassis: 1 Bova, 1 Dennis, 1 Iveco, 1 LDV, 1 MAN,
2 Mercedes, 3 Volvo.
Bodies: 2 Berkhof, 1 Beulas, 1 Bova, 1 LDV,
1 Mellor, 2 Plaxton, 1 Van Hool.
Ops incl: school contracts, excursions & tours,
private hire.

DAISH'S TRAVEL

DEVONSHIRE HOTEL, PARKHILL ROAD,
TORQUAY TQ1 2DY
Tel: 0844 846 4680
Web site: www.daishs.com
Fleet: 15 single-deck coach
Chassis: 1 Bova, 14 Volvo.
Ops incl: excursions & tours, private hire,
continental tours
Livery: White with Blue/Brown.

DARTLINE COACHES

LANGDONS BUSINESS PARK,
CLYST ST MARY, EXETER EX5 1AF
Tel: 01392 872900
Fax: 01392 872909

E-mail: info@dartline-coaches.co.uk
Web site: www.dartline-coaches.co.uk
Dirs: David Dart, Dave Hounslow **Ops Dir:**
Kevin Busby
Fleet: 45 - single-deck coach, midibus, midicoach,
minibus
Chassis: 3 Bova, 5 Dennis, 6 Optare, 1 Scania,
10 Volvo.
Bodies: 1 Berkhof, 3 Bova, 1 Caetano, 1 Irizar, 14
Plaxton, 1 Sunsundegui, 1 Van Hool.
Ops incl: local bus services, school contracts,
excursions & tours, private hire.
Livery: White/Green
Ticket System: Almex.

DOWN MOTORS & OTTER COACHES

1 MILL STREET, OTTERY ST MARY EX11 1AB
Tel: 01404 812002
Fax: 01404 811128
Partners: W M Down, A G Down, C P Down
Fleet: 10 - 8 single-deck coach, 2 midicoach.
Chassis: 1 Bedford, 1 Bova, 4 Dennis, 1 Iveco,
1 MAN, 1 Mercedes, 1 Toyota.
Bodies: 1 Beulas, 1 Bova, 4 Caetano, 1 Duple,
1 Mercedes, 2 Plaxton.
Ops incl: school contracts, excursions & tours,
private hire.
Livery: Ivory/red

C J DOWN

THE GARAGE, MARY TAVY, TAVISTOCK
PL19 9PA
Tel: 01822 664925
Fax: 01822 810242
E-mail: downscoaches@aol.com
Web site: www.cjdowncoachhiretavistock.co.uk
Proprietors: Mr & Mrs. C J Down **Ops Man:**
W J Wakem **Chief Eng:** W J Lashbrook
Fleet: 21 - 19 single-deck coach, 2 midicoach.
Chassis: 1 MAN, 1 Mercedes, 19 Volvo.
Bodies: 10 Jonckheere, 1 Marcopolo, 9 Plaxton,
1 Other.
Ops incl: school contracts, excursions & tours,
private hire.
Livery: Cream

EASTWARD COACHES

Ceased trading.

FILERS TRAVEL LTD

SLADE LODGE, SLADE ROAD, ILFRACOMBE
EX34 8LB
Tel: 01271 863819 **Fax:** 01271 867281
E-mail: info@filers.co.uk
Web site: www.filers.co.uk
Dirs: Royston J Filer, Irene H Filer
Office Man: Christina King
Ch Eng: George Rogers
Fleet: 23 - 10 single-deck bus, 10 single-deck
coach, 1 midibus, 1 minibus, 1 minicoach.
Chassis: 4 Bova, 2 Dennis, 2 Enterprise, 1 Iveco,
1 MAN, 2 Mercedes, 2 Optare, 1 Scania, 2
Transbus, 2 Volkswagen, 3 Volvo, 1 Other.
Bodies: 4 Bova, 1 Caetano, 1 Irizar, 2 Mercedes, 1
Noge, 2 Optare, 5 Plaxton, 1 Sitcar, 1 Volvo,
5 Other.
Ops incl: local bus services, excursions & tours,
private hire, school contracts, continental tours.
Livery: White/Royal Blue/Gold
Ticket system: Almex

Legend (symbols)

- Vehicle suitable for disabled
- Toilet-drop facilities available
- Recovery service available
- Open top vehicle(s)
- Seat belt-fitted Vehicle
- Coach(es) with galley facilities
- Air-conditioned vehicle(s)
- Coaches with toilet facilities
- **R24** 24 hour recovery service
- Replacement vehicle available
- Vintage Coach(es) available
- Hybrid Buses

FIRST DEVON & CORNWALL LTD
THE RIDE, CHELSON MEADOW,
PLYMOUTH PL9 7JT
Tel: 01752 495250
Fax: 01752 495230
E-mail: firstdevonandcornwall@firstgroup.com
Web site: www.firstgroup.com
Reg Man Dir: Justin Davies
Reg Finance & Planning Dir: Amelia Price
Service Delivery Dir South Coast: Chris
Bainbridge
Reg Eng Standards Dir: Chris Jones
Reg Commercial & Business Growth Dir:
Marc Reddy **Reg Man Devon & Cornwall:**
Robbie Lamerton
Fleet Engineer: Simon Marsh
Fleet: 279 – 106 double-deck bus, 145 single-
deck bus, 18 single-deck coach, 7 open-top bus,
3 articulated bus.
Chassis: 132 Alexander Dennis, 1 Enterprise,
2 Ford, 5 Leyland, 8 Mercedes, 19 Optare, 112
Volvo.
Bodies: 63 Alexander Dennis, 25 East Lancs,
3 Mercedes, 33 Northern Counties, 19 Optare,
83 Plaxton, 3 Van Hool, 48 Wright, 2 Other.
Ops incl: local bus services, school contracts,
excursions & tours, private hire, express,
continental tours.
Livery: FirstGroup UK Bus
Ticket System: Almex

GREY CARS COACHES OF TORBAY
6/7 DANEHEATH BUSINESS PARK,
HEATHFIELD, NEWTON ABBOT
TQ12 6TL
Tel: 01626 833038
Fax: 01626 835920
E-mail: garage@greycars.com
Web site: www.greycars.com
Man Dir: Duncan Millman
Dir: Bruce Millman **Ops Manager:** Colin Holt
Fleet: 18 – 16 single-deck coach, 1 midicoach,
1 minibus.
Chassis: 1 Dennis, 1 Mercedes, 1 Toyota, 15 Volvo.
Bodies: 3 Berkhof, 1 Caetano, 1 Jonckheere,
1 Mercedes, 8 Plaxton, 4 Van Hool.
Ops incl: school contracts, excursions & tours,
private hire.
Livery: Grey/Yellow/Turquoise

GUSCOTT'S COACHES LTD
THE GARAGE, CROFT GATE, HALWILL,
BEAWORTHY EX21 5TL
Tel: 01409 221661
Fax: 01409 221435
Dirs: C D Guscott, T Guscott.
Fleet: 5 single-deck coach.
Chassis: 5 Volvo.
Bodies: 1 Caetano, 1 Jonckheere, 3 Plaxton.
Ops incl: local bus services, school contracts,
private hire.
Livery: Cream/Blue/Red

HARVEY'S BUS LTD
UNIT 5, STATION ROAD,
MORETONHAMPSTEAD TQ13 8SA
Tel: 01647 441221
Web site: www.harveysbus.com
Dirs: P Denton, M Murray.
Fleet incl: midicoach, minibus, minicoach
Ops incl: school contracts, private hire
Livery: White with Blue

HEARDS COACHES
FORE STREET, HARTLAND, BIDEFORD
EX39 6BD
Tel: 01237 441789
E-mail: info@heardscoaches.co.uk
Web Site: www.heardscoaches.co.uk
Fleet Name: Heards Coaches
Dirs: G Heard, B Heard.
Fleet: 19 – 18 single-deck coach, 1 midicoach.
Chassis: Dennis, MAN, Mercedes, Scania, Volvo.
Ops incl: school contracts, private hire.
Livery: Cream

HEMMINGS COACHES LTD
POWLERS PIECE GARAGE, EAST PUTFORD,
HOLSWORTHY EX22 7XW
Tel: 01237 451282
Fax: 01237 451920
E-mail: hemmingscoaches@aol.com
Web site: www.hemmingscoaches.co.uk
Dirs: Ken & Linda Hemmings.
Fleet: 8 – 6 single-deck coach, 1 minibus,
1 minicoach.
Chassis: 1 MAN, 3 Mercedes, 1 Scania, 2 Setra,
1 Volvo.
Bodies: 2 Berkhof, 5 Mercedes, 1 Noge.
Ops incl: excursions & tours, private hire,
continental tours.
Livery: Gold

HILLS SERVICES LTD
THE GARAGE, STIBB CROSS, LANGTREE,
TORRINGTON EX38 8LH
Tel: 01805 601102, 601203
Fax: 01805 601103
E-mail: hills.servicesltd@btinternet.com
Web site: www.hillsholidays.co.uk
Dirs: David J Hearn, Mrs D Hearn, Mrs
M E Hearn
Fleet: 30 – 13 single-deck coach, 5 midicoach,
12 minibus.
Chassis: 3 Bova, 2 DAF, 1 Ford Transit, 10 LDV,
6 Mercedes, 8 Volvo.
Bodies: 3 Bova, 10 LDV, 6 Neoplan, 2 Plaxton,
6 Van Hool, 3 Other.
Ops incl: excursions & tours, private hire, school
contracts.
Livery: White with Orange, Green

HOOKWAYS
Ceased trading since LRB 2011 went to press.

IVYBRIDGE & DISTRICT COMMUNITY
TRANSPORT
Ceased operations.

KINGDOMS TOURS LTD
WESTFIELD GARAGE, EXETER ROAD,
TIVERTON EX16 5NZ
Tel: 01884 252373
Fax: 01884 252646
E-mail: kingdoms-tours@supanet.com
Web site: www.kingdom-tours.co.uk
Dirs: Steven Kingdom, Russell Kingdom,
Ronald Kingdom
Fleet: 23 – 10 single-deck coach, 5 midicoach,
6 minibus, 2 minicoach.
Chassis: 1 Bova, 1 DAF, 4 Iveco, 11 Mercedes,
2 Scania, 4 Volvo.
Bodies: 2 Beulas, 2 Berkhof, 1 Bova, 1 Carlyle,
1 Irizar, 10 Mercedes, 4 Van Hool, 2 Other.
Ops incl: local bus services, school contracts,
excursions & tours, private hire, express,
continental tours.
Livery: White/Red/Orange

MID DEVON COACHES
STATION ROAD, BOW, CREDITON EX17 6JD
Tel/Fax: 01363 82200
E-mail: enquiries@middevoncoaches.co.uk
Web site: www.middevoncoaches.co.uk
Prop: Mrs L A Hamilton
Fleet: 22 – 18 single-deck coach, 2 minicoach,
2 minibus.
Chassis: 2 DAF, 3 Ford, 3 Ford Transit, 5 Leyland,
4 Scania, 2 Toyota, 2 Volvo.
Bodies: 2 Bova, 2 Caetano, 1 Irizar, 2 Jonckheere,
10 Plaxton.
Ops incl: school contracts, excursions & tours,
private hire, continental tours.
Livery: Green/Cream.

PARAMOUNT COACHES LTD
6 VENN CRESCENT, HARTLEY, PLYMOUTH
PL3 5PJ
Tel: 01752 767255
Fax: 01752 767255
Prop: B M Couch **Touring Man:** Brian Madge
Fleet: 7 minibus.
Chassis: 4 LDV, 2 Mercedes, 1 Volkswagen.
Ops incl: excursions & tours, private hire, school
contracts.
Associated company: Eastward Coaches
(see above)

PARKS OF HAMILTON
BURRINGTON WAY, PLYMOUTH PL5 3LS
Tel: 01752 794545/790565
Fax: 01752 777931
Web site: www.parksofhamilton.co.uk
Chairman: D I Park **Dir:** John Bettinson
Fleet: 31 – single-deck coach, double-deck coach,
sleeper coach.

Chassis: Neoplan, Volvo.
Ops incl: express, continental tours, band buses.
Liveries: White with Red and Yellow lining,
National Express.
A division of Parks of Hamilton (see South
Lanarkshire)

PLYMOUTH CITYBUS LTD
MILEHOUSE, PLYMOUTH PL3 4AA
Tel: 0845 077 2223
Fax: 01752 567209
Recovery: 01752 264215
E-mail: customer.services@plymouthbus.co.uk
Web site: www.plymouthbus.co.uk
Fleet Names: Citybus, Citycoach.
Man Dir: Andrew Wickham **Ops Dir:** Tom
Piggott **Eng Dir:** Karl Duncan **Fin Cont:** Iain
Perring.
Fleet: 190 - 37 double-deck bus, 123 single-deck
bus, 11 single-deck coach, 19 midibus.
Chassis: 22 Alexander Dennis, 75 Dennis, 25
Mercedes, 4 Optare, 13 Transbus, 51 Volvo.
Bodies: 13 Alexander, 22 Alexander Dennis, 24
East Lancs, 15 Mercedes, 4 Optare, 96 Plaxton, 13
Transbus, 3 Wright.
Ops incl: local bus services, excursions & tours,
private hire, continental tours, school contracts.
Liveries: Buses: Red/White; **Coaches:** Two
tone Blue.
Ticket system: ERG
A subsidiary of the Go-Ahead Group

POWELLS COACHES
2 BARRIS, LAPFORD, CREDITON EX17 6PT
Tel/Fax: 01363 83468
Props: James P Powell, Mrs D M Powell, W R
Powell
Fleet: 4 single-deck coach
Chassis: 1 DAF, 3 Volvo.
Bodies: 2 Jonckheere, 2 Van Hool.
Ops incl: school contracts, excursions & tours,
private hire.

RADMORES COACHES
4 WOODFORD CRESCENT, PLYMPTON PL7
4QY
Tel/Fax: 01752 335391
Owner: John Williams **Man:** Sarah Hale
Fleet Name: Radmores Coaches
Fleet: 3 - 1 midibus, 2 midicoach.

Ops incl: local bus services, school contracts,
excursions & tours, private hire.
Livery: Red/Gold

RAYS COACHES
88 KINGS TAMERTON ROAD, ST BUDEAUX
PL5 2BW
Tel: 01752 369000

REDWOODS TRAVEL
UNIT 3, STATION ROAD INDUSTRIAL PARK,
HEMYOCK, CULLOMPTON EX15 3SE
Tel: 01823 680288
Fax: 01823 681096
E-mail: info@redwoodstravel.com
Web site: www.redwoodstravel.com
Dirs: Paul Redwood, Jacquie Redwood **Ch Eng:**
Garrie Morrissey.
Fleet: 24 – 15 single-deck coach, 1 midicoach,
8 minibus.
Chassis: 2 LDV, 4 MAN, 5 Mercedes, 1 Renault,
4 Scania, 8 Volvo.
Bodies: 5 Jonckheere, 2 LDV, 5 Mercedes, 3
Noge, 1 Plaxton, 4 Scania, 2 UVG, 2 Other.
Ops incl: local bus services, school contracts,
excursions & tours, private hire, continental tours
Livery: White/Red/Green
Ticket System: Wayfarer

RIVER LINK
5 LOWER STREET, DARTMOUTH TQ6 9AJ
Tel: 01803 834488
Fax: 01803 835248
E-mail: sales@riverlink.co.uk
Web site: www.riverlink.co.uk
Chairman: Sir William McAlpine **Dirs:** David
Allan, John Butt, Norman Christy **Co Sec:** Philip
Smallwood **Group Gen Man:** Andrew Pooley
Tran Man: Michael Palmer
Fleet: 7 - 2 double-deck bus, 1 single-deck bus, 2
open-top bus, 2 midibus.
Chassis: 3 Bristol, 1 Dennis, 1 Leyland, 2
Mercedes.
Ops incl: local bus services, private hire.
Livery: Dark Blue/Ivory
Ticket System: Almex.

SEWARDS COACHES
GLENDALE, DALWOOD, AXMINSTER
X13 7EJ

Tel/Fax: 01404 881343
Partners: Richard M Seward, Ivy A Seward,
Catherine E Seward
Fleet: 19 - 11 single-deck coach, 1 midibus,
5 midicoach, 2 minicoach.
Chassis: 2 Bova, 1 DAF, 5 Dennis, 1 Iveco,
1 Leyland, 2 MAN, 4 Mercedes, 1 Renault, 1 Temsa,
1 Toyota.
Bodies: 1 Berkhof, 2 Bova, 3 Caetano, 1 Hispano,
1 Marcopolo, 4 Plaxton, 1 Sitcar, 1 UVG, 5 Other
Ops incl: local bus services, school contracts,
private hire.
Livery: Cream with Orange/Green

SHEARINGS HOLIDAYS
BARTON HILL WAY, TORQUAY TQ2 8JG
Tel: 01803 326016
Fax: 01803 316059
Depot Man: David Braund
See Shearings Holidays, Greater Manchester

STAGECOACH SOUTH WEST
BELGRAVE ROAD, EXETER EX1 2LB
Tel: 01392 427711
Fax: 01392 889727
E-mail: southwest.enquiries@stagecoachbus.
com
Web site: www.stagecoachbus.com
Man Dir: Ms Michelle Hargreaves **Ops Dir:**
Richard Stevens **Ops Man:** Richard McAllister
Eng Man: Adrian Noel
Fleet: 377- 140 double-deck bus, 170 single-deck
bus, 2 single-deck coach, 65 midibus.
Chassis: 104 Alexander Dennis, 91 Dennis,
1 Leyland, 12 MAN, 10 Mercedes, 65 Optare,
10 Scania, 48 Transbus, 38 Volvo.
Bodies: 120 Alexander, 133 Alexander Dennis,
1 Caetano, 3 Marshall, 7 Northern Counties,
65 Optare, 13 Plaxton, 41 Transbus.
Ops incl: local bus services, school contracts.
Livery: Stagecoach UK Bus
Ticket System: ERG EP5000

STREETS COACHWAYS LTD
THE OLD AERODROME, CHIVENOR,
BARNSTAPLE EX31 4AY
Tel: 01271 815069
Fax: 01271 817333
E-mail: lyn@streetscoachways.co.uk
Dirs: M Street, S M Street
Fleet: 12 - 5 single-deck coach, 1 midibus,
1 midicoach, 5 minibus.
Chassis: 1 Bova, 1 DAF, 2 Dennis, 5 LDV, 1 MAN,
2 Mercedes.
Ops incl: private hire, school contracts.

TALLY HO! COACHES LTD
STATION YARD INDUSTRIAL ESTATE,
KINGSBRIDGE TQ7 1ES
Tel: 01548 853081
Fax: 01548 853602
E-mail: info@tallyhocoaches.com
Web site: www.tallyhocoaches.com
Dir: Don McIntosh **Head of Transport:**
Steve Pengelly **Head of Engineering:**
Adam Wilson
Fleet: 49 – 2 double-deck bus, 16 single-deck
bus, 25 single-deck coach, 6 minibus.
Ops incl: local bus services, school contracts,
excursions & tours, private hire.
Livery: Blue/White
Ticket system: Almex

TARGET TRAVEL
EAGLE ROAD, LANGAGE BUSINESS PARK,
PLYMOUTH PL7 5JY
Tel: 01752 242000
Fax: 01752 345700
E-mail: admin@targettravel.info
Web site: www.targettravel.co.uk
Ops incl: local bus services, private hire
Livery: Green/White

TAVISTOCK COMMUNITY TRANSPORT
See Cornwall

TAW & TORRIDGE COACHES LTD
GRANGE LANE, MERTON, OKEHAMPTON
EX20 3ED
Tel: 01805 603400
Fax: 01805 603559
Recovery: 01805 603400
E-mail: enquiries@tawandtorridge.co.uk
Web site: www.tawandtorridge.co.uk
Man Dir: Tony Hunt **Dir/Ops Man:** Mark Hunt
Dir/Co Sec: Linda Hunt **Dir:** Tracey Laughton
Fleet Eng/Dir: Chris Laughton.
Fleet: 44 - 34 single-deck coach, 9 minibus, 1
midicoach
Chassis: 1 DAF, 8 Dennis, 3 Ford Transit, 1 LDV, 3
MAN, 5 Mercedes, 19 Volvo, 3 Other.
Bodies: 1 Berkhof, 7 Jonckheere, 7 Mercedes, 7
Plaxton, 1 UVG, 5 Van Hool, 8 Wadham Stringer, 2
Volvo, 3 Other.

Ops incl: school contracts, excursions & tours,
private hire, continental tours.
Livery: Blue/Silver

T.T. COACHES LTD
HACCHE LANE, SOUTH MOLTON EX36 3EH
Tel: 01769 572139 **Fax:** 01769 574182
E-mail: info@ttcoaches.co.uk
Dirs: Tony Hunt, Mark Hunt, Christopher
Laughton
Fleet: 18 – single-deck bus, single-deck coach,
midibus, midicoach, minibus, minicoach.
Chassis: 3 Dennis, 11 Mercedes, 4 Optare.
Bodies: 1 Berkhof, 2 Jonckheere, 11 Mercedes,
4 Optare.
Ops incl: local bus services, school contracts,
excursions & tours, private hire, continental tours.
Livery: Blue
Ticket system: Almex
Formerly T.W. Coaches Ltd

TURNERS TOURS
BACK LANE INDUSTRIAL ESTATE,
CHULMLEIGH EX18 7AA
Tel: 01769 580242
Fax: 01769 581281
E-mail: coaches@turnerstours.co.uk
Web site: www.turnerstours.co.uk
Dirs: S L Gilson, P C Gilson.
Fleet: 32 - 15 single-deck coach, 10 single-deck

bus, 2 midibus, 1 midicoach, 4 minibus.
Chassis: Dennis, LDV, Mercedes, Volvo.
Bodies: Alexander, Caetano, Jonckheere, Marshall,
Mercedes, Plaxton, Reeve Burgess.
Ops incl: local bus services, school contracts,
excursions & tours, private hire, express,
continental tours.
Livery: Cream.
Ticket System: Almex

WESTERN GREYHOUND LTD
See Cornwall

WILLS MINI COACHES
Ceased trading since LRB 2011 went to press.

WOOD BROTHERS TRAVEL LTD
WHITECLEAVES QUARRY, PLYMOUTH ROAD,
BUCKFASTLEIGH TQ11 0DQ
Tel: 01364 642666
Fax: 01364 643870
E-mail: woodbrotherstravel@hotmail.co.uk
Dirs: David Wood, Roger Wood, Adrian Carter
Co Sec: Sue Wood
Fleet: 10 - 6 single-deck coach, 3 midicoach, 1
minicoach.
Chassis: 1 Alexander Dennis, 3 Dennis, 3
Mercedes, 1 Volkswagen, 2 Volvo.
Bodies: 1 Autobus, 1 Optare, 7 Plaxton, 1 Other.
Ops incl: school contracts, private hire.
Livery: Yellow and Black on White.

DORSET, BOURNEMOUTH, POOLE

BARRY'S COACHES LTD
9 CAMBRIDGE ROAD, GRANBY INDUSTRIAL
ESTATE, WEYMOUTH DT4 9TJ
Tel: 01305 784850
Fax: 01305 782252
E-mail: barryscoaches@hotmail.co.uk
Web site: www.barryscoachesdorset.co.uk
Fleet: 25 – 22 single-deck coach, 1 double-deck
coach, 2 midicoach.
Man Dir: Mrs M Newsam
Fleet Eng: Mr G Newsam
Chassis: 2 MAN, 2 Mercedes, 14 Scania, 7 Volvo.
Ops incl: school contracts, excursions & tours,
private hire, continental tours.
Livery: White/Blue/Yellow

BLUEBIRD COACHES
(WEYMOUTH) LTD
450 CHICKERELL ROAD,
WEYMOUTH DT3 4DH
Tel: 01305 786262
Fax: 01305 766223
Recovery: 01305 786262/07771 561060
E-mail: martyn@bluebirdcoaches.com
Web site: www.bluebirdcoaches.com
Dirs: Martyn Hoare, Stephen Hoare.
Fleet: 22 - 20 single-deck coach, 1 midicoach,
1 minibus.
Chassis: 7 DAF, 1 Mercedes, 2 Neoplan,
1 Volkswagen, 11 Volvo.
Bodies: 7 Bova, 1 Caetano, 3 Jonckheere,
2 Neoplan, 4 Plaxton, 5 Van Hool.
Ops incl: school contracts, excursions & tours,
private hire, continental tours.
Livery: White/Blue/Orange

CAVENDISH LINER LTD
BANBURY ROAD, NUFFIELD INDUSTRIAL
ESTATE, POOLE BH17 0GA
Tel: 01202 660620
Fax: 01202 660220
E-mail: sales@cavendishliner.com
Web site: www.cavendishliner.com
Fleet: 15 – double-deck bus, single-deck bus,
single-deck coach, double-deck coach, midicoach,
minicoach.
Ops incl: schools contracts, private hire
Livery: Grey/Black

COACH HOUSE TRAVEL
*Business acquired by the Go-Ahead Group since LRB
2011 went to press.*

DAMORY COACHES
See Go South Coast Ltd

DOLPHIN COACHES LTD
UNIT 6, STONE LANE INDUSTRIAL ESTATE,
WIMBORNE MINSTER
BH21 1HB
Tel: 01202 883134   **Fax:** 01202 883132
E-mail: markself@dolphincoaches.co.uk
Web site: www.dolphincoaches.co.uk
Man Dir: T J Hann
Fin Dir: Mrs S Hann
Ops Man: M R Self
Fleet: 10 – 9 single-deck coach, 1 midibus.
Chassis: 3 Bova, 1 Dennis, 1 MAN, 1 Optare,
4 Scania
Bodies: 3 Bova, 1 Caetano, 1 Noge, 1 Optare,
4 Van Hool

Ops incl: local bus services, school contracts,
excursions & tours, private hire, express,
continental tours.
Livery: Cream & Blue
Ticket System: Wayfarer

DORSET COUNTY COUNCIL –
DORSET PASSENGER TRANSPORT
DPT GARAGE, GROVE TRADING ESTATE,
DORCHESTER DT1 1ST
Tel: 01305 224540
Fax: 01305 225166
E-mail: K.R.Clark@dorsetcc.gov.uk
Ops Man: David Besant
Fleet Sup: Kevin Clark
Fleet: 103 – 4 single-deck coach, 6 single-
deck bus, 22 midibus, 68 minibus, 3 wheelchair
accessible cars
Chassis: 2 Dennis, 30 Fiat, 7 Iveco, 1 Leyland,
23 Mercedes, 21 Optare, 3 Peugeot, 9 Renault,
6 Scania, 1 Volvo.
Bodies: 3 Expert, 30 Fiat, 7 Irisbus, 6 Irizar,
23 Mercedes, 21 Optare, 4 Plaxton, 9 Renault.
Ops incl: school contracts, welfare contracts,
adult day centre transport, school excursions,
park & ride.
Livery: Silver/Green (large vehicles: Yellow)

EXCELSIOR COACHES LTD
CENTRAL BUSINESS PARK,
BOURNEMOUTH BH1 3SJ
Tel: 01202 652222 **Fax:** 01202 652223
E-mail: coaches@excelsior-coaches.com
Web site: www.excelsior-coaches.com
Man Dir: Kathy Tilbury

Fleet: 40 - 36 coach, 2 midicoach, 2 minibus.
Chassis: 6 Mercedes, 34 Volvo.
Bodies: 17 Caetano, 2 Esker, 2 Jonckheere, 2 Mercedes, 9 Plaxton, 4 Sunsundegui, 4 Volvo.
Ops incl: school contracts, private hire, express, continental tours.
Liveries: Cream, National Express

FIRST HAMPSHIRE & DORSET LTD
See Hampshire

GO SOUTH COAST LTD
TOWNGATE HOUSE, 2-8 PARKSTONE ROAD, POOLE BH15 2PR
Tel: 01202 680888
Fax: 01202 670244
E-mail: alex.carter@gosouthcoast.co.uk
Web site: www.damorycoach.co.uk, www.wdbus.co.uk, www.go-ahead.com
Fleet Names: Damory Coaches, More, Purbeck Breezers, Wilts & Dorset
Chairman: David Brown
Man Dir: Alex Carter
Eng Dir: Steve Hamilton
Fin Dir: Matt Dolphin
Divisional Dirs: Marc Morgan Huws, Ed Wills
Fleet: 625 - 252 double-deck bus, 125 single-deck bus, 91 single-deck coach, 1 articulated bus, 12 open top bus, 137 midibus, 7 minibus.
Chassis: 2 Bristol, 104 DAF, 49 Dennis, 2 Ford, 4 Iveco, 5 LDV, 33 Leyland, 1 MAN, 50 Mercedes, 99 Optare, 106 Scania, 2 Toyota, 168 Volvo.
Bodies: 10 Alexander Dennis, 2 Autobus, 4 Beulas, 1 Bova, 6 Caetano, 2 ECW, 56 East Lancs, 2 Ford, 12 Ikarus, 4 Irizar, 2 Jonckheere, 5 LDV, 25 Leyland, 47 Mercedes, 41 Northern Counties, 153 Optare, 76 Plaxton, 73 Scania, 27 Transbus, 22 Van Hool, 55 Wright.
Ops incl: local bus services, school contracts.
Liveries: Damory: Blue/Black; **Wilts & Dorset:** Red/White/Black, Red/Blue
Ticket System: Wayfarer TGX
Part of the Go-Ahead Group

MIKE HALFORD COACHES
KISEM, NORTH MILLS, BRIDPORT DT6 3AH
Tel/Fax: 01308 421106
Prop: M G Halford
Fleet: 8 - 3 midibus, 3 midicoach, 2 minibus.
Chassis: 8 Mercedes.
Ops incl: local bus services, private hire, school contracts.

HERRINGTON COACHES LTD
MANOR FARM, SANDLEHEATH ROAD, ALDERHOLT, FORDINGBRIDGE SP6 3EG
Tel: 01425 652842
E-mail: herringtoncoaches@live.co.uk
Web site: www.herringtoncoaches.com
Props: Alan Herrington, Mrs Janet Herrington.
Fleet: 5 - 3 single-deck coach, 2 midicoach.
Chassis: 2 Mercedes, 2 Scania, 1 Volvo.
Bodies: 1 Jonckheere, 2 Van Hool, 2 Other.
Ops incl: local bus services, school contracts, private hire.
Livery: Red/Grey
Ticket System: Setright

HIGHCLIFFE COACH HOLIDAYS
312 LYMINGTON ROAD, HIGHCLIFFE, CHRISTCHURCH BH23 5ET
Tel: 01425 271111

Web site: www.highcliffecoachholidays.co.uk
Fleet: 2 single-deck coach.
Chassis: 1 Volvo, 1 Setra.
Ops incl: excursions & tours, continental tours.

HOMEWARD BOUND
137 LYNWOOD DRIVE, WIMBORNE BH21 1UU
Tel: 01202 884491
E-mail: enquiries@homewardboundtravel.co.uk
Web site: www.homewardboundtravel.co.uk
Prop: Louisa Fairhead
Fleet: 3 minicoach
Chassis: 3 Renault
Ops incl: school contracts, excursions & tours, private hire, continental tours.
Livery: Silver/Green/Purple

LAGUNA HOLIDAYS
LAGUNA HOTEL, 6 SUFFOLK ROAD SOUTH, BOURNEMOUTH BH2 6AZ
Tel: 01202 767022
Web site: www.lagunaholidays.com
Fleet: 11 – 1 double-deck coach, 10 single-deck coach
Chassis: 1 Ayats, 9 Scania, 1 Setra.
Bodies: 1 Ayats, 9 Irizar, 1 Setra.
Ops incl: excursions & tours, private hire.
Livery: White with Red Lettering

LINKRIDER COACHES LTD
FLOWER MEADOW, HAYCRAFTS LANE, HARMANS CROSS, SWANAGE BH19 3EB
Tel: 01929 477344
Fax: 01929 477345
E-mail: linkridercoaches@btconnect.com
Web site: www.linkridercoaches.co.uk
Fleet Names: Linkrider Coaches, South Dorset Coaches
Dirs: Nick & Anne Hubbard
Ops Man: Ben Banks **Ch Eng:** Barry Goodwin.
Fleet incl: single-deck coach, midicoach.
Chassis: Alexander Dennis, Bova, Mercedes, Setra, Toyota.
Bodies: Alexander Dennis, Bova, Mercedes, Setra.
Ops incl: local bus services, school contracts, excursions & tours, continental tours.

POWELLS COACHES
THORNFORD GARAGE, THORNFORD DT9 6QN
Tel: 01935 872390
Fleet: 2 single-deck coach.
Ops incl: excursions & tours, private hire.
Livery: Red/White.

SEAVIEW COACHES (POOLE) LTD
10-12 FANCY ROAD, POOLE BH12 4QZ
Tel: 01202 741439 **Fax:** 01202 740241
E-mail: info@seaviewcoaches.com
Web site: www.seaviewcoaches.com
Man Dir: David Tarr
Fleet: 24 - 20 single-deck coach, 2 minibus, 2 minicoach.
Chassis: 1 Ford Transit, 1 Irisbus, 11 MAN, 5 Mercedes, 4 Neoplan, 2 Temsa.
Bodies: 7 Beulas, 4 Neoplan, 6 Noge, 2 Temsa, 5 Other.
Ops incl: school contracts, excursions & tours, private hire.
Livery: Silver with Blue/Red

SHAFTESBURY & DISTRICT MOTOR SERVICES LTD
UNIT 2, MELBURY WORKSHOPS, CANN COMMON, SHAFTESBURY SP7 0EB
Tel/Fax: 01747 854359
E-mail: info@sdbuses.co.uk
Web site: www.sdbuses.co.uk
Dir: Roger Brown **Co Sec:** Liam Stacey
Fleet: 16 - 5 double-deck bus, 5 single-deck bus, 5 single-deck coach, 1 minicoach.
Chassis: 5 AEC, 4 Leyland, 3 Mercedes, 1 Toyota, 2 Volvo.
Bodies: 1 Caetano, 1 Duple, 1 Jonckheere, 1 MCW, 1 Optare, 4 Plaxton, 1 Wadham Stringer, 5 Other.
Ops incl: local bus services, school contracts, private hire.
Livery: Red/Cream/Maroon
Ticket System: Wayfarer Saver

SHAMROCK BUSES LTD
Ceased operations since LRB 2011 went to press.

SHORELINE BUS & COACH TRAVEL
13 CHESHIRE DRIVE, BOURNEMOUTH BH8 0JU
Tel/Fax/Recovery: 01202 391285
E-mail: shoreline@shorelinetravel.co.uk
Web site: www.shorelinetravel.co.uk
Prop: Trevor Shore
Tran Man: Shirley Shore.
Fleet: 4 single-deck coach.
Chassis: 2 DAF, 1 Scania, 1 Volvo.
Bodies: 1 Plaxton, 3 Van Hool.
Ops incl: local bus services, school contracts, excursions & tours, private hire.
Livery: Red.

SOUTH WEST COACHES LTD
UNIT 17, TRADECROFT INDUSTRIAL ESTATE, PORTLAND DT5 2LN
Tel: 01305 823039
See Somerset

SOVEREIGN COACHES
PINE LODGE, SIDMOUTH ROAD, ROUSDON, LYME REGIS DT7 3RD
Tel: 01297 23000
E-mail: sov_coaches@btinternet.com
Web site: www.sovereigncoaches.co.uk
Partners: Richard C Keech, Mrs Cynthia M Keech.
Fleet: 8 - 5 midicoach, 3 minicoach.
Chassis: 2 Iveco, 1 LDV, 4 Mercedes, 1 Toyota.
Bodies: 1 Autobus, 1 Esker, 1 Indcar, 1 LDV, 2 Onyx, 1 Plaxton, 1 Other.
Ops incl: school contracts, excursions & tours, private hire.
Livery: White/Red

DAVID THOMPSON TOURS LTD
NEWLYN, 11 LINCOLN AVENUE, CHRISTCHURCH BH23 2SG
Tel: 01202 490333
Fax: 01202 480026
Web site: www.thompsonstours.co.uk
Dir: David Thompson
Ops incl: local bus services, excursions & tours, private hire, continental tours.
Livery: White with Blue Lettering

TRAVEL GUEST
63 PINEVALE CRESCENT, REDHILL,
BOURNEMOUTH BH10 6BG
Tel: 01202 383643
Web site: www.dorsetsprinter.com
Fleet Name: Dorset Sprinter
Ops incl: local bus services, private hire

WILTS & DORSET BUS COMPANY LTD
See Go South Coast Ltd

YELLOW BUSES
🚍 ⬚ ♿ ❄ 🅃
YEOMANS WAY, BOURNEMOUTH
BH8 0BQ
Tel: 01202 636000
Fax: 01202 636001

E-mail: mail@yellowbuses.co.uk
Web site: www.bybus.co.uk
Man Dir: D ALott
Eng Dir: GCCorrie
Fin Dir & Co Sec: A Smith
Head of Marketing: Mrs J Wilkinson
Ops Man: M Conroy
Fleet: 146 - 47 double-deck bus, 76 single-deck
bus, 18 single-deck coach, 3 open top bus,
2 training vehicles.
Chassis: 12 Alexander Dennis, 1 DAF, 43 Dennis,
29 Optare, 2 Scania, 53 Volvo.
Bodies: 5 Alexander Dennis, 10 Caetano,
58 East Lancs, 1 Jonckheere, 29 Optare,
15 Plaxton, 18 Wright, 4 Other.
Ops incl: local bus services, school contracts,
express.

Livery: Yellow
Ticket System: Wayfarer TGX200
A subsidiary of RATP Dev UK Ltd

2ⁿᵈ & 4ᵗʰ LIMITED
5 HEATHFIELD WAY, WEST MOORS,
FERNDOWN BH22 0DA
Tel/Fax: 01202 870724
E-mail: nwiain@aol.com
Web site: www.2and4th.com
Man Dir: Lian Newman
Dir: Gillian Newman.
Fleet: 2 - 1 midicoach, 1 minibus.
Chassis: 1 Fiat, 1 Mercedes.
Ops incl: school contracts, excursion & tour,
private hire, express.
Livery: White

♿ Vehicle suitable for disabled	⬚ Seat belt-fitted Vehicle	R24 24 hour recovery service
🅃 Toilet-drop facilities available	🍽 Coach(es) with galley facilities	❌ Replacement vehicle available
R Recovery service available	❄ Air-conditioned vehicle(s)	🚌 Vintage Coach(es) available
🚍 Open top vehicle(s)	⛟ Coaches with toilet facilities	⬚ Hybrid Buses

ALFA TRAVEL LTD
See Alfa Travel, Lancashire

ARRIVA NORTH EAST
See Tyne & Wear

BROWNS OF DURHAM
Ceased operations since LRB 2011 went to press

CLASSIC COACHES LTD
♿ ⬚ ❄ ❌ 🅃
CLASSIC HOUSE, MORRISON ROAD,
ANNFIELD PLAIN, STANLEY DH9 7RX
Tel: 01207 282288
Fax: 01207 281333
E-mail: ian.shipley@tgmgroup.co.uk
Web site: www.classic-coaches.co.uk
Man Dir: Ian Shipley
Tran Man: John Shipley
Ch Eng: Eric Bowerbank
Fleet: 67 - 4 double-deck bus, 4 single-deck bus,
35 single-deck coach, 5 double-deck coach,
9 midibus, 10 minibus.
Chassis: 1 Alexander Dennis, 1 Ayats, 1 DAF,
4 Leyland, 10 Mercedes, 8 Optare, 16 Scania,
1 VDL, 23 Volvo.
Bodies: 1 Alexander Dennis, 1 Ayats, 8 Berkhof,
12 Caetano, 1 ECW, 2 East Lancs, 5 Irizar,
1 Jonckheere, 1 Northern Counties, 8 Optare,
11 Plaxton, 6 Van Hool, 10 Other.
Ops incl: local bus services, school contracts,
excursions & tours, private hire, express,
continental tours
Livery: Red
Part of the TGM Group, a subsidiary of Arriva

COCHRANE'S
♿ ⬚ R24
4 FARADAY ROAD, NORTH EAST
INDUSTRIAL ESTATE, PETERLEE SR8 5AP
Tel: 0191 586 2136
Fax: 0191 586 5566
Fleet Name: Cochrane's Kelvin Travel
Owner: I P Cochrane
Fleet: 8 - 7 single-deck bus, 1 midicoach.

Chassis: 1 Bedford, 3 Bova, 1 DAF, 1 Mercedes,
2 Volvo.
Bodies: 3 Bova, 1 Caetano, 1 Duple, 1 Plaxton,
1 Van Hool, 1 Other.
Ops incl: school contracts.
Livery: Orange/Black.
Ticket System: Setright.

COMPASS ROYSTON TRAVEL LTD
⛟ 🍽 ♿ R24 ❌ 🅃
BOWESFIELD LANE INDUSTRIAL ESTATE,
STOCKTON-ON-TEES TS18 3EG
Tel: 01642 606644
Fax: 01642 608617
Web site: www.compassroyston.com
Man Dir: G Walton **Trans Man:** M Metcalfe.
Fleet: 65 – 1 single-deck bus, 1 double-deck
coach, 49 single-deck coach, 12 midibus,
1 midicoach, 1 minibus.
Chassis: Ayats, Ford, Mercedes, Neoplan, Optare,
Setra, Volvo.
Bodies: Ayats, Berkhof, Jonckheere, Mercedes,
Optare, Neoplan, Plaxton, Setra, Van Hool, Wright.
Ops incl: local bus services, excursions & tours,
private hire, express, continental tours, school
contracts.
Livery: White with Blue/Yellow.
Associated with Procters Coaches, North
Yorkshire

DURHAM CITY COACHES LTD
⛟ ♿ 🍽 ❄ ❌ 🅃
BRANDON LANE, BRANDON,
URHAM DH7 8PG
Tel: 0191 378 0540
Fax: 0191 378 1985
E-mail: sales@durhamcitycoaches.co.uk
Web site: www.durhamcitycoaches.co.uk
Man Dir: Michael Lightfoot **Dir:** Christine
Lightfoot.
Fleet: 17 - 13 single-deck coach, 4 midicoach.
Chassis: 3 Bova, 5 Mercedes, 9 Volvo.
Ops incl: excursions & tours, private hire,
continental tours, school contracts.
Livery: Black/Red/Gold

ENTERPRISE TRAVEL
⛟ 🍽 ♿ ❄ ❌ 🅃
19 PINE GROVE, DARLINGTON DL3 8JF
Tel/Fax: 01325 286924
E-mail: coachhire@aol.com
Web site: www.enterprisecoachhire.co.uk
Dirs: B R Brown, Mrs B M Brown
Fleet: 6 - 5 single-deck coach, 1 minicoach.
Chassis: 1 DAF, 1 Dennis, 1 MAN, 1 Mercedes,
1 Scania, 1 Toyota.
Bodies: 2 Berkhof, 1 Bova, 1 Caetano, 1 Setra,
1 Van Hool.
Ops incl: excursions & tours, private hire, school
contracts.
Livery: White with Red/Green reliefs.

GARDINERS NMC TRAVEL
⬚ ⛟ ❄ R ❌
COULSON STREET, SPENNYMOOR DL16 7RS
Tel: 01388 818235   **Fax:** 01388 811466
E-mail: info@gardinerstravel.co.uk
Web site: www.nmctours.co.uk
Man Dir: John Gardiner **Tran Man:** Harry Revel.
Fleet: 10 – 9 single-deck coach, 1 double-deck
coach.
Chassis: 6 DAF, 1 Mercedes, 1 Scania, 2 Setra.
Ops incl: excursions & tours, private hire,
continental tours.
Livery: White with Orange/Black.
Ticket system: AES

GARNETT'S COACHES
⬚ ⛟ ❄
UNIT E1, ROMAN WAY INDUSTRIAL ESTATE,
TINDALE CRESCENT, BISHOP AUCKLAND
DL14 9AW
Tel: 01388 604419 **Fax:** 01388 609549
E-mail: bookings@garnettscoaches.com
Web site: www.garnettscoaches.com
Fleet Ops Man: Paul Garnett
Fleet: 40 - 13 double-deck bus, 21 single-deck
coach, 3 double-deck coach, 3 midicoach.
Ops incl: school contracts, excursions & tours,
private hire, continental tours.
Livery: Yellow/Red/Black.

GO NORTH EAST
See Tyne & Wear

GRIERSONS COACHES
♿ 🍴

SEDGEFIELD ROAD GARAGE, FISHBURN,
STOCKTON-ON-TEES TS21 4DD
Tel: 01740 620209
Fax: 01740 621243
Web site: www.griersonscoachhire.co.uk
Props: C & D Grierson.
Fleet: 20 - 5 double-deck bus, 6 single-deck bus,
4 single-deck coach, 1 midicoach, 4 minibus.
Chassis: 1 DAF, 1 Ford, 1 Ford Transit, 2 Freight
Rover, 2 Mercedes, 1 Scania, 13 Volvo.
Bodies: 1 Carlyle, 3 Jonckheere, 2 Mercedes,
13 Plaxton, 1 Reeve Burgess, 1 Van Hool.
Ops incl: excursions & tours, private hire,
express, continental tours.
Livery: Blue/Red.

HODGSONS COACH OPERATORS LTD
♿ ♨ ✈ 🔧

16 GALGATE, BARNARD CASTLE
DL12 8BG
Tel: 01833 630730
Fax: 01833 630830
E-mail: hodgsonscoaches@btconnect.com
Web site: www.hodgsonscoachtravel.co.uk
Man Dir: Keith Hodgson
Ops Man: Mark Hodgson.
Fleet: 20 – 2 single-deck bus, 12 single-deck
coach, 3 midicoach, 3 minibus.
Chassis: 1 Bova, 4 Dennis, 1 Irisbus, 1 LDV,
3 Mercedes, 1 Optare, 2 Volkswagen, 7 Volvo.
Bodies: 1 Beulas, 1 Bova, 2 Jonckheere, 1 LDV,
1 Optare, 12 Plaxton, 2 Others.
Ops incl: local bus services, school contracts,
excursions & tours, private hire, continental tours.
Livery: White/Blue.
Ticket System: Wayfarer Saver.

HUMBLES COACHES
♨ ♨

UP YONDER, ROBSON STREET, SHILDON
DL4 1EB
Tel: 01388 772772
Fax: 01388 772211
E-mail: malcolm.humble@sky.com
Dirs: Malcolm Humble, Mrs Pamela West.
Fleet: 2 midicoach.
Chassis: 2 Mercedes.
Ops incl: school contracts, excursions & tours,
private hire.
Livery: White

HUNTER BROS LTD
THE GARAGE, TANTOBIE, STANLEY
DH9 9TG
Tel: 01207 232392
Fax: 01207 290575
Ops incl: local bus services.
Livery: Black/White.

J & C COACHES
♿ 🍴 ♨ 🔧 T

COACH DEPOT, GROAT DRIVE, AYCLIFFE
INDUSTRIAL PARK, NEWTON AYCLIFFE
DL5 6HY
Tel: 01325 312705
Fax: 01325 320385
Web site: www.jandccoaches.co.uk
Snr Partner: J N Jones
Partners: A Jones, N Jones, D Jones.
Fleet: 10 - 3 single-deck coach, 1 double-deck

coach, 3 midibus, 2 midicoach, 1 minibus.
Ops incl: school contracts, excursions & tours,
private hire, continental tours.
Livery: various

JSB TRAVEL
♿

13 HILLSIDE ROAD, COUNDON
DL14 8LS
Tel: 07900 426206
Web site: www.jsbtravel.co.uk
Ops incl: local bus services, private hire.
Fleet: midibus, minibus.
Chassis: Mercedes, Optare.
Livery: Maroon/White.

JAYLINE BAND SERVICES
♿ 🍴 ❄

1 HACKWORTH ROAD, NORTH WEST
INDUSTRIAL ESTATE, PETERLEE
SR8 2JQ
Tel: 0750 314 2222
E-mail: jaylinetravel@hotmail.com
Web site: jaylinetravel.com
Prop: Jason Rogers **Dir:** Neil Tait.
Fleet: 6 - 2 single-deck band coach,
4 double-deck band coach.
Chassis: 2 Scania, 2 Setra, 2 Volvo.
Bodies: Berkhof, Jonckheere, Setra, Van Hool.
Ops incl: private hire (band buses, film crews)
Livery: Blue

KINGSLEY COACHES LTD
See Tyne & Wear

LEE'S COACHES LTD
♨ ♿ 🍴 ❄ 🔧

MILL ROAD GARAGE, LITTLEBURN
INDUSTRIAL ESTATE, LANGLEY MOOR
DH7 8HE
Tel: 0191 378 0653
Fax: 0191 378 9086
E-mail: info@leescoaches.co.uk
Web site: www.leescoaches.co.uk
Man Dir: Malcolm Lee **Dir:** Colin Lee
Co Sec: Mrs Jean Lee **Eng:** David Welch
Fleet: 16 - 15 singe-deck coach, 1 minibus
Chassis: 1 EOS, 1 LDV, 1 MAN, 1 Mercedes,
12 Volvo.
Bodies: 3 Berkhof, 1 Bova, 2 Caetano,
2 Jonckheere, 1 Neoplan, 1 Plaxton, 1 Sitcar,
4 Van Hool, 1 Volvo.
Ops incl: school contracts, excursions & tours,
private hire, continental tours
Livery: Blue/Silver

MAUDES COACHES
♨ 🍴 🔧

REDWELL GARAGE, HARMIRE ROAD,
BARNARD CASTLE DL12 8QJ
Tel: 01833 637341 **Fax:** 01833 631888
Prop: Stephen Maude
Fleet: 7 - 4 single-deck coach, 2 midicoach,
1 minibus.
Chassis: 1 Dennis, 1 LDV, 2 Mercedes, 3 Volvo.
Bodies: 1 Berkhof, 1 LDV, 3 Plaxton, 1 Van Hool,
1 Other.
Ops incl: local bus services, school contracts,
excursions & tours, private hire.
Livery: Red/White.

METRO COACHES
♨

THE CONIFERS, DARLINGTON ROAD,
STOCKTON-ON-TEES TS21 1PE

Tel: 01642 219555
E-mail: info@coachiremiddlesbrough.co.uk
Web site: www.coachhirestockton.co.uk

NORTON MINI TRAVEL
♿

5 PLUMER DRIVE, NORTON TS20 1HF
Tel: 01642 555832
Owner: R Spears
Fleet: 2 minicoach.
Chassis: 1 Iveco, 1 Mercedes.
Ops incl: private hire, school contracts.
Livery: White/Purple.

RICHARDSON COACHES
♿

3 OXFORD ROAD, HARTLEPOOL
TS25 5SS
Tel/Fax: 01429 272235
Man Dir/Ch Eng: T Richardson
Dir/Co Sec/Traf Man: D Richardson.
Fleet: 9 - 3 single-deck coach, 2 midicoach,
4 minibus.
Chassis: 4 Ford, 2 Leyland, 2 Mercedes, 1 Scania.
Bodies: 4 Ford, 5 Plaxton.
Ops incl: excursions & tours, private hire.
Livery: Green/Red/White.

ROBERTS TOURS
♿ 🍴 ♨ ❄

36 NORTH ROAD WEST, WINGATE
TS28 5AP
Tel: 01429 838268
Fax: 01429 838228
E-mail: robertstours@aol.com
Web site: www.robertstours.co.uk
Dirs: T G Roberts, D Roberts, C A Harper.
Fleet: 10 single-deck coach.
Chassis: 4 Bova, 1 DAF, 2 Leyland, 1 Scania,
2 Volvo.
Bodies: 4 Bova, 1 Jonckheere, 3 Plaxton,
2 Van Hool.
Ops incl: excursions & tours, private hire,
express, school contracts.
Livery: Cream/Green.

SCARLET BAND
♨ ♿ ♨

WELFARE GARAGE, STATION ROAD,
WEST CORNFORTH, FERRYHILL
DL17 9LA
Tel: 01740 654247
Fax: 01740 656068
E-mail: s.band@btconnect.com
Web site: www.scarletbandbuses.co.uk
Dirs: Graeme Torrance **Traffic Man:** Andrew
Dolan **Fleet Eng:** George Lambert
Fleet: 27 - 1 double-deck bus, 2 single-deck bus,
3 single-deck coach, 9 midibus, 12 minibus.
Chassis: 5 Leyland, 11 Mercedes, 9 Optare,
2 Volvo.
Bodies: 1 Alexander Dennis, 1 Bova,
11 Mercedes, 9 Optare, 3 Plaxton, 2 Volvo.
Ops incl: local bus services, school contracts,
excursions & tours, private hire.
Livery: Red and Cream with Scarlet Band
Ticket System: Wayfarer 3

SHERBURN VILLAGE COACHES
♨ 🍴 ♿ ❄ 🔧

FRONT STREET, SHERBURN VILLAGE
DH6 1QY
Tel: 0191 372 1531
Fax: 0191 372 1531
E-mail: sherburncoaches@btconnect.com

Prop: John Cousins.
Fleet: 7 - 2 single-deck coach, 3 midibus, 2 midicoach.
Chassis: 1 MAN, 4 Mercedes, 2 Volvo.
Bodies: 1 Autobus, 1 Berkhof, 1 Caetano, 3 Plaxton, 1 Wadham Stringer.
Ops incl: local bus services, excursions & tours, private hire.
Livery: Red/White
Ticket System: AES.

SIESTA INTERNATIONAL HOLIDAYS LTD

NEWPORT SOUTH BUSINESS PARK, LAMPORT STREET, MIDDLESBROUGH TS1 5QL
Tel: 01642 257920
Fax: 01642 219153
Recovery: 07739 679957
E-mail: sales@siestaholidays.co.uk
Web site: www.siestaholidays.co.uk
Chairman: Paul R Herbert
Dirs: C Herbert, J Herbert, J Cofton
Ops Mans: K Keelan, J Potter
Fleet: 9 - 2 single-deck coach, 6 double-deck coach, 1 minibus.
Chassis: 1 Ford Transit, 8 Scania.
Bodies: 8 Berkhof, 1 Ford.
Ops incl: excursions & tours, private hire, continental tours.
Livery: Metallic Blue.

SNOWDON COACHES

SEASIDE LANE, EASINGTON SR8 3TW
Tel: 0191 527 0535
Fax: 0191 527 3280
E-mail: snowdoncoaches@gmail.com
Web site: www.snowdoncoaches.co.uk
Props: Alan Snowdon, Andrew Snowdon.
Fleet: 11 single-deck coach.
Chassis: 2 DAF, 9 Volvo.

Bodies: 7 Plaxton, 4 Van Hool.
Ops incl: private hire, school contracts.
Livery: White

STAGECOACH TRANSIT

CHURCH ROAD, STOCKTON ON TEES TS18 2HW
Tel: 01642 602112
Web site: www.stagecoachbus.com
Man Dir: John Conroy
Fleet: See Stagecoach North East (Tyne & Wear)
Ops incl: local bus services
Livery: Stagecoach UK Bus

STANLEY TRAVEL

THE BUS STATION, STANLEY DH9 OTD
Tel: 01207 237424
Fax: 01207 233233
Web site: www.minicoachhire.co.uk
Dirs: Andrew Scott, Ian Scott.
Fleet: 20 - 2 double-deck bus, 6 single-deck coach, 1 midibus, 3 midicoach 6 minibus, 2 minicoach.
Ops incl: local bus services, school contracts, private hire, excursions & tours.
Livery: White/Orange

TEES VALLEY LUXURY COACHES LTD

EAGLESCLIFFE LOGISTICS CENTRE, DURHAM LANE, EAGLESCLIFFE, STOCKTON-ON-TEES TS16 0RW
Tel: 01642 781150
Fax: 01642 780666
E-mail: info@teesvalleycoachtravel.co.uk
Web site: www.teesvalleycoachtravel.co.uk
Fleet Name: Tees Valley Coach Travel
Fleet incl: double-deck bus, single-deck bus, single-deck coach, midibus.
Ops incl: local bus services, school contracts, private hire
Livery: Blue/White

TOWN & COUNTRY MOTOR SERVICES LTD

Ceased operations since LRB 2011 went to press

PAUL WATSON TRAVEL

BRIDGE HOUSE, MOOR ROAD, STAINDROP, DARLINGTON DL2 3LF
Tel/Fax: 01833 660471
E-mail: paul.watson9@btconnect.com
Web site: www.paulwatsontravel.co.uk
Dir: Paul Watson
Co Sec: Joanne Watson.
Fleet: 5 - 2 single-deck coach, 1 midicoach, 2 minibus.
Chassis: 1 Ford Transit, 1 LDV, 1 Mercedes, 2 Volvo.
Ops incl: school contracts, excursions & tours, private hire, continental tours.
Livery: White

WEARDALE MOTOR SERVICES LTD

39 EAST END, STANHOPE DL13 2YQ
Tel: 01388 528235
Fax: 01388 526080
E-mail: enquiries@weardalemotorservices.co.uk
Web site: www.weardale-travel.co.uk
Dirs: Messrs Gibson
Ops Man: C Adams.
Fleet: 42 - 15 double-deck bus, 3 single-deck bus, 12 single-deck coach, 8 midibus, 2 midicoach, 2 minibus.
Chassis: Bova, DAF, Irisbus, Leyland, LDV, MAN, Mercedes, Neoplan, Optare, Scania, Volvo.
Bodies: Alexander, Berkhof, Beulas, Bova, Ikarus, Mercedes, Neoplan, Optare, Plaxton, Van Hool, Wright.
Ops incl: local bus services, excursions & tours, school contracts, private hire, express, continental tours.
Livery: Red/White
Ticket System: Wayfarer.

East Riding of Yorkshire, City of Kingston Upon Hull

ABBEY COACHWAYS LTD

MEADOWCROFT GARAGE, LOW STREET, CARLTON, GOOLE DN14 9PH
Tel: 01405 860337
Fax: 01405 869433
Dirs: Mrs L E Baker, S J Stockdale.
Fleet: 5 - 4 single-deck coaches, 1 double-deck coach.
Chassis: 1 MAN, 1 Scania, 3 Volvo.
Bodies: 2 Jonckheere, 3 Plaxton.
Ops incl: school contracts, private hire
Livery: Blue/White

ACKLAMS COACHES LTD

BARMSTON CLOSE, BEVERLEY HU17 0LA
Tel: 01482 887666
Fax: 01482 874949
E-mail: alanacklam@hotmail.com
Web site: www.acklamscoaches.co.uk
Prop: Paul Acklam
Fleet: 20 – 4 double-deck bus, 6 single-deck coach, 3 midibus, 1 midicoach, 6 minibus.
Chassis: 1 Dennis, 1 Ford Transit, 4 LDV, 1 Mazda, 1 Mercedes, 3 Optare, 1 Transbus, 8 Volvo.
Bodies: Alexander, Ford, Optare, Plaxton, Transbus.
Ops incl: local bus services, school contracts, private hire.
Livery: Red/Grey

BARNETTS FAIRWAY RHODES COACH TRAVEL

308 WINCOLMLEE, HULL HU2 0QE
Tel: 01482 328473
Fleet: 17 – 9 double-deck bus, 1 double-deck coach, 6 single-deck coach, 1 midicoach.
Chassis: Bova, DAF, Dennis, Leyland, MCW, Neoplan, Toyota, Volvo.
Ops incl: school contracts, private hire.

JIM BELL COACHES LTD

27 CROWLE STREET, HEDON ROAD, HULL HU9 1RH
Tel: 01482 307572 **Fax:** 01482 307574
E-mail: jim@jimbellcoaches.com

Web site: www.jimbellcoaches.com
Man Dir: Jim Bell
Fleet: 23 – 4 single-deck bus, 8 single-deck coach, 4 midicoach, 7 minibus.
Chassis: Alexander Dennis, Irisbus, LDV, Mercedes, Temsa, Vauxhall, Volvo.
Ops incl: school contracts, private hire.
Livery: White with logos.

CAB EXECUTIVE TRAVEL

21 PARADISE PLACE, GOOLE DN14 5DL
Tel: 01405 765599
Fax: 01405 720880
E-mail: info@cab-travel.com
Web site: www.cab-travel.com
Fleet: 5 – 3 single-deck coaches, 1 midicoach, 1 minibus.
Chassis: 2 Mercedes, 3 Setra.
Ops incl: excursions & tours, private hire, continental tours.

CAIRNGORM COACH TRAVEL

35 AIRE STREET, GOOLE DN14 5QW
Tel: 01405 761334
Web site: www.cairngorm-travel.co.uk
Fleet: 7 single-deck coach.
Chassis: 6 Neoplan, 1 Scania.
Bodies: 1 Berkhof, 6 Neoplan.
Ops incl: excursions & tours, continental tours.
Livery: Blue

CT PLUS (YORKSHIRE) CIC

GREENS INDUSTRIAL PARK, CALDER VALE ROAD, WAKEFIELD WF1 5PF
Tel: 01924 377084
Fax: 01924 365324
E-mail: info@hctgroup.org
Web site: www.hctgroup.org
Ch Exec: Dai Powell **Dep Ch Exec:** Jude Winter **Ch Fin Off:** Douglas Downie
Ch Ops Off: Jon McColl
Fleet (East Riding): 6 single-deck bus.
Chassis: 6 BMC.
Bodies: 6 BMC.
Ops incl: Hull Park & Ride.
Livery: Park & Ride: Black.
A subsidiary of the HCT Group – see CT Plus Ltd (London & Middlesex)

R DRURY COACHES

6 BLENHEIM DRIVE, GOOLE DN14 6LP
Tel/Fax: 01405 763440
E-mail: rdrurycoaches@aol.com
Dirs: Roland Drury, Eileen Drury, Richard Wilson.
Fleet: 6 - 4 single-deck coach, 1 midibus, 1 midicoach
Chassis: 3 Mercedes, 3 Volvo.
Bodies: 6 Plaxton.
Ops incl: school contracts, private hire.
Livery: Green/White

EAST YORKSHIRE MOTOR SERVICES LTD

R24

252 ANLABY ROAD, HULL HU3 2RS
Tel: 01482 327142
Fax: 01482 212040
E-mail: enquiries@eyms.co.uk
Web site: www.eyms.co.uk
Chairman: Peter Shipp **Fin Dir:** Peter Harrison
Comm Man: Bob Rackley
Ch Eng: David Heptinstall
Co Sec: Paul Leeman **Ops Man:** Ray Hill
Marketing Man: Claire Robinson.
Fleet: 322 - 172 double-deck bus, 86 single-deck bus, 23 single-deck coach, 8 open-top bus, 33 midibus.
Chassis: 23 Alexander Dennis, 2 AEC, 1 Bedford, 1 Bristol, 29 Dennis, 6 Enterprise, 10 Leyland, 12 MAN, 11 Mercedes, 17 Optare, 1 Transbus, 269 Volvo.
Bodies: 55 Alexander Dennis, 3 Berkhof, 10 Caetano, 1 Duple, 1 ECW, 2 East Lancs, 2 Mercedes, 51 Northern Counties, 24 Optare, 1 Park Royal, 61 Plaxton, 13 Transbus, 1 Willowbrook, 1 Volvo, 96 Wright.
Ops incl: local bus services, school contracts, excursion & tours, private hire, express, continental tours.
Livery: Burgundy/Cream.
Ticket System: Wayfarer TGX150 (TGX200 from Dec 2011)

ELLIE ROSE TRAVEL LTD

UNIT 2, BANKSIDE INDUSTRIAL ESTATE, VALLETTA STREET, HEDON ROAD, HULL HU9 5NP
Tel: 01482 890616
Fax: 01482 899359
E-mail: jasonreid@ellierosetravel.karoo.co.uk
Chairman & Dir: James Houghton
Man Dir: Jason Reid.
Fleet: 65 - 30 double-deck bus, 10 single-deck bus, 17 single-deck coach, 1 open top bus, 3 midibus, 4 minibus.
Chassis: 3 DAF, 3 LDV, 25 MCW, 14 Volvo, 20 Other.
Bodies: 25 MCW, 14 Plaxton, 26 Other.
Ops incl: school contracts, private hire.
Livery: White.
Ticket system: Wayfarer.

LORDS COACHES

5 HOLMES LANE, BILTON, HULL HU11 4EX
Tel: 01482 321655
E-mail: lordscoaches@hotmail.com
Web site: www.lordscoaches.co.uk
Prop: N Lord
Fleet: 9 – 2 double-deck bus, 6 single-deck coach, 1 midibus, 1 midicoach.

Chassis: I Irisbus, I Mercedes, 7 Volvo.
Ops incl: local bus services, school contracts, excursions & tours, private hire.
Livery: White/Blue.

NATIONAL HOLIDAYS

THE TRAVEL CENTRE, SPRINGFIELD WAY, ANLABY, HULL HU10 6RJ
Tel: 01482 572572
Fax: 01482 569004
E-mail: s.hart@nationalholidays.com
Web site: www.nationalholidays.com
Man Dir: G Rogers
Ops Man: A Hutchinson Traffic Man: P Joyce.
Fleet: 102 single-deck coach.
Chassis: 45 Setra, 57 Volvo.
Bodies: 2 Jonckheere, 15 Plaxton, 45 Setra, 40 Transbus.
Ops incl: excursions & tours.
Livery: White & Blue
Subsidiary company of Shearings Holidays, see Greater Manchester

PEARSON COACHES LTD

9 HEADLANDS ROAD, ALDBROUGH, HU11 4RR
Tel: 01964 527260
Fax: 01964 527774
E-mail: enquiries@pearsonscoaches.co.uk
Web site: www.pearsonscoaches.co.uk
Dirs: Mrs V Pearson, S Colley

Fleet: 11 - 5 single-deck coach, I minibus, 5 minicoach.
Chassis: 6 Mercedes, 5 Volvo.
Bodies: I Mercedes, I Plaxton, I UVG, 4 Van Hool, 4 Other.
Ops incl: local bus services, school contracts, excursions & tours, private hire.
Livery: Grey with Red & Burgundy stripes.
Ticket system: Wayfarer 2

SHAW'S OF WHITLEY

WHITLEY FARM, SILVER STREET, WHITLEY, GOOLE DN14 0JG
Tel: 01977 661214
Fax: 01977 662036
Recovery: 07802 249878
E-mail: info@shawsofwhitley.co.uk
Web site: www.shawsofwhitley.co.uk
Prop: Mrs Marjorie Shaw
Ops Man: Philip Shaw
Fleet: 5 - I double-deck bus, 4 single-deck coach.
Chassis: I MAN, 2 Setra, I Van Hool, I Volvo.
Bodies incl: I Mercedes, 2 Setra, I Van Hool.
Ops incl: excursions & tours, private hire, express, continental tours.
Livery: Various.

STAGECOACH EAST MIDLANDS

PO BOX 15, DEACON ROAD, LINCOLN LN2 4JB
Tel: 01522 522255

Fax: 01522 538229
Fleet Name: Stagecoach in Hull
Web site: www.stagecoachbus.com
Man Dir: Gary Nolan
Eng Dir: John Taylor
Comm Dir: Dave Skepper
Ops Dir: Richard Kay.
Fleet: 498 - 230 double-deck bus, 251 single-deck bus, 9 single-deck coach, 8 open top bus.
Chassis: 294 Alexander Dennis, 6 DAF, I Leyland, 51 MAN, 21 Optare, 14 Scania, 111 Volvo.
Bodies: 335 Alexander Dennis, 63 East Lancs, 5 Jonckheere, 11 Northern Counties, 21 Optare, 33 Plaxton, 12 Transbus, 18 Wright.
Ops incl: local bus services.
Livery: Stagecoach UK Bus
Ticket System: ERG TP5000.

SWEYNE COACHES

LONGSHORE, REEDNESS ROAD, SWINEFLEET DN14 8ER
Tel: 01405 704263
E-mail: mail@sweyne.co.uk
Web site: www.sweyne.co.uk
Fleet: 13 - 4 double-deck bus, 4 single-deck bus, 5 single-deck coach.
Chassis: 7 DAF, 2 Dennis, 4 Leyland.
Bodies: 4 Alexander, 5 Ikarus, 2 Plaxton, 2 Van Hool.
Ops incl: local bus services, school contracts, private hire.
Livery: Blue/White/Gold.

BARCROFT TOURS & EVENTS

247 LONDON ROAD, ST LEONARDS ON SEA TN37 6LU
Tel: 01424 200201   Fax: 01424 200206
Recovery: 07977 004371
E-mail: info@barcrofttours.co.uk
Web site: www.barcrofttours.co.uk
Fleet: 2 single-deck coach.
Chassis: I Scania, I Volvo.
Bodies: I Caetano, I Irizar.
Ops incl: excursions & tours, private hire, continental tours.
Livery: White

THE BIG LEMON CIC

PROTRAN HOUSE, BOUNDARY ROAD, BLACK ROCK, BRIGHTON BN2 5TJ
Tel/Fax: 01273 681681
E-mail: lemonbus@thebiglemon.com
Web site: www.thebiglemon.com
Fleet: 11 - 6 single-deck bus, 2 single-deck coach, 3 midibus.
Chassis: 3 Dennis, 3 Mercedes, 5 Volvo.
Bodies: 3 Alexander, 3 East Lancs, I Marshall, 3 Plaxton, I Other.
Ops incl: local bus services, private hire, excursions.
Livery: Yellow

BRIGHTON & HOVE BUS & COACH COMPANY

43 CONWAY STREET, HOVE BN3 3LT
Tel: 01273 886200
Fax: 01273 822073
E-mail: info@buses.co.uk
Web site: www.buses.co.uk

Fleet Name: Brighton & Hove
Chairman: David Brown Man Dir: Roger French Fin Dir: Philip Woodgate
Ops Dir: Mike Best Eng Dir: Adrian Mitchell
Fleet: 288 - 235 double-deck bus, 42 single-deck bus, 7 single-deck coach, 4 articulated bus.
Chassis: I AEC, 103 Alexander Dennis, I Bristol, I Optare, 148 Scania, 34 Volvo.
Bodies: 7 Alexander, I ECW, 149 East Lancs, 7 Irizar, I Optare, I Park Royal, 57 Plaxton, 31 Scania, 34 Wright.
Ops incl: local bus services, school contracts, excursions & tours, private hire, continental tours.
Livery: Red/Cream/Black
Ticket System: ERG
A subsidiary of the Go-Ahead Group

BRIGHTONIAN COACHES

3 THE AVENUE, BRIGHTON BN2 4GF
Tel: 01273 696195
Props: Laurence R Walker, Susan M Walker.
Fleet: 2 coach.
Chassis: 2 Volvo.
Bodies: I Plaxton, I Van Hool.
Ops incl: school contracts, private hire.
Livery: White

C & S COACH TRAVEL LTD

Ceased trading since LRB 2011 went to press. Operations were concentrated within the Countryliner Group.

COASTAL COACHES

Ceased trading since LRB 2011 went to press.

COUNTRYLINER (SUSSEX) LTD

A Countryliner Group company — see Surrey

CUCKMERE COMMUNITY BUS LTD

THE OLD RECTORY, LITLINGTON, POLEGATE BN26 5RB
Tel: 01323 870920
E-mail: candpayers@mistral.co.uk
Web site: www.cuckmerebus.freeuk.com
Chairman: Mrs B Smith Organiser: P Ayers
Deputy Organiser: J Bunce
Co Sec: Mrs S de Angeli
Treasurer: A Cottingham
Fleet: 7 minibus
Chassis: 7 Mercedes.
Bodies: I Alexander, 2 Mellor, 2 Mercedes, 2 Other.
Ops incl: local bus services, private hire.
Livery: Green/Cream
Ticket system: Wayfarer TGX 150

L J EDWARDS COACH HIRE

BELLBANKS CORNER, MILL ROAD, HAILSHAM BN27 2HR
Tel: 01323 440622
Fax: 01323 442555
E-mail: info@ljedwards.co.uk
Web site: www.ljedwards.co.uk
Prop: John Edwards
Gen Man: Antony Burkill Co Acct: David Maynard
Fleet: 12 - 6 single-deck coach, 4 midicoach, 2 minibus.
Chassis: 6 Bova, 2 Mercedes, I Renault, 2 Toyota, I Volkswagen.
Bodies: 6 Bova, 2 Caetano, 2 Mercedes, 2 Other.
Ops incl: school contracts, excursions & tours, private hire, continental tours.
Livery: White with Red detail

EMPRESS COACHES LTD

10/11 ST MARGARETS ROAD, ST LEONARDS-ON-SEA TN37 6EH
Tel/Fax: 01424 430621
E-mail: info@empresscoaches.com
Web site: www.empresscoaches.com
Dir: Stephen Dine
Ch Eng: Bill Sweetman
Fleet: 10 - 2 midicoach, 6 minibus, 2 minicoach.
Chassis: 3 Ford Transit, 6 Mercedes, 1 Other.
Bodies: 2 Autobus, 1 Mellor, 2 Optare, 5 Other.
Ops incl: school contracts, private hire.
Livery: Claret/Cream

HAMS TRAVEL

THE WHITE HOUSE, LONDON ROAD, FLIMWELL TN5 7PL
Tel: 01580 879537 **Fax:** 01580 879629
E-mail: info@hamstravel.co.uk
Web site: www.hamstravel.co.uk
Fleet incl: double-deck bus, double-deck coach, single-deck coach, midicoach, minibus.
Chassis: Alexander Dennis, Dennis, Ford Transit, Leyland, LDV, Mercedes, Scania, Volvo.
Ops incl: local bus services, excursions & tours, school contracts, private hire.
Livery: Red/Orange/Brown.

J G COACHES LTD

BUTTONS FARM, MERES LANE, CROSS IN HAND, HEATHFIELD TN21 0TY
Tel: 01435 862435
Fax: 01435 864765
E-mail: jesse@jgcoaches.com
Web site: www.jgcoaches.wordpress.com
Prop: J Gorwyn
Fleet: 10 single-deck coach.
Chassis: 9 DAF, 1 Scania.
Ops incl: school contracts, private hire.
Livery: White with Blue.

OCEAN COACHES

19 STONERY CLOSE, PORTSLADE BN41 2TD
Tel/Fax: 01273 278385
Recovery: 07887 815798
Web site: www.oceancoaches.net
E-mail: info@oceancoaches.net
Prop: Peter Woodcock.
Fleet: 1 single-deck coach.
Chassis: Volvo.
Body: Ikarus.
Ops incl: private hire, school contracts, excursions & tours.
Livery: Blue/White

PAVILION COACHES

144 NEVILL AVENUE, HOVE BN3 7NH
Tel: 01273 732405
E-mail: nicky2168@hotmail.com
Web-site: www.pavilioncoaches.co.uk
Joint owners: Peter Hammer, Nicky Hammer.
Fleet: 1 single-deck coach.
Chassis: 1 Volvo.
Bodies: 1 Plaxton.
Ops incl: excursions & tours, private hire, continental tours

RAMBLER COACHES

WESTRIDGE MANOR, WHITWORTH ROAD, HASTINGS TN37 7PZ
Tel: 01424 752505
Fax: 01424 751815
Partners: Colin Rowland, J Goodwin.
Fleet: 37 – 2 double-deck bus, 5 single-deck bus, 24 single-deck coach, 2 midibus, 3 midicoach, 1 minicoach.
Chassis: 2 Dennis, 1 Leyland, 6 Mercedes, 28 Volvo.
Bodies: 6 Alexander, 2 Berkhof, 1 Hispano, 2 Jonckheere, 1 Northern Counties, 18 Plaxton, 2 Van Hool, 2 Volvo, 3 Other.
Ops incl: local bus services, school contracts, excursions & tours, private hire, continental tours.
Livery: White, Green/Black.
Ticket System: Wayfarer.

RDH SERVICES

UNIT 27, MOREHOUSE FARM BUSINESS CENTRE, DITCHLING ROAD, WIVELSFIELD RH17 7RE
Tel: 01444 470000
Fax: 01444 470002
E-mail: info@rdhservices.co.uk
Web site: www.rdhservices.co.uk
Props: T Hawthorne, D Hunnisett.
Fleet: 11 – 9 single-deck coach, 2 midicoach.
Chassis: 4 Dennis, 1 Leyland, 2 Mercedes, 4 Volvo.
Ops incl: private hire.

REGENCY COACHES LTD

UPPER STONEHAM FARM, LEWES BN8 5RH
Tel: 01273 442579
Web site: www.regencycoacheslewes.co.uk
Fleet: 17 - 5 single-deck coach, 1 double-deck coach, 8 midicoach, 3 minibus.
Ops incl: school contracts, excursions & tours, private hire.

RENOWN COACHES LTD

1A BEECHING ROAD, BEXHILL-ON-SEA TN39 3LG
Tel: 01424 210744
Fax: 01424 212651
E-mail: renowncoaches@yahoo.co.uk
Web Site: www.renowncoaches.co.uk

Man Dir: Christian Harmer
Fleet: 41 - 10 double-deck bus, 23 single-deck bus, 2 single-deck coach, 5 midibus, 1 midicoach.
Ops incl: local bus services, school contracts, excursions & tours, private hire.
Livery: Green/Cream.

STAGECOACH IN EAST KENT & EAST SUSSEX

BUS STATION, ST GEORGE'S LANE, CANTERBURY CT1 2SY
Tel: 01227 828103
Fax: 01227 828150
Web site: www.stagecoachbus.com/eastkent
Fleet Names: Stagecoach in Eastbourne, Stagecoach in Hastings
Man Dir: Phil Medlicott
Ops Dir: Neil Instrall
Eng Dir: Jason Bush
Comm Dir: Jeremy Cooper.
Fleet: 415 - 169 double-deck bus, 65 single-deck bus, 16 single-deck coach, 102 midibus, 63 minibus.
Chassis: 170 Alexander Dennis, 10 DAF, 21 MAN, 65 Optare, 76 Scania, 73 Volvo.
Bodies: 318 Alexander Dennis, 14 Caetano, 10 Marshall/MCV, 65 Optare, 2 Plaxton, 6 Wright.
Ops incl: local bus services, school contracts.
Livery: Stagecoach UK Bus; National Express (White).
Ticket System: ERG TP5000.

SUSSEX COUNTRY COACH HIRE

Ceased trading.

WISE COACHES LTD

74 HIGH STREET, HAILSHAM BN27 1AU
Tel: 01323 844321
E-mail: info@wisecoaches.co.uk
Web site: www.wisecoaches.co.uk
Fleet: 2 single-deck coach.
Chassis: 2 DAF.
Bodies: 1 Ikarus, 1 Ovi.
Ops incl: excursions & tours, private hire, school contracts.
Livery: Red/Silver

♿ Vehicle suitable for disabled	🔒 Seat belt-fitted Vehicle	R24 24 hour recovery service
T Toilet-drop facilities available	🍽 Coach(es) with galley facilities	Replacement vehicle available
R Recovery service available	❄ Air-conditioned vehicle(s)	Vintage Coach(es) available
Open top vehicle(s)	Coaches with toilet facilities	Hybrid Buses

The Little Red Book 2012 - in association with Transport Benevolent Fund

AMBER COACHES LTD

UNIT 4A, RAWRETH INDUSTRIAL ESTATE, RAWRETH LANE, RAYLEIGH SS6 9RL
Tel: 01268 786550
E-mail: ambercoachesltd@gmail.com
Web site: www.ambercoaches.com
Fleet: 24 – 4 double-deck bus, 17 single-deck coach, 1 midicoach, 2 minibus.
Chassis: Autosan, Bova, DAF, Dennis, LDV, Mercedes, Volvo.
Ops incl: school contracts, private hire, excursions & tours.
Livery: White/Orange.

ANITA'S COACH & MINIBUS HIRE LTD

15 AIRWAYS HOUSE, FIRST AVENUE, STANSTED AIRPORT CM24 1RY
Tel: 01279 661551
Fax: 01279 661771
E-mail: anitas.coaches@btconnect.com
Web site: www.anitascoaches.com
Dirs: E A S Wheeler, Mrs V A Wyatt.
Fleet: 8 - 6 single-deck coach, 1 midicoach, 1 minicoach.
Chassis: 4 Bova, 1 Iveco, 1 Mercedes, 2 Volvo.
Bodies: 4 Bova, 1 Caetano, 1 Volvo, 2 Other.
Ops incl: school contracts, private hire, continental tours.

APT COACHES LTD

UNIT 27, RAWRETH INDUSTRIAL ESTATE, RAWRETH LANE, RAYLEIGH SS6 9RL
Tel: 01268 783878
Fax: 01268 782656
E-mail: admin@aptcoaches.co.uk
Web site: www.aptcoaches.co.uk
Fleet Name: APT Travel
Man Dir: Peter Thorn
Fleet: 14 – 2 double-deck bus, 12 single-deck coach.
Chassis: 1 Bova, 1 Leyland, 1 Mercedes, 1 Neoplan, 7 Scania, 2 Volvo.
Bodies: 1 Bova, 1 Caetano, 7 Irizar, 1 Mercedes, 1 Neoplan, 2 Other.
Ops incl: school contracts, excursions & tours, private hire, continental tours
Livery: White/Pink

ARRIVA SOUTHEND LTD

20 SHORT STREET, SOUTHEND ON SEA, SS2 5BY
Tel: 01622 697000
Fax: 01702 697001
Web site: www.arrivabus.co.uk
Regional Man Dir: Heath Williams
Comm Dir: Kevin Hawkins
Fin Dir: Beverley Lawson
A division of Arriva Southern Counties - See Kent

B J S TRAVEL

61A HIGH STREET, GREAT WAKERING SS3 0EF
Tel: 01702 219403
Prop: Brian Snow
Fleet: 1 single-deck coach.
Chassis: 1 Scania.
Bodies: 1 Irizar.
Ops incl: school contracts, private hire.
Livery: White, Red & Gold.

BLUE DIAMOND COACHES

37 HOLMES MEADOW, HARLOW CM19 5SG
Tel: 01279 427524 **Fax:** 01279 427525
E-mail: beau.aukett@ntlworld.com
Prop: J. Robilliard **Sec:** A. Aukett.
Fleet: 4 - 3 midibus, 1 minibus.
Ops incl: school contracts, private hire.
Livery: Blue/White.

BLUE TRIANGLE LTD

18 MERTON HIGH STREET, LONDON SW19 1DN
Tel: 020 8545 6100 **Fax:** 020 8545 6101
E-mail: enquiries@go-ahead-london.com
Web site: www.go-ahead-london.com
Ch Exec: John Trayner **Eng Dir:** Phil Margrave
Fin Dir: Paul Reeves **Ops Dir:** David Cutts
Fleet: 51 – 25 double-deck bus, 26 single-deck bus.
Chassis: 21 Alexander Dennis, 3 Dennis, 2 Transbus, 25 Volvo.
Bodies: 21 Alexander Dennis, 2 MCV, 10 Plaxton, 2 Transbus, 16 Wright.
Ops incl: local bus services, school contracts, private hire.
Livery: Red
Ticket System: TfL Prestige
Part of the Go-Ahead Group

BORDACOACH

25B, EASTWOOD ROAD, RAYLEIGH SS6 7JD
Tel: 01268 747608
Prop: David Stubbington
Fleet: 1 single-deck coach.
Chassis: 1 Volvo.
Body: 1 Van Hool.
Ops incl: excursions & tours, private hire.
Livery: White & Blue

BRENTWOOD COACHES

79 WASH ROAD, HUTTON, BRENTWOOD CM13 1DL
Tel: 01277 233144 **Fax:** 01277 201386
E-mail: brentwoodcoach@tiscali.co.uk
Web site: www.brentwoodcoach.co.uk
Prop: A J Brenson **Ch Eng:** K Wright
Sec: Mrs P Alexander **Traf Man:** B Pierce.
Fleet: 10 – 8 single-deck coach, 2 midicoach.
Chassis: 2 Mercedes, 2 Setra, 6 Volvo.
Bodies: Caetano, Plaxton, Setra.
Ops incl: excursions & tours, private hire, school contracts, continental tours.
Livery: White/Brown/Orange/Yellow.
Ticket System: Almex.

C I CLUB CLASS TRAVEL

Ceased trading since LRB 2011 went to press.

C N ENTERPRISES LTD

Ceased trading since LRB 2011 went to press.

CEDRIC COACHES LTD

A120 NORTH, ARDLEIGH, COLCHESTER CO7 7SL
Tel: 01206 231212 **Fax:** 01206 231029
E-mail: info@cedriccoaches.com

Web site: www.cedriccoaches.co.uk
Dirs: Stephen Peck, Alan Short
Fleet: 20 - 10 double-deck bus, 8 single-deck coach, 1 double-deck coach, 1 minicoach.
Chassis: 2 Bova, 4 DAF, 7 Leyland, 2 Scania, 1 Toyota, 4 Volvo.
Bodies: 2 Berkhof, 2 Bova, 1 Caetano, 6 ECW, 2 Irizar, 2 Jonckheere, 1 Northern Counties, 3 Optare, 1 Van Hool.
Ops incl: local bus services, school contracts, private hire.
Livery: White/Yellow/Orange/Red
Ticket system: Wayfarer

CENTREBUS LTD

CUSTOM HOUSE, HAROLDS ROAD, HARLOW CM19 5BJ
Tel: 0844 357 6520
Fax: 01279 417809
E-mail: info@centrebus.com
Web site: www.lutonbus.com
Man Dir: Peter Harvey **Ops Dir:** Neil Harris.
Fleet (Essex): 21 – 9 single-deck bus, 12 midibus.
Chassis: 5 Alexander Dennis, 7 Dennis, 1 MAN, 1 Optare, 4 Scania, 3 Transbus.
Bodies: 1 Alexander Dennis, 4 MCV, 3 Marshall, 2 Optare, 2 Plaxton, 3 Transbus, 6 Wright.
Ops incl: local bus services.
Livery: Blue/Orange/White
Ticket system: Wayfarer 3
Part of the Centrebus Group

CHADWELL HEATH COACHES

30 REYNOLDS AVENUE, CHADWELL HEATH RM6 4NT
Tel: 020 8590 7505
Fax: 020 8597 8883
Props: John Thompson, Lynn Thompson.
Fleet: 3 single-deck coach.
Chassis: 1 Leyland, 2 Volvo.
Ops incl: excursions & tours, private hire, school contracts.
Livery: Country cream.

CHARIOTS OF ESSEX LTD

1 ONE TREE HILL, STANFORD-LE-HOPE SS17 9NH
Tel: 01268 581444
Fax: 01268 581555
E-mail: chariotsofessex@btconnect.com
Web site: www.chariots-coaches.co.uk
Man Dir: K T Flavin **Dir:** W J Collier.
Fleet: 11 – 5 single-deck coach, 2 midicoach, 2 minibus, 1 minicoach.
Chassis: DAF, Iveco, LDV, Mercedes, Renault, Scania, Toyota, Volvo.
Bodies: Caetano, Jonckheere, Van Hool.
Ops incl: school contracts, private hire, express.
Livery: Orange/Yellow
Ticket system: Wayfarer

CLINTONA MINICOACHES

MAGPIE LANE, LITTLE WARLEY, BRENTWOOD CM13 JDZ
Tel: 01277 215526
Fax: 01277 200038
E-mail: info@clintona.co.uk
Web site: www.clintona.co.uk

Fleet Name: Clintona
Partners: Robin Staines, Barbara Staines.
Fleet: 18 - 5 midibus, 6 midicoach, 5 minibus, 2 minicoach.
Chassis: 1 Ford Transit, 3 LDV, 14 Mercedes.
Ops incl: local bus services, school contracts, private hire.
Livery: White/Blue.
Ticket System: Wayfarer 2

COOKS COACHES

607 LONDON ROAD, WESTCLIFF-ON-SEA
SS0 9PE
Tel: 01702 344702 **Fax:** 01702 436887
E-mail: info@cookscoaches.co.uk
Web site: www.cookscoaches.co.uk
Prop: W E Cook
Fleet: 13 single-deck coach.
Chassis: 12 Bova, 1 Volvo.
Bodies: 1 Berkhof, 12 Bova.
Ops incl: excursions & tours, private hire, continental tours.
Livery: Red & White

COUNTY COACHES

2 CRESCENT ROAD, BRENTWOOD
CM14 5JR
Tel: 01277 201505
Fax: 01277 225918
E-mail: enquiries@countycoaches.com
Web site: www.countycoaches.com
Off Man: C A Jee **Tran Man:** R J Pratt.
Fleet: 9 – 7 single-deck coach, 2 midibus.
Chassis: 1 Ayats, 2 Mercedes, 6 Volvo.
Bodies: 1 Ayats, 1 Berkhof, 2 Caetano, 1 Jonckheere, 2 Plaxton, 2 Van Hool.
Ops incl: school contracts, excursions & tours, private hire.
Livery: Green/White

CRUSADER HOLIDAYS

CRUSADER BUSINESS PARK, STEPHENSON
ROAD WEST, CLACTON-ON-SEA CO15 4HP
Tel: 01255 425453 **Fax:** 01255 222683
Recovery: 01255 431777
E-mail: info@crusader-holidays.co.uk
Web site: www.crusader-holidays.co.uk
CEO: Martyn Burke
Fleet: 14 - 12 single-deck coach, 2 minibus.
Chassis/Bodies: 12 Setra.
Ops incl: excursions & tours, continental tours, private hire.
Livery: White/Blue/Red

CUNNINGHAM CARRIAGE COMPANY
Ceased operations since LRB 2011 went to press

DOCKLANDS BUSES LTD
See London

DONS COACHES (DUNMOW) LTD

PARSONAGE DOWNS, GREAT DUNMOW
CM6 2AT
Tel: 01371 872644 **Fax:** 01371 876055
E-mail: info@donscoaches.fsnet.co.uk
Web: www.donscoaches.co.uk
Dir: S D Harvey **Man:** Jamie Bishop.
Fleet: 20 - 7 double-deck bus, 1 single-deck bus, 11 single-deck coach, 1 midicoach.
Chassis: 1 Ayats, 3 Bova, 5 Dennis, 7 Leyland, 2 Neoplan.

Bodies: 6 Alexander, 1 Ayats, 3 Bova, 1 Caetano, 1 Duple, 1 Jonckheere, 1 Marcopolo, 2 Neoplan, 4 Plaxton.
Ops incl: private hire, school contracts.
Livery: Red/Yellow/Blue

EDS MINIBUS & COACH HIRE
257 PRINCESS MARGARET ROAD, EAST
TILBURY RM18 8SB
Tel/Fax: 01375 858049
Props: E Sammons, Mrs S Sammons.
Fleet: 2 - 1 midicoach, 1 minibus.
Chassis: Iveco, Toyota.
Ops incl: Private hire, excursions & tours

ENSIGN BUS COMPANY LTD

JULIETTE CLOSE, PURFLEET INDUSTRIAL
PARK, PURFLEET RM15 4YF
Tel: 01708 865656
Fax: 01708 864340
E-mail: sales@ensignbus.com
Web site: www.ensignbus.com
Chairman: Peter Newman
Comm Dir: Ross Newman **City Sightseeing Dir:** Steve Newman **Eng Dir:** Brian Longley
Fin Man: Tony Astle **Comm Man:** John Lupton
Eng Man: Roger Jackson
Fleet: 86 - 30 double-deck bus, 27 single-deck bus, 2 open-top bus, 27 heritage vehicles.
Chassis (main fleet): 1 Alexander Dennis, 1 DAF, 36 Dennis, 21 Volvo.
Bodies (main fleet): 1 Alexander Dennis, 22 Alexander, 20 Marshall, 10 Optare, 4 Plaxton, 1 UVG, 1 Wright.
Ops incl: local bus services, private hire.
Livery: Blue/Silver
Ticket System: Wayfarer TGX150

EXCALIBUR COACH TRAVEL

44 MOUNTVIEW CRESCENT, ST LAWRENCE
BAY, SOUTHMINSTER CM0 7NR
Tel: 01621 779980 **Fax:** 01621 778928
E-mail: info@excalibur-travel.com
Web site: www.excalibur-travel.com
Prop: Trevor Wynn
Fleet: 2 minibus.
Chassis: 1 Ford Transit, 1 LDV.
Ops incl: private hire, school contracts.

FARGOLINK

ALLVIEWS, SCHOOL ROAD, RAYNE,
BRAINTREE CM7 6SS
Tel: 01376 343179
E-mail: enquiries@fargocoachlines.co.uk
Web site: www.fargocoachlines.co.uk
Prop: L J Smith
Fleet: 21 minibus.
Ops incl: private hire.
Livery: White

FERRERS COACHES LTD
Ceased operations since LRB 2011 went to press

FIRST EAST OF ENGLAND
(formerly FIRST ESSEX BUSES)

WESTWAY, CHELMSFORD CM1 3AR
Tel: 0845 602 0121
Web site: www.firstgroup.com
Regional Man Dir: Nigel Barrett **Regional Eng Dir:** Mick Brannigan **Regional Comm Dir:** Steve Wickers **Regional Fin Planning Dir:** David Marshall
Fleet (Essex): 349 - 62 double-deck bus, 234 single-deck bus, 8 single-deck coach, 42 midibus, 3 minibus.
Chassis: 1 AEC, 25 Alexander Dennis, 7 BMC, 141 Dennis, 2 Enterprise, 4 Leyland, 3 Mercedes, 22 Optare, 62 Scania, 8 Transbus, 74 Volvo.
Bodies: 20 Alexander, 25 Alexander Dennis, 7 BMC, 19 East Lancs, 24 Marshall, 22 Optare, 35 Northern Counties, 1 Park Royal, 87 Plaxton, 5 Scania, 8 Transbus, 96 Wright.
Ops incl: local bus services, school contracts.
Livery: FirstGroup UK Bus
Ticket System: Wayfarer

FIRST LONDON
See London & Middlesex

FLAGFINDERS
267 COGGESHALL ROAD, BRAINTREE
CM7 9EF
Tel: 01376 320501 **Fax:** 01376 331127
E-mail: enquiries@flagfinders.com
Web site: www.flagfinders.com
Ops incl: local bus services, private hire, school contracts, excursions & tours.
Livery: White

FLORIDA COACHES

LITTLE STUBLEYS FARM, SUDBURY ROAD,
HALSTEAD CO9 2BB
Tel: 01787 477701
Fax: 01787 475209
E-mail: info@coachcompany.co.uk
Web site: www.coachcompany.co.uk
Man Dir: Patrick Keeble **Ops Man:** Murray
Dean **Office Man:** Lisa Whellem.
Fleet: 15 – 3 double-deck bus, 2 single-deck bus,
7 single-deck coach, 1 double-deck coach,
1 midicoach.
Chassis: 1 BMC, 2 Dennis, 2 Leyland, 4 MAN,
1 Neoplan, 1 Renault, 2 Setra, 2 Volvo.
Bodies: 2 Alexander Dennis, 1 Beulas, 1 BMC,
1 Caetano, 1 East Lancs, 1 Jonckheere, 1 Neoplan,
2 Noge, 1 Northern Counties, 2 Setra, 2 Other.
Ops incl: local bus services, school contracts,
excursions & tours, private hire, continental tours.
Livery: Various
Ticket System: Almex

FORDS COACHES

THE GARAGE, FAMBRIDGE ROAD,
ALTHORNE CM3 6BZ
Tel: 01621 740326
Fax: 01621 742781
E-mail: info@fordscoaches.co.uk
Web site: www.fordscoaches.co.uk
Partners: Anthony A W Ford, Anthony W Ford.
Fleet: 22 - 10 double-deck bus, 1 single-deck bus,
7 single-deck coach, 3 double-deck coach,
1 midicoach.
Chassis: 1 Alexander Dennis, 1 Ayats, 1 Bedford,
1 BMC, 2 Dennis, 1 Iveco, 7 Leyland, 4 Scania,
2 Van Hool.
Bodies: 5 Alexander Dennis, 1 Ayats, 1 Beulas,
2 Berkhof, 1 BMC, 1 Caetano, 4 ECW, 1 Optare,
1 Plaxton, 3 Van Hool.
Ops incl: local bus services, school contracts,
excursions & tours, private hire.
Livery: White/Multi-colour stripe
Ticket system: Wayfarer

GALLEON TRAVEL LTD

TYLERS CROSS YARD, BROADLEY COMMON
EN9 2DH
Tel: 0845 894 4747
Fax: 0845 894 4748
E-mail: sales@galleontravel.co.uk
Web site: www.galleontravel.co.uk
Man Dir: M Bowden-Scott.
Fleet: 4 - 2 single-deck coach, 1 double-deck
coach, 1 midicoach
Chassis: 1 Ayats, 1 Mercedes, 2 Scania.
Bodies: 1 Ayats, 2 Irizar, 1 Plaxton.
Ops incl: private hire.
Liveries: Maroon, White

GATWICK FLYER LTD

DANES ROAD, ROMFORD RM7 0HL
Tel: 01708 730555
Fax: 01708 751231
Web site: www.gatwickflyer.co.uk
Fleet Names: Gatwick Flyer, Stansted Flyer.
Fleet: 10 – 7 midicoach, 3 minibus.
Chassis: 3 Ford Transit, 7 Mercedes.
Ops incl: airport express.

GENIAL TRAVEL
Ceased operations since LRB 2011 went to press

PETER GODWARD COACHES

UNITS 3&4, MILLS COURT, SWINBOURNE
ROAD, BURNT MILLS INDUSTRIAL ESTATE,
BASILDON SS13 1EH
Tel: 01268 591834
Fax: 01268 591835
E-mail: peter.godward@virgin.net
Props: P R Godward **(Ops)**,
J Godward **(Ops)**,
Mrs A M Godward **(Co Sec)**
Fleet: 13 – 3 double-deck bus, 10 single-deck
coach.
Chassis: 3 Irisbus, 7 Scania, 3 Volvo.
Bodies: 3 Beulas, 1 Caetano, 3 East Lancs, 5 Irizar,
1 Scania Omni Express.
Ops incl: school contracts, excursions & tours,
private hire, express, continental tours.
Livery: White or Yellow with Blue/Orange.

GOLDEN BOY COACHES
See Hertfordshire

GOODWIN'S COACHES
Ceased operations since LRB 2011 went to press

GRAHAM'S COACHES LTD

STATION ROAD, KELVEDON
CO5 9NP
Tel: 01376 570150
Fax: 01376 570657
E-mail: info@grahamscoaches.ltd.uk
Web site: www.grahamscoaches.com
Prop: G Ellis.
Fleet: 8 – 2 single-deck coach, 1 midibus,
2 midicoach, 2 minibus, 1 minicoach.
Livery: White/Blue.

HAILSTONE TRAVEL LTD

82 BRACKLEY CRESCENT, BASILDON
SS13 1RA
Tel: 0845 388 3848
Fax: 0845 388 3856
E-mail: info@hailstonetravel.co.uk
Web site: www.hailstonetravel.co.uk
Dirs: Mrs Tina Hailstone, Lawrence Hailstone.
Fleet: 7 – 6 midicoach, 1 minibus.
Chassis: 1 Iveco, 6 Mercedes.
Ops incl: school contracts, excursions & tours,
private hire
Livery: White

HARDY MILES COACHES LTD
Ceased operations since LRB 2011 went to press

HEDINGHAM & DISTRICT
OMNIBUSES LTD

WETHERSFIELD ROAD, SIBLE
HEDINGHAM CO9 3LB
Tel: 01787 460621
Fax: 01787 462852
E-mail: services@hedingham.co.uk
Web site: www.hedingham.co.uk
Man Dir: R J MacGregor
Dirs: D R MacGregor, C M MacGregor.
Fleet: 98 - 44 double-deck bus, 41 single-deck
bus, 13 single-deck coach.
Chassis: 31 ADL/Dennis/Transbus, 15 Leyland,
57 Volvo.
Bodies: 38 Alexander Dennis, 11 ECW, 1 East
Lancs, 13 Northern Counties, 20 Plaxton,
3 Wright, 5 Other.

Ops incl: local bus services, school contracts,
excursions & tours, private hire.
Livery: Red/Cream.
Ticket System: Wayfarer TGX

IMPERIAL BUS CO LTD

COMPOUND 6, MILL FARM ESTATE,
WHALEBONE LANE NORTH, ROMFORD,
RM6 5QT
Tel: 0208 597 7368
Web site: www.imperialbus.co.uk
Man Dir: M Biddell
Fleet: 24 - 14 double-deck bus,
10 single-deck bus.
Chassis: 6 AEC, 10 Dennis, 6 Leyland,
2 MCW.
Bodies: 1 ECW, 1 Leyland, 2 MCW, 4 Marshall,
4 Northern Counties, 7 Park Royal, 5 Plaxton.
Ops incl: local bus services, school contracts,
private hire
Livery: Green.

JACKSONS COACHES

BICKNACRE HOUSE, LEIGHAMS ROAD,
BICKNACRE CM3 4HF
Tel: 01245 320598
E-mail: info@jacksoncoaches.com
Web site: www.jacksoncoaches.com
Fleet: 8 – 5 single-deck coach, 3 midicoach.
Ops incl: school contracts, private hire,
excursions & tours.
Livery: White

KB COACHES

AVON, CRANFIELD PARK ROAD,
WICKFORD SS12 9EP
Tel/Fax: 01268 734558
E-mail: raykbcoaches@aol.com
Prop: Ray Bourgein
Fleet: 5 single-deck coach.
Chassis: 1 Ayats, 1 Iveco, 2 Setra, 1 Volvo.
Bodies: 1 Ayats, 1 Beulas, 2 Setra, 1 Van Hool.
Ops incl: school contracts, excursions & tours,
private hire.
Livery: Blue

KELLY'S TRAVEL

58 SHOOTERS DRIVE, NAZEING
EN9 2QD
Tel: 01992 892232
Fax: 01992 892232
Web site: www.coaching-essex.com
Fleet: 6 single-deck coach.
Chassis: Mercedes, Setra.
Ops incl: school contracts, private hire,
continental tours.
Livery: White.

KINGS COACHES

364 LONDON ROAD, STANWAY,
COLCHESTER CO3 8LT
Tel: 01206 210332
Fax: 01206 213861
E-mail: info@kings-coaches.co.uk
Web site: www.kings-coaches.co.uk
Prop: Andrew B Cousins.
Fleet: 7 single-deck coach.
Chassis: 6 Bova, 1 Van Hool.
Bodies: 6 Bova, 1 Van Hool.
Ops incl: excursions & tours, private hire.
Livery: Green/Cream

KIRBYS COACHES (RAYLEIGH) LTD

2 PRINCESS ROAD, RAYLEIGH SS6 8HR
Tel: 01268 777777 **Fax:** 01702 202555
E-mail: kirbyscoaches@hotmail.co.uk
Web site: www.kirbyscoaches.co.uk
Dir: Edward Kirby **Co Sec:** Elizabeth Kirby.
Fleet: 10 single-deck coach.
Chassis/Bodies: 10 Setra.
Ops incl: excursions & tours, private hire,
continental tours.
Livery: Lilac/Turquoise

LINKFAST LTD t/a S&M COACHES

*Ceased operations since LRB 2011 went to press,
but operations may recommence.*

LODGE COACHES

THE GARAGE, HIGH EASTER, CHELMSFORD
CM1 4QR
Tel: 01245 231262
Fax: 01245 231825
E-mail: Robert.lodge@lodgecoaches.co.uk
Web site: www.lodgecoaches.co.uk
Dirs: R C Lodge, A D Lodge, C J Lodge
Ch Eng: Paul Hartley
Fleet: 26 - 7 double-deck bus, 2 single-deck bus
11 single-deck coach, 1 minibus, 4 vintage coach.
Chassis: 4 Bedford, 3 Dennis, 7 Leyland, 1 MAN,
3 Mercedes, 2 Optare, 1 Scania, 5 Setra.
Bodies: 2 Alexander Dennis, 2 Berkhof, 4 Duple.
5 ECW, 2 Mercedes, 3 Optare, 2 Plaxton, 5 Setra,
1 Van Hool.
Ops incl: local bus services, school contracts,
excursions & tours, private hire, continental tours.
Livery: Blue/Cream
Ticket System: Wayfarer

MIKES COACHES

Ceased operations since LRB 2011 went to press.

W. H. NELSON COACHES (WICKFORD) LTD

THE COACH STATION, BRUCE GROVE,
WICKFORD SS11 8BZ
Tel: 01268 767870
Fax: 01268 735307
E-mail: info@nibsbus.com
Web site: www.nibsbus.com
Man Dir: Steve Nelson
Fleet Name: Nelsons Independent Bus Services
Fleet: 27 - 24 double-deck bus, 2 single-deck bus,
1 midibus.
Chassis: 7 Dennis, 1 Leyland, 1 Optare, 18 Scania.
Bodies: 10 Alexander, 11 East Lancs, 1 ECW,
3 Optare, 2 Plaxton.
Ops incl: local bus services, school contracts.
Livery: Yellow/Red.

NETWORK COLCHESTER LTD

UNIT 4 HEATH BUSINESS PARK, GRANGE
WAY, COLCHESTER CO2 8GH
Tel: 01206 877620
Fax: 01206 790393
Web site: www.networkcolchester.co.uk
Regional Dir: R Dorr **Ops Man:** A Mears.
Fleet Name: Network Colchester
Fleet: 42 - 19 double-deck bus, 23 single-deck
bus.
Chassis: 5 Alexander Dennis, 2 DAF, 15 Dennis,
9 Scania, 11 Volvo.
Bodies: 5 Alexander Dennis, 9 Alexander,

7 Caetano, 12 East Lancs, 3 Northern Counties,
2 Optare, 5 Plaxton.
Ops incl: local bus services, excursions & tours,
school contracts, private hire, continental tours.
Livery: Blue/Yellow on White base
Network Colchester is a subsidiary of TGM
Group Ltd, part of Arriva. See TGM entry below
and main TGM entry under London & Middlesex.

NEW HORIZON TRAVEL LTD

FRATING ROAD, FRATING, CO7 7HN
Tel: 01206 255255
Fax: 01206 255033
E-mail: nhtltd@aol.com
Web Site: www.horizonbus.co.uk
Man Dir: R Connor.
Fleet: 18 - 8 double-deck bus, 3 single-deck bus,
2 single-deck coach, 2 midicoach, 2 minibus,
1 minicoach.
Chassis: 3 DAF, 4 Dennis, 1 Ford Transit,
4 Mercedes, 6 Volvo.
Ops incl: local bus services, school contracts,
excursions & tours, private hire
Livery: White, with Blue, Red, Yellow

OLYMPIAN & SM COACHES

9 BURNT MILL, ELIZABETH WAY, HARLOW
CM20 2HT
Tel: 01279 426266/868868
Fax: 01279 431438
E-mail: info@smcoaches.co.uk
Web site: www.smcoaches.com
Fleet Names: Olympian, Road Runner,
SM Coaches.
Fleet: 40 - double-deck bus, single-deck bus,
single-deck coach, minibus.
Ops incl: local bus services, school contracts,
excursions & tours, private hire, express
continental tours.

P & M COACHES

1A BEEDELL AVENUE, WICKFORD SS11 8RP
Tel: 01268 203479
Web site: www.pmcoacheswickford.co.uk
Fleet: 4 - 3 single-deck coach, 1 midibus.
Livery: White

PHILLIPS COACHES

117B HULLBRIDGE ROAD, SOUTH
WOODHAM FERRERS CM3 5LL
Tel/Fax: 01245 323039
Prop: L Phillips
Fleet: 6 - single-deck coach, midibus, minibus,
minicoach.
Ops incl: excursions & tours, private hire, school
contracts.
Livery: Cream/Maroon.

RAYLEIGH ROADWAYS LTD

13 RIVERSIDE HOUSE, LOWER SOUTHEND
ROAD, WICKFORD SS11 8BB
Tel: 01268 765240
Fax: 01268 570221
E-mail: info@rayleighroadways.co.uk
Web site: www.rayleighroadways.co.uk
Props: K & Mrs W Nash
Fleet: 7 - 6 single-deck coaches, 1 minicoach.
Chassis: 1 Dennis, 1 Iveco, 2 MAN, 1 Neoplan,
2 Volvo.
Ops incl: school contracts, private hire,
excursions & tours, continental tours.

REGAL BUSWAYS LTD

LANDVIEW, COOKSMILL GREEN,
CHELMSFORD CM1 3SR
Tel: 01245 249001
E-mail: info@regalbusways.com
Web site: www.regalbusways.com
Man Dir: Adrian McGarry **Ops Dir:** Lee
Whitehead **Dir:** Mandy McGarry.
Fleet Names: Essex Pullman, Regal Busways.
Fleet: 42 - 6 double-deck bus, 23 single-deck bus,
13 midibus.
Chassis: 1 Alexander Dennis, 17 Dennis,
7 Leyland, 3 MAN, 14 Optare.
Bodies: 4 Alexander Dennis, 3 ECW, 3 Leyland,
1 MCV, 14 Optare, 15 Plaxton, 2 Wright.
Ops incl: local bus services, private hire, school
contracts.
Livery: Maroon/Cream
Ticket system: ERG

RELIANCE LUXURY COACHES

54 BROOK ROAD, BENFLEET SS7 5JF
Tel/Fax: 01268 758426
Web site: www.reliancecoaches-essex.co.uk
Prop: Martyn J Titchen
Fleet: 4 - 1 double-deck coach, 3 single-deck
coach
Chassis: 1 MAN, 3 Scania.
Bodies: 1 Jonckheere Monaco, 3 Irizar Century
Club.
Ops incl: school contracts, excursions & tours,
private hire.
Livery: White/Red/Yellow/Orange.

RICHMOND'S COACHES

THE GARAGE, HIGH STREET, BARLEY,
ROYSTON SG8 8JA
Tel: 01763 848226 **Fax:** 01763 848105
E-mail: postbox@richmonds-coaches.co.uk
Web site: www.richmonds-coaches.co.uk
Dirs: David Richmond, Michael Richmond,
Andrew Richmond **Sales & Marketing Man:**
Rick Ellis **Asst Ops Man:** Craig Ellis **Ch Eng:**
Patrick Granville **Exc & Tours Man:** Natalie
Richmond.
Fleet: 25 - 12 single-deck coach, 2 double-deck
coach, 4 midicoach, 5 minibus, 2 minicoach.
Chassis: Bova, DAF, Mercedes, Optare, Van Hool,
VDL, Volvo.
Bodies: Bova, Optare, Plaxton, Sitcar, Van Hool.
Ops incl: local bus services, school contracts,
excursions & tours, private hire, continental tours.
Livery: Cream/Brown
Ticket System: Wayfarer 3

STAGECOACH LONDON

See London & Middlesex

STALLION COACHES

Ceased operations since LRB 2011 went to press

STAN'S COACHES

THE COACH HOUSE, BECKINGHAM ROAD,
GREAT TOTHAM, MALDON CM9 8DY
Tel: 01621 891959 **Fax:** 01621 891365
Web site: www.stans-coaches.co.uk
Props: S J Porter, Mrs J Porter.
Fleet: 9 - 7 single-deck coach, 2 minibus.
Ops incl: excursions & tours, school contracts,
private hire, continental tours.
Livery: White with Blue/Grey stripes.

STEPHENSONS OF ESSEX LTD

RIVERSIDE INDUSTRIAL ESTATE, SOUTH
STREET, ROCHFORD SS4 1BS
Tel: 01702 541511
Fax: 01702 549461
E-mail: sales@stephensonsofessex.com
Web site: www.stephensonsofessex.com
Man Dir: Bill Hiron **Fin Dir:** Lyn Watson.
Fleet: 74 - 44 double-deck bus, 21 single-deck
bus, 3 single-deck coach, 6 midibus.
Chassis: 12 Alexander Dennis, 9 Dennis,
27 Leyland, 6 Optare, 5 Scania, 15 Volvo.
Bodies: 22 Alexander, 9 Alexander Dennis, 3 East
Lancs, 23 Northern Counties, 9 Optare, 8 Plaxton.
Ops incl: local bus services, school contracts,
private hire.
Livery: White/Green
Ticket System: Wayfarer 3
See also Suffolk

SUPREME COACHES

REAR OF SOUTHERN COUNTIES,
SOUTHEND ROAD, RETTENDON COMMON,
CHELMSFORD CM3 8DZ
Tel: 01702 401541
Fax: 01702 401480
E-mail: info@supremecoaches.co.uk
Web site: www.supremetravel.co.uk
Man Dir: John Bridge
Fleet Eng: Toby Lyster-Bridge.
Fleet: 13 - 5 double-deck bus, 7 single-deck
coach, 1 midicoach.
Chassis: 6 MCW, 1 Mercedes, 5 Scania, 1 Setra,
1 Volvo.
Ops incl: school contracts, excursions & tours,
private hire, continental tours.
Livery: Red/White/Blue

THE SWALLOW COACH CO LTD

1 BARLOW WAY SOUTH, RAINHAM
RM13 8BT
Tel: 01708 630555
Fax: 01708 555135
E-mail: kevin@swallowcoach.co.uk
Web site: www.swallowcoach.com
Chairman: D R Webb **Man Dir:** K I Webb
Sec: Mrs S D Webb.
Fleet: 24 - 18 single-deck coach, 2 double-deck
coach, 2 midicoach, 1 minibus, 1 minicoach.
Chassis: 1 Dennis, 1 Ford Transit, 10 MAN,

2 Mercedes, 5 Neoplan, 2 Scania, 1 Setra, 2 Toyota,
4 Volvo.
Bodies: Berkhof, Caetano, Irizar, Jonckheere,
Marcopolo, Mercedes, Neoplan, Noge, Plaxton,
Scania, Setra.
Ops incl: Private hire.
Livery: White.

TALISMAN COACH LINES

THE COACH STATION, HARWICH ROAD,
GREAT BROMLEY, COLCHESTER CO7 7UL
Tel: 01206 252472
Fax: 01206 251742
E-mail: sales@talismancoachlines.co.uk
Web site: www.talismancoachlines.com
Man Dir: Terry Smith
Fleet incl: 20 - 4 double-deck bus, 14 single-
deck coach, 2 open-top bus.
Chassis: 1 AEC, 1 Bristol, 1 Daimler, 3 Leyland,
2 Scania, 12 Setra.
Bodies: 1 Alexander, 2 ECW, 2 Irizar, 2 Leyland,
1 Park Royal, 12 Setra.
Ops incl: excursions & tours, private hire,
continental tours.
Livery: Blue/Silver/Yellow

TGM GROUP LTD

FOURTH AVENUE, HARLOW CM20 1DU
Tel: 01279 400905
Fax: 01279 682268
Recovery: 07770 873614
Web site: www.harlowbus.com
Regional Director: R Dorr
Area Eng Man: M Sayer.
Ops incl: local bus services, school contracts.
Harlow, Stansted and Network Colchester
operations form TGM Group East. A subsidiary
of Arriva. For main TGM entry see London &
Middlesex.

TURNERS OF ESSEX

SUDBURY ROAD, LITTLE MAPLESTEAD,
HALSTEAD CO9 2SE
Tel: 01787 479132
Fax: 01787 479147
E-mail: enquiries@turnersofessex.co.uk
Web site: www.turnersofessex.co.uk
Fleet incl: double-deck bus, single-deck bus,
single-deck coach, midibus, midicoach, minibus.
Ops incl: school contracts, excursions & tours,

private hire, continental tours.
Livery: White with multicoloured logos.

TWH BUS AND COACH SERVICES

THE ACADEMY, LANGSTON ROAD,
LOUGHTON IG10 3TQ
Tel: 07734 851705
E-mail: chris@travelwithhunny.com
Web site: www.travelwithhunny.com
Prop: Chris Hunn
Ops incl: local bus services, school contracts,
private hire.
Fleet incl: double deck bus, single deck bus,
midibus.

VICEROY OF ESSEX LTD

12 BRIDGE STREET, SAFFRON WALDEN
CB10 1BU
Tel: 01799 508010
Fax: 01799 510774
E-mail: viceroycoach@btconnect.com
Web site: www.viceroycoaches.co.uk
Man Dir: A R Moore **Man Dir/Eng:** S A Moore
Ops Man: A L Moore.
Fleet: 12 - 1 single-deck bus, 6 single-deck coach,
4 midibus, 1 minicoach.
Chassis: 1 BMC, 1 Bova, 1 DAF, 1 Dennis, 1 Iveco,
2 Mercedes, 2 Optare, 3 Scania.
Ops incl: local bus services, school contracts,
excursions & tours, private hire, continental tours.
Livery: White
Ticket System: Wayfarer 3

WALDEN TRAVEL LTD

126 THAXTED ROAD, SAFFRON WALDEN
CB11 3BJ
Tel/Fax: 01799 516878
Man Dir: Peter Blanchard
Non-Exec Dirs: John Wilson, David Grimmett.
Fleet: 7 - 4 single-deck coach, 3 midibus.
Chassis: 2 Dennis, 3 Mercedes, 2 Volvo
Bodies: 1 Jonckheere, 6 Plaxton.
Ops incl: local bus services, school contracts,
excursions & tours, private hire.
Livery: White
Ticket System: ERG

WEST'S COACHES LTD

See London

GLOUCESTERSHIRE

ALEXCARS LTD

11 LOVE LANE INDUSTRIAL ESTATE,
CIRENCESTER GL7 1YG
Tel: 01285 653985
Fax: 01285 652964
E-mail: info@alexcars.co.uk
Web site: www.alexcars.co.uk
Man Dir & Ops Man: Rod Hibberd
Dirs: Will Jarvis **(Tran Man),** Jenny Jarvis
(Co Sec), Ben Jarvis
(Accounts Man),
Barbara Hibberd
Ch Eng: Steve Hall.
Fleet: 23 - 15 single-deck coach, 2 midicoach,
2 minibus, 3 minicoach, 1 vintage.
Chassis: 1 Bedford (vintage), 1 Dennis, 2 Iveco,
1 MAN, 4 Mercedes, 11 Scania, 3 Toyota, 2
Volkswagen.

Bodies: 3 Caetano, 1 Duple (vintage), 2 Indcar,
11 Irizar, 4 Mercedes, 1 Wadham Stringer.
Ops incl: school contracts, excursions & tours,
private hire, continental tours.
Livery: Duo Blue

BAKERS COACHES

COTSWOLD BUSINESS VILLAGE,
MORETON-IN-THE-MARSH GL56 0JQ
Tel: 0845 688 7707, 01608 652178
Fax: 0845 688 7660
E-mail: enquiries@bakerscoaches.co.uk
Web site: www.bakerscoaches.co.uk
Dir: Mike Baker
Ops Man: Dave Goodall.
Fleet: 17 - 14 single-deck coach, 2 midicoach,
1 minibus.
Chassis: 2 Dennis, 2 Iveco, 3 Mercedes, 1 Scania,

2 Transbus, 7 Volvo.
Bodies: Alexander, Irizar, Plaxton, Sitcar.
Ops incl: local bus services, excursions & tours,
school contracts, private hire, continental tours.
Livery: White/Red

B. E.W. BEAVIS/BEAVIS HOLIDAYS

BUSSAGE GARAGE, BUSSAGE, STROUD
GL6 8BA
Tel: 01453 882297
Fax: 01453 731019
E-mail: admin@beavisholidays.co.uk
Web site: www.beavisholidays.co.uk
Partners: Brian Beavis, Mrs Anita Baxter.
Fleet: 8 - 5 single-deck coach, 1 midicoach,
1 minibus, 1 minicoach.
Chassis: 1 DAF, 4 Neoplan, 1 Scania, 1 Toyota,
1 Volkswagen.

Bodies: 1 Caetano, 1 EOS, 1 Irizar, 4 Neoplan, 1 Volkswagen.
Ops incl: excursions & tours, private hire, school contracts.
Livery: Gold/Orange/Red/Yellow.

BENNETT'S COACHES

EASTERN AVENUE, GLOUCESTER GL4 4LP
Tel: 01452 527809
Fax: 01452 384448
E-mail: info@bennettscoaches.co.uk
Web site: www.bennettscoaches.co.uk
Senior Partner: Peter Bennett
Ops Man: Gavin Bennett
Sales Man: Paul O'Connor.
Fleet: 37 - 5 double-deck bus, 14 single-deck bus, 16 single-deck coach.
Chassis: 4 DAF, 1 MAN, 17 Mercedes, 3 Neoplan, 3 Optare, 9 Volvo.
Bodies: 5 Alexander, 6 Caetano, 1 Ikarus, 15 Mercedes, 3 Neoplan, 3 Optare, 4 Van Hool.
Ops incl: local bus services, school contracts, express, private hire.
Livery: Blue/Orange or Silver; National Express.

JAMES BEVAN (LYDNEY) LTD

UNIT 1, MEAD LANE INDUSTRIAL ESTATE, LYDNEY GL15 5DA
Tel: 01594 842859
Fax: 01594 845615
E-mail: enquiries@jamesbevancoaches.co.uk
Web site: www.jamesbevancoaches.com
Man Dir: James Bevan
Ops Dir: J Zimmerman
Eng Dir: M Zimmerman.
Fleet: 13 - 2 single-deck bus, 5 single-deck coach, 5 midibus, 1 midicoach.
Chassis: 5 Dennis, 2 Mercedes, 1 Optare, 1 Setra, 4 Volvo.
Bodies: 1 Alexander, 1 Optare, 3 Plaxton, 1 Setra, 2 Sunsundegui, 3 UVG, 2 Wadham Stringer.
Ops incl: local bus services, school contracts, private hire.
Livery: Silver
Ticket System: Wayfarer

CASTLEWAYS LTD

CASTLE HOUSE, GREET ROAD, WINCHCOMBE GL54 5PU
Tel: 01242 603715
Fax: 01242 604454
E-mail: castleways@epinet.co.uk
Web site: www.castleways.co.uk
Man Dir: John Fogarty
Dir: Mrs Rowena McCubbin
Ch Eng: Trevor Wood.
Fleet: 14 - 4 single-deck bus, 8 single-deck coach, 1 midibus, 1 midicoach.
Chassis: 1 Bova, 1 Dennis, 2 Mercedes, 2 Optare, 4 Setra, 1 Temsa, 1 Toyota, 2 Volvo.
Bodies: 1 Bova, 1 Caetano, 2 Mercedes, 2 Optare, 2 Plaxton, 4 Setra, 1 Sunsundegui, 1 Temsa.
Ops incl: local bus services, school contracts, private hire.
Livery: Dark Blue/Silver/Gold
Ticket System: Wayfarer

CATHEDRAL COACHES LTD

18 QUAY STREET, GLOUCESTER GL1 2JS
Tel: 01452 524591

Fax: 01452 524595
E-mail: info@cathedralcoaches.fsnet.co.uk
Web site: www.cathedralcoaches.co.uk
Dirs: Irene Chandler, Paul Chandler.
Fleet: 9 - 5 single-deck coach, 2 midicoach, 2 minicoach.
Chassis: 1 DAF, 3 Dennis, 3 Mercedes, 1 Toyota, 1 Volvo.
Bodies: 2 Caetano, 1 Optare, 5 Plaxton, 1 Reeve Burgess.
Ops incl: school contracts, private hire.
Livery: Blue/Grey/Red/White

COLEFORDIAN (WILLETTS) LTD

CROWN PARK ESTATE, EDENWALL ROAD, COALWAY, COLEFORD GL16 7HW
Tel: 01594 810080
Fax: 01594 834480
E-mail: colefordian@tiscali.co.uk
Web site: www.colefordian.co.uk
Man Dir: Paul Willetts.
Fleet: 8 single-deck coach.
Ops incl: excursions & tours, school contracts, private hire, continental tours.

COTSWOLD GREEN LTD

UNIT 27A, NAILSWORTH MILLS ESTATE, AVERNING ROAD, NAILSWORTH GL6 0DS
Tel: 01453 835153
Web site: www.cotswoldgreen.com
Fleet: 17 - 12 single-deck bus, 5 midibus.
Chassis: 10 Dennis, 1 MAN, 4 Mercedes, 1 Optare, 1 Volvo.
Bodies: 5 Alexander, 2 Caetano, 2 East Lancs, 1 Northern Counties, 1 Optare, 6 Plaxton.
Ops incl: local bus services, school contracts.
Livery: Green/White.

EAGLE LINE TRAVEL

ANDOVERSFORD TRADING ESTATE, ANDOVERSFORD GL54 4LB
Tel/Fax: 01242 820535
E-mail: brian@eaglelinetravel.co.uk
Web site: www.eagleline.co.uk
Man Dirs: Brian Davis, Martin Davis, Wayne Hodges
Ch Eng: Tony Mezzone.
Fleet: 22 - 10 single-deck coach, 2 double-deck coach, 2 midibus, 4 midicoach, 2 minicoach, 2 minibus.
Chassis: 2 DAF, 2 Dennis, 4 Ford Transit, 6 Mercedes, 1 Neoplan, 1 Scania, 1 Toyota, 5 Volvo.
Bodies: 2 Autobus, 2 Berkhof, 1 Caetano, 2 Mercedes, 4 Ford Transit, 1 Neoplan, 2 Plaxton, 6 Van Hool, 2 Volkswagen.
Ops incl: school contracts, excursions & tours, private hire, continental tours.
Livery: Dark Blue/Silver/Silver Blue

EBLEY COACHES LTD

UNIT 27, NAILSWORTH MILLS ESTATE, AVENING ROAD, NAILSWORTH GL6 0BS
Tel/Fax: 01453 839333
E-mail: enquiries@ebleyexcursions.co.uk
Web site: www.ebleyexcursions.co.uk
Dirs: C C Levitt, G A Jones.
Fleet incl: single-deck bus, single-deck coach.
Ops incl: school contracts, excursions & tours, private hire.
Livery: White.

DAVID FIELD

WHEATSTONE HOUSE, WATERY LANE, NEWENT GL18 1PY
Tel: 01531 820979
Web site: www.davidfieldtravel.co.uk
Prop: David Field MSOE, MIRTE
Fleet: 8 - 6 single-deck coach, 1 midicoach, 1 minicoach.
Chassis: 1 DAF, 1 Dennis, 1 Iveco, 1 Leyland, 2 Mercedes, 1 Setra, 1 Toyota.
Ops incl: school contracts, private hire.
Livery: Black/White
Ticket System: Setright

GRINDLES COACHES LTD

4 DOCKHAM ROAD, CINDERFORD GL14 2DD
Tel: 01594 822110
Fax: 01594 824575
E-mail: admin@grindlescoaches.co.uk
Web site: www.grindlescoaches.co.uk
Man Dir: P R Grindle **Co Sec:** W H R Grindle.
Fleet: 11 - 9 single-deck coach, 1 midicoach, 1 minicoach.
Chassis: 7 DAF, 2 Mercedes, 2 Setra.
Bodies: 1 Mercedes, 1 Plaxton, 2 Setra, 7 Van Hool.
Ops incl: local bus services, private hire.
Livery: White with Gold

JACKIES COACHES

THE OLD AIRFIELD, MORETON VALENCE, GLOUCESTER GL2 7NG
Tel: 01452 720666
Props: D & J Pratt
Fleet: 10 - 7 single-deck coaches, 3 midibuses
Chassis: DAF, Fiat, Leyland, MAN, Mercedes, Volvo.
Ops incl: local bus services, school contracts, private hire.

MARCHANTS COACHES

61 CLARENCE STREET, CHELTENHAM GL50 3LB
Tel: 01242 257714
Fax: 01242 251360
E-mail: sales@marchants-coaches.com
Web site: www.marchants-coaches.com
Man Dir: Roger Marchant
Dir/Ops/Tran Man: Richard Marchant
Ch Eng: Russell Marchant
Co Sec: Mrs Jean Ellis.
Fleet: 28 - 6 double-deck bus, 5 single-deck bus, 13 single-deck coach, 2 double-deck coach, 1 midibus, 1 midicoach.
Chassis: 2 DAF, 4 Leyland, 1 Mercedes, 2 Neoplan, 1 Optare, 17 Volvo.
Bodies: 2 Alexander, 1 ECW, 1 East Lancs, 4 Jonckheere, 2 Neoplan, 3 Optare, 11 Plaxton, 4 Wright.
Ops incl: local bus services, school contracts, excursions & tours, private hire, continental tours.
Livery: Red/Gold
Ticket System: Wayfarer

PULHAM & SONS (COACHES) LTD

STATION ROAD GARAGE, BOURTON ON THE WATER, GL54 2EN
Tel: 01451 820369 **Fax:** 01451 821721
E-mail: info@pulhamscoaches.com
Man Dir: Andrew Pulham.

Web site: www.pulhamscoaches.com
Fleet: 29 – 22 single-deck coach, 3 midibus, 4 midicoach.
Chassis: 1 Dennis, 1 Leyland, 3 Mercedes, 3 Optare, 1 Toyota, 20 Volvo.
Bodies: 1 Caetano, 3 Optare, 22 Plaxton, 3 Van Hool.
Ops incl: local bus services, school contracts, excursions & tours, private hire.
Livery: Red & Cream

ROVER EUROPEAN LTD
THE COACH HOUSE, THE STREET, HORSLEY, STROUD GL6 0PU
Tel: 01453 832121
Fax: 01453 832722
E-mail: info@rovereuropean.co.uk
Web site: www.rovereuropean.co.uk
Man Dir: David Hand **Dir:** Carole Hand.
Fleet: 9 - 8 single-deck coach, 1 minicoach.
Chassis: 6 Bova, 2 Dennis, 1 Mercedes.
Bodies: 6 Bova, 2 Plaxton.
Ops incl: school contracts, excursions & tours, private hire, continental tours.
Livery: Cream base with Light Blue/Dark Blue/Orange.

STAGECOACH WEST
3RD FLOOR, 65 LONDON ROAD, GLOUCESTER GL1 3HF
Tel: 01452 418630
Fax: 01452 304857
E-Mail: west@stagecoachbus.com

Web site: www.stagecoachbus.com
Man Dir: Ian Manning
Eng Dir: Peter Sheldon
Ops Dir: Sholto Thomas
Comm Man: Craig Lockley.
Fleet: 236 - 99 double-deck bus, 22 single-deck bus, 5 single-deck coach, 91 midibus, 19 minibus.
Chassis: 156 Alexander Dennis, 15 MAN, 2 Mercedes, 18 Optare, 22 Scania, 23 Volvo.
Bodies: 192 Alexander Dennis, 6 Caetano, 3 Northern Counties, 18 Optare, 17 Plaxton.
Ops incl: local bus services, school contracts, private hire, express.
Liveries: Stagecoach UK Bus, National Express.
Ticket System: ERG

SWANBROOK TRANSPORT LTD
GOLDEN VALLEY, STAVERTON, CHELTENHAM GL51 0TE
Tel: 01452 712386
Fax: 01452 859217
E-mail: enquiries@swanbrook.co.uk
Web site: www.swanbrook.co.uk
Fleet Name: Swanbrook
Man Dir: K J Thomas
Eng Dir: J A Thomas
Ops Dir: Mrs K J West
Ops Man: M Dowle.
Fleet: 24 - 9 double-deck bus, 1 single-deck bus, 5 single-deck coach, 9 midibus.
Chassis: 5 Leyland, 3 MCW, 6 Mercedes, 3 Optare, 7 Volvo.
Bodies: 7 Alexander Dennis, 1 East Lancs, 3 MCW, 3 Optare, 7 Plaxton, 2 Van Hool, 1 Other.

Ops incl: local bus services, school contracts, private hire.
Livery: Purple & Green
Ticket System: Wayfarer II

F R WILLETTS & CO (YORKLEY) LTD
DEAN RISE, MAIN ROAD, PILLOWELL GL15 4QY
Tel: 01594 562511
Fax: 01594 564373
Man Dir: Geoff Willetts
Sec: Sue Willetts.
Fleet: 4 - 3 single-deck coach, 1 midicoach.
Chassis: 1 Dennis, 1 Leyland, 1 Mercedes, 1 Volvo.
Bodies: 4 Plaxton.
Ops incl: local bus services, school contracts, excursions & tours, private hire.
Livery: Red
Ticket System: Setright

MAL WITTS EXECUTIVE TRAVEL
Ceased operations since LRB 2011 went to press

GEORGE YOUNG'S COACHES LTD
HOLME BUNGALOW, GLEBE ROAD, NEWENT GL18 1BJ
Tel: 01989 763889
Fleet incl: single-deck bus, single-deck coach, midibus, midicoach, minibus
Ops incl: local bus services, school contracts, private hire.
Livery: White with Red/Black

ADLINGTON TAXIS AND MINICOACHES
Ceased operations since LRB 2011 went to press.

ARRIVA NORTH WEST & WALES
73 ORMSKIRK ROAD, AINTREE, LIVERPOOL L9 5AE
Tel: 0151 522 2800
Fax: 0151 525 9556
Web site: www.arriva.co.uk
Regional Man Dir: Phil Stone **Reg Fin Dir:** Simon Mills **Reg Eng Dir:** Phil Cummins **Area Man Dir (Merseyside):** Howard Farrall **Area Man Dir (Manchester):** John Rimmer **Area Man Dir (Wales):** Michael Morton
Fleet: 1209 - 187 double-deck bus, 873 single-deck bus, 11 articulated bus, 129 midibus, 8 open-top bus, 1 minibus.
Chassis: 49 Alexander Dennis, 517 DAF/VDL, 347 Dennis, 7 Leyland, 5 MAN, 11 Mercedes, 53 Optare, 64 Scania, 156 Volvo.
Bodies: 178 Alexander Dennis, 4 ECW, 38 East Lancs, 10 Ikarus, 64 Marshall/MCV, 11 Mercedes, 74 Northern Counties, 53 Optare, 276 Plaxton, 3 Scania, 498 Wright.
Ops incl: local bus services, school contracts.
Livery: Arriva UK Bus
Ticket System: Wayfarer TGX

BATTERSBY'S COACHES
73 BRIDGEWATER ROAD, WALKDEN M28 3AF
Tel/Fax: 0161 790 2842
Dirs: R W Griffiths, S J Griffiths.
Fleet: 1 single-deck coach.
Chassis: 1 Setra.
Ops incl: private hire, school contracts.

BLUEBIRD BUS & COACH
ALEXANDER HOUSE, GREENGATE, MIDDLETON M24 1RU
Tel: 0844 504 0144
Fax: 0844 504 0145
Web site: www.bluebirdbus.co.uk
Gen Man: Michael T G Dunstan
Fleet: 44 – 1 double-deck bus, 43 single-deck bus.
Chassis: 25 Alexander Dennis, 1 MAN, 4 Optare, 9 Transbus, 4 Volvo, 2 Other.
Bodies: 3 Caetano, 2 East Lancs, 9 MCV, 4 Optare, 12 Plaxton, 14 Transbus.
Ops incl: local bus services.
Livery: Two tone Blue
Ticket system: ERG

R BULLOCK & CO (TRANSPORT) LTD
COMMERCIAL GARAGE, STOCKPORT ROAD, CHEADLE SK8 2AG
Tel: 0161 428 5265
Fax: 0161 428 9074
Web site: www.bullockscoaches.co.uk
Fleet: 45 – 18 double-deck bus, 5 single-deck bus, 19 single-deck coach, 1 midicoach, 2 minicoach.
Chassis: Irisbus, Leyland, Mercedes, Scania, Toyota, Volvo.
Bodies: Alexander, Caetano, East Lancs, Irizar, Northern Counties, Optare, Plaxton, Scania, Vehixel.
Ops incl: local bus services, school contracts, excursions & tours, private hire
Livery: Red/White.

BU-VAL BUSES LTD
Ceased operations since LRB 2011 went to press.

LES BYWATER & SONS LTD
SPARTH BOTTOMS ROAD, ROCHDALE OL11 4HT
Tel: 01706 648573
Man Dir: MT Bywater **Dir:** N L Bywater.
Fleet: 3 - 1 single-deck coach, 1 midicoach, 1 minibus.
Chassis: 1 Dennis, 2 Iveco.
Bodies: 1 Duple, 2 Robin Hood.
Ops incl: private hire, school contracts.
Livery: White/Blue/Black.

CARSVILLE COACHES
51A HIGHER ROAD, URMSTON M41 9AP
Tel: 0161 748 2698
Fax: 0161 747 2694
Recovery: 07812 964367
E-mail: janetcarsville@hotmail.com
Man Dir: D Nickson **Man:** Mrs J Nickson.
Fleet: 10 – 8 single-deck coach, 1 double-deck coach, 1 minibus.
Chassis: 1 Ford, 1 Ford Transit, 1 Iveco, 1 MAN, 5 Scania, 1 Volvo.
Bodies: 1 Ayats, 5 Irizar, 4 Plaxton.
Ops incl: private hire, excursions & tours, school contracts, continental tours.
Livery: White/Purple.

COACH OPTIONS
768 MANCHESTER ROAD, CASTLETON, ROCHDALE OL11 3AW
Tel: 01706 713966
Fax: 01706 759996
E-mail: coach.options@freeuk.com
Web site: www.optionstours.co.uk
Dir: Paul Stone
Fleet: 10 - 6 single-deck coach, 2 midicoach, 2 minibus.
Chassis: 2 Bova, 1 Ford Transit, 4 Mercedes, 2 Scania, 1 Van Hool.
Ops incl: school contracts, excursions & tours, private hire, continental tours.
Livery: Blue

COURTESY COACHES LTD
P.O. BOX 632, OLDHAM OL1 9HN
Tel: 0845 045 0344
Fax: 0161 287 3344
E-mail: sales@courtesycoaches.co.uk
Web site: www.courtesycoaches.co.uk
Fleet Names: Hartshead Travel, Hebble Travel, Yelloway.
Ops incl: private hire, excursions & tours, continental tours.
Livery: White with multicolour logos.

CROPPER COACHES
Ceased trading since LRB 2011 went to press.

DAM EXPRESS
Ceased trading since LRB 2011 went to press.

ELLEN SMITH (TOURS) LTD
MANDALE PARK, CORPORATION ROAD, ROCHDALE OL11 4HJ
Tel: 01706 345000
Fax: 01706 345970
E-mail: p.targett@ellensmith.co.uk
Web site: www.ellensmith.co.uk
Man Dir: Paul Targett
Fleet: 6 - 4 single-deck coach, 2 minibus
Chassis: 2 Bova, 1 Iveco, 1 Mercedes, 2 VW.
Bodies: 1 Beulas, 2 Bova, 1 Mercedes.
Ops incl: excursions & tours, private hire.
Livery: Black/Orange.

ELITE SERVICES LTD
UNITS 3/6, ADSWOOD ROAD INDUSTRIAL ESTATE, ADSWOOD ROAD, STOCKPORT SK3 8LF
Tel: 0161 480 0617
Fax: 0161 480 3099
Dirs: Dave Nickson
Fleet: 21 - 2 double-deck bus, 17 single-deck coach, 2 double-deck coach.
Chassis: 1 Ayats, 1 Ford, 15 Scania, 2 Volvo.
Ops incl: local bus service, excursions & tours, private hire, continental tours, school contracts.
Livery: White/Purple/Pink

FINGLANDS COACHWAYS LTD
261 WILMSLOW ROAD, RUSHOLME, MANCHESTER M14 5LJ
Tel: 0161 224 3341
Fax: 0161 257 3154
E-mail: enquiry@finglands.co.uk
Web site: www.finglands.co.uk
Fleet Name: Finglands
Chairman: Peter Shipp **Fin Dir:** Peter Harrison
Man Dir: David Shurden **Fleet Eng:** Tim Jenkins.
Fleet: 50 - 33 double-deck bus, 9 single-deck bus, 8 single-deck coach.
Chassis: 5 Alexander Dennis, 4 Dennis, 41 Volvo.
Bodies: 18 Alexander, 14 Northern Counties, 12 Plaxton, 2 Volvo, 4 Wright.
Ops incl: local bus services, school contracts, private hire.
Livery: White with Brown/Orange
Ticket System: Wayfarer TGX150
Subsidiary of East Yorkshire Motor Services Ltd – see East Riding

FIRST IN MANCHESTER
WALLSHAW STREET, OLDHAM OL1 3TR
Tel: 0161 627 2929
Fax: 0161 627 5845
Fleet Name: First
Regional Man Dir: Dave Alexander **Man Dir:** Richard Soper **Fin Dir:** Martin Wilson **Service Delivery Dir:** Ken Poole **Network Dir:** Simon Bennett
Fleet: 881 - 249 double-deck bus, 572 single-deck bus, 41 midibus, 19 articulated bus.
Chassis: 13 BMC, 135 Dennis, 23 Irisbus, 2 Leyland, 63 Mercedes, 76 Optare, 95 Scania, 474 Volvo.
Ops incl: local bus services, school contracts, private hire.
Livery: FirstGroup UK Bus
Ticket System: ERG TP4004
Includes First in Cheshire and The Wirral

FREEBIRD
Business acquired by Swans Travel since LRB 2011 went to press.

GO-GOODWINS COACHES

♿ ♻ ☺ ⚁ ⚀

LYNTOWN TRADING ESTATE, 186 OLD
WELLINGTON ROAD, ECCLES, MANCHESTER
M30 9QG
Tel: 0161 789 4545 **Fax:** 0161 789 0939
E-mail: info@gogoodwins.co.uk
Web site: www.gogoodwins.co.uk
Prop: Geoff Goodwin **Co Sec:** Suzanne
Goodwin.
Fleet: 26 – 17 single-deck bus, 4 single-deck
coach, 5 midibus
Chassis: 3 Alexander Dennis, 1 DAF, 2 Dennis,
3 Irisbus, 1 Mercedes, 12 Optare, 1 Van Hool,
1 Volvo, 2 Wrightbus.
Ops incl: local bus services, school contracts,
private hire.
Livery: Blue/White/Red

GPD TRAVEL

27 HARTFORD AVENUE, HEYWOOD
OL10 4XM
Tel: 01706 622297
Fax: 01706 361494
E-mail: janinedawson@hotmail.co.uk
Web site: www.gpdtravel.co.uk
Proprietor: Gary Dawson
Fleet: 5 – 4 single-deck coach, 1 midicoach.
Chassis: 1 Mercedes-Benz, 4 Volvo.
Ops incl: school contracts, excursions & tours,
private hire, continental tours.
Livery: White with red lettering

GRAYWAY COACHES

♻ ♿ ☺ ⚁

237 MANCHESTER ROAD, INCE,
WIGAN WN2 2AE
Tel: 01942 243165 **Fax:** 01942 824807
E-mail: enquiries@grayway.co.uk
Web site: www.grayway.co.uk
Proprietors: Janet Gray, Michael Gray.
Fleet: 34 – 27 single-deck coach, 5 midicoach,
2 minicoach.
Chassis: 2 DAF, 7 Mercedes, 3 VDL, 22 Volvo.
Bodies: 18 Jonckheere, 2 Plaxton, 9 Van Hool,
5 Other.
Ops incl: school contracts, excursions & tours,
private hire, continental tours.
Livery: Cream/Orange/Red

HAYTON'S EXECUTIVE TRAVEL LTD

♻ ♿ ⚁ ☺ ═ ⚑

VELOS HOUSE, UNIT 3, FROXMER STREET,
GORTON, MANCHESTER M19 2HS
Tel: 0161 223 3103 **Fax:** 0161 223 9528
Web site: www.haytonstravel.co.uk
Prop: Barry Hayton **Dir/Sec:** Barry A Hayton.
Fleet: 47 – 5 single-deck bus, 31 single-deck
coach, 1 double-deck coach, 9 midibus, 1 minibus,
1 midicoach.
Chassis: DAF, Dennis, Enterprise, MAN,
Mercedes, Optare, Scania, Setra, Volvo.
Bodies: Alexander, Berkhof, Caetano, Ikarus,
Jonckheere, Marcopolo, Optare, Plaxton, Setra,
Van Hool.

Ops incl: local bus services, school contracts,
excursions & tours, private hire, express,
continental tours.
Livery: White, National Express.

HEALINGS INTERNATIONAL COACHES

♿ ♻ ☺

251 HIGGINSHAW LANE, ROYTON, OLDHAM
OL2 6HW
Tel: 0161 624 8975 **Fax:** 0161 652 0320
Web site: www.healingstravel.co.uk
Partners: Philip Healing, Richard Healing.
Fleet: 7 – 5 single-deck coach, 1 midicoach,
1 minicoach.
Chassis: 1 DAF, 1 Mercedes, 1 Scania, 1 Toyota,
1 Volvo, 2 Duple 425
Ops incl: school contracts, excursions & tours,
private hire, continental tours.
Livery: White with coloured decals

JONES EXECUTIVE COACHES LTD

♿ ♻ ☺ ═

THE COACH STATION, SHARP STREET,
WALKDEN, MANCHESTER M28 3LX
Tel: 0161 790 9495 **Fax:** 0161 790 9400
Web site: www.jonesexecutive.co.uk
E-mail: simon@jonesexecutive.co.uk
Man Dir: Simon Jones
Fleet: 7 single-deck coach.
Chassis: 2 DAF, 2 Iveco, 2 Scania, 1 Volvo.
Bodies: 2 Beulas, 5 Van Hool.
Ops incl: school contracts, private hire.
Livery: White

JPT BUSES

♿

THE COACH HOUSE, JOSHUA LANE,
MIDDLETON, MANCHESTER M24 2AZ
Tel: 0161 643 4182 **Fax:** 0161 653 3404
E-mail: info@jptbuses.co.uk
Web site: www.jptbuses.co.uk
Fleet Name: JPT
Fleet: 48 – 20 double-deck bus, 23 single-deck
bus, 5 midibus.
Chassis: Alexander Dennis, Dennis, Enterprise,
MAN, Optare, Scania, Volvo.
Bodies: Alexander, Alexander Dennis, East Lancs,
Optare, Plaxton, Wright
Ops incl: local bus services.
Livery: Blue/Yellow

LAINTON COACHES LTD t/a ASHALL'S COACHES

♿ ♻ ☺

UNIT 11, FROXMER STREET, GORTON,
MANCHESTER M18 8EF
Tel: 0161 231 7777 **Fax:** 0161 231 7787
E-mail: info@ashallscoaches.co.uk
Web site: www.ashallscoaches.co.uk
Dirs: James A Ashall, Aaron Ashworth.
Fleet: 13 – 1 single-deck bus, 11 single-deck
coach, 1 midicoach.
Chassis: 1 DAF, 1 Mercedes, 1 Optare, 3 Scania,
7 Volvo.

Bodies: 2 Caetano, 1 Duple, 3 Irizar,
1 Jonckheere, 1 Optare, 4 Plaxton, 1 Van Hool.
Ops incl: school contracts, private hire
(UK only).
Livery: White
Ticket System: Wayfarer 2

LAMBS

♿ ♻ ☺

BUXTON STREET, HAZEL GROVE,
STOCKPORT SK7 4BB
Tel: 0161 456 1515 **Fax:** 0161 483 5011
E-mail: lambs139@aol.com
Web site: www.lambscoaches.net
Dirs: Geoffrey Lamb, Graham Lamb,
Mrs Christine Lamb.
Fleet: 6 single-deck coach, 1 midicoach.
Chassis: 3 DAF, 2 Mercedes, 1 Scania, 1 Volvo.
Bodies: 1 Plaxton, 1 Setra, 5 Van Hool.
Ops incl: private hire, school contracts.
Livery: White/Blue

MARPLE MINI COACHES

♿ ═

5 GROSVENOR ROAD, MARPLE
K6 6PR
Tel: 0161 881 9111
Owner: G W Cross.
Fleet: 2 minicoach.
Chassis: Ford Transit, LDV.
Ops incl: school contracts, private hire.
Livery: White/Gold.

MAYNE COACHES LTD

♻ ♿ ☺ ═ ⚑

MARSH HOUSE LANE, WARRINGTON
WA1 7ET
Tel: 01925 445588 **Fax:** 01925 232300
E-mail: coaches@mayne.co.uk
Web site: www.mayne.co.uk
Dirs: S B Mayne **(Chairman & Man Dir)**,
D Mayne **(Co Sec)**, C S Mayne, S L Mayne
Gen Man: R W Vernon **Sales Mans:** A J Dykes,
D Williams **Eng Dir:** C F Pannel
Eng Man: E Sutcliffe **Traffic Man:** J Drake
Fleet: 42 – 4 double-deck bus, 38 single-deck
coach.
Chassis: 2 Alexander Dennis, 2 Dennis, 4 Bova,
1 Leyland, 26 Scania, 7 Volvo.
Bodies: 4 Bova, 4 East Lancs, 19 Irizar, 10 Plaxton,
3 Scania, 2 UVG.
Ops incl: local bus services, school contracts,
excursions & tours, private hire.
Livery: Cream/Red

MAYTREE TRAVEL LTD

♿

UNIT D1, SMETHURST LANE, BOLTON
BL4 0DB
Tel: 01204 665671
E-mail: customerservices@maytreetravel.co.uk
Web site: www.maytreetravel.co.uk
Dir: G Hawthorne
Fleet: 29 – 1 double-deck bus, 16 single-deck
bus, 12 midibus.

&#9855;	Vehicle suitable for disabled	&#9851;	Seat belt-fitted Vehicle
&#9873;	Toilet-drop facilities available	&#9857;	Coach(es) with galley facilities
R	Recovery service available	&#9286;	Air-conditioned vehicle(s)
&#9552;	Open top vehicle(s)	&#9786;	Coaches with toilet facilities

R24	24 hour recovery service
&#9552;	Replacement vehicle available
&#9552;	Vintage Coach(es) available
&#9478;	Hybrid Buses

Chassis: 8 Alexander Dennis, 15 Optare, 1 Volvo, 5 Wrightbus.
Bodies: 1 Alexander, 8 Alexander Dennis, 15 Optare, 5 Wrightbus.
Ops incl: local bus services.
Livery: White with Green.

METROLINK
See Section 5 – Tram and Bus Rapid Transit Systems

DAVID PLATT COACHES & MINITRAVEL OF LEES
8 THE WOODS, GROTTON, SADDLEWORTH, OLDHAM OL4 4LP
Tel/Fax: 0161 633 4845
Prop: David Platt
Fleet: 2 - 1 single-deck coach, 1 minicoach.
Chassis: 1 Bedford, 1 Toyota.
Bodies: 1 Caetano, 1 Plaxton.
Ops incl: private hire.
Livery: Aqua/White

SELWYNS TRAVEL SERVICES
ROOM 1, MULTI STOREY CAR PARK, TERMINAL 2, MANCHESTER AIRPORT M90 1QX
Tel: 0161 930 8884 **Fax:** 0161 499 9157
E-mail: info@selwyns.co.uk
Web site: www.selwyns.co.uk
Fleet: See Selwyns Travel Services, Cheshire.
Ops incl: local bus services, school contracts, private hire.
Livery: White/Blue/Orange/Green
Ticket System: Wayfarer
See also Selwyns Travel Services, Runcorn (Cheshire)

SHEARINGS HOLIDAYS
MIRY LANE, WIGAN WN3 4AG
Tel: 01942 244246 **Fax:** 01942 242518
Web site: www.shearings.com
Fleet Names: Shearings Holidays, Caledonian Travel, Euro Tourer, Grand Tourer, National Holidays (see East Riding).
Chairman: Bernard Norman
Ch Exec: Dennis Wormwell **Man Dir:** Ruth Connor **Man Dir (Hotels)** Vince Flower
Fin Dir: David Newbold **Tran Dir:** Chris Brown **Eng Dir:** Mick Forbes
Group HR Dir: Jane Burke.
Fleet (Shearings): 172 - 167 single-deck coach, 5 minibus.
Chassis: 5 Ford Transit, 90 Setra, 77 Volvo.
Bodies: 5 Ford, 7 Jonckheere, 9 Plaxton, 90 Setra, 16 Transbus, 45 Van Hool.
Ops incl: excursions & tours, private hire, continental tours.
Livery: Blue or Gold

SOUTH LANCS TRAVEL
UNIT 22/23, CHANTERS INDUSTRIAL ESTATE, ATHERTON M46 9BF
Tel: 01942 888893 **Fax:** 01942 894010
E-mail: southlancs@btconnect.com
Web site: www.southlancs.com
Man Dir: Martin Bott **Eng Dir:** D A Stewart
Tran Man: W Peach.
Fleet: 49 – 2 double-deck bus, 33 single-deck bus, 14 midibus.
Chassis: 15 Dennis, 4 MAN, 4 Mercedes, 14 Optare, 11 Scania, 1 Volvo.
Bodies: 1 Alexander, 3 Caetano, 1 East Lancs, 3 Marshall, 16 Optare, 12 Plaxton, 2 Scania, 1 UVG, 12 Wright.
Ops incl: local bus services, school contracts.
Livery: Yellow/Blue
Ticket System: Wayfarer TGX

SPEEDWELLBUS LTD
RAGLAN STREET, HYDE SK14 2DX
Tel: 0161 367 8588 **Fax:** 0161 367 8589
E-mail: enquiries@speedwellbus.com
Web site: www.speedwellbus.com
Fleet: 26 - 4 double-deck bus, 7 single-deck bus, 15 midibus.
Chassis: Dennis, Enterprise, Leyland, Mercedes, Optare.
Bodies: Alexander, Marshall, Northern Counties, Optare, Plaxton.
Ops incl: local bus services, school contracts
Livery: White/Green

STAGECOACH MANCHESTER
HYDE ROAD, MANCHESTER M41 5DR
Tel: 0161 273 3377 **Fax:** 0161 276 2594
E-mail: manchester.enquiries@stagecoachbus.com
Web site: www.stagecoachbus.com/manchester
Man Dir: Christopher Bowles **Ops Dir:** Vacant
Comm Dir: Ray Cossins **Eng Dir:** Peter Sumner
Fleet: 675 - 510 double-deck bus, 94 single-deck bus, 49 midibus, 22 minibus.
Chassis: 425 Alexander Dennis, 2 DAF, 81 Dennis, 93 MAN, 2 Mercedes, 22 Optare, 2 Scania, 3 Transbus, 45 Volvo.
Bodies: 619 Alexander Dennis, 15 East Lancs, 5 Northern Counties, 24 Optare, 9 Plaxton, 3 Transbus.
Ops incl: local bus services, school contracts.
Livery: Stagecoach UK Bus
Ticket System: ERG

STOTT'S TOURS (OLDHAM) LTD
144 LEES ROAD, OLDHAM OL4 1HT
Tel: 0161 624 4200 **Fax:** 0161 628 2969
Web site: www.stottstours.com

Props: A Stott, G Stott, S Stott.
Fleet: 38 - 23 double-deck bus, 1 single-deck bus, 3 single-deck coach, 11 midibus.
Chassis: Leyland, MCW, Mercedes, Optare, Scania, Volvo.
Ops incl: local bus services, school contracts.
Livery: Cream/Red/Black.

SWANS TRAVEL
STANLEY HOUSE, BROADGATE, CHADDERTON, OLDHAM OL9 9XA
Tel: 0161 681 0999
Fax: 0161 681 0777
E-mail: enquiries@swanstravel.com
Web site: www.swanstravel.com
Man Dir: Kieran Swindells
Ops Man: Reno Peers **Eng Man:** David Midgeley.
Ops incl: local bus services, private hire.
Livery: White with Blue/Yellow.
Incorporating Freebird, Bury.

TYRER BUS
See Lancashire

VIKING COACHES
DOCTOR FOLD FARM, DOCTOR FOLD LANE, BIRCH, HEYWOOD OL10 2QE
Tel: 01706 368999
Fax: 01706 620011
E-mail: vikingcoaches@btconnect.com
Web site: www.viking-coaches.com
Owners: A Warburton, Ms A Warburton.
Fleet: 4 single-deck coach.
Chassis: Iveco, Volvo.
Bodies: Beulas, Plaxton, Van Hool.
Ops incl: excursions & tours, private hire, continental tours, school contracts.
Livery: Viking Ship.

WRIGLEY'S COACHES LTD
4 FIDDLERS LANE, IRLAM M44 6QE
Tel: 0161 775 2414
Fax: 0161 775 1558
E-mail: sales@wrigleyscoaches.com
Web site: www.wrigleyscoaches.com
Man Dir: Colin Wrigley
Co Sec/Dir: Lesley Wrigley
Ops Man: Alan Grice.
Fleet: 8 - 1 double-deck bus, 4 single-deck coach, 2 double-deck coach, 1 minicoach.
Chassis: 1 Leyland, 2 MAN, 1 Neoplan, 1 Setra, 1 Toyota, 2 Volvo.
Bodies: 1 Alexander, 1 Caetano, 3 Neoplan, 1 Plaxton, 1 Setra, 1 Van Hool.
Ops incl: private hire, school contracts.
Livery: Blue/White

HAMPSHIRE, PORTSMOUTH, SOUTHAMPTON

AIRLYNX EXPRESS
TEN ACRES, STONEHAM LANE, EASTLEIGH SO50 9HT
Tel: 02380 687371 **Fax:** 02380 617190
E-mail: us@airlynxexpress.co.uk
Web site: www.airlynxexpress.co.uk
Dir: Gary Gregory **Co Sec:** Sharon Lucas.
Fleet: 9 - midicoach, minibus, minicoach.
Chassis: Ford Transit, Mercedes, Renault, Volkswagen.

Ops incl: private hire, school contracts.
Livery: Blue/Yellow

ALTONIAN COACHES LTD
1A WESTBROOK WALK, MARKET SQUARE, ALTON GU34 1HZ
Tel: 01420 84845 **Fax:** 01420 541429
E-mail: sales@altoniancoaches.co.uk
Web site: www.altoniancoaches.co.uk
Man Dir: Derek Wheeler **Depot Man:** David

Butcher **Tours Man:** Ian McKee.
Fleet: 20 - 13 single-deck coach, 2 midicoach, 3 minibus, 2 minicoach.
Chassis: 1 Ayats, 1 Bova, 1 BMC, 1 Daimler, 1 Irisbus, 1 Iveco, 1 King Long, 3 LDV, 2 MAN, 3 Mercedes, 2 Renault, 1 Scania, 2 Volvo.
Ops incl: school contracts, excursions & tours, private hire, continental tours.
Livery: Blue & Orange
Associated with Wheelers Travel Ltd, Southampton

AMK CHAUFFEUR DRIVE LTD

♿ ✈ ⛴

MILL LANE, PASSFIELD, LIPHOOK GU30 7RP
Tel: 01428 751675
Fax: 01428 751677
E-mail: info@amkxl.com
Web site: www.amkxl.com
Man Dir: G Fraser **Fin Dir:** M Dummer.
Fleet: 78 - 65 minibus, 3 midibus, 10 minicoach.
Ops incl: local bus services, school contracts, excursions & tours, private hire.

AMPORT & DISTRICT COACHES LTD

Ⓜ ✈ ⏸ ⛴

EASTFIELD HOUSE, AMESBURY ROAD, THRUXTON, ANDOVER SP11 8ED
Tel: 01264 772307
Fax: 01264 773020
E-mail: tedd@onetel.net
Dirs: P J Tedd, A M Tedd, N B Tedd.
Fleet: 9 - 7 single-deck coach, 2 midicoach.
Chassis: 2 Mercedes, 3 Scania, 1 Setra, 3 Volvo.
Bodies: 1 Autobus, 3 Berkhof, 1 Esker, 2 Plaxton, 1 Setra, 1 Van Hool.
Ops incl: private hire, continental tours, school contracts.
Livery: White/Brown/Orange

ANGELA COACHES LTD

Ⓜ ✈ ⏸ ⛴ Ⓣ

OAKTREE HOUSE, LOWFORD, BURSLEDON, SOUTHAMPTON SO31 8ES
Tel: 02380 403170
Fax: 02380 406487
E-mail: robert@angelacoaches.com
Web site: www.angelacoaches.com
Man Dir: M J Pressley **Co Sec:** Mrs H M Pressley **Ops Dir:** R J Pressley **Ch Eng:** D Evans
Ops Man: J Davies.
Fleet: 11- 5 single-deck coach, 1 midicoach, 5 minicoach.
Chassis: 2 Iveco, 6 MAN, 1 Mercedes, 2 Toyota.
Bodies: 1 Beulas, 2 Caetano, 2 Indcar, 5 Neoplan, 1 Other.
Ops incl: school contracts, excursions & tours, private hire, continental tours.
Livery: Red/White

AVENSIS COACH TRAVEL LTD

Ⓜ ✈ ⛴ ⏸

29 PREMIER WAY, ABBEY PARK INDUSTRIAL ESTATE, ROMSEY SO51 9DQ
Tel: 01794 515260 **Fax:** 01794 512260
E-mail: info@avensiscoaches.co.uk
Web site: www.avensiscoaches.co.uk
Dirs: Graham Humby, Simon Humby.
Fleet: 8 single-deck coach.
Chassis: 8 Scania.
Bodies: 8 Irizar.
Ops incl: excursions & tours, private hire, continental tours.
Livery: Yellow/Purple

BLACK & WHITE MOTORWAYS LTD

✈ Ⓜ ▭ ⏸ ▭ ⚊

31 STONEY LANE, WINCHESTER SO22 6DP
Tel: 01962 883398
Fax: 01962 620169
Recovery: 07810 772074
E-mail: info@bwmotorways.co.uk
Web site: www.bwmotorways.co.uk
Dirs: Peter Bailey, Eve Bailey **Ch Eng:** Michael Elliott.
Fleet: 10 - 5 double-deck bus, 5 single-deck bus.
Chassis: 1 Bristol, 1 Daimler, 8 Dennis.

Bodies: 1 Alexander Dennis, 1 ECW, 3 East Lancs, 2 Plaxton, 3 UVG.
Ops incl: local bus services, school contracts, excursions & tours, private hire.
Livery: Black & White
Ticket System: Setright

BLACK VELVET TRAVEL LTD

SUITE A, BINNING HOUSE, 4A HIGH STREET EASTLEIGH S050 5LA
Tel: 02380 612288
Fax: 02380 644881
E-mail: talk2us@velvetbus.co.uk
Web site: www.velvetbus.co.uk
Chairman: Terry Stockley **Comp Sec:** Rosalind Stockley **Man Dir:** Phil Stockley
Ops Man: Taz Keeley **Dir:** David Huber.
Fleet: 10 - 6 double-deck bus. 4 single-deck bus.
Chassis: 4 DAF, 3 Leyland, 3 Volvo.
Bodies: 3 Alexander Dennis, 4 East Lancs, 3 Northern Counties.
Ops incl: local bus services, private hire.
Livery: Purple
Ticket System: Wayfarer 3

A. S. BONE & SONS LTD

LONDON ROAD, HOOK RG27 9EQ
Tel: 01256 761388, 762106
Fleet Name: Newnham Coaches
Man Dir: J E Bone **Co Sec:** Mrs M Bone.
Fleet: 7 - 6 double-deck bus, 1 single-deck bus.
Chassis: 1 Dennis, 2 Leyland, 2 MCW, 1 Scania.
Ops incl: private hire.
Livery: Cream/Blue.

BRIJAN TOURS LTD

✈ Ⓡ Ⓡ24 ⚊

THE COACH STATION, UNITS 4/5, BOTTINGS INDUSTRIAL ESTATE, CURDRIDGE SO30 2DY
Tel: 01489 788138
Fax: 01489 789395
Recovery: 07711 435189
E-mail: info@brijantours.com
Web site: www.brijantours.com
Man Dir: Brian Botley **Co Sec:** Janet Botley
Ops Man: Brian Bedford **Fleet Eng:** Ben Cresswell **Asst Man:** David Thompson.
Fleet: 24 - 11 double-deck bus, 6 single-deck bus, 7 single-deck coach.
Chassis: 9 Dennis, 1 Iveco, 8 Leyland, 2 MCW, 2 Scania, 1 Volvo.
Ops incl: local bus services, school contracts, excursions & tours, private hire, continental tours.
Livery: Cream/Burgundy.
Ticket system: Wayfarer

CLEGG & BROOKING LTD

Ⓜ ✈ ⛴ ⏸

WHITE HORSE SERVICE STATION, MIDDLE WALLOP, STOCKBRIDGE SO20 8DZ
Tel: 01264 781283
Fax: 01264 781679
E-mail: cleggandbrooking@btconnect.com
Web site: www.cbcoaches.co.uk
Dirs: Kevin Brooking, Jeanette Cook, John Cook, Sarah Glasspool.
Fleet: 11 - 7 single-deck coach, 1 midicoach, 3 minicoach.
Chassis: 2 Dennis, 2 Mercedes, 4 Scania, 2 Toyota, 2 Volvo.
Bodies: 1 Berkhof, 4 Caetano, 2 Irizar, 2 Plaxton, 1 Sitcar, 1 Sunsundegui.
Ops incl: local bus services, private hire, school contracts.
Livery: Blue/Grey

COLISEUM COACHES LTD

Ⓜ ⏸ ✈ ⛴ Ⓣ

BOTLEY ROAD GARAGE, WEST END, SOUTHAMPTON SO30 3JA
Tel: 02380 472377 **Fax:** 02380 476537
E-mail: info@coliseumcoaches.co.uk
Web site: www.coliseumcoaches.co.uk
Props: David Pitter, Kerry Pitter
Ops Man: Mark Pitter **Ch Eng:** Dave Rowsell.
Fleet: 11 – 10 single-deck coach, 1 minicoach.
Chassis: 10 MAN, 1 Mercedes.
Bodies: 3 Beulas, 1 Mercedes, 7 Neoplan.
Ops incl: excursions & tours, private hire.
Livery: Silver

COOPERS COACHES

✈

31-35 LAKE ROAD, WOOLSTON SO19 9EB
Tel: 023 8039 3393 **Fax:** 023 8044 4929
E-mail: cooperscoaches@yahoo.co.uk
Props: Stephen & Ellen Cooper.
Fleet: 6 - 4 single-deck coach, 2 minibus.
Chassis: 1 DAF, 1 Dennis, 1 Ford Transit, 2 Scania, 1 Volvo.
Bodies: 1 Berkhof, 1 Caetano, 1 Ikarus, 1 Plaxton, 1 Scania.
Ops incl: local bus services, school contracts, private hire.

COUNTRYLINER GROUP

See Surrey

COUNTYWIDE TOP TRAVEL

♿ ✈ Ⓜ ⏸ ⛴ ⚊

169 NEW GREENHAM PARK, THATCHAM RG19 6HN
Tel: 01256 780079 **Fax:** 01635 821128
E-mail: info@countywidetoptravel.co.uk
Web site: www.countywidetoptravel.co.uk
Dir: Simon Weaver
Fleet: See Weavaway Travel, Berkshire.
Liveries: Black, Blue & Black
A subsidiary of Weavaway Travel, Berkshire

COUNTYWIDE TRAVEL (FLEET) LTD

♿ ✈

BOWENHURST FARM, CRONDALL FARNHAM, GU10 5RP
Tel: 01252 851009 **Fax:** 01252 852009
E-mail: info@fleetbuzz.co.uk
Web site: www.fleetbuzz.co.uk
Fleet Name: Fleet Buzz
Man Dir: John C Chadwick
Fleet: 22 - 4 single-deck bus, 16 midibus, 2 minibus.
Chassis: 2 Alexander Dennis, 1 Iveco, 2 LDV, 9 Mercedes, 8 Optare.
Bodies: 2 Caetano, 2 LDV, 1 Mellor, 9 Mercedes, 8 Optare.
Ops incl: local bus services,
Livery: Black & Yellow
Ticket system: Wayfarer III

EASSONS COACHES LTD

✈ Ⓜ ⛴

44 WODEHOUSE ROAD, ITCHEN, SOUTHAMPTON SO19 2EQ
Tel: 023 8044 8153
Fax: 023 8044 1635
Dirs: D H Easson, R A Easson.
Fleet: 7 - 5 single-deck coach, 2 midicoach.
Chassis: 2 Mercedes, 1 Neoplan, 3 Setra, 1 Volvo.
Bodies: 1 Neoplan, 1 Plaxton, 3 Setra, 2 Sitcar.
Ops incl: excursions & tours, private hire.
Livery: Cream & Khaki Brown

EMSWORTH & DISTRICT MOTOR SERVICES LTD

THE BUS GARAGE, CLOVELLY ROAD, SOUTHBOURNE PO10 8PE
Tel: 01243 378337
Fax: 01243 389424
E-mail: caren@emsworthanddistrict.co.uk
Web site: www.emsworthanddistrict.co.uk
Man Dir: Paul Lea
Fleet: 36 - 3 double-deck bus, 22 single-deck bus, 10 single-deck coach, 1 minibus.
Chassis: Alexander Dennis, Bova, DAF, Dennis, Ford Transit, Leyland, Mercedes, Van Hool.
Ops incl: local bus services, school contracts, excursions & tours, private hire, continental tours
Livery: Green/Silver.
Ticket system: Wayfarer

FIRST HAMPSHIRE & DORSET LTD

EMPRESS ROAD, SOUTHAMPTON SO14 0JW
Tel: 0870 010 6022 **Fax:** 023 8071 4891
E-mail: hampshire-dorset.csc@firstgroup.com
Web site: www.firstgroup.com
Reg Man Dir: Justin Davies **Reg Finance & Planning Dir:** Amelia Price **Service Delivery Dir South Coast:** Chris Bainbridge **Comm & Business Growth Dir:** Marc Reddy **Reg Eng Standards Dir:** Chris Jones.
Fleet: 382 - 69 double-deck bus, 264 single-deck bus, 5 single-deck coach, 44 midibus.
Chassis: 4 Alexander Dennis, 16 BMC, 142 Dennis, 6 Leyland, 29 Mercedes, 15 Optare, 29 Scania, 141 Volvo.
Bodies: 4 Alexander Dennis, 31 Alexander, 6 BMC, 1 Caetano, 10 East Lancs, 11 Marshall, 30 Northern Counties, 15 Optare, 147 Plaxton, 22 Scania, 6 UVG, 89 Wright.
Ops incl: local bus services, school contracts, private hire.
Livery: FirstGroup UK Bus

GEMINI TRAVEL SOUTHAMPTON LTD

NORTH ROAD, MARCHWOOD INDUSTRIAL PARK, MARCHWOOD, SOUTHAMPTON SO40 4BL
Tel: 02380 660066 **Fax:** 02380 871308
E-mail: info@travel-gemini.co.uk
Web site: www.travel-gemini.co.uk
Dirs: Ken Hatch, Mark Bennett
Gen Man: Nigel Smith.
Fleet: 10 - 2 single-deck coach, 5 midicoach, 3 minicoach.
Chassis: 2 Ford, 1 LDV, 5 Mercedes, 2 Volvo.
Bodies: 1 LDV, 3 Optare, 2 Plaxton, 4 other.
Ops incl: private hire, school contracts.
Livery: White/Blue

GO SOUTH COAST LTD

TOWNGATE HOUSE, 2-8 PARKSTONE ROAD, POOLE BH15 2PR
Tel: 01202 680888 **Fax:** 01202 670244
E-mail: alex.carter@gosouthcoast.co.uk
Web site: www.bluestarbus.co.uk, www.go-ahead.com
Fleet Names: Bluestar, Marchwood Motorways, Unilink..
Chairman: David Brown **Man Dir:** Alex Carter
Eng Dir: Steve Hamilton **Fin Dir:** Matt Dolphin
Divisional Dirs: Marc Morgan Huws, Ed Wills.
Fleet: 625 - 252 double-deck bus, 125 single-deck bus, 91 single-deck coach, 1 articulated bus,

12 open top bus, 137 midibus, 7 minibus.
Chassis: 2 Bristol, 104 DAF, 49 Dennis, 2 Ford, 4 Iveco, 5 LDV, 33 Leyland, 1 MAN, 50 Mercedes, 99 Optare, 106 Scania, 2 Toyota, 168 Volvo.
Bodies: 10 Alexander Dennis, 2 Autobus, 4 Beulas, 1 Bova, 6 Caetano, 2 ECW, 56 East Lancs, 2 Ford, 12 Ikarus, 4 Irizar, 2 Jonckheere, 5 LDV, 25 Leyland, 47 Mercedes, 41 Northern Counties, 153 Optare, 76 Plaxton, 73 Scania, 27 Transbus, 22 Van Hool, 55 Wright.
Ops incl: local bus services, school contracts.
Liveries: Bluestar, Marchwood: Blue;
Unilink: Blue/White.
Ticket System: Wayfarer TGX
Part of the Go-Ahead Group

GREYHOUND UK LTD

FIRSTGROUP PLC, EMPRESS ROAD, SOUTHAMPTON SO14 0JW
Tel: 0900 096 0000
E-mail: support@greyhounduk.com
Web site: www.greyhounduk.com
Fleet: 11 single-deck coach.
Chassis: 11 Scania.
Bodies: 11 Irizar.
A subsidiary of FirstGroup

HERRINGTON COACHES LTD

See Dorset

HYTHE & WATERSIDE COACHES LTD

1A THE HIGH STREET, HYTHE SO45 6AG
Tel: 02380 844788 **Fax:** 02380 207284
E-mail: enquiries@watersidetours.co.uk
Web site: www.watersidetours.co.uk
Fleet Name: Waterside Tours
Man Dir: Roy Barker **Dirs:** Pamela Barker, Jackie Withey **(Co Sec).**
Fleet: 7 – 4 single-deck coach, 2 midicoach, 1 minibus.
Chassis: 3 Mercedes, 1 Scania, 3 Volvo.
Bodies: 3 Berkhof, 2 Esker, 1 Mercedes, 1 Scania.
Ops incl: school contracts, excursions & tours, private hire, continental tours.
Livery: Burgundy & Gold.

KING ALFRED MOTOR SERVICES LTD

UNIT 6, THE GRAINSTORE, PENTON MEWSEY, ANDOVER SP11 0RG
Tel: 01962 620169
Recovery: 07825 224723
E-mail: kingalfredmotorservices@ntlworld.com
Web site: www.kingalfredmotorservices.co.uk
Dirs: Peter Bailey, Eve Bailey **Eng:** Graham True.
Fleet: 16 – 5 double-deck bus, 4 single-deck bus, 3 single-deck coach, 2 double-deck coach, 2 open-top bus.
Chassis: 4 AEC, 2 Bristol, 1 DAF, 2 Daimler, 4 Dennis, 2 Leyland, 1 Neoplan.
Bodies: 2 ECW, 1 East Lancs, 1 MCW, 1 Neoplan, 1 Northern Counties, 3 Park Royal, 4 Plaxton, 1 UVG, 2 Wadham Stringer.
Ops incl: local bus services, school contracts, excursions & tours, private hire.
Livery: Apple Green/Pale Yellow
Ticket System: Setright

LUCKETTS TRAVEL

BROADCUT, WALLINGTON, FAREHAM PO16 8TB
Tel: 01329 823755 **Fax:** 01329 823855
E-mail: contact@lucketts.co.uk

Web site: www.lucketts.co.uk
Chairman: David Luckett **Joint Man Dirs:** Steven Luckett, Ian Luckett **Eng Dir:** Mark Jordan
Ops Man: Tony Harper.
Fleet: 61 – 1 single-deck bus, 47 single-deck coach, 1 double-deck coach, 4 midicoach, 8 minibus.
Chassis: 2 Bova, 5 Dennis, 12 Mercedes, 1 Neoplan, 1 Optare, 35 Scania, 3 Toyota, 2 Volvo.
Bodies: 5 Berkhof, 2 Bova, 17 Caetano, 2 Hispano, 18 Irizar, 9 Mercedes, 1 Neoplan, 1 Optare, 4 Plaxton, 2 Scania.
Ops incl: school contracts, excursions & tours, private hire, express, continental tours.
Liveries: Grey/White/Orange, National Express.

MARCHWOOD MOTORWAYS

See Go South Coast Ltd

MERVYN'S COACHES

THE NEW COACH HOUSE, INNERSDOWN, MICHELDEVER, WINCHESTER SO21 3BW
Tel/Fax: 01962 774574
E-mail: mervynscoaches@btconnect.com
Web site: www.mervynscoaches.com
Partners: M Annetts, C L Annetts, L Porter, J Annetts.
Fleet: 6 - 4 single-deck coach, 1 midicoach, 1 minicoach.
Chassis: 2 Bedford, 4 Volvo.
Bodies: 1 Duple, 3 Plaxton, 1 Van Hool, 1 Other.
Ops incl: local bus services, school contracts, excursions & tours, private hire.
Livery: Brown/Cream
Ticket System: Setright

MORTONS TRAVEL

UNIT 11, BERRY COURT BUSINESS PARK, BRAMLEY ROAD, LITTLE LONDON, TADLEY RG26 5AT
Tel: 01256 889082 **Fax:** 01256 889083
Recovery: 07917 202895
E-mail: enquiries@mortonstravel.com
Web site: www.mortonstravel.com
Prop: Adrian Morton
Fleet incl: double-deck bus, single-deck bus, single-deck coach, double-deck coach, open top bus, midicoach, minicoach.
Ops incl: school contracts, excursions & tours, private hire, continental tours.
Livery: Green & Silver, White & Green

PIKE'S COACHES LTD

77 SCOTT CLOSE, WALWORTH INDUSTRIAL ESTATE, ANDOVER SP10 5NU
Tel: 01264 312702 **Fax:** 01264 334329
Web site: www.pikecoaches-andover.co.uk
Props: J S Pike, Jenny Pike, C Pike, R Pike.
Fleet: 15 - 4 double-deck bus, 5 single-deck coach, 2 midicoach, 4 minibus.
Chassis: Bristol, Ford Transit, Iveco, Mercedes, Volvo.
Bodies: Mercedes, Plaxton, ECW.
Ops incl: local bus services, school contracts, excursions & tours, private hire, continental tours.
Livery: White.
Ticket System: Setright.

PRINCESS COACHES LTD

PRINCESS COACH GARAGE, BOTLEY ROAD, WEST END, SOUTHAMPTON SO30 3HA

Tel: 023 8047 2150 **Fax:** 023 8039 9944
E-mail: admin@princesscoaches.com
Web site: www.princesscoaches.co.uk
Man Dir: Peter Brown **Gen Man:** Jamie Brown
Co Sec: Yvonne Barfoot
Chair/Dir: Denise Brown.
Fleet: 16 - 14 single-deck coach, 1 midicoach,
1 minibus.
Chassis: 2 Mercedes, 14 Scania.
Bodies: 14 Irizar, 1 Optare, 1 Sitcar.
Ops incl: school contracts, private hire.
Livery: White with multi-coloured flashes.

SOLENT BLUE LINE
See Go South Coast Ltd

SOLENT COACHES LTD
♿🅿️🍴❄️R24📞
BROOKSIDE GARAGE, CROW LANE,
RINGWOOD BH24 3EA
Tel: 01425 473188
Fax: 01425 473669
Recovery: 0784 326 6720/1
E-mail: enquiries@solentcoaches.co.uk
Web site: www.solentcoaches.co.uk
Man Dir/Co Sec: John Skew **Dir/Ch Eng:**
Paul Skew.
Fleet: 9 - 7 single-deck coach, 1 minibus,
1 midicoach.
Chassis: 1 Mercedes, 6 Scania, 1 Setra, 1 Toyota.
Bodies: 1 Caetano, 2 Irizar, 1 Mercedes, 1 Setra,
4 Van Hool.
Ops incl: excursions & tours, private hire,
continental tours, school contracts.
Livery: White/Blue

STAGECOACH IN HAMPSHIRE
♿
THE BUS STATION, FESTIVAL PLACE,
CHURCHILL WAY, BASINGSTOKE RG21 7BE
Tel: 0871 200 2233
Fax: 01243 755888
E-mail: south.enquiries@stagecoachbus.com
Web site: www.stagecoachbus/com/hampshire
Man Dir: Andrew Dyer **Eng Dir:**
Richard Alexander **Fin Dir:** Martin Stoggell
Div Man: Matthew Callow.
Fleet: 161 - 42 double-deck bus, 103 single-deck
bus, 16 midibus.
Chassis: 75 Alexander Dennis, 41 Dennis,

5 Mercedes, 11 Optare, 2 Transbus, 27 Volvo.
Bodies: 56 Alexander, 75 Alexander Dennis,
11 Optare, 17 Plaxton, 2 Transbus.
Ops incl: local bus services, school contracts.
Livery: Stagecoach UK Bus
Ticket System: Wayfarer.

STAGECOACH IN HANTS & SURREY
HALIMOTE ROAD, ALDERSHOT GU11 1NJ
Tel: 0871 200 2233
Fax: 01243 755888
E-mail: south.enquiries@stagecoachbus.com
Web site: www.stagecoachbus.com
Man Dir: Andrew Dyer **Eng Dir:**
Richard Alexander **Fin Dir:** Martin Stoggell.
Fleet: 89 - 15 double-deck bus, 58 single-deck
bus, 16 midibus.
Chassis: 17 Alexander Dennis, 13 Dennis,
20 MAN, 2 Mercedes, 14 Optare, 4 Transbus,
19 Volvo.
Bodies: 19 Alexander, 37 Alexander Dennis,
9 Northern Counties, 14 Optare, 6 Plaxton,
4 Transbus.
Ops incl: local bus services, school contracts.
Livery: Stagecoach UK Bus
Ticket System: Wayfarer

TEST VALLEY TRAVEL LTD
♿
BANNISTER BARN, NEWTON LANE,
WHITEPARISH SP5 2QQ
Tel/Fax: 01794 884555
Dirs: Mr J M Norman, Mrs A N Norman.
E-mail: falconlomax@hotmail.co.uk
Fleet: 3 minibus.
Chassis/Bodies: 3 LDV.
Ops incl: private hire, school contracts.
Livery: Green/Gold/White

TRUEMANS COACHES (FLEET) LTD
♿🅿️❄️
TRUEMANS END, LYNCHFORD ROAD, ASH
VALE, GU12 5PQ
Tel: 01252 373303
Fax: 01252 373393
Dir: Richard Trueman
Fleet: 15 single deck coach.
Chassis: 5 Iveco, 10 MAN.
Bodies: 5 Beulas, 6 Neoplan, 4 Plaxton.
Ops incl: school contracts, private hire,

excursions & tours, continental tours.
Livery: Electric Blue

VISION TRAVEL
♿🅿️❄️
3A SPUR ROAD, COSHAM, PORTSMOUTH
PO6 3DY
Tel: 02392 359168 **Fax:** 02392 361253
E-mail: visiontravels@aol.com
Web site: www.visiontravel.co.uk
Dir: Peter Sharpe
Fleet: 37 - 29 single-deck coach, 2 double-deck
coach, 4 midicoach, 2 minibus.
Ops incl: school contracts, excursions & tours,
private hire, continental tours.
Livery: Yellow/Red/White

WHEELERS TRAVEL LTD
♿🅿️❄️📞T
UNIT 9, GROVE FARM, UPPER NORTHAM
DRIVE, HEDGE END, SOUTHAMPTON SO30
4BG
Tel: 02380 471800
Fax: 02380 470414
E-mail: sales@wheelerstravel.co.uk
Web site: www.wheelerstravel.co.uk
Man Dir: Derek Wheeler **Gen Man:** Paul
Barker **Traffic Man:** Keith Trenchard
Assistant Traffic Man: Nigel Taylor.
Fleet: 22
Chassis: 1 Ayats, 1 Bova, 2 Iveco, 1 King Long,
5 LDV, 5 Mercedes, 2 Renault, 2 Scania, 3 Volvo.
Bodies: 1 Ayats, 2 Beulas, 1 Esker, 2 Indcar,
2 Marcopolo, 1 Noge, 2 Plaxton, 1 Van Hool.
Ops incl: private hire, excursions & tours, school
contracts, continental tours.
Livery: Blue Body, Orange Mirrors

XELABUS LTD
♿🅿️❄️
2 TRAFALGAR CLOSE, CHANDLERS FORD
BUSINESS PARK, CHANDLERS FORD
SO53 4BW
Tel: 02380 275000
Fax: 02380 274414
Web site: www.xelabus.info
Man Dir: Gareth Blair
Ops incl: local bus services, school contracts,
sightseeing tours, private hire.
Livery: Green

BOWYER'S COACHES
♿
QUARRY GARAGE, PETERCHURCH HR2 0TF
Tel: 01981 550206
Prop: Fernley C. Anning, Anthony H. Anning.
Fleet: 9 - 5 single-deck coach, 4 minibus.
Chassis: Bedford, LDV.
Ops incl: local bus services, private hire, school
contracts.
Livery: White/Red.

BROMYARD OMNIBUS COMPANY
Operations transferred to Village Green Motor
Services.

COACH COMPANIONS LTD
Ceased trading since LRB 2011 went to press.

D R M BUS AND CONTRACT SERVICES
♿
THE COACH GARAGE, BROMYARD HR7 4NT
Tel: 01885 483219

Prop: David R. Morris
Fleet: single-deck bus
Chassis: Scania, Volvo.
Ops incl: local bus services, school contracts.
Livery: Blue/Silver-White
Ticket System: Wayfarer 3

FIRST MIDLANDS
♿♿
HERON LODGE, LONDON ROAD,
WORCESTER WR5 2EU
Tel: 08450 100 111 **Fax:** 01905 351104
Regional Man Dir: Nigel Barrett **Regional
Eng Dir:** Mick Brannigan **Regional Comm
Dir:** Steve Wickers **Regional Fin Planning
Dir:** David Marshall.
Fleet Name: First Wyvern
Fleet (Worcestershire & Hereford):
160 – 9 double-deck bus, 127 single-deck bus,
2 single-deck coach, 22 midibus.
Chassis: 44 Alexander Dennis, 1 BMC,
69 Dennis, 1 Leyland, 23 Optare, 5 Transbus,

17 Volvo.
Bodies: 4 Alexander, 44 Alexander Dennis,
1 BMC, 5 Caetano, 23 Optare, 56 Plaxton,
5 Transbus, 22 Wright.
Ops incl: local bus services, school contracts.
Livery: FirstGroup UK Bus
Ticket System: Wayfarer

GOLDEN PIONEER TRAVEL
🅿️🍴♿❄️
BRANDON, REDHILL, HEREFORD HR2 8BH
Tel: 01432 274307 **Fax:** 01432 275809
E-mail: crockbrey@aol.com
Web site: www.goldenpioneertravel.com
Prop: Bryan Crockett **Dir:** J Crockett.
Fleet: 3 single-deck coach.
Chassis incl: King Long.
Bodies incl: Van Hool.
Ops incl: excursions & tours, private hire,
continental tours.
Livery: Black/Gold/Red/Green/Yellow

GOLD STAR TRAVEL
See Worcestershire

P.W. JONES COACHES
HILBREY GARAGE, BURLEY GATE, HEREFORD
HR1 3QL
Tel: 01432 820214
Fax: 01432 820521
Recovery: 01432 820214
E-mail: coaches@p.w.jones.com
Owner: Philip Jones
Fleet: 19 – 16 single-deck coach, 1 midicoach,
2 minibus.
Chassis: 1 Bova, 9 Dennis, 1 LDV, 1 MAN,
1 Mercedes, 2 Neoplan, 1 Toyota, 3 Volvo.
Bodies: 1 Bova, 1 Caetano, 1 LDV, 2 Mercedes,
14 Plaxton.
Ops incl: school contracts, excursions & tours,
private hire, continental tours.
Livery: Multi Colours

LUGG VALLEY PRIMROSE TRAVEL LTD
SOUTHERN AVENUE, LEOMINSTER HR6 OQF
Tel: 01432 344341
Fax: 01432 356206
E-mail: sales@luggvalleytravel.co.uk
Man Dir: N D Yeomans **Ops Man:** I Davies
Chief Eng: D W Jones.
Fleet: 26 – 4 single-deck bus, 8 single-deck coach,
13 midibus, 1 midicoach.
Chassis: 5 Dennis, 1 Mercedes, 13 Optare,
2 Scania, 5 Volvo.
Bodies: 1 Berkhof, 1 Carlyle, 1 Duple, 1 Esker,
2 Irizar, 1 Jonckheere, 13 Optare, 6 Plaxton.
Ops incl: local bus services, school contracts,
excursions & tours, private hire
Livery: Green/Cream/Orange
Ticket System: ERG

M & S COACHES OF HEREFORDSHIRE LTD
UNIT 3, BRIERLEY WAY, SOUTHERN AVENUE,
LEOMINSTER HR6 0QF
Tel: 01568 612803

E-mail: maurice@mscoaches.co.uk
Web site: www.mscoaches.co.uk
Dirs: Maurice Peruffo, Mrs Susan Peruffo,
Les Allen.
Fleet: 10 – 6 midicoach, 4 minicoach.
Chassis: 1 BMC, 7 Mercedes, 2 Toyota.
Bodies: 1 BMC, 2 Caetano, 1 Esker, 3 Optare,
1 Sitcar, 2 Unvi.
Ops incl: school contracts, private hire,
continental tours.
Livery: White with Red/Black lettering

NEWBURY COACHES
LOWER ROAD TRADING ESTATE,
LEDBURY HR8 2DJ
Tel: 01531 633483
Fax: 01531 633650
Livery: Blue/White.

NICK MADDY COACHES
171 WIDEMARSH STREET, HEREFORD
HR4 9HE
Tel: 01432 266211 **Fax:** 01432 356645
Prop: Nick Maddy
Fleet: 5 – 1 single-deck bus, 4 minibus.
Chassis: 2 Iveco, 2 LDV, 1 Optare.
Ops incl: local bus services, school contracts,
private hire.

SARGEANTS BROS LTD
MILL STREET, KINGTON HR5 3AL
Tel: 01544 230481
Fax: 01544 231892
E-mail: mike@sargeantsbros.com
Web site: www.sargeantsbros.com
Man Dir: Michael Sargeant **Man:** David Lloyd.
Fleet: 22 – 1 double-deck bus, 4 single-deck bus,
5 single-deck coach, 7 midibus, 5 minibus.
Chassis: 1 Blue Bird, 1 DAF, 1 Dennis, 2 Ford
Transit, 1 LDV, 9 Mercedes, 2 Plaxton, 2 Van Hool,
5 Other.
Bodies: 1 Autobus, 2 Jonckheere, 1 LDV,
9 Optare, 2 Plaxton, 2 Van Hool, 6 Other.
Ops incl: local bus services, school contracts,
private hire.

Livery: Red
Ticket System: ERG

SMITHS MOTORS (LEDBURY) LTD
COACH GARAGE, HOMEND, LEDBURY
HR8 1BA
Tel: 01531 632953
Dirs: F W B Sterry, M Sterry.
Ops incl: private hire, continental tours.
Livery: White with Green/Blue/Red stripe.
Ticket System: Setright.

STAGECOACH IN SOUTH WALES
See Torfaen

VILLAGE GREEN MOTOR SERVICES
LYSANDER YARD, CANTERBURY ROAD,
SHOBDON, LEOMINSTER HR6 9NN
Tel: 01568 709053
Ops incl: school contracts, private hire.
Livery: Green

YEOMANS CANYON TRAVEL LTD
THE TRAVEL CENTRE, OLD SCHOOL LANE,
HEREFORD HR1 1EX
Tel: 01432 356201
Fax: 01432 356206
E-mail: sales@yeomanstravel.co.uk
Web site: www.yeomanscoachholidays.com
Man Dir: N D Yeomans
Ops Man: I Davies
Ch Eng: C Taylor.
Fleet: 40 – 4 single-deck bus, 26 single-deck
coach, 9 midibus, 1 midicoach.
Chassis: 2 BMC, 10 Dennis, 1 Neoplan, 9 Optare,
9 Scania, 9 Volvo.
Bodies: 1 Berkhof, 2 BMC, 7 Caetano, 1 Duple,
2 Irizar, 2 Marcopolo, 1 Marshall/MCV, 1 Neoplan,
1 Northern Counties, 9 Optare, 11 Plaxton,
2 Van Hool.
Ops incl: local bus services, school contracts,
excursions & tours, private hire, express,
continental tours.
Livery: Green/Cream/Orange
Ticket System: ERG

HERTFORDSHIRE

A R TRAVEL LTD
34 ROESTOCK LANE, COLNEY HEATH,
ST ALBANS AL4 0PR
Tel: 01727 822404 **Fax:** 01727 821566
E-mail: artravelltd@hotmail.com
Web site: www.artravelltd.co.uk
Dir: Terry Hill
Fleet: 4 – 1 midicoach, 3 minicoach.
Chassis: 4 Mercedes.
Ops incl: school contracts, excursions & tours,
private hire.
Livery: Silver & White

ARRIVA THE SHIRES LTD
See Bedfordshire

CENTREBUS LTD
ALBANY HOUSE, PIN GREEN, WEDGEWOOD
WAY, STEVENAGE SG1 4PX
Tel: 0844 357 6520
E-mail: info@centrebus.com
Web site: www.centrebus.com
Fleet (Hertfordshire): 23 – 1 single-deck bus,
22 midibus.

Chassis: 2 Dennis, 16 Optare, 1 Scania, 4 VDL.
Bodies: 1 Alexander, 1 East Lancs, 16 Optare,
5 Plaxton.
Ops incl: local bus services.
Livery: Blue/Orange/White.
Ticket System: Wayfarer 3.
Part of the Centrebus Group

CHAMBERS COACHES (STEVENAGE) LTD
JACKS MILL PARK, GREAT NORTH ROAD,
GRAVELEY, HITCHIN SG4 7EG
Tel: 01438 352920
Fax: 01462 486616
E-mail: chamberscoaches@btconnect.com
Web site: www.chamberscoaches.com
Man Dir: Martin Chambers
Dir & Comp Sec: Debra Tidey.
Fleet: 26 – 22 single-deck coach, 3 midicoach,
1 minicoach.
Chassis: 1 BMC, 12 Dennis, 3 Iveco, 1 LDV,
2 Mercedes, 2 Toyota, 1 VDL.
Bodies incl: 1 BMC, 2 Marcopolo, 2 Mercedes,
15 Plaxton, 1 Wadham Stringer.

Ops incl: school contacts, private hire.
Livery: White/Red/Blue

COZY TRAVEL LTD
661 SAUNDERS CLOSE, GREEN LANE,
LETCHWORTH SG6 1PF
Tel: 01462 481707
Fax: 01462 673875
E-mail: info@cozys.co.uk
Web site: www.cozys.co.uk
Fleet Name: Cozy's.
Dirs: N Powell, G Powell, B Powell.
Fleet: 17 – 2 double-deck bus, 2 single-deck bus,
8 single-deck coach, 1 double-deck coach,
2 midibus, 2 minicoach.
Chassis: 2 Dennis, 2 Iveco, 1 MAN, 1 Mercedes,
1 Neoplan, 2 Optare, 2 Scania, 1 Toyota, 5 Volvo.
Bodies: 2 Alexander Dennis, 2 East Lancs, 2 Irizar,
1 Jonckheere, 1 Mercedes, 1 Neoplan, 1 Noge,
2 Optare, 2 Plaxton, 3 Other.
Ops incl: local bus services, private hire, school
contracts, excursions & tours, continental tours.
Livery: White/Multicoloured.

GOLDEN BOY COACHES (JETSIE LTD)

JOHN TERENCE HOUSE, GEDDINGS ROAD, HODDESDON EN11 0NT
Tel: 0800 731 4378
Fax: 01992 450957
E-mail: sales@goldenboy.co.uk
Web site: www.goldenboy.co.uk
Joint Man Dirs: G A McIntyre, T P McIntyre
Tran Man: G Jaikens **Ch Eng:** P Murdoch.
Fleet: 33 - 18 single-deck coach, 12 midicoach, 3 minicoach.
Chassis: 2 MAN, 16 Mercedes, 15 Volvo.
Bodies: 1 Euro, 1 Mercedes, 3 Optare, 9 Plaxton, 1 Sitcar, 18 Van Hool.
Ops incl: private hire, school contracts, excursions & tours, continental tours.
Livery: Black/Red/Gold.
Ticket System: Wayfarer

GRAVES COACHES & MINIBUSES

134 WINFORD DRIVE, BROXBOURNE EN10 6PN
Tel/Fax: 01992 445556
E-mail: m.graves@btinternet.com
Prop: Michael Graves
Fleet: 2 - 1 minicoach, 1 minibus.
Chassis: 1 Mercedes, 1 Toyota.
Bodies: 1 Caetano, 1 Mercedes.
Ops incl: private hire, school contracts.

GROVE COACHES

101 MANDEVILLE ROAD, HERTFORD SG13 8JL
Tel: 01992 583417
Fleet Name: Pride of Hertford
Driver/operator: R A Bowers
Fleet: 1 single-deck coach.
Chassis: Volvo.
Body: Plaxton.
Ops incl: private hire, school contracts.
Livery: Brown/Orange

KENZIES COACHES LTD

6 ANGLE LANE, SHEPRETH SG8 6QH
Tel: 01763 260288
Fax: 01763 262012
Fleet: 20 single-deck coach.
Chassis: 2 Bedford, 18 Volvo.
Bodies: 6 Plaxton, 14 Van Hool.
Ops incl: private hire, school contracts.
Livery: Blue with logos.

LITTLE JIM'S BUSES

5 WILLIAM FISKE HOUSE, CASTLE STREET, BERKHAMSTED HP4 2HF
Tel: 01442 870029
E-mail: littlejimbuses@aol.com
Prop: James H Petty
Fleet: 3 - 2 single-deck bus, 1 midicoach.
Chassis: 1 Dennis, 2 Mercedes.
Bodies: 1 Alexander Dennis, 1 Mercedes, 1 Optare.
Ops incl: local bus services, school contracts, excursions & tours, private hire.
Livery: Various.
Ticket System: Almex

LWB LTD

9 ELTON WAY, WATFORD WD25 8HH

Tel: 01923 247444 **Fax:** 01923 817066
Fleet Name: Cantabrica Coaches
Web site: www.cantabricacoaches.co.uk
Gen Man: Colin Brown **Ops Man:** Paul Cram.
Fleet: 14 - 12 single-deck coach, 2 minicoach.
Chassis: 1 LDV, 1 Peugeot, 12 Volvo.
Bodies: 12 Berkhof, 2 Other.
Ops incl: excursions & tours, private hire, continental tours.
Livery: Blue with Red relief

MARSHALLS COACHES

UNIT 4, FIRBANK WAY, LEIGHTON BUZZARD LU7 4YP
Tel: 01525 376077
Fax: 01525 850967
E-mail: info@marshalls-coaches.co.uk
Web site: www.marshalls-coaches.co.uk
Prop: Glen Marshall
Fleet: 34 - 6 double-deck bus, 24 single-deck coach, 2 double-deck coach, 2 midicoach.
Chassis: 2 Bova, 1 Bristol, 4 Dennis, 1 Iveco, 2 Leyland, 3 MAN, 2 Mercedes, 1 Neoplan, 1 Scania, 17 Volvo.
Bodies: 3 Ayats, 1 Beulas, 2 Bova, 1 Mercedes, 1 Neoplan, 17 Plaxton, 1 Scania, 7 Other.
Ops incl: private hire, school contracts.
Livery: Blue/Multicoloured.

MASTER TRAVEL COACHES

9-12 PEARTREE FARM, WELWYN GARDEN CITY AL7 3UW
Tel: 01707 334040
Fax: 01707 334366
E-mail: mastertravel@btclick.com
Partners: R J Goulden, S Goulden.
Fleet: 16 - 1 single-deck bus, 13 single-deck coach, 2 minibus.
Chassis: 1 BMC, 4 Dennis, 2 Ford Transit, 3 Mercedes, 1 Neoplan, 2 Scania, 1 Optare, 1 Autosan, 1 Volvo.
Bodies: 1 Berkhof, 1 BMC, 1 Caetano, 2 Irizar, 2 Marcopolo, 1 Neoplan, 1 Northern Counties, 1 Optare, 1 UGV, 4 other.
Ops incl: school contracts, private hire.
Livery: White/Blue, White

MERIDIAN LINE TRAVEL

UNIT 2, WIRELESS STATION PARK, CHESTNUT LANE, BASSINGBOURN, ROYSTON SG8 5JH
Tel: 01763 241999
Fax: 01763 245697
E-mail: enquiries@mltravel.co.uk
Web site: www.mltravel.co.uk
Ops incl: school contracts, private hire, excursions & tours.
Livery: White/Multicolour.

MINIBUS SERVICES LTD

773 ST ALBANS ROAD, WATFORD WD25 9LA
Tel: 01923 663432
Fax: 01923 337347
E-mail: minibusservices@btconnect.com
Props: Russell Crowson, Gillian Crowson.
Fleet: 4 - 1 single-deck coach, 1 minibus, 2 midicoach.
Chassis: 1 Ford Transit, 1 Mercedes, 1 Toyota, 1 Volvo.
Bodies: include Caetano, Plaxton.
Ops incl: school contracts, private hire

MULLANY'S COACHES

BROOKDELL TRANSPORT YARD, ST ALBANS ROAD, WATFORD WD25 0GB
Tel: 01923 279991
Fax: 01923 682212
E-mail: coachbookings@mullanyscoaches.com
Web site: www.mullanyscoaches.com, www.mullanysbuses.com
Dir: Kevin Crawford
Fleet: double-deck bus, single-deck bus, single-deck coach, midibus.
Ops incl: local bus services, school contracts, private hire.
Livery: Buses: Red and Blue; **Coaches:** White with Blue Lettering.
Associated with J J Kavanagh & Sons, Urlingford – see Republic of Ireland.

PARKSIDE TRAVEL LTD

PARADISE WILDLIFE PARK, WHITE STUBBS LANE, BROXBOURNE EN10 7QA
Tel: 01992 444477
Fax: 01992 465441
Fleet Name: Parkside Travel
Dirs: P C Sampson, G F Sampson.
Fleet: 7 minibus.
Chassis: 7 Ford Transit.
Ops incl: school contracts, private hire.
Livery: Light Blue

PROVENCE PRIVATE HIRE (P.P.H. COACHES)

HEATH FARM LANE, ST ALBANS AL3 5AE
Tel: 01727 864988
Fax: 01727 855275
E-mail: office@pphcoaches.com
Web site: www.pphcoaches.com
Dirs: A K Hayes, R F Hayes
Ch Eng: D Higgins.
Fleet: 30 - 2 double-deck bus, 19 single-deck coach, 3 double-deck coach, 4 midicoach, 2 minibus.
Chassis: 1 Bova, 1 DAF, 4 Dennis, 2 LDV, 3 Leyland, 1 MCW, 3 Mercedes, 9 Scania, 1 Toyota, 5 Volvo.
Bodies: 1 Bova, 2 Caetano, 1 Duple, 3 East Lancs, 1 Hispano, 6 Irizar, 1 MCW, 1 Mercedes, 3 Optare, 8 Plaxton, 2 UVG, 1 Van Hool.
Ops incl: school contracts, excursions & tours, private hire, continental tours.
Livery: Yellow.

REG'S COACHES LTD

113 - 115 CODICOTE ROAD, WELWYN AL6 9TY
Tel: 01483 822000
Fax: 01483 822003
E-mail: regscoaches@btconnect.com
Web site: www.regscoaches.co.uk
Man Dir: Mr T Hunt. **Dir:** Mrs B Hunt.
Fleet: 18 - 2 single-deck bus, 13 single-deck coach, 3 midicoach.
Chassis: 7 Dennis, 1 Mercedes, 1 Optare, 8 Volvo, 1 Other.
Bodies: 1 Berkhof, 1 Mercedes, 1 Northern Counties, 1 Optare, 10 Plaxton, 1 Sitcar, 2 Van Hool, 1 Wright.
Ops incl: local bus services, school contracts, excursions & tours, private hire.
Livery: Multi Coloured
Ticket System: Wayfarer 2/Almex

REYNOLDS DIPLOMAT COACHES

285 LOWER HIGH STREET, WATFORD
WD17 2HY
Tel: 01923 296877 **Fax:** 01923 210020
E-mail: enquiries@reynoldscoaches.com
Web site: www.reynoldscoaches.com
Partners: Richard Reynolds, Mrs Susan Reynolds.
Fleet: 17 - 12 single-deck coach, 2 double-deck coach, 1 midicoach, 2 minicoach.
Chassis incl: 3 Scania, 6 Setra, 1 Toyota, 3 Volvo.
Bodies incl: 1 Caetano, 3 Jonckheere, 6 Setra, 3 Van Hool.
Ops incl: excursions & tours, private hire, continental tours, school contracts.
Livery: Gold

PETER REYNOLDS COACHES

SPRING COTTAGES, ELTON WAY, BUSHEY,
WATFORD WD2 8HB
Tel: 01923 841174
Web site: www.peterreynoldscoaches.co.uk
Prop: P J Reynolds
Fleet: single-deck bus, single-deck coach, midicoach.
Ops incl: local bus services, school contracts, private hire.
Livery: White

RICHMOND'S COACHES

THE GARAGE, HIGH STREET, BARLEY,
ROYSTON SG8 8JA
Tel: 01763 848226 **Fax:** 01763 848105
E-mail: postbox@richmonds-coaches.co.uk
Web site: www.richmonds-coaches.co.uk
Dirs: David Richmond, Michael Richmond, Andrew Richmond **Sales & Marketing Man:** Rick Ellis **Asst Ops Man:** Craig Ellis **Ch Eng:** Patrick Granville **Exc & Tours Man:** Natalie Richmond.
Fleet: 25 – 12 single-deck coach, 2 double-deck coach, 4 midicoach, 5 minibus, 2 minicoach.
Chassis: Bova, DAF, Mercedes, Optare, Van Hool, VDL, Volvo.
Bodies: Bova, Optare, Plaxton, Sitcar, Van Hool.
Ops incl: local bus services, school contracts, excursions & tours, private hire, continental tours.
Livery: Cream/Brown
Ticket System: Wayfarer 3

SMITH BUNTINGFORD

CLAREMONT, BALDOCK ROAD,
BUNTINGFORD SG9 9DJ
Tel/Fax: 01763 271516
Prop: Graham H Smith
Fleet Eng: Stewart C Smith.
Fleet: 6 minicoach.
Chassis: 1 Ford Transit, 3 Mercedes, 1 Renault, 1 Vauxhall
Bodies: 1 Autobus, 1 Courtside, 1 Ford, 1 Mellor, 1 Stanford.
Ops incl: private hire, school contracts
Livery: White/Orange

SMITHS OF TRING

THE GARAGE, WIGGINTON HP23 6EJ
Tel: 01442 322555 **Fax:** 08707 627292
Dirs: G A Smith (**Man Dir**), Mrs S N Smith, J Smith.
Fleet: 8 - 6 single-deck coach, 1 midicoach, 1 minicoach.
Chassis: 2 Mercedes, 6 Volvo.
Bodies: 2 Mercedes, 1 Plaxton, 1 Reeve Burgess.
Ops incl: local bus services, excursions & tours, private hire, continental tours.
Livery: Red/Cream.

SOUTH MIMMS TRAVEL LTD

WARRENGATE ROAD, NORTH MYMMS
AL9 7TU
Tel: 01707 322555 **Fax:** 08707 627292
E-mail: office@southmimmstravel.com
Web site: www.southmimmstravel.co.uk
Man Dir: S J Griffiths.
Fleet: 18 single-deck coach.
Chassis incl: Dennis, MCW, Neoplan, Volvo.
Bodies incl: Berkhof, Bova, MCW, Neoplan, Plaxton.
Ops incl: school contracts, excursions & tours, private hire, continental tours.
Livery: Red/Black/Gold

SULLIVAN BUSES LTD

FIRST FLOOR, DEARDS HOUSE ST ALBANS
ROAD, POTTERS BAR EN6 3NE
Tel: 01707 646803 **Fax:** 01707 646804
E-mail: admin@sullivanbuses.com
Web site: www.sullivanbuses.com
Man Dir: Dean Sullivan **Fleet Eng:** Neal Hogg.
Fleet: 46 - 32 double-deck bus, 7 single-deck bus, 7 midibus.
Chassis: 5 Alexander Dennis, 5 AEC, 14 Dennis, 4 Leyland, 7 MCW, 6 Transbus, 10 Volvo.
Bodies: 5 Alexander Dennis, 5 Alexander, 4 Caetano, 1 Duple, 8 East Lancs, 2 MCW, 1 Northern Counties, 9 Park Royal, 7 Plaxton, 3 Transbus, 1 Wright.
Ops incl: local bus services, private hire, rail replacement
Livery: Red
Ticket system: Wayfarer TGX

TATES COACHES

44 HIGH STREET, MARKYATE AL3 8PA
Tel: 01582 840297 **Fax:** 01582 840014
E-mail: info@tatescoaches.co.uk
Web site: www.tatescoaches.co.uk
Dirs: A M Tate, A J Tate, S W Tate.
Fleet: 9 single-deck coach.
Chassis: 1 Bova, 1 DAF, 1 Dennis, 1 EOS, 1 MAN, 2 Mercedes, 2 Scania.
Bodies: 1 Bova, 1 Caetano, 1 Hispano, 2 Irizar, 2 Neoplan, 1 Van Hool, 1 Wadham Stringer.
Ops incl: school contracts, excursions & tours, private hire, continental tours.
Livery: Blue/Cream/Orange

TERRY'S COACHES

45 HOMEFIELD ROAD, HEMEL HEMPSTEAD
HP1 4BZ
Tel: 01442 265850
Web site: www.terrysminibuses.co.uk
Dirs: Terry Bunyan, Shirley Bunyan.
Fleet: 5 - 1 midibus, 2 midicoach, 2 minicoach.
Chassis: 1 Iveco, 1 LDV, 2 Mercedes.
Bodies: 1 Leicester, 2 Optare, 2 other.
Ops incl: school contracts, private hire.
Livery: Blue/White

THREE STAR COACHES.COM

UNIT 1, GUARDIAN BUSINESS PARK,
DALLOW ROAD, LUTON LU1 1NA
Tel: 01582 722626 **Fax:** 01582 484034
E-mail: sales@threestarcoaches.com
Web Site: www.threestarcoaches.com
Man Dir: Colin Dudley, **Ops Man:** Kevin Green
Ch Eng: Michael Nallaby **Co Sec:** Isabelle Dudley.
Fleet: 14 – 1 single-deck bus, 7 single-deck coach, 2 double-deck coach, 4 midicoach.
Chassis: 2 Ayats, 3 Dennis, 6 Mercedes, 1 Optare, 1 Scania, 1 Volvo.
Bodies: 2 Ayats, 4 Berkhof, 1 Mercedes, 1 Optare, 4 Plaxton, 2 Other.
Ops incl: school contracts, excursions & tours, private hire.
Livery: Blue

TIMEBUS TRAVEL

See London

UNICORN COACHES

PO BOX 45, HATFIELD AL9 5LD
Tel: 0845 658 5000
E-mail: unicorncoaches@aol.com
Web site: www.unicorncoaches.com
Man Dir: Mrs J E Pleshette
Gen Man: S T Saltmarsh.
Fleet: 4 – 2 single-deck coach, 2 minibus.
Chassis: 2 Setra, 2 Volkswagen.
Ops incl: private hire, continental tours.
Livery: White

UNO LTD

GYPSY MOTH AVENUE, HATFIELD BUSINESS
PARK, HATFIELD AL10 9BS
Tel: 01707 255764
Web site: www.unobus.info
Man Dir: Jim Thorpe **Fin Dir:** Alistair Moffat
Fleet: 91 - 10 double deck bus, 66 single deck bus, 15 midibus.
Chassis: 4 Alexander Dennis, 7 DAF, 20 Dennis, 22 Mercedes, 11 Optare, 9 Scania, 18 Transbus.
Bodies: 4 Caetano, 6 East Lancs, 22 Mercedes, 12 Optare, 15 Plaxton, 4 Scania, 18 Transbus, 10 Wright.
Ops incl: local bus services, school contracts.
Livery: Pink/Purple.
Ticket System: Wayfarer 3 Inform.

🦽 Vehicle suitable for disabled	🪑 Seat belt-fitted Vehicle	R24 24 hour recovery service
🚽 Toilet-drop facilities available	🍴 Coach(es) with galley facilities	🔧 Replacement vehicle available
R Recovery service available	❄ Air-conditioned vehicle(s)	🚌 Vintage Coach(es) available
🚌 Open top vehicle(s)	🚻 Coaches with toilet facilities	Hybrid Buses

A L S TRAVEL
SPITHEAD BUSINESS CENTRE, NEWPORT
ROAD, LAKE, SANDOWN PO36 9PH
Tel: 01983 401900
E-mail: als.travel@unicombox.co.uk
Web site: www.alstravel.co.uk
Fleet: 11 – 10 single-deck coach, 1 midicoach.
Chassis: 1 BMC, 1 Bova, 1 Dennis, 1 Neoplan,
2 Setra, 5 Volvo.
Ops incl: school contracts, excursions & tours,
private hire.

GANGES COACHES
77 PLACE ROAD, COWES PO31 7AE
Tel: 01983 296666 **Fax:** 01983 293822
E-mail: info@gangescoaches.com
Web site: www.gangescoaches.com
Prop: John Gange
Fleet: 6 - 2 single-deck coach, 3 midicoach,
1 minibus.
Chassis: 1 Bedford, 1 Leyland, 3 Mercedes,
1 Renault.
Bodies: 1 Duple, 2 Plaxton, 3 other.
Ops incl: private hire
Livery: Red/Cream and Blue/Cream

GO SOUTH COAST LTD
TOWNGATE HOUSE, 2-8 PARKSTONE ROAD,
POOLE BH15 2PR
Tel: 01202 680888 **Fax:** 01202 670244
E-mail: alex.carter@gosouthcoast.co.uk
Web site: www.islandbuses.info
www.go-ahead.com
Fleet Names: Southern Vectis, Fountain
Coaches, Island Breezers, Moss Motor Tours,
West Wight Bus & Coach, Wightrollers.
Chairman: David Brown **Man Dir:** Alex Carter

Eng Dir: Steve Hamilton **Fin Dir:** Matt Dolphin
Divisional Dirs: Marc Morgan Huws, Ed Wills.
Fleet: 625 - 252 double-deck bus, 125 single-
deck bus, 91 single-deck coach, 1 articulated bus,
12 open top bus, 137 midibus, 7 minibus.
Chassis: 2 Bristol, 104 DAF, 49 Dennis, 2 Ford,
4 Iveco, 5 LDV, 33 Leyland, 1 MAN, 50 Mercedes,
99 Optare, 106 Scania, 2 Toyota, 168 Volvo.
Bodies: 10 Alexander Dennis, 2 Autobus,
4 Beulas, 1 Bova, 6 Caetano, 2 ECW, 56 East Lancs,
2 Ford, 12 Ikarus, 4 Irizar, 2 Jonckheere, 5 LDV,
25 Leyland, 47 Mercedes, 41 Northern Counties,
153 Optare, 76 Plaxton, 73 Scania, 27 Transbus,
22 Van Hool, 55 Wright.
Ops incl: local bus services, school contracts.
Livery: Green
Ticket System: Wayfarer TGX
Part of the Go-Ahead Group

KARDAN TRAVEL LTD
1ST FLOOR, 35A ST JAMES STREET,
NEWPORT PO30 1LG
Tel: 01983 520995 **Fax:** 01983 821288
E-mail: info@kardan.co.uk
Web site: www.kardan.co.uk
Dirs: R Hodgson, L Hodgson.
Fleet: 5 single-deck coach.
Chassis: 3 Setra, 2 Volvo.
Bodies: 2 Plaxton, 3 Setra.
Ops incl: excursions & tours, private hire,
continental tours.
Livery: Yellow/White

A & M A ROBINSON SEAVIEW
SERVICES LTD
SEAFIELD GARAFE, COLLEGE FARM
INDUSTRIAL ESTATE, FAULKNER LANE,

SANDOWN PO36 9AZ
Tel: 01983 407070
Fax: 01983 407045
Recovery: 07739 237361
E-mail: info@seaview-services.co.uk
Web site: www.seaview-services.com
Chairman: Philip Robinson
Ops Man: Lorraine Bunce
Ch Engs: Peter Brand, Jim Wood
Ch Body Eng: Dennis Bunce.
Fleet: 9 - 8 single-deck coach, 1 midicoach.
Chassis: 1 Setra, 1 Toyota, 7 Volvo.
Bodies: 2 Caetano, 4 Plaxton, 1 Setra,
2 Van Hool.
Ops incl: school contracts, excursions
& tours, private hire, continental tours,
express.
Livery: Silver/Green/Red

THE SOUTHERN VECTIS
OMNIBUS CO LTD
See Go South Coast Ltd

WIGHTROLLERS
Business acquired by Go South Coast Ltd

JOHN WOODHAMS VINTAGE TOURS
WOODSTOCK, GROVE ROAD, RYDE
PO33 3LH
Tel: 01983 812147
E-mail: vintagetours@btconnect.com
Web site: www.vintage-tours.co.uk
Prop: John Woodhams
Fleet: 3 midicoach.
Chassis: 3 Bedford.
Bodies: 3 Duple.
Ops incl: excursions & tours, private hire
Livery: Two tone Green

AMB TRAVEL/ASHFORD MINIBUSES
45 KINGSNORTH ROAD, ASHFORD TN23 6JB
Tel: 01233 626952
Fax: 01233 620117
E-mail: enquiries@amb-travel.co.uk
Web site: www.ashford-minibuses.co.uk
Fleet: 12 – 3 single-deck coach, 3 midicoach,
6 minibus.
Chassis: Mercedes, Setra.
Ops incl: private hire.
Livery: Yellow.

ARRIVA SOUTHERN COUNTIES
INVICTA HOUSE, ARMSTRONG ROAD,
MAIDSTONE ME15 6TX
Tel: 01622 697000
Fax: 01622 697001
Web site: www.arriva.co.uk
Fleet Names: Arriva Kent & Sussex, Arriva
Kent Thameside, Arriva Medway Towns, Arriva
Southend, New Enterprise Coaches.
Regional Man Dir: Heath Williams **Comm
Dir:** Kevin Hawkins **Fin Dir:** Beverley Lawson.
Fleet: 656 – 137 double-deck bus, 447 single-
deck bus, 18 single-deck coach, 54 midibus.
Chassis: 139 Alexander Dennis, 86 DAF, 220
Dennis, 6 Leyland, 13 Mercedes, 8 Optare,
11 Scania, 1 Setra, 37 VDL, 122 Volvo.
Bodies: 22 Alexander, 138 Alexander Dennis,

2 Caetano, 19 East Lancs, 1 Ikarus, 1 Irizar,
3 Mercedes, 8 Optare, 47 Northern Counties,
225 Plaxton, 1 Setra, 60 Transbus, 3 Van Hool,
124 Wright.
Ops incl: local bus services, school contracts,
excursions & tours, express, continental tours,
private hire.
Liveries: Arriva UK Bus, TfL Red, White/Red/Blue
(New Enterprise).
Ticket System: Wayfarer 3 & TGX150, TfL
Prestige.

ASM COACHES
8 THE OAZE, WHITSTABLE CT5 4TQ
Tel: 01227 280254
E-mail: info@asmcoaches.co.uk
Web site: www.asmcoaches.co.uk
Prop/Tran Man: Steve Morrish
Fleet: 3 minicoach.
Chassis: 1 Fiat, 1 Iveco, 1 Mercedes.
Ops incl: school contracts, private hire.
Livery: White/Silver

AUTOCAR BUS & COACH SERVICES
LTD
64 WHETSTED ROAD, FIVE OAK GREEN,
TONBRIDGE TN12 6RT
Tel: 01892 833830 **Fax:** 01892 836977
Dir: Julian Brown **Ops Dir:** Eric Baldock.

Fleet: 22 – 5 double-deck bus, 8 single-deck bus,
4 single-deck coach, 4 midibus, 1 open-top bus
Chassis: 2 AEC, 1 Alexander Dennis, 1 DAF,
6 Dennis, 4 Leyland, 2 Mercedes, 2 Optare,
1 Scania, 3 Volvo.
Bodies: 5 Alexander, 1 Alexander Dennis, 2 East
Lancs, 1 Leyland, 1 Marshall, 2 Optare, 2 Park
Royal, 5 Plaxton, 1 Wadham Stringer, 2 Wright.
Ops incl: local bus services, private hire.
Livery: White/Purple/Pink
Ticket System: Wayfarer 2

BAYLISS EXECUTIVE TRAVEL LTD
MINTERS INDUSTRIAL ESTATE, SOUTHWALL
ROAD, DEAL CT14 9PZ
Tel: 01304 363600
E-mail: enquiries@baylissexecutivetravel.co.uk
Web site: www.baylissexecutivetravel.co.uk
Dir: A Bayliss
Fleet: 5 – 4 single-deck coach, 1 minibus.
Chassis: 1 Mercedes, 1 Scania, 1 Volkswagen,
2 Volvo.
Ops incl: excursions & tours, private hire.
Livery: White.

BRITANNIA COACHES
HOLLOW WOOD ROAD, DOVER CT17 0UB
Tel: 01304 228111 **Fax:** 01304 215350
E-mail: enq@britannia-coaches.co.uk

Web site: www.britannia-coaches.co.uk.
Partners: Barry Watson, Danny Lawson.
Fleet: 19 minicoach.
Chassis: 1 Ford, 9 Mercedes, 9 Renault.
Ops incl: private hire, school contracts,
excursions & tours.
Livery: White with Blue/Red

BROOKLINE COACHES LTD

THE STREET, RYARSH, WEST MALLING
ME19 5LQ
Tel: 01732 845656
Fax: 01732 221577
E-mail: info@brooklinecoaches.co.uk
Web site: www.brooklinecoaches.co.uk
Dirs: D Brooks, R Brooks.
Fleet: 8 – double-deck bus, double-deck coach,
single-deck coach, midicoach.
Ops incl: school contracts, private hire,
excursions & tours, continental tours.
Livery: Green/Cream

BROWNS COACHES

Ceased operations since LRB 2011 went to press.

BUZZLINES TRAVEL LTD

LYMPNE INDUSTRIAL PARK, LYMPNE
CT21 4LR
Tel: 01303 261870
Fax: 01303 230093
Recovery: 07767 475625
E-mail: sales@buzzlines.co.uk
Web site: www.buzzlinestravel.co.uk
Man Dir: Nigel Busbridge
Co Sec: Mrs Kathryn Busbridge.
Fleet: 36 – single-deck coach, double-deck coach,
midicoach, minibus, minicoach.
Chassis incl: 5 Ford Transit, 2 Mercedes,
9 Scania, 8 Setra, 3 Toyota.
Ops incl: excursions & tours, private hire,
London commuter express, continental tours.
Livery: White with Blue.

BZEE BUS & TRAVEL LTD

UNIT 2F, DEACON TRADING ESTATE,
FORSTAL ROAD, AYLESFORD ME20 7SP
Tel: 01622 882288
Fax: 01622 718070
Dirs: D Quick, N Kemp.
Associated with Nu-Venture Coaches Ltd

CAROL PETERS TRAVEL

TIMBERYARD INDUSTRIAL ESTATE,
MANSTON ROAD, RAMSGATE CT12 6HJ
Tel: 01843 591007
Fax: 01843 586466
Web site: www.carolpeters.co.uk
Props: C Howe, P Howe.
Fleet: 8 – 5 single-deck coach, 2 midicoach,
1 minibus.
Chassis: Mercedes, Setra, Toyota, Volvo.
Ops incl: private hire, excursions & tours,
continental tours.
Livery: White

CENTAUR COACHES & MINICOACHES

188 HALFWAY STREET, SIDCUP DA15 8DJ
Tel: 020 8300 3001
Fax: 020 8302 5959
Man Dir: M. Sims **Dirs:** P Sims, S Durrant.
E-mail: matt@minicoaches.com

Web site: www.minicoaches.com
Fleet: 107 – incl 7 single-deck bus, 12 midibus,
22 midicoach, 41 minibus, 20 minicoach.
Chassis incl: 25 Ford Transit, 17 LDV,
12 Mercedes.
Bodies incl: Alexander Dennis, Mercedes, Reeve
Burgess.
Ops incl: private hire, school contracts,
excursions & tours.

CENTRAL EXECUTIVE TRAVEL

177 LOWER ROAD, DOVER CT17 1RE
Tel: 01304 823030 **Fax:** 01304 828092
E-mail: phull4321@aol.com
Web site: www.centralexectravel.co.uk
Prop: P Hull.
Fleet: 2 minibus.
Chassis: 2 Mercedes.
Ops incl: private hire, school contracts.
Livery: White with Blue.

CHALKWELL COACH HIRE & TOURS

195 CHALKWELL ROAD, SITTINGBOURNE
ME10 1BJ
Tel: 01795 423982 **Fax:** 01795 431855
E-mail: coachhire@chalkwell.co.uk
Web site: www.chalkwell.co.uk
Fleet Name: Chalkwell
Man Dir: Clive Eglinton **Gen Man:** Martyn
Cleaver.
Fleet: 53 – 5 double-deck bus, 22 single-deck
coach, 16 midibus, 2 midicoach, 7 minibus,
1 minicoach.
Chassis: 1 DAF, 11 Dennis, 6 Mercedes,
9 Optare, 6 Renault, 7 Scania, 13 Volvo.
Bodies: 5 Alexander, 7 Irizar, 4 Jonckheere,
9 Optare, 14 Plaxton, 3 UVG, 3 Wadham Stringer,
9 Other.
Ops incl: local bus services, school contracts,
excursions & tours, private hire, London
commuter express, continental tours.
Livery: White/Red/Black
Ticket System: Almex

COUNTRYLINER GROUP

See Surrey

COUNTRYWIDE TRAVEL SERVICES
LTD t/a DAWNEY HOLIDAYS

Ceased operations since LRB 2011 went to press.

CROSSKEYS COACHES LTD

CROSSKEYS BUSINESS PARK, CAESARS WAY,
FOLKESTONE CT19 4AL
Tel: 01303 272625 **Fax:** 01303 274085
E-mail: coachire@crosskeys.uk.com
Web site: www.crosskeys.uk.com
Dir: Alan Johnson
Fleet: 20 - 3 single-deck bus, 16 single-deck
coach, 1 minibus.
Chassis: 5 Alexander Dennis, 8 Bova, 1 Leyland
National, 1 Mercedes, 2 Setra, 1 Van Hool, 2 Volvo.
Bodies: 2 Alexander Dennis, 8 Bova,
1 Jonckheere, 1 Leyland National, 4 Plaxton,
2 Setra, 1 Van Hool, 1 Other.
Ops incl: school contracts, excursions & tours,
private hire, continental tours.
Livery: Orange

DJ COACHES LTD

7 MARK LANE, GRAVESEND DA12 2QB
Tel: 01634 560319
E-mail: enquiries@djcoaches.co.uk
Web site: www.djcoaches.co.uk
Fleet: 22 – 12 single-deck coach, 6 midicoach,
4 minicoach.
Chassis: Mercedes, Scania, Setra, Volvo.
Ops incl: private hire.
Livery: White with Orange.

EASTONWAYS LTD

MANSTON ROAD, RAMSGATE CT12 6HJ
Tel: 01843 588944 **Fax:** 01843 582300
E-mail: info@eastonways.co.uk
Web site: www.eastonways.co.uk
Man Dir: D Austin **Co Sec:** Mrs Y M Easton
Gen Man: S Bishop.
Fleet: 29 - 6 double-deck bus, 15 single-deck bus,
1 single-deck coach, 4 midibus, 3 minicoach.
Chassis incl: 15 Alexander Dennis.
Ops incl: local bus services, school contracts,
private hire, continental tours.
Livery: Coaches: Blue/Silver; **Buses:** Red.
Ticket System: Wayfarer.

EUROLINK FOKESTONE

GREATWORTH, CANTERBURY ROAD,
ETCHINGHILL, FOLKESTONE CT18 8BS
Tel: 01303 862767

Fax: 01303 862484
E-mail: eurolinkcoaches@btconnect.com
Partners: Andy Williams, Lyn Williams.
Fleet: 5 - 3 midicoach, 2 minicoach.
Chassis: 1 Ford, 1 MAN, 3 Mercedes.
Bodies: 1 Caetano, 1 Ferqui, 1 Unvi, 2 other.
Ops incl: school contracts, private hire.
Livery: White/Grey/Orange

FARLEIGH COACHES
UNIT E, HOO INDUSTRIAL ESTATE,
VICARAGE LANE, HOO, ROCHESTER ME3 9LB
Tel: 01634 201065
Fax: 01634 254009
Web site: www.farleighcoaches.com
Prop: D R Smith
Ops incl: local bus services, school contracts,
private hire.
Livery: White/Yellow/Red/Black.

FERRYMAN TRAVEL
57 RECTORY LANE NORTH, LEYBOURNE
ME19 5HD
Tel/Fax: 01732 843396
E-mail: sales@ferryman.co.uk
Web site: www.ferryman.co.uk
Fleet: 3 minibus.
Chassis: 1 Ford Transit, 1 Iveco, 1 LDV.
Ops incl: school contracts, excursions & tours,
private hire, continental tours.
Livery: White

G & S TRAVEL
Ceased operations since LRB 2011 went to press.

GO-COACH HIRE LTD
VESTRY ROAD ESTATE, OTFORD TN14 5EL
Tel: 01732 469800
E-mail: info@go-coach.co.uk
Web site: www.go-coach.co.uk
Fleet: 8 – double-deck bus, single-deck bus,
single-deck coach.
Ops incl: local bus services, school contracts,
private hire.
Livery: Yellow/Purple.

GRIFFIN BUS
Ceased operations since LRB 2011 went to press

JEWELS TOURS
56 NEW ROAD, GRAVESEND DA11 0AD
Tel: 01474 334434
Fax: 01474 322622
E-mail: jeweltours@btconnect.com
Web site: www.jewelstours.co.uk
Dirs: J Loynes, M Hafner.
Fleet: 2 single-deck coach.
Chassis: Scania.
Bodies: Irizar.
Ops incl: private hire, excursions & tours,
continental tours.
Livery: Blue

KENT COACH TOURS LTD
THE COACH STATION, MALCOLM SARGENT
ROAD, ASHFORD TN23 6JW
Tel/Recovery: 01233 627330
Fax: 01233 612977
E-mail: sales@kentcoachtours.co.uk
Web site: www.kentcoachtours.co.uk
Dirs: David Farmer, Ann Farmer, Andrew Farmer

(Co Sec), Brian Farmer **(Ch Eng)**.
Fleet: 10 - 6 single-deck coach, 4 midibus.
Chassis: 1 Alexander Dennis, 1 Irisbus, 3
Mercedes, 1 Optare, 4 Volvo.
Bodies: 1 Optare, 9 Plaxton.
Ops incl: local bus services, school contracts,
excursions & tours, private hire.
Livery: Two Tone Blue.
Ticket System: Wayfarer

KENT COUNTY COUNCIL
PASSENGER SERVICES, FORSTAL ROAD,
AYLESFORD ME20 7HB
Tel: 01622 605935
Fax: 01622 790338
Fleet Name: Kent Top Travel
Ops Man: Andy Bates.
Fleet: 48 - 2 double-deck bus, 12 single-deck
bus, 4 single-deck coach, 2 midibus, 1 midicoach,
27 minibus.
Chassis: 5 Dennis, 27 Iveco, 4 Leyland,
3 Mercedes, 4 Optare, 1 Volvo.
Bodies: 1 Alexander, 1 Caetano, 27 Euromotive,
7 Leicester, 2 Leyland, 4 Optare, 6 Plaxton.
Ops incl: local bus services, school contracts,
private hire.
Livery: Red on White.
Ticket System: Almex.

THE KINGS FERRY LTD
THE TRAVEL CENTRE, GILLINGHAM ME8
6HW
Tel: 01634 377577
Fax: 01634 370656
E-mail: sales@thekingsferry.co.uk
Web site: www.thekingsferry.co.uk
Ops Dir: Ian Fraser **Comm Dir:** Danny Elford
Head of Ops: Nadene Curley
Eng Man: Mick Keohane.
Fleet: 63 – 2 single-deck bus, 50 single-deck
coach, 6 double-deck coach, 2 midicoach,
3 minicoach.
Chassis: 1 Alexander Dennis, 2 DAF, 3 MAN,
15 Mercedes, 1 Optare, 16 Scania, 25 Volvo.
Bodies: 6 Berkhof, 32 Caetano, 1 Castrosua,
9 Irizar, 4 Mercedes, 3 Noge, 1 Optare, 1 Plaxton,
4 Sunsundegui, 2 Van Hool.
Ops incl: local bus services, school contracts,
private hire, express, continental tours.
Livery: Yellow with Green stripe
Part of the National Express Group

KINGSMAN INTERNATIONAL TRAVEL
57 BRAMLEY AVENUE, FAVERSHAM
ME13 8LP
Tel: 01795 501746
Fax: 01795 536798
E-mail: jonathanamancini@tiscali.co.uk
Web site:
www.kingsmaninternationalme13.co.uk
Props: J A Mancini, J Mancini.
Fleet: 9 - single-deck coach, midibus, midicoach,
minibus.
Chassis: BMC, Mercedes, Neoplan, Setra.
Bodies: Mercedes, Neoplan, Plaxton.
Ops incl: local bus services, excursions & tours,
private hire, continental tours.

LEHANE TRAVEL LTD
BREDLANDS LANE, STURRY CT2 0HD
Tel: 01227 710493

E-mail: info@lehanetravel.co.uk
Web site: www.lehanetravel.co.uk
Fleet: 14 – 12 single-deck coach, 2 midicoach.
Ops incl: school contracts, private hire.
Livery: Blue/White.

LEO'S PRIDE LTD
259 CANTERBURY ROAD, HERNE BAY
CT6 7HD
Tel: 01227 363636
E-mail: leospride@lineone.net
Web site: www.leospride.co.uk
Fleet: 6 single-deck coach.
Chassis: 1 MAN, 2 Neoplan, 3 Scania.
Ops incl: private hire.
Livery: Light Green

LOGANS TOURS LTD
Ceased operations since LRB 2011 went to press.

LONDON BUS COMPANY LTD
UNITS 1-4, NORTHFLEET INDUSTRIAL
ESTATE, LOWER ROAD, NORTHFLEET
DA11 9SN
Tel: 01474 361199
Fax: 01474 361188
E-mail: info@thelondonbuscompany.co.uk
Web site: www.thelondonbuscompany.co.uk
Man Dir: Roger Wright
Fleet: double-deck bus, single-deck bus, heritage
vehicles.
Ops incl: private hire.
Livery: Red

MANNS TRAVEL LTD
ENTERPRISE HOUSE, NORFOLK ROAD,
GRAVESEND DA12 2AX
Tel: 01474 358194
Web site: www.mannstravel.co.uk
Fleet: single-deck coach, midicoach, minibus.
Ops incl: school contracts, excursions & tours,
private hire, continental tours.
Livery: White with Red/Yellow/Blue

NEW ENTERPRISE COACHES
CANNON LANE, TONBRIDGE
TN9 1PP
Tel: 01732 350509
Fax: 01732 357716
Prop: Arriva Southern Counties
Man Dir: Heath Williams
Gen Man: Chris Lawrence
Eng Man: Andy Weber.
Fleet: Included within Arriva Southern Counties.
Ops incl: local bus services, school contracts,
excursions & tours, private hire, continental tours.
Livery: White/Red/Blue.
Ticket System: Wayfarer II.

NU-VENTURE COACHES LTD
UNIT 2F, DEACON TRADING ESTATE,
FORSTAL ROAD, AYLESFORD ME20 7SP
Tel: 01622 882288
Fax: 01622 718070
E-mail: nuventurecoachesltd@yahoo.co.uk
Web site: www.nu-venture.co.uk
Dir: D Quick **Co Sec:** N Kemp.
Ops incl: local bus services, school contracts,
private hire, excursions & tours.
Livery: Two Tone Green
Ticket System: Wayfarer 3

POYNTERS COACHES LTD

WYE COACH DEPOT, WYE TN25 5BX
Tel: 01233 812002
Fax: 01233 813210
Recovery: 07770 874631
E-mail: poyntercoaches@aol.com
Man Dir: B Poynter **Ch Eng:** B Poynter.
Fleet: 17 - 1 double-deck bus, 7 single-deck bus,
5 single-deck coach, 3 midibus, 1 minicoach.
Chassis: 2 Bova, 1 Leyland, 4 Mercedes, 10 Volvo.
Ops incl: local bus services, school contracts,
excursions & tours, private hire, continental tours.
Livery: White
Ticket System: Wayfarer

R. K. F. TRAVEL

22 BROMPTON FARM ROAD, ROCHESTER
ME2 3QY
Tel/Fax: 01634 715897
Dir: Ray Fraser.
Fleet: 1 minibus.
Chassis: 1 Mercedes.
Ops incl: private hire.

THE RAINHAM COACH COMPANY

1A SPRINGFIELD ROAD, GILLINGHAM
ME7 1YJ
Tel & Recovery: 01634 852020
Fax: 01634 582020
E-mail: info@rainhamcoach.co.uk
Web site: www.rainhamcoach.co.uk
Senior Partner: David Graham
Gen Man: Richard Graham **Traffic Man:** Louise
Salisbury **Ch Eng:** Geoff Birdock.
Fleet: 21 - 4 midicoach, 17 minicoach.
Chassis: 1 Ford Transit, 20 Mercedes.
Ops incl: school contracts, excursions & tours,
private hire.
Livery: White/Magenta/Grey

RED ROUTE BUSES LTD

GRANBY COACHWORKS, GROVE ROAD,
NORTHFLEET DA11 9AX
Tel: 0800 234 6842
Fax: 01424 358475
E-mail: enquiries@redroutebuses.co.uk
Web site: www.redroutebuses.co.uk
Ops Dir: Jason Mee **Eng Dir:** Terry Mee
Tran Man: Peter Brown.
Fleet: 16 - 9 double-deck bus, 2 single-deck bus,
3 single-deck coach, 1 minibus, 1 open top bus.
Chassis: 5 AEC Routemaster, 2 DAF, 1 Daimler,
1 Dennis, 2 Leyland, 1 MCW, 1 Mercedes, 3 Volvo.
Ops incl: local bus services, school contracts,
private hire
Livery: Red/White
Ticket System: Wayfarer Saver

REGENT COACHES

UNIT 16, ST AUGUSTINE'S BUSINESS PARK,
SWALECLIFFE CT5 2QJ
Tel: 01227 794345
Fax: 01227 795127
E-mail: info@regentcoaches.com
Web site: www.regentcoaches.co.uk
Partners: Paul Regent, Kerry Regent
Tran Man: Colin MacDonald **Workshop Man:**
Robert Wildish **Office Man:** Sam Regent **Asst
Tran Man:** Nigel Andrews.
Fleet: 23 – 3 midibus, 10 midicoach, 8 minibus.

Chassis: 2 Alexander Dennis, 1 Ayats,
1 Enterprise, 4 Irisbus, 4 Iveco, 2 LDV, 7 Mercedes,
2 Renault.
Ops incl: local bus services, school contracts,
excursions & tours, private hire, continental tours.
Livery: Ivory with Red/Orange lettering.
Ticket system: Ticketer

RELIANCE TRAVEL

UNIT 8, NORFOLK ROAD, GRAVESEND
DA12 2PS
Tel: 01474 322002
Fax: 01474 536998
E-mail: info@reliance-travel.co.uk
Web site: www.reliance-travel.co.uk
Gen Man: D Hockley
Fleet: 16 single-deck coach.
Chassis: 12 Irisbus, 4 Mercedes.
Ops incl: private hire, London commuter
express.
Livery: Red/Cream
Associated with Redwing Coaches (see London)

ROUNDABOUT BUSES LTD

PO BOX 221, BEXLEYHEATH DA7 9AN
Tel: 0844 357 4598
Fax: 07092 131054
E-mail: info@roundaboutbuses.co.uk
Web site: www.roundaboutbuses.co.uk
Man Dir: Glyn Matthews
Dir: Robert Woodruff
Ops Man: Ian Evans **Comm Man:** Thomas
White.
Fleet: 17 – 2 double-deck bus, 5 single-deck bus,
10 single-deck coach.
Chassis: 2 Alexander Dennis, 5 Dennis, 10 Volvo.
Bodies: 2 Alexander Dennis, 15 Plaxton.
Ops incl: local bus services, express.
Livery: Green/Cream.
Ticket System: Wayfarer.

SCOTLAND & BATES

HEATH ROAD, APPLEDORE, ASHFORD
TN26 2AJ
Tel: 01233 758325
Fax: 01233 758611
E-mail: info@scotlandandbates.co.uk
Web site: www.scotlandandbates.co.uk
Partners: Mr R M Bates, Mrs G A Bates.
Fleet: 17 single-deck coach.
Chassis: 17 Volvo.
Bodies: 17 Van Hool.
Ops incl: private hire.
Livery: Cream/Brown/Orange

SEATH COACHES

THE FIELDINGS, STONEHEAP ROAD,
EAST STUDDAL, DOVER CT15 5BU
Tel: 01304 620825
Fax: 01304 620825
Prop: Philip J Seath
Fleet: 4 - single-deck coach, midicoach, minibus.
Chassis: Ford Transit, MAN, Volvo.
Ops incl: school contracts, private hire.
Livery: White/Blue

SPOT HIRE TRAVEL

STATION APPROACH, BEARSTED STATION,
WARE STREET, MAIDSTONE ME14 4PH
Tel: 01622 736660

Fax: 01622 630406
E-mail: sales@spothire.co.uk
Web site: www.spothire.co.uk
Prop: Ross Young
Tours & Excursions Man: Ms Jodie Follett.
Fleet: 9 - 3 single-deck coach, 3 midicoach,
3 minicoach.
Chassis: 1 Ford, 5 Mercedes, 3 Volvo
Bodies: 3 Esker, 1 Jonckheere, 2 Van Hool,
3 Other.
Ops incl: excursions & tours.
Livery: Cream with three stripes

STAGECOACH IN EAST KENT
& EAST SUSSEX

BUS STATION, ST GEORGE'S LANE,
CANTERBURY CT1 2SY
Tel: 01227 828103
Fax: 01227 828150
Web site: www.stagecoachbus.com/eastkent
Fleet Name: Stagecoach in East Kent
Man Dir: Phil Medlicott
Ops Dir: Neil Instrall
Eng Dir: Jason Bush
Comm Dir: Jeremy Cooper.
Fleet: 415 - 169 double-deck bus, 65 single-deck
bus, 16 single-deck coach, 102 midibus, 63 minibus.
Chassis: 170 Alexander Dennis, 10 DAF,
21 MAN, 65 Optare, 76 Scania, 73 Volvo.
Bodies: 318 Alexander Dennis, 14 Caetano,
10 Marshall/MCV, 65 Optare, 2 Plaxton, 6 Wright.
Ops incl: local bus services, school contracts.
Liveries: Stagecoach UK Bus; National Express.
Ticket System: ERG TP5000.

STREAMLINE (KENT) LTD

WEST STATION APPROACH,
MAIDSTONE ME16 8RJ
Tel: 01622 750000
Fax: 01622 752978
E-mail: coaches@streamline.travel
Web site: www.streamline.travel
Man Dir: Ron Parker **Co Sec:** Angela Parker.
Fleet: 8 - 2 midicoach, 6 minibus.
Chassis: Ford, Iveco, Mercedes, Volkswagen.
Ops incl: school contracts, excursions & tours,
private hire, continental tours.
Livery: Silver/Blue.

THOMSETT'S COACHES

50 GOLF ROAD, DEAL
CT14 6QB
Tel/Fax: 01304 374731
E-mail: thomsettscoaches@fsmail.net
Web site: www.thomsettscoaches.com
Prop: S J Thomsett
Fleet: 4 - 3 single-deck coach, 1 midicoach.
Chassis: 1 MAN, 3 Scania.
Bodies: 1 Caetano, 3 Van Hool.
Ops incl: school contracts, private hire.
Livery: White/Black

TRACKS VEHICLE SERVICES LTD

THE FLOTS, BROOKLAND, ROMNEY MARSH
TN29 9TF
Tel: 0845 130 0936
Fax: 01797 344135
E-mail: info@tracks-travel.com
Web site: www.tracks-travel.com
Man Dir: Andrew Toms.
Ops incl: private hire, continental tours.

TRAVELMASTERS

 ♿ ⚙ ✱ R24 ✆ T

DORSET ROAD INDUSTRIAL ESTATE,
DORSET ROAD, SHEERNESS ME12 1LT
Tel: 01795 660066 **Fax:** 01795 660033
Recovery: 07850 848008
Dirs: T Lambkin, C Smith.
Fleet: double-deck bus, single-deck bus,
single-deck coach, double-deck coach, midibus,
midicoach, minibus.
Chassis: Alexander Dennis, Dennis, Leyland,
Mercedes, Scania, Volvo.
Ops incl: school contracts, excursions & tours,
private hire, continental tours.
Livery: Yellow/Blue

VIKING MINICOACHES

Ceased operations since LRB 2011 went to press.

WESTERHAM COACHES

 ♿ ⚙ ✱

15 BARROW GREEN ROAD, OXTED RH8 0NJ
Tel: 01883 713633
Fax: 01883 730079
E-mail: info@skinners.travel
Web site: www.skinners.travel
Partners: Stephen Skinner, Deborah Skinner.
Fleet: 14 - 11 single-deck coach, 2 midicoach,
1 minicoach.
Chassis: 4 Alexander Dennis, 1 MAN,
2 Mercedes, 7 Setra.
Bodies: 1 Duple, 1 Mercedes, 4 Neoplan,
1 Optare, 7 Setra.
Ops incl: excursions & tours, private hire, school
contracts, continental tours.
Livery: Brown & Cream
Part of Skinners of Oxted – see Surrey

WEST KENT BUSES

 ♿

THE COACH STATION, LONDON ROAD,
WEST KINGSDOWN TN15 6AR
Tel: 01474 855444
Fax: 01474 855454
E-mail: info@westkentbuses.co.uk
Web site: www.westkentbuses.co.uk
Proprietor: Stuart Gilkes **Ch Eng:** Paul Jones
Tran Man: Jason Tilley **Depot Eng:** Alexandra
Pretious.
Fleet: 8 - 5 double-deck bus, 3 single-deck coach.
Chassis: 4 Leyland, 4 Volvo.
Bodies: 2 Alexander Dennis, 3 Leyland,
3 Van Hool.
Ops incl: local bus services, private hire.
Livery: Dark Red/Cream
Ticket System: Wayfarer

LANCASHIRE, BLACKBURN & DARWEN, BLACKPOOL

ADLINGTON TAXIS & MINICOACHES

See Greater Manchester

ALFA TRAVEL

 ♿ ✱ ✱

EUXTON LANE, EUXTON, CHORLEY PR7 6AF
Tel: 0845 130 5777 **Fax:** 0845 130 3777
E-mail: req@alfatravel .co.uk
Web site: www.alfatravel.co.uk
Man Dir: Paul Sawbridge **Fin Dir:** Peter
Sawbridge **Head of Ops:** Neil McMurdy
Ops Man: Tom Smith **Eng Man:** Peter Tetlow.
Fleet: 42 single-deck coach.
Chassis: 13 Alexander Dennis, 5 Mercedes,
24 Volvo.
Bodies: 5 Mercedes, 37 Plaxton.
Ops incl: excursions & tours, private hire,
continental tours.
Livery: Cream

ARRIVA NORTH WEST & WALES

See Merseyside

ASPDEN'S COACHES

 ✱ ✱ R ✆

LANCASTER STREET, BLACKBURN BB2 1UA.
Tel: 01254 52020 **Fax:** 01254 57474
E-mail: aspdens@holmeswood.uk.com
Web site: www.holmeswood.uk.com
Dirs: J F Aspinall, M Aspinall, C H Aspinall,
D E Aspinall, M F Aspinall, M J Forshaw
Ops Man: M E Bostock **Tours Man:**
J Bostock-Gibson **Ch Eng:** M Boniface.
Fleet: see Holmeswood Coaches
Ops incl: local bus services, excursions & tours,
private hire, continental tours, school contracts.
Livery: Green
(Subsidiary of Holmeswood Coaches, Lancashire)

BATTERSBY SILVER GREY COACHES

 ♿ ✱ ✱ ✱ ✱ ✆ T

THE COACH & TRAVEL CENTRE,
MIDDLEGATE, WHITE LUND BUSINESS PARK,
MORECAMBE LA3 3PE
Tel: 01524 380000
Fax: 01524 380800
E-mail: info@battersbys.co.uk
Web site: www.battersbys.co.uk
Chairman & Director: James A Harrison
Director & Co Sec: M F Harrison.
Fleet: 27 - 20 single-deck coach, 7 midicoach.
Chassis: 7 Mercedes, 20 Volvo.
Bodies: 2 Jonckheere, 1 Mercedes, 23 Plaxton,
1 Van Hool.

Ops incl: local bus services, excursions & tours,
private hire, continental tours, school contracts.
Livery: White
Ticket system: Wayfarer

BLACKPOOL TRANSPORT SERVICES LTD

 ♿ ⚙ ✱ T

RIGBY ROAD, BLACKPOOL FY1 5DD
Tel: 01253 473001 **Fax:** 01253 473101
E-mail:
debbie.vallance@blackpooltransport.com
Web site: www.blackpooltransport.com
Fleet Name: Metro Coastlines
Man Dir: Trevor Roberts **Eng Dir:** Dave Hislop
Fin Dir: Sue Kennerley
Ops Man: Guy Thornton
Fleet: 213 - 65 double-deck bus, 31 single-deck
bus, 4 open top bus, 51 midibus, 62 tram.
Chassis: 40 Dennis, 23 Leyland, 68 Optare,
20 Volvo, 62 Tram.
Bodies: 17 ECW, 46 East Lancs, 6 Northern
Counties, 68 Optare, 9 Plaxton, 5 Wright.
Ops incl: local bus services, tram services.
Livery: Yellow plus route branded route colours.
Ticket System: Wayfarer/Almex A90
See also Section 5 – Tram and Bus Rapid Transit
Systems

BRADSHAWS TRAVEL

 ♿ ✱

46 WESTBOURNE ROAD, KNOTT END ON
SEA, POULTON-LE-FYLDE FY6 0BS
Tel/Fax: 01253 810058
Proprietor: Mrs Jill Swift
Fleet: 10 - 7 single-deck coach, 2 minibus,
1 minicoach.
Chassis: 1 DAF, 1 Dennis, 1 LDV, 3 Leyland,
1 Mercedes, 3 Volvo.
Bodies: 1 LDV, 6 Plaxton, 2 Van Hool, 1 Other.
Ops incl: private hire, school contracts.
Livery: White/Yellow
Ticket System: Almex

COACH OPTIONS

See Greater Manchester

COASTAL COACHES

 ♿ ✱ ✱ ✱ ✱

65 CHURCH STREET, WARTON, PRESTON
PR4 1BD
Tel: 01772 635820
Web site: www.coastalcoaches.co.uk
Props: W Holder, Mrs H Holder.

Fleet: 20 – 2 single-deck coach, 8 midibus,
8 midicoach, 2 minicoach
Chassis: 10 Mercedes, 8 Optare, 2 Setra
Ops incl: local bus services, private hire
Livery: Blue & White

COLRAY COACHES

 ♿ ✱ ✱ ✱ ✱

14 PRESTBURY AVENUE, BLACKPOOL
FY4 1PT
Tel: 01253 202076
Dirs: Geoffrey Shaw, V Shaw.
Fleet: 5 – single-deck coach, midibus, midicoach.
Chassis: 1 Mercedes, 1 Setra, 2 Toyota, 1 Volvo.
Bodies: 1 Caetano, 1 Mercedes, 1 Plaxton,
1 Setra
Ops incl: excursions & tours, school contracts,
private hire, continental tours.
Livery: White/Blue

COSGROVE'S TOURS

133 WOODPLUMPTON ROAD, PRESTON
PR2 3LF
Tel: 01772 460748
Web site: www.cosgroveafton.co.uk
Fleet: 5 single-deck coach.
Chassis: 3 DAF, 1 Mercedes, 1 VDL.
Bodies: 1 Mercedes, 4 Van Hool
Ops incl: excursions & tours, private hire
Livery: White with logos

EAVESWAY TRAVEL LTD

 ♿ ✱ ✱ ✱ ✱ ✆ T

BRYN SIDE, BRYN ROAD, ASHTON-IN-
MAKERFIELD WN4 8BT
Tel: 01942 727985 **Fax:** 01942 271234
E-mail: sales@eaveswaytravel.com
Web site: www.eaveswaytravel.com
Man Dir: Mike Eaves **Dir:** Phil Rogers
Ops Man: Tim Presley **Service Man:** Mick
Mullen.
Fleet: 30 – 20 double-deck coach, 10 single-deck
coach.
Chassis: 1 DAF, 29 Van Hool.
Bodies: 30 Van Hool.
Ops incl: express, private hire.
Livery: Silver/Blue/Green.

JOHN FISHWICK & SONS

 ♿ ✱ ✱ ✱ ✱ ✱

GOLDEN HILL LANE, LEYLAND PR25 3LE
Tel: 01772 421207
Fax: 01772 622407
E-mail: enquiries@fishwicks.co.uk

Web site: www.fishwicks.co.uk
Dirs: John C Brindle, James F Hustler.
Fleet: 35 - 7 double-deck bus, 25 single-deck bus, 3 single-deck coach.
Chassis: 10 DAF, 1 Dennis, 5 Leyland, 1 Van Hool, 16 VDL, 2 Volvo.
Bodies: 7 Alexander Dennis, 3 Plaxton, 3 Van Hool, 22 Wright.
Ops incl: local bus services, school contracts, excursions & tours, private hire, continental tours.
Livery: Green.
Ticket System: Wayfarer.

FLIGHTS HALLMARK
See West Midlands

GPD TRAVEL

27 HARTFORD AVENUE, HEYWOOD OL10 4XH
Tel: 01706 622297
Fax: 01706 361494
Props: Gary Dawson, Janine Dawson
Fleet: 4 - 3 single-deck coach, 1 minicoach.
Chassis: 1 Mercedes, 3 Volvo.
Bodies: 1 Caetano, 2 Plaxton, 1 Other.
Ops incl: school contracts, excursions & tours, private hire, continental tours.
Livery: Red/Gold stripes.

G-LINE HOLIDAYS LTD
54 ST DAVIDS ROAD SOUTH, ST ANNE'S ON SEA FY8 1TS
Tel: 01253 725999
Fax: 01253 781843
Web site: www.g-linecoaches.co.uk
E-mail: info@g-linecoaches.co.uk
Dirs: Mr E W Bradshaw, Mrs P H Jenkinson, Mr A W Bradshaw.
Fleet: 10 single-deck coach
Chassis: 2 DAF, 3 Van Hool, 5 Volvo.
Bodies: 5 Plaxton, 5 Van Hool.
Ops incl: excursions & tours, private hire, continental tours.
Livery: White, Maroon & Gold

JEFF GRIFFITHS COACHES
Ceased trading since LRB 2011 went to press.

HEALINGS INTERNATIONAL COACHES
See Greater Manchester

HODDER MOTOR SERVICES LTD
3 ALDERFORD CLOSE, CLITHEROE BB7 2QP
Tel: 01200 422473
Fax: 01200 422590
E-mail: hoddercoaches@hotmail.co.uk
Dir: Paul Hodgson **Co Sec:** Janice Hodgson
Fleet: 2 single-deck coach.
Chassis: 1 Neoplan, 1 Volvo.
Body: 1 Neoplan, 1 Van Hool.
Ops incl: school contracts, private hire,

excursions & tours.
Livery: Silver/Grey

HODSONS COACHES
LINK 59 BUSINESS PARK, DEANFIELD WAY, CLITHEROE BB7 1QU
Tel: 01200 429220
E-mail: info@hodsonscoaches.com
Web site: www.hodsonscoaches.com
Prop: M Hodson
Fleet: 20 – single-deck coach, midicoach, minibus.
Ops incl: school contracts, private hire, excursions & tours.
Livery: White

HOLMESWOOD COACHES LTD
SANDY WAY, HOLMESWOOD, ORMSKIRK L40 1UB
Tel: 01704 821245
Fax: 01704 822090
E-mail: sales@holmeswood.uk.com
Web site: www.holmeswood.uk.com
Dirs: J F Aspinall, M Aspinall, D G Aspinall, C H Aspinall, M F Aspinall, M J Aspinall.
Fleet Names: Aspden's Coaches; Bostock's Coaches; Holmeswood Coaches; John Flanagan Coaches, Walker's Coaches.
Fleet: 149 - 14 double-deck bus, 108 single-deck coach, 2 double-deck coach, 17 midibus, 8 midicoach.
Chassis: 1 Alexander Dennis, 4 DAF, 7 Dennis, 2 Enterprise, 35 Iveco, 9 Leyland, 38 MAN, 3 Mercedes, 3 Neoplan, 13 Optare, 12 Scania, 6 VDL, 14 Volvo.
Bodies: 3 Alexander, 1 Alexander Dennis, 6 Berkhof, 28 Beulas, 3 Caetano, 1 ECW, 6 East Lancs, 1 Hispano, 3 Ikarus, 6 Indcar, 2 Jonckheere, 2 Leyland, 48 Marcopolo, 3 Neoplan, 2 Noge, 2 Northern Counties, 13 Optare, 12 Plaxton, 8 Van Hool.
Ops incl: local bus services, school contracts, excursions & tours, private hire, continental tours.
Livery: Green
Ticket system: Wayfarer
Holmeswood Group Companies:
Aspden's Coaches, Blackburn (see Lancashire)
Bostock's Coaches, Congleton (see Cheshire)
Walker's & Flanagan's Coaches (see Cheshire)

JACKSONS COACHES
JACKSON HOUSE, BURTON ROAD, BLACKPOOL FY4 4NW
Tel: 01253 792222
Fax: 01253 692070
Web site: www.jacksonscoachesblackpool.co.uk
Partner: Jon Paul Jackson
Fleet: 4 single-deck coach.
Chassis: 1 Iveco, 2 Scania, 1 Volvo.
Bodies: 1 Irizar, 2 Plaxton, 1 Van Hool.
Ops incl: school contracts, private hire, excursions & tours, continental tours.
Livery: White/Blue.
Ticket System: Setright

KIRKBY LONSDALE COACH HIRE LTD
OLD STATION YARD, WARTON ROAD, CARNFORTH LA5 9EU
Tel: 01524 733831
Fax: 01524 733821
E-mail: sutton@klch.bbfree.co.uk
Web site: www.klcoachhire.co.uk
Dir: Stephen Sutton **Ops Man:** Matthew Sutton
Fleet: 25 – 1 single-deck bus, 7 single-deck coach, 11 midibus, 5 midicoach, 1 minicoach.
Ops incl: local bus services, school contracts, private hire.
Livery: White/Maroon
Ticket System: Wayfarer TGX

LAKELAND COACHES
SMITHY ROW, HURST GREEN, CLITHEROE BB7 9QA
Tel: 01254 826007
Fleet: 9 – 7 single-deck coach, 2 midicoach.
Chassis: 2 Mercedes, 2 Scania, 5 Volvo.
Bodies: 2 Irizar, 1 Jonckheere, 3 Plaxton, 3 Van Hool.
Ops incl: excursions & tours, private hire.

NORTH WEST COACHES & LIMOS
HILLHOUSE INTERNATIONAL BUSINESS PARK, WEST ROAD, THORNTON CLEVELEYS FY5 4DQ
Tel: 01253 855000
Fax: 01253 522845
Recovery: 07850 500015
E-mail: stewart.farrel@tiscali.co.uk
Web site: www.northwestcoaches.co.uk
Owner/Operator: Stuart J Farrell
Ops Man: Paul Portisman
Head Fitter: John Keen.
Fleet: 18 - 1 double-deck coach, 3 single-deck coach, 2 midibus, 5 midicoach, 7 minibus.
Chassis: 1 DAF, 1 Iveco, 5 Mercedes, 1 Neoplan, 8 Renault, 2 Volvo.
Ops incl: local bus services, excursions & tours, school contracts, private hire

OLYMPIA TRAVEL UK LTD
44 ARGYLE STREET, HINDLEY, WIGAN WN2 3PH
Tel: 01942 522322
Fax: 01942 255845
Recovery: 07736 329133
E-mail: olympia@coach-hire.net
Web site: www.olympiatravel.co.uk
Props: Joseph Lewis, Shaun Lewis.
Fleet: 19 – double-deck bus, single-deck coach, midicoach, minibus, minicoach.
Chassis: 4 Mercedes, 15 Volvo.
Bodies: 1 East Lancs, 4 Jonckheere, 2 Mercedes, 6 Plaxton, 6 Van Hool, 1 Other.
Ops incl: local bus services, school contracts, excursions & tours, private hire, continental tours.
Livery: White with blue stripes
Ticket System: Wayfarer

PRESTON BUS LTD

♿ ♻ R24

221 DEEPDALE ROAD, PRESTON
PR1 6NY
Tel: 01772 253671
Fax: 01772 555840
Recovery: 01772 253671
E-mail: customer.care@prestonbus.co.uk
Web site: www.prestonbus.co.uk
Man Dir: Bob Dunn
Ops Man: John Asquith.
Fleet: 90 – 36 double-deck bus, 12 single-deck bus, 42 midibus.
Chassis: 22 Dennis, 13 Leyland, 1 Mercedes, 42 Optare, 12 Scania.
Bodies: 2 Alexander, 29 East Lancs, 7 Leyland, 1 Mercedes, 4 Northern Counties, 42 Optare, 5 Plaxton.
Ops incl: local bus services, school contracts.
Livery: Blue/Cream
Ticket System: Wayfarer TGX150
A subsidiary of Rotala

REDLINE TRAVEL

♿ ♻ ♨ ⬚

GREENBANK, HOWICK CROSS LANE, PENWORTHAM, PRESTON PR1 0NS
Tel: 01772 747877
Fax: 01772 747878
E-mail: enquiries@redlinetravel.co.uk
Web site: www.redlinetravel.co.uk
Props: R G H & S R Nuttall.
Fleet: 19 – 8 double-deck bus, 2 single-deck bus, 9 single-deck coach.
Chassis: 1 Scania, 18 Volvo.
Bodies: 5 Alexander, 1 Caetano, 5 East Lancs, 1 Irizar, 3 Jonckheere, 2 Plaxton, 2 Van Hool.
Ops incl: school contracts, private hire, excursions & tours.
Livery: Red/White/Green

REEVES COACH SERVICES

♻ ♨ ⬚ ⬚

34 MONKS DRIVE, WITHNELL, CHORLEY PR6 8SG
Tel/Fax: 01254 830545
E-mail: info@reevescoachholidays.com
Web site: www.reevescoachholidays.com
Prop: John E Reeves.
Fleet: 1 single-deck coach.
Chassis/Body: Setra.
Ops incl: excursions & tours, continental tours.
Livery: Blue

RIGBY'S EXECUTIVE COACHES LTD

♻ ♨ ♨ ⬚ ⬚ ⬚ ⬚

MOORFIELD INDUSTRIAL ESTATE, MOORFIELD DRIVE, ALTHAM, ACCRINGTON BB5 5WG
Tel: 01254 388866
Fax: 01254 232505
Web site: www.rigbyscoaches.co.uk
Man Dir: Derek Moorhouse
Eng Dir: Mel Mellor
Dir/Tran Man: Andrew Knowles.
Fleet: 23 – 20 single-deck coach, 2 minibus, 1 minicoach.
Chassis: 1 Ford Transit, 2 Mercedes, 1 Scania, 19 Volvo.
Bodies: 2 Berkhof, 1 Irizar, 2 Jonckheere, 1 Reeve Burgess, 16 Van Hool, 1 Wright.
Ops incl: school contracts, excursions & tours, private hire.
Livery: Orange
Ticket System: Almex

ROBINSONS HOLIDAYS

♻ ♨ ♨ ⬚ ⬚ ⬚

PARK GARAGE, GREAT HARWOOD BB6 7SP
Tel: 01254 889900 **Fax:** 01254 884708
E-mail: info@robinsons-holidays.co.uk
Web site: www.robinsons-holidays.co.uk
Dirs: D D Lord, J E Bannister **(Sec)**, J McMillan
Ops Man: C Skeen **Engineer:** P Godwin **Off Man:** B Cooke **Sales Man:** G Holdsworth.
Fleet: 17 single-deck coach.
Chassis: 1 MAN, 6 Neoplan, 10 Volvo.
Bodies: 3 Jonckheere, 6 Neoplan, 1 Noge, 5 Plaxton, 2 Sunsundegui.
Ops incl: excursions & tours, private hire, continental tours, school contracts.
Livery: Dark Blue

ROSSENDALE TRANSPORT LTD

♿ ♻ ♨ ♨ ⬚ ⬚

KNOWSLEY PARK WAY, HASLINGDEN BB4 4RS
Tel: 01706 390520
Fax: 01706 390530
Web site: www.rossendalebus.co.uk
E-mail: info@rossendalebus.co.uk
Man Dir: Alastair Nuttall **Comm Dir:** Barry Drelincourt.
Fleet: 110 - 16 double-deck bus, 48 single-deck bus, 3 single-deck coach, 43 midibus.
Chassis: 1 Bova, 48 Dennis, 3 MAN, 23 Optare, 35 Volvo.
Bodies: 4 Alexander, 1 Bova, 5 Caetano, 20 East Lancs, 3 MCV, 2 Marshall, 13 Northern Counties, 23 Optare, 22 Plaxton, 17 Wright.
Ops incl: local bus services, school contracts, private hire, express, continental tours.
Livery: White/Red/Cream.
Ticket System: Wayfarer TGX

SANDGROUNDER COACHES

Ceased trading since LRB 2011 went to press.

STAGECOACH CUMBRIA AND NORTH LANCASHIRE

♿ ▭ ♻

BROADACRE HOUSE, 16-20 LOWTHER STREET, CARLISLE CA3 8DA
Tel: 01524 422217
Fax: 01772 255757
E-mail: northwest.enquiries@stagecoachbus.com
Web site: www.stagecoachbus.com
Fleet Names: Stagecoach in Cumbria, Stagecoach in Lancaster.
Man Dir: Nigel Winter **Eng Dir:** Paul W Lee
Comm Man: James Mellor
Fleet: 311 - 103 double-deck bus, 145 single-deck bus, 10 single-deck coach, 53 midibus.
Chassis: 36 Alexander Dennis, 71 Dennis, 11 Leyland, 39 MAN, 56 Optare, 12 Scania, 86 Volvo.
Ops incl: local bus services, school contracts, excursions & tours, private hire, express.
Livery: Stagecoach UK Bus
Ticket System: Wayfarer TGX

STAGECOACH MERSEYSIDE AND SOUTH LANCASHIRE

♿ ▭ ♻

COMMERCIAL OFFICES, CENTRAL BUS STATION, TITHEBARN STREET, PRESTON PR1 1YU
Tel: 01772 884484 **Fax:** 01772 255757
E-mail: northwest.enquiries@stagecoachbus.com

Web site: www.stagecoachbus.com
Fleet Name: Stagecoach in Cumbria/Lancashire
Man Dir: Elisabeth Tasker **Eng Dir:** Paul W Lee
Ops Dir: Les Burton
Comm Man: James Mellor.
Fleet: 361 - 100 double-deck bus, 218 single-deck bus, 2 single-deck coach, 41 midibus.
Chassis: 39 Alexander Dennis, 114 Dennis, 2 Leyland, 52 MAN, 51 Optare, 33 Scania, 70 Volvo.
Ops incl: local bus services, school contracts, excursions & tours, private hire, express.
Livery: Stagecoach UK Bus
Ticket System: Wayfarer TGX

TRANSDEV BURNLEY & PENDLE

♿

QUEENSGATE BUS DEPOT, COLNE ROAD, BURNLEY BB10 1HH
Tel: 0845 604 0110
E-mail: enquire@burnleyandpendle.co.uk
Web site: www.lancashirebus.co.uk
Fleet Names: Mainline, Starship, The Witch Way.
Prop: Blazefield Holdings Ltd.
Man Dir: Russell Revill **Business Dir:** Douglas Robertson **Marketing Dir:** Nigel Eggleton.
Fleet: 94 – 32 double-deck bus, 56 single-deck bus, 2 single-deck coach, 4 midibus.
Chassis: 10 Leyland, 23 Optare, 5 Scania, 6 Volvo.
Bodies: 8 Alexander, 5 ECW, 1 East Lancs, 2 Leyland, 1 Northern Counties, 23 Optare, 2 Plaxton, 52 Wright.
Livery: Red/Cream.
Ticket System: ERG.
(Part of the Blazefield group which is owned by Veolia Transdev)

TRANSDEV LANCASHIRE UNITED

INTACK GARAGE, WHITEBIRK ROAD, INTACK, BLACKBURN BB1 3JD
Tel: 0845 272 7272 **Fax:** 01234 693964
E-mail: enquire@lancashireunited.co.uk
Web site: www.lancashireunited.co.uk
Fleet Names: Spot On, The Lancashire Way.
Prop: Blazefield Holdings Ltd
Man Dir: Russell Revill **Business Dir:** John Threlfall **Marketing Dir:** Nigel Eggleton.
Fleet: 117 - 36 double-deck bus, 69 single-deck bus, 12 midibus.
Chassis: 12 Dennis, 25 Leyland, 8 Optare, 72 Volvo.
Bodies: 1 Alexander, 17 ECW, 3 Leyland, 5 Northern Counties, 8 Optare, 22 Plaxton, 61 Wright.
Livery: Blue/Cream.
Ticket System: ERG.
(Part of the Blazefield group which is owned by Veolia Transdev)

THE TRAVELLERS CHOICE

♿ ♻ ♨ ♨ ⬚ ⬚ ⬚

THE COACH & TRAVEL CENTRE, SCOTLAND ROAD, CARNFORTH LA5 9RQ
Tel: 01524 720033
Fax: 01524 720044
E-mail: info@travellerschoice.co.uk
Web site: www.travellerschoice.co.uk
Chairman: R Shaw **Man Dirs:** J Shaw, D Shaw
Co Sec: P Shaw **Dir:** M Shaw.
Fleet: 97 – 79 single-deck coach, 3 midibus, 9 midicoach, 5 minibus, 1 minicoach.
Chassis: 1 Ford Transit, 1 King Long, 11 Mercedes, 3 Optare, 6 Scania, 2 Volkswagen, 73 Volvo.

Bodies: 6 Berkhof, 6 Caetano, 3 Esker, 1 Irizar, 43 Jonckheere, 1 King Long, 8 Mercedes, 4 Optare, 12 Plaxton, 14 Sunsundegui, 2 Volkswagen, 5 Other.
Ops incl: local bus services, school contracts, excursions & tours, private hire, continental tours, express.
Liveries: White with blue/yellow/red stripe, National Express.

R S TYRER LTD
168 CHORLEY ROAD, ADLINGTON PR6 9LQ
Tel: 01257 480979
Web site: www.tyrerscoaches.co.uk
Fleet: 16 – 5 double-deck bus, 7 single-deck coach, 2 double-deck coach, 2 midicoach.
Chassis: DAF, Scania, Volvo.
Bodies: Alexander, East Lancs, Northern Counties, Optare, Plaxton, Van Hool.
Ops incl: school contracts, excursions & tours, private hire, continental tours.
Livery: Blue & White

TYRER TOURS LTD
16 KIRBY ROAD, LOMESHAYE INDUSTRIAL ESTATE, NELSON BB9 6RS
Tel: 0845 130 1716
Fax: 01282 615541
E-mail: ask@tyrerbus.myzen.co.uk
Fleet Name: Tyrer Bus
Dir: R Tyrer
Fleet: 37 - 1 double-deck bus, 2 single-deck bus, 34 midibus.
Chassis: 1 Alexander Dennis, 2 Dennis, 2 Mercedes, 31 Optare, 1 Volvo.
Ops incl: local bus services.
Livery: White with Blue/Gold.

WALTONS COACH HIRE LTD
NAZE LANE EAST, FRECKLETON, PRESTON PR4 1UN
Tel: 01772 634563
E-mail: jill@waltonscoaches.co.uk
Web site: www.waltonscoaches.co.uk

Man Dir: P Walton
Fleet: 22 - 6 double-deck bus, 8 single-deck coach, 7 midicoach, 1 minicoach.
Ops incl: school contracts, private hire, excursions & tours.
Livery: Blue/Grey/Yellow.

WALTON SWIFT LTD
ROMANWAY INDUSTRIAL ESTATE, LONGRIDGE ROAD, PRESTON PR2 5BB
Tel: 01772 709100
Fax: 01772 702102
E-mail: walton.swift@btconnect.com
Web site: www.waltonswift.co.uk
Fleet: 29 – 9 double-deck bus, 3 single-deck bus, 16 single-deck coach, 1 minibus.
Chassis: DAF, King Long, Leyland, Neoplan, Scania, Setra, VDL, Volvo.
Ops incl: school contracts, private hire, excursions & tours, continental tours.
Liveries: Blue/White; Black.

LEICESTERSHIRE, CITY OF LEICESTER, RUTLAND

ABBEY TRAVEL
RMC YARD, THURMASTON FOOTPATH, HUMBERSTONE LANE, LEICESTER LE4 9JU
Tel: 0116 246 1755 **Fax:** 0116 246 1755
Recovery: 07900 438428
Web site: www.abbeytravel.org.uk
Partners: Bryan A Garratt, Pauline Garratt (Co Sec), Paul Garratt.
Fleet: 27 – 10 double-deck bus, 15 single-deck coach, 1 midibus, 1 minibus.
Chassis: 2 Bova, 4 Dennis, 1 LDV, 1 Leyland, 4 MAN, 8 MCW, 2 Mercedes, 5 Volvo.
Bodies: Alexander, Berkhof, Bova, Caetano, Hispano, Jonckheere, MCW, Neoplan, Noge, Plaxton, Van Hool.
Ops incl: local bus services, school contracts, excursions & tours, private hire, continental tours.
Livery: White/Green/Red

ARRIVA MIDLANDS LTD
852 MELTON ROAD, LEICESTER LE4 8BT
Tel: 0116 264 0400 **Fax:** 0116 260 5605
E-mail: myattk.midlands@arriva.co.uk
Web site: www.arriva.co.uk
Regional Man Dir: R A Hind **Fin Dir:** J Barlow
Ops Dir: A Lloyd **Eng Dir:** M Evans **Area Business Man (Leicestershire):** S Smith.
Fleet: 642 - 133 double-deck bus, 147 single-deck bus, 5 articulated bus, 218 midibus, 139 minibus.
Chassis: 1 Bova, 115 DAF, 182 Dennis, 4 Leyland, 35 Mercedes, 83 Optare, 49 Scania, 56 VDL, 117 Volvo.
Bodies: 57 Alexander Dennis, 1 Caetano, 65 East Lancs, 2 Marshall, 29 Mercedes, 9 Northern Counties, 83 Optare, 131 Plaxton, 42 Scania, 8 UVG, 202 Wright, 13 Other.
Ops incl: local bus services, private hire, express.
Livery: Arriva, Wardles (Red/White, Red/Cream)
Ticket System: Wayfarer 150 & 200

AUSDEN CLARK GROUP
DYSART WAY, LEICESTER LE1 2JY
Tel: 0116 262 9492 **Fax:** 0116 251 5551
Recovery: 0116 262 9492

E-mail: afrost@ausdenclark.co.uk
Web site: www.ausdenclark.co.uk
Man Dir: Paul Ausden-Clark **Dir:** Danny Smith
Gen Man: Susan Ward **Ops Man:** Adam Frost
Tran Man: Les Gent-Watts.
Fleet: 75 – 10 double-deck bus, 12 double-deck coach, 45 single-deck coach, 6 midicoach, 1 minibus, 1 minicoach.
Chassis: 1 MAN, 8 Mercedes, 66 Scania.
Bodies: 3 Alexander, 15 Berkhof, 7 East Lancs, 1 Esker, 1 Excel, 1 Ferqui, 7 Irizar, 2 Mercedes, 2 Plaxton, 1 Unvi, 35 Van Hool, 2 Other.
Ops incl: local bus services, school contracts, excursions & tours, private hire, express, continental tours.
Livery: Pink/Black/Purple on Metallic Silver.

CENTREBUS LIMITED
37 WENLOCK WAY, LEICESTER LE4 9HU
Tel: 0844 351 1120
Fax: 0116 276 7221
E-mail: info@centrebus.com
Web Site: www.centrebus.info
Dirs: Peter Harvey, Mark O Mahony
Comm Dir: David Shelley
Ops Dir (Leic): Neil Harris
Fin Controller: Chris Holmes.
Fleet (Leicestershire): 75 – 11 double-deck bus, 28 single-deck bus, 34 midibus, 2 minibus.
Chassis: 39 Dennis, 3 Leyland, 11 Mercedes, 9 Optare, 8 Scania, 3 VDL, 2 Volvo.
Bodies: 16 Alexander, 9 East Lancs, 3 Northern Counties, 9 Optare, 29 Plaxton, 1 Reeve Burgess, 4 Scania, 3 Wright.
Ops Inc: local bus services.
Livery: Blue/Orange/White
Part of the Centrebus Group

COACHCARE TRAVEL
MURRAYFIELD ROAD, LEICESTER LE3 1UW
Tel: 0116 287 7728
E-mail: coachcaretravel@fsmail.net
Web site: www.coachcaretravel.co.uk
Dir: R Sankar
Fleet: 17 - 1 single-deck bus, 6 single-deck coach, 6 minibus, 3 midicoach, 1 minibus.
Ops incl: local bus services, excursions & tours, private hire.
Livery: White with Red.

COACHMASTER
10A PINFOLD ROAD, THURMASTON, LEICESTER LE4 8BF
Tel: 0116 269 3717
Dirs: R Powell, L Watson.
Fleet: 8 – 7 single-deck coaches, 1 midicoach.
Chassis: Irisbus, Scania, Volvo.
Ops incl: private hire, express.
Liveries: White, National Express.
Associated with Thurmaston Bus

CONFIDENCE BUS & COACH LTD
30 SPALDING STREET, LEICESTER LE5 4PH
Tel/Fax: 0116 276 2171
E-mail: confidencebus@btclick.com
Web site: www.confidencebus.co.uk
Man Dir: K M Williams **Tran Man:** A Harris
Ch Eng: R Allen **Sec:** Mrs M Daines.
Fleet: 26 - 18 double-deck bus, 8 single-deck coach.
Chassis: 1 AEC, 1 Alexander Dennis, 20 Leyland, 4 Volvo.
Bodies: 1 Alexander Dennis, 1 Duple, 11 ECW, 2 Optare, 1 Park Royal, 6 Plaxton, 3 Roe, 1 Van Hool.
Ops incl: school contracts, private hire.
Livery: Buses: Black/Grey; **Coaches:** Black/Red.
Ticket System: Setright

COUNTY MINI COACHES
Ceased operations since LRB 2011 went to press

COUNTRY HOPPER
213 MELBOURNE ROAD, IBSTOCK LE67 6NQ
Tel: 01530 260888
Fleet: 6 – 5 double-deck bus, 1 single-deck bus.
Ops incl: school contracts.
Livery: Green/Cream.

FIRST MIDLANDS
PO BOX 8324, LEICESTER LE41 9BF
Tel: 08450 100 111 **Fax:** 0116 268 9198
Fleet Name: First Leicester
Regional Man Dir: Nigel Barrett

The Little Red Book 2012 - in association with Transport Benevolent Fund

Regional Eng Dir: Mick Brannigan
Regional Comm Dir: Steve Wickers
Regional Fin Planning Dir: David Marshall.
Fleet (Leicester): 102 – 66 double-deck bus, 36 single-deck bus.
Chassis: 102 Volvo.
Bodies: 47 Alexander, 55 Wright.
Ops incl: local bus services, school contracts, excursions & tours, private hire, express, continental tours.
Livery: FirstGroup UK Bus.
Ticket System: Wayfarer 3

KINCHBUS LTD

SULLIVAN WAY, SWINGBRIDGE ROAD, LOUGHBOROUGH LE11 5QS
Tel: 01509 815637
E-mail: customer.services@kinchbus.co.uk
Web site: www.kinchbus.co.uk
Ops Man: James Cheatle
Fleet: 32 - 2 double-deck bus, 20 single-deck bus, 3 midibus, 7 minibus.
Chassis: 2 Dennis, 2 Leyland, 14 Optare, 8 Scania, 6 Volvo.
Bodies: 2 ECW, 14 Optare, 8 Plaxton, 8 Wright.
Ops incl: local bus services, school contracts.
Livery: Blue/Yellow
Ticket System: Wayfarer
Part of the Wellglade Group

MACPHERSON COACHES LTD

THE GARAGE, HILL STREET, DONISTHORPE, SWADLINCOTE DE12 7PL
Tel: 01530 270226
Fax: 01530 273669
E-mail: travel@macphersoncoaches.co.uk
Web site: www.macphersoncoaches.co.uk
Man Dir: D C N MacPherson
Traffic Man: R Gadsby
Fleet Eng: C Underwood.
Fleet: 14 - 4 double-deck bus, 7 single-deck coach, 1 midibus, 1 midicoach, 1 minicoach.
Chassis: 1 Dennis, 4 Leyland, 3 Mercedes, 6 Setra.
Bodies: 3 Alexander Dennis, 2 Caetano, 1 East Lancs, 1 Mercedes, 6 Setra, 1 Other.
Ops incl: local bus services, school contracts, excursions & tours, private hire, continental tours.
Livery: Red & Cream.
Ticket System: Wayfarer.

NESBIT BROS LTD

BURROUGH ROAD, SOMERBY, MELTON MOWBRAY LE14 2PP
Tel: 01664 454284   **Fax:** 01664 454106
Dirs: I Foster, J Townsend.
Fleet: 14 single-deck coach.
Chassis: 14 Volvo.
Bodies: 7 Plaxton, 7 Van Hool.
Ops incl: school contracts, private hire

NJ TRAVEL SERVICES

5 NEW ZEALAND LANE, QUENIBOROUGH, LEICESTER LE7 3FU
Tel: 0116 276 9456
Fax: 0116 276 1969
E-mail: coaches9@btconnect.com
Prop: Nigel Jackson
Fleet: 8 - 4 double-deck bus, 2 single-deck bus, 2 single-deck coach.
Chassis: 1 Bova, 1 MAN, 4 MCW, 1 Toyota.
Bodies: 1 Bova, 4 MCW, 2 Plaxton.

Ops incl: local bus services, school contracts, private hire.
Livery: Blue/Red
Ticket System: Wayfarer

NOTTINGHAM CITY COACHES

BUILDING 3, ASHBY ROAD CENTRAL, SHEPSHED, LOUGHBOROUGH LE12 9BS
Tel: 01509 506188
Fax: 01509 506388
E-mail: coachhire@moseleygroup.co.uk
Web site: www.nottinghamcitycoaches.co.uk
Prop: A H Moseley   **Chairman:** K Lower
Chief Exec: P J Harper   **Co Sec:** R Graham
Ops Man: N Carver-Smith
Fleet: 9 single-deck coach
Chassis: 1 Bova, 5 Iveco, 3 Volvo.
Bodies: 3 Bova, 5 Beulas, 3 Plaxton.
Ops incl: school contracts, excursions & tours, private hire, continental tours.
Livery: Gold/Green.
Subsidiary of the Bowen Travel Group – see Staffordshire.

REDFERN TRAVEL LTD

See Nottinghamshire

ROBERTS TOURS LTD

THE LIMES, MIDLAND ROAD, HUGGLESCOTE LE67 2FX
Tel: 01530 817444
Fax: 01530 817666
Recovery: 07785 572526
E-mail: info@robertscoaches.co.uk
Web site: www.robertsholidays.co.uk
Man Dir: Jonathan Hunt
Ops Man: Andrew Lomas
Chief Eng: Mick Crawford.
Bodies: 2 East Lancs, 1 ECW, 6 Jonckheere, 1 LDV, 20 MCW, 3 Optare, 4 Van Hool, 2 Other.
Ops incl: local bus services, school contracts, excursions & tours, private hire, continental tours
Livery: White with Vinyls.
Ticket System: Wayfarer 3

THURMASTON BUS LTD

12 PINFOLD ROAD, THURMASTON, LEICESTER LE4 8AS
Tel: 0116 269 3707
Fax: 0116 260 4020
Web site: www.thurmastonbus.com
Dirs: L Watson, M O'Mahony.
Ops incl: local bus services, school contracts.
Livery: White with Blue
See also Coachmaster, Thurmaston

TRAVEL-WRIGHT

Ceased trading since LRB 2011 went to press.

VEOLIA TRANSPORT (ENGLAND) PLC

UNIT 5, GRANGE FARM BUSINESS PARK, GRANGE ROAD, HUGGLESCOTE LE67 2BT
Tel: 01530 832399
Fax: 01530 836128
E-mail: info@pauljamescoaches.co.uk
Web site: www.pauljamescoaches.co.uk
Gen Man: Wayne Smith
Fleet: 55 – 16 single-deck bus, 8 single-deck coach, 30 midibus.
Chassis: 2 Dennis, 4 MAN, 5 Mercedes, 22 Optare, 2 Setra, 20 Volvo.

Bodies: 1 Alexander, 1 Caetano 2 East Lancs, 3 MCV, 22 Optare, 24 Plaxton, 2 Setra.
Ops incl: excursions & tours, private hire, local bus services, school contracts, continental tours.
Livery: Red/White (Veolia); Red/Cream (Paul James); Brands.
Ticket System: Wayfarer 3
Formerly Paul James Coaches

WEST END TRAVEL/RUTLAND TRAVEL

LAKESIDE BUS & COACH CENTRE, DIXON DRIVE, LEICESTER ROAD, MELTON MOWBRAY LE13 0DA
Tel: 01664 563498
Fax: 01664 568568
Web site: www.westendandrutlandtravel.co.uk
Fleet: single-deck coach, midicoach, minibus.
Ops incl: school contracts, excursions & tours, private hire.
Livery: White with Maroon Flashes.
Bus operations transferred to Centrebus in 2011.

WIDE HORIZON COACHES LTD

48 COVENTRY ROAD, BURBAGE, HINCKLEY LE10 2HP
Tel: 01455 615915
Fax: 01455 230767
Partners: Reg Clarke, Jon Clarke.
Fleet: 12 - 2 double-deck bus, 7 single-deck coach, 2 midibus, 1 midicoach.
Chassis: 2 Iveco, 2 Leyland, 4 Mercedes, 1 Neoplan, 1 Setra, 1 Van Hool, 1 Volvo.
Ops incl: local bus services, excursions & tours, school contracts, private hire, continental tours.
Livery: White

PAUL S WINSON COACHES LTD

ROYAL WAY, BELTON PARK, LOUGHBOROUGH LE11 5XR
Tel: 01509 232354
Fax: 01509 265110
Recovery: 01509 237999
E-mail: sales@winsoncoaches.co.uk
Web site: www.winsoncoaches.co.uk
Man Dir: Paul S Winson   **Ch Eng:** Paul B Winson   **Ops Man/Co Sec:** Anthony J Winson.
Fleet: 30 – 8 double-deck bus, 5 single-deck bus, 13 single-deck coach, 2 midibus, 2 midicoach.
Chassis: 4 Alexander Dennis, 6 Bova, 1 DAF, 3 Dennis, 4 Leyland, 4 Mercedes, 1 Scania, 7 Volvo.
Ops incl: local bus services, school contracts, excursions & tours, private hire, continental tours.
Livery: Red/White/Blue.
Ticket system: Wayfarer

WOODS COACHES LTD

223 GLOUCESTER CRESCENT, WIGSTON LE18 4YR
Tel: 0116 278 6374
Fax: 0116 247 7693
E-mail: sales@woods-coaches.co.uk
Web site: www.woodscoaches.com
Man Dir: Kevin Brown   **Co Sec:** Jacqui Bates
Eng Dir: Ian Trigg   **Traffic Man:** Bill Tanser
Ops Man: Peter Skinner.
Fleet: 14 - 13 single-deck coach, 1 midicoach.
Chassis: 1 Mercedes, 4 Neoplan, 9 Volvo.
Bodies: 1 Mercedes, 4 Neoplan, 9 Plaxton.
Ops incl: school contracts, excursions & tours, private hire, continental tours.
Livery: Blue base – Orange/Yellow/White relief.

APPLEBYS COACH TRAVEL

MAIN ROAD, CONISHOLME, LOUTH LN11 7LT

Tel: 01507 357900
Fax: 01507 357910
Recovery: 07764 278466
E-mail: coach@applebyscoaches.co.uk
Web site: www.applebyscoaches.co.uk
Tran Man: Neil Warne **Man Dir:** Rob Lyng
Group Ops Man: Nick Tetley
Fleet Eng: David Hoy.
Fleet: 17 – 13 single-deck coach, 4 minibus
Chassis: 1 Dennis, 12 Scania, 4 Volkswagen.
Bodies: 8 Irizar, 4 Volkswagen, 5 Other.
Ops incl: excursions & tours, private hire, continental tours.
Subsidiary of the Bowen Travel Group - see Staffordshire

BARNARD COACHES

STATION ROAD, KIRTON LINDSEY, GAINSBOROUGH DN21 4BD

Tel: 01652 648381
Fax: 01652 640377
E-mail: bookings@barnardcoaches.co.uk
Web site: www.barnardcoaches.co.uk
Fleet: 20 – 1 double-deck bus, 19 single-deck coach.
Chassis: 3 DAF, 1 Dennis, 1 Leyland, 8 Scania, 7 Volvo.
Bodies: 1 Duple, 6 Irizar, 1 Leyland, 8 Plaxton, 4 Van Hool.
Ops incl: school contracts, private hire, excursions & tours.
Livery: White with Red.

MARK BLAND TRAVEL LTD

ESSENDINE ROAD, RYHALL, STAMFORD PE9 4JN

Tel: 01780 751671
Fax: 01780 763198
E-mail: info@markblandtravel.com
Fleet: 14 – 1 double-deck bus, 1 single-deck bus, 11 single-deck coach, 1 midibus.
Chassis: 4 DAF, 1 Dennis, 1 Leyland, 1 Mercedes, 3 Scania, 4 Volvo.
Ops incl: local bus services, school contracts.
Livery: Red/Cream

BRYLAINE TRAVEL LTD

291 LONDON ROAD, BOSTON PE21 7DD

Tel: 01205 364087
Fax: 01205 359504
E-mail: enquiries@brylaine.co.uk
Web site: www.brylaine.co.uk
Man Dir: Brian W Gregg, Elaine R Gregg
Co Sec: Susan E Bradshaw **Eng Dir:** Brian P Gregg **Ops Dir:** Malcolm P Wheatley.
Fleet: 46 - 18 double-deck bus, 14 single-deck bus, 14 midibus.
Chassis: 3 BMC, 6 DAF, 8 Dennis, 3 Leyland, 2 MCW, 14 Optare, 2 VDL, 8 Volvo.
Ops incl: local bus services, school contracts.
Liveries: Red/Blue/Yellow, Lincolnshire Inter-Connect.
Ticket system: Wayfarer

JW CARNELL LTD

Ceased operations since LRB 2011 went to press

CENTREBUS LTD

TOLLEMARCHE ROAD SOUTH, SPITALGATE LEVEL, GRANTHAM NG31 7UH

Tel: 0844 351 1120
E-mail: info@centrebus.com
Web site: www.granthambus.com
Fleet (Lincolnshire): 30 - 8 double-deck bus, 9 single-deck bus, 13 midibus.
Chassis: 1 Alexander Dennis, 11 Dennis, 5 Leyland, 1 Mercedes, 10 Optare, 2 Volvo.
Bodies: 1 Alexander Dennis, 2 Alexander, 2 East Lancs, 2 Leyland, 1 MCV, 4 Northern Counties, 10 Optare, 6 Plaxton, 2 UVG.
Ops incl: local bus services, school contracts.
Livery: Blue/Orange/White
Part of the Centrebus Group. See also Kimes Buses.

CROPLEY COACHES

MAIN ROAD, FOSDYKE, BOSTON PE20 2BH

Tel: 01205 260226
Fax: 01205 260246
Web site: www.cropleycoach.co.uk
E-mail: enquiries@cropleycoach.co.uk
Man Dir: John Cropley **Co Sec:** Mrs Sandra Cropley **Ch Eng:** Chris Cropley.
Fleet: 13 - 12 single-deck coach, 1 midicoach.
Chassis: 1 Toyota, 12 Volvo.
Bodies: 1 Caetano, 1 Plaxton, 11 Sunsundegui
Ops incl: local bus services, school contracts, excursions & tours, private hire, continental tours.
Livery: Turquoise & White

DELAINE BUSES LTD

8 SPALDING ROAD, BOURNE PE10 9LE

Tel: 01778 422866   **Fax:** 01778 425593
Web site: www.delainebuses.com
Chairman: I Delaine-Smith **Man Dir:** A Delaine-Smith **Dirs:** M Delaine-Smith, K Delaine-Smith **Sec:** Miss J A Delaine-Smith.
Fleet: 20 - 15 double-deck bus, 5 single-deck bus.
Chassis: 20 Volvo.
Bodies: 14 East Lancs, 6 Wright.
Ops incl: local bus services.
Livery: Light/Dark Blue & Cream.
Ticket System: Almex A90

DICKINSON'S COACHES

BROADGATE, WRANGLE, BOSTON, PE22 9DY

Tel/Fax: 01205 870333
E-mail: enquiries@dickinsons-coaches.co.uk
Web site: www.dickinsons-coaches.co.uk
Fleet: 11 – 1 double-deck bus, 7 single-deck coach, 3 midicoach.
Chassis: 1 Alexander Dennis, 4 Dennis, 3 Mercedes, 1 Scania, 2 Volvo.
Ops incl: school contracts, private hire, excursions & tours.
Livery: White with Orange/Green.

EAGRE COACHES LTD

See Wilfreda Beehive – South Yorkshire

W H FOWLER & SONS (COACHES) LTD

155 DOG DROVE SOUTH, HOLBEACH DROVE, SPALDING PE12 0SD

Tel: 01406 330232

Fax: 01406 330923
E-mail: andrew@fowlerstravel.com
Web site: www.fowlerstravel.com
Fleet Name: Fowlers Travel
Man Dir: John Fowler **Co Sec:** Jackie Fowler
Dir: Andrew Fowler.
Fleet: 20 - 7 double-deck bus, 3 single-deck bus, 10 single-deck coach, 1 minibus.
Chassis: 1 DAF, 2 Leyland, 1 Mercedes, 15 Volvo.
Bodies: 5 Alexander Dennis, 1 Berkhof, 2 Jonckheere, 1 Northern Counties, 11 Plaxton.
Ops incl: local bus services, school contracts, excursions & tours, private hire.
Livery: Cream/Orange/Red
Ticket System: Wayfarer

GRAYSCROFT BUS SERVICES LTD

15A VICTORIA ROAD, MABLETHORPE LN12 2AF

Tel: 01507 473236
Fax: 01507 477073
E-mail: Grayscroft.ltd@btconnect.com
Web site: www.grayscroft.co.uk
Dirs: C W Barker, N Barker, N W Barker.
Fleet: 16 - 5 double-deck bus, 9 single-deck coach, 2 minibus.
Chassis: 4 Mercedes, 1 Neoplan, 11 Volvo.
Bodies: 1 Hispano, 3 Jonckheere, 3 Mercedes, 5 Northern Counties, 2 Plaxton, 3 Van Hool.
Ops incl: local bus services, school contracts, excursions & tours, private hire.
Livery: Cream, Blue & Orange
Ticket system: Wayfarer

PHIL HAINES COACHES

RALPHS LANE, FRAMPTON WEST, BOSTON PE20 1QU

Tel/Fax: 01205 722359
Props: N A & S Haines.
Fleet: 15 – 8 single-deck coach, 1 midicoach, 6 minibus.
Ops incl: local bus services, school contracts, private hire.
Livery: White.

HODSON'S COACHES LTD

SAXILBY ENTERPRISE PARK, SKELLINGTHORPE ROAD, SAXILBY, LINCOLN LN1 2LR

Tel: 01522 706030
Fax: 01522 706031
E-mail: sales@hodsoncoaches.co.uk
Web Site: www.hodsoncoaches.co.uk
Man Dir: Alistair Gooseman **Ops Dir:** Tim Gooseman **Dir:** Sue Gooseman.
Fleet: 11 - 4 single-deck coach, 2 midicoach, 5 minibus.
Chassis: 1 LDV, 6 Mercedes, 3 Setra, 1 Vauxhall.
Ops incl: school contracts, excursions & tours, private hire, continental tours.
Livery: Lemon/Purple
Ticket system: Almex

HORNSBY TRAVEL SERVICES LTD

51 ASHBY HIGH STREET, SCUNTHORPE DN16 2NB

Tel: 01724 282255
Fax: 01274 282788
E-mail: office@hornsbytravel.co.uk

Lincolnshire

Web site: www.hornsbytravel.co.uk
Man Dir: Raymond Hornsby
Gen Man: Nicholas Hornsby
Ch Eng: Rob Andrew.
Fleet: 30 - 3 double-deck bus, 17 single-deck bus, 8 single-deck coach, 1 midicoach, 1 minibus.
Chassis: Alexander Dennis, BMC, Dennis, Ford Transit, Mercedes, Volvo.
Bodies: Alexander Dennis, BMC, Mercedes, Plaxton.
Ops incl: local bus services, school contracts, excursions & tours, private hire.
Livery: Blue/Silver.
Ticket System: ERG

F HUNT COACH HIRE LTD

2/3 WEST STREET, ALFORD
LN13 9DG
Tel/Fax: 01507 463000
E-mail: travel.office@hunts-coaches.co.uk
Web site: www.hunts-coaches.co.uk
Fleet Name: Hunts Travel
Dirs: Michael Hunt, Charles Hunt, Dave Eales.
Fleet: 20 - 1 double-deck bus, 2 single-deck bus, 11 single-deck coach, 2 midibus, 3 midicoach, 1 minicoach.
Chassis: 1 Iveco, 5 Mercedes, 1 Optare, 13 Volvo.
Bodies: 2 Mercedes, 1 Northern Counties, 2 Optare, 2 Plaxton, 9 Van Hool, 3 Wright, 1 Other.
Ops incl: local bus services, school contracts,

excursions & tours, private hire, express, continental tours.
Livery: White/Red/Grey
Ticket System: Almex

KIMES BUSES

3 SLEAFORD ROAD, FOLKINGHAM, SLEAFORD NG34 0SB
Tel: 01529 497251
Fax: 01529 497554
E-mail: enquiries@kimesbuses.co.uk
Web site: www.kimesbuses.co.uk
Traffic Man: Angela Cliff
Fleet: 26 - 14 double-deck bus, 12 single-deck bus.
Chassis: 7 DAF, 6 Dennis, 7 Leyland, 1 Optare, 1 Scania, 4 VDL.
Bodies: 9 Alexander, 4 East Lancs, 1 Ikarus, 3 Northern Counties, 1 Optare, 1 Plaxton, 7 Wright.
Ops incl: local bus services, school contracts, excursions & tours, private hire.
Livery: Cream/Green
Ticket System: Almex
A subsidiary of Centrebus

LAWTON'S EXECUTIVE COACHES

LAST MOORINGS, EAST FEN LANE, STICKNEY, BOSTON PE22 8DE
Tel: 01205480462
Fax: 01205 480709
Recovery: 07879 444085

E-mail: info@lawtonscoaches.co.uk
Web site: www.lawtonscoaches.co.uk
Props: Geoff & Liz Lawton.
Fleet: 9 – 4 double-deck bus, 5 single-deck coach.
Chassis: 2 Bova, 2 Leyland, 2 Scania, 1 Setra, 2 Volvo
Bodies: 2 Bova, 2 East Lancs, 2 ECW, 1 Jonckheere, 1 Plaxton, 1 Setra.
Ops incl: school contracts, excursions & tours, private hire.
Livery: White

LOVEDEN TRAVEL

16 NORTH ROAD, LEADENHAM LN5 0PG
Tel: 01400 273838
Fax: 01400 272587
E-mail: enquiries@loveden-travel.com
Web site: www.loveden-travel.com
Ops incl: school contracts, private hire, excursions & tours.
Livery: White

MEMORY LANE COACHES

ELM HOUSE, OLD BOLINGBROKE, SPILSBY PE23 4HF
Tel: 01790 763394
Prop: John B Dorey
Fleet: 3 - 2 single-deck coach, 1 minibus.
Chassis: 2 Dennis, 1 Mercedes.
Bodies: 2 Plaxton, 1 Other.
Ops incl: school contracts, private hire.
Livery: White/Green/Red.

PC COACHES OF LINCOLN LTD

17 CROFTON ROAD, LINCOLN LN3 4NL
Tel: 01522 533605
Fax: 01522 560402
Man Dir: Peter Smith
Ops Dir: Miss Sarah Smith
Dir International Ops: Chris Bristow.
Fleet: 67 - 16 double-deck bus, 3 single-deck bus, 37 single-deck coach, 4 midibus, 1 midicoach, 6 minibus.
Chassis: 1 Alexander Dennis, 1 Ford Transit, 1 LDV, 3 Mercedes, 4 Optare, 57 Scania.
Bodies: 1 Alexander Dennis, 2 Berkhof, 18 East Lancs, 25 Irizar, 1 Jonckheere, 3 LDV, 4 Optare, 6 Plaxton, 3 Van Hool, 1 Wright, 4 Other.
Ops incl: local bus services, school contracts, private hire, continental tours.
Livery: White/Maroon/Red

ROY PHILLIPS

69 STATION ROAD, RUSKINGTON
NG34 9DF
Tel: 01526 832279
Prop: R Phillips.
Fleet: 6 single-deck coach.
Chassis: 1 Leyland, 5 Volvo.
Bodies: 1 Jonckheere, 2 Plaxton, 3 Van Hool.
Ops incl: private hire, school contracts.

PRESTIGE COACHES

3 PETHLEY LANE, POINTON,
SLEAFORD NG34 0ND
Tel: 01529 241122
E-mail: enquiries@prestige-coaches.com
Web site: www.prestige-coaches.com
Props: L & R Robbins.
Fleet: 3 single-deck coach.
Chassis: 3 Scania.
Bodies: 3 Irizar.
Ops incl: excursions & tours, private hire, continental tours.
Livery: Blue & Yellow

PULFREYS COACHES

1 WILKINSON ROAD, FOSTON,
GRANTHAM NG32 2JX
Tel: 01476 564144
Dir: Andrew Pulfrey.
Fleet: 4 - 2 single-deck coach, 1 midibus, 1 minibus.
Chassis: 1 Dennis, 1 Iveco, 2 Mercedes.
Bodies: 1 Beulas, 2 Plaxton, 1 Other.
Ops incl: school contracts, excursions & tours, private hire, continental tours.
Livery: Blue/White
Ticket System: Wayfarer

RADLEY COACH TRAVEL

THE TRAVEL OFFICE, 11 CHAPEL COURT,
BRIGG DN20 8JZ
Tel: 01652 653583   **Fax:** 01652 656020
Fleet Name: Radley Holidays
E-mail: radleytravel@aol.com
Web site: www.radleytravel.co.uk
Owner: Kevin Radley.
Fleet: 2 single-deck coach.
Chassis: 4 Scania.
Bodies: 1 Berkhof, 1 Irizar, 2 Scania Omni Express.

Ops incl: excursions & tours, private hire, continental tours.
Livery: Maroon/Gold

REDFERN TRAVEL LTD

See Nottinghamshire

SLEAFORDIAN COACHES

PRIDE PARKWAY, EAST ROAD,
SLEAFORD NG34 8GL
Tel: 01529 303333
Fax: 01529 303324
E-mail: office@sleafordian.co.uk
Web site: www.sleafordian.co.uk
Dirs: Mark Broughton
(Man Dir), Mrs Lisa Broughton, Don
Broughton **(Co Sec),** Mrs Jean Broughton
Chief Eng: Phil Kerr.
Fleet: 27 - 12 double-deck bus, 11 single-deck coach, 3 midibus, 1 midicoach.
Chassis: 2 Dennis, 10 Leyland, 2 Mercedes, 1 Neoplan, 2 Optare, 10 Volvo.
Ops incl: local bus services, school contracts, excursions & tours, private hire, continental tours.
Livery: White/Orange/Blue
Ticket System: Wayfarer TGX, Setright

SMITHS COACHES, CORBY GLEN

THE GREEN, CORBY GLEN NG33 4NP
Tel: 01476 550285
Fax: 01476 550032
Partners: H J and Mary J Smith.
Ops incl: excursions & tours, private hire, continental tours, school contracts.
Livery: Blue/White.

STAGECOACH EAST MIDLANDS

PO BOX 15, DEACON ROAD,
LINCOLN LN2 4JB
Tel: 0845 605 0605
Fax: 01522 538229
E-mail: eastmidlands.enquiries@
stagecoachbus.com
Web site: www.stagecoachbus.com
Fleet Name: Stagecoach in Lincolnshire.
Man Dir: Gary Nolan
Eng Dir: John Taylor
Comm Dir: Dave Skepper
Ops Dir: Richard Kay.
Fleet: 498 - 230 double-deck bus, 251 single-deck bus, 9 single-deck coach, 8 open top bus.
Chassis: 294 Alexander Dennis, 6 DAF, 1 Leyland, 51 MAN, 21 Optare, 14 Scania, 111 Volvo.
Bodies: 335 Alexander Dennis, 63 East Lancs, 5 Jonckheere, 11 Northern Counties, 21 Optare, 33 Plaxton, 12 Transbus, 18 Wright.
Ops incl: local bus services.
Livery: Stagecoach UK Bus
Ticket System: ERG TP5000.

TOURMASTER COACHES LTD

ALDERLANDS, JAMES ROAD, CROWLAND,
PETERBOROUGH PE6 0AA
Tel: 01733 211710   **Fax:** 01733 2113369
Recovery: 01733 211639
E-mail: tourmaster@btconnect.com
Prop: David Dinsey
Fleet: 12 - 1 double-deck bus, 11 single-deck coach.

Chassis: 3 DAF, 1 Dennis, 3 Leyland, 5 Volvo.
Bodies: 1 Berkhof, 3 Bova, 1 Jonckheere, 3 Van Hool, 1 Volvo, 3 Other.
Ops incl: school contracts, private hire.
Livery: Blue/Red/Turquoise.

TRANSLINC

JARVIS HOUSE, 157 SADLER ROAD,
LINCOLN LN6 3RS
Tel: 01522 503400
Fax: 01522 503406
E-mail: logistics@translinc.co.uk
Web site: www.translinc.co.uk
Man Dir: Paul Roberts
Fleet: 193 - 18 single-deck coach, 19 midibus, 136 minibus, 20 minicoach (8 seats & under).
Chassis: 16 Citroen, 2 DAF, 10 Dennis, 8 Fiat, 104 Iveco, 7 LDV, 20 Mercedes, 2 Optare, 13 Renault, 2 Scania, 4 Toyota, 1 Volkswagen, 4 Volvo.
Ops incl: local bus services, school contracts, excursions & tours, private hire, express.

A C WILLIAMS LTD

ERMINE STREET, ANCASTER, GRANTHAM
NG32 3QN
Tel: 01400 230833
Fax: 01400 230296
Recovery: 01400 230491
E-mail: coaches@acwilliams.co.uk
Web site: www.acwcoaches.co.uk
Man Dir: A D C Williams
Dirs: Mrs M Williams, Mrs A Parker
Coach Man: Ian Mansell.
Fleet: 20 - 4 double-deck bus, 14 single-deck coach, 1 double-deck coach, 1 midicoach.
Chassis: 2 Alexander Dennis, 1 DAF, 2 Leyland, 1 MAN, 5 Scania, 2 Setra, 1 Toyota, 6 Volvo.
Bodies: 1 Alexander Dennis, 1 Caetano, 2 East Lancs, 1 ECW, 5 Irizar, 1 Neoplan, 2 Setra, 7 Van Hool.
Ops incl: school contracts, excursions & tours, private hire, continental tours.
Livery: White

For information regarding advertising

in the next edition, contact:

Graham Middleton

Tel: 01780 484632

Fax: 01780 763388

E-mail: graham.middleton@

ianallanpublishing.co.uk

Ian Allan
PUBLISHING

**Riverdene Business Park, Molesey
Road, Hersham, Surrey KT12 4RG
Tel: 01932 266600 Fax: 01932 266601**

This section includes those operators in the London and Middlesex postal areas, as well as operators who have asked to appear under this heading. Other operators within Greater London with a non-London postal address, eg Kingston, Surrey; Bromley, Kent; etc, may be found under their respective postal counties.

AA, KNIGHTS OF THE ROAD
Ceased trading since LRB 2011 went to press.

ABELLIO LONDON LTD
301 CAMBERWELL NEW ROAD, LONDON SE5 0TF
Tel: 020 7788 8550
Fax: 020 7805 3510
E-mail: customer.care@abellio.co.uk
Web site: www.abellio.co.uk
Man Dir: Tony Wilson **Ops Dir:** Bill Weatherley
Eng Dir: Steve Hamilton
Fin Dir: Ross Hanley.
Fleet (London): 521 - 293 double-deck bus, 183 single-deck bus, 45 midibus.
Chassis: 235 Alexander Dennis, 173 Dennis, 35 Transbus, 73 Volvo, 5 Wrightbus.
Bodies: 235 Alexander Dennis, 116 Alexander, 32 Caetano, 3 East Lancs, 34 Plaxton, 23 Transbus, 78 Wright.
Ops incl: local bus services
Livery: Red
Ticket system: TfL Prestige

ABELLIO LONDON WEST LTD
See Surrey

ANDERSON TRAVEL GROUP
178A TOWER BRIDGE ROAD, LONDON SE1 3LS
Tel: 020 7403 8118
Fax: 020 7403 8421
E-mail: sales@andersontravel.co.uk
Web site: www.andersontravel.co.uk
Man Dir: Mark Anderson
Comm Man: Keith Payne **Ops Man:** Peter Gilbert.
Fleet: 28 - 22 single-deck coach, 4 midicoach, 2 minibus.
Chassis incl: 8 Bova, 8 Mercedes, 1 Volkswagen, 8 Volvo.
Bodies incl: 8 Bova, 4 Mercedes, 9 Plaxton, 1 Sitcar.
Ops incl: school contracts, excursions & tours, private hire, express, continental tours.
Livery: White with Green lettering
See also London Mini Coaches

ARRIVA LONDON
16 WATSONS ROAD LONDON N22 7TZ
Tel: 020 8271 0101
Fax: 020 8271 0120
Web site: arrivabus.co.uk
Man Dir: Bob Scowen **Comm Dir:** Peter Batty
Ops Dir: Jeff Quantrell **Eng Dir:** Tony Ward.
Fleet: 1820 - 1398 double-deck bus, 160 single-deck bus, 180 midibus, 82 articulated bus.
Chassis: 8 AEC, 323 Alexander Dennis, 515 DAF, 101 Dennis, 82 Mercedes, 25 Transbus, 83 VDL, 418 Volvo, 267 Wrightbus.
Bodies: 322 Alexander, 402 Alexander Dennis, 82 Mercedes, 8 Park Royal, 87 Plaxton, 201 Transbus, 723 Wright
Ops incl: local bus services, private hire.
Livery: Red
Ticket System: TfL Prestige

ASHFORD LUXURY COACHES
Ceased operations since LRB 2011 went to press. Name acquired by London Mini Coaches.

ATBUS LTD
41 MANOR ROAD, ASHFORD TW15 2SL
Tel: 07949 140437 **Fax:** 01784 241094
E-mail: info@atbus.co.uk
Man Dir: Andrew Tanner **Co Sec:** Clifford Tanner.
Ops incl: school contracts, rail replacement.
Livery: Red with Grey Stripe
Ticket System: Wayfarer

ATLAS COACHES LTD
52-63 PALMERSTON ROAD, WEALDSTONE HA3 7RW
Tel: 020 8863 8883 **Fax:** 020 863 4443
E-mail: info@atlascoaches.co.uk
Web site: www.atlascoaches.co.uk
Fleet: 9 – 7 single-deck coach, 2 midicoach.
Chassis: 1 Mercedes, 1 Scania, 6 Volvo, 1 Other.
Ops incl: school contracts, private hire, excursions & tours, continental tours.
Livery: White with Pale Blue

BACK ROADS TOURING CO LTD
LEVEL 2, 107 POWER ROAD, CHISWICK, LONDON W4 5PY
Tel: 020 8987 0990 **Fax:** 020 8994 0888
E-mail: info@backroadstouring.co.uk
Web site: www.backroadstouring.co.uk
Man Dir: Bruce Cherry **Fin Dir:** Erika Harcz
Ops Dir: Alex Newmann.
Fleet: 14 minibus.
Chassis: 13 Mercedes, 1 Renault.
Ops incl: excursions & tours, private hire, continental tours.
Livery: White

BEAR BUSES
54 FAGGS ROAD, FELTHAM TW14 0LG
Tel: 020 8867 0617
Prop: G Massiah.
Fleet: 6 double-deck bus
Ops incl: school contracts, private hire.

BEECHES TRAVEL
23 POWDER MILL LANE, WHITTON, TWICKENHAM TW2 6EE
Tel/Fax: 020 8898 7048
E-mail: info@beeches-travel.co.uk
Web site: www.beeches-travel.co.uk
Prop: C Miller.
Fleet: 3 minicoach.
Chassis: 1 Ford Transit, 1 Iveco, 1 Mercedes.
Ops incl: school contracts, excursions & tours, private hire.
Livery: White/Yellow.

BESSWAY TRAVEL LTD
THE IMPACT BUSINESS PARK, 7-9 WADSWORTH ROAD, PERIVALE, GREENFORD UB6 7JD
Tel: 020 8997 1297
Fax: 020 8998 6853
E-mail: info@besswaytravel.co.uk
Web site: www.besswaytravel.co.uk
Prop: Michael Heffernan.
Fleet: 11 - 3 single-deck coach, 2 midicoach, 2 minicoach, 4 minibus.
Chassis: 2 Iveco, 2 LDV, 4 Mercedes, 2 Scania, 1 Volvo.
Bodies: 3 Crest, 1 Excel, 3 Ferqui, 2 Plaxton, 2 Scania.
Ops incl: private hire, school contracts.
Livery: White with Blue/Red

BIG BUS COMPANY
GROSVENOR GARDENS HOUSE, 35-37 GROSVENOR GARDENS, LONDON SW1W 0BS
Tel: 020 7233 8722
Fax: 020 7233 8766
E-mail: info@bigbustours.com
Web site: www.bigbustours.com
Fleet: 93 open-top bus.
Chassis: 31 Dennis, 25 Leyland, 11 MCW, 26 Volvo.
Bodies: 22 Alexander, 19 Duple, 22 East Lancs, 3 Leyland, 11 MCW, 16 Optare.
Ops incl: excursions & tours, private hire.
Livery: Burgundy/Cream
Ticket system: Almex

BLUE TRIANGLE LTD
18 MERTON HIGH STREET, LONDON SW19 1DN
Tel: 020 8545 6100
Fax: 020 8545 6101
E-mail: enquiries@go-ahead-london.com
Web site: www.go-ahead-london.com
Ch Exec: John Trayner
Eng Dir: Phil Margrave
Fin Dir: Paul Reeves
Ops Dir: David Cutts.
Fleet: 51 – 25 double-deck bus, 26 single-deck bus.
Chassis: 21 Alexander Dennis, 3 Dennis, 2 Transbus, 25 Volvo.
Bodies: 21 Alexander Dennis, 2 MCV, 10 Plaxton, 2 Transbus, 16 Wright.
Ops incl: local bus services, school contracts, private hire.
Livery: Red
Ticket System: TfL Prestige
Part of the Go-Ahead Group

BM COACHES
SHACKLES DOCK, SILVERDALE ROAD, HAYES UB3 3BN
Tel: 0845 555 7711
Fax: 0845 555 7722
E-mail: info@bmcoaches.co.uk
Web site: www.bmcoaches.co.uk
Fleet: 38 – double-deck coach, single-deck coach, midicoach, minibus, minicoach.
Chassis: Mercedes, Scania, Temsa, Van Hool, VDL, Volvo.
Ops incl: excursions & tours, private hire.

BRENTONS OF BLACKHEATH

♿ 🔧 ⛽ ❄ 🔧

27 FORDMILL ROAD, CATFORD, LONDON
SE6 3JL
Tel: 020 8698 6834
Fax: 020 8461 0110
E-mail: davee@brentonsofblackheath.co.uk
Web site: www.brentonsselfdrivehire.co.uk
Prop: C Clark **Ch Eng:** I Powell.
Fleet: 12 - 9 single-deck coach, I midicoach,
2 minicoach.
Chassis: I Leyland, 2 Mercedes, I Toyota,
2 Van Hool, 6 Volvo.
Ops incl: school contracts, private hire.
Livery: County Cream

BRYANS OF ENFIELD

🚌 🔧 ⛽ 🔧

19 WETHERLEY ROAD, ENFIELD EN2 0NS
Tel: 020 8366 0062
Owner: B. Nash.
Fleet: 6 - 3 double-deck bus, I single-deck bus,
I single-deck coach, I double-deck coach.
Chassis: I AEC, I DAF, 2 Daimler, I Leyland,
I MCW.
Bodies: I ECW, 2 MCW, 2 Park Royal,
I Van Hool.
Ops incl: school contracts, private hire.
Livery: Red.

CABIN COACHES

♿ 🚌 🍽 ❄ 🔧

I PARSONAGE CLOSE, HAYES UB3 2LZ
Tel: 020 8573 1100
Fax: 020 8573 8604
E-mail: info@cabincoaches.com
Web site: www.cabincoaches.com
Prop: P Martin.
Fleet: 4 - 3 single-deck coach, I midicoach.
Chassis: I BMC, 3 Scania.
Bodies: I BMC, 2 Irizar, I Van Hool.
Ops incl: excursions & tours, school contracts,
private hire.
Livery: White with Purple/Light Blue

CARAVELLE COACHES

🔧

9 CHESTNUT AVENUE, EDGWARE HA8 7RA
Tel/Fax: 020 8952 4025
E-mail: caravelle@aol.com
Prop: Harvey Lawrence
Fleet: 2 - I midibus, I minibus.
Chassis: I Ford Transit, I Mercedes.
Bodies: I Mellor, I Other
Ops incl: school contracts, excursions & tours,
private hire.

CAVALIER TRAVEL SERVICES

Ceased trading since LRB 2011 went to press.

CENTAUR COACHES & MINICOACHES

♿ 🔧 🚌 🍽 ❄ 🔧

188 HALFWAY STREET, SIDCUP DA15 8DJ
Tel: 020 8300 3001
Fax: 020 8302 5959

E-mail: matt@minicoaches.com
Web site: www.minicoaches.com
Man Dir: M Sims **Dirs:** P Sims, S Durrant.
Fleet: 107 – incl 7 single-deck bus, 12 midibus,
22 midicoach, 41 minibus, 20 minicoach.
Chassis incl: 25 Ford Transit, 17 LDV,
12 Mercedes.
Bodies incl: Alexander Dennis, Mercedes, Reeve
Burgess.
Ops incl: private hire, school contracts,
excursions & tours.

CHALFONT COACHES
OF HARROW LTD

🔧 🚌 R 🔧

200 FEATHERSTONE ROAD,
SOUTHALL UB2 5AQ
Tel: 020 8843 2323
Fax: 020 8574 0939
E-mail: chalfontcoaches@btopenworld.com
Web site: www.chalfontcoaches.co.uk
Man Dir: C J Shears **Dirs:** I Shears, M Shears
Ops Man: P Williams **Ch Eng:** R Arents
Co Sec: G Shears.
Fleet: 18 - 16 single-deck coach, 2 minibus.
Chassis: I Bova, I LDV, I Mercedes, 15 Volvo.
Bodies: I Bova, 15 Van Hool, 2 Other.
Ops incl: school contracts, excursions & tours,
private hire, express, continental tours.
Livery: Mauve/White

CHALFONT LINE LTD

♿ 🔧 ❄

4 PROVIDENCE ROAD, WEST DRAYTON
UB7 8HJ
Tel: 01895 459540
Fax: 01895 459549
E-mail: info@chalfont-line.co.uk
Web site: www.chalfont-line.co.uk
Chairman: T J Reynolds **Man Dir:** R Chadija
Dir: M Kerr **Tran Man:** Lynn Young.
Fleet: 84 minibus.
Chassis: 64 DAF, 6 Ford Transit, 8 Mercedes,
6 Renault.
Ops incl: school contracts, excursions & tours,
private hire, continental tours.
Livery: White/Green

CITY CIRCLE (UK) LTD

♿ 🚌 🍽 ❄

WEST LONDON COACH CENTRE,
NORTH HYDE GARDENS, HAYES UB4 3QT
Tel: 020 8561 2112
Fax: 020 8561 2010
E-mail: go@citycircleuk.com
Web site: www.citycircleuk.com
Man Dir: Neil Pegg
Fin Dir: Johnson Mitchell.
Fleet: 34 single-deck coach, minicoach.
Chassis: Mercedes, Neoplan, Setra, Van Hool,
VDL, Volvo.
Bodies: Jonckheere, Mercedes, Neoplan, Setra,
Van Hool.
Ops incl: excursions & tours, private hire.
Livery: White with Red/Grey

CLARKES OF LONDON

🚌 🔧 ❄ 🍽 🔧 🔧

KANGLEY BRIDGE ROAD, LOWER
SYDENHAM, LONDON SE26 5AT
Tel: 020 8778 6697
Fax: 020 8778 0389
E-mail: info@clarkescoaches.co.uk
Web site: www.clarkescoaches.co.uk
Man Dir: Mrs D Newman
Comm Dir: J Devacmaker **Fin Dir:** S Reeve
Fleet: 55 - 51 single-deck coach, 4 midicoach.
Chassis: 11 Mercedes, 9 Setra, 31 Scania,
4 Toyota.
Bodies: 7 Berkhof, 4 Caetano, 24 Irizar,
11 Mercedes, 9 Setra.
Ops incl: excursions & tours, private hire,
express, continental tours.
Livery: Green/Silver.

COACHES EXCETERA

🔧 🚌 🍽 ❄

120 BEDDINGTON LANE, CROYDON
CR9 4ND
Tel: 020 8665 5561
Fax: 020 8664 8694
E-mail: info@coachesetc.com
Web site: www.coachesetc.com
Man Dir: Alex Mazza **Gen Man:** Richard Hill.
Fleet: single-deck coach, midicoach, minibus,
minicoach.
Chassis: Mercedes, Scania, Setra, Volvo.
Livery: White with logo.

COLLINS COACHES LTD

Ceased trading since LRB 2011 went to press.

CONISTON COACHES LTD

🚌 🔧 ❄

88 CONISTON ROAD, BROMLEY BR1 4JB
Tel/Fax: 020 8460 3432
E-mail: ricksmock@oal.com
Web site: www.conistoncoaches.co.uk
Dir: Richard Smock,
Fleet: 5 - 5 single-deck coach,
Chassis: 5 Volvo.
Bodies: I Caetano, 4 Plaxton.
Ops incl: private hire, school contracts.
Livery: White/Red.

COUNTY COACHES

See Essex

DAVID CORBEL OF LONDON LTD

🚌 🔧 🍽 ❄

6 CAMROSE AVENUE, EDGWARE HA8 6EG
Tel: 020 8952 1300
Fax: 020 8952 8641
E-mail: corbeloflondon@aol.com
Web site: www.corbel-coaches.com
Dir: Robert Whelan,
Fleet: 10 single-deck coach,
Chassis: 3 Scania, 7 Volvo.
Bodies: 3 Irizar, 7 Plaxton.
Ops incl: school contracts, private hire.
Livery: Pink/Blue.

London and Middlesex

♿	Vehicle suitable for disabled	🔧	Seat belt-fitted Vehicle	R24	24 hour recovery service
🍽	Toilet-drop facilities available	🍽	Coach(es) with galley facilities	🔧	Replacement vehicle available
R	Recovery service available	❄	Air-conditioned vehicle(s)	⛽	Vintage Coach(es) available
⛽	Open top vehicle(s)	🚌	Coaches with toilet facilities	🔧	Hybrid Buses

CROWN COACHES

68 CANON ROAD, BICKLEY BR1 2SP
Tel: 020 8313 3020
Fleet: 1 minibus.
Chassis: Ford Transit.
Ops incl: school contracts, private hire.

CRYSTALS COACHES LTD

1 ELKSTONE ROAD, LONDON W10 5NT
Tel: 020 8960 8800
Ops Man: G. Betts.
Fleet: 30 - 15 minibus, 15 minicoach.
Chassis: Ford Transit, Freight Rover, Mercedes.
Ops incl: local bus services, school contracts, private hire.

CT PLUS LTD

5th FLOOR, 88 OLD STREET, LONDON, EC1V 9HU
Tel: 020 7275 2400
Fax: 020 7275 2450
E-mail: info@hctgroup.org
Web site: www.hctgroup.org
Ch Exec: Dai Powell **Dep Ch Exec:** Jude Winter **Ch Fin Off:** Douglas Downie
Ch Ops Off: Jon McColl,
Fleet (London): 84 - 27 double deck bus, 13 single-deck bus, 35 midibus, 9 minibus.
Chassis: 11 Alexander Dennis, 13 Dennis, 22 Optare, 10 Scania, 3 Transbus, 3 Volkswagen.
Bodies: 4 Alexander Dennis, 3 Bluebird, 21 Caetano, 20 East Lancs, 22 Optare, 1 Plaxton, 10 Scania, 3 Transbus.
Ops incl: local bus services
Livery: Red/Yellow
See also operations in East Riding, West Yorkshire.
Ticket System: TfL Prestige

CUMFI-LUX COACHES

69 CORWELL LANE, HILLINGDON UB8 3DE
Tel: 020 8561 6948 **Fax:** 020 8569 3809
Prop: N R Farrow
(Traf Man) Sec: Mrs T K Lovell.
Fleet: 1 single-deck coach.
Chassis: Scania.
Ops incl: excursions & tours, private hire.
Livery: Orange/White (coach); White (minibuses).

DANS LUXURY TRAVEL LTD

ROYAL FOREST COACH HOUSE, 109 MAYBANK ROAD, LONDON E18 1EZ
Tel: 020 8505 8833
Fax: 020 8519 1937
Man Dir: D Brown **Dir:** S A Brown.
Fleet: 28 - single-deck coach, midicoach, minicoach.
Chassis: 4 Ford Transit, 15 Mercedes, 1 Toyota, 8 Volvo.
Ops incl: school contracts, excursions & tours, private hire, continental tours.
Livery: White with Blue/Red

DAVIAN COACHES LTD

1-3 BECKET ROAD, EDMONTON, LONDON N18 3PN
Tel: 020 8807 1515
Fax: 020 8807 2323
E-mail: daviancoaches@btconnect.com

Web site: www.daviancoaches.co.uk
Man Dir: Darren Wardle **Dir & Co Sec:** Judy Wardle **Comm Man:** David Bee
Transport Man: Richard Window.
Fleet: 20 - 11 single-deck coach, 9 minibus.
Chassis: 2 Autosan, 1 BMC, 1 Iveco, 2 King Long, 8 LDV, 1 Mercedes, 4 Scania, 1 Volvo.
Bodies: 1 Beulas, 1 BMC, 4 Irizar, 8 LDV, 1 Mercedes, 1 Plaxton.
Ops incl: excursions & tours, school contracts, private hire, continental tours.
Livery: White

DOCKLANDS BUSES LTD

18 MERTON HIGH STREET, LONDON SW19 1DN
Tel: 020 8545 6100 **Fax:** 020 8545 6101
E-mail: enquiries@go-ahead-london.com
Web site: www.go-ahead-london.com
Ch Exec: John Trayner **Eng Dir:** Phil Margrave
Fin Dir: Paul Reeves **Ops Dir:** David Cutts.
Fleet: 65 – 25 double-deck bus, 40 single-deck bus.
Chassis: 30 Alexander Dennis, 10 Dennis, 14 Scania, 11 Volvo.
Bodies: 10 Alexander Dennis, 5 East Lancs, 21 MCV, 11 Plaxton, 9 Scania, 9 Wright.
Ops incl: local bus services, school contracts, private hire.
Livery: Red
Ticket System: TfL Prestige
A subsidiary of the Go Ahead Group

DOCKLANDS COACHES LTD

FACTORY ROAD, SILVERTOWN E16 2EW
Tel: 020 7474 8130
Dir: F Cheroomi.
Fleet: 13 – single-deck coach, midicoach, minicoach, minibus.
Chassis: Mercedes.
Ops incl: school contracts, private hire.
Livery: Blue with White/Red

EAST LONDON BUS GROUP

Now under Stagecoach ownership as Stagecoach London

EASYBUS LTD

HAMILTON HOUSE, NORTH CIRCULAR ROAD, LONDON NW10 7PX
Web site: www.easybus.co.uk
Man Dir: Jonathan Crick.
Fleet: 31 minibus.
Chassis: 31 Mercedes.
Bodies: 30 Ferqui, 1 Mercedes.
Operations: Express.
Livery: Orange
Buses are also provided by Arriva The Shires (see Bedfordshire).

P & J ELLIS LTD

UNIT 3, RADFORD ESTATE, OLD OAK LANE, LONDON NW10 6UA
Tel: 020 8961 1141 **Fax:** 020 8965 5995
E-mail: enquiries@pjellis.co.uk
Web site: www.pjellis.co.uk
Dirs: Matthew Ellis, J Ellis.
Fleet: 16 - 15 single-deck coach, 1 midicoach.
Chassis: 1 Mercedes, 15 Volvo.
Bodies: 13 Jonckheere, 1 Plaxton, 2 Sunsundegui.
Ops incl: excursions & tours, private hire, continental tours.
Livery: White with Red lettering.

ELTHAM EXECUTIVE CHARTER LTD

21-23 CROWN WOODS WAY, LONDON SE9 2NL
Tel: 020 8850 2011
Fax: 020 8850 5210
E-mail: enquiries@eec-minicoaches.co.uk
Web site: www.eec-minicoaches.co.uk
Dirs: Ray Lawrence, Jill Lawrence, Fiona Lawrence.
Fleet: 6 - 3 midicoach, 1 minibus, 2 minicoach.
Chassis: 1 Ford, 5 Iveco.
Bodies: 3 Indcar, 1 Optare, 2 Other.
Ops incl: private hire.
Livery: White with blue and gold graphics

EMPRESS OF LONDON

3 CORBRIDGE CRESCENT, LONDON E2 9DS
Tel: 020 7739 5454
Fax: 020 7729 0237
E-mail: info@empresscoaches.co.uk
Web site: www.empresscoaches.co.uk
Dir: C Clark.
Fleet: single-deck coach, midicoach.
Chassis: Mercedes, Toyota, Volvo.
Bodies: Caetano, Ferqui, Plaxton.
Ops incl: private hire.
Livery: Cream.

EXCALIBUR COACHES

NYES WHARF, FRENSHAM STREET, LONDON SE15 6TH
Tel: 020 7358 1441
Fax: 020 7358 1661
E-mail: office@excaliburcoaches.com
Web site: www.excaliburcoaches.com
Man Dir: Mark Jewell.
Fleet: 25 single-deck coach.
Chassis: 20 Scania, 5 Volvo.
Bodies: 2 Caetano, 19 Irizar, 1 Plaxton, 1 Van Hool, 2 Volvo.
Ops incl: school contracts, excursions & tours, private hire, express, continental tours.
Livery: Blue

FALCON TRAVEL

123 NUTTY LANE, SHEPPERTON TW17 0RQ
Tel: 01932 787752
Fax: 01932 785521
Prop: A Risby.
Fleet: 4 - 3 single-deck coach, 1 minicoach.
Chassis: 1 Mercedes, 3 Volvo.
Bodies: 1 Sitcar, 3 Van Hool.
Ops incl: private hire, school contracts, excursions & tours.
Livery: White/Black/Crimson

FELLSON COACHES

41 STAINFORTH ROAD, ILFORD IG2 7EJ
Tel: 020 8599 7019
Prop: R J Fell.
Fleet: 2 single-deck coach.
Chassis: 2 Volvo.
Ops incl: private hire.

FIRST LONDON

3RD FLOOR, MACMILLAN HOUSE, PADDINGTON STATION, LONDON W2 1TY
Tel: 020 7298 7300
Fax: 020 7706 8789
Web site: www.firstgroup.co.uk
Man Dir: Adrian Jones.

The Little Red Book 2012 - in association with Transport Benevolent Fund

Fleet: 1272 - 758 double-deck bus, 396 single-deck bus, 8 single-deck coach, 54 midibus, 54 articulated bus, 1 minibus, 1 open-top bus.
Chassis: 12 AEC, 366 Alexander Dennis, 265 Dennis, 59 Mercedes, 5 Scania, 171 Transbus, 5 VDL, 377 Volvo, 9 Wrightbus.
Bodies: 1 Alexander, 366 Alexander Dennis, 5 Berkhof, 53 Caetano, 178 Marshall, 58 Mercedes, 3 Northern Counties, 12 Park Royal, 90 Plaxton, 135 Transbus, 371 Wright.
Ops incl: local bus services, school contracts, private hire.
Livery: Red with Yellow.
Ticket System: TfL Prestige

FLIGHTS HALLMARK
See West Midlands, West Sussex

FORESTDALE COACHES LTD
68 VINEY BANK, COURTWOOD LANE, FORESTDALE, ADDINGTON CR0 9JT
Tel/Fax: 020 8651 1359
Chairman/Man Dir: V J Holub
Co Sec: Mrs P R Holub.
Fleet: 1 single-deck coach.
Chassis/Body: Bova.
Ops incl: excursions & tours, private hire, continental tours.
Livery: Red with Gold sign writing

GOLDENSTAND SOUTHERN
13 WAXLOW ROAD, LONDON NW10 7NY
Tel: 020 8961 9974/5
Fax: 020 8961 9949
E-mail: info@goldenstand.com
Web site: www.goldenstand.com
Dir: John Chivrall.
Fleet: 6 single-deck coach.
Chassis: 5 Scania, 1 Volvo.
Ops incl: school contracts, excursions & tours, private hire.
Livery: Red/White

GOLDEN TOURS
123-151 BUCKINGHAM PALACE ROAD, LONDON SW1W 9SH
Tel: 020 7233 7030   **Fax:** 020 7233 7039
Web site: www.goldentours.com
Fleet: 17 open-top bus.
Chassis: 14 Dennis, 3 Volvo.
Bodies: 14 Alexander, 3 Optare.
Ops incl: sightseeing tours.
Livery: Multicoloured.

THE GOLD STANDARD
94A HORSENDEN LANE NORTH, GREENFORD UB6 7QH
Tel: 0845 388 0045
E-mail: paul@luxuryminicoaches.co.uk
Web site: www.luxuryminicoach.co.uk
Prop: Paul Grant.
Fleet: 1 minicoach.
Chassis: Mercedes.
Ops incl: excursions & tours, private hire.

A GREEN COACHES LTD
357A HOE STREET, WALTHAMSTOW, LONDON E17 9AP
Tel: 020 8520 1138
Fax: 020 8520 1139

Recovery: 07563 551679
E-mail: agreencoaches357@aol.com
Web site: www.agreencoaches.co.uk
Fleet Name: Greens of London.
Dirs: Keith Richards, Ms Janis Grover.
Fleet: 5 single-deck coach.
Chassis: 1 Scania, 4 Volvo.
Ops incl: school contracts, private hire, continental tours.
Livery: White.

GRIFFIN EXECUTIVE TRAVEL
47 WALLINGFORD ROAD, UXBRIDGE UB8 2XS
Tel: 01895 430851
E-mail: info@griffinexecutive.com
Web site: www.griffinexecutive.com
Dir: G Griffin.
Fleet: 2 single-deck coach
Chassis: Temsa
Bodies: Temsa
Ops incl: private hire.

GUIDELINE COACHES LONDON LTD
49 WINDERS ROAD, LONDON SW11 3HE
Tel: 020 7228 3515
Fax: 020 7228 0290
Web site: www.guidelinecoaches.co.uk
Dirs: Philip Bruton, Janet Bruton, Thomas McKechnie.
Fleet: 5 - 4 single-deck coach. 1 minicoach.
Chassis: 4 Scania, 1 Toyota.
Bodies: 1 Caetano, 4 Irizar.
Ops incl: excursions & tours, private hire, continental tours, school contracts.
Livery: 2 White/two-tone Blue, 1 White, 2 England sponsors.

HAMILTON OF UXBRIDGE
589-591 UXBRIDGE ROAD, HAYES END UB4 8HP
Tel: 01895 232266
Fax: 01895 810454
Prop: D L Bennett.
Fleet: 9 - 8 single-deck coach, 1 midicoach.
Chassis: 1 Neoplan, 1 Toyota, 7 Volvo.
Bodies: 1 Berkhof, 5 Caetano, 1 Jonckheere, 1 Neoplan, 1 Sunsundegui.
Ops incl: private hire, express, continental tours.

HEARNS COACHES
801 KENTON LANE, HARROW WEALD HA3 6AH
Tel: 020 8954 0444
Fax: 020 8954 5959
E-mail: admin@hearns-coaches.co.uk
Web site: www.hearns-coaches.co.uk
Prop: R J Hearn **Ops Man:** Ged Newham
Ch Eng: Dave Berry.
Fleet: 33 - 29 single-deck coach, 2 midicoach, 2 minicoach.
Chassis: 2 MAN, 9 Mercedes, 2 Neoplan, 9 Scania, 11 Setra.
Ops incl: private hire, school contracts, excursions & tours, continental tours.
Livery: Blue

JOHN HOUGHTON LUXURY MINI COACHES
2 ELGAR AVENUE, EALING, LONDON W5 3JU
Tel: 020 8567 0056

Fax: 020 8567 5781
E-mail: john@luxuryminicoaches.co.uk
Web site: www.luxuryminicoaches.co.uk
Man Dir: John Houghton **Co Sec:** M Houghton.
Fleet: 2 minicoach.
Chassis: 2 Mercedes.
Ops incl: private hire
Livery: White

HOUNSLOW MINI COACHES
2 VINEYARD ROAD, HIGH STREET, FELTHAM TW13 4HQ
Tel: 020 8890 8429
Fax: 020 8893 1736
E-mail: hounslowminicoaches@btconnect.com
Web site: www.hounslowminicoaches.co.uk
Prop: G J Cooke-Willing.
Fleet: 7 - 6 minibus, 1 minicoach
Chassis: 1 Iveco, 6 Mercedes.
Ops incl: school contracts, private hire.

HOUSTON'S OF LONDON
Ceased trading since LRB 2011 went to press.

VIC HUGHES & SON LTD
61 FERN GROVE, FELTHAM TW14 9AY
Tel: 020 8831 0770
Fax: 020 8831 0660
Man Dir: V B Hughes **Co Sec:** Mrs V Hughes
Dir: K Hughes.
Fleet: 12 - 6 midicoach, 6 minibus.
Chassis: LDV, Mercedes.
Ops incl: school contracts, excursions & tours, private hire.
Livery: White/Black.

IMPACT OF LONDON
7-9 WADSWORTH ROAD, GREENFORD UB6 7JZ
Tel: 020 8601 3555 **Fax:** 020 8601 3502
E-mail: info@impactgroup.co.uk
Web site: www.impactgroup.co.uk
Dir: A Hill **Gen Mans:** A Palmer, M O'Conner
Engs: H Louis, L Singh.
Fleet: 85 – 1 double-deck bus, 14 single-deck coach, 2 midibus, 25 midicoach, 43 minibus.
Chassis: Alexander Dennis, DAF, Dennis, Iveco, LDV, Leyland, Mercedes, Scania, Volvo.
Ops incl: excursions & tours, private hire, express, continental tours, school contracts.
Livery: White.

IMPERIAL COACHES LTD
80 SCOTTS ROAD, SOUTHALL UB2 5DE
Tel: 020 8574 0028 **Fax:** 020 8574 0061
E-mail: imperialcoaches1@hotmail.com
Web site: www.imperialcoaches.co.uk
Fleet: 8 – 3 double-deck coach, 5 single-deck coach.
Chassis: 8 Volvo.
Bodies: 3 Optare, 5 Van Hool.
Ops incl: school contracts, excursions & tours, private hire.
Livery: White/Silver.

INTERNATIONAL COACH LINES
19 NURSERY ROAD, THORNTON HEATH CR7 8RE
Tel: 020 8684 8308
Fax: 020 8689 3483
Recovery: 07738 282840

E-mail: louise@internationalcoachlines.co.uk
Web site: www.internationalcoaches.co.uk
Fleet Name: I.C.L.
Dirs: Sue Wood, Louise Gaynor.
Fleet: 23 - 2 double-deck bus, 6 single-deck coach, I double-deck coach, 14 minibus.
Chassis: 2 AEC, 4 Ford Transit, 3 Iveco, 7 LDV, 2 Scania, 2 Setra, 3 Volvo.
Bodies: I Berkhof, I Jonckheere, 7 LDV, 2 Park Royal, 2 Plaxton, I Scania, 2 Setra, 8 Other.
Ops incl: school contracts, private hire, continental tours.
Livery: Blue/White.

J & D EUROTRAVEL
58 WEALD LANE, HARROW WEALD HA3 5EX
Tel: 020 8861 1829
Fax: 020 8424 2585
E-mail: jdetravel1@aol.com
Man Dir: J T Thomas.
Fleet: 9 - 3 single-deck coach, 3 midicoach, 3 minibus.
Ops incl: school contracts, excursions & tours, private hire, express, continental tours.
Livery: White

THE KINGS FERRY
See Kent

LEOLINE TRAVEL
UPPER SUNBURY ROAD, HAMPTON TW12 2DW
Tel: 020 8941 3370
Fax: 020 8941 3372
E-mail: leolinecoaches@aol.com
Web site: www.leolinetravel.co.uk
Prop: David Baker **Ops Man:** Judy Dale.
Fleet: 6 - 5 single-deck coach, I midicoach.
Chassis: 3 Iveco, I Toyota, 2 Volvo.
Bodies: 3 Beulas, I Caetano, 2 Van Hool.
Ops incl: excursions & tours, private hire, school contracts.
Livery: Blue/Orange

LEWIS TRAVEL
UNIT 2, BUILDING 3, ASHLEIGH COMMERCIAL ESTATE, 86 WESTMOOR STREET, CHARLTON SE7 8NQ
Tel: 020 8858 0031
Fax: 020 8858 7631
E-mail: info@lewistravel.co.uk
Web site: www.lewistravel.co.uk
Fleet: 14 - 9 single-deck coach, 3 minibus, 2 minicoach.
Chassis: DAF, Mercedes, Volvo.
Ops incl: school contracts, excursions & tours, private hire, continental tours.
Livery: incl. Red

LINK LINE COACHES LTD
I WROTTESLEY ROAD, LONDON NW10 5XA
Tel: 020 8965 2221
Fax: 020 8961 3680
E-mail: info@linkline-coaches.co.uk
Web site: www.linkline-coaches.co.uk
Ops Dir: T J Russell.
Fleet: 10 - 8 midibus, 2 minibus.
Chassis: 2 Alexander Dennis, 6 Dennis, I Mercedes, I Optare.
Bodies: I Alexander Dennis, 7 Caetano,

I Optare, I Other.
Ops incl: contracts, private hire.
Livery: White.
A subsidiary of TGM Group Ltd, part of Arriva

THE LITTLE BUS COMPANY
HOME FARM, ALDENHAM ROAD, ELSTREE WD6 3AZ
Tel: 020 8953 0202
Fax: 020 8953 9553
E-mail: enquiry@littlebus.co.uk
Web site: www.littlebus.co.uk
Prop: Jeremy Reese.
Fleet: 7 minibus.
Chassis: 5 LDV, 2 Ford Transit.
Ops incl: school contracts, private hire.

LONDON CENTRAL BUS CO LTD
LONDON GENERAL TRANSPORT SERVICES LTD
18 MERTON HIGH STREET, LONDON SW19 1DN
Tel: 020 8545 6100
Fax: 020 8545 6101
E-mail: enquiries@go-ahead-london.com
Web site: www.go-ahead-london.com
Fleet Names: London Central, London General.
Ch Exec: John Trayner **Eng Dir:** Phil Margrave
Fin Dir: Paul Reeves **Ops Dir:** David Cutts.
Fleet: 1497 - 1029 double-deck bus, 377 single-deck bus, 91 articulated bus.
Chassis: 373 Alexander Dennis, 111 Dennis, 141 Mercedes, 14 Scania, 843 Volvo, 15 Wrightbus.
Bodies: 276 Alexander Dennis, 17 East Lancs, 6 MCV, 141 Mercedes, 94 Optare, 438 Plaxton, 524 Wright.
Ops incl: local bus services, school contracts, excursions & tours, private hire.
Livery: Red
Ticket System: TfL Prestige.
Subsidiaries of the Go-Ahead Group.

LONDON MINI COACHES LTD
UNIT 23, AIRLINKS INDUSTRIAL ESTATE, SPITFIRE WAY, HESTON TW5 9NR
Tel: 020 8589 0795
Fax: 020 8589 0796
E-mail: info@lmcoaches.co.uk
Web site: www.lmcoaches.co.uk
Fleet Names: London Mini Coaches, Windsorian.
Man Dir: Mark Anderson.
Fleet: 18 - single-deck coach, midicoach, minicoach.
Chassis: Mercedes, Temsa.
Bodies: Ferqui, Sitcar, Temsa.
Ops incl: school contracts, private hire, excursions & tours.
Liveries: Silver/Maroon (London Mini Coaches); Blue/White (Windsorian).
A subsidiary of the Anderson Travel Group.

LONDON SOVEREIGN
APPROACH ROAD, EDGWARE, MIDDLESEX HA8 7AN
Tel: 020 8238 5500 **Fax:** 020 8238 5519
E-mail: customerservices@londonsovereign.co.uk
Web site: www.transdevplc.co.uk
Fleet: 127 – 72 double-deck bus, 48 single-deck bus, 7 midibus.
Chassis: 14 Alexander Dennis, 28 Dennis,

48 Scania, 13 Transbus, 24 Volvo.
Bodies: I Alexander, 14 Alexander Dennis, 41 East Lancs, 38 Plaxton, 20 Scania, 13 Transbus.
Ops Incl: local bus services, private hire.
Livery: Red
Ticket System: TfL Prestige.
A subsidiary of the Veolia-Transdev Group

LONDON TRAMLINK
See Section 5 – Tram and Bus Rapid Transit Systems.

LONDON UNITED BUSWAYS LTD
BUSWAYS HOUSE, WELLINGTON ROAD, TWICKENHAM TW2 5NX
Tel: 020 8400 6665
Fax: 020 8943 2688
E-mail: customer@lonutd.co.uk
Web site: www.londonutd.co.uk
Man Dir: Richard Casling **Human Res Dir:** Karen Fuller **Eng Dir:** Les Birchley **Comm Man:** Steffan Evans. **Fleet:** 937 - 475 double-deck bus, 436 single-deck bus, 26 midibus.
Chassis: I AEC, 226 Alexander Dennis, 149 Dennis, 7 MAN, 52 Optare, 222 Scania, 155 Transbus, 125 Volvo.
Bodies: 113 Alexander, 226 Alexander Dennis, 78 East Lancs, 59 Optare, I Park Royal, 132 Plaxton, 186 Scania, 139 Transbus, 3 Wright.
Ops Incl: local bus services, private hire.
Livery: Red
Ticket system: TfL Prestige.
A subsidiary of RATP Dev UK Ltd

M C H MINIBUSES LTD
47 WALLINGFORD ROAD, UXBRIDGE UB8 2XS
Tel: 01895 230643 **Fax:** 01895 234891
E-mail: info@mchbuses.demon.co.uk
Web site: www.mch-coaches.co.uk
Fleet: 40 - double-deck coach, single-deck coach, midicoach, midicoach, minibus.
Chassis incl: Irisbus, King Long, Mercedes, Neoplan, Setra.
Ops incl: excursions & tours, private hire, continental tours.
Livery: White with Blue

MEMORY LANE VINTAGE OMNIBUS SERVICES
78 LILLIBROOKE CRESCENT, MAIDENHEAD SL6 3XQ
Tel: 01628 825050 **Fax:** 01628 825851
E-mail: admin@memorylane.co.uk
Web site: www.memorylane.co.uk
Prop: M J Clarke.
Fleet: 6 - 3 double-deck bus, 3 single-deck bus.
Chassis: 6 AEC.
Bodies: 2 ECW, 3 Park Royal, I Willowbrook.
Ops incl: private hire.
Livery: Original operators

METROBUS LTD
See West Sussex

METROLINE TRAVEL LTD
COMFORT DELGRO HOUSE, 3rd FLOOR, 329 EDGWARE ROAD, CRICKLEWOOD, LONDON NW2 6JP
Tel: 020 8218 8888
Fax: 020 8218 8899

E-mail: info@metroline.co.uk
Web site: www.metroline.co.uk
Chief Exec Off: Jaspal Singh **Ch Op Officer:**
Sean O'Shea **Fin Dir:** Damian Rowbotham
Eng Dir: Ian Foster.
Fleet: 1261 - 910 double-deck bus,
324 single-deck bus, 1 open top bus, 26 midibus.
Chassis: 3 AEC, 417 Alexander Dennis,
220 Dennis, 38 MAN, 5 Optare, 33 Scania,
169 Transbus, 374 Volvo.
Bodies: 50 Alexander, 409 Alexander Dennis,
33 East Lancs, 48 MCV, 5 Optare, 3 Park Royal,
281 Plaxton, 363 Transbus, 69 Wright.
Ops incl: local bus services, school contracts,
private hire.
Livery: Red
Ticket System: TfL Prestige.
A subsidiary of the Comfort Delgro Group

MT P CHARTER COACHES
Ceased trading since LRB 2011 went to press.

NEW BHARAT COACHES LTD
1A PRIORY WAY, SOUTHALL UB2 5EB
Tel: 020 8574 6817 **Fax:** 020 8813 9555
E-mail: bharatcoaches@aol.com
Web site: www.newbharat.co.uk
Dir: Surjit Singh Dhaliwal
Ch Eng: Alan Littlemore.
Fleet: 10 – 2 double-deck coach, 6 single-deck
coach, 2 midicoach.
Chassis: 2 Mercedes, 8 Volvo.
Ops incl: school contracts, excursions & tours,
private hire, express, continental tours.
Livery: Red/Yellow/Blue on white base.

NEWBOURNE COACHES
R24
FIRBANK WAY, LEIGHTON BUZZARD
LU7 4YP
Tel: 020 7837 6663
Fax: 01525 850967
E-mail: info@marshalls-coaches.co.uk
Web site: www.marshalls-coaches.co.uk
Prop: G R Marshall **Ops Man:** Ian White
Ch Eng: Bob Barnard.
Fleet: See Marshalls Coaches
Ops incl: private hire, school contracts, local bus
services.
Livery: Blue/Multicoloured.
A subsidiary of Marshalls Coaches - see
Bedfordshire.

OFJ CONNECTIONS LTD
BUILDING 16300 MT2, ELECTRA AVENUE,
HEATHROW AIRPORT, HOUNSLOW,
MIDDLESEX, TW6 2DN
Tel: 020 8754 7375 **Fax:** 020 8759 6589
E-mail: enquiries@ofjbus.com
Web site: www.ofjbus.com
Ops Inc: school contracts, private hire, airport
transfers.
Livery: White
A subsidiary of TGM Group Ltd, part of Arriva

THE ORIGINAL LONDON TOUR
JEWS ROW, LONDON SW18 1TB
Tel: 020 8877 1722 **Fax:** 020 8877 1968
E-mail: info@theoriginaltour.com
Web site: www.theoriginaltour.com
Man Dir: Colin Atkins **Ops Dir:** Alistair Fraser
Head of Comm Devt: Ms N Crump.
Fleet: 93 open-top bus.

Chassis: 14 DAF, 38 Leyland, 21 MCW, 20 Volvo.
Bodies: 38 Alexander, 10 Ayats, 10 East Lancs,
21 MCW, 14 Plaxton.
Ops incl: London Sightseeing Tours.
Livery: Red/Cream.
A subsidiary of Arriva

P & A TRAVEL
62 SOUTH PARK TERRACE, ILFORD IG1 1YB
Tel: 020 8478 2621
Web site: www.pandatravelilford.co.uk
Dir: A Peart.
Fleet: 2 single-deck coach.
Chassis: Volvo.
Bodies: Jonckheere.
Ops incl: private hire.
Livery: White

REDWING COACHES
10 DYLAN ROAD, LONDON SE24 0HL
Tel: 020 7733 1124 **Fax:** 020 7733 5194
E-mail: redwingsales@redwing-coaches.co.uk.
Web site: www.redwing-coaches.co.uk.
Gen Man: Paul Hockley **Ops Man:** Nigel Taylor
Asst Gen Man: Colin Miller **Ch Eng:** Robbie
Hodgekiss.
Fleet: 61 – 56 single-deck coach, 1 midicoach,
4 minicoach.
Chassis: 34 Mercedes, 7 Neoplan, 20 Setra.
Bodies: 4 Ferqui, 30 Mercedes, 7 Neoplan,
20 Setra.
Ops incl: excursions & tours, private hire,
continental tours.
Livery: Red/Cream
A subsidiary of Addison Lee PLC

ROUNDABOUT BUSES LTD
See Kent.

ROYALE EUROPEAN COACHES
PHOENIX DISTRIBUTION PARK, PHOENIX
WAY, HESTON TW5 9NB
Tel: 020 8754 0322 **Fax:** 020 8897 9583
E-mail: royaleeuropean@aol.com
Web site: www.royaleeuropean.co.uk
Prop: J Kent.
Fleet: 8 – double-deck coach, single-deck coach,
midicoach.
Chassis: Mercedes, Neoplan, Volvo.
Ops incl: private hire.
Livery: Red/Grey/White

SILVERDALE LONDON LTD
UNIT 11, SHAKESPEARE INDUSTRIAL ESTATE,
SHAKESPEARE STREET, WATFORD WD24 5RR
Tel: 01923 248170
Fax: 01923 223793
E-mail: silverdalelondon@aol.com
Web site: www.silverdalelondon.co.uk
Dirs: John Doherty, Shaun Doherty, Robert
Green **Tran Man:** Richard Cassell.
Ops incl: school contracts, excursions & tours,
private hire, express, continental tours.
Livery: White/Red
A subsidiary of Silverdale Tours - see
Nottinghamshire.

SOUTHGATE & FINCHLEY COACHES LTD
231A COLNEY HATCH LANE, LONDON
N11 3DG
Tel: 020 8368 0040 **Fax:** 020 8361 1934

E-mail: bookingsoffice@btconnect.com
Web site:
www.southgate-finchley-coaches.co.uk
Man Dir: M P Rice **Dirs:** Mrs V M Rice
(Co Sec), P. M Rice, Mrs E B Scrivens.
Fleet: 24 - 23 single-deck coach, 1 minibus.
Chassis: 1 Iveco, 23 Volvo.
Bodies: 5 Jonckheere, 18 Plaxton, 1 Other.
Ops incl: school contracts, excursions and tours,
private hire.
Livery: Yellow/Blue/Orange

SPEEDICARS GROUP
COULGATE STREET, BROCKLEY SE4 2RW
Tel: 020 8694 2244 **Fax:** 020 7732 1102
E-mail: info@speedicars.co.uk
Web site: www.speedicars.co.uk
Bookings Consultant: Mike Luther.
Fleet: single-deck coach, midicoach, minicoach.
Chassis: Mercedes, Setra, Volkswagen.
Ops incl: private hire.
Livery: White with Blue.

STAGECOACH LONDON
WEST HAM GARAGE, STEPHENSON STREET,
CANNING TOWN, LONDON E16 4SA
Tel: 020 7055 9600 **Fax:** 020 7055 9762
E-mail: PR.London@stagecoachlondon.com
Web site: www.stagecoachbus.com
Man Dir: Mark Threapleton.
Fleet: 1464 – 1174 double-deck bus,
241 single-deck bus, 49 midibus.
Chassis: 11 AEC, 300 Alexander Dennis,
529 Dennis, 19 Optare, 174 Scania, 441 Transbus.
Bodies: 511 Alexander, 311 Alexander Dennis,
19 Optare, 11 Park Royal, 18 Plaxton, 174 Scania,
441 Transbus.
Operations: local bus services.
Livery: Red
Ticket System: TfL Prestige.

SUNBURY COACHES
204A CHARLTON ROAD, SHEPPERTON
TW17 0SJ
Tel: 01932 785153 **Fax:** 01932 789937
E-mail: sunburycoaches@tiscali.co.uk
Dirs: P Jones, D Jones.
Fleet: 6 - 4 single-deck coach, 1 midicoach,
1 minicoach.
Chassis: 2 DAF, 3 Iveco, 1 Toyota.
Bodies: 3 Beulas, 1 Caetano, 1 Plaxton,
1 Van Hool.
Ops incl: school contracts, excursions & tours,
private hire.
Livery: White/Turquoise/Navy Blue.

TGM GROUP LTD
BUILDING 16300 MT2, ELECTRA AVENUE,
HEATHROW AIRPORT, HOUNSLOW
TW6 2DN
Tel: 020 8757 4700 **Fax:** 020 8757 4799
E-mail: info@tellings.co.uk
Web site: www.tellingsgoldenmiller.co.uk
Fleet Name: Tellings Golden Miller.
Group Man Dir: Paul Churchman **Regional
Man Dir (South):** Matt Clayson **Group Eng
Dir:** Richard Telling **Fin Dir/Co Sec:** Basil Taylor.
Ops incl: school contracts, excursions & tours,
private hire, express, continental tours.
Livery: White/Blue/Yellow
A subsidiary of Arriva

TIMEBUS TRAVEL

7 BOLEYN DRIVE, St ALBANS AL1 2BP
Tel: 01727 866248
Web site: www.timebus.co.uk
Fleet Name: Timebus.
Prop: David Pring.
Fleet: 15 - 12 double-deck bus, 1 single-deck bus, 2 open-top bus.
Chassis: 15 AEC.
Bodies: 1 Metro-Cammell, 13 Park Royal, 1 Weymann.
Ops incl: private hire
Livery: Red with grey lining

TRINA COACHES LTD

80 GLOUCESTER PLACE, LONDON
W1U 6HL
Tel: 020 7935 7688
Fleet: 6 – 5 single-deck coach, 1 midicoach.
Chassis: 1 Toyota, 1 Van Hool, 4 Volvo.
Bodies: 1 Caetano, 5 Van Hool.
Ops incl: excursions & tours.
Livery: Silver/Blue.

VENTURE TRANSPORT (HENDON) (1965) LTD

307 PINNER ROAD, HARROW
HA14HG
Tel: 020 8427 0101
Fax: 020 8427 1707
Ops incl: private hire.
A subsidiary of Hearns Coaches, Harrow Weald

WESTBUS COACH SERVICES LTD

27A SPRING GROVE ROAD, HOUNSLOW
TW3 4BE
Tel: 020 8572 6348
Fax: 020 8570 2234
Recovery: 020 8572 6348
E-mail: reservations@westbus.co.uk
Web site: www.westbus.co.uk
Gen Man: Tim Miles
Ops Man: Chris Shaw
Ch Eng: Graham Bessant.
Fleet: 37 – 3 double-deck bus, 29 single-deck coach, 2 double-deck coach, 3 midicoach.

Chassis: DAF, Mercedes, Scania, Setra, Van Hool, VDL, Volvo.
Bodies: Alexander, Berkhof, Irizar, Setra, Sitcar, Van Hool.
Ops incl: private hire, continental tours, excursions & tours, school contracts.
Livery: Red/Beige
Part of the Comfort Delgro Corporation

WEST'S COACHES LTD

198/200 HIGH ROAD, WOODFORD GREEN, IG8 9EF
Tel: 020 8504 9747
Fax: 020 8559 1085
E-mail: info@westscoaches.myzen.co.uk
Web site: www.westscoaches.co.uk
Dirs: R L West, Mrs E J M West, Mrs M M West.
Fleet: 15 single-deck coach.
Chassis: 8 Alexander Dennis, 1 Iveco, 6 Volvo.
Bodies: 1 Caetano, 2 Marcopolo, 11 Plaxton, 1 UVG.
Ops incl: excursions & tours, private hire, school contracts, continental tours.
Livery: Red/White/Blue

WESTWAY COACH SERVICES LTD

7A RAINBOW INDUSTRIAL ESTATE, STATION APPROACH, RAYNES PARK, LONDON SW20 0JY
Tel: 020 8944 1277
Fax: 020 8947 5339
E-mail: info@westway-coaches.co.uk
Web site: www.westwaycoachservices.com
Prop: David West
Ops Man: Peter Minnette
Coach Services Man: Kevin Pates.
Fleet: 24 - 11 single-deck coach, 11 double-deck coach, 2 midicoach, 1 minicoach.
Chassis: 1 EOS, 3 Mercedes, 1 Van Hool, 20 Volvo.
Bodies: 1 EOS, 5 Jonckheere, 2 Plaxton, 2 Sitcar, 16 Van Hool, 1 Other.
Ops incl: school contracts, excursions & tours, private hire, continental tours.
Livery: Blue/Orange

WINGS LUXURY TRAVEL LTD

47 WALLINGFORD ROAD, UXBRIDGE
UB8 2XS
Tel: 01895 239999
Fax: 01895 270022
E-mail: info@wingstravel.co.uk
Web site: www.wings-luxury-coach-hire.co.uk
Chairman: F L Gritt
Gen Man: W Gritt
Ops Man: S Hughes.
Fleet: 14 - 7 midicoach, 4 minicoach, 3 minibus.
Chassis: 14 Mercedes.
Ops Incl: school contracts, excursions and tours, private hire.
Livery: White

A1A LTD
373 CLEVELAND STREET, BIRKENHEAD
CH41 4JW
Tel: 0151 650 1616 **Fax:** 0151 650 0007
Web site: www.a1atravel.co.uk
Prop: Barbara Ashworth.
Fleet: 14 - 1 single-deck bus, 2 midibus,
11 minibus.
Chassis: Dennis, Ford, LDV, Mercedes,
Volkswagen.
Ops incl: local bus services, school contracts,
private hire.
Livery: White/Blue

A2B TRAVEL UK LTD
PRENTON WAY, NORTH CHESHIRE TRADING
ESTATE, PRENTON CH43 3DU
Tel: 0151 609 0600 **Fax:** 0151 609 0601
E-mail: info@a2b-travel.com
Web site: www.a2b-travel.com
Dirs: G Evans, D Evans.
Fleet: 25 - 2 single-deck coach, 9 midibus,
2 midicoach, 12 minibus
Chassis: 1 Dennis, 1 Iveco, 9 LDV, 5 Mercedes,
9 Optare.
Ops incl: school contracts, private hire,
excursions & tours.
Livery: White/Blue

ACE TRAVEL NORTH WEST LTD
BARCLAY TRADING ESTATE, WAREING
ROAD, AINTREE L9 7AU
Tel: 0151 203 3920
Fleet: 28 – double-deck bus, single-deck bus,
open-top bus, midibus.
Ops incl: local bus services, Liverpool sightseeing
tours.
Liveries: Maroon/Cream, City Sightseeing.

AINTREE COACHLINE
11 CLARE ROAD, BOOTLE L20 9LY
Tel: 0151 922 8630
Fax: 0151 933 6994
Fleet: 42 – double-deck bus, single-deck bus,
single-deck coach, midibus.
Ops incl: local bus services, school contracts,
private hire.
Livery: Red/Cream.
Incorporating Helms of Eastham.

ALS COACHES LTD
400 CELEVELAND STREET, BIRKENHEAD
CH41 8EQ
Tel: 0151 6530222
Fax: 0151 6700509
Fleet Name: Happy Al's
Man Dir: T A Cullinan **Gen Man:** M Cullinan
Tran Man: C Cullinan.
Fleet: 73 - 51 double-deck bus, 9 single-deck bus,
13 single-deck coach.
Chassis: 1 Bova, 7 DAF, 1 Leyland, 64 Volvo.
Ops incl: school contracts, private hire,
excursions & tours.
Ticket System: Wayfarer
Livery: Red/Gold

ARRIVA NORTH WEST & WALES
73 ORMSKIRK ROAD, AINTREE,
LIVERPOOL L9 5AE
Tel: 0151 522 2800

Fax: 0151 525 9556
Web site: www.arriva.co.uk
Regional Man Dir: Phil Stone **Reg Fin Dir:**
Simon Mills **Reg Eng Dir:** Phil Cummins
Area Man Dir (Merseyside): Howard Farrall
Area Man Dir (Manchester): John Rimmer
Area Man Dir (Wales): Michael Morton.
Fleet: 1209 - 187 double-deck bus, 873 single-
deck bus, 11 articulated bus, 129 midibus,
8 open-top bus, 1 minibus.
Chassis: 49 Alexander Dennis, 517 DAF/VDL,
347 Dennis, 7 Leyland, 5 MAN, 11 Mercedes,
53 Optare, 64 Scania, 156 Volvo
Bodies: 178 Alexander Dennis, 4 ECW, 38 East
Lancs, 10 Ikarus, 64 Marshall/MCV, 11 Mercedes,
74 Northern Counties, 53 Optare, 276 Plaxton,
3 Scania, 498 Wright.
Ops incl: local bus services, school contracts.
Livery: Arriva UK Bus
Ticket System: Wayfarer TGX

G. ASHTON COACHES
WATERY LANE, ST HELENS WA9 3JA
Tel: 01744 733275
Fax: 01744 454122
E-mail: enquiries@gashtoncoachholidays.co.uk
Web site: www.gashtoncoachholidays.co.uk
Prop: Simon Ashton.
Fleet: 6- 4 single-deck coach, 1 double-deck
coach, 1 midicoach.
Chassis: 2 Scania, 1 Toyota, 2 Van Hool, 1 VDL.
Bodies: 1 Berkhof, 1 Caetano, 2 Irizar, 2 Van Hool.
Ops incl: excursions & tours, private hire,
continental tours.
Livery: Multicoloured

AVON BUSES LTD
10 BROOKWAY, NORTH CHESHIRE TRADING
ESTATE, PRENTON CH43 3DT
Tel: 0151 608 8000
Fax: 0151 608 9955
Props: Larry Smith, George Lewis
Ops Man: George Lewis.
Fleet: 36 – 35 single-deck bus, 1 midibus.
Chassis: 11 Alexander Dennis, 20 Dennis,
1 Enterprise, 4 Volvo.
Ops incl: local bus services, school contracts,
excursions & tours, private hire.
Livery: Cream with Blue and Gold stripe.
Ticket System: Wayfarer.

BLUELINE TRAVEL
54 STATION ROAD, MAGHULL
L31 3DB
Tel: 0151 526 5050
Fax: 0151 526 2727
E-mail: blueline5050@hotmail.com
Web site: www.bluelineuk.com
Prop: C P Carr.
Fleet: 12 – 3 double-deck bus, 3 single-deck
coach, 2 midicoach, 2 minibus.
Ops incl: private hire, school contracts.
Livery: White

CUMFYBUS LTD
178 CAMBRIDGE ROAD, SOUTHPORT
PR9 7LW
Tel: 01704 227321
Fax: 01704 505781

E-mail: info@cumfybus.co.uk
Web site: www.cumfybus.co.uk
Man Dir: M R Vickers **Admin:** Mrs P Lyon.
Fleet: 104 – 2 double-deck bus, 12 single-deck
bus, 65 midibus, 25 minibus.
Chassis: 8 DAF, 4 Dennis, 2 Leyland, 87 Optare,
3 Renault.
Bodies: 4 Caetano, 8 East Lancs, 2 Leyland,
87 Optare, 3 Other.
Ops incl: local bus services, school contracts.
Livery: Yellow

EAZIBUS
OLD HALL ROAD, BROMBOROUGH,
WIRRAL CH62 3PE
Tel: 07977 470577
Fleet: 15 – 5 single-deck bus, 8 midibus,
2 minibus.
Chassis: 5 Alexander Dennis, 2 LDV, 8 Optare.
Ops incl: local bus services.
Livery: White

FIRST MANCHESTER LTD
THE PEBBLES, LIVERPOOL ROAD,
CHESTER CH2 1AE
Tel: 08708 500 868 **Fax:** 01782 592541
Web site: www.firstgroup.com
Fleet Name: First in Chester and the Wirral
See Greater Manchester

FIVE STAR TRAVEL
SNAPE GATE, FOX'S BANK LANE,
WHISTON, PRESCOT L35 3SS
Tel: 0151 481 0000
Fax: 0151 493 9999
E-mail: admin@fivestar.freeserve.co.uk
Web site: www.fivestartravel.co.uk
Prop: Phil Riley.
Fleet: 2 single-deck coach.
Chassis: 2 DAF.
Bodies: 2 Bova.
Ops incl: excursions & tours, private hire,
continental tours.
Livery: White

FORMBY COACHWAYS LTD
38 STEPHENSON WAY, FORMBY
L37 8EG
Tel: 01704 834448
Fax: 01704 878820
Fleet Name: Freshfield Coaches.
Man Dir: K W Bradley **Sec:** D A Bradley.
Fleet: 1 minicoach.
Chassis/Body: Mercedes.
Ops incl: school contracts, private hire.
Livery: Green/Silver

HARDINGS TOURS LTD
A subsidiary of Selwyn's Travel – see Cheshire

HATTON'S TRAVEL
WALKERS LANE, ST HELENS WA9 4AF
Tel: 01744 822818
E-mail: enquiries@hattonstravel.co.uk
Web site: www.hattonstravel.co.uk
Fleet: 26 – double-deck bus, single-deck bus,
single-deck coach, midibus.
Ops incl: local bus services, school contracts,
private hire, excursions & tours, continental tours.
Livery: White with Blue/Red

HUYTON TRAVEL LTD
37 WILSON ROAD, LIVERPOOL L36 6AN
Tel: 0151 449 3868
E-mail: info@huytontravel.co.uk
Web site: www.huytontravel.co.uk
Fleet Name: HTL Buses.
Fleet: 46 – 5 single-deck bus, 23 midibus, 18 minibus.
Chassis: Alexander Dennis, Dennis, Mercedes, Optare, Renault, Transbus, Volkswagen.
Bodies: Alexander Dennis, Alexander, Koch, Marshall, Optare, Plaxton, Rohill, Transbus.
Ops incl: local bus services, school contracts.
Livery: Green

IMPERA BUS & COACH LTD
21 TARRAN WAY NORTH, TARRAN INDUSTRIAL ESTATE, WIRRAL CH46 4UA
Tel: 0151 641 0897
Web site: www.imperbuscoachwirral.co.uk
Fleet: single-deck bus.
Ops incl: local bus services.

MAGHULL COACHES LTD
1 CANAL STREET, BOOTLE L20 8AE
Tel: 0151 922 4284
Fax: 0151 9227521
E-mail: maghullcoaches@tiscali.co.uk
Web site: www.maghullcoaches.co.uk
Dirs: B Reilly, C Reilly, J Reilly, A Meek
Fleet Eng: P Bucknall.
Fleet: 44 – double-deck bus, double-deck coach, single-deck coach, open-top bus, midibus, midicoach, minibus.
Chassis: Bedford, Dennis, LDV, Leyland, MAN, MCW, Mercedes, Neoplan, Scania, Volvo.
Ops incl: school contracts, private hire, sightseeing tours.
Livery: Wed/Orange/White.

MAYPOLE COACHES
Ceased operations since LRB 2011 went to press.

GAVIN MURRAY & ELLISONS TRAVEL SERVICES
QUEENS GARAGE, 61 BOUNDARY ROAD, ST HELENS WA10 2LX
Tel: 0800 917 4917
Fax: 01744 24402
Web site: www.ellisonstravel.com
Dirs: A Magowan, M Magowan.

Fleet: 23 – 20 single-deck coach, 3 midicoach.
Chassis: 6 VDL Bova, 4 Mercedes, 4 Neoplan, 5 Van Hool, 4 Volvo.
Bodies: 6 VDL Bova, 4 Jonckheere, 1 Mercedes, 4 Neoplan, 5 Van Hool, 2 Other.
Ops incl: private hire.
Livery: Silver

DAVID OGDEN COACHES
BAXTERS LANE, SUTTON, ST HELENS WA9 3DH
Tel: 01744 606176
Fax: 01744 822146
E-mail: reservations@davidogdenholidays.co.uk
Web site: www.davidogdenholidays.co.uk
Prop: John David Ogden
Co Sec: Carol Ogden.
Fleet: 19 – 5 single-deck bus, 12 single-deck coach, 2 minibus.
Chassis: 1 Bova, 7 DAF, 1 Dennis, 2 EOS, 1 Ford Transit, 1 Leyland, 2 Mercedes, 2 Optare, 1 Temsa, 1 Van Hool.
Ops incl: school contracts, excursions & tours, private hire, continental tours.
Livery: Red/White/Blue.

PEOPLES BUS LTD
CUSTOMER SERVICE CENTRE, PO BOX 57, LIVERPOOL L9 8YZ
Tel: 0151 523 4010
Fax: 0151 523 4010
Recovery: 07885 417847
E-mail: enquiries@peoplesbus.com
Web site: www.peoplesbus.com
Man Dir: Andrew Cawley.
Ops incl: local bus services, school contracts, private hire.
Fleet: 21 – 10 double-deck bus, 8 single-deck bus, 1 single-deck coach, 1 articulated bus, 1 minibus.
Chassis: 6 Dennis, 1 Leyland, 3 Optare, 1 Scania, 10 Volvo.
Bodies: 13 Alexander Dennis, 1 Irizar, 2 Northern Counties, 3 Optare, 2 Wright.
Ops incl: local bus services, school contracts, private hire.
Livery: Blue/Pink.
Ticket System: Wayfarer.

SANDGROUNDER COACHES
Ceased trading since LRB 2011 went to press.

STAGECOACH MERSEYSIDE AND SOUTH LANCASHIRE
GILMOSS DEPOT, EAST LANCASHIRE ROAD, LIVERPOOL L11 0BB
Tel: 0151 330 6200   **Fax:** 0151 330 6210
E-mail: enquiries.merseyside@stagecoachbus.com
Web site: www.stagecoachbus.com
Fleet Name: Stagecoach in Merseyside
Man Dir: Elisabeth Tasker **Eng Dir:** Paul W Lee
Ops Dir: Les Burton **Ops Man:** James Byrne.
Fleet: 361 - 100 double-deck bus, 218 single-deck bus, 2 single-deck coach, 41 midibus.
Chassis: 39 Alexander Dennis, 114 Dennis, 2 Leyland, 52 MAN, 51 Optare, 33 Scania, 70 Volvo.
Ops incl: local bus services, school contracts, excursions & tours, private hire, express.
Livery: Stagecoach UK Bus
Ticket System: Wayfarer TGX

STRAWBERRY
ROLLING SOLUTIONS LTD, 2 LOCK STREET, ST HELENS WA9 1HS
Tel: 01744 612856
E-mail: oliverhowarth@strawberrybus.co.uk
Web site: www.strawberrybus.co.uk
Dirs: O S Howarth, L Howarth, D Reeves.
Fleet: 18 single-deck bus.
Chassis: 16 Dennis, 2 Scania.
Bodies: 12 Alexander, 4 Plaxton, 2 Wright.
Ops incl: local bus services, school contracts.
Livery: Lime Green and Red
Ticket System: Wayfarer

SUPERTRAVEL OMNIBUS LTD
GATEACRE HOUSE, GOODLASS ROAD, SPEKE, LIVERPOOL L24 9HJ
Tel: 0151 486 3994   **Fax:** 0151 448 1216
E-mail: info@supertravelltd.com
Web site: www.supertravelltd.com
Man Dir: Graham Bolderson.
Fleet: single-deck bus, midibus, minibus.
Chassis: 12 Dennis, 2 MAN, 13 Optare, 1 Renault.
Bodies: 5 Alexander, 13 Optare, 9 Plaxton, 1 Other.
Ops incl: local bus services, school contracts, private hire.
Livery: White with Purple

NORFOLK

AMBASSADOR TRAVEL (ANGLIA) LTD
R24
JAMES WATT CLOSE, GAPTON HALL INDUSTRIAL ESTATE, GREAT YARMOUTH NR14 7RG
Tel/Recovery: 01493 440350
Fax: 01493 440367
E-mail: ambassador-travel@hotmail.co.uk
Fleet Name: Ambassador Travel
Chairman: R Green **Man Dir:** M C Green
Ops Man: B Picton **Dep Ops Man:** M Pleasants.
Fleet: 45 - 1 double-deck bus, 2 single-deck bus, 38 single-deck coach, 4 midibus.
Chassis: 7 Scania, 32 Volvo, 6 Other.
Bodies: 33 Plaxton, 6 Scania, 6 Other.
Ops incl: local bus services, school contracts, private hire, express.
Livery: Various.
Ticket System: Setright/Almex/Wayfarer

ANGLIAN COACHES LTD
See Suffolk

CHENERY TRAVEL
THE GARAGE, DICKLEBURGH, DISS IP21 4NJ
Tel: 01379 741221
Fax: 01379 740728
Recovery: 01379 741656
E-mail: julia@chenerytravel.co.uk
Web site: www.chenerytravel.co.uk
Dir: Mrs P G Garnham
Gen Man: Mrs J M McGraffin.
Fleet: 21 single-deck coach.
Chassis: 1 Bedford, 17 Setra, 3 Volvo.
Bodies: 1 Duple, 3 Jonckheere, 17 Setra.
Ops incl: school contracts, excursions & tours, private hire, express, continental tours.
Liveries: Silver/Blue, National Express.

COACH SERVICES LTD
1A HOWLETT WAY, THETFORD IP24 1HZ
Tel: 01842 821509   **Fax:** 01842 766581
E-mail: info@coachservicesltd.com
Web site: www.coachservicesltd.com
Man Dir: Allen Crawford **Tran Man:** Robert Crawford **Ops Man:** Thomas Crawford.
Fleet: 37 - 1 double-deck bus, 12 single-deck bus, 20 single-deck coach, 4 minibus.
Chassis: 1 AEC Routemaster, 1 Alexander Dennis, 1 DAF, 2 Dennis, 4 Ford Transit, 1 MAN, 6 Mercedes, 10 Scania, 11 Volvo.
Bodies: 1 Alexander Dennis, 6 Irizar, 4 Jonckheere, 1 Neoplan, 5 Optare, 1 Park Royal, 5 Plaxton, 2 Scania, 3 Van Hool, 3 Wright.
Ops incl: local bus services, school contracts, excursions & tours, private hire.
Livery: White
Ticket System: Almex

CRUSADER HOLIDAYS
See Essex

D-WAY TRAVEL
See Suffolk

EASTONS COACHES
THE OLD COACH HOUSE, PARISH ROAD,
STRATTON STRAWLESS, NORWICH
NR10 5LR
Tel: 01603 754253
Fax: 01603 754133
E-mail: info@eastonsholidays.co.uk
Web site: www.eastonsholidays.co.uk
Dirs: Robert Easton, Derek Easton.
Fleet: 14 - 1 single-deck bus, 11 single-deck
coach, 1 vintage.
Chassis incl: 3 Bova, 1 Mercedes, 1 Scania,
3 Setra, 3 Van Hool.
Ops incl: local bus services, excursions & tours,
school contracts, private hire, continental tours.
Livery: Purple
Ticket System: Almex

EUROSUN COACHES
25 REGENT ROAD, LOWESTOFT NR32 1PA
Tel: 01520 501015
Fax: 01502 589382
E-mail: eurosuncoaches@hotmail.com
Web site: www.eurosuncoaches.co.uk
Dirs: Phil Overy, Jack Overy Ch Eng: Adam
Goffin Sales & Marketing Man: Tony Porter.
Fleet: 19 - 16 single-deck coach, 3 double-deck
coach.
Chassis: 7 DAF, 4 Leyland, 3 MAN, 2 Mercedes,
5 Neoplan.
Bodies: 3 Bova, 2 Leyland, 5 Neoplan, 6 Plaxton,
2 Van Hool, 1 other.
Ops incl: school contracts, excursions & tours,
private hire, continental tours.
Livery: Red and Gold

FARELINE COACH SERVICES
See Suffolk

FIRST EAST OF ENGLAND
(formerly FIRST EASTERN COUNTIES)
ROUEN HOUSE, ROUEN ROAD,
NORWICH NR1 1RB
Tel: 0845 602 0121 Fax: 01603 615439
Web site: www.firstgroup.com
Regional Man Dir: Nigel Barrett Regional
Eng Dir: Mick Brannigan Regional Comm
Dir: Steve Wickers Regional Fin Planning
Dir: David Marshall.
Fleet (Norfolk & Suffolk): 314 - 144 double-
deck bus, 151 single-deck bus, 4 single-deck coach,
15 midibus.
Chassis: 2 AEC, 106 Dennis, 1 Leyland,
14 Optare, 52 Scania, 139 Volvo.
Bodies: 17 Alexander, 6 Alexander Dennis,
7 Northern Counties, 14 Optare, 2 Park Royal,
132 Plaxton, 20 Transbus, 116 Wright.
Ops incl: local bus services, school contract,
private hire.
Livery: FirstGroup UK Bus.
Ticket System: Wayfarer 3

FREESTONES COACHES LTD
GREEN LANE, BEETLEY, DEREHAM NR20 4DL
Tel: 01362 860236

Fax: 01362 860276
Dir: Mrs Gloria Feeke Ops Man: Robert Tibbles
Co Sec: Gary Feeke.
E-mail: enquiries@freestonescoaches.co.uk
Web site: www.freestonescoaches.co.uk
Fleet: 11 - 1 single-deck bus, 9 single-deck coach,
1 minibus.
Chassis: 1 BMC, 2 Iveco, 1 Mercedes, 2 Scania
1 Volkswagen, 4 Volvo.
Bodies: 2 Beulas, 1 BMC, 1 Hispano, 1 Irizar,
1 Plaxton, 4 Van Hool.
Ops incl: local bus services, excursions & tours,
school contracts, private hire, continental tours.

D&H HARROD (COACHES) LTD
BEXWELL AERODROME, DOWNHAM
MARKET PE38 9LU
Tel: 01366 381111
Fax: 01366 382010
E-mail: info@harrodscoaches.co.uk
Web site: www.harrodcoaches.co.uk
Prop: Derek Harrod Ops Man: Paul Harrod.
Fleet: 11 – 10 single-deck coach, 1 midicoach.
Chassis: 1 Dennis, 1 Mercedes, 9 Volvo.
Bodies: Jonckheere, Mercedes, Plaxton, UVG,
Van Hool.
Ops incl: local bus services, school contracts,
excursions & tours, private hire, continental tours.
Liveries: Gold/Cream & Blue

KONECTBUS LTD
JOHN GOSHAWK ROAD, DEREHAM
NR19 1SY
Tel: 01362 851210
Fax: 01362 851215
E-mail: feedback@konectbus.co.uk
Web site: www.konectbus.co.uk
Man Dir: Steve Challis Ops & Comm Dir:
Julian Patterson Eng Dir: Andrew Warnes.
Fleet: 47 - 15 double-deck bus, 32 single-deck
bus.
Chassis: 5 Alexander Dennis, 3 Leyland,
31 Optare, 5 VDL, 3 Volvo.
Bodies: 7 Alexander Dennis, 1 Mellor, 31 Optare,
3 Plaxton, 5 Wright.
Ops incl: local bus services
Livery: Blue/Yellow/Grey
Ticket System: Wayfarer TGX
A subsidiary of the Go-Ahead Group.

MATTHEWS COACHES
50 WESTGATE STREET, SHOULDHAM,
KING'S LYNN PE33 0BN
Tel: 01366 347220
Fax: 01366 347293
E-mail: john@matthewscoaches.co.uk
Man Dir: John Lloyd.
Fleet: 7 - 6 single-deck coach, 1 minibus
Chassis: 1 DAF, 2 Dennis, 1 Iveco, 1 LDV,
1 Leyland, 1 Volvo.
Bodies: 1 Beulas, 1 Duple, 1 Jonckheere, 1 LDV,
2 Plaxton, 1 Van Hool.
Ops incl: school contracts, excursions & tours,
private hire.
Livery: White/Blue

NEAVES COACHES
THE STREET, CATFIELD, GREAT YARMOUTH
NR29 5AA
Tel: 01692 580383
Fax: 01692 582977

Recovery: 07810 504082
E-mail: info@neavescoaches.com
Web site: www.neavescoaches.com
Man Dir: Mrs Daphne Holburn
Gen Man: Richard Hipkiss.
Fleet: 8 – 2 single-deck bus, 4 single-deck coach,
1 midicoach, 1 minibus.
Chassis: 1 DAF, 1 Dennis, 2 Mercedes, 2 Optare,
2 Volvo.
Bodies: 2 Mercedes, 2 Optare, 2 Plaxton,
1 Van Hool, 1 Other.
Ops incl: local bus services, school contracts,
excursions & tours, private hire.
Livery: White, Red & Grey
Ticket System: Wayfarer

NORFOLK GREEN
HAMLIN WAY, KINGS LYNN PE31 6HA
Tel: 01553 776980 Fax: 01553 770891
E-mail: enquiries@norfolkgreen.co.uk
Web site: www.norfolkgreen.co.uk
Man Dir: Ben Colson Dir: Keith Shayshutt
Fleet Eng: Nigel Firth Ops Man: Richard
Pengelly Accountant: Simon Carr.
Fleet: 73 – 9 double-deck bus, 28 single-deck
bus, 36 midibus.
Chassis: 9 DAF, 1 Dennis, 9 Irisbus, 54 Optare.
Bodies: 1 Alexander, 9 Irisbus, 63 Optare.
Ops incl: local bus services
Livery: two-tone Green
Ticket System: Wayfarer TGX

PEELINGS COACHES
THE GARAGE, CLAY HILL, TITTLESHALL,
KING'S LYNN PE32 2RQ
Tel/Fax: 01328 701531
E-mail: info@peelings-coaches.co.uk
Web site: www.peelings-coaches.co.uk
Prop: Jonathan Joplin Comp Sec: Ruth Joplin
Ch Eng: Jonathan Sayer.
Fleet: 6 - single-deck coach.
Chassis: 1 Dennis, 1 Iveco, 4 Volvo.
Bodies: 1 Beulas, 1 Jonckheere, 4 Plaxton.
Ops incl: local bus services, school contracts,
excursions & tours, private hire, express.
Livery: White/Blue/Silver
Ticket System: Setright

REYNOLDS COACHES LTD
THE GARAGE, ORMESBY ROAD, CAISTER-
ON-SEA, GREAT YARMOUTH NR30 5QJ
Tel: 01493 720312 Fax: 01493 721512
E-mail: info@reynolds-coaches.co.uk
Web site: www.reynolds-coaches.com
Man Dir: Charles Reynolds Tours Dir: Mrs
Julie Reynolds Co Sec: Mrs Grace Reynolds
Ch Eng: Jeffrey Buckle.
Fleet: 22 – 15 single-deck coach, 6 midicoach,
1 minicoach.
Chassis: 1 Bova, 8 Dennis, 1 EOS, 1 Iveco,
1 MAN, 2 Mercedes, 4 Toyota, 4 Volvo.
Bodies: 2 Beulas, 1 Bova, 4 Caetano, 1 Duple,
2 Mercedes, 9 Plaxton, 3 Van Hool.
Ops incl: school contracts, excursions & tours,
private hire, continental tours.
Livery: Silver.

SANDERS COACHES LTD
HEATH DRIVE, HEMPSTEAD ROAD
INDUSTRIAL ESTATE, HOLT NR25 6ER
Tel: 01263 712800 Fax: 01263 710920

E-mail: info@sanderscoaches.com
Web site: www.sanderscoaches.com
Man Dir: Charles Sanders Ops Dir: Paul
Sanders Head of Tours & Finance: Carole
Willimott Fleet Eng: Andrew Sanders.
Fleet: 92 - 10 double-deck bus, 31 single-deck
bus, 1 open-top bus, 26 single-deck coach,
16 midibus, 6 midicoach, 2 minibus.
Chassis: 2 Bova, 40 DAF, 6 Dennis, 1 Leyland,
16 Mercedes, 5 Optare, 10 Scania, 2 Setra, 3 VDL,
7 Volvo.
Bodies: 1 Alexander, 2 Bova, 12 East Lancs,
13 Ikarus, 2 Mercedes, 10 Optare, 22 Plaxton,
9 Scania, 2 Setra, 14 Van Hool, 4 Wright.
Ops incl: local bus services, school contracts,
excursions & tours, private hire, continental tours.
Livery: Orange/Yellow/Blue
Ticket System: Wayfarer

H SEMMENCE & CO LTD
34 NORWICH ROAD, WYMONDHAM
NR18 0NS
Tel: 01953 602135
Fax: 01953 605867
E-mail: sales@semmence.co.uk
Web site: www.semmence.co.uk
Man Dir: Sean Green.
Fleet: 29 – 26 single-deck coach, 3 midicoach.
Chassis: 15 Dennis, 3 Mercedes, 3 Scania, 8 Volvo.
Bodies: 1 Caetano, 6 Duple, 20 Plaxton,
2 Van Hool
Ops incl: local bus services, school contracts,
excursions & tours, express, private hire.
Livery: White.
Ticket System: Wayfarer
(Associated with Ambassador Travel)

SIMONDS COACH & TRAVEL
R24
ROSWALD HOUSE, OAK DRIVE,
DISS IP22 4GX
Tel/Recovery: 01379 647300
Fax: 01379 647350
E-mail: info@simonds.co.uk
Web site: www.simonds.co.uk
Chairman: D O Simonds
Man Dir: M S Simonds
Dir: R S Simonds
Eng Dir: A P Tant.
Fleet: 48 – 17 single-deck bus, 27 single-deck
coach, 1 midicoach, 3 minicoach.
Chassis: 1 Ford, 2 Ford Transit, 9 MAN,
6 Mercedes, 1 Optare, 1 Van Hool, 28 Volvo.
Bodies: 1 Alexander Dennis, 1 Jonckheere,
7 MCV, 1 Mercedes, 4 Optare, 11 Plaxton,
23 Van Hool.
Ops incl: local bus services, school contracts,
excursions & tours, private hire, continental tours.
Livery: White base with Red/Gold leaves.
Ticket system: Wayfarer TGX/Paycell

SPRATTS COACHES LTD
THE GARAGE, WRENINGHAM, NORWICH
NR16 1AZ
Tel: 01508 489262
Fax: 01508 489404
E-mail: sprattscoaches@btconnect.com
Web site: www.sprattscoaches.co.uk
Dirs: Richard Spratt, Christine Bilham.
Fleet: 12 - 8 single-deck coach, 3 midicoach,
1 vintage.
Chassis: 1 Bova, 2 MAN, 1 Mercedes, 1 Optare,
5 Scania, 1 Volvo.

Bodies: 1 Berkhof, 1 Beulas, 1 Bova, 1 Caetano,
6 Van Hool, 1 Other.
Ops incl: school contracts, excursions & tours,
private hire, continental tours.
Livery: White

SUNBEAM COACHES LTD
WESTGATE STREET, HEVINGHAM,
NORWICH NR10 5NH
Tel/Fax: 01603 754211
E-mail: sunbeamcoaches@aol.com
Web site: www.sunbeamluxurycoachesnorwich.
co.uk
Man Dir: G M Coldham.
Fleet: 6 – 1 single-deck bus, 4 single-deck coach,
1 minicoach.
Chassis: 1 Dennis, 2 MAN, 1 Mercedes,
1 Toyota, 1 Volvo.
Bodies: 1 Caetano, 2 Neoplan, 2 Plaxton,
1 Van Hool.
Ops incl: local bus service, school contracts,
private hire, excursions & tours.
Livery: White with Orange/Blue/Yellow

UPWELL & DISTRICT COACHES
THE COACH DEPOT, SCHOOL ROAD,
UPWELL PE14 9EW
Tel & Fax: 01945 773461
Partners: Caroline Parsons, William Hircock.
Fleet: 2 single-deck coach, 1 midicoach.
Chassis: 1 Alexander Dennis, 1 Mercedes,
1 Scania.
Ops incl: excursions & tours, private hire, school
contracts.
Livery: Red/White/Blue.

Icon	Description	Icon	Description	Icon	Description
♿	Vehicle suitable for disabled	💺	Seat belt-fitted Vehicle	R24	24 hour recovery service
T	Toilet-drop facilities available	🍴	Coach(es) with galley facilities	🔧	Replacement vehicle available
R	Recovery service available	❄	Air-conditioned vehicle(s)	🚌	Vintage Coach(es) available
🚍	Open top vehicle(s)	🚻	Coaches with toilet facilities	🌿	Hybrid Buses

---

NORTH AND NORTH EAST LINCOLNSHIRE

APPLEBYS COACH TRAVEL
R
MAIN STREET, CONISHOLME, LOUTH
LN11 7LT
Tel: 01507 357900
Fax: 01507 357910
Recovery: 07764 278466
E-mail: coach@applebyscoaches.co.uk
Web site: www.applebyscoaches.co.uk
Tran Man: Neil Warne Man Dir: Rob Lyng
Group Ops Man: Nick Tetley
Fleet Eng: David Hoy.
Fleet: 17 – 13 single-deck coach, 4 minibus.
Chassis: 1 Dennis, 12 Scania, 4 Volkswagen.
Bodies: 8 Irizar, 4 Volkswagen, 5 Other.
Ops incl: excursions & tours, private hire,
continental tours.
A subsidiary of the Bowen Travel Group - see
Staffordshire.

BLACK & WHITE COACHES
22B HEBDEN ROAD, SCUNTHORPE
DN15 8DT
Tel: 01724 843355
Fax: 01724 853749

E-mail: blackwhite.coaches@btconnect.com
Web site: www.bwcoaches.co.uk
Fleet: 8 – 4 single-deck coach, 1 midibus,
3 midicoach.
Ops incl: school contracts, private hire.
Livery: Black/White

EMMERSON COACHES LTD
BLUESTONE LANE, IMMINGHAM DN40 2EL
Tel: 01469 578166
Fax: 01469 575278
E-mail: emmersoncoaches@tiscali.co.uk
Web site: www.emmersoncoaches.com
Dir: Alan Brumby.
Fleet: 8 single-deck coach.
Chassis: 1 EOS, 1 Leyland, 1 MAN, 3 Mercedes,
2 Volvo.
Bodies: 1 EOS, 1 Ikarus, 2 Mercedes, 1 Neoplan,
1 Noge, 1 Plaxton, 1 Van Hool.
Ops incl: school contracts, private hire.
Livery: White, Orange & Brown.

EXPERT COACH SERVICES LTD
Ceased trading since LRB 2011 went to press

BEN GEORGE TRAVEL LTD
39 ESTATE AVENUE, BROUGHTON,
BRIGG DN20 0JZ
Tel: 01652 654681
Fax: 01652 650224
E-mail: s.p.easton@btinternet.com
Dirs: Stephen & John Easton.
Fleet: 2 single-deck coach, 1 minicoach.
Chassis: 1 Dennis, 1 Toyota, 1 Volvo.
Bodies: 1 Caetano, 1 Plaxton, 1 Van Hool.
Ops incl: school contracts, private hire.
Livery: Red/White/Blue

HOLLOWAY COACHES LTD
COTTAGE BECK ROAD, SCUNTHORPE
DN16 1TP
Tel: 01724 282277, 281177 Fax: 01724 289945
Man Dir: F S Holloway Dir: P A Holloway.
Fleet: 26 – 13 double-deck bus, 6 single-deck bus,
6 single-deck coach, 1 midicoach.
Chassis: 2 DAF, 9 Leyland, 1 Mercedes, 14 Volvo.
Bodies: 14 Alexander, 1 East Lancs, 4 Northern
Counties, 7 Plaxton.

Ops incl: local bus services, school contracts, excursions & tours, express.
Liveries: Red/White/Blue, Yellow (school buses).

HORNSBY TRAVEL SERVICES LTD
♿🚍❄T
51 ASHBY HIGH STREET, SCUNTHORPE
DN16 2NB
Tel: 01724 282255 **Fax:** 01274 282788
E-mail: office@hornsbytravel.co.uk
Web site: www.hornsbytravel.co.uk
Man Dir: Raymond Hornsby **Gen Man:**
Nicholas Hornsby **Ch Eng:** Rob Andrew.
Fleet: 30 - 3 double-deck bus, 17 single-deck bus,
8 single-deck coach, 1 midicoach, 1 minibus.
Chassis: Alexander Dennis, BMC, Dennis, Ford
Transit, Mercedes, Volvo.
Bodies: Alexander Dennis, BMC, Mercedes,
Plaxton.
Ops incl: local bus services, school contracts,
excursions & tours, private hire.
Livery: Blue/Silver.
Ticket System: ERG

JOHNSONS COACHES
♿
THORNTON ROAD, GOXHILL DN19 7HN
Tel: 01469 530267
Prop: N L Johnson.
Fleet: 7 – 5 single-deck coach, 2 midibus.
Chassis: 2 Mercedes, 5 Volvo.
Ops incl: local bus services, school contracts,
private hire.

MILLMAN COACHES
🚍♿
17 WILTON ROAD, HUMBERSTON,
GRIMSBY DN36 4AW
Tel: 01472 210297 **Fax:** 01472 595915
E-mail: enquiries@millmancoaches.co.uk

Web site: www.millmancoaches.co.uk
Partners: David Millman, Amanda J Millman.
Fleet: 9 - 6 single-deck coach, 3 midicoach.
Chassis: 2 Dennis, 1 Mercedes, 6 Volvo.
Bodies: 1 Duple, 5 Jonckheere, 1 Mercedes,
2 Plaxton.
Ops incl: private hire, school contracts.
Livery: White/Blue/Yellow

RADLEY COACH TRAVEL
♿🚍❄
THE TRAVEL OFFICE, 11 CHAPEL COURT,
BRIGG DN20 8JZ
Tel: 01652 653583 **Fax:** 01652 656020
Fleet Name: Radley Holidays
E-mail: radleytravel@aol.com
Web site: www.radleytravel.co.uk
Owner: Kevin Radley.
Fleet: 2 single-deck coach.
Chassis: 4 Scania.
Bodies: 1 Berkhof, 1 Irizar, 2 Scania Omni
Express.
Ops incl: excursions & tours, private hire,
continental tours.
Livery: Maroon/Gold

SELWYN MOTORS
♿
WESTGATE, SANDTOFT ROAD, BELTON
DN9 1QA
Tel: 01427 872334
Prop: B S Dodd.
Fleet: 3 – 1 double-deck bus, 2 single-deck coach.
Ops incl: local bus service, school contracts.
Livery: Red/Grey

SHERWOOD TRAVEL
♿🚍❄
19 QUEENS ROAD, IMMINGHAM DN40 1QR
Tel: 01469 571140 **Fax:** 01469 574937

E-mail: enquiries@sherwoodtravel.co.uk
Web site: www.sherwoodtravel.co.uk
Dirs: Stuart Oakland, Jane Oakland,
Lucy Oakland.
Fleet: 9 - 5 single-deck coach, 2 midibus,
2 minicoach.
Chassis: 4 Mercedes, 1 Scania, 4 Volvo.
Ops incl: local bus services, school contracts,
excursions & tours, private hire.

SOLID ENTERTAINMENTS
Ceased trading since LRB 2011 went to press

STAGECOACH EAST MIDLANDS
♿🚌🚍🚍T
PO BOX 15, DEACON ROAD,
LINCOLN LN2 4JB
Tel: 0845 605 0605
Fax: 01522 538229
E-mail:
eastmidlands.enquiries@stagecoachbus.com
Web site: www.stagecoachbus.com
Fleet Name: Stagecoach in Grimsby-
Cleethorpes.
Man Dir: Gary Nolan
Eng Dir: John Taylor
Comm Dir: Dave Skepper
Ops Dir: Richard Kay.
Fleet: 498 - 230 double-deck bus, 251 single-
deck bus, 9 single-deck coach, 8 open top bus.
Chassis: 294 Alexander Dennis, 6 DAF, 1 Leyland,
51 MAN, 21 Optare, 14 Scania, 111 Volvo.
Bodies: 335 Alexander Dennis, 63 East Lancs,
5 Jonckheere, 11 Northern Counties, 21 Optare,
33 Plaxton, 12 Transbus, 18 Wright.
Ops incl: local bus services.
Livery: Stagecoach UK Bus
Ticket System: ERG TP5000.

NORTH YORKSHIRE, DARLINGTON, MIDDLESBROUGH, REDCAR & CLEVELAND, YORK

ABBEY COACHWAYS LTD
♿❄
MEADOWCROFT GARAGE, LOW STREET,
CARLTON, GOOLE DN14 9PH
Tel: 01405 860337
Fax: 01405 869433
Dirs: Mrs L E Baker, S J Stockdale.
Fleet: 5 - 4 single-deck coaches, 1 double-deck
coach.
Chassis: 1 MAN, 1 Scania, 3 Volvo.
Bodies: 2 Jonckheere, 3 Plaxton.
Ops incl: school contracts, private hire.
Livery: Blue/White

G. ABBOTT & SONS
🚌♿❄🅿R24♿
AUMANS HOUSE, LEEMING,
NORTHALLERTON DL7 9RZ
Tel: 01677 422858/422571
Fax: 01677 424971
Fleet Name: Abbotts of Leeming
Partners: David C Abbott, Clifford G Abbot.
Fleet: 89 - 59 single-deck coach, 1 double-deck
coach, 12 midibus, 4 midicoach, 13 minibus.
Chassis: 1 Bedford, 8 DAF, 1 Fiat, 4 Ford Transit,
6 LDV, 15 Leyland, 14 Mercedes, 4 Optare,
16 Scania, 4 Van Hool, 16 Volvo.
Bodies: 2 Caetano, 14 Duple, 1 Euro, 1 Ford,
2 Ikarus, 9 Irizar, 6 LDV, 3 Mercedes, 4 Optare,
20 Plaxton, 3 Reeve Burgess, 6 Sunsundegui,
1 Transbus, 10 Van Hool, 7 Other.
Ops incl: local bus services, school contracts,

excursions & tours, private hire, express,
continental tours.
Livery: Orange/Cream/Red.

ARRIVA YORKSHIRE LTD
♿
24 BARNSLEY ROAD, WAKEFIELD WF1 5JX
Tel: 01924 231300
Fax: 01924 200106
Regional Man Dir: Nigel Featham **Fin Dir:**
David Cocker **Eng Dir:** Neil Craig **Head of
Ops:** Colin Newbury.
Fleet: 327 - 137 double-deck bus, 111 single-
deck bus, 79 midibus.
Chassis: 31 Alexander Dennis, 99 DAF, 62
Dennis, 13 Optare, 35 VDL, 79 Volvo, 8 Wrightbus.
Bodies: 31 Alexander Dennis, 103 Alexander,
14 East Lancs, 6 Ikarus, 3 Northern Counties,
71 Optare, 5 Plaxton, 49 Wright.
Ops incl: local bus services.
Livery: Arriva UK Bus.

H ATKINSON & SONS (INGLEBY) LTD
🚍♿❄🅿T
NORWOOD GARAGE, INGLEBY ARNCLIFFE,
NORTHALLERTON DL6 3LN
Tel: 01609 882222 **Fax:** 01609 882476
E-mail: office@atkinsoncoaches.co.uk
Web site: www.atkinsoncoaches.co.uk
Dirs: M T Atkinson, D Atkinson, R Atkinson.
Fleet: 11 - 10 single-deck coach, 1 midicoach.
Chassis: 2 Bova, 2 Irisbus, 2 MAN, 1 Scania,

2 Setra, 2 Volvo.
Bodies: 2 Beulas, 2 Bova, 1 Indcar, 1 Irizar,
1 Jonckheere, 1 Plaxton, 2 Setra, 1 Van Hool.
Ops Incl: schools contracts, excursions & tours,
private hire, continental tours.
Livery: Yellow with Maroon/Gold

BALDRY'S COACHES
♿🚌
LEYLANDII, SELBY ROAD,
HOLME-ON-SPALDING-MOOR YO43 4HB
Tel/Fax: 01430 860992
E-mail: baldryscoaches@live.co.uk
Prop: A Baldry.
Fleet: 5 single-deck coach.
Chassis: 1 AEC, 4 Bedford.
Bodies: Duple, Plaxton.
Ops incl: school contracts, excursions & tours,
private hire.
Livery: Two-tone Green.

BEECROFT COACHES
🚍🍴
POST OFFICE, FEWSTON HG3 1SG
Tel/Fax: 01943 880206
Prop: D Beecroft.
Fleet: 1 single-deck coach.
Chassis: 1 Dennis.
Bodies: 1 Caetano.
Ops incl: school contracts, excursions & tours,
private hire, continental tours.
Livery: Green/Orange/White.

BIBBY'S OF INGLETON LTD

INGLETON INDUSTRIAL ESTATE, NEW ROAD,
INGLETON LA6 3NU
Tel: 01524 241330
Fax: 01524 242216
E-mail: enquiries@bibbys.co.uk
Web site: www.bibbys.co.uk
Man Dir: P Bibby **Co Sec:** Mrs S Holcroft
Ch Eng: M Stephenson.
Fleet: 29 - 19 single-deck coach, 4 midicoach,
2 minicoach, 3 minibus, 1 vintage.
Chassis: 1 Bedford, 14 DAF, 1 Ford Transit, 2 LDV,
6 Mercedes, 1 Temsa, 4 VDL.
Bodies: 1 Duple, 1 Ford, 7 Ikarus, 2 LDV,
2 Plaxton, 1 Temsa, 11 Van Hool, 4 Other.
Ops incl: school contracts, excursions & tours,
private hire, continental tours.
Livery: Blue/Grey/Red with white stripes.

BOTTERILLS MINIBUSES

HIGH STREET GARAGE, THORNTON LE
DALE, PICKERING YO18 7QW
Tel: 01751 474210
E-mail: botterills@hotmail.com
Web site: www.botterills.org.uk
Fleet: 4 minibus.
Chassis/Bodies: 4 Mercedes.
Ops incl: local bus services, school contracts,
private hire.
Livery: White

EDDIE BROWN TOURS LTD

UNIT 370, THORP ARCH TRADING ESTATE,
WETHERBY, YORK LS23 7EG
Tel: 01423 321248 **Fax:** 01423 326213
Recovery: 07736 692702
E-mail: enquiries@eddiebrowntours.com
Web site: www.eddiebrowntours.com
Dir: Philip Brown **Dir/Co Sec:** Mrs Deirdre
Brown **Ch Eng:** John Firth
Ops Man: John Bywater.
Fleet: 43 – 3 double-deck bus, 31 single-deck
coach, 9 midicoach.
Chassis: 4 Dennis, 2 MAN, 10 Mercedes,
2 Scania, 25 Volvo.
Bodies: 3 East Lancs, 36 Plaxton, 4 Van Hool.
Ops incl: local bus services, school contracts,
excursions & tours, private hire, continental tours.
Livery: White Base with Red/Orange/Maroon

BURRELLS (BARNARD CASTLE
COACHES)

SOUTH VIEW GARAGE, NEWSHAM,
RICHMOND DL11 7RA
Tel: 01833 621302 **Fax:** 01833 621431
E-mail: alburrell@hotmail.com
Dirs: Alan Burrell, Mrs Sandra Burrell.
Fleet: 6 - 5 single-deck coach, 1 minibus.
Chassis: 1 Leyland, 1 Mercedes, 4 Volvo.
Bodies: 1 Duple, 1 Mercedes, 4 Van Hool.
Ops incl: school contracts, excursions & tours,
private hire, express, continental tours.
Livery: Yellow/White

CHARTER COACH LTD

Ceased trading since LRB 2011 went to press.

COASTAL AND COUNTRY COACHES

THE GARAGE, FAIRFIELD WAY, WHITBY
BUSINESS PARK, WHITBY YO22 4PU
Tel: 01947 602922 **Fax:** 01947 600830
E-mail: enquiries@coastalandcountry.co.uk
Web site: www.coastalandcountry.co.uk
Man Dir: C Vasey **Dir:** J Vasey **Ch Eng:** A Caley.
Fleet: 19 - 14 single-deck coach, 1 open-top bus,
2 midibus, 2 midicoach.
Chassis: 1 Bedford, 1 Leyland, 4 Mercedes,
13 Volvo.
Bodies: 1 Berkhof, 1 Duple, 1 ECW, 13 Plaxton,
2 Van Hool, 1 Other.
Ops incl: local bus services, school contracts,
excursions & tours, private hire.
Livery: White/Blue.
Ticket system: Wayfarer

COLLINS COACHES

CLIFFE SERVICE STATION, YORK ROAD,
CLIFFE, SELBY YO8 6NN
Tel: 01757 638591
Fax: 01757 630196
E-mail: collins.coaches@hotmail.co.uk
Web site: www.collinscoaches.co.uk
Prop: Alan Collins.
Fleet: 4 - 3 single-deck coach, 1 midicoach.
Chassis: 1 Mercedes, 3 Volvo.
Bodies: 1 Plaxton, 3 Van Hool.
Ops incl: local bus service, school contracts,
private hire.
Livery: White

JOHN DODSWORTH (COACHES) LTD

WETHERBY ROAD, BOROUGHBRIDGE
YO5 9HS
Tel: 01423 322236
Fax: 01423 324682
Dir: John Dodsworth.
Fleet: 10 - 9 single-deck coach, 1 minibus.
Chassis: 1 Mercedes, 4 Setra, 1 VDL, 4 Volvo.
Bodies: 4 Plaxton, 4 Setra, 1 Van Hool, 1 Other.
Ops incl: excursions & tours, private hire,
continental tours, school contracts.
Livery: Cream/Orange.

FIRST YORK

45 TANNER ROW, YORK YO1 6JP
Tel: 01904 883000
Fax: 01904 883057
Web site: www.firstgroup.com
Regional Man Dir: Dave Alexander
Service Delivery Dir: Bob Hamilton
Strategic Devt Dir: Richard Soper
Business Efficiency Man: Ian Humphreys
Fleet: 98 – 12 double-deck bus, 60 single-deck
bus, 26 articulated bus.
Chassis: 15 Mercedes, 83 Volvo.
Bodies: 12 Alexander, 15 Mercedes, 71 Wright.
Ops incl: local bus services, school contracts.
Livery: FirstGroup UK Bus.
Ticket System: Wayfarer.

HANDLEY'S COACHES

NORTH ROAD, MIDDLEHAM, LEYBURN
DL8 4PJ
Tel: 01969 623216
Fax: 01969 624546
Dirs: Mr M Anderson, Mrs J Anderson,
Mr E Bowes, Mrs L Cooke.
Fleet: 11 - 5 single-deck coach, 1 midibus,
4 midicoach, 1 minicoach.
Chassis: 1 Leyland, 6 Mercedes, 2 Scania, 2 Volvo.
Bodies: 1 Autobus, 1 Crest, 1 Irizar, 1 Jonckheere,

1 Optare, 5 Plaxton, 1 Van Hool.
Ops incl: private hire, school contracts.
Livery: White

HARGREAVES COACHES

BRIDGE HOUSE, HEBDEN, SKIPTON
BD23 5DE
Tel: 01756 752567 **Fax:** 01756 753768
E-mail: info@hargreaves.coaches.co.uk
Web site: www.hargreavescoaches.co.uk
Prop: Andrew C Howick.
Fleet: 7 - 3 single-deck coach, 1 double-deck
coach, 2 midicoach, 1 minibus.
Chassis: 1 Ayats, 3 MAN, 2 Mercedes,
1 Van Hool.
Bodies incl: 1 Ayats, 1 LDV, 2 Mercedes,
1 Neoplan, 1 Noge, 1 Van Hool.
Ops incl: local bus services, school contracts,
excursions & tours, private hire, continental tours.
Livery: Silver/Pink/White

HARROGATE COACH TRAVEL LTD
(CONNEXIONS BUSES)

6 ST THOMAS'S WAY, GREEN HAMMERTON,
YORK YO26 8BE
Tel: 01423 339600
Fax: 01423 339785
Web site: www.connexionsbuses.com
E-mail: harrogatecoach@aol.com
Fleet Name: Connexions Buses.
Man Dir: Craig Temple **Fin Dir:** Julie Temple.
Fleet: 20 - 4 double-deck bus, 11 single-deck bus,
5 midibus.
Chassis: 1 Leyland, 5 Optare, 14 Scania.
Bodies: 7 Alexander Dennis, 2 East Lancs,
2 Northern Counties, 5 Optare, 2 Scania,
2 Wright.
Ops incl: local bus services, school contracts,
private hire.
Livery: Green/White
Ticket System: Wayfarer TGX 150

HODGSON & SON

STILLINGTON ROAD, EASINGWOLD
YO61 3ET
Tel: 01347 822011
E-mail: info@hodgsonandson.co.uk
Web site: www.hodgsonandson.co.uk
Fleet: 4 – 1 midibus, 2 midicoach, 1 minibus.
Chassis: 4 Mercedes.
Ops incl: local bus services, school contracts,
private hire.
Livery: White with Red.

P & D A HOPWOOD

22 MAIN STREET, ASKHAM BRYAN, YORK
YO23 3QU
Tel: 01904 707394
Dirs: P Hopwood, D A Hopwood, R C Baker,
A J Baker.
Fleet: 2 single-deck coach.
Chassis: 2 Dennis.
Bodies: 1 Duple, 1 Plaxton.
Ops incl: school contracts, private hire.

W P & M HUTCHINSON

ROXBY HOUSE, YORK ROAD, EASINGWOLD
YO61 3EF
Tel: 01347 821853
Fleet: 28 – single-deck coach, midibus, midicoach,
minibus, minicoach.

Chassis: Mercedes, Neoplan.
Ops incl: local bus services, school contracts, private hire.
Livery: White with Blue/Yellow.

INGLEBY'S LUXURY COACHES LTD
24 HOSPITAL FIELDS ROAD, FULFORD ROAD, YORK YO10 4DZ
Tel: 01904 637620
Fax: 01904 612944
Dir: C Ingleby **Fleet Eng:** R Atkinson
Ops: A Evans.
Fleet: 13 - 7 single-deck coach, 2 midicoach, 4 minibus.
Chassis: I Bova, 6 Mercedes, 3 VDL, 3 Volvo.
Bodies: I Bova, I Mercedes, I Plaxton, I Sitcar, 6 Van Hool, 3 Other.
Ops incl: school contracts, private hire.
Livery: Blue/Cream

J. R. TRAVEL
Ceased operations since LRB 2011 went to press

KINGS LUXURY COACHES
FERRY ROAD, MIDDLESBROUGH TS2 IPL
Tel: 01642 243687 **Fax:** 01642 213109
E-mail: enquiries@kingscoaches.co.uk
Web site: www.kingscoaches.co.uk
Prop: Ken King.
Fleet: 7 - 2 double-deck coach, 5 single-deck coach.
Chassis: 2 Scania, 3 Setra, 2 Volvo.
Bodies: I Jonckheere, 3 Setra, 3 Van Hool.
Ops incl: private hire, continental tours.
Livery: Cream with Orange/Black.

LEVEN VALLEY COACHES
TILBURY ROAD, SOUTH BANK, MIDDLESBROUGH TS6 6AW
Tel: 01642 722068
Prop: P Thompson.
Fleet: 10 midibus.
Chassis: 7 Alexander Dennis, 3 Optare.
Bodies: 7 Alexander Dennis, 3 Optare.
Ops incl: local bus services.
Livery: Red/Yellow

PENNINE MOTOR SERVICES
BROUGHTON ROAD, SKIPTON BD23 ITE
Tel: 01756 795515
E-mail: penninemotors@btconnect.com
Web site: www.pennine-bus.co.uk
Props: M Simpson, N Simpson.
Fleet: 17 midibus.
Chassis: 17 Dennis.
Bodies: Plaxton, Wright.
Ops incl: local bus services.
Livery: Orange/Black

PERRY'S COACHES
RICCAL DRIVE, YORK ROAD INDUSTRIAL PARK, MALTON YO17 6YE
Tel: 01653 690500
Fax: 01653 690800
Web site: www.perrystravel.com
E-mail: info@perrystravel.com
Partners: D J Perry **(Gen Man/Ch Eng)**, Mrs A Holtby **(Co Sec).**
Fleet: 20 - 11 single-deck coach, 7 midicoach, 3 minicoach.
Chassis: 11 Mercedes, 4 VDL, 5 Volvo.

Bodies: I Jonckheere, 9 Plaxton, 2 Sitcar, 5 Van Hool, 4 Other.
Ops incl: school contracts, excursions & tours, private hire, continental tours.
Livery: Red/Yellow/White.

PROCTERS COACHES (NORTH YORKSHIRE) LTD
TUTIN ROAD, LEEMING BAR INDUSTRIAL ESTATE, LEEMING BAR, NORTHALLERTON DL7 9UJ
Tel: 01677 425203 **Fax:** 01677 426550
E-mail: enquiries@procterscoaches.co.uk
Web site: www.procterscoaches.com
Fleet Names: Procters Coaches, Dales & District.
Man Dir: Kevin J Procter **Fleet Eng:** Philip Kenyon **Tran Man:** Andrew Fryatt.
Fleet: 58 – 2 single-deck bus, 26 single-deck coach, 2 double-deck coach, 20 midibus, I midicoach, 7 minibus.
Chassis: Alexander Dennis, DAF, Dennis, Ford Transit, Irisbus, LDV, MAN, Mercedes, Optare, Scania, Setra, Van Hool, VDL, Volvo.
Bodies: Alexander, Autobus, Berkhof, Caetano, Fast, Irizar, Jonckheere, Optare, Plaxton, Setra, Van Hool, Wright.
Ops incl: local bus services, school contracts, excursions & tours, private hire, continental tours.
Livery: White with Blue/Yellow.
Ticket System: Wayfarer 3

RELIANCE MOTOR SERVICES
RELIANCE GARAGE, YORK ROAD, SUTTON-ON-THE-FOREST, YORK YO61 IES
Tel/Fax: 01904 768262
E-mail: reliance.motors@btconnnect.com
Web site: www.reliancemotorservices.co.uk
Prop: John H Duff.
Fleet: 10 - 4 double-deck bus, 6 single-deck bus.
Chassis: 10 Volvo.
Bodies: I Alexander Dennis, 2 East Lancs, 7 Wright.
Ops incl: local bus services, school contracts.
Livery: Cream/Green
Ticket System: Wayfarer TGX 150

SCARBOROUGH & DISTRICT
BARRY'S LANE, SCARBOROUGH YO12 4HA
Tel: 01723 500064
Fax: 01723 370064
E-mail: sd@eyms.co.uk
Web site: www.eyms.co.uk
Chairman: Peter Shipp **Fin Dir:** Peter Harrison
Comm Man: Bob Rackley **Ch Eng:** David Heptinstall **Co Sec:** Paul Leeman
Ops Man: Ray Hill
Marketing Man: Claire Robinson.
Ops incl: local bus services, school contracts, excursions & tours, private hire, express, continental tours.
Livery: Burgundy/Cream
Ticket system: Wayfarer TGX150
A division of East Yorkshire Motor Services Ltd (see East Riding)

SHAW'S OF WHITLEY
WHITLEY FARM, SILVER STREET, WHITLEY, GOOLE DN14 0JG

Tel: 01977 661214 **Fax:** 01977 662036
Recovery: 07802 249878
E-mail: info@shawsofwhitley.co.uk
Web site: www.shawsofwhitley.co.uk
Prop: Mrs Marjorie Shaw **Ops Man:** Philip Shaw.
Fleet: 5 – I double-deck bus, 4 single-deck coach.
Chassis: I MAN, 2 Setra, I Van Hool, I Volvo.
Bodies incl: I Mercedes, 2 Setra, I Van Hool.
Ops incl: excursions & tours, private hire, express, continental tours.
Livery: Various.

SIESTA INTERNATIONAL HOLIDAYS LTD
NEWPORT SOUTH BUSINESS PARK, LAMPORT STREET, MIDDLESBROUGH TS1 5QL
Tel: 01642 257920
Fax: 01642 219153
Recovery: 07739 679957
E-mail: sales@siestaholidays.co.uk
Web site: www.siestaholidays.co.uk
Chairman: Paul R Herbert
Dirs: C Herbert, J Herbert, J Cofton
Ops Mans: K Keelan, J Potter.
Fleet: 9 - 2 single-deck coach, 6 double-deck coach, I minibus.
Chassis: I Ford Transit, 8 Scania.
Bodies: 8 Berkhof, I Ford.
Ops incl: excursions & tours, private hire, continental tours.
Livery: Metallic Blue.

JOHN SMITH & SONS LTD
THE AIRFIELD, DALTON, THIRSK YO7 3HE
Tel/Recovery: 01845 577250
Fax: 01845 577752
E-mail: admin@johnsmithandsons.net
Web site: www.johnsmithandsons.net
Man Dir: Neville Smith **Ops Man:** John Smith
Ch Eng: Ivan Smith **Co Sec:** Sarah Smith.
Fleet: 22 - I single-deck bus, 13 single-deck coach, 3 midibus, 3 midicoach, I minicoach, I vintage coach.
Chassis: 10 DAF, 2 Dennis, I Leyland, I MAN, 6 Mercedes, 2 Neoplan.
Bodies: I Berkhof, I Duple, 6 Mercedes, 5 Neoplan, 5 Plaxton, 3 Van Hool.
Ops incl: local bus services, school contracts, excursions & tours, private hire, continental tours.
Livery: Green/Cream/Gold
Ticket system: Wayfarer

STEPHENSONS OF EASINGWOLD LTD
MOOR LANE INDUSTRIAL ESTATE, THOLTHORPE, YORK YO61 ISR
Tel: 01347 838990
Fax: 01347 830189
E-mail: sales@stephensonsofeasingwold.co.uk
Web site: www.stephensonsofeasingwold.co.uk
Chairman: Harry J Stephenson
Man Dir/Co Sec: David A Stephenson.
Fleet: 59 - 10 double-deck bus, 9 single-deck bus, 35 single-deck coach, 5 midibus.
Chassis: 4 Alexander Dennis, I DAF, 7 Leyland, 5 Mercedes, 10 Scania, 32 Volvo.
Bodies: I Jonckheere, 27 Plaxton, 3 Van Hool, 4 Wright, 14 Other.
Ops incl: local bus services, school contracts, private hire.
Livery: Red/Orange/Cream/Gold
Ticket system: Wayfarer

STEVE STOCKDALE COACHES
(Validford Ltd t/a)

76 GREEN LANE, SELBY YO8 9AW
Tel: 01757 703549 **Fax:** 01757 210956
Dirs: S Stockdale, J Stockdale, Julie O'Neill
(Co Sec).
Fleet: 5 - 2 double-deck bus, 3 single-deck coach
Chassis: 1 Leyland, 1 Scania, 3 Volvo.
Bodies: 1 East Lancs, 1 ECW, 2 Jonckheere,
1 Van Hool.
Ops incl: school contracts, private hire.
Livery: Red/White.

TEES VALLEY STAGE CARRIAGE

6 WHISTABLE GARDENS, REDCAR TS10 4GE
Tel: 01642 498622
E-mail: wayne@stagecarriage.co.uk
Web site: www.eastcleveland.co.uk
Props: W Brown, I Peacock.
Fleet: 6 - 3 double-deck bus, 3 single-deck coach.
Chassis: 1 Bova, 1 Leyland, 1 Mercedes, 3 Volvo.
Bodies: 1 Bova, 2 East Lancs, 1 Northern
Counties, 1 Plaxton, 1 Other.
Ops incl: local bus services, school contracts,
excursions & tours, private hire.

THORNES INDEPENDENT LTD

THE COACH STATION, HULL ROAD,
HEMINGBOROUGH, SELBY YO8 6QG
Tel: 01757 630777 **Fax:** 01757 630666
Web site: www.thornes.info
E-mail: coaches@thornes.info
Man Dir: Philip Thornes **Co Sec:** Mrs Christine
Thornes **Ops Dir:** Ms Jane Thornes
Ch Eng: Steven Cotton.
Fleet: 18 - 2 double-deck bus, 1 single-deck bus,
7 single-deck coach, 2 midicoach, 6 heritage.
Chassis: 2 AEC, 1 Beadle, 1 Bedford, 1 Bristol,
1 DAF, 2 Dennis, 1 Leyland, 2 Mercedes, 1 Seddon,
6 Volvo.
Bodies: 1 Beadle, 2 Duple, 3 East Lancs,
1 Harrington, 1 Optare, 10 Plaxton.
Ops incl: local bus services, school contracts,
excursions & tours, private hire, continental tours.
Livery: Blue/Grey
Ticket System: Wayfarer

TRANSDEV HARROGATE & DISTRICT

PROSPECT PARK, BROUGHTON WAY,
STARBECK, HARROGATE HG2 7NY

Tel: 01423 566061 **Fax:** 01423 885670
E-mail: enquire@harrogateanddistrict.co.uk
Web site: www.harrogatebus.co.uk
Fleet Names: Harrogate & District, The 36.
Ch Exec: Martin Gilbert **Fin Dir:** Jim Wallace
Marketing Dir: Nigel Eggleton.
Fleet: 77 - 23 double-deck bus, 31 single-deck
bus, 11 single-deck coach, 12 midibus.
Chassis: 11 Dennis, 2 Leyland, 64 Volvo.
Bodies: 2 Alexander, 2 Leyland, 14 Plaxton,
59 Wright.
Ops incl: local bus services, school contracts.
Livery: Red/Cream.
Ticket System: Wayfarer 3
(Part of Transdev Blazefield)

TRANSDEV YORK

11-12 STONEBOW HOUSE, STONEBOW,
YORK YO1 7NP
Tel: 01904 633990
Fax: 01904 655587
E-mail: info@transdevyork.co.uk
Web sites: www.yorkbus.co.uk
Fleet Names: Transdev York, York City
Sightseeing
Chief Exec: Martin Gilbert **Fin Dir:** Jim Wallace
Marketing Dir: Nigel Eggleton.
Fleet: 25 - 2 double-deck bus, 9 single-deck bus,
8 open-top bus, 6 midibus.
Chassis: 3 Dennis, 4 Leyland, 3 MCW, 12 Optare,
3 Volvo.
Bodies: 3 Alexander, 4 East Lancs, 3 MCW,
12 Optare, 3 Wright.
Ops incl: local bus services, city sightseeing tours,
school contracts.
Livery: Red
Ticket System: Almex A90/Wayfarer TGX150
(Part of Transdev Blazefield)

TRANSDEV YORKSHIRE COASTLINER

BUS STATION, RAILWAY STREET, MALTON
YO17 7NR
Tel: 01653 692556 **Fax:** 01653 695341
E-mail: enquire@coastliner.co.uk
Web site: www.yorkbus.co.uk
Ops Man: Brian Kneeshaw.
Fleet: 20 double-deck bus.
Chassis: 20 Volvo.
Bodies: 20 Wright.
Ops incl: local bus services.
Livery: Cream/Blue.

Ticket System: Wayfarer 3
(Part of Transdev Blazefield)

WINN BROS

8 MILL HILL CLOSE, BROMPTON,
NORTHALLERTON DL6 2QP
Tel: 01609 773520 **Fax:** 01609 775234
Fleet: 12 – 7 single-deck coach, 1 midibus,
2 midicoach, 2 minibus.
Chassis: Bova, LDV, Mercedes, Setra, Toyota,
Volvo.
Ops incl: school contracts, private hire.

WISTONIAN COACHES

PLANTATION GARAGE, CAWOOD ROAD,
WISTOW, SELBY YO8 0XB
Tel/Fax: 01757 269303
Partners: John Firth, Gordon Firth.
Fleet: 6 - 4 single-deck coach, 2 midicoach
Chassis: 1 Bedford, 1 Mercedes, 4 Volvo.
Bodies: 6 Plaxton.
Ops incl: private hire.
Livery: Cream with Red/Orange/Yellow stripes.

YORK PULLMAN BUS CO LTD

WETHERBY ROAD, RUFFORTH, YORK
YO23 3QA
Tel: 01904 622992
Fax: 01904 622993
Recovery: 07753 670742
E-mail: sales@yorkpullmanbus.co.uk
Web site: www.yorkpullmanbus.co.uk
Man Dir: Tom James **Co Sec:** Maxine James
Coaching Man: Kevin Walker **Comm Man:**
Richard Startup **Chief Eng:** Paul Hirst
Sales Man: Chloe Fenton.
Fleet: 105 – incl 15 double-deck bus, 15 single-
deck bus, 40 single-deck coach, 10 open-top bus,
10 midicoach, 5 minibus.
Chassis: 2 AEC, 1 Bedford, 1 BMC, 2 Bristol,
5 DAF, 4 Dennis, 1 Ford, 6 Iveco, 35 Leyland,
2 MAN, 6 Mercedes, 3 Scania, 1 Toyota, 50 Volvo.
Bodies: 1 Berkhof, 1 Beulas, 1 BMC, 1 Caetano,
1 Duple, 5 ECW, 4 East Lancs, 1 Ikarus, 1 Irizar,
1 Jonckheere, 40 Plaxton, 2 Sitcar, 10 Van Hool.
Ops incl: local bus services, school contracts,
excursions & tours, private hire, express,
continental tours.
Livery: Maroon, Cream & Yellow
Ticket system: Wayfarer 3

NORTHAMPTONSHIRE

GEOFF AMOS COACHES LTD
Ceased trading since LRB 2011 went to press

L F BOWEN LTD t/a
JEFFS COACHES LTD

STATION ROAD, HELMDON, BRACKLEY
NN13 5QT
Tel: 01295 768292
Fax: 01295 760365
E-mail: admin@jeffscoaches.com
Web site: www.bowenscoaches.com
Chairman: Kevin Lower **Chief Executive
Officer:** R Graham **Man Dir (Coaching):**
R Lyng **Group Ops Man:** N G Tetley **Group
Eng Man:** D Hoy **Fin Dir:** S Beech **Man Dir
(Retail):** M Stones **Property Dir:** N Ellis
Dirs: A H Moseley, C J Padbury, K G York.
Fleet: 58 - 8 double-deck bus, 1 single-deck

bus, 47 single-deck coach, 2 midicoach.
Chassis: 4 Dennis, 6 Iveco, 8 Leyland,
2 Toyota, 38 Volvo.
Bodies: 6 Beulas, 23 Caetano, 8 Jonckheere,
8 Leyland, 9 Plaxton, 2 Van Hool, 2 other.
Ops incl: school contracts, excursions &
tours.
Livery: White /Red/Green/Silver
A subsidiary of the Bowen Travel Group – see
Staffordshire.

L F BOWEN LTD t/a YORKS COACHES

SHORT LANE, COGENHOE,
NORTHAMPTON NN7 1LE
Tel: 01604 890210 **Fax:** 01604 891153
E-mail: yorksco@yorks-travel.co.uk
Web site: www.yorkscoaches.com
Chairman: Kevin Lower **Chief Executive**

Officer: R Graham **Man Dir (Coaching):**
R Lyng **Group Ops Man:** N G Tetley **Group
Eng Man:** D Hoy **Fin Dir:** S Beech **Man Dir
(Retail):** M Stones **Property Dir:** N Ellis
Dirs: A H Moseley, C J Padbury, K G York.
Fleet: 27 – 3 double-deck bus, 22 single-deck
coach, 2 midicoach.
Chassis: 2 Dennis, 2 Iveco, 3 Leyland, 5 MAN,
1 Scania, 2 Setra, 2 Toyota, 10 Volvo.
Bodies: 2 Beulas, 2 Caetano, 3 ECW, 1 Irizar,
2 Marcopolo, 5 Noge, 9 Plaxton, 2 Setra,
1 Van Hool.
Ops incl: local bus services, excursions &
tours, school contracts, private hire, express,
continental tours.
Livery: Silver
Ticket System: Almex
A subsidiary of the Bowen Travel Group – see
Staffordshire.

Legend

Symbol	Description	Symbol	Description	Symbol	Description
♿	Vehicle suitable for disabled	🚏	Seat belt-fitted Vehicle	R24	24 hour recovery service
T	Toilet-drop facilities available	🍴	Coach(es) with galley facilities	↘	Replacement vehicle available
R	Recovery service available	❄	Air-conditioned vehicle(s)	▭	Vintage Coach(es) available
▭	Open top vehicle(s)	♿♿	Coaches with toilet facilities	🍃	Hybrid Buses

CENTREBUS LTD

UNIT 5, SOUTH FOLDS ROAD, CORBY
NN18 9EU
Tel: 0844 351 1120
E-mail: info@centrebus.com
Web site: www.centrebus.info
Ops incl: local bus services, school contracts.
Livery: Blue/Orange

COUNTRY LION (NORTHAMPTON) LTD

OXWICH CLOSE, BRACKMILLS,
NORTHAMPTON NN4 7BH
Tel: 01604 754566
Fax: 01604 664062
Web site: www.countrylion.co.uk
Dir: A J Bull.
Fleet: 49 – 9 double-deck bus, 2 single-deck
bus, 28 single-deck coach, 10 midicoach.
Chassis: 2 Alexander Dennis, 1 Bristol,
7 Dennis, 1 Ford, 5 Irisbus, 3 Iveco, 3 Leyland,
7 Mercedes, 1 Scania, 2 Setra, 1 Toyota,
15 Volvo.
Bodies: Alexander, Beulas, Caetano, Duple,
East Lancs, ECW, Irizar, Marshall, Optare,
Plaxton, Wadham Stringer.
Ops incl: local bus services, school contracts,
excursions & tours, continental tours, private
hire.

FIRST MIDLANDS

ST JAMES' ROAD, NORTHAMPTON
NN5 5TD
Tel: 08450 100 111
Fax: 01604 590522
Fleet Name: First Northampton
Regional Man Dir: Nigel Barrett **Regional
Eng Dir:** Mick Brannigan **Regional Comm
Dir:** Steve Wickers **Regional Fin Planning
Dir:** David Marshall.
Fleet (Northampton): 48 - 7 double-deck
bus, 34 single-deck bus, 4 articulated bus,
3 midibus.
Chassis: 4 BMC, 2 Dennis, 3 Optare, 39 Volvo.
Bodies: 4 Alexander, 4 BMC, 1 East Lancs,
3 Optare, 2 Plaxton, 34 Wright.
Ops incl: local bus services, school contracts,
private hire.
Livery: FirstGroup UK Bus
Ticket System: Wayfarer 3

GOODE COACHES

47 BURFORD AVENUE, NORTHAMPTON
NN3 6AF
Tel: 01604 862700
Tel (night): 01604 645369
Prop & Ch Eng: David W L Goode
Traffic Man: Andrew J Wall
Fleet: 4 single-deck coach.
Chassis: 1 DAF, 3 Leyland
Bodies: 1 Ikarus, 3 Van Hool
Ops incl: school contracts, private hire.

HAMILTON'S COACHES

3 FOX STREET, ROTHWELL,
KETTERING NN14 6AN
Tel: 01536 710344   **Fax:** 01536 712244
Recovery: 07887 945564
E-mail: hamiltonscoaches@googlemail.com
Prop: Minesh Uka.
Fleet: 20 - 11 double-deck bus, 8 single-deck
coach, 1 double-deck coach.
Chassis: 6 MCW, 14 Volvo.
Bodies: 1 Jonckheere, 6 MCW, 5 Northern
Counties, 8 Plaxton.
Ops incl: local bus services, school contracts,
excursions & tours, private hire, continental
tours.
Livery: White with Yellow, Orange & Red
stripes

J & M B TRAVEL

2 THE JAMB, CORBY NN17 1AY
Tel: 01536 202660
Fax: 01536 406299
E-mail: info@jambtravel.co.uk
Web site: www.jambtravel.co.uk
Props: Jackie Burton, Michael Burton.
Fleet: 6 - 5 single-deck coach, 1 midicoach.
Chassis: 2 Bova, 3 DAF, 1 Mercedes.
Bodies: 2 Bova, 1 Caetano, 1 Ikarus,
1 Marshall, 1 Van Hool.
Ops incl: school contracts, excursions &
tours, private hire.
Livery: Silver

R S LAWMAN COACHES LTD

7 ROBINSON WAY, KETTERING
NN16 8PT
Tel: 01536 517664
Fax: 01536 513474
E-mail: lawmans.coaches@tiscali.co.uk
Web site: www.lawmanscoaches.co.uk
Fleet: 10 single-deck coach, 2 midicoach,
3 minibus.
Chassis: Bova, LDV, Mercedes, Volvo.
Ops incl: school contracts, private hire,
excursions & tours.
Livery: White with Green/Orange

MERIDIAN BUS

23 MILLBROOK CLOSE, ST JAMES,
NORTHAMPTON NN5 5JF
Tel: 01604 590480
Web site: www.meridianbus.co.uk
Fleet: 6 midibus.
Chassis: 2 Mercedes, 4 Optare.
Ops incl: local bus services.
Livery: Red/Blue/White

R B TRAVEL

ISHAM ROAD, PYTCHLEY
NN4 1EW

Prop: Roger Bull.
Tel/Fax: 01536 791066
Fleet: 10 single-deck coach.

RODGER'S COACHES LTD

102 KETTERING ROAD, WELDON
NN17 3JG
Tel: 01536 200500
Fax: 01536 407407
Recovery: 01536 200500
E-mail: enquiries@rodgerscoaches.co.uk
Web site: www.rodgerscoaches.co.uk
Props: James Rodger, Linda Rodger.
Fleet: 22 - 14 double-deck bus, 8 single-deck
coach.
Ops incl: school contracts, private hire,
excursions & tours.
Livery: White/Red

SOUL BROTHERS

See Buckinghamshire

STAGECOACH MIDLANDS

ROTHERSTHORPE AVENUE,
NORTHAMPTON NN4 8UT
Tel: 08456 001314
Fax: 01622 662286
E-mail: midlands.enquiries@stagecoachbus.
com
Web site: www.stagecoachbus.com
Regional Man Dir: Bob Montgomery
Man Dir: Steve Burd **Ops Dir:** Liz Esnouf
Eng Dir: Keith Dyball.
Fleet (Northants): 168 - 63 double-deck
bus, 60 single-deck bus, 45 midibus.
Chassis: 17 Alexander Dennis, 45 Dennis,
21 MAN, 45 Optare, 18 Scania, 23 Volvo.
Ops incl: local bus services, school contracts,
private hire, express.
Livery: Stagecoach UK Bus
Ticket System: ERG

ADAMSON'S COACHES
8 PORLOCK COURT, NORTHBURN CHASE,
CRAMLINGTON NE23 3TT
Tel/Fax: 01670 734050
Recovery: 07721 633351
E-mail: adamsonscoaches@btconnect.com
Web site: www.adamsonscoaches.co.uk
Prop: Allen Mullen
Ch Eng: Paul Mullen
Co Sec: Mrs Wendy Mullen.
Fleet: 3 single-deck coach.
Chassis: 3 DAF.
Bodies: 3 Van Hool.
Ops incl: excursions & tours, private hire.
Livery: White/Rosewood

ARRIVA NORTH EAST
See Tyne & Wear.

HENRY COOPER
See Tyne & Wear.

COOPER'S TOURMASTER LTD
RIVERSIDE, KITTYBREWSTER BRIDGE,
BEDLINGTON NE22 7BS
Tel: 01670 824900
Fax: 01670 824800
E-mail: helen@cooperstourmaster.co.uk
Web site: www.cooperstourmaster.co.uk
Fleet: 19 - 1 double-deck bus, 2 single-deck bus,
14 single-deck coach, 1 minibus, 1 minicoach.
Ops incl: school contracts, private hire,
excursions & tours.
Livery: Blue & Orange

CRAIGGS TRAVEL EUROPEAN
1 CENTRAL AVENUE, AMBLE, MORPETH
NE65 0NQ
Tel/Fax: 01665 710614
E-mail: classicalholiday@tiscali.co.uk
Partners: Joan Craiggs, Ian Craiggs
Man: Lawrence Craiggs.
Fleet: 3 single-deck coach, 1 minibus.
Chassis: 1 DAF, 1 LDV, 1 Setra, 1 Volvo.
Bodies: 1 LDV, 1 Plaxton, 1 Setra, 1 Van Hool.
Ops incl: excursions & tours, private hire,
continental tours.
Livery: Red

DREADNOUGHT COACHES
198 ALLERBURN LEA, ALNWICK
NE66 2QR
Tel: 01665 603022
E-mail: info@dreadnoughtcoaches.co.uk
Web site: www.dreadnoughtcoaches.co.uk
Prop: Claire Gilroy **Ch Eng:** Paul Fuller.
Fleet: 8 – 6 double-deck bus, 2 single-deck bus.
Chassis: 2 AEC, 4 Bristol, 2 Dennis, 1 Leyland.
Ops incl: local bus services, excursions & tours,
private hire.
Livery: Red & Cream
Ticket System: Setright

GLEN VALLEY TOURS LTD
STATION ROAD, WOOLER NE71 6SP
Tel: 01668 281578
Fax: 01668 281169
E-mail: enquiries@glenvalley.co.uk
Web site: www.glenvalley.co.uk
Ops incl: local bus services, school contracts,

private hire, excursions & tours.
Livery: Green & White

GO NORTH EAST
See Tyne & Wear.

HILLARYS COACHES
20 CASTLE VIEW, PRUDHOE
NE42 6NG
Tel/Fax: 01661 832560
Props: Lawrence Hillary.
Fleet: 5 - 3 single-deck bus, 1 midicoach,
1 minibus.
Chassis: 1 Ford, 1 MAN, 1 Mercedes, 1 Toyota,
1 Volkswagen.
Ops incl: school contracts, excursions & tours,
private hire.

JEWITTS COACHES
CHOLLERFORD BUNGALOW,
CHOLLERFORD, HEXHAM NE46 4EW
Tel: 01434 681325
Fax: 01434 681517
Web site: www.jewittscoaches.co.uk
Fleet: 5 – 2 single-deck coach, 3 midicoach.
Ops incl: school contracts, excursions & tours,
private hire, continental tours.
Livery: White with Blue/Red.

LONGSTAFF'S COACHES
UNIT 107, COQUET ENTERPRISE PARK,
AMBLE, MORPETH NE65 0PE
Tel: 01665 713300
Fax: 01665 710987
E-mail: fred@longstaffcoaches.co.uk
Web site: www.longstaffcoaches.co.uk
Dirs: Frederick Longstaff, Edward Longstaff.
Fleet: 7 – 5 single-deck coach, 2 midicoach.
Chassis: Mercedes, Neoplan, Volvo.
Bodies: Jonckheere, Neoplan, Plaxton, Sitcar,
Van Hool.
Ops incl: school contracts, excursions & tours,
private hire, continental tours.
Livery: White.

PERRYMAN'S BUSES LTD
RAMPARTS BUSINESS PARK, NORTH ROAD,
BERWICK UPON TWEED TD15 1TX
Tel: 01289 308719
Fax: 01289 309970
Web site: www.perrymansbuses.com
Dirs: R J Perryman L M Perryman.
Fleet: 30 - 15 single-deck bus, 5 single-deck
coach, 6 midibus, 4 minibus.
Chassis: 2 Alexander Dennis, 1 Ford, 4 MAN,
11 Mercedes, 12 Optare.
Bodies: 2 Alexander Dennis, 4 MCV, 12 Optare,
10 Plaxton.
Ops incl: local bus services, school contracts,
private hire.
Livery: White with Red/Blue.
Ticket System: Wayfarer TGX.

ROTHBURY MOTORS
HAWTHORN CLOSE, LIONHEART
ENTERPRISE PARK, ALNWICK NE66 2HT
Tel: 01665 606616
E-mail: rothburymotors@btconnect.com
Web site: www.rothburymotors.co.uk
Ops incl: local bus services, school contracts,

private hire, excursions & tours.
Livery: White with Blue Lettering

ROWELL COACHES
3B DUKES WAY, PRUDHOE NE42 6PQ
Tel: 01661 832316
Fax: 01661 834485
E-mail: sales@rowellcoaches.co.uk
Web site: www.rowellcoaches.co.uk
Dirs: Mr S Gardiner, Mrs B Gardiner.
Fleet: 7 single-deck coach.
Chassis: 6 Bova, 1 Leyland.
Ops incl: school contracts, excursions & tours,
private hire.
Livery: White

SERENE TRAVEL
Ceased trading

HOWARD SNAITH COACHES
THE COACH HOUSE, BRIERLEY GARDENS,
OTTERBURN NE19 1HB
Tel: 01830 520609
Fax: 01830 520462
E-mail: howardsnaith@btconnect.com
Web site: www.howardsnaith.co.uk
Fleet: 75 – single-deck bus, single-deck coach,
midibus, midicoach, minibus, minicoach.
Chassis: Alexander Dennis, DAF, Ford, LDV,
Mercedes, Volvo.
Ops incl: local bus services, school contracts,
private hire, excursions & tours, continental tours.
Livery: White with Blue/Pink

STAGECOACH NORTH EAST
See Tyne & Wear.

TRAVELSURE
67 MAIN STREET, SEAHOUSES NE68 7TN
Tel: 01668 219291
Fax: 01668 721381
E-mail: travelsure@travelsure.co.uk
Web site: www.travelsure.co.uk
Props: Barrie Patterson, Karen Patterson.
Fleet: 25 - 5 single-deck bus, 11 single-deck
coach, 1 midibus, 3 midicoach, 5 minibus.
Chassis: 2 Alexander Dennis, 1 DAF, 3 Dennis,
4 Irisbus, 2 Iveco, 1 LDV, 5 Mercedes, 1 Optare,
3 Renault, 1 Scania, 3 Setra.
Bodies: 2 Alexander Dennis, 6 Beulas, 1 Caetano,
1 Irizar, 1 LDV, 1 Mellor, 1 Optare, 3 Plaxton,
3 Setra, 1 Sitcar, 1 Van Hool, 4 Other.
Ops incl: local bus services, school contracts,
excursions & tours, private hire.
Livery: Blue.
Ticket System: Wayfarer

TYNEDALE GROUP TRAVEL
TOWNFOOT GARAGE, HALTWHISTLE
NE49 0EJ
Tel: 01434 322944
Fax: 01434 322955
E-mail: admin@tynedalegrouptravel.co.uk
Web site: www.tynedalegrouptravel.co.uk
Partner: Andy Sinclair.
Fleet: 4 - 3 single-deck coach, 1 minicoach.
Chassis: 1 Mercedes, 3 Neoplan.
Bodies: 3 Neoplan, 1 Other.
Ops incl: local bus services, school contracts,

excursions & tours, private hire, continental tours.

TYNE VALLEY COACHES LTD
♿ ⚙ ❄ ⑪
ACOMB, HEXHAM NE46 4QT
Tel: 01434 602217
Fax: 01434 604150
E-mail: alistair@tynevalleycoaches.co.uk
Web site: www.tynevalleycoaches.co.uk
Dir: Mrs K M Weir.
Fleet: 20 - 2 single-deck bus, 18 single-deck coach.
Chassis: 2 DAF, 13 Leyland, 5 Volvo.
Bodies: 3 Duple, 1 East Lancs, 1 Optare, 14 Plaxton, 1 Van Hool.
Ops incl: local bus services, school contracts, private hire.
Livery: Blue/Silver
Ticket System: AES

TREVOR BAILEY TRAVEL LTD
⚙ ⑪ ❄ ⑪
26 FOREST STREET, KIRKBY IN ASHFIELD NG17 7DT
Tel: 01623 759400
Web site: www.trevorbaileytravel.co.uk
Man Dir: T Bailey **Ch Eng:** G Payne
Fleet: single-deck coach.
Ops incl: school contracts, private hire, excursions & tours.

BELLAMY COACHES LTD
Ceased trading since LRB 2011 went to press.

BUTLER BROTHERS COACHES
⑪ ⚙ ❄ ⚒
60 VERNON ROAD, KIRKBY IN ASHFIELD NG17 8ED
Tel: 01623 753260 **Fax:** 01623 754581
E-mail: butlerscoaches@btconnect.com
Web site: www.butlerscoaches.co.uk
Dirs: Robert Butler, Anita Butler, James Butler.
Fleet: 9 - 1 double-deck bus, 7 single-deck coach, 1 midicoach.
Chassis: 2 DAF, 3 Dennis, 1 Leyland, 2 MAN, 1 Volvo.
Bodies: 1 Berkhof, 2 Caetano, 1 East Lancs, 2 Plaxton, 3 Van Hool.
Ops incl: school contracts, excursions & tours, private hire, continental tours.
Livery: Dual Blue
Ticket System: Wayfarer

DUNN MOTOR TRACTION (YOUR BUS)
See Derbyshire

GILL'S TRAVEL
106 ILKESTON ROAD, TROWELL, NOTTINGHAM NG9 3PX
Tel: 0115 944 1400
E-mail: info@gills-travel.co.uk
Web site: www.gills-travel.co.uk
Fleet incl: single-deck bus
Ops incl: local bus services, school contracts
Livery: Yellow

GOSPEL'S COACHES
⚙ ⑪ ❄ ⚒
THE AERODROME, WATNALL ROAD, HUCKNALL NG15 6EN
Tel: 0115 963 3894

Dirs: T Gospel, G Gospel, G T Gospel
Fleet: 4 - 2 double-deck bus, 2 single-deck coach.
Chassis: 2 Leyland, 2 Volvo.
Bodies: 1 Alexander, 1 Northern Counties, 2 Plaxton.
Ops incl: excursions & tours, private hire, school contracts.
Livery: White/Blue.

HENSHAWS COACHES
⑪ ⚙ ❄
57 PYE HILL ROAD, JACKSDALE NG16 5LR
Tel: 01:773 607909
E-mail: paul@henshawscoaches.co.uk
Web site: www.henshawscoaches.co.uk
Prop: Paul Henshaw
Fleet: 5 - 4 single-deck coach, 1 midicoach
Chassis: 1 BMC, 1 Bova, 1 DAF, 2 Mercedes
Bodies: 1 BMC, 1 Bova, 2 Mercedes, 1 Van Hool.
Ops incl: excursions & tours, private hire, school contracts, continental tours.
Livery: White/Orange

JOHNSON BROS TOURS LTD
♿ ⚙ ⑪ ⑪ ▭ ❄ R R24 ⚒ T
GREEN ACRES, GREEN LANE, HODTHORPE, WORKSOP S80 4XR
Tel/Recovery: 01909 720337 / 721847
Fax: 01909 722886
E-mail: lee@johnsonstours.co.uk
Web site: www.johnsonstours.co.uk
Dirs: C A Johnson, S Johnson, A Johnson, L Johnson, S Johnson **Ops Man:** S Smallshaw
Fleet: 118 - 70 double-deck bus, 4 single-deck bus, 30 single-deck coach, 4 double-deck coach, 4 midibus, 2 midicoach, 1 minibus, 3 minicoach.
Chassis incl: 2 Alexander Dennis, 1 Ayats, 3 Bova, 30 Bristol, 2 DAF, 2 Ford Transit, 6 Irisbus, 4 Iveco, 4 MAN, 4 Mercedes, 6 Neoplan, 6 Scania, 3 Van Hool, 20 Volvo.
Bodies: 1 Ayats, 6 Beulas, 2 Berkhof, 3 Bova, 2 Caetano, 30 ECW, 5 East Lancs, 6 Irizar, 4 Jonckheere, 6 Neoplan, 30 Northern Counties, 25 Plaxton, 6 Scania, 2 Sunsundegui, 3 Van Hool, 1 Volvo.
Ops incl: local bus services, school contracts, excursions & tours, private hire, express, continental tours.
Livery: Blue Fade with Stars
Ticket System: ITSO
See also Redfern Travel Ltd

K & S COACHES
♿ ⚙
21 CLIFTON GROVE, MANSFIELD NG18 4HY
Tel/Fax: 01623 656768
Prop: K & Sue Burnside.
Fleet: 2 - 1 midicoach, 1 minicoach.
Chassis: Ford Transit, Mercedes.
Ops incl: school contracts, excursions & tours, private hire.
Livery: White/Red/Grey.

KETTLEWELL (RETFORD) LTD
⑪ ⚙ ⑪ ▭ ❄ ⚒ T
GROVE STREET, RETFORD DN22 6LA
Tel: 01777 860360 **Fax:** 01777 710351
E-mail: info@kettlewellscoaches.co.uk
Web site: www.kettlewellscoaches.co.uk
Man Dir: Paul Kettlewell **Chairman:** Aubrey Kettlewell **Tours Dir:** Christine Kettlewell
PA to Man Dir: Margaret Burton **PA to Tours Dir:** Jane Bushby **Ops Man:** Tony Bradley
Fleet: 13 - 2 double-deck coach, 10 single-deck coach, 1 minicoach.
Chassis: 1 Dennis, 1 MAN, 1 Mercedes, 9 Scania, 1 Volvo.
Bodies: 1 East Lancs, 9 Irizar, 1 Jonckheere, 1 Mercedes, 1 Neoplan.
Ops incl: local bus services, school contracts, excursions & tours, private hire, continental tours.
Livery: White
Ticket System: Wayfarer

McEWENS TRAVEL
⚙ ⑪ ❄ R R24 T
MILLENNIUM BUSINESS PARK, CHESTERFIELD ROAD, MANSFIELD NG19 7JX
Tel: 01623 646733 **Fax:** 01623 621366
E-mail: mcewentravel@hotmail.co.uk
Web site: www.mcewenscoaches.co.uk
Dirs: J McEwen, Mrs T McEwen
Ops Man: A Poyser **Comm Man:** C Elkin
Fleet: 20 – 8 double-deck bus, 10 single-deck coach, 1 midicoach, 1 minibus.
Chassis incl: 1 Bedford, 1 Irisbus, 1 LDV, 8 Leyland, 1 MAN
Bodies: 1 Beulas, 1 Berkhof, 1 East Lancs, 1 Irizar, 2 Jonckheere, 1 LDV, 1 Marcopolo, 7 Northern Counties, 5 Plaxton.
Ops incl: school contracts, excursions & tours, private hire, continental tours.
Livery: Red & White

MARSHALLS OF SUTTON-ON-TRENT LTD

11 MAIN STREET, SUTTON-ON-TRENT
NG23 6PF
Tel: 01636 821138
Fax: 01636 822227
E-mail: office@marshallscoaches.co.uk
Web site: www.marshalls-coaches.co.uk
Man Dir: John Marshall **Eng Dir:** Paul Marshall
Financial Dir: Sally Sloan
Ops Dir: Kenneth Tagg
Fleet: 27 - 10 double-deck bus, 7 single-deck bus,
6 single-deck coach, 1 double-deck coach,
3 midicoach.
Chassis: 1 Dennis, 1 Iveco, 3 Leyland, 1 MAN,
1 Mercedes, 1 Neoplan, 7 Optare, 12 Volvo.
Bodies: 7 Alexander, 2 Berkhof, 2 East Lancs,
1 Indcar, 1 Mercedes, 1 Neoplan, 7 Optare,
4 Plaxton, 1 Transbus, 1 Wright.
Ops incl: local bus services, school contracts,
excursions & tours, private hire, continental tours.
Livery: Blue/Cream.
Ticket System: Wayfarer

C.W. MOXON LTD

MALTBY ROAD, OLDCOTES, WORKSOP
S81 8JN
Tel: 01909 730345
Fax: 01909 733670
E-mail: enquiries@moxons-tours.co.uk
Web site: www.moxons.co.uk
Fleet Name: Moxons Coaches.
Dirs: Mrs L Marlow, Mrs M Moxon
Co Sec: Mrs J Holder **Ch Eng:** M Marlow.
Fleet: 15 - 3 double-deck bus, 12 single-deck
coach.
Chassis: 2 Bedford, 3 Bristol, 7 DAF, 2 Leyland,
1 Iveco.
Bodies: 2 Bova, 1 Duple, 1 EOS, 3 MCW,
5 Plaxton, 3 Van Hool.
Ops incl: excursions & tours, private hire,
continental tours, school contracts.
Livery: Cream/Red.

NOTTINGHAM CITY TRANSPORT

LOWER PARLIAMENT STREET,
NOTTINGHAM NG1 1GG
Tel: 0115 950 5745
Fax: 0115 950 4425
E-mail:
shiela.swift@nctx.co.uk, info@nctx.co.uk
Web site: www.nctx.co.uk
Chairman: Brian Parbutt
Man Dir: Mark Fowles
Eng Dir: Barry Baxter
Fin Dir/Co Sec: Rob Hicklin
Marketing & Communications Dir:
Nicola Tidy
Comm Man: Barrie Burch
Fleet Eng: Farrell Smith
Fleet: 355 - 193 double-deck bus, 93 single-deck
bus, 5 articulated bus, 64 midibus.
Chassis: 46 Dennis, 98 Optare, 209 Scania.
Bodies: 137 East Lancs, 161 Optare, 55 Scania,
5 Wright.
Ops incl: local bus services.
Livery: Multi-Branded
Ticket system: Almex

NOTTINGHAM EXPRESS TRANSIT

See section 5 - Tram and Bus Rapid Transit
Systems

PREMIERE TRAVEL LTD

TRENT WHARF, MEADOW LANE,
NOTTINGHAM NG2 3HR
Tel: 0115 985 1111
Fax: 0115 986 3366
E-mail: info@premierebuses.co.uk
Web sites: www.premierebuses.co.uk
Man Dir: Stephen Greaves
Fleet: 93 – 6 double-deck bus, 45 single-deck bus,
15 single-deck coach, 25 midibus, 2 minibus.
Chassis: Alexander Dennis, BMC, Dennis, LDV,
MAN, Mercedes, Optare, Scania, Volvo.
Ops incl: local bus services, private hire, school
contracts.
Livery: Red/Silver

REDFERN TRAVEL LTD

THE SIDINGS, DEBDALE LANE,
MANSFIELD WOODHOUSE,
MANSFIELD NG19 7FE
Tel/Recovery: 01623 627653
Fax: 01909 625787
E-mail: andy@redferntravelltd.co.uk
Web site: www.johnsonstours.co.uk
Dirs: C A Johnson, S Johnson, A Johnson,
L Johnson, S Johnson
Ops Man: A Moran
Fleet: 118 - 70 double-deck bus, 4 single-deck
bus, 30 single-deck coach, 4 double-deck coach,
4 midibus, 2 midicoach, 1 minibus, 3 minicoach.
Chassis incl: 2 Alexander Dennis, 1 Ayats,
3 Bova, 30 Bristol, 2 DAF, 2 Ford Transit, 6 Irisbus,
4 Iveco, 4 MAN, 4 Mercedes, 6 Neoplan, 6 Scania,
3 Van Hool, 20 Volvo.
Bodies: 1 Ayats, 6 Beulas, 2 Berkhof, 3 Bova,
2 Caetano, 30 ECW, 5 East Lancs, 6 Irizar,
4 Jonckheere, 6 Neoplan, 30 Northern Counties,
25 Plaxton, 6 Scania, 2 Sunsundegui, 3 Van Hool,
1 Volvo.
Ops incl: local bus services, excursions & tours,
private hire, express, continental tours, school
contracts.
Livery: Green Fade/Stars
Ticket System: ITSO
(Subsidiary of Johnson Bros Tours Ltd)

SHARPE & SONS (NOTTINGHAM) LTD

UNIT 10, CANALSIDE INDUSTRIAL PARK,
CROPWELL BISHOP, NOTTINGHAM
NG12 3BE
Tel/Recovery: 0115 989 4466
Fax: 0115 989 4666
E-mail:
trevor.sharpe@sharpesofnottingham.com
Web site: www.sharpesofnottingham.com
Fleet Name: Sharpes of Nottingham
Man Dir: Trevor Sharpe
Ops Dir: James Sharpe
Dirs: Russell Sharpe, Neil Sharpe
Fin Dir: Simon Sharpe
Fleet: 34 - 12 double-deck bus, 3 single-deck
bus, 15 single-deck coach, 2 double-deck coach,
2 minibus.
Chassis: 2 Ford Transit, 5 MCW, 3 Van Hool,
4 VDL, 23 Volvo.
Bodies: 10 Alexander Dennis, 4 Berkhof,
2 Ford, 5 MCW, 13 Van Hool.
Ops incl: local bus services, school contracts,
excursions & tours, private hire, continental tours.
Livery: Silver with Two Tone Blue relief.
Ticket System: Wayfarer

SILVERDALE TOURS LTD

LITTLE TENNIS STREET SOUTH,
NOTTINGHAM NG2 4EU
Tel: 0115 912 1000
Fax: 0115 912 1558
E-mail: info@silverdaletours.co.uk
Web site: www.silverdaletours.co.uk
Dirs: Shaun Doherty, John Doherty
Fleet: 39 - 6 double-deck bus, 3 single-deck bus,
26 single-deck coach, 2 double-deck coach,
2 midicoach.
Chassis: 2 Ayats, 2 DAF, 3 Leyland National,
2 Mercedes, 30 Volvo.
Bodies: 5 Beulas, 19 Caetano, 3 Jonckheere,
3 Leyland National, 8 Plaxton, 1 Van Hool.
Ops incl: local bus services, private hire, express,
school contracts, continental tours.
Livery: Yellow/Red/Black

SKILLS MOTOR COACHES LTD

BELGRAVE ROAD, BULWELL,
NOTTINGHAM NG6 8LY
Tel: 0115 977 0080
Fax: 0115 977 7439
E-mail: pete.hallam@skills.co.uk
Web site: www.skills.co.uk
Man Dir: Nigel Skill
Fin Dir: Simon Skill
Ops Dir: Peter Hallam
Fleet: 48 - 14 double-deck bus, 30 single-deck
coach, 4 midicoach.
Chassis: 1 Bova, 2 MAN, 4 Mercedes, 1 Optare,
16 Setra, 25 Volvo.
Bodies: 9 Alexander, 1 Bova, 5 East Lancs,
7 Jonckheere, 1 Optare, 3 Plaxton, 16 Setra,
6 Van Hool.
Ops incl: school contracts, excursions & tours,
private hire, continental tours.
Livery: Green

STAGECOACH EAST MIDLANDS

PO BOX 15, DEACON ROAD,
LINCOLN LN2 4JB
Tel: 0845 605 0605
Fax: 01522 538229
E-mail:
eastmidlands.enquiries@stagecoachbus.com
Web site: www.stagecoachbus.com
Fleet Names: Stagecoach in Bassetlaw,
Stagecoach in Mansfield, Stagecoach in Newark.
Man Dir: Gary Nolan
Eng Dir: John Taylor
Comm Dir: Dave Skepper
Ops Dir: Richard Kay.
Fleet: 498 - 230 double-deck bus, 251 single-
deck bus, 9 single-deck coach, 8 open top bus.
Chassis: 294 Alexander Dennis, 6 DAF, 1 Leyland,
51 MAN, 21 Optare, 14 Scania, 111 Volvo.
Bodies: 335 Alexander Dennis, 63 East Lancs,
5 Jonckheere, 11 Northern Counties,
21 Optare, 33 Plaxton, 12 Transbus,
18 Wright.
Ops incl: local bus services.
Livery: Stagecoach UK Bus
Ticket System: ERG TP5000.

TIGER EUROPEAN

UNIT E PRIVATE ROAD, NO.4 COLWICK
INDUSTRIAL ESTATE, NOTTINGHAM
NG2 2JT
Tel: 01159 404040
Fax: 01159 404030

E-mail: info@tiger-european.com
Web site: www.tiger-european.com
Dirs: Mr G Golaz, Mrs B Golaz.
Fleet: 15 - 2 double-deck bus, 3 single-deck bus, 3 single-deck coach, 1 double-deck coach, 1 midicoach, 5 minibus
Chassis: 4 Ford, 1 LDV, 3 Leyland, 1 MAN, 1 MCV, 2 Mercedes, 3 Volvo.
Bodies: 1 Caetano, 2 Jonckheere, 2 Leyland, 1 Marshall/MCV, 1 Plaxton, 8 Other.
Ops incl: School contracts, private hire

TRANSIT EXPRESS TRAVEL
Ceased trading since LRB 2011 went to press.

TRAVEL WRIGHT LTD
BRUNEL BUSINESS PARK, JESSOP CLOSE, NEWARK NG24 2AG
Tel: 01636 703813
Fax: 01636 674641
E-mail: info@travelwright.fsnet.co.uk
Web site: www.travelwright.co.uk.
Dirs: D C Wright, C A Wright, T D Wright

Dir/Co Sec: Mrs P J Allen
Ch Eng: D Walker
Fleet: 33 – 1 double-deck bus, 3 single-deck bus, 21 single-deck coach, 7 midibus, 1 midicoach.
Chassis: Dennis, MAN, Mercedes, Optare, Setra, Volvo.
Bodies: Berkhof, Caetano, Mercedes, Neoplan, Noge, Optare, Plaxton, Setra, Van Hool.
Ops incl: local bus services, school contracts, excursions & tours, private hire, continental tours.
Livery: Cream/Red/Black.
Ticket System: Wayfarer

UNITY COACHES
BECK GARAGE, CLAYWORTH DN22 9AG
Tel: 07777 817556
E-mail: info@unity-coaches.com
Web site: www.unity-coaches.com
Partners: F Marriott, Mrs J Marriott.
Fleet: single-deck coach, midibus, midicoach, minicoach.
Chassis: Mercedes, Scania, Setra.
Livery: White with Orange.

VEOLIA TRANSPORT ENGLAND PLC
Operations in Nottinghamshire ceased since LRB 2011 went to press

WALLIS COACHWAYS
100 KIRKLINGTON ROAD, BILSTHORPE NG22 8SP
Tel: 01623 870655
Fax: 01623 870655
Prop: Stephen Wallis
Fleet: 2 - 1 midibus, 1 midicoach.
Chassis: 1 Mercedes, 1 Toyota
Ops incl: school contracts, private hire
Livery: White
Ticket system: Almex

ABINGDON COACHES
169, NEW GREENHAM PARK, THATCHAM RG19 6HN
Tel: 01235 420520
Fax: 01635 821128
E-mail: info@abingdoncoaches.co.uk
Web site: www.abingdoncoaches.co.uk
Dir: Simon Weaver.
Fleet: see Weavaway Travel, Berkshire.
Ops incl: private hire.
Livery: Blue
A subsidiary of Weavaway Travel, Berkshire

BAKERS COMMERCIAL SERVICES
COTSWOLD BUSINESS VILLAGE, MORETON-IN-THE-MARSH GL56 0JQ
Tel: 0845 688 7707
Fax: 0845 688 7660
E-mail: enquiries@bakerscoaches.co.uk
Web site: www.bakerscoaches.co.uk
Dir: Mike Baker **Ops Man:** Dave Goodall.
Fleet: 17 - 14 single-deck coach, 2 midicoach, 1 minibus.
Chassis: 2 Dennis, 2 Iveco, 3 Mercedes, 1 Scania, 2 Transbus, 7 Volvo.
Bodies: Alexander, Irizar, Plaxton, Sitcar.
Ops incl: local bus services, excursions & tours, school contracts, private hire, continental tours.
Livery: White/Red

BANBURYSHIRE CTA LTD
UNIT 17, BEAUMONT BUSINESS CENTRE, BEAUMONT CLOSE, BANBURY OX16 7TN
Tel: 01295 273086
Fax: 01295 273086
E-mail: bcta@msn.com
Fleet Name: Cherwell District Dial-A-Ride.
Fleet: 12 minibus.
Chassis: 1 Iveco, 2 LDV, 8 Mercedes, 1 Renault.
Ops incl: local bus services, private hire.

BLUNSDON'S COACH TRAVEL
13 HAMBLESIDE, BICESTER OX26 2GA

Tel: 01993 811320
Fax: 01993 811416
E-mail: blunsdonsct@talktalk.net
Prop: Michael Blunsdon.
Fleet: 6 single-deck coach.
Chassis: 2 Dennis, 2 Mercedes, 1 Neoplan, 1 Volvo.
Bodies: 2 Hispano, 1 Mercedes, 1 Neoplan. 3 Plaxton.
Ops incl: private hire, excursions & tours, school contracts.
Livery: White

CHARLTON-ON-OTMOOR SERVICES
THE GARAGE, CHARLTON-ON-OTMOOR OX5 2UQ
Tel: 01865 331249
Fax: 01865 316189
Fleet: 22 - 1 double-deck bus, 17 single-deck coach, 1 midibus, 1 midicoach, 2 minibus.
Chassis: Leyland, Mercedes, Volvo.
Ops incl: local bus services, school contracts, private hire.
Livery: Blue

CHENEY COACHES LTD
THORPE MEAD, BANBURY OX16 4RZ
Tel: 01295 254254
Fax: 01295 271990
E-mail: travel@cheneycoaches.co.uk
Web site: www.cheneycoaches.co.uk
Chairman: G W Peace **Man Dir:** M R Peace
Co Sec: S A Peace **Dir:** A G Peace
Fleet Eng: Tony Piotrowski.
Fleet: 43 - 34 single-deck coach, 9 minibus.
Chassis: 2 Citroen, 5 Ford Transit, 2 Mercedes, 1 Neoplan, 1 Peugeot, 15 Scania, 17 Volvo.
Bodies: 1 Berkhof, 15 Jonckheere, 2 Mercedes, 1 Neoplan, 3 Plaxton, 15 Van Hool.
Ops incl: school contracts, private hire, continental tours.
Livery: White/Red/Blue

GRAYLINE COACHES
STATION APPROACH, BICESTER OX26 6HU

Tel: 01869 246461
Fax: 01869 240087
Recovery: 07980 796028
E-mail: alan@grayline.co.uk
Web site: www.grayline.co.uk
Dir/Co Sec: Alan Gray **Dir:** Brian Gray
Ops Man: Paul Gray **Traffic Man:** Stuart Gray
Fleet Eng: Geoff Willoughby.
Fleet: 19 –11 single-deck coach, 8 midibus.
Chassis: 1 Alexander Dennis, 1 Bedford, 5 Iveco, 1 MAN, 2 Mercedes, 3 Optare, 3 Volvo, 3 Other.
Bodies: 2 Alexander Dennis, 5 Beulas, 1 Mercedes, 3 Optare, 5 Plaxton, 3 Wright.
Ops incl: local bus services, school contracts, excursions & tours, private hire, continental tours.
Livery: Red/White/Blue
Ticket System: Wayfarer 3

HEYFORDIAN TRAVEL LTD
MURDOCK ROAD, BICESTER OX26 4PP
Tel: 01869 241500 **Fax:** 01869 360011
E-mail: info@heyfordian.co.uk
Web site: www.heyfordian.travel
Dir: Graham Smith.
Fleet: 83 – 13 double-deck bus, 45 single-deck coach, 2 double-deck coach, 20 midibus, 1 midicoach, 2 minicoach.
Chassis: 4 Alexander Dennis, 2 Ayats, 2 DAF, 6 Dennis, 2 Enterprise, 7 Leyland, 3 MAN, 4 Mercedes, 11 Optare, 7 Scania, 1 Toyota, 39 Volvo.
Bodies: 4 Alexander Dennis, 2 Ayats, 2 Caetano, 7 ECW, 3 East Lancs, 32 Jonckheere, 1 Mercedes, 13 Optare, 14 Plaxton, 2 Sunsundegui, 6 Van Hool, 1 Volvo, 1 Other.
Ops incl: local bus services, school contracts, excursions & tours, private hire, continental tours.
Livery: White/Red/Orange/Black.
Ticket System: Wayfarer.

McLEANS COACHES
GATEWAY HOUSE, WINDRUSH PARK ROAD, WITNEY OX29 7EY
Tel: 01993 771445
Fax: 01993 779556

E-mail: info@mcleanscoaches.co.uk
Web site: www.mcleanscoaches.co.uk
Dirs: Roger Alder, Mark Hepden
Man: Paul Skidmore **Ch Eng:** Paul Rose.
Fleet: 26 - 25 single-deck coach, 1 midicoach.
Chassis: 2 Bova, 2 Dennis, 1 EOS, 1 Iveco, 20 Volvo.
Bodies: 1 Berkhof, 2 Bova, 3 Caetano, 1 EOS, 1 Ikarus, 1 Indcar, 2 Jonckheere, 13 Plaxton, 2 Van Hool.
Ops incl: school contracts, excursions & tours, private hire, continental tours.
Livery: White/Red.

OXFORD BUS COMPANY

COWLEY HOUSE, WATLINGTON ROAD, OXFORD OX4 6GA
Tel: 01865 785400 **Fax:** 01865 774611
E-mail: info@oxfordbus.co.uk
Web site: www.oxfordbus.co.uk
Fleet Names: Brookes Bus, City, Oxford Espress, Park & Ride, The Airline.
Man Dir: Philip Kirk **Ops Dir:** Louisa Weeks
Eng Dir: Ray Woodhouse **Fin & Comm Dir:** Helen Fowweather
Fleet: 153 – 68 double-deck bus, 48 single-deck bus, 37 single-deck coach.
Chassis: 17 Alexander Dennis, 20 Dennis, 48 Mercedes, 43 Scania, 25 Volvo.
Bodies: 68 Alexander Dennis, 12 Irizar, 6 Jonckheere, 48 Mercedes, 19 Plaxton.
Ops incl: local bus services, express.
Liveries: Red (City bus) Green (Oxford Espress/ Park & Ride) Blue (Brookes Bus, The Airline)
Ticket System: ERG
A subsidiary of the Go-Ahead Group

PEARCES PRIVATE HIRE LTD

TOWER ROAD INDUSTRIAL ESTATE, BERINSFIELD, WALLINGFORD OX10 7LN
Tel: 01865 340560
Fax: 01865 341582
Web site: www.coachhireoxford.com
Props: Clive Pearce, Martin Pearce.
Fleet: 12 - 8 single-deck coach, 2 midicoach, 2 minicoach.
Chassis: 2 Alexander Dennis, 6 Irisbus, 4 Toyota.
Bodies: 4 Caetano, 8 Plaxton.
Ops incl: school contracts, excursions and tours, private hire.
Livery: White with Yellow/Black

PLASTOWS COACHES

134 LONDON ROAD, WHEATLEY OX33 1JH
Tel: 01865 872270
Fax: 01865 875066
E-mail: plastowscoaches@btconnect.com
Web site: www.plastows.co.uk
Fleet: 9 single-deck coach.
Chassis: 9 Volvo.
Bodies: 9 Jonckheere.
Ops incl: private hire, school contracts.
Livery: White with Yellow/Orange.

RH TRANSPORT SERVICES

NORTH BUNGALOW, DOWNS ROAD, WITNEY OX29 0SY
Tel: 01993 869100
E-mail: rhbuses@googlemail.com
Web sites: www.rhbuses.com
www.rhcoaches.com

Props: A & A Hutt.
Fleet: 44 - 9 double-deck bus, 2 single-deck bus, 1 double-deck coach, 10 single-deck coach, 18 midibus, 4 minibus.
Ops incl: local bus services, school contracts, private hire
Livery: Blue & Cream

STAGECOACH IN OXFORDSHIRE

HORSPATH ROAD, COWLEY, OXFORD OX4 2RY
Tel: 01865 772250
Fax: 01865 405500
E-mail: oxford.enquiries@stagecoachbus.com
Web site: www.stagecoachbus.com/ warwickshire
Man Dir: Martin Sutton **Service Delivery Dir:** Paul O'Callaghan **Fleet Man:** Simon Weaver
Comm Man: Andy Hamer
Fleet: 156 - 61 double-deck bus, 53 single-deck bus, 5 single-deck coach, 26 double-deck coach, 11 midibus.
Chassis: 29 Alexander Dennis, 8 Dennis, 31 MAN, 11 Optare, 30 Scania, 9 Transbus, 26 Van Hool, 12 Volvo.
Bodies: 31 Alexander, 70 Alexander Dennis, 11 Optare, 5 Plaxton, 13 Transbus, 26 Van Hool.
Ops incl: local bus services, express, school contracts.
Livery: Stagecoach UK Bus
Ticket system: Wayfarer 3

TAPPINS COACHES

COLLETT ROAD, SOUTHMEAD PARK, DIDCOT OX11 7ET
Tel: 01235 819393
Fax: 01235 816464
E-mail: coaches@tappins.co.uk
Web site: www.tappins.co.uk
Man Dir: Graham Smith **Comp Sec:** Jeremy Smith **Dirs:** Andrew Smith, Roland Smith.
Fleet: 50 - 45 single-deck coach, 2 double-deck coach, 1 midibus, 2 midicoach.
Chassis: 1 Dennis, 1 Neoplan, 1 Optare, 1 Scania, 2 Toyota, 44 Volvo.
Bodies: 1 Berkhof, 2 Caetano, 3 Jonckheere, 1 Optare, 1 Neoplan, 26 Plaxton, 16 Van Hool.
Ops incl: local bus services, school contracts, excursions & tours, private hire, express.
Livery: Orange/Black
Ticket System: Wayfarer.
A subsidiary of Heyfordian Travel

TOM TAPPIN LTD

No 1 SHOP, OXFORD RAILWAY STATION, PARK END STREET, OXFORD OX1 1HS
Tel: 01865 790522
Fax: 01865 202154
E-mail: info@citysightseeingoxford.com
Web site: www.citysightseeingoxford.com
Fleet Names: Guide Friday, City Sightseeing Oxford.
Chairman: Bill Allen **Gen Man:** Jane Marshall
Ops Man: Vacant **Transport Man:** Thomas Knowles.
Fleet: 11 open top bus.
Chassis: 4 Dennis, 5 Leyland, 2 Volvo.
Bodies: 5 Alexander Dennis, 6 East Lancs.
Ops incl: open top city sightseeing tours, private hire.
Livery: City Sightseeing Red with pictorial vinyls.
Ticket System: Casio

TEX COACHES

UNIT A, COTEFIELD FARM, OXFORD ROAD, BODICOTE OX15 4AQ
Tel: 01295 251579
Fax: 01295 673800
E-mail: sales@texcoaches.co.uk
Web site: www.texcoaches.co.uk
Dirs: Graham Harris, Alicicica Harris, Danielle Harris, Gemma Harris, Kyle Harris, Geoff Coles.
Fleet: 17 – 4 single-deck bus, 8 single-deck coach, 1 midicoach, 4 minibus.
Chassis: 8 Alexander Dennis, 2 Ford Transit, 1 Iveco, 2 MAN, 2 Mercedes, 2 Volvo.
Ops incl: local bus services, school contracts, private hire.
Livery: White & Burgundy
Ticket System: Almex

THAMES TRAVEL

WYNDHAM HOUSE, LESTER WAY, WALLINGFORD OX10 9TD
Tel: 01491 837988
Fax: 01491 838562
E-mail: office@thames-travel.co.uk
Web site: www.thames-travel.co.uk
Man Dir: John Wright.
Fleet: 43 - 5 double-deck bus, 18 single-deck bus, 20 midibus.
Chassis: 11 Alexander Dennis, 14 MAN, 8 Optare, 8 Scania, 1 Transbus, 1 Volvo.
Bodies: 1 Alexander, 9 Alexander Dennis, 5 East Lancs, 16 MCV, 8 Optare, 3 Scania, 1 Transbus.
Ops incl: local bus services, school contracts.
Livery: Green/Blue
Ticket system: Wayfarer
A subsidiary of the Go-Ahead Group

WHITES COACHES

90 COLWELL ROAD, BERINSFIELD, WALLINGFORD OX10 7NU
Tel: 01865 340516
E-mail: sue@whitescoaches.com
Web site: www.whitescoaches.com
Props: D Bainbridge, N Bland.
Fleet: 14 - 4 single-deck coach, 8 midibus, 2 midicoach.
Chassis: 4 Alexander Dennis, 2 Mercedes, 8 Optare.
Ops incl: local bus services, school contracts, excursions & tours, private hire.
Liveries: Buses – Yellow; Coaches: White with Red/Blue.

WORTHS MOTOR SERVICES LTD

ENSTONE, CHIPPING NORTON OX7 4LQ
Tel: 01608 677322
Fax: 01608 677298
E-mail: enquiries@worthscoaches.co.uk
Web site: www.worthscoaches.co.uk
Dirs: Richard Worth, Paul Worth.
Fleet: 14 - 1 double-deck bus, 11 single-deck coach, 1 midibus, 1 midicoach.
Chassis: 1 Dennis, 1 Mercedes, 12 Volvo.
Bodies: 1 Caetano, 1 Ferqui, 1 Jonckheere, 1 Northern Counties, 10 Plaxton.
Ops incl: school contracts, continental tours, private hire.
Livery: Silver/Blue
Ticket System: Wayfarer

ARRIVA MIDLANDS LTD

852 MELTON ROAD, LEICESTER LE4 8BT
Tel: 0116 264 0400
Fax: 0116 260 5605
E-mail: myattk.midlands@arriva.co.uk
Web site: www.arriva.co.uk
Regional Man Dir: R A Hind **Fin Dir:** J Barlow
Ops Dir: A Lloyd **Eng Dir:** M Evans **Area Business Man (Shropshire):** G Frost.
Fleet: 642 - 133 double-deck bus, 147 single-deck bus, 5 articulated bus, 218 midibus, 139 minibus.
Chassis: 1 Bova, 115 DAF, 182 Dennis, 4 Leyland, 35 Mercedes, 83 Optare, 49 Scania, 56 VDL, 117 Volvo.
Bodies: 57 Alexander Dennis, 1 Caetano, 65 East Lancs, 2 Marshall, 29 Mercedes, 9 Northern Counties, 83 Optare, 131 Plaxton, 42 Scania, 8 UVG, 202 Wright, 13 Other.
Ops incl: local bus services, school contracts, private hire, express.
Livery: Arriva, Wardles (Red/White, Red/Cream)
Ticket System: Wayfarer 150 & 200

BOULTONS OF SHROPSHIRE LTD

SUNNYSIDE, CARDINGTON, CHURCH STRETTON SY6 7JZ
Tel: 01694 771226
Fax: 01694 771296
Dir: Mick Boulton.
E-mail: info@boultonsofshropshire.co.uk
Web site: www.boultonsofshropshire.co.uk
Fleet: 19 - 3 single-deck bus, 10 single-deck coach, 1 midibus, 4 midicoach, 1 minibus.
Chassis incl: 4 Alexander Dennis, 2 Autosan, 5 DAF, 7 Mercedes, 1 Optare.
Bodies: 4 Alexander Dennis, 2 BMC, 5 Bova, 7 Mercedes, 1 Optare.
Ops incl: local bus services, school contracts, private hire.
Livery: Cream/Brown/Orange
Ticket System: Microfare

A T BROWN (COACHES) LTD

FREEMAIN HOUSE, HORTON ENTERPRISE PARK, HORTON WOOD 50, TELFORD TF1 7GZ
Tel: 01952 605331
Fax: 01952 608011
Recovery: 07983 562340
E-mail: enquiries@atbrowncoaches.co.uk
Web site: www.atbrowncoaches.co.uk
Dir: Ewen MacLeod.
Fleet: 23 - 22 single-deck coach, 1 minibus.
Chassis: 1 Bova, 8 DAF, 4 Dennis, 5 Iveco, 4 MAN, 1 Mercedes.
Bodies: 2 Berkhof, 5 Beulas, 1 Bova, 4 Caetano, 2 Ikarus, 1 Mercedes, 2 Neoplan, 3 Plaxton, 1 UVG, 2 Van Hool.
Ops incl: school contracts, private hire.
Livery: Sky Blue/Navy.

CARADOC COACHES LTD

2 NURSERY FIELDS, RUSHBURY ROAD, RUSHBURY, CHURCH STRETTON SY6 7DY
Tel: 01694 724522
Fax: 01694 771632
E-mail: graham.caradoc@btinternet.com
Web site: www caradoccoaches.co.uk

Prop: Mr & Mrs Graham Gough.
Fleet: 10 - 4 single-deck coach, 5 minibus, 1 minicoach.
Chassis: 2 LDV, 3 Mercedes, 1 Neoplan, 2 Scania, 2 Volvo.
Bodies: 2 Berkhof, 3 Mercedes, 1 Neoplan, 1 Optare, 1 Plaxton, 2 Volvo.
Ops incl: local bus services, school contracts, excursions & tours, private hire, continental tours.

COURTESY TRAVEL

2 WOODFIELD AVENUE, SHREWSBURY SY3 8HT
Tel/Fax/Recovery: 01743 358209
E-mail: courtesy@talktalkbusiness.net
Prop: W J Amies.
Fleet: 2 - 1 minicoach, 1 midicoach.
Chassis: 1 LDV, 1 Mercedes.
Bodies: 1 Autobus, 1 LDV.
Ops incl: excursions & tours, private hire.
Livery: White/Blue

ELCOCK REISEN

THE MADDOCKS, MADELEY, TELFORD TF7 5HA
Tel: 01952 585712
Fax: 01952 582577
Man Dir: J C Elcock **Dir:** J H Prince.
E-mail: debbie@elcockreisen.co.uk
Web site: www.elcockreisen.co.uk
Fleet: 33 - 27 single-deck coach, 4 midicoach, 2 minicoach.
Chassis: 6 Mercedes, 27 Volvo.
Bodies: 1 Autobus, 3 Esker, 13 Plaxton, 16 Van Hool.
Ops incl: school contracts, excursions & tours, private hire, continental tours.
Livery: Silver/Red/Gold.

HAPPY DAYS COACHES

See Staffordshire

HOLMES GROUP TRAVEL

CHAPEL HOUSE, 6 STAFFORD ROAD, NEWPORT TF10 7LY
Tel: 01952 820477

Fax: 01952 270607
Fax: 07831 258084
Dir: C Holmes.
Fleet: 4 - 2 single-deck coach, 1 midicoach, 1 minibus.
Chassis: 2 Iveco, 2 Scania.
Bodies: 1 Berkhof, 1 Indcar, 1 Irizar, 1 Other.
Ops incl: excursions & tours, private hire.
Livery: White with flag emblem

HORROCKS BUS LTD

IVY HOUSE, BROCKTON, LYDBURY NORTH SY7 8BA
Tel: 01588 680364
Prop: A P Horrocks.
Fleet: 11 - 4 single-deck bus, 2 single-deck coach, 2 midibus, 2 midicoach, 1 minibus.
Chassis: 5 Dennis, 5 Mercedes, 1 Volvo.
Ops incl: school contracts, private hire
Livery: White/Blue

LAKESIDE COACHES LTD

THE COACH CENTRE, ELLESMERE BUSINESS PARK, ELLESMERE SY12 0EW
Tel: 01691 622761
Fax: 01691 623694
E-mail: mailbox@lakesidecoaches.co.uk
Web site: www.lakesidecoaches.co.uk
Man Dir: John Davies **Dirs:** Dorothy Davies, Gareth Davies **Gen Man:** Neal Hall.
Fleet: 22 - single-deck coach, midicoach, minicoach
Chassis: 1 Alexander Dennis, 1 DAF, 4 Mercedes, 3 Toyota, 13 Volvo.
Bodies: 6 Caetano, 3 Mercedes, 1 Optare, 10 Plaxton, 1 Sunsundegui, 1 Van Hool.
Ops incl: excursions & tours, private hire, school contracts.
Livery: Green/White

LONGMYND TRAVEL LTD

THE COACH DEPOT, LEA CROSS, SHREWSBURY SY5 8HX
Tel: 01743 861999
Fax: 01743 861901
E-mail: info@longmyndtravel.co.uk
Web Site: www.longmyndtravel.co.uk

Dirs: T G Evans, F J Evans, V M Sheppard-Evans, D M Sheppard.
Fleet: 22 - 19 single-deck coach, 2 midicoach, 1 minibus.
Chassis: 3 DAF, 1 Iveco, 1 Mercedes, 1 Toyota, 16 Volvo.
Bodies: 3 Bova, 1 Caetano, 16 Plaxton, 1 Sunsundegui, 1 Other.
Ops incl: school contracts, private hire.
Livery: White/Red

M & J TRAVEL
COACH GARAGE, NEWCASTLE, CRAVEN ARMS SY7 8QL
Tel: 01588 640273
Prop: W M Price.
Fleet: 14 - 7 single-deck coach, 2 midicoach, 5 minibus.
Chassis: 1 Bova, 1 DAF, 4 LDV, 2 Mercedes, 1 Toyota, 5 Volvo.
Ops incl: school contracts, excursions & tours, private hire, continental tours.
Livery: White/Black/Gold.
Ticket System: Setright.

M P MINICOACHES LTD
14 REDBURN CLOSE, KETLEY GRANGE, TELFORD TF2 0EE
Tel: 01952 415607
Fax: 01952 619188
E-mail: mpminicoaches@hotmail.co.uk
Web site: www.mpmcoaches.co.uk
Fleet Name: MPM of Telford.
Prop: Mark Perkins.
Fleet: 3 - 1 midicoach, 2 minicoach.
Chassis: 1 Iveco, 2 Mercedes.
Bodies: 1 Crest, 1 Onyx, 1 Plaxton.
Ops incl: school contracts, private hire.
Livery: Two-tone Blue

MINSTERLEY MOTORS
STIPERSTONES, MINSTERLEY, SHREWSBURY SY5 0LZ
Tel: 01743 791208   Fax: 01743 790101
E-mail: john@minsterleymotors.co.uk
Web site: www.minsterleymotors.co.uk
Dirs: John B Jones, Carl Evans.
Fleet: 23 - 8 single-deck bus, 12 single-deck coach, 3 midicoach.

Chassis: 3 Mercedes, 6 Scania, 14 Volvo.
Bodies: 5 Berkhof, 7 Caetano, 3 Mercedes, 5 Plaxton, 2 Volvo, 1 Wright.
Ops incl: local bus services, school contracts, excursions & tours, private hire, continental tours.
Livery: 2 Tone Blue/White
Ticket system: Wayfarer

N.C.B. MOTORS LTD
EDSTASTON GARAGE, WEM, SHREWSBURY SY4 5RF
Tel: 01939 232379
Fax: 01939 234892
E-mail: paul@ncb-motors.co.uk
Web site: www.ncb-motors.co.uk
Dirs: Paul R Brown, Derek N Brown.
Fleet: 14 single-deck coach.
Chassis: 14 Volvo.
Bodies: 8 Jonckheere, 5 Plaxton, 1 Van Hool.
Ops incl: private hire, school contracts.
Livery: Brown/Cream

OWENS COACHES LTD
36 BEATRICE STREET, OSWESTRY SY11 1QG
Tel: 01691 652126
Fax: 01691 670047
E-mail: mike@owenstravel.co.uk
Web site: www.owenstravel.co.uk
Dir: Michael Owen Ops Man: Peter Worthy.
Fleet: 22 - 3 single-deck bus, 16 single-deck coach, 3 midicoach.
Chassis: 3 BMC, 2 Dennis, 1 Irisbus, 1 Iveco, 4 MAN, 5 Mercedes, 1 Scania, 5 Volvo.
Bodies: 2 Ayats, 1 Beulas, 2 Berkhof, 3 BMC, 2 Mercedes, 1 Noge, 8 Plaxton, 1 UVG, 2 Van Hool.
Ops incl: local bus services, excursions & tours, private hire, continental tours, school contracts.
Livery: White with Blue/Red stripes.
Ticket System: Wayfarer

R & B TRAVEL
PLEASANT VIEW, KNOWLE, CLEE HILL, LUDLOW SY8 3NE
Tel/Fax: 01584 890770
E-mail: radnorradnor@supanet.com
Prop: A T Radnor, Mrs L Radnor.
Fleet: 15 - 3 single-deck coach, 4 midibus, 3 midicoach, 5 minibus.
Chassis: 1 Bedford, 1 Duple 425, 3 LDV, 1 MAN,

1 Mercedes, 5 Optare, 1 Renault, 1 Scania, 1 Toyota.
Ops incl: local bus services, school contracts, private hire, excursions & tours.
Livery: Grey, Orange and Red over Grey or White
Ticket System: Wayfarer

RIVERSIDE COACHWAYS LTD
HEATH HILL, DAWLEY TF4 2JU
Tel: 01952 505490 Fax: 01952 505590
Prop: K H Pollen.
Fleet: 8 - 1 double-deck bus, 5 single-deck coach, 1 midicoach, 1 minibus.
Chassis: 1 Dennis, 1 Ford, 1 Leyland, 1 Mercedes, 1 Scania, 3 Volvo.
Ops Incl: private hire, school contracts.
Livery: Blue/Silver and Blue/White

SHROPSHIRE COUNTY COUNCIL
INTEGRATED TRANSPORT UNIT, 107 LONGDEN ROAD, SHREWSBURY SY3 9DS
Tel: 01743 245300
Fax: 01743 253279
E-mail: peter.ralphs@shropshire-cc.gov.uk
Web site: www.shropshireonline.gov.uk
Fleet Name: Fleet Operations.
Ch Exec: Carolyn Downs Gen Man Transport: Adrian Millard
Fleet Ops Off: Peter Ralphs.
Fleet: 79 - 2 midibus, 77 minibus.
Ops incl: local bus services, school contracts.
Livery: White
Ticket system: Almex

WORTHEN MOTORS/TRAVEL
BENTHALL STONE FARM BUILDINGS, ALDERBURY ROAD, FORD, SHREWSBURY SY5 9NA
Tel: 01743 861360
Fax: 01743 851356
E-mail: jackie@worthentravel.freeserve.co.uk
Prop: D A Pye Sec: J Davies.
Fleet: 8 single-deck coach.
Chassis: 1 Bova, 4 DAF, 1 Dennis, 1 Leyland, 1 Volvo.
Ops incl: school contracts, excursions & tours, private hire.
Livery: White/Blue

SOMERSET, BATH & N E SOMERSET, N SOMERSET

A1 TRAVEL
Ceased trading since LRB 2011 went to press.

ARLEEN COACH HIRE & SERVICES LTD
14 BATH ROAD, PEASEDOWN ST JOHN, BATH BA2 8DH
Tel: 01761 434625
Fax: 01761 436578
E-mail: enquiries@arleen.co.uk
Web site: www.arleen.co.uk
Chairman: Alan Spiller
Co Sec: Mrs Mary Spiller
Dir/Office Man: Ms Carol Spiller
Dir/Ops Man: Justin Spiller
Ch Eng: Kristian Spiller.
Fleet: 18 - 13 single-deck coach, 2 midibus, 3 midicoach.
Chassis: 2 Alexander Dennis, 6 DAF, 2 Leyland, 3 Mercedes, 2 Neoplan, 3 Volvo.

Bodies: 1 Alexander Dennis, 1 Berkhof, 3 Duple, 4 Mercedes, 2 Neoplan, 1 Optare, 4 Plaxton, 1 Van Hool, 1 Wadham Stringer.
Ops incl: school contracts, excursions & tours, private hire, continental tours.
Livery: Red/White/Blue

AXE VALE COACHES LTD
BIDDISHAM, AXBRIDGE BS26 2RD
Tel: 01934 750321   Fax: 01934 750334
E-mail: enquiries@axevale.com
Web site: www.axevale.com
Partners: C P Bailey, J I Bailey, J Bailey.
Fleet: 13 - 12 single-deck coach, 1 midibus.
Chassis: 1 Autosan, 8 Bova, 1 DAF, 1 Dennis, 1 Mercedes, 1 Volvo.
Bodies: 8 Bova, 3 Plaxton, 1 UVG, 1 Other.
Ops incl: local bus services, school contracts, excursions & tours, private hire, continental tours.

Livery: White
Ticket system: Setright

BAKERS COACHES YEOVIL
8 BUCKLAND ROAD, PEN MILL TRADING ESTATE, YEOVIL BA21 5EA
Tel: 01935 312316   Fax: 01935 410423
Recovery: 01935 428401
E-mail: enquiries@bakerscoaches-somerset.co.uk
Web site: www.bakerscoaches-somerset.co.uk
Dir: S Baker.
Fleet: 13 - 10 single-deck coach, 2 midicoach, 1 minicoach.
Chassis: DAF, Ford Transit, Iveco, Volvo.
Bodies: Beulas, Jonckheere, Mercedes, Van Hool.
Ops incl: school contracts, excursions & tours, private hire, continental tours.
Livery: White

BAKERS DOLPHIN COACH TRAVEL

⚇ ⓘⅡ ⚇ ❄

48 LOCKING ROAD, WESTON-SUPER-MARE BS23 3DN
Tel: 01934 415000
Fax: 01934 641162
E-mail: coach.hire@bakersdolphin.com
Web site: www.bakersdolphin.com
Chairman: John Baker **Man Dir:** Max Fletcher
Ch Eng: Mark Vearncombe **Marketing Dir:** Amanda Harrington **Fin Dir:** Steve Hunt
Ops Man: Chris Rubery.
Fleet: 75 - 68 single-deck coach, 3 double-deck coach, 1 midicoach, 2 minibus, 1 minicoach
Chassis: 4 Bedford, 1 Bova, 1 Dennis, 5 Iveco, 2 LDV, 15 Leyland, 2 Mercedes, 45 Volvo.
Bodies: 5 Beulas, 1 Bova, 3 Jonckheere, 2 LDV, 1 Mercedes, 1 Optare, 34 Plaxton, 28 Van Hool.
Ops incl: local bus services, excursions & tours, private hire, express, continental tours, school contracts.
Livery: Blue/White/Green/Yellow.
Ticket System: Setright

BATH BUS COMPANY

🚎

6 NORTH PARADE, BATH BA1 1LF
Tel: 01225 330444
Fax: 01225 330727
E-mail: hq@bathbuscompany.com
Web site: www.bathbuscompany.com
Man Dir: Martin Curtis **Dir:** Dr. Mike Walker
Eng Dir: Collin Brougham-Field **Co Sec/Dir:** Rob Bromley **Com Dir:** Keith Tazewell.
Fleet: 11 double-deck bus, 7 single-deck bus, 3 minibus.
Chassis: 1 AEC, 6 Bristol, 6 Dennis, 3 Leyland-DAB, 3 Leyland, 3 MCW, 4 Mercedes.
Bodies: 1 Alexander, 6 ECW, 1 Leyland, 3 MCW, 1 Park Royal, 3 Plaxton, 6 Wright.
Ops incl: local bus services, excursions & tours, private hire.
Livery: Red/Primrose.
Ticket System: Wayfarer/BBC punch system.
A subsidiary of RATP Dev UK Ltd

BATH CONNECT

Fleet Name: UniConnect
A subsidiary of Wessex Connect – see Bristol

BERKELEY COACH & TRAVEL

⚇ ⚇ ❄ T

HAM LANE, PAULTON BS39 7PL
Tel & Fax: 01761 413196
E-mail: mail@berkeleycoachandtravel.co.uk
Web Site: www.berkeleycoachandtravel.co.uk
Proprietor: Mr Tim Pow
Fleet: 5 - 4 single-deck coach, 1 minicoach.
Chassis: Mercedes, Volvo.
Bodies: Optare, Van Hool.
Ops incl: school contracts, private hire.
Livery: Silver

BERRY'S COACHES (TAUNTON) LTD

♿ ⚇ ⚇ ⓘⅡ ❄ ⚑ T

CORNISHWAY WEST, NEW WELLINGTON ROAD, TAUNTON TA1 5NB
Tel: 01823 331356
Fax: 01823 322347
E-mail: info@berryscoaches.co.uk
Web site: www.berryscoaches.co.uk
Dir: SA Berry.
Fleet: 34 - 29 single-deck coach, 5 double-deck coach.
Chassis: 34 Volvo.
Bodies: 2 Jonckheere, 1 Plaxton, 31 Van Hool.
Ops incl: local bus services, school contracts, excursions & tours, private hire, express, continental tours.
Livery: White/Red/Orange
Ticket system: Manual

BLAGDON LIONESS COACHES LTD

⚇ ❄ R

MENDIP GARAGE, BLAGDON BS40 7TL
Tel: 01761 462250   **Fax:** 01761 463237
Recovery: 01761 462250
Dir: T M Lyons **Gen Man:** M A Lyons.
Fleet: 3 - 2 single-deck coach, 1 minibus.
Chassis: 1 Bova, 1 Leyland, 1 Mercedes.
Bodies: 1 Bova, 2 Plaxton.
Ops incl: local bus services, excursions & tours, private hire, school contracts.
Livery: White
Ticket System: Wayfarer

BLUE IRIS COACHES

⚇ ⚇ ⚑ ❄ T

25 CLEVEDON ROAD, NAILSEA BS48 1EH
Tel: 01275 851121
Fax: 01275 856522
E-mail: enquiry@blueiris.co.uk
Web site: www.blueiris.co.uk
Dirs: Philip Hatherall, Tony Spiller.
Fleet: 17 - 2 single-deck bus, 9 single-deck coach, 6 midicoach.
Chassis: 2 Optare, 9 Scania, 6 Toyota.
Bodies: 1 Berkhof, 6 Caetano, 6 Irizar, 2 Optare, 2 Van Hool.
Ops incl: local bus services, school contracts, private hire, continental tours.
Livery: 2-tone Blue/White.
Ticket System: Wayfarer

BUGLERS COACHES LTD

♿ ⚇ ❄

29 VICTORIA BUILDINGS, LOWER BRISTOL ROAD, BATH BA2 3EH
Tel: 01225 444422 **Fax:** 01225 466665
E-mail: info@buglercoaches.co.uk
Web site: www.buglercoaches.co.uk
Prop: Computer Village Group.
Ops Incl: local bus services, private hire, excursions & tours, school contracts.
Livery: Red/White/Yellow

CENTURION TRAVEL LTD

⚇ ⚇ ❄ ⚑

WEST ROAD GARAGE, WELTON, MIDSOMER NORTON, RADSTOCK BA3 2TP
Tel: 01761 417392
Fax: 01761 417369
E-mail: coach-hire@centuriontravel.co.uk
Web site: www.centuriontravel.co.uk
Man Dir: Martin Spiller.
Fleet: 22 - 18 single-deck coach, 1 midibus, 3 midicoach.
Chassis: 2 Bedford, 2 Bova, 4 DAF, 4 Dennis, 2 Leyland, 5 Mercedes, 1 Scania, 1 Temsa, 2 Volvo.
Bodies: 1 Autobus, 1 Berkhof, 2 Bova, 1 Caetano, 3 Duple, 1 Esker, 1 Irizar, 3 Jonckheere, 1 Marcopolo, 2 Optare, 3 Plaxton, 2 Van Hool
Ops incl: school contracts, private hire, continental tours.
Livery: Red/Cream/Burgundy

CLAPTON COACHES

⚇ ⓘⅡ

1 HAYDON ESTATE, RADSTOCK BA3 3RD
Tel: 01761 431936
Fax: 01761 431935
E-mail: claptonholidays@btconnect.com
Dirs: S C Lippet, M C Lippet.
Fleet: 11 - 6 single-deck coach, 5 minicoach.
Ops incl: excursions & tours, private hire, continental tours.
Livery: Lilac

COOMBS TRAVEL

♿ ⚇ ❄ ⚑ T

COOMBS HOUSE, SEARLE CRESCENT, WESTON-SUPER-MARE BS23 3YX
Tel: 01934 428555 **Fax:** 01934 428559
E-mail: coombscoaches@aol.com
Dirs: Brian F Coombs, Ruth A Coombs
Ops Man: Mrs June Carroll
Admin: Mrs M Lillie.
Fleet: 30 - 1 double-deck bus, 18 single-deck coach, 6 midicoach, 5 minibus.
Chassis incl: 3 Dennis, 3 Ford Transit, 5 Mercedes, 8 Scania.
Bodies incl: 8 Plaxton, 2 Scania, 3 Van Hool
Ops incl: local bus services, school contracts, excursions & tours, private hire.
Livery: Yellow/White
Ticket system: Wayfarer

FIRST BRISTOL, SOMERSET & AVON

♿ ⚇

ENTERPRISE HOUSE, EASTON ROAD, BRISTOL BS5 0DZ
Tel: 0117 955 8211 **Fax:** 0117 955 1248
Web site: www.firstgroup.com
Reg Man Dir: Justin Davies **Reg Finance & Planning Dir:** Amelia Price **Service Delivery Dir:** Tony McNiff **Comm & Business Growth Dir:** Marc Reddy **Reg Eng Standards Dir:** Chris Jones

♿	Vehicle suitable for disabled	⚇	Seat belt-fitted Vehicle	**R24**	24 hour recovery service
T	Toilet-drop facilities available	ⓘⅡ	Coach(es) with galley facilities	⚑	Replacement vehicle available
R	Recovery service available	❄	Air-conditioned vehicle(s)	🚎	Vintage Coach(es) available
🚎	Open top vehicle(s)	⚇	Coaches with toilet facilities	⚇	Hybrid Buses

Fleet: 600 - 214 double-deck bus, 336 single-deck bus, 8 single-deck coach, 9 articulated bus, 21 midibus, 12 minibus.
Chassis: 20 Alexander Dennis, 192 Dennis, 12 Mercedes, 21 Optare, 2 Scania, 1 VDL, 352 Volvo.
Ops incl: local bus services, school contracts.
Livery: FirstGroup UK Bus
Ticket System: Wayfarer

FROME MINIBUSES LTD
GEORGES GROUND, FROME BA11 4RP
Tel: 01373 471474
Fax: 01373 455294
Man Dir: Andrew Young.
Ops incl: local bus services.
Livery: White.

HATCH GREEN COACHES
HATCH GREEN GARAGE, HATCH BEAUCHAMP, TAUNTON TA3 6TN
Tel: 01823 480338
Fax: 01823 480500
E-mail: info@hatchgreencoaches.com
Web site: www.hatchgreencoaches.co.uk
Fleet incl: midibus, midicoach, minicoach.
Ops incl: local bus services, school contracts, private hire.
Livery: White/Grey/Black

HUTTON COACH HIRE
95 MOORLAND ROAD, WESTON-SUPER-MARE BS23 4HS
Tel: 01934 618292
Fax: 01934 641362
E-mail: jnjlawrence@onetel.com
Owner: John Lawrence Man: Wendy Dover.
Fleet: 5 - 3 single-deck coach, 2 midibus.
Chassis: 1 Alexander Dennis, 1 DAF, 1 MAN, 1 Mercedes, 1 Volvo.
Bodies: 1 Autobus, 1 Caetano, 1 UVG, 2 Van Hool.
Ops incl: school contracts, excursions & tours, private hire.
Livery: White with orange/green logo

NORTH SOMERSET COACHES
See Bristol

QUANTOCK MOTOR SERVICES LTD
THE OLD COAL YARD, BROADGAUGE BUSINESS PARK, BISHOPS LYDEARD, TAUNTON TA4 3BU
Tel: 01823 430202
Fax: 01823 431664
E-mail: sales@quantockmotorservices.co.uk
Web site: www.quantockmotorservices.co.uk
Man Dir: Steve Morris Dir: Liz Ranson
Gen Man: Peter McNaughton Fleet Eng: Paul Smith Supervisor: William Ricketts.
Fleet: double-deck bus, single-deck bus, single-deck coach, open-top bus, minibus, heritage vehicles.
Ops incl: local bus services, private hire, school contracts, excursions & tours, express.
Livery: Red
Ticket system: Wayfarer 2/3

RIDLERS LTD
JURY ROAD GARAGE, DULVERTON TA22 9EJ
Tel: 01398 323398
Fax: 01398 324398

E-mail: info@ridlers.co.uk
Web site: www.ridlers.co.uk
Man Dir: Gary Ridler Dir: Sarah Ridler
ps Man: Mark Jamieson.
Fleet: 18 - 15 single-deck coach, 3 minicoach.
Chassis: 5 Dennis, 1 Iveco, 2 Leyland, 1 Mercedes, 6 Scania, 2 Toyota, 1 Volvo.
Bodies: 2 Caetano, 5 Duple, 2 Irizar, 1 Jonckheere, 5 Plaxton, 3 Van Hool.
Ops incl: local bus services, school contracts, excursions & tours, private hire, continental tours.
Livery: White/Red/Silver.
Ticket system: Almex

SMITH'S COACHES (B E & G W SMITH)
BYFIELDS, PYLLE BA4 6TA
Tel: 01749 830126
Fax: 01749 830888
Prop: Graham Smith.
Fleet: 14 single-deck coach.
Chassis: 3 Bedford, 3 Leyland, 8 Volvo.
Bodies: 14 Plaxton.
Ops incl: school contracts, private hire.
Livery: Maroon/Cream

SOMERBUS LIMITED
64 BROOKSIDE, PAULTON, BRISTOL BS39 7YR
Tel/Fax: 01761 415456
E-mail: somerbus@tinyworld.co.uk
Web site: www.myweb.tiscali.co.uk/somerbus
Dir: Tim Jennings.
Fleet: 5 - 2 single-deck bus, 3 midibus.
Chassis: 1 Mercedes, 4 Optare.
Bodies: 1 MCV, 4 Optare.
Ops incl: local bus services, school contracts.
Ticket system: Wayfarer

SOUTH WEST COACHES LTD
SOUTHGATE ROAD, WINCANTON BA9 9EB
Tel: 01963 33124
Fax: 01963 31599
E-mail: info@southwestcoaches.co.uk
Web site: www.southwestcoaches.co.uk
Man Dir: Alan Graham Co Sec: Mrs Sandra Graham Comm Dir: Steve Caine
Ops Dir: P Fairey Eng Man: K Jeffrey
Ops Man: L Trahar.
Fleet: 95 - 31 single-deck bus, 46 single-deck coach, 12 midibus, 6 minibus.
Chassis: 1 BMC, 2 DAF, 12 Dennis, 3 Ford, 2 LDV, 8 Leyland, 6 MAN, 21 Mercedes, 8 Setra, 1 Volkswagen, 31 Volvo.
Bodies: 6 Alexander Dennis, 5 Berkhof, 1 BMC, 7 Caetano, 1 Duple, 5 Irizar, 5 Jonckheere, 2 LDV, 5 MCV, 7 Mercedes, 7 Optare, 19 Plaxton, 8 Setra, 3 Van Hool, 4 Wright, 11 Other.
Ops incl: local bus services, school contracts, excursions & tours, private hire, continental tours.
Livery: Red, White & Blue
Ticket Systems: Wayfarer, Almex

STAGECOACH SOUTH WEST
(formerly COOKS COACHES)
BELGRAVE ROAD, EXETER EX1 2LB
Tel: 01392 427711
Fax: 01392 889727
E-mail: southwest.enquiries@stagecoachbus.com
Web site: www.stagecoachbus.com

Officers: See Stagecoach South West (Devon)
Fleet: See Stagecoach South West (Devon)
Ops incl: local bus services, school contracts.
Livery: Stagecoach UK Bus

STONES OF BATH
LOWER BRISTOL ROAD, BATH BA2 3DR
Tel: 01225 422267
Fax: 01225 442209
E-mail: info@hattscoaches.com
Web site: www.stonescoaches.co.uk
A subsidiary of Hatts Coaches, Wiltshire.

TAYLORS COACH TRAVEL LTD
BOUNDARY WAY, LUFTON TRADING ESTATE, YEOVIL BA22 8HZ
Tel: 01935 423177
Fax: 01935 427775
E-mail: info@taylorscoachtravel.co.uk
Web site: www.taylorscoachtravel.co.uk
Man Dir: D D J Elliott Co Sec: Mrs T R Elliott
Eng Dir: D Porter Ops Dir: M D Kirkland.
Fleet: 46 - 34 single-deck coach, 7 midicoach, 5 minibus.
Chassis: 2 Autosan, 2 Bova, 4 BMC, 3 DAF, 3 Dennis, 4 Irisbus, 4 Iveco, 2 LDV, 6 Leyland, 1 Mercedes, 15 Volvo.
Bodies: 2 Autosan, 3 Alexander, 4 BMC, 2 Bova, 2 Duple, 3 Indcar, 2 Leyland, 1 Mercedes, 10 Plaxton, 1 Reeve Burgess, 12 Van Hool, 3 Vehixel, 1 Wadham Stringer.
Ops incl: local bus services, private hire, school contracts, excursions & tours, continental tours.
Livery: Burgundy/White/Yellow/Gold
Ticket system: Wayfarer

TRAVELINE
Ceased operations since LRB 2011 went to press

WEBBER BUS
UNIT 8C, BEECH BUSINESS PARK, BRISTOL ROAD, BRIDGWATER TA6 4FF
Tel: 0800 096 3039
Fax: 01278 455250
E-mail: sales@webberbus.com
Web site: www.webberbus.com
Fleet Names: Easy Link, Village Link.
Man Dir: Tim Gardner
Eng & Ops Dir: David Webber.
Fleet: 38 - 25 single-deck coach, 3 midicoach, 7 minibus, 3 midibus.
Chassis incl: 2 Bova, 1 DAF, 5 Ford Transit, 5 Irisbus, 2 LDV, 4 Optare.
Bodies incl: 2 Bova, 4 Optare, 11 Plaxton, 4 Van Hool.
Ops incl: local bus services, Taunton Park & Ride, school contracts, excursions & tours, private hire.
Ticket system: Wayfarer

ANDERSON COACHES LTD
36 BONET LANE, BRINSWORTH, ROTHERHAM S60 5NE
Tel: 01709 364750
Web site: www.andersoncoachesrotherham.co.uk
Fleet: 4 - 3 single-deck coach, I minibus.
Chassis: 2 Dennis, I LDV, I MAN.
Ops incl: excursions & tours, private hire

ASHLEY TRAVEL LTD t/a GRANT & McALLIN
RENISHAW SERVICE STATION, RENISHAW S21 3WF
Tel: 0114 251 1234
Fax: 0114 251 1900
Web site: www.ashleytravelsheffield.co.uk
Dirs: R Atack (**Gen Man/Traf Man**) T F Atack (**Ch Eng/Sec**).
Fleet: 7 single-deck coach.
Chassis: 7 Volvo.
Bodies: I Berkhof, I Jonckheere, 2 Plaxton, 3 Van Hool.
Ops incl: excursions & tours, private hire.
Livery: Turquoise/Blue/White.

BUCKLEYS TOURS LTD
THORNE ROAD, BLAXTON, DONCASTER DN9 3AX
Tel: 01302 770379
E-mail: info@buckleysholidays.co.uk
Web site: www.buckleysholidays.co.uk
Man Dir: Richard Buckley.
Fleet: 6 single-deck coach.
Chassis: 3 DAF, I Mercedes, 2 Neoplan.
Ops incl: private hire, excursions & tours.
Livery: Orange

BURDETTS COACHES LTD
8 STATION ROAD, MOSBOROUGH, SHEFFIELD S20 5AD
Tel: 0114 321 4597
Fax: 0114 247 5733
Web site: www.burdettscoachessheffield.co.uk
Fleet: 4 single-deck coach.
Chassis: 4 Volvo.
Bodies: 4 Van Hool.
Ops incl: school contracts, excursions & tours, private hire

BYRAN TOURS LTD
Ceased trading since LRB 2011 went to press.

CENTRAL TRAVEL
313 COLEFORD ROAD, DARNALL, SHEFFIELD S9 5NF
Tel: 0114 276 7000
Fax: 0114 275 9060
Recovery: 0114 276 9869
E-mail: paulharrison4@btconnect.com
Web site: www.centraltravelsheffield.co.uk
Props: Paul Harrison, Joy Harrison.
Fleet: 34 – 4 single-deck bus, 8 single-deck coach, 2 midibus, 2 midicoach, 10 minibus, 8 minicoach.
Chassis incl: I Bova, 2 Dennis, 5 Ford Transit, 3 Mercedes, I Neoplan, I Optare, I Peugeot, I Renault, 3 Setra, I Volvo.
Ops incl: school contracts, excursions & tours, private hire, continental tours.

CLARKSONS HOLIDAYS
See Wilfreda Beehive.

COOPERS TOURS LTD
14 BRIDGE STREET, KILLAMARSH S21 1AH
Tel: 0114 248 2859
Fax: 0114 248 3867
E-mail: sales@cooperstours.co.uk
Web site: www.coopers-coach-tours.co.uk
Dirs: Alan Cooper, Graham Cooper.
Fleet: 30 - 4 double-deck bus, 3 single-deck bus, 21 single-deck coach, 2 minibus.
Ops incl: excursions & tours, private hire, continental tours.
Livery: Yellow/White.

ELLENDERS COACHES
71 HURLFIELD AVENUE, SHEFFIELD S12 2TL
Tel: 0114 321 9364
Web site: www.ellenderscoachessheffield.co.uk
Partners: P J D. Ellender, C S Ellender.
Fleet: I single-deck coach.
Chassis: Volvo.
Bodies: Jonckheere.
Ops incl: excursions & tours, private hire, continental tours, school contracts.

EXPRESSWAY COACHES
DERWENT WAY, WATH WEST INDUSTRIAL ESTATE, WATH ON DEARNE, ROTHERHAM S63 6EX
Tel: 01709 875358
Fax: 01709 879919
E-mail: expresswaycoaches@btconnect.com
Dirs: Peter Regan.
Fleet: 16 - I single-deck bus 4 single-deck coach, 5 midicoach, 6 minicoach.
Chassis: I Alexander Dennis, I MAN, 11 Mercedes, I Volkswagen, 2 Volvo.
Bodies: I Alexander Dennis, 8 Mercedes, I Neoplan, 5 Plaxton, I Other.
Ops incl: local bus service, private hire, continental tours, school contracts, excursions & tours.
Livery: Orange/Yellow/White
Ticket system: Wayfarer II

FIRST SOUTH YORKSHIRE
MIDLAND ROAD, ROTHERHAM S61 1TF
Tel: 01709 566000
Fax: 01709 566063
E-mail: enquiries@firstgroup.com
Web site: www.firstgroup.com
Regional Man Dir: Dave Alexander
Service Delivery Dir: Bob Hamilton
Strategic Devt Dir: Richard Soper
Business Efficiency Man: Ian Humphreys.
Fleet: 526 - 235 double-deck bus, 281 single-deck bus, 10 midibus.
Chassis: 15 Dennis, 10 Optare, 6 Scania, 495 Volvo.
Ops incl: local bus services, school contracts.
Livery: FirstGroup UK Bus.
Ticket System: Wayfarer 3

L. FURNESS & SONS
Ceased trading since LRB 2011 went to press.

GEE-VEE TRAVEL
7 KENDRAY STREET, BARNSLEY S70 1DB
Tel: 01226 287403
Fax: 01226 284783
E-mail: info@geeveetravel.co.uk
Web site: www.geeveetravel.co.uk
Prop: Gordon Clark.
Fleet: 13 single-deck coach.
Chassis: 12 DAF, I Setra.
Bodies: 12 Bova, I Setra.
Ops incl: excursions & tours, private hire, continental tours.
Livery: Blue/White/Yellow

W GORDON & SONS
CHESTERTON ROAD, EASTWOOD TRADING ESTATE, ROTHERHAM S65 1SU
Tel: 01709 363913
Fax: 01709 830570
Dir: D Gordon.
Fleet: 10 – 9 single-deck coach, I midicoach.
Chassis: 4 MAN, 6 Volvo.
Bodies: Neoplan, Plaxton, Sunsundegui, Unvi, Van Hool.
Ops incl: school contracts, excursions & tours, private hire.
Livery: Red/Ivory

GRAYS TRAVEL GROUP
30-32 SHEFFIELD ROAD, HOYLAND COMMON S74 0DQ
Tel: 01226 743109
Fax: 01226 749430
E-mail: chris@graystravel.co.uk
Web site: www.graystravel.co.uk
Man Dir: S Gray **Ch Eng:** P Winter.
Fleet: 10 - 7 single-deck coach, I midicoach, I minibus, I minicoach.
Chassis: I Bova, 6 DAF, 2 Dennis, I Toyota.
Bodies: I Berkhof, I Caetano, 2 Duple, 6 Plaxton.
Ops incl: excursions & tours, private hire, school contracts.
Livery: White/Blue/Yellow.

HEATON'S OF SHEFFIELD LTD
31 SUSSEX STREET, SHEFFIELD S3 7YY
Tel/Fax: 0114 230 9184
E-mail: info@heatonscoachhire.com
Web site: www.heatonscoachhire.com
Fleet: 10 - 4 single-deck coach, 2 midicoach, 4 minicoach.
Chassis: I Ford, 4 Mercedes, 5 Setra.
Bodies: 4 Mercedes, I Plaxton, 5 Setra.
Ops incl: school contracts, excursions & tours.
Livery: White.

ISLE COACHES
97 HIGH STREET, OWSTON FERRY DN9 1RL
Tel: 01427 728227
Props: J & C Bannister **Ch Eng:** E Scotford
Sec: Jill Bannister.
Fleet: 14 - 9 double-deck bus, 5 single-deck bus.
Ops incl: local bus services, school contracts.
Livery: Blue/Cream.
Ticket System: Almex.

JEMS TRAVEL
Ceased trading since LRB 2011 went to press.

JOHNSON BROS TOURS LTD

GREEN ACRES, GREEN LANE,
HODTHORPE, WORKSOP S80 4XR
Tel/Recovery: 01909 720337 / 721847
Fax: 01909 722886
E-mail: lee@johnsonstours.co.uk
Web site: www.johnsonstours.co.uk
Dirs: C A Johnson, S Johnson, A Johnson,
L Johnson, S Johnson **Ops Man:** S Smallshaw.
Fleet: 118 - 70 double-deck bus, 4 single-
deck bus, 30 single-deck coach, 4 double-deck
coach, 4 midibus, 2 midicoach, 1 minibus, 3
minicoach.
Chassis incl: 2 Alexander Dennis, 1 Ayats,
3 Bova, 30 Bristol, 2 DAF, 2 Ford Transit,
6 Irisbus, 4 Iveco, 4 MAN, 4 Mercedes,
6 Neoplan, 6 Scania, 3 Van Hool, 20 Volvo.
Bodies: 1 Ayats, 6 Beulas, 2 Berkhof, 3 Bova,
2 Caetano, 30 ECW, 5 East Lancs, 6 Irizar,
4 Jonckheere, 6 Neoplan, 30 Northern
Counties, 25 Plaxton, 6 Scania, 2 Sunsundegui,
3 Van Hool, 1 Volvo.
Ops incl: local bus services, school contracts,
excursions & tours, private hire, express,
continental tours.
Livery: Blue Fade with Stars
Ticket System: ITSO
See also Redfern Travel Ltd
(Nottinghamshire)

JOURNEYS-DESTINATION

42-45 WILSON STREET, NEEPSEND,
SHEFFIELD S3 8DD
Tel: 0800 298 1938
Fax: 0114 242 0885
E-mail: info@journeys-destination.com
Web site: www.journeys-destination.com
Prop: Mrs Patricia R Russell.
Fleet: 3 minibus.
Chassis: 2 Iveco, 1 LDV.
Ops incl: school contracts, excursions &
tours, private hire.

K. M. MOTORS LTD

WILSON GROVE, LUNDWOOD,
BARNSLEY S71 5JS
Tel: 01226 245564
Fax: 01226 213004
Man Dir: Keith Meynell.
Fleet: 11 - 8 single-deck coach, 3 minibus.
Chassis: 5 Bova, 1 Ford Transit, 2 Mercedes,
3 Scania.
Bodies: 5 Bova, 1 Constable, 1 Ford,
1 Mercedes, 3 Van Hool.
Ops incl: excursions & tours, continental
tours, private hire.
Livery: Gold/Maroon/White.

LADYLINE

47 BERNARD STREET, RAWMARSH
S62 5NR
Tel: 01709 522422
Fax: 01709 525558
Owner: C B Goodridge.
Fleet: 6 single-deck coach.
Chassis: 2 AEC, 3 Bova, 1 DAF.
Bodies: 3 Bova, 1 Caetano, 2 Plaxton.
Ops incl: local bus services, school contracts,
excursions & tours, private hire, continental
tours.
Livery: Blue/Silver.

LINBURG BUS & COACH

UNIT 7, 35 CATLEY ROAD, DARNALL,
SHEFFIELD S9 5JF
Tel: 0114 261 9172
Fax: 0114 256 1159
E-mail: info@linburg.co.uk
Web site: www.linburg.co.uk
Dirs: John Hadaway, Gill Dawson.
Fleet: 21 – 8 double-deck bus, 13 single-deck
coach.
Chassis: 9 DAF, 11 Leyland, 1 Volvo.
Ops incl: school contracts, private hire,
express.
Livery: White/Multi
Ticket System: Wayfarer 2

MALCYS

Ceased trading since LRB 2011 went to press.

WALTER MARTIN COACHES

57 OLD PARK AVENUE, GREENHILL,
SHEFFIELD S8 7DQ
Tel: 0114 274 5004
E-mail: info@waltermartincoaches.co.uk
Web site: www.waltermartincoaches.co.uk
Prop: John Martin, June Martin.
Fleet: 3 coach.
Chassis: 3 Volvo.
Ops incl: excursions & tours, private hire.

MASS BRIGHT BUS

HOUGHTON ROAD, ANSTON,
SHEFFIELD S25 4JJ
Tel: 01909 550480
Fax: 01909 550486
Recovery: 01909 550480
Fleet Name: Brightbus
Man Dir: Mick Strafford
Co Sec: Carol Morton
Eng Man: Richard Harrison.
Fleet: 51 double-deck bus.
Chassis: 9 DAF, 13 Dennis, 18 Leyland,
1 MCW, 10 Scania.
Bodies: 18 Alexander, 13 Duple, 1 MCW,
10 Northern Counties, 9 Optare.
Ops incl: local bus services, school contracts.
Livery: Green

J A MAXFIELD & SONS LTD

172 AUGHTON ROAD, AUGHTON,
SHEFFIELD S26 3XE
Tel: 0114 287 2622
Fax: 0114 287 5003
E-mail: info@maxfieldstravel.co.uk
Web site: www.maxfieldstravel.co.uk
Fleet: single-deck coach, minicoach.
Ops incl: excursions & tours, private hire.
Livery: Yellow with Orange/Green

MOSLEYS TOURS

LEES HALL ROAD, THORNHILL LEES,
DEWSBURY WF12 9EQ.
Tel: 01226 382243
Fax: 01924 458665
Dirs: A Gath-Bragg, J R Bragg
Gen Man: P R Emerton.
Fleet: 3 - 2 single-deck coach, 1 midicoach.
Chassis: 1 Dennis, 1 Leyland, 1 Volvo.
Ops incl: school contracts, private hire,

continental tours, excursions and tours,
express.
Livery: Grey/Cream

NIELSEN TRAVEL SERVICE

23 WINN GROVE, MIDDLEWOOD,
SHEFFIELD S6 1UW
Tel/Fax: 0114 234 2961
E-mail: niel@nielsentravel.co.uk
Web site: www.nielsentravel.co.uk
Fleet: 2 minibus
Chassis: 2 Mercedes.
Ops incl: school contracts, private hire,
excursions & tours.

JOHN POWELL TRAVEL LTD

UNIT 2, 6 HELLABY LANE, HELLABY,
ROTHERHAM S66 8HA
Tel: 01709 700900
Fax: 01709 701521
E-mail: jane@johnpowelltravel.co.uk
Dir: Ian Powell **Co Sec:** Jane Powell
Chief Eng: Ian Slater
Office Man: Lynn Oliver.
Fleet: 35 – 6 double-deck bus, 18 single-deck
bus, 9 single-deck coach, 1 midicoach.
Chassis: 10 Alexander Dennis, 1 BMC,
4 Dennis, 2 Iveco, 2 MCW, 4 Optare, 7 Volvo,
3 Other.
Ops incl: local bus services, school contracts,
private hire.
Livery: Blue/Yellow/Orange
Ticket system: Wayfarer III

RED LINE BUSES

TOP SCAFF YARD, SHAWFIELD ROAD,
CARLTON INDUSTRIAL ESTATE, BARNSLEY
S71 3HS
Tel: 07525 070527
E-mail: redline08@hotmail.co.uk
Web site: www.red-line-buses.co.uk
Prop: S McDermott
Fleet: 7 single-deck bus.
Chassis: 6 Dennis, 1 Optare.
Bodies: 2 East Lancs, 1 Optare, 4 Plaxton.
Ops incl: local bus services, school contracts.
Livery: Red/White

ROYLES TRAVEL

114 TUNWELL AVENUE, SHEFFIELD
S5 9FG
Tel: 0114 245 4519
Fax: 0114 257 8585
E-mail: enquire@roylestravel.co.uk
Web site: www.roylestravel.co.uk
Partners: Ricky Eales, Roy Eales.
Fleet: 2 single-deck coach.
Chassis: 1 Bova, 1 Iveco.
Bodies: 1 Beulas, 1 Bova.
Ops incl: excursions & tours, private hire.

SLEIGHTS COACHES

COACH HOUSE, MAIN STREET,
MEXBOROUGH S64 9DU
Tel: 01709 584561
Fax: 01709 582016
Owner: J. Sleight.
Fleet: 3 single-deck coach.
Chassis: DAF.
Bodies: Jonckheere.
Ops incl: excursions & tours, private hire,

continental tours, school contracts.
Livery: Orange/Cream

STAGECOACH YORKSHIRE
UNIT 4 ELDON ARCADE, BARNSLEY
S70 4PP
Tel: 01226 202555
Fax: 01226 346715
E-mail: Yorkshire.enquiries@stagecoach.com
Web site: www.stagecoachbus.com
Man Dir: Paul Lynch
Eng Dir: Joe Gilchrist
Ops Dir: Sue Hayes
Comm Dir: Rupert Cox.
Fleet: 224 – 21 double-deck bus,
181 single-deck bus, 22 midibus.
Chassis: 30 Alexander Dennis, 13 DAF,
36 Dennis, 79 MAN, 22 Optare, 7 Scania,
46 Volvo.
Fleet excludes Chesterfield, Sheffield
– see separate entries.
Ops incl: local bus services, school contracts,
private hire.
Livery: Stagecoach UK Bus
Ticket system: Wayfarer

STAGECOACH SHEFFIELD
GREEN LANE, ECCLESFIELD, SHEFFIELD
S35 9WY
Tel: 0114 246 5555
Fax: 0114 257 0343
E-mail: Sheffield.enquiries@stagecoachbus.
com
Web site: www.stagecoachbus.com
Man Dir: Paul Lynch
Eng Dir: Joe Gilchrist
Ops Dir: Sue Hayes
Comm Dir: Rupert Cox.
Fleet (Sheffield): 80 – 15 double-deck bus,
55 single-deck bus, 10 midibus.
Chassis: 11 Alexander Dennis, 44 MAN,
10 Optare, 15 Scania.
Livery: Stagecoach UK Bus.
Ticket machines: Wayfarer.

STAGECOACH SUPERTRAM
See Section 5 – Trams and Bus Rapid Transit
Systems.

SWIFTS HAPPY DAYS TRAVEL
THORNE ROAD, BLAXTON,
DONCASTER DN9 3AX
Tel/Fax: 01302 770999
A subsidiary of Buckley's Tours.

TATE'S TRAVEL GROUP
WHALEY ROAD, BARNSLEY
S75 1HT
Tel: 01226 205800
Fax: 01226 390048
E-mail: info@tates-travel.com
Web site: www.tates-travel.com
Props: Graham Mallinson, Scott Woolley.
Fleet: 56 –1 double-deck bus, 43 single-deck
bus, 5 single-deck coach, 4 midibus, 3 minibus.
Chassis: Alexander Dennis, DAF, Dennis, LDV,
Leyland, Mercedes, Volvo.
Bodies: Alexander, Alexander Dennis,
Caetano, Ikarus, Plaxton, Van Hool, Wright.
Ops incl: local bus services, private hire,
excursions & tours.
Livery: Blue/White.

TM TRAVEL LTD
HALFWAY BUS GARAGE, STATION ROAD,
HALFWAY S20 3GZ
Tel: 0114 263 3890
Fax: 0114 263 3899
Web site: www.tmtravel.co.uk
E-mail: info@tmtravel.co.uk
Gen Man: Paul Hopkinson
Ops Man: Paul Harding
Eng Man: Mark Clare
Tran Man: Gary Paterson.
Fleet: 83 – 26 double-deck bus, 18 single-
deck bus, 5 single-deck coach, 33 midibus,
1 minicoach.
Chassis: 3 Dennis, 12 Leyland, 3 MAN,
1 Mercedes, 38 Optare, 3 Scania, 12 VDL,
11 Volvo.
Bodies: 19 Alexander Dennis, 1 ECW,
7 East Lancs, 1 Ikarus, 1 Northern Counties,
38 Optare, 16 Plaxton.
Ops incl: local bus services, school contracts,
private hire.
Livery: Red & Cream
Ticket system: Parkeon.
Part of the Wellglade Group

TRAVELGREEN COACHES
CANDA LODGE, HAMPOLE BALK LANE,
SKELLOW, DONCASTER DN6 8LF
Tel/Recovery: 01302 722227
Fax: 01302 727999
E-mail: travelgreen@btconnect.com
Web site: www.travelgreen.co.uk
Dir: David Green.
Fleet: 7 – 1 double-deck bus, 2 midicoach,
4 minicoach.
Chassis: 1 AEC, 6 Mercedes.
Bodies: 1 Mercedes, 2 Optare, 1 Park Royal,
2 Plaxton.
Ops incl: excursions & tours, private hire,
continental tours.
Livery: Maroon/White

VEOLIA TRANSPORT
ENGLAND PLC
*Operations in South Yorkshire have ceased since
LRB 2011 went to press.*

WILFREDA BEEHIVE
APEX HOUSE, CHURCH LANE,
ADWICK-LE-STREET, DONCASTER
DN6 7AY
Tel: 01302 330330
Fax: 01302 330204
E-mail: sales@wilfreda.co.uk
Web site: www.wilfreda.co.uk
Man Dir: Mrs S M Scholey DL
Dirs: P G Haxby, N G Haxby
Ops Man: 1 Kaye **Ch Eng:** P Whitaker.
Fleet: 43 - 3 double-deck bus, 4 single-deck
bus, 21 single-deck coach, 10 midibus,
3 midicoach, 2 minicoach.
Chassis: 4 BMC, 1 Iveco, 4 MAN,
15 Mercedes, 18 Scania, 1 Van Hool.
Bodies: 5 Beulas, 4 BMC, 18 Irizar,
5 Mercedes, 7 Optare, 3 Plaxton, 1 Van Hool.
Ops incl: school contracts, excursions &
tours, private hire, continental tours.
Livery: Blue & Silver
Ticket System: Wayfarer TGX150
Incorporating Clarksons Holidays, Eagre
Coaches.

WILKINSONS TRAVEL
2 REDSCOPE CRESCENT, KIMBERWORTH
PARK, ROTHERHAM S61 3LX
Tel: 01709 553403
Fax: 01709 550550
Owner: M D Wilkinson.
Fleet: 9 - 2 single-deck coach, 3 minibus,
4 minicoach.
Chassis: AEC, Volvo.
Bodies: Berkhof, Duple, Ikarus, Jonckheere.
Ops incl: excursions & tours, private hire,
continental tours, school contracts.

WILLIAMSONS OF ROTHERHAM
19 VICTORIA STREET, CATCLIFFE
S60 5SJ
Tel: 01709 366856
Fax: 01709 828241
Prop: P Williamson.
Fleet: 3 single-deck coach.
Chassis: 1 Bedford, 1 DAF, 1 Leyland.
Bodies: 1 Duple, 1 Leyland, 1 Van Hool.
Ops incl: school contracts, excursions &
tours, private hire, continental tours.
Livery: White.

WILSON'S COACHES
PLOT 5, BANKWOOD LANE INDUSTRIAL
ESTATE, ROSSINGTON, DONCASTER
DN11 0PS
Tel: 01302 866193
E-mail: info@wilson-tours.co.uk
Web site: www.wilson-tours.co.uk
Prop: E Wilson.
Fleet: 3 single-deck coach.
Chassis: 1 EOS, 2 Volvo.
Bodies: 1 Berkhof, 2 Van Hool.
Ops incl: excursions & tours, private hire,
continental tours.

WOMBWELL COACH TOURS LTD
1 CEMETARY ROAD, WOMBWELL,
BARNSLEY S73 8HZ
Tel: 01226 753903
Fleet: single-deck coach, midicoach, minibus.
Ops incl: school contracts, excursions &
tours, private hire.
Livery: White with Blue

WOODS COACHES
NEW LODGE, WAKEFIELD ROAD,
BARNSLEY S71 1PA
Tel: 01226 286830
E-mail: contact@woodscoachesbarnsley.
co.uk
Web site: www.woodscoaches.co.uk
Fleet: 4 single-deck coach.
Chassis: 4 VDL.
Bodies: 4 Van Hool.
Ops incl: excursions & tours, private hire.
Livery: White with Blue/Yellow

YORKSHIRE ROSE COACHES
28 BRANKSOME AVENUE, BARNSLEY
S70 6XH
Tel: 0808 166 2924
Web site: www.yorkshireroseholidays.co.uk
Fleet: 5 – 4 single-deck coaches, 1 midicoach.
Chassis: 1 DAF, 1 Mercedes, 3 Volvo.
Bodies: 1 Unvi, 3 Van Hool, 1 Volvo.
Ops incl: private hire, excursions & tours.
Livery: White with Blue/Red

South Yorkshire

ACE TRAVEL

10 BIDDULPH PARK, IRONSTONE ROAD, BURNTWOOD WS7 1LG
Tel: 01543 279068
Prop: G E Elson.
Fleet: 2 – 1 single-deck coach, 1 midicoach.
Chassis: 1 Dennis, 1 Toyota.
Ops incl: excursions & tours, private hire, continental tours, school contracts.

ARRIVA MIDLANDS LTD

852 MELTON ROAD, LEICESTER LE4 8BT
Tel: 0116 264 0400
Fax: 0116 260 5605
E-mail: myattk.midlands@arriva.co.uk
Web site: www.arriva.co.uk
Fleet Names: Arriva, Wardles
Regional Man Dir: R A Hind
Fin Dir: J Barlow **Ops Dir:** A Lloyd **Eng Dir:** M Evans **Area Business Man (Staffordshire):** K Walker.
Fleet: 642 - 133 double-deck bus, 147 single-deck bus, 5 articulated bus, 218 midibus, 139 minibus.
Chassis: 1 Bova, 115 DAF, 182 Dennis, 4 Leyland, 35 Mercedes, 83 Optare, 49 Scania, 56 VDL, 117 Volvo.
Bodies: 57 Alexander Dennis, 1 Caetano, 65 East Lancs, 2 Marshall, 29 Mercedes, 9 Northern Counties, 83 Optare, 131 Plaxton, 42 Scania, 8 UVG, 202 Wright, 13 Other.
Ops incl: local bus services, school contracts, private hire, express.
Livery: Arriva, Wardles (Red/White, Red/Cream)
Ticket System: Wayfarer 150 & 200

BAKERS COACHES

THE COACH TRAVEL CENTRE, PROSPECT WAY, VICTORIA BUSINESS PARK, BIDDULPH ST8 7PL
Tel: 01782 522101
Fax: 01782 522363
E-mail: sales@bakerscoaches.com
Web site: www.bakerscoaches.com
Man Dir: Philip Baker **Ops Man:** Dave Machin
Eng Comm Man: Garry Burgoyne.
Fleet: 56 - 15 single-deck bus, 15 single-deck coach, 25 midibus, 1 midicoach.
Chassis: 5 Alexander Dennis, 3 DAF, 6 Enterprise, 10 Mercedes, 5 Optare, 9 Scania, 18 Volvo.
Bodies: 12 Alexander Dennis, 3 Berkhof, 2 Caetano, 2 Irizar, 2 Jonckheere, 5 Optare, 24 Plaxton, 2 Van Hool, 6 Wright.
Ops incl: local bus services, school contracts, excursions & tours, private hire, continental tours.
Livery: Coach – Green/White; **Bus** – Yellow/Blue
Ticket System: Wayfarer TGX150

BENNETTS TRAVEL (CRANBERRY) LTD

CRANBERRY, COTES HEATH ST21 6SQ
Tel: 01782 791468
Prop/Gen Man: J P McDonnell.
Fleet: 27 – single-deck bus, single-deck coach, midibus, minibus.
Chassis: Bedford, Ford Transit, Leyland, Mercedes.
Bodies: Mercedes, Plaxton.
Ops incl: local bus services, excursions & tours, private hire.
Livery: Blue/White

L F BOWEN LTD

104 MARINER, LICHFIELD ROAD INDUSTRIAL ESTATE, TAMWORTH B79 7UL
Tel: 01827 300000
Fax: 01827 300009
E-mail: coachhire@bowenstravel.com
Web site: www.bowenstravel.com
Chairman: Kevin Lower **Chief Executive Officer:** R Graham **Man Dir (Coaching):** R Lyng **Group Ops Man:** N G Tetley **Group Eng Man:** D Hoy **Fin Dir:** S Beech **Man Dir (Retail):** N Stones **Property Dir:** N Ellis **Dirs:** A H Moseley, C J Padbury, K G York
Fleet: 39 - 27 single-deck coach, 2 midicoach, 10 minibus.
Chassis: 10 MAN, 15 Scania, 2 Toyota, 10 Volkswagen, 2 Volvo.
Bodies: 15 Irizar, 2 Marcopolo. 8 Noge, 2 Plaxton.
Ops incl: school contracts, private hire, express, continental tours, excursions & tours.
Livery: Silver/sun emblem
Bowen Group Companies:
Applebys Coach Travel, Louth (see Lincolnshire)
Jeffs Coaches, Helmdon (see Northamptonshire)
Nottingham City Coaches, Shepshed (see Leicestershire)
Woottens, Chesham (see Buckinghamshire)
Yorks Coaches, Cogenhoe (see Northamptonshire)

TERRY BUSHELL TRAVEL

14 DERBY STREET, BURTON-UPON-TRENT DE14 2LA
Tel/Fax: 01283 538242
E-mail: info@terrybushelltravel.co.uk
Web site: www.terrybushelltravel.co.uk
Prop: Terry Bushell
Fleet: 3 - 2 single-deck coach, 1 minicoach.
Chassis: 2 Mercedes, 1 Volvo.
Bodies: 1 Mercedes, 1 Neoplan, 1 Van Hool.
Ops incl: excursions & tours, private hire, continental tours.
Livery: Red/Poppy/Gold

CLOWES COACHES

See Derbyshire

COPELAND TOURS (STOKE-ON-TRENT) LTD

1009 UTTOXETER ROAD, MEIR, STOKE ON TRENT, ST3 6HE
Tel: 01782 324466
Fax: 01782 319401
Recovery: 01782 324466
E-mail: mb@copelandstours.co.uk
Web site: www.copelandstours.co.uk
Chairman/Man Dir: J E M Burn
Dir: Mrs P Burn **Ch Eng:** J C Burn
Co Sec: J E M Burn.
Fleet: 26 - 1 single-deck bus, 22 single-deck coach, 2 midibus, 1 midicoach.
Chassis: 1 AEC, 14 DAF, 1 Dennis, 7 Leyland, 1 MAN, 2 Mercedes.
Bodies: 1 Duple, 1 Jonckheere, 1 Marshall, 17 Plaxton, 4 Van Hool, 2 Wadham Stringer.
Ops incl: local bus services, school contracts, excursions & tours, private hire, express, continental tours.
Livery: Blue-Blue/Orange.
Ticket System: Wayfarer.

CRUSADE TRAVEL LTD

THE COACHYARD, BUXTON ESTATES, PENKRIDGE ST19 5RP
Tel: 01785 714124
Fax: 01543 579678
E-mail: enquiries@crusade-travel.com
Web site: www.crusade-travel.com
Ops Man: Gavin Pardoe
Fleet: 3 single-deck coach, 3 midicoach, 2 minibus, 1 minicoach.
Chassis: 1 MAN, 6 Mercedes, 2 Volvo.
Ops incl: school contracts, excursions & tours, private hire.
Livery: White.

D & G COACH AND BUS LTD

See Cheshire. Staffordshire operations sold to Wardle (Arriva Midlands) in August 2011.

D H CARS OF DENSTONE LTD

9 HAWTHORN CLOSE, DENSTONE, UTTOXETER ST14 5HB
Tel: 01889 590819
Fax: 01889 591888
Dir: Donald Handley **Sec:** Alison Williams.
Fleet: 2 - 1 single-deck coach, 1 minicoach.
Chassis: 1 Mercedes, 1 Scania.
Bodies: 1 Crest, 1 Irizar.
Ops incl: private hire.
Livery: White with Gold/Blue lining.

FIRST MIDLANDS

ADDERLEY GREEN GARAGE, DIVIDY ROAD, STOKE ON TRENT ST3 0AJ
Tel: 08708 500 868
Fax: 01782 592541
Fleet Name: First Potteries
Regional Man Dir: Nigel Barrett **Regional Eng Dir:** Mick Brannigan **Regional Comm Dir:** Steve Wickers **Regional Fin Planning Dir:** David Marshall
Fleet (Potteries): 183 – 9 double-deck bus, 149 single-deck bus, 25 midibus.
Chassis: 53 Dennis, 8 Leyland, 25 Optare, 96 Scania, 1 Volvo.
Bodies: 18 Alexander, 5 Leyland, 15 Marshall, 25 Optare, 20 Plaxton, 17 Scania, 4 UVG, 79 Wright.
Ops incl: local bus services, school contracts.
Livery: FirstGroup UK Bus

GOLDEN GREEN TRAVEL

COWBROOK LANE, GAWSWORTH, MACCLESFIELD SK11 0JH
Tel: 01260 223453
E-mail: goldengreentravel@hotmail.com
Web site: www.goldengreentravel.co.uk
Partners: John Worth, Gill Worth, Derek J Lownds.
Fleet: 11 single-deck coaches.
Chassis and Bodies: Mercedes
Ops incl: local bus services, school contracts, excursions & tours, private hire.

HAPPY DAYS COACHES

GREYFRIARS COACH STATION, GREYFRIARS WAY, STAFFORD ST16 2SH
Tel/Recovery: 01785 229797
Fax: 01785 229790
E-mail: info@happydayscoaches.co.uk

The Little Red Book 2012 - in association with *tbf* Transport Benevolent Fund

Web site: www.happydayscoaches.co.uk
Joint Man Dirs: Richard Austin, Neil Austin
Dir: Brian Austin.
Fleet: 29 - 25 single-deck coach, 3 minicoach,
1 minibus.
Chassis: 3 DAF, 4 Mercedes, 5 Scania, 17 Volvo.
Bodies: 2 Bova, 2 Irizar, 1 Jonckheere, 12 Plaxton,
2 Scania, 10 Van Hool.
Ops incl: local bus services, excursions & tours,
private hire, express, school contracts, continental
tours.
Livery: Rising Sun
Ticket System: Setright
Also at Bronington, Shropshire.

HEARTLANDS TRAVEL LTD
INVINCIBLE TRAVEL
LICHFIELD ROAD INDUSTRIAL ESTATE,
TAMWORTH B79 7XE
Tel: 01827 311313
Fax: 01827 271327
E-mail: info@heartlandstravel.co.uk
Web site: www.heartlandstravel.co.uk
Fleet Names: Heartlands Bus,
Heartlands Travel, Invincible Travel, Tamworth
Coach Company.
Fleet: 22 - 2 double-deck bus, 10 single-deck bus,
4 single-deck coach, 5 midibus, 1 minibus..
Ops incl: local bus services, school contracts,
private hire
Livery: Blue/White.

HOLLINSHEAD COACHES LTD
BEMERSLEY ROAD, KNYPERSLEY
ST8 7PZ
Tel: 01782 512209
Fleet: 10 single-deck coach.
Chassis: 1 DAF, 2 Leyland, 7 Volvo.
Ops incl: school contracts, excursions & tours,
private hire.
Livery: Red/Cream.

JOSEPHS MINI COACHES
171 CRACKLEY BANK, CHESTERTON,
NEWCASTLE-UNDER-LYME ST5 7AB
Tel: 01782 564944
Prop: Joseph Windsor.
Fleet: 2 – 1 minibus, 1 minicoach.
Chassis/Bodies: Mercedes.
Ops incl: private hire.
Livery: White

LEONS COACH TRAVEL
(STAFFORD) LTD
PATON DRIVE, TOLLGATE PARK,
BEACONSIDE, STAFFORD
ST16 3EF
Tel: 01785 244575
Fax: 01785 258444
E-mail: info@leons.co.uk
Web site: www.leons.co.uk
Dirs: A Douglas, R L Douglas, L H Douglas
Co Sec: S Douglas.
Fleet: 30 - 23 single-deck coach, 2 midibus,
2 midicoach, 2 minibus, 1 minicoach.
Chassis: 1 DAF, 2 Ford Transit, 1 Iveco,
5 Mercedes, 11 MAN, 4 Scania, 6 Volvo.
Bodies: 1 Bova, 2 Irizar, 6 Plaxton, 2 Mellor,
3 Mercedes, 13 Van Hool.
Ops incl: school contracts, excursions & tours,
private hire, continental tours.
Livery: Burgundy

MIDLAND CLASSIC LTD
UNIT 5, 290 STANTON ROAD, BURTON-ON-
TRENT DE15 9SQ
Tel/Fax: 01283 500228
E-mail: info@midlandclassic.com
Web site: www.midlandclassic.com
Dirs: James Boddice, Julian H Peddle,
David B Reeves, John Mitcheson.
Fleet: 16 – 7 double-deck bus, 9 single-deck bus.
Chassis: 1 AEC, 11 Alexander Dennis, 1 MCW,
3 Volvo.
Bodies: 5 Alexander Dennis, 1 East Lancs,
1 MCW, 5 Plaxton, 3 Wright, 1 Other.
Ops incl: local bus services, private hire.
Livery: LT Red/Stevensons Yellow.
Ticket System: Wayfarer 3.

PARAGON TRAVEL LTD
Ceased operations since LRB 2011 went to press.

PARRYS INTERNATIONAL TOURS LTD
LANDYWOOD GREEN, CHESLYN HAY
WS6 7QX
Tel: 01922 414576   **Fax:** 01922 413416
E-mail: info@parrys-international.co.uk
Web site: www.parrys-international.co.uk
Man Dir: David Parry
Fleet: 16 - 13 single-deck coach, 3 minicoach.
Chassis: 3 Mercedes, 13 Van Hool.
Bodies: 3 Mercedes, 13 Van Hool.
Ops incl: excursions & tours.
Livery: Red/Gold

PLANTS LUXURY TRAVEL LTD
167 TEAN ROAD, CHEADLE ST10 1LS
Tel: 01538 753561
Fax: 01538 757025
E-mail: julie.plant@plantsluxurytravel.co.uk
Web site: www.plantsluxurytravel.co.uk
Partners: T J Plant, M P Plant.
Fleet: 4 - 1 midicoach, 3 minicoach.
Chassis: 3 Mercedes, 1 Toyota.
Ops incl: private hire, school contracts.
Livery: Silver with Burgundy/Gold/Mustard
stripes.

F PROCTER & SON LTD
DEWSBURY ROAD, FENTON ST4 2TE
Tel: 01782 846031
Fax: 01782 744732
Web site: www.proctersholidays.com
Dirs: R Walker, J Walker.
Fleet: 16
Chassis: 2 Bova, 5 DAF, 1 Iveco, 6 Leyland, 2
Scania.
Ops incl: local bus services, school contracts,
excursions & tours, private hire.
Livery: Blue/White.
Ticket System: Wayfarer

ROBIN HOOD TRAVEL LTD
HIGHWAY GARAGE, MACCLESFIELD ROAD,
LEEK ST13 8PS
Tel: 01538 306618
Fax: 01538 306069
E-mail: info@robinhoodtravel.co.uk
Web site: www.robinhoodtravel.co.uk
Fleet: 12 - 3 single-deck bus, 7 single-deck coach,
1 midicoach, 1 minicoach.
Ops incl: school contracts, excursions & tours,

private hire, continental tours.
Livery: Green/Gold stars

SHIRE TRAVEL INTERNATIONAL LTD
UNIT 9, MARKET HALL STREET, CANNOCK
WS11 1EB
Tel/Fax: 01543 871605
E-mail: hire@shiretravel.co.uk
Web site: www.shiretravel.co.uk
Dir: Robert Garrington **Comp Sec:** Michelle
Wassell.
Fleet: 9 - 3 single-deck coach, 1 midibus,
5 minibus.
Chassis incl: 1 Scania, 2 Setra, 5 Mercedes.
Bodies: 1 Irizar, 6 Mercedes, 2 Setra.
Ops incl: private hire, school contracts,
excursions & tours, continental tours.
Livery: White/Red + end three lions flag

SOLUS COACH TRAVEL LTD
LICHFIELD ROAD INDUSTRIAL ESTATE,
TAMWORTH B79 7TA
Tel: 01827 51736
Fax: 0871 900 4124
Recovery: 01785 222666
E-mail: info@soluscoaches.co.uk
Web site: www.soluscoaches.co.uk
Man Dir: Andy Garratt **Co Sec:** Lucy Garratt
Ch Eng: Graham Hopkins **Ops Man:** Dave
Wakelin **Fin Dir:** David Baldwin.
Fleet: 24 – single-deck bus, single-deck coach,
midibus, minibus, midicoach, minicoach.
Chassis incl: 2 Bova, 4 DAF, 8 Ford Transit,
1 Mercedes, 3 Scania, 1 Setra, 4 Temsa.
Bodies incl: 2 Bova, 3 Irizar, 1 Mercedes,
1 Plaxton, 1 Scania, 1 Setra, 4 Van Hool, 4 Volvo,
1 Other.
Ops incl: local bus services, school contracts,
excursions & tours, private hire, continental tours.
Livery: Red/Black/Grey
Ticket System: Wayfarer

STANWAYS COACHES
ODLUMS GARAGE, KNUTSFORD ROAD,
RODE HEATH, STOKE-ON-TRENT ST7 3QT
Tel: 01270 884242
Fax: 01270 884262
E-mail: stanwayscoaches@yahoo.co.uk
Partners: David Elliot, Paul Richman.
Fleet: 11 - 1 single-deck bus, 8 single-deck coach,
2 midibus.
Chassis: 1 DAF, 3 Dennis, 4 Leyland, 1 Optare,
1 Scania, 4 Volvo.
Bodies: 1 Alexander Dennis, 1 Berkhof,
1 Caetano, 1 Duple, 3 Plaxton, 4 Other.
Ops incl: local bus services, school contracts,
private hire.
Livery: various
Ticket System: Wayfarer

STODDARDS LTD
GREENHILL GARAGE, LEEK ROAD, CHEADLE
ST10 1JF
Tel: 01538 752253   **Fax:** 01538 750375
E-mail: info@stoddards.co.uk
Web site: www.stoddards.co.uk
Man/Fin Dir: J A Stoddard **Driver
Operations/IT:** P H Stoddard **Vehicles/
Operations:** P M Stoddard **Co Sec:** B H
Stoddard.
Fleet: 4 single-deck coach.

Chassis: 4 DAF.
Bodies: 4 Bova.
Ops incl: excursions & tours, private hire, school contracts.
Livery: Silver/Blue

SWIFTSURE TRAVEL

UNIT 6, 290 STANTON ROAD, BURTON-UPON-TRENT DE15 9SQ
Tel: 01283 512974 **Fax:** 01283 516728
E-mail: info@swiftsure-travel.co.uk
Web site: www.swiftsure-travel.co.uk
Man Dir: Richard Hackett **Dirs:** Julian Peddle, Brian Kershaw **Co Sec:** Kathleen Hackett.
Fleet: 6 - 4 single-deck coach, 2 midicoach.
Chassis: 1 Bova, 1 DAF, 2 Mercedes,

1 Scania, 1 Toyota.
Bodies: 1 Bova, 1 Caetano, 2 Optare, 1 Scania, 1 Van Hool.
Ops incl: school contracts, excursions & tours, express, private hire.
Livery: White/Blue/Green

TAMWORTH COACH CO

See Heartlands Travel

WARDLE TRANSPORT

MOSSFIELD ROAD, ADDERLEY GREEN ST3 5BW
Tel: 01782 827282
Now a subsidiary of Arriva Midlands, including former Staffordshire operations of D & G Coach & Bus Hire. See Arriva Midlands.

WARRINGTON COACHES

See Derbyshire

WINTS COACHES

MONTANA, WETTON ROAD, BUTTERTON ST13 7ST
Tel/Fax: 01538 713938
Web site: www.wintscoachesleek.co.uk
Props: Andrew Wint, Maxine Wint.
Fleet: 10 - 8 single-deck coach, 2 minicoach.
Chassis: 1 DAF, 1 Dennis, 6 Mercedes, 1 Optare, 1 Volvo.
Bodies: 1 Bova, 6 Mercedes, 1 Neoplan, 1 Optare, 1 Plaxton.
Ops incl: school contracts, excursions & tours, private hire, continental tours.

SUFFOLK

ANGLIAN BUS LTD

BECCLES BUSINESS PARK, BECCLES NR34 7TH
Tel: 01502 711109
Fax: 01502 711161
E-mail: office@angliancoaches.co.uk
Web site: www.anglianbus.co.uk
Fleet: 75 - 6 double-deck bus, 33 single-deck bus, 1 single-deck coach, 35 midibus.
Chassis: 2 Dennis, 8 Mercedes, 27 Optare, 32 Scania, 2 Volvo, 4 Wright.
Bodies: 2 Alexander, 1 Mercedes, 27 Optare, 8 Plaxton, 32 Scania, 1 Wadham Stringer, 9 Wright.
Ops incl: local bus services, school contracts.
Livery: Yellow with blue stripes
Ticket System: Wayfarer 3

AWAYDAYS LTD, t/a GEMINI TRAVEL

UNIT 20, STERLING COMPLEX, FARTHING ROAD, IPSWICH IP1 5AP
Tel: 01473 462721 **Fax:** 01473 462731
E-mail: info@geminiofipswich.co.uk
Web site: www.geminiofipswich.co.uk
Dir: Ed Nicholls
Fleet: 7 - 2 midicoach, 1 minibus, 4 minicoach.
Chassis: 6 Mercedes, 1 Renault.
Bodies: 1 Mellor, 5 Optare, 1 Reeve Burgess.
Ops incl: excursions & tours, private hire, school contracts, continental tours.
Livery: Red/White
See also Far East Travel

BEESTONS (HADLEIGH) LTD

THE COACH DEPOT, IPSWICH ROAD, HADLEIGH IP7 6BG
Tel: 01473 823243 **Fax:** 01473 823608
E-mail: info@beestons.co.uk
Web site: www.beestons.co.uk
Man Dir: P R Munson

Co Sec: S J Munson
Ops Man: T Munson.
Fleet: 35 - 11 double-deck bus, 8 single-deck bus, 8 single-deck coach, 2 double-deck coach, 5 minibus, 1 minicoach.
Chassis: 6 Mercedes, 13 Scania, 2 Van Hool, 14 Volvo.
Bodies: 1 Alexander, 6 East Lancs, 2 Northern Counties, 1 Optare, 6 Plaxton, 2 Scania, 10 Van Hool, 7 Wright.
Ops incl: local bus services, school contracts, excursions & tours, private hire.
Liveries: Buses: Blue; Coaches: Black/Gold.
Ticket System: Wayfarer 3

BURTONS COACHES

Ceased trading since LRB 2011 went to press. Bus operations were acquired by Stephensons of Essex.

CARTERS COACH SERVICES

LONDON ROAD, CAPEL ST MARY, IPSWICH IP9 2JT
Tel: 01473 378018
E-mail: enquiries@cartersbusdepot.demon.co.uk
Web site: www.carterscoachservices.co.uk
Fleet: 22 - 8 double-deck bus, 5 single-deck bus, 4 midibus, 5 heritage.
Chassis (main fleet): 3 Alexander Dennis, 9 Dennis, 1 Enterprise, 1 VDL, 3 Volvo.
Bodies (main fleet): 6 Alexander, 3 Alexander Dennis, 1 East Lancs, 1 MCV, 2 Northern Counties, 4 Plaxton.
Ops incl: local bus services, school contracts, private hire.
Livery: Red/Yellow/Black

H C CHAMBERS & SON LTD

KNOWLE HOUSE, HIGH STREET, BURES CO8 5AB
Tel: 01787 227233 **Fax:** 01787 227042

Recovery: 07770 886834
E-mail: info@chamberscoaches.co.uk
Web site: www.chamberscoaches.co.uk
Ops Dir: Alec Chambers
Eng Dir: Robert Chambers.
Fleet: 30 - 20 double-deck bus, 5 single-deck bus, 4 single-deck coach, 1 minibus
Chassis: 4 Dennis, 3 Mercedes, 23 Volvo.
Bodies: 17 Alexander, 2 Mercedes, 8 Northern Counties, 1 Plaxton, 1 Van Hool, 1 Wright.
Ops incl: local bus services, excursions & tours, private hire.
Livery: Red
Ticket System: Wayfarer

CONSTABLE COACHES LTD

See parent company – Beestons (Hadleigh) Ltd

CUTTINGS COACHES

Ceased trading since LRB 2011 went to press

D-WAY TRAVEL

THE COACH CENTRE, OLD HARLESTON ROAD, EARSHAM, BUNGAY NR35 2AF
Tel: 01986 895375
Fax: 05600 751425
E-mail: david@dwaytravel.com
Web site: www.dwaytravel.com
Prop: David Thompson
Ops Man: Dale Jermy.
Fleet: 10 - 7 single-deck coach, 1 minibus, 1 minicoach, 1 midicoach.
Chassis incl: 1 Ford Transit, 5 MAN, 2 Mercedes, 1 Peugeot, 1 Volvo.
Ops incl: school contracts, excursions & tours, private hire, continental tours.
Livery: White/Multi Colours

FAR EAST TRAVEL

UNIT 20, STERLING COMPLEX, FARTHING ROAD, IPSWICH IP1 5AP

The Little Red Book 2012 - in association with *tbf* Transport Benevolent Fund

Suffolk

Tel: 01473 462721
Fax: 01473 462731
E-mail: info@geminiofipswich.co.uk
Web site: www.geminiofipswich.co.uk
Man Dir: Ed Nicholls.
Fleet: 6 midibus
Chassis: 4 Mercedes, 2 Optare.
Bodies: 2 Optare, 4 Plaxton.
Ops incl: local bus services, school contracts.
Livery: Red/White
Ticket System: Wayfarer
Associated with Awaydays Ltd, t/a Gemini
Travel

FARELINE BUS & COACH SERVICES

OLD ROSES, SYLEHAM ROAD, WINGFIELD,
EYE IP21 5RF
Tel: 01379 668151
Prop: Jeff Morss.
Fleet: I single-deck coach.
Chassis: I Bedford.
Body: I Plaxton.
Ops incl: local bus services, school contracts,
excursions & tours, private hire.
Livery: Blue/Cream
Ticket System: Setright Mk 3

FELIX OF LONG MELFORD

8 WINDMILL HILL, LONG MELFORD,
SUDBURY CO10 9AD
Tel: 01787 310574, 372125
Fax: 01787 310584
Web site: www.felixcoaches.co.uk
Fleet: 20 – 3 midibus, 3 midicoach, 7 minibus,
3 minicoach, 4 heritage.
Chassis (main fleet): I MAN, 15 Mercedes.
Bodies (main fleet): I Caetano, 3 Esker,
5 Mercedes, 3 Plaxton, 4 Other.
Ops incl: local bus services, school contracts,
excursions & tours, private hire
Livery: White with Red/Black

FIRST EAST OF ENGLAND (formerly
FIRST EASTERN COUNTIES)

ROUEN HOUSE, ROUEN ROAD, NORWICH
NR1 1RB
Tel: 0845 602 0121
Fax: 01603 615439

Web site: www.firstgroup.com
Regional Man Dir: Nigel Barrett
Regional Eng Dir: Mick Brannigan
Regional Comm Dir: Steve Wickers
Regional Fin Planning Dir: David Marshall.
Fleet (Norfolk & Suffolk): 314 - 144
double-deck bus, 151 single-deck bus,
4 single-deck coach, 15 midibus.
Chassis: 2 AEC, 106 Dennis, I Leyland,
14 Optare, 52 Scania, 139 Volvo.
Bodies: 17 Alexander, 6 Alexander Dennis,
7 Northern Counties, 14 Optare, 2 Park
Royal, 132 Plaxton, 20 Transbus, 116 Wright.
Ops incl: local bus services, school contract,
private hire.
Livery: FirstGroup UK Bus.
Ticket System: Wayfarer 3

FORGET-ME-NOT (TRAVEL) LTD

CHAPEL ROAD, OTLEY, IPSWICH IP6 9NT
Tel: 01473 890268
Fax: 01473 890748
E-mail: sales@forgetmenot-travel.co.uk
Web site: www.forgetmenottravel.co.uk
Fleet Name: Soames
Dirs: A F Soames, Mrs M A Soames
(Co Sec), A M Soames (Ch Eng).
Fleet: 17 - 16 single-deck coach, I midicoach.
Chassis: I Mercedes, 16 Volvo.
Bodies: I Jonckheere, I Optare, 11 Plaxton,
I Transbus, 3 Van Hool.
Ops incl: private hire, school contracts.
Livery: Three tone Blue

GALLOWAY EUROPEAN
COACHLINES LTD

DENTERS HILL, MENDLESHAM,
STOWMARKET IP14 5RR
Tel: 01449 766323
Fax: 01449 766241
E-mail: david@gallowayeuropean.co.uk
Web: www.gallowayeuropean.com
Man Dir: David Cattermole
Comm Dir: John Miles Fin Dir: Roger
Stedman Fleet Man: Andy Kemp
Ops Man: Richard Smith
Comm Man: Liz Palfrey
Training Man: Ian Brain.
Fleet: 44 - 2 double-deck bus, 14 single-deck

bus, 25 single-deck coach, 3 midicoach.
Chassis: 28 DAF/VDL, 12 Mercedes, I Scania,
2 Setra, I Temsa.
Bodies: 4 Ikarus, 2 Mercedes, 3 Optare,
13 Plaxton, I Scania, 2 Setra, I UVG,
14 Van Hool, 4 Wright.
Ops incl: local bus services, school contracts,
excursions & tours, private hire, express,
continental tours.
Livery: Multi Globe & Star based.
Ticket System: Wayfarer 3.

HARLEQUIN TRAVEL

77 LANERCOST WAY, IPSWICH IP2 9DP
Tel: 01473 407408
E-mail: paul.lewis80@ntlworld.com
Web site: www.harlequin-travel.co.uk
Dirs: P D Lewis, Mrs L M Lewis.
Fleet: 3 - 2 midicoach, I minibus.
Chassis: 2 Mercedes, I Peugeot.
Bodies incl: I Autobus, I Plaxton.
Ops incl: school contracts, private hire.
Livery: Maroon/White

IPSWICH BUSES LTD

7 CONSTANTINE ROAD, IPSWICH
IP1 2DL
Tel: 01473 232600
Fax: 01473 232062
Recovery: 01473 344817
E-mail: info@ipswichbuses.co.uk
Web site: www.ipswichbuses.co.uk
Man Dir: Malcolm Robson
Chair: Paul West.
Fleet: 71 - 32 double-deck bus, I open-top
bus, 33 single-deck bus, 5 midibus.
Chassis: 10 DAF, 26 Dennis, 6 Leyland,
9 Optare, 11 Scania, 5 Transbus, I VDL, 3 Volvo.
Bodies: 9 Alexander, 3 ECW, 37 East Lancs,
15 Optare, I Roe, 6 Scania Omnicity.
Ops incl: local bus services, school contracts.
Livery: Green/White
Ticket System: Ticketer

LAMBERT'S COACHES
(BECCLES) LTD

UNIT 4A, MOOR BUSINESS PARK,
BENACRE ROAD, BECCLES NR34 7TQ
Tel: 01502 717579
Fax: 01502 711209
E-mail: lorraine@lambertscoaches.co.uk
Web site: www.lambertscoaches.co.uk
Chairman: D M Reade Dir: Miss L K Reade.
Fleet: 7 single-deck coach.
Chassis: 5 DAF, 2 Volvo.
Bodies: 7 Van Hool.
Ops incl: private hire, school contracts.
Livery: White with Blue Signwriting

MIL-KEN TRAVEL LTD

11 LYNN ROAD, LITTLEPORT, ELY
CB6 1QG
Tel: 01353 860705
Fax: 01353 863222
E-mail: milken@btconnect.com
Web-site: www.milkentravel.com
Man Dir: Jason Miller
Ops Man: David Edmondson
Fleet Eng: Ian Martin.
Fleet: 33 - 30 single-deck coach, I minibus,
2 minicoach.
Chassis: I LDV, 2 Mercedes, 30 Volvo.

Bodies: 2 Jonckheere, 1 LDV, 22 Plaxton, 1 Sitcar, 1 Unvi, 3 Van Hool, 3 Volvo.
Ops incl: school contracts, private hire.
Livery: White with Red, Blue, Yellow.

MINIBUS & COACH HIRE (EAST ANGLIA) LTD

LINGS FARM, BLACKSMITHS LANE, FORWARD GREEN, EARL STONHAM IP14 5ET.
Tel: 01449 711117
Fax: 01449 711977
Dirs: Mrs L J Eustace, S Eustace.
Fleet: 11 - 3 single-deck coach, 8 minibus.
Chassis: 3 Bedford, 1 Iveco, 6 LDV, 1 Nissan.
Ops incl: local bus services, school contracts, excursions & tours, private hire.

MULLEYS MOTORWAYS LTD

STOW ROAD, IXWORTH, BURY ST EDMUNDS IP31 2JB.
Tel: 01359 230234
Fax: 01359 232451
E-mail: enquiries@mulleys.co.uk
Web site: www.mulleys.co.uk
Dir/Co Sec: Jayne D Munson
Man Dir: David J Munson
Ops Man: Daniel Munson.
Fleet: 43 - 9 double-deck bus, 6 single-deck bus, 17 single-deck coach, 1 double-deck coach, 2 midicoach, 7 midibus, 1 minibus.
Chassis: 3 BMC, 1 Ford Transit, 1 Irisbus, 2 Iveco, 10 Leyland, 8 Mercedes, 6 Scania, 2 Setra, 10 Volvo.
Bodies: 5 Alexander, 3 BMC, 2 Beulas, 3 ECW, 3 East Lancs, 1 Euro, 1 Ford, 1 Indcar, 1 Irizar, 7 Jonckheere, 1 Northern Counties, 6 Plaxton, 2 Setra, 2 Transbus, 5 Van Hool.
Ops incl: local bus services, school contracts, excursions & tours, private hire, continental tours.
Livery: Orange/Silver.
Ticket System: Wayfarer.

NIGHTINGALES OF BECCLES LTD

BENACRE ROAD, ELLOUGH, BECCLES NR34 7TD
Tel: 01502 476048
Ops incl: local bus services, school contracts. A subsidiary of Souls Coaches Ltd (see Buckinghamshire)

ROUTESPEK COACH HIRE LTD

3 ELMS CLOSE, EARSHAM, NR BUNGAY NR35 2TD
Tel/Fax: 01968 893035
Dirs: Mr K Reeve, Mrs R Reeve.
Fleet: 4 - 1 double-deck bus, 3 single-deck coach.
Chassis: 1 Bristol, 2 Leyland, 1 Volvo.
Bodies: 1 ECW, 3 Van Hool.
Ops incl: local bus service, school contracts, private hire.
Livery: Fawn
Ticket System: hand m/c

B R SHREEVE & SONS LTD

HADENHAM ROAD, LOWESTOFT NR33 7NF
Tel: 01502 532000
Fax: 01502 532009
E-mail: info@bellecoaches.co.uk

Web site: www.bellecoaches.co.uk
Fleet Name: Belle Coaches.
Joint Man Dirs: Ken Shreeve, Robert Shreeve **Dir:** John Shreeve
Co Sec: Susan Speed.
Fleet: 44 - 37 single-deck coach, 3 midicoach, 4 minibus.
Chassis: 2 Ford Transit, 3 MAN, 5 Mercedes, 9 Scania, 15 Setra, 1 Toyota, 2 Volkswagen, 7 Volvo.
Bodies: 1 Caetano, 3 Mercedes, 6 Plaxton, 2 Scania, 18 Setra, 9 Van Hool, 5 Other.
Ops incl: school contracts, excursions & tours, private hire, continental tours.
Livery: Blue

SQUIRRELL'S COACHES LTD

THE COACH HOUSE, THE CAUSEWAY, HITCHAM, IPSWICH IP7 7NF
Tel/Fax: 01449 740582
E-mail: info@squirrellscoaches.co.uk
Web site: www.squirrellscoaches.co.uk
Dirs: R J Squirrell, J A Squirrell.
Fleet: 7 - 5 single-deck coach, 2 midicoach.
Chassis: 1 Leyland, 2 Mercedes, 4 Volvo.
Bodies: 1 Autobus, 1 Reeve Burgess, 5 Van Hool.
Ops incl: school contracts, private hire.
Livery: Silver/Black/Orange

STEPHENSONS OF ESSEX LTD

DUDDERY HILL, HAVERHILL CB9 8DR
Tel: 01440 704583
Fax: 01702 549461
E-mail: sales@stephensonsofessex.com
Web site: www.stephensonsofessex.com
Man Dir: Bill Hiron
Fin Dir: Lyn Watson.
Fleet: 74 - 44 double-deck bus, 21 single-deck bus, 3 single-deck coach, 6 midibus.
Chassis: 12 Alexander Dennis, 9 Dennis, 27 Leyland, 6 Optare, 5 Scania, 15 Volvo.
Bodies: 22 Alexander, 9 Alexander Dennis, 3 East Lancs, 23 Northern Counties, 9 Optare, 8 Plaxton.

Ops incl: local bus services, school contracts, private hire.
Livery: White/Green
Ticket System: Wayfarer 3
See also Essex

WHINCOP'S COACHES

THE GARAGE, PEASENHALL, SAXMUNDHAM IP17 2HJ
Tel: 01728 660233
Fax: 01728 660156
Owner: Paul S Whincop.
Fleet: 10 single-deck coach.
Chassis: 10 Volvo.
Bodies: 2 Jonckheere, 6 Plaxton, 2 Van Hool.
Ops incl: school contracts, excursions & tours, private hire.

The Little Red Book 2012 - in association with Transport Benevolent Fund

ABELLIO WEST LONDON LTD

301 CAMBERWELL ROAD, LONDON
SE5 0TF
Tel: 020 7788 8550
Fax: 020 7805 3502
E-mail: customer.care@abellio.co.uk
Web site: www.abellio.co.uk
Fleet Name: Abellio Surrey
Man Dir: Tony Wilson.
Fleet (Surrey): 52 – 17 single-deck bus,
35 midibus.
Chassis: 4 Alexander Dennis, 22 Dennis,
7 Optare, 19 Transbus.
Bodies: 4 Alexander Dennis, 15 East Lancs,
7 Optare, 7 Plaxton, 19 Transbus.
Ops incl: local bus services.
Livery: Red/White
A division of the Abellio Group

ALLENBY COACH HIRE LTD

415 LIMPSFIELD ROAD, WARLINGHAM
CR6 9HA
Tel: 01883 330095
Fax: 01883 818546
E-mail: enquiries@allenbycoachhire.co.uk
Web site: www.allenbycoachhire.co.uk
Fleet: 8 – 5 midicoach, 3 minicoach.
Chassis: 1 Ford Transit, 1 King Long, 5 Mercedes,
1 Toyota.
Ops incl: school contracts, private hire.
Livery: Silver/Maroon

ARRIVA SOUTHERN COUNTIES

FRIARY BUS STATION, GUILDFORD
GU1 4YP
Tel: 01483 505693
Fleet Name: Arriva serving Guildford & West
Surrey.
Man Dir: Heath Williams
Comm Dir: Kevin Hawkins **Fin Dir:** Beverley
Lawson.
Fleet: see Arriva Southern Counties (Kent)
Ops incl: local bus services.
Livery: Arriva UK Bus.
Ticket System: Wayfarer 3

BANSTEAD COACHES LTD

1 SHRUBLAND ROAD, BANSTEAD
SM7 2ES
Tel: 01737 354322
Fax: 01737 371090
E-mail: sales@bansteadcoaches.co.uk
Web site: www.bansteadcoaches.co.uk
Dirs: D C Haynes, C J Haynes, M C Haynes.
Fleet: 18 - 16 single-deck coach, 2 midicoach.
Chassis: 1 Bedford, 3 Mercedes,
1 Neoplan, 2 Toyota, 2 Volvo.
Bodies: 3 Berkhof, 2 Caetano, 5 Mercedes,
1 Neoplan, 7 Plaxton.
Ops incl: school contracts, private hire.
Livery: Pink/White.

BUSES4U

EAST SURREY RURAL TRANSPORT
PARTNERSHIP, TANDRIDGE DISTRICT
COUNCIL, STATION ROAD EAST, OXTED
RH8 0BT
Tel: 01730 815518
Web site: www.buses4u.org.uk

CALL-A-COACH

CAPRI HOUSE, WALTON-ON-THAMES
KT12 2LY
Tel: 01932 223838
Fax: 01932 269109
E-mail: callacoach@aol.com
Owner: Arthur Freakes.
Fleet: 6 – 2 single-deck coach, 2 midicoach,
2 minicoach
Chassis: 1 Bova, 1 DAF, 2 LDV, 1 Mercedes,
1 Van Hool.
Ops incl: school contracts, excursions & tours,
private hire.
Livery: White

CHEAM COACHES

Ceased operations since LRB 2011 went to press

CHIVERS COACHES LTD

CLARENDON HOUSE, 35 POUND STREET,
CARSHALTON SM5 3PG
Tel: 020 3 535 5759
E-mail: enquiries@chiverscoaches.co.uk
Web site: www.chiverscoaches.co.uk
Dirs: Lynne Lucas, Melanie Chivers.
Fleet: 3 - 2 single-deck coach, 1 midicoach.
Chassis: 1 Mercedes, 2 Volvo.
Bodies: 2 Van Hool, 1 Other.
Ops Incl: private hire, school contracts.
Livery: White with blue graphics

COUNTRYLINER GROUP

GB HOUSE, MERROW LANE, GUILDFORD
GU4 7BQ
Tel: 0844 477 1623 **Fax:** 01483 506913
E-mail: info@countryliner-coaches.com
Web site: www.countryliner-coaches.co.uk
Dirs: R Hodgetts, R Belcher **Gen Man:**
N Hatcher **Ops Man:** M Bishop
Eng Man: G Mills.
Fleet: double-deck bus, double-deck coach,
single-deck bus, single-deck coach, midibus,
midicoach.
Chassis: Alexander Dennis, DAF, Leyland, MAN,
Marshall, MCW, Mercedes, Neoplan, Optare,
Scania, Volvo.
Bodies: Berkhof, Caetano, ECW, East Lancs,
Hispano, Marshall/MCV, Mercedes, Neoplan,
Northern Counties, Plaxton, Van Hool.
Ops incl: local bus services, school contracts,
private hire.
Livery: Green/White.
Ticket System: Wayfarer

CRUISERS LIMITED

UNIT M, KINGSFIELD BUSINESS CENTRE,
REDHILL RH1 4DP
Tel: 01737 770036
Fax: 01737 770046
E-mail: enq@cruisersltd.co.uk
Web site: www.cruisersltd.co.uk
Dir: M J Walter.
Fleet: 18 - single-deck bus, single-deck coach,
minibus, minicoach.
Chassis: Dennis, LDV, Mercedes, Volvo.
Ops incl: local bus services, school contracts,
private hire.
Livery: Various Metallic
Ticket System: Almex

EPSOM COACHES GROUP

ROY RICHMOND WAY, EPSOM KT19 9AF
Tel: 01372 731700
Fax: 01372 731740
E-mail: sales@epsomcoaches.com
Web site: www.epsomcoaches.com
Fleet Names: Epsom Coaches, Quality Line.
Man Dir: Andrew Richmond **Comm Dir:**
Steve Whiteway **Ch Eng:** John Huxford **Coach
Service Man:** John Fowler **Bus Services Man:**
Jonathan Ball **Ch Eng:** 1 Norman
Fin Controller: Nilesh Mandvia **Office
Man:** Melanie Cox **Training Man:** Terry
Torch **Performance & Planning Man:** Huw
Barrington.
Fleet: 97 - 12 double-deck bus, 63 single-deck
bus, 22 single-deck coach.
Chassis: 30 Alexander Dennis, 45 Optare,
20 Setra, 2 Volvo.
Bodies: 30 Alexander Dennis, 45 Optare,
20 Setra, 2 Volvo.
Ops incl: local bus services, excursions & tours,
private hire, express, continental tours.
Livery: Buses: Red; **Coaches:** Maroon/Cream,
National Express.
Ticket system: Prestige

FARNHAM COACHES

See Safeguard Coaches

HARDINGS COACHES

WELLWOOD, WELLHOUSE LANE,
BETCHWORTH RH3 7HH
Tel: 01737 842103
Fax: 01737 842831
E-mail: sales@bookhardings.com
Web site: www.minibushiresurrey.com
Fleet: 11 - 6 single-deck coach, 5 midicoach.
Chassis: 4 Mercedes, 2 Scania, 1 Toyota, 3 Volvo.
Bodies: 2 Berkhof, 1 Caetano, 2 Irizar,
2 Jonckheere, 1 Mercedes, 1 Plaxton, 2 Other.
Ops incl: private hire.
Livery: White/Orange.

HARWOOD'S COACHES

51 ELLESMERE ROAD, WEYBRIDGE
KT13 0HW
Tel: 01932 842073 **Fax:** 01932 843901
E-mail: gillian.harwood@btinternet.com
Prop: Gillian Harwood.
Fleet: 3 single-deck coach.
Chassis: 3 Volvo.
Bodies: 3 Van Hool.
Ops incl: school contracts, private hire.
Livery: Red/Beige/Brown.

HILLS OF HERSHAM

129 BURWOOD ROAD HERSHAM KT12 4AN
Tel: 01932 254795
Fax: 01932 222671
E-mail: info@hillscoachesofhersham.co.uk
Web site: www.hillscoachesofhersham.co.uk
Dir: D Hill
Fleet: 7 - 6 single-deck coach, 1 midicoach.
Chassis: 1 Irisbus, 1 Iveco, 1 Mercedes, 4 Volvo.
Bodies: 2 Beulas, 1 Jonckheere, 1 Plaxton,
1 Sitcar, 2 Van Hool.
Ops incl: school contracts, private hire.
Livery: White/Red

MAYDAY TRAVEL LTD

ANCHOR BUSINESS PARK,
102 BEDDINGTON LANE, CROYDON
CR0 4YX
Tel: 020 8680 5111
Fax: 020 8680 8624
E-mail: info@maydaytravel.co.uk
Web site: www.coachhirelondon.co.uk
Fleet: single-deck coach, midibus, minibus.
Ops incl: private hire, excursions & tours,
continental tours.
Livery: Silver/White/Blue

M&E COACHES

11 VAUX CRESCENT, HERSHAM
KT12 4HE
Tel: 01932 244664
Prop/Gen Man: M W Oram
Sec: Mrs A E Oram.
Fleet: 5 – 3 midicoach, 2 minibus.
Chassis: 1 Ford Transit, 2 Mercedes, 2 Toyota.
Ops incl: school contracts, excursions &
private hire.
Livery: Blue/White.

MEMORY LANE VINTAGE OMNIBUS SERVICES

78 LILLIBROOKE CRESCENT,
MAIDENHEAD SL6 3XQ
Tel: 01628 825050
Fax: 01628 825851
E-mail: admin@memorylane.co.uk
Web site: www.memorylane.co.uk
Prop: M J Clarke.
Fleet: 6 - 3 double-deck bus, 3 single-deck bus
Chassis: 6 AEC.
Bodies: 2 ECW, 3 Park Royal, 1 Willowbrook.
Ops incl: private hire.
Livery: Original operators

MERTON COMMUNITY TRANSPORT

JUSTIN PLAZA 3, SUITE 3, LONDON ROAD,
MITCHAM CR4 4BE
Tel: 020 8648 7727
E-mail: mertonct@ukonline.co.uk

METROBUS LTD

See West Sussex

PICKERING COACHES

12 HAYSBRIDGE COTTAGES, WHITE WOOD
LANE, SOUTH GODSTONE RHG 8JN
Tel/Fax: 01342 843731
Props: R Pickering, Ms D Pickering.
Fleet: 5 single-deck coach.
Chassis: 5 Volvo.
Bodies: 1 Jonckheere, 4 Van Hool.
Ops incl: private hire, school contracts.

REPTON'S COACHES

GUILDFORD ROAD, LITTLE BOOKHAM
KT23 4HB
Tel: 01372 452330
Web site: www.reptonscoaches.com
Fleet: 6 – 5 single-deck coach, 1 midicoach.
Chassis: 2 DAF, 1 Mercedes, 1 Van Hool, 2 Volvo.
Ops incl: local bus services, school contracts,
private hire, excursions & tours.
Livery: Blue/Cream.

SAFEGUARD COACHES LTD

GUILDFORD PARK ROAD, GUILDFORD
GU2 7TH
Tel: 01483 561103
Fax: 01483 455865
E-mail: sales@safeguardcoaches.co.uk
Web site: www.safeguardcoaches.co.uk
Man Dir: Andrew Halliday **Ops Man:** Mike
Wescombe **Eng Man:** Brett Lambley.
Fleet: 39 - 11 single-deck bus, 25 single-deck
coach, 3 midicoach.
Chassis: 1 AEC, 6 Dennis, 4 Mercedes, 7 Optare,
2 Setra, 19 Volvo.
Bodies: 3 East Lancs, 1 Hispano, 1 Mercedes,
8 Optare, 14 Plaxton, 2 Setra, 9 Van Hool, 1 Other.
Ops incl: local bus services, school contracts,
private hire.
Livery: Red/Cream.
Ticket System: Wayfarer TGX 150
(Incorporating Farnham Coaches)

SKINNERS OF OXTED

15 BARROW GREEN ROAD, OXTED RH8 0NJ
Tel: 01883 713633
Fax: 01883 730079
E-mail: info@skinners.travel
Web site: www.skinners.travel
Partners: Stephen Skinner, Deborah Skinner.
Fleet: 14 - 11 single-deck coach, 2 midicoach,
1 minicoach.
Chassis: 4 Alexander Dennis, 1 MAN,
2 Mercedes, 7 Setra.
Bodies: 1 Duple, 1 Mercedes, 4 Neoplan,
1 Optare, 7 Setra.
Ops incl: excursions & tours, private hire, school
contracts, continental tours.
Livery: Brown & Cream
(Incorporating Westerham Coaches)

STAGECOACH IN HANTS & SURREY

See Hampshire

SUNRAY TRAVEL LTD

79 ASHLEY ROAD, EPSOM KT18 5BN
Tel: 01372 740400
Fax: 01372 800778
E-mail: enquiries@gosunray.com
Fleet Name: Go Sunray.com
Dir: Noel Millier,
Fleet: single-deck bus, single-deck coach
Ops incl: school contracts, excursions & tours,
private hire, continental tours.
Livery: Blue with yellow/orange/red sun rays

SURELINE COACHES

UNIT 8, MARTLANDS INDUSTRIAL ESTATE,
SMARTS HEATH LANE, MAYFORD, WOKING
GU22 0RQ
Tel: 01483 234649
Fax: 01483 236464
E-mail: sureline@btconnect.com
Prop: J R McCracken
Fleet: 9 - 5 single-deck coach, 1 minibus,
3 minicoach.
Chassis: 2 Bova, 3 MAN, 1 Mercedes, 2 Setra,
1 Toyota.
Bodies: 2 Bova, 2 Caetano, 1 Neoplan, 2 Setra,
1 Other.
Ops incl: excursions & tours, private hire, school
contracts.
Livery: White with Red lettering.

SURREY CONNECT

GATWICK COACH CENTRE, OLD
BRIGHTON ROAD, LOWFIELD HEATH,
CRAWLEY RH4 0PR
Tel: 01293 596831
See Flights Hallmark, West Sussex

SUTTON COMMUNITY TRANSPORT

UNIT 3, BROOKMEAD, JESSOPS WAY,
CROYDON CR0 4TS
Tel: 020 8683 3944
Web site: www.suttonct.co.uk
Ch Exec: Mike Skinner **Training & Ops Man:**
Karen Golding **Admin Man:** Sharon Sadler
Acc Officer: Emma Weaver **Senior Driver:**
Owen Wright **Dirs:** Philip Hewitt **(Chair)**,
Tony Pattison **(Vice Chair)** Oumouly Ba, Peter
Morley, Bob Harris, Sue Robson, Peter Talboys,
Andrew Theobald, Brian Wilson, Pam Wilson.
Fleet: 17 minibus.
Chassis/Bodies: LDV, Mercedes, Optare,
Volkswagen.
Ops incl: school contracts, excursions & tours,
private hire.
Livery: White with purple logo

TELLINGS GOLDEN MILLER COACHES LTD

See Middlesex

EDWARD THOMAS & SON

442 CHESSINGTON ROAD, EPSOM, SURREY
KT19 9EJ
Tel: 020 8397 4276 **Fax:** 020 8397 5276
E-mail: edwardthomasandson@btconnect.com
Web site: www.edwardthomasandson.co.uk
Owner: Ivan Thomas **Ch Eng:** Manny Seager
Ops Man: Neil Seager,
Fleet: 33 - 1 double-deck bus, 4 single-deck bus,
28 single-deck coach
Ops incl: local bus services, school contracts,
private hire.
Livery: Green/Cream

W H MOTORS

See West Sussex

WESTERHAM COACHES

See Skinners of Oxted

WOKING COMMUNITY TRANSPORT

MOORCROFT, OLD SCHOOL PLACE,
WESTFIELD, WOKING GU22 9LY
Tel: 01483 744800 **Fax:** 01483 757115
E-mail: enquiries@wokingbustler.co.uk
Web site: www.wokingbustler.org.uk
Fleet Name: Woking Bustler
Chairman: Jacquie Chamberlain **Ch Exec:** Vic
Clare **Sec:** Sheila Rapley **Dir of Fin:** Ron Bell,
Fleet: 28 minibus
Ops incl: local bus services, private hire
Livery: Yellow

Surrey

Legend

Vehicle suitable for disabled		Seat belt-fitted Vehicle		**R24**	24 hour recovery service	
Toilet-drop facilities available		Coach(es) with galley facilities			Replacement vehicle available	
Recovery service available		Air-conditioned vehicle(s)			Vintage Coache(s) available	
Open top vehicle(s)		Coaches with toilet facilities			Hybrid Buses	

TYNE & WEAR

A & J COACHES OF WASHINGTON
6 SKIRLAW CLOSE, GLEBE VILLAGE,
WASHINGTON NE38 7RE
Tel: 0191 417 2564 **Fax:** 0191 415 4672
Recovery: 07702 068063
E-mail: info@ajcoaches.co.uk
Man Dir: Ian Ashman **Co Sec:** Jean Ashman.
Fleet: 1 single-deck coach.
Chassis: 1 Volvo.
Bodies: 1 Plaxton.
Ops incl: school contracts, private hire.
Livery: Blue/White

A LINE COACHES
UNIT 1, PELAW INDUSTRIAL ESTATE,
GATESHEAD NE10 0UW
Tel/Fax: 0191 495 2424
Recovery: 07984 501243
E-mail: enquiries@a-linecoaches.co.uk
Web site: www.a-linecoaches.co.uk
Partners: David C Annis, Leslie B Annis.
Fleet: 9 – 1 double-deck bus, 4 single-deck bus,
2 single-deck coach, 2 midibus.
Ops incl: local bus services, school contracts,
excursions & tours, private hire, continental tours.
Livery: Red/White
Ticket System: AES 2000 Datafare

ALTONA COACH SERVICES LTD
LIDDELL TERRACE, KIBBLESWORTH,
GATESHEAD NE11 0XJ
Tel: 0191 469 2193 **Fax:** 0191 469 3025
Fleet Name: Altona Travel
Prop: A C Hunter **Ops Man:** A I Hunter
Office Man: R Dudding.
Fleet: 9 - 5 single-deck coach, 2 midicoach,
2 minicoach.
Chassis: 1 DAF, 1 Dennis, 2 Mercedes, 1 Toyota,
3 Volvo.
Bodies: 2 Caetano, 2 Duple, 1 LAG, 2 Plaxton,
1 Robin Hood, 1 Bus Craft Impala.
Ops incl: excursions & tours, private hire,
continental tours.
Livery: Two tone Blue and Orange.

ARRIVA NORTH EAST
ADMIRAL WAY, DOXFORD INTERNATIONAL
BUSINESS PARK, SUNDERLAND SR3 3XP
Tel: 0191 520 4200 **Fax:** 0191 520 4222
Web site: www.arriva.co.uk
Regional Man Dir: Nigel Featham
Area Man Dir: Iain McInroy
Eng Dir: John Greaves **Fin Dir:** Dave Barry.
Fleet: 612 - 110 double-deck bus, 326 single-
deck bus, 14 single-deck coach, 162 minibus.
Chassis: 42 Alexander Dennis, 117 DAF,
122 Dennis, 3 Leyland, 27 Mercedes, 76 Optare,
55 Scania, 21 Temsa, 3 Transbus, 84 VDL, 63 Volvo.
Bodies: 38 Alexander, 42 Alexander Dennis,
50 East Lancs, 9 Ikarus, 43 Northern Counties,

102 Optare, 175 Plaxton, 19 Scania, 21 Temsa,
3 Transbus, 109 Wright.
Ops incl: local bus services, school contracts,
private hire, express.
Livery: Arriva UK Bus.
Ticket System: Wayfarer 3

COACHLINERS OF TYNESIDE
16 BRANDLING COURT, SOUTH SHIELDS
NE34 8PA
Tel/Fax: 0191 427 1515
E-mail: coachliners@yahoo.co.uk
Prop: John Dorothy.
Fleet: 2 midicoach.
Chassis: 2 Mercedes.
Bodies: 2 Plaxton.
Ops incl: school contracts, excursions & tours,
private hire.
Livery: White with red stripes

HENRY COOPER
LANE END GARAGE, ANNITSFORD
NE23 7BD
Tel: 0191 250 0260 **Fax:** 0191 250 1820
E-mail: graham@henrycoopercoaches.com
Web site: www.henrycoopercoaches.com
Partners: Graham, Lily, Pamela Greaves.
Fleet: 8 – 1 double-deck bus, 1 single-deck bus,
6 single-deck coach.
Chassis: 1 AEC, 1 Leyland National, 6 Volvo.
Bodies: 1 Park Royal, 1 Leyland National,
6 Plaxton.
Ops incl: school contracts, private hire.
Livery: Orange/Cream.

ERB SERVICES LTD
Business acquired by Stanley Travel – see Durham

GO NORTH EAST
117 QUEEN STREET, GATESHEAD NE8 2UA
Tel: 0191 420 5050 **Fax:** 0191 420 0225
E-mail: customerservices@gonortheast.co.uk
Web site: www.simplygo.com
Man Dir: P G Huntley **Ops Dir:** K Carr **Fin
Dir:** G C McPherson **Comm Dir:** M P Harris.
Fleet: 691 - 150 double-deck bus, 412 single-
deck bus, 19 single-deck coach, 106 midibus,
4 articulated bus.
Chassis: 6 Alexander Dennis, 1 Blue Bird,
30 DAF, 157 Dennis, 32 Leyland, 63 Mercedes,
25 Optare, 137 Scania, 52 Transbus, 21 VDL,
167 Volvo.
Bodies: 5 Alexander, 6 Alexander Dennis,
22 Caetano, 52 East Lancs, 63 Mercedes,
86 Northern Counties, 25 Optare, 132 Plaxton,
41 Scania, 60 Transbus, 201 Wright.
Ops incl: local bus services, school contracts,
express.
Livery: Various route brands, National Express.
Ticket System: Wayfarer 3

JIM HUGHES COACHES LTD
WEAR STREET, LOW SOUTHWICK,
SUNDERLAND SR5 2BH
Tel: 0191 548 9600
Fax: 0191 549 3728
E-mail: jhcoaches@hotmail.co.uk
Man Dir: James Hughes **Dir:** Valerie Hughes
Sec: Jean Fisher **Ch Eng:** Stephen McGuinness.
Fleet: 7 single-deck coach.
Chassis: 1 MAN, 1 Mercedes, 5 Volvo.
Bodies: 3 Plaxton, 2 Setra, 2 Van Hool.
Ops incl: excursions & tours, private hire,
continental tours.
Livery: White with Red/Orange.

KINGSLEY COACHES LTD
UNIT 20, PENSHAW WAY, PORTOBELLO
INDUSTRIAL ESTATE, BIRTLEY
DH3 2SA
Tel: 0191 492 1299
Fax: 0191 410 9281
E-mail: accounts@kingsleycoaches.co.uk
Dir: David Kingsley (senior)
Ch Eng: David Kingsley (junior)
Co Sec: Mrs Eileen Kingsley.
Fleet: 20 - 8 double-deck bus, 4 single-deck bus,
1 double-deck coach, 4 single-deck coach,
1 midicoach, 2 minibus.
Chassis: 2 Freight Rover, 1 Iveco, 1 Leyland,
2 MAN, 8 MCW, 1 Optare, 1 Scania, 1 Van Hool,
3 Volvo.
Bodies: 1 Berkhof, 1 Jonckheere, 1 Leicester,
2 LDV, 2 Marshall/MCV, 8 MCW, 1 Optare,
2 Plaxton, 2 Van Hool.
Ops incl: local bus services, school contracts,
excursions & tours, private hire.
Livery: Blue/White.
Ticket System: Wayfarer

PRIORY COACH & BUS LTD
59 CHURCH WAY, NORTH SHIELDS
NE29 0AD
Tel/Fax: 0191 257 0283
E-mail: info@priorycoaches.com
Web site: www.priorycoaches.com
Dirs: S Kirkpatrick, P Harris, I Fenwick, L Stewart.
Fleet: 10 - 9 single-deck coach, 1 minibus.
Chassis: 1 LDV, 1 Leyland, 8 Volvo.
Bodies: 1 Berkhof, 1 Caetano, 2 Plaxton,
4 Van Hool, 1 Other.
Ops incl: excursions & tours, private hire, school
contracts.
Livery: White/Blue vinyls

ROWLANDS GILL COACHES & TAXIS
1 THORNEY VIEW, ROWLANDS GILL, TYNE &
WEAR NE39 1QL
Tel: 01207 543118
E-mail: ashleycoaches@aol.com
Prop: David Murphy

Tyne & Wear

STAGECOACH NORTH EAST

WHEATSHEAF, NORTH BRIDGE STREET,
SUNDERLAND SR5 1AQ
Tel: 0191 567 5251
Fax: 0191 566 0202
E-mail: northeast.enquiries@stagecoachbus.com
Web site: www.stagecoachbus.com
Man Dir: John Conroy **Ops Dir:** Vacant **Eng Dir:** David Kirsopp **Comm Dir:** Robin Knight.
Fleet: 472 – 101 double-deck bus, 227 single-deck bus, 5 open top bus, 139 midibus.
Chassis: 202 Alexander Dennis, 5 Leyland, 229 MAN, 36 Volvo.
Bodies: 452 Alexander Dennis, 19 Northern Counties, 1 Plaxton.
Ops incl: local bus services, school contracts.
Livery: Stagecoach UK Bus
Ticket System: ERG TP5000

THIRLWELL'S COACHES

MILLERS BRIDGE, WHICKHAM BANK,
SWALWELL, NEWCASTLE NE16 3BP
Tel/Fax: 0191 488 4948
E-mail: enquiries@thirlwellcoaches.co.uk
Web site: www.thirlwellcoaches.co.uk
Fleet: 7 – 6 single-deck coach, 1 midicoach.
Chassis: 1 Mercedes, 6 Volvo.

Bodies: 4 Plaxton, 2 Van Hool, 1 Other.
Ops incl: excursions & tours, private hire.
Livery: Red & Grey

VEOLIA TRANSPORT ENGLAND PLC
Operations in Tyne & Wear ceased since LRB 2011 went to press.

YOURBUS (DURHAM) LTD
COLLIERY LANE, HETTON-LE-HOLE,
HOUGHTON LE SPRING DH5 0BG
In process of acquiring some Veolia operations in Tyne & Wear as LRB 2012 goes to press.
See also Dunn Motor Traction (Derbyshire)

WARWICKSHIRE

A-LINE COACHES

BRANDON ROAD, BINLEY, COVENTRY
CV3 2JD
Tel: 024 7645 0808
Fax: 024 7645 6434
E-mail: office@a-linecoaches.com
Web site: www.a-linecoaches.com
Dirs: B Haywood, K Prosser
Fleet: 23 - 1 single-deck bus, 13 single-deck coach, 6 midibus, 2 minibus, 1 minicoach.
Chassis: 5 Bova, 1 DAF, 3 Mercedes, 2 Optare, 2 Scania, 10 Volvo.
Bodies: 5 Alexander, 2 Berkhof, 5 Bova, 1 Jonckheere, 3 Optare, 5 Plaxton, 2 Other.
Ops incl: local bus services, private hire, school contracts.
Livery: White

CATTERALLS COACHES

74 COVENTRY STREET, SOUTHAM
CV47 0EA
Tel: 01926 813192
Fax: 01926 813915
Recovery: 01926 813192
E-mail: info@travelcatteralls.co.uk
Web site: www.travelcatteralls.co.uk
Dir: Paul Catterall.
Fleet: 35 – 2 double-deck bus, 30 single-deck coach, 2 double-deck coach, 1 midicoach.
Ops incl: local bus services, school contracts, excursions & tours, private hire, continental tours.
Livery: Blue, Yellow and White

CHAPEL END COACHES

WILSON HOUSE, 3 OASTON ROAD,
NUNEATON CV11 6JX
Tel: 024 7635 4588
Fax: 024 7635 6406
E-mail: chapelendcoaches@btconnect.com
Web site: www.chapelendcoaches.co.uk
Man Dir/Trans Man: Ian Wilson
Dir/Sec: Mrs Tracey Wilson.
Fleet: 11 single-deck coaches.
Ops incl: local bus services, excursions & tours, private hire, continental tours, school contracts.
Livery: White/Red/Black

MIKE DE COURCEY TRAVEL LTD
See West Midlands.

MARTIN'S OF TYSOE
20 OXHILL ROAD, MIDDLE TYSOE

CV35 0SX
Tel: 01295 680642
Prop: Martin Thomas.

MIDLAND RED COACHES/WHEELS HERITAGE

Postal Office, 23 Broad Street, Brinklow,
Warwickshire CV23 0LS
Tel: 02476 633624, 07733 884914
Fax: 02476 354900
E-mail: buses@wheels.co.uk
Web site: www.wheels.co.uk
Props: Ashley Wakelin, Rob Paramour.
Fleet: vintage vehicles.
Ops incl: private hire, excursions & tours, bus driver experiences.
Livery: Midland Red

SKYLINERS LTD

19 BOND STREET, NUNEATON
CV11 4NX
Tel: 024 7632 5682
Fax: 024 7635 4626
E-mail: haydn@skyliners.co.uk
Dir: Haydon J Dawkins.
Fleet: 1 double-deck coach.
Body: Neoplan.
Ops incl: excursions & tours, private hire, continental tours.

STAGECOACH IN WARWICKSHIRE

RAILWAY TERRACE, RUGBY
CV21 3HS
Tel: 01788 562036   **Fax:** 01788 566094
E-mail: warksenquiries@stagecoachbus.com
Web site: www.stagecoachbus.com/warwickshire
Man Dir: Steve Burd
Ops Dir: Liz Esnouf
Eng Dir: Keith Dyball
Comm Mgr: Clive Jones
Marketing Man: Adam Rideout.
Fleet (Warwickshire): 206 - 45 double-deck bus, 131 single-deck bus, 21 single-deck coach, 31 midibus.
Chassis: 42 Alexander Dennis, 50 Dennis, 1 Leyland, 14 MAN, 36 Optare, 14 Scania, 71 Volvo.
Ops incl: local bus services, school contracts, private hire, express.
Livery: Stagecoach UK Bus
Ticket System: ERG
Part of Stagecoach Midlands – see also Northamptonshire

NOTES

ADAMS TOURS

75 SANDBANK, BLOXWICH, WALSALL
WS3 2HL
Tel/Fax: 01922 406469
Prop: David Adams.
Fleet: 7 - 4 single-deck coach, 3 midicoach.
Chassis: 4 DAF, 3 Mercedes.
Bodies: 2 Autobus, 1 Plaxton, 4 Van Hool.
Ops incl: private hire, school contracts, excursions & tours.
Livery: Cream.

AIRPARKS SERVICES LTD

WILLOW HOUSE, PINEWOOD BUSINESS PARK, COLESHILL ROAD, MARSTON GREEN, BIRMINGHAM B37 7HJ
Tel: 0121 717 5300
Fax: 0121 788 0778
E-mail: david.rowe@airparks.co.ik
Web site: www.airparks.co.uk
Ops Dir: Paul Humphrey **Group Fleet Man:** David Rowe **Trans Man:** Matt Lawton
Co Sec: Elisabeth Hirlemann.
Fleet: 32 - 27 single-deck bus, 5 minibus.
Chassis: 11 Alexandra Dennis, 4 Ford Transit, 16 MAN, 1 Volkswagen.
Bodies: 11 Alexander Dennis, 16 MCV
Ops incl: local bus services, private hire, - car park to airport shuttle.

AM-PM TRAVEL

Operations ceased since LRB 2011 went to press

B B COACHES LTD

22 VICTORIA AVENUE, HALESOWEN
B62 9BL
Tel: 0121 422 4501
Fax: 0121 602 2040
Dirs: Mick Bird, Barbara Blewitt.
Fleet: 1 single-deck coach.
Chassis: Volvo.
Bodies: Plaxton.
Ops incl: excursions & tours, private hire
Livery: Cream

BEACON COACHES

24 CHICHESTER GROVE, CHELMSLEY WOOD
B37 5RZ
Tel: 0121 783 2221
Fax: 0121 680 2582
E-mail: enquiries@beaconcoaches.co.uk
Web site: www.beaconcoaches.co.uk
Fleet: 6 - 2 double-deck coach, 1 midicoach, 1 minicoach, 2 minibus.
Chassis: 1 MAN, 2 Scania, 1 Toyota, LDV.
Bodies incl: 3 Jonckheere.
Ops incl: excursions & tours, private hire, school contracts, continental tours.
Livery: White /Red/Grey.

BIRMINGHAM INTERNATIONAL COACHES LTD

10 FORTNUM CLOSE, TILE CROSS, BIRMINGHAM B33 0JT
Tel: 0121 783 4004
Fax: 0121 785 0967
E-mail: Birmingham.intl@btconnect.com
Web site: www.
birminghaminternationalcoaches.co.uk

Dirs: M Watkiss, A Watkiss, N Watkiss.
Fleet: 11 – 1 double-deck bus, 10 single-deck coach.
Chassis: 11 DAF.
Bodies: 10 Bova, 1 Optare.
Ops incl: school contracts, excursions & tours, private hire, continental tours.
Livery: Grey/Red

L F BOWEN LTD

See Staffordshire

CENTRAL BUSES LTD

UNIT 14A, TAMEBRIDGE INDUSTRIAL ESTATE, ALDRIDGE ROAD, BIRMINGHAM B42 2TX
Tel: 0121 356 3487 **Fax:** 0870 199 2923
E-mail: email@centralbuses.com
Web site: www.centralbuses.com
Man Dir: Geoff Cross
Fleet: 16 – 2 double-deck bus, 14 single-deck bus.
Chassis: 8 Alexander Dennis, 6 Dennis, 2 Volvo.
Bodies: 2 Alexander, 8 Alexander Dennis, 6 Plaxton.
Ops incl: local bus services, school contracts.
Livery: Red/Grey
Ticket System: Wayfarer TGX200

CENTRAL CONNECT

BEACON HOUSE, LONG ACRE, BIRMINGHAM B7 5JJ
Tel: 0121 322 2222 **Fax:** 0121 322 2718
Recovery: 07973 939103
E-mail: buses@connectbuses.com
Web site: www.connectbuses.net
Fleet: single-deck bus, single-deck coach, minibus.
Chassis: Dennis, Enterprise, LDV, MAN, Neoplan, Setra, Volvo.
Bodies: Caetano, Duple, Neoplan, Plaxton, Setra, Van Hool.
Ops incl: local bus services, school contracts, excursions & tours, private hire, express, continental tours
Livery: White with Blue, Red
Ticket System: Wayfarer TGX
Part of Rotala PLC - Incorporating Birmingham Motor Traction, North Birmingham Busways & Zak's Bus & Coach Services.

DEN CANEY COACHES LTD

THE COACH STATION, STONE HOUSE LANE, BARTLEY GREEN, BIRMINGHAM B32 3AH
Tel: 0121 427 2078
Fax: 0121 427 8905
E-mail: enquiry@dencaneycoaches.co.uk
Web site: www.dencaneycoaches.co.uk
Man Dir: D Stevens **Dir:** M Stevens
Ch Eng: A Doggett **Ops Man:** J Clarke
Administrator: Mrs D Johnston.
Fleet: 9 single-deck coach
Chassis: Dennis, Leyland, Toyota, Volvo
Ops incl: private hire, school contracts

CHAUFFEURS OF BIRMINGHAM

CREST HOUSE, 7 HIGHFIELD ROAD, EDGBASTON, BIRMINGHAM B15 3ED.
Tel: 0121 456 3355
E-mail: enquiries@c-o-b.co.uk
Web site: www.chauffeursbirmingham.co.uk
Fleet incl: single-deck coach, midicoach, minicoach.

CLARIBEL COACHES LTD

10 FORTNUM CLOSE, TILE CROSS, BIRMINGHAM B33 0JT
Tel: 0121 789 7878
Fax: 0121 785 0967
E-mail: Birmingham.intl@btconnect.com
Web site: www.claribelcoaches.co.uk
Dirs: M J Watkiss, M Watkiss, A Watkiss, N Watkiss.
Fleet: 24 - 2 double-deck bus, 22 single-deck bus.
Chassis: DAF, VDL.
Bodies: 1 East Lancs, 1 Optare, 22 Wright.
Ops incl: local bus services, school contracts, private hire.
Livery: Blue/White.
Ticket System: Wayfarer TGX

COURTESY TRAVEL

See Shropshire

N N CRESSWELL

See Worcestershire

DAIMLER

99 SAREHOLE ROAD, BIRMINGHAM B28 8ED
Tel: 0121 778 2837
Fax: 0121 702 2843
E-mail: roy@daimlertours.wanadoo.co.uk
Prop: Roy Picken.
Fleet: 1 single-deck coach.
Chassis/Body: 1 Neoplan.
Ops incl: excursions & tours.
Livery: White/Burgundy

MIKE DE COURCEY TRAVEL LTD

ROWLEY DRIVE, COVENTRY
CV3 4FG
Tel: 024 7630 2656
Fax: 024 7663 9276
Web site: www.traveldecourcey.com
Fleet Name: Travel De Courcey
Man Dir: Mike de Courcey **Co Sec:** Adrian de Courcey **Gen Man:** Bob Wildman
Fleet Eng: Neville Collins
Bus Man: Mick Rossiter
Coach Man: John Bowns.
Fleet: 90 - 31 double-deck bus, 29 single-deck bus, 30 single-deck coach.
Chassis: 8 Alexander Dennis, 1 Daimler, 2 Dennis, 3 Leyland, 30 MAN, 10 MCW, 6 Mercedes, 6 Scania, 24 Volvo.
Bodies: 11 Alexander Dennis, 14 Caetano, 4 East Lancs, 1 Jonckheere, 5 Marcopolo, 27 Marshall/MCV, 11 MCW, 6 Mercedes, 3 Northern Counties, 2 Optare, 6 Plaxton.
Ops incl: local bus services, school contracts, excursions & tours, private hire, express.
Livery: White/Blue/Orange.
Ticket System: Parkeon Wayfarer TGX

DIAMOND BUS LTD

CROSS QUAYS BUSINESS PARK, HALLBRIDGE WAY, TIVIDALE, OLDBURY, B69 3HW
Tel: 0121 557 7337
Fax: 0121 520 4999
Web site: www.diamondbuses.com
Fleet Names: Black Diamond, Red Diamond.
Fleet incl: single-deck bus, midibus.
Man Dir: Scott Dunn.

Ops incl: local bus services.
Livery: Red/Black
Part of Rotala PLC

DIRECT COACH TOURS
68 BERKELEY ROAD EAST, HAYMILLS,
BIRMINGHAM B25 8NP
Tel: 0121 772 0664
Fax: 0121 773 8649
Tours Man: Brian Bourne.
Fleet: 7 - 6 single-deck coach, 1 midicoach.
Chassis: 1 Toyota, 6 Volvo.
Bodies: 1 Caetano, 6 Plaxton.
Ops incl: excursions & tours, private hire.

ENDEAVOUR COACHES LTD
30 PLUME STREET, ASTON, BIRMINGHAM
B6 7RT
Tel: 0121 326 4994
Fax: 0121 326 4999
E-mail: enquiries@endeavourcoaches.co.uk
Web site: www.endeavourcoaches.co.uk
Dirs: J Mitchell, G Mitchell, D Mitchell.
Fleet: 14 – 10 single-deck coach, 4 minibus.
Chassis: 2 Ford Transit, 2 Freight Rover, 1 MAN,
2 VDL, 7 Volvo.
Bodies incl: 2 Bova, 1 Marcopolo, 7 Van Hool.
Ops incl: school contracts, excursions & tours,
private hire, continental tours.
Livery: Silver

EUROLINERS
See Worcestershire

FLIGHTS HALLMARK LTD
BEACON HOUSE, LONG ACRE,
BIRMINGHAM B7 5JJ
Tel: 0121 322 2222
Fax: 0121 322 2224
Recovery: 0121 322 2710
E-mail: sales@flightshallmark.com
Web site: www.flightshallmark.com
Chairman: John Gunn **Ch Exec:** Kim Taylor
Man Dir: Simon Dunn **Dir:** Geoff Flight
Eng Man: Dave Russell **Bus Dev Man:** Anthony
Goozee **Comm Man:** Ian Pollard
Ops Mans: Paul Williams (coach), Steve Elms
(bus)
Fleet: double-deck bus, single-deck bus, single-
deck coach, midicoach.
Chassis: DAF, Dennis, LDV, MAN, Mercedes,
Optare, Toyota, Volvo.
Bodies incl: Alexander, Caetano, Jonckheere, MCW,
Mercedes, Neoplan, Optare, Plaxton, Sunsundegui,
Van Hool, Wright.
Ops incl: local bus services, school contracts,
excursions & tours, private hire, express,
continental tours.
Ticket system: Wayfarer, ERG
Part of Rotala PLC

J. R. HOLYHEAD INTERNATIONAL
32 CROSS STREET, WILLENHALL WV13 1PG
Tel: 01902 607364
Fax: 01902 609772
Owner: J. R. Holyhead.
Fleet: 5 single-deck coach.
Chassis: 2 Bova, 3 Volvo.
Bodies: 2 Bova, 3 Plaxton.
Ops incl: excursions & tours, private hire,
express, continental tours.
Livery: White.

JOHNSONS COACH & BUS TRAVEL
LIVERIDGE HOUSE, LIVERIDGE HILL,
HENLEY-IN-ARDEN, SOLIHULL
B95 5QS
Tel: 01564 797000   **Fax:** 01564 797050
E-mail: info@johnsonscoaches.co.uk
Web site: www.johnsonscoaches.co.uk
Dirs: Peter Johnson, John Johnson.
Fleet: 84 – 3 double-deck bus, 26 single-deck
bus, 40 single-deck coach, 1 midicoach, 11 minibus,
3 minicoach.
Chassis: 38 Bova, 3 DAF, 4 Dennis, 11 Ford,
22 Optare, 6 Scania.
Bodies: 38 Bova, 2 East Lancs, 1 Ikarus, 3 Irizar,
22 Optare, 4 Transbus, 14 Other.
Ops incl: local bus services, school contracts,
excursions & tours, private hire, express,
continental tours.
Livery: Yellow/Blue/White
Ticket system: Wayfarer TGX150

JOSEPHS MINI COACHES
See Staffordshire

KEN MILLER TRAVEL
10 CHURCHILL ROAD, SHENSTONE
WS14 0LP
Tel: 01827 60494
Fax: 01827 60494
Recovery: 07976 303951
E-mail: ken.m.traveluk@amserve.net
Fleetname: Ken Miller Recovery.
Prop: Ken Miller.
Fleet: 2 single-deck bus, 2 minibus.
Chassis: LDV, Volvo.
Ops incl: school contracts, private hire, express,
continental tours.
Livery: Blue/Silver
Ticket system: Wayfarer.

KINGSNORTON COACHES
40 BISHOPS GATE, NORTHFIELD,
BIRMINGHAM B31 4AJ
Tel: 0121 550 8519
Fax: 0121 501 6554
E-mail: info@kingsnortoncoaches.co.uk
Web site: www.kingsnortoncoaches.co.uk
Prop: Richard Egan
Fleet: 23 – 1 midibus, 1 midicoach, 20 minibus,
1 minicoach.
Chassis: 1 Iveco, 20 LDV, 1 MAN, 1 Mercedes.
Ops incl: school contracts, excursions & tours,
private hire.
Livery: Red/White

KINGSWINFORD COACHWAYS
HIGH STREET, PENSNETT, BRIERLEY HILL
DY6 8XB
Tel: 01384 401626
Fax: 01384 401580
Recovery: 07831 148626
Dir: David William Edmunds **Ch Eng:**
Robert Lamesdale **Sec:** Robert Morgan
Advisor: David Moor.
Fleet: 7 - 6 single-deck coach, 1 midibus.
Chassis: 6 Volvo.
Body: 2 Plaxton, 1 Reeve Burgess, 4 Van Hool
Ops incl: school contracts, private hire.
Livery: White/Yellow/Red.

LAKESIDE COACHES LTD
See Shropshire

MEADWAY PRIVATE HIRE LTD
28-32 BERKELEY ROAD, HAY MILLS,
BIRMINGHAM B25 8NG
Tel: 0121 773 8389, 8380
Fax: 0121 693 7171
E-mail: meadwaycoaches@btconnect.com
Web site: www.meadwaycoaches.co.uk
Fleet Name: Meadway Coaches.
Fleet: single-deck coach, minibus.
Chassis: Alexander Dennis, DAF, Mercedes, Volvo.
Ops incl: private hire, school contracts.

MIDLAND BUS
PLANETARY ROAD, WEDNESFIELD,
WOLVERHAMPTON WV13 3SW
Tel: 01902 305181
Fax: 01902 307454
E-mail: info@midlandbus.net
Web site: www.midlandbus.net
Fleet Name: Midland
Man Dir: David Reeves
Ops Dir: Shaz Ali
Fleet: 70 – 51 single-deck bus, 19 midibus.
Chassis: 45 Dennis, 23 Optare, 2 VDL.
Ops incl: local bus services
Livery: Blue/White
Associated with D&G Coach & Bus Ltd – see
Cheshire

MIDLAND METRO
See Section 5 – Tram and Bus Rapid Transit
Systems.

NASH COACHES LTD
83 RAGLAN ROAD, SMETHWICK B66 3TT
Tel: 0121 558 0024
Fax: 0121 558 0907
E-mail: info@nashcoaches.co.uk
Web site: www.nashcoaches.co.uk
Dirs: Ian Powell, Miss Linda Powell.
Fleet: 8 – 6 single-deck coach, 2 midicoach.
Chassis: 5 Mercedes, 1 Toyota, 2 Volvo.
Bodies: 1 Berkhof, 1 Caetano, 2 Neoplan,
1 Plaxton, 2 Setra, 1 Van Hool.
Ops incl: excursions & tours, private hire,
express, continental tours, school contracts.
Livery: Multi coloured.

NATIONAL EXPRESS LTD
1 HAGLEY ROAD, EDGBASTON,
BIRMINGHAM B16 8TG
Tel: 0121 625 1122
Fax: 0121 456 1397
E-mail: reception@nationalexpress.com
Web site: www.nationalexpress.com
Man Dir: Andrew Cleaves.
Ops incl: express.
Livery: Red/White/Blue.
Ticket System: Pre-sale, Wayfarer.

NATIONAL EXPRESS WEST
MIDLANDS
51 BORDESLEY GREEN, BIRMINGHAM
B9 4BZ
Tel: 0121 254 7200
Fax: 0121 254 7277
Web site: www.travelwm.co.uk
Man Dir: Neil Barker
Fin Dir: Peter Coates
Eng Dir: Jack Henry
Marketing & Dev Dir: Martin Hancock.

Fleet: 1700 - 929 double-deck bus, 31 articulated bus, 689 single-deck bus, 51 minibus.
Chassis: DAF, Dennis, Mercedes, Optare, Scania, Volvo.
Bodies: Alexander, Mercedes, Optare, Plaxton, Scania, Wright.
Ops incl: local bus services, school contracts, private hire.
Livery: Red/White/Blue

NEWBURY TRAVEL

NEWBURY LANE, OLDBURY B69 1HF
Tel: 0121 552 3262
Fax: 0121 552 0230
E-mail: newburytravel@aol.com
Web site: www.newburytravel.co.uk
Man Dir: David Greenhouse
Ch Eng: Chris Phillips.
Fleet: 11 - 5 single-deck coach, 3 midicoach, 3 minicoach.
Chassis: 1 Ford Transit, 2 LDV, 3 Mercedes, 5 Volvo.
Bodies: 1 Berkhof, 3 Mercedes, 4 Van Hool.
Ops incl: school contracts, private hire.
Livery: White

PROSPECT COACHES (WEST) LTD

81 HIGH STREET, LYE, STOURBRIDGE DY9 8NG
Tel: 01384 895436
Fax: 01384 898654
E-mail: enquiries@prospectcoaches.co.uk
Web site: www.prospectcoaches.co.uk
Man Dirs: Geoffrey Watts, Roslynd A D Hadley
Tran Man: Nathan Hadley
Ops Man: David Price
Garage Man: Martin Hadley.
Fleet: 34 single-deck coach.
Chassis: 30 Alexander Dennis, 1 Neoplan, 3 Volvo.
Bodies: 1 Marcopolo, 1 Neoplan, 32 Plaxton.
Ops incl: school contracts, private hire.
Livery: Silver with Red/Blue/White stripes.

HARRY SHAW

MILL HOUSE, MILL LANE, BINLEY, COVENTRY CV3 2DU
Tel: 024 7665 0650
Fax: 024 7663 5684
E-mail: john@harryshaw.co.uk
Web site: www.harryshaw.co.uk
Fleet: 21 - 19 single-deck coach, 1 midicoach, 1 minibus.
Chassis: 1 Bova, 1 DAF, 2 Dennis, 2 Mercedes, 4 Scania, 2 Setra, 9 Volvo.
Bodies: 5 Berkhof, 1 Bova, 1 Excel, 1 Ikarus, 3 Irizar, 1 Jonckheere, 1 Mercedes, 2 Setra, 3 Van Hool, 2 Wadham Stringer.
Ops incl: local bus services, excursions & tours, school contracts, private hire, continental tours.
Livery: Orange

SHEARINGS HOLIDAYS

BAYTON ROAD, EXHALL CV7 9EJ
Tel: 024 7664 4633
Fax: 024 7636 0304
Gen Man: Carol Carpenter.
See also Shearings Holidays, Greater Manchester.

SILVERLINE LANDFLIGHT LTD

ARGENT HOUSE, VULCAN ROAD, SOLIHULL B91 2JY
Tel: 0121 705 5555
Fax: 0121 709 0556
E-mail: silverline@landflight.co.uk
Web site: www.landflight.co.uk
Man Dir: M E Breakwell
Ops Dir: R G Knott **Bus Dev Dir:** W J Matthews
Eng Man: R J Nowlan.
Fleet: 16 - 6 single-deck bus, 7 single-deck coach, 3 midicoach.
Chassis: 1 DAF, 1 Dennis, 2 MAN, 7 Mercedes, 2 Scania, 3 Toyota.
Bodies: 3 Caetano, 2 Esker, 2 Irizar, 2 Neoplan, 5 Optare, 2 Scania.
Ops incl: local bus services, private hire, continental tours.
Livery: Silver/Blue
Ticket System: Parkeon/ITSO

SOLUS COACH TRAVEL LTD

See Staffordshire

STAGECOACH IN WARWICKSHIRE

See Warwickshire

T. N. C. COACHES

257 CHESTER ROAD, CASTLE BROMWICH B36 0ET
Tel: 0121 747 5722
Fax: 0121 747 5722
Dirs: N T Cunningham, K M Cunningham.
Fleet: 5 - 2 single-deck coach, 3 minibus.
Chassis: 1 DAF, 1 Leyland, 3 LDV.
Bodies: Duple. Van Hool.
Ops incl: school contracts, excursions & tours, private hire.

TERRYS COACH HIRE

21 PANDORA ROAD, COVENTRY CV2 2FU
Tel/Fax: 024 7636 2975
E-mail: enquiries@terrys-coaches.co.uk
Web site: www.terrys-coaches.co.uk
Prop: T Hall **Ops Man:** L Hall
Chief Engs: D Harrison, J Hall
Co Sec: S Hall.
Fleet: 12 single-deck coach.
Chassis: 1 Leyland, 6 MAN, 2 Neoplan, 3 Volvo.
Bodies: 1 Jonckheere, 2 Neoplan, 5 Noge, 4 Plaxton.
Ops incl: excursions & tours, private hire, continental tours.
Livery: Gold/Green leaf

THE TRANSPORT MUSEUM, WYTHALL

See Worcestershire

TRAVEL EXPRESS LTD

30 COTON ROAD, PENN, WOLVERHAMPTON WV41 5AT
Tel/Fax: 01902 330653
E-mail: kishan.chumber@sky.com
Props: Kishan Chumber, Nirmal Chumber.
Fleet: 10 - 10 single-deck bus.
Chassis incl: 9 Alexander Dennis.
Bodies: 6 Carlyle, 3 Duple, 1 Reeve Burgess.
Ops incl: local bus service.
Livery: mixed
Ticket System: Wayfarer

WEST MIDLANDS SPECIAL NEEDS TRANSPORT

80 PARK ROAD, ASTON, BIRMINGHAM B6 5PL
Tel: 0121 327 8128
Fax: 0121 327 9559
E-mail: enquiries@ringandride.org
Web site: www.ringandride.org
Fleet Name: Ring and Ride.
Chief Executive: Peter Maggs.
Fleet: 300 minibus.

WHITTLE COACH & BUS LTD

See Worcestershire

WICKSONS TRAVEL

COPPICE ROAD, BROWNHILLS, WALSALL WS8 7DG
Tel: 01543 372247
Fax: 01543 374271
E-mail: enquiries@wicksons.co.uk
Web site: www.wicksons.co.uk
Dirs: Martin Wickson, Ann Wickson (Co Sec)
Ch Eng: Graham Roe.
Fleet: 11 - 10 single-deck coach, 1 minicoach.
Chassis: 3 Bova, 1 Mercedes, 6 Other.
Bodies: 7 Van Hool, 4 Other.
Ops incl: school contracts, excursions & tours, private hire, continental tours.
Livery: White/Orange/Blue

WINDSOR-GRAY TRAVEL

186 GRIFFITHS DRIVE, WEDNESFIELD, WOLVERHAMPTON WV11 2JR
Tel: 01902 722392
Fax: 01902 722339
E-Mail: grahamwgt@hotmail.co.uk
Owner: Graham Williams.
Fleet: 1 midicoach.
Chassis: 1 Dennis.
Bodies: 1 Duple.
Ops incl: private hire, excursions & tours.
Livery: Cream/Brown/Orange.

YARDLEY TRAVEL LTD

68 BERKELEY ROAD EAST, HAY MILLS, BIRMINGHAM B25 8NP
Tel: 0121 773 3700
Fax: 0121 773 8649
E-mail: info@yardleytravel.co.uk
Web site: www.yardleytravel.co.uk
Dirs: Mr Mohammed Saleem, Mrs Tasneem Saleem.
Fleet: 11 - 8 coach, 3 midicoach.
Chassis: Volvo.
Bodies: Plaxton.
Ops incl: school contracts, excursions & tours, excursions & tours, private hire.
Livery: White/Yellow/Black.

YOUNGS OF ROMSLEY

MALVERN VIEW, DAYHOUSE BANK, ROMSLEY, HALESOWEN B62 0EU
Tel/Fax: 01562 710717
E-mail: roger@youngscoaches.eclipse.co.uk
Prop: R J Young
Fleet: 3 - 1 single-deck coach, 1 midicoach, 1 minicoach
Chassis: 1 Iveco, 2 Mercedes.
Ops incl: excursions & tours, private hire, continental tours.
Livery: Bronze & Yellow

ARUN COACHES

1 NORFOLK TERRACE, HORSHAM RH12 1DA
Tel: 01403 272999 **Fax:** 01403 272777
Prop/Ch Eng: H. Miller.
Fleet: 2 single-deck coach.
Chassis: 2 Hestair/Duple.
Bodies: 2 Duple.
Ops incl: private hire.
Livery: Red/Gold.

COMPASS TRAVEL

FARADAY CLOSE, WORTHING BN13 3RB
Tel: 01903 690025 **Fax:** 01903 690015
E-mail: office@compass-travel.co.uk
Web site: www.compass-travel.co.uk
Man Dir: Chris Chatfield **Ops Dir:** Tim Clarke
Eng Dir: Malcolm Gallichan **Co Sec:** Roger Cotterell.
Fleet: 47 - 30 single-deck bus, 10 single-deck coach, 4 midibus, 2 midicoach, 1 minibus.
Chassis: 25 Alexander Dennis, 4 DAF, 1 Ford Transit, 4 Mercedes, 7 Optare, 4 Scania, 2 Volvo.
Bodies: 25 Alexander Dennis, 1 Ikarus, 3 Irizar, 3 MCW, 4 Optare, 2 Plaxton, 6 Van Hool, 3 Other.
Ops incl: local bus services, school contracts, private hire.
Livery: White/Burgundy.
Ticket System: Wayfarer

COUNTRYLINER GROUP

See Surrey

CRAWLEY LUXURY

STEPHENSON WAY, THREE BRIDGES RH10 1TN
Tel: 01293 521007 **Fax:** 01293 522450
E-mail: crawleylux@aol.com
Fleet Name: Crawley Luxury Coaches.
Dirs: David Brown, Darren Brown, Gavin Brown
Ops Man: Stephen Burse.
Fleet: 56 - 2 double-deck bus, 52 single-deck coach, 2 minibus.
Chassis: 1 Bedford, 1 LDV, 1 Mercedes, 53 Volvo.
Bodies: 2 Alexander, 3 Berkhof, 1 Duple, 1 LDV, 49 Plaxton.
Ops incl: private hire, school contracts.
Livery: Cream/Green/Grey.

FLIGHTS HALLMARK LTD

GATWICK COACH CENTRE, OLD BRIGHTON ROAD, LOWFIELD HEATH, CRAWLEY RH1 0PR
Tel: 01293 596831 **Fax:** 01293 596837
E-mail: gatwick@flightshallmark.com
Web site: www.connectbuses.org
Chairman: S Dunn **Gen Man:** D Dow
Ops incl: school contracts, excursions & tours, private hire, express.
Part of Rotala PLC

HERITAGE TRAVEL

STAR ROAD, PARTRIDGE GREEN RH13 8RD
Tel: 0800 652 5251
E-mail: info@heritagecoaches.com
Web site: www.heritage-coaches.com
Fleet: 30 - 3 double-deck buses, 3 single-deck buses, 14 single-deck coach, 10 double-deck coach.

Ops incl: school contracts, excursions & tours, private hire.

METROBUS LTD

WHEATSTONE CLOSE, CRAWLEY RH10 9UA
Tel: 01293 449192
Fax: 01293 404281
E-mail: info@metrobus.co.uk
Web site: www.metrobus.co.uk
Man Dir: Alan Eatwell **Fin Dir:** Kevin Lavender
Ops Dir: Kevin Carey
Ch Eng: Les Bishop.
Fleet: 479 - 167 double-deck bus, 62 single-deck bus, 248 midibus, 2 minibus.
Chassis: 21 Alexander Dennis, 134 Dennis, 23 MAN, 2 Optare, 269 Scania.
Bodies: 33 Alexander Dennis, 18 Caetano, 160 East Lancs, 32 Marshall/MCV, 32 Optare, 33 Plaxton, 105 Scania, 36 Transbus.
Ops incl: local bus services.
Livery: Two Tone Blue (Home Counties), Red (London).
Ticket Systems: Parkeon, TfL Prestige.
Part of the Go-Ahead Group

PAVILION COACHES

See East Sussex

RICHARDSON TRAVEL LTD

RUSSELL HOUSE, BEPTON ROAD, MIDHURST GU29 9NB
Tel: 01730 813304
Fax: 01730 815985
E-mail: sales@richardson-travel.co.uk
Web site: www.richardson-travel.co.uk
Dir: C Richardson.
Fleet: 18 - 4 double-deck bus, 5 single-deck bus, 7 single-deck coach, 2 midicoach.
Chassis: 2 Mercedes, 16 Volvo.
Bodies: 6 Alexander Dennis, 2 East Lancs, 9 Plaxton, 1 Wright.
Ops incl: local bus services, school contracts, excursions & tours, private hire, continental tours.
Livery: Blue

ROADMARK TRAVEL LTD

UNIT 15, GERSTON BUSINESS PARK, GREYFRIARS LANE, STORRINGTON, PULBOROUGH RH20 4HE
Tel: 01903 741233
Fax: 01903 741232
E-mail: coaches@roadmarktravel.co.uk
Web site: www.roadmarktravel.co.uk
Man Dir: David Coster
Co Sec: Leslie Anderson.
Fleet: 2 single-deck coach.
Chassis: 2 Mercedes.
Bodies: 2 Mercedes.
Ops incl: excursions & tours, private hire, continental tours.
Livery: White/Blue

RUTHERFORDS TRAVEL

BRAMFIELD HOUSE, CHURCH LANE, EASTERGATE, CHICHESTER PO20 3UZ
Tel: 01243 543673
E-mail: rutherfordstravel@hotmail.co.uk
Owner: George Bell.

Fleet: 12 single-deck coach.
Chassis: 2 Dennis, 8 Leyland, 1 MAN, 1 Scania.
Bodies: 1 Duple, 1 Noge, 8 Plaxton, 2 Wadham Stringer.
Ops incl: private hire, school contracts.
Livery: White

SOUTHDOWN PSV LTD

SILVERWOOD, SNOW HILL, COPTHORNE RH10 3EN
Tel: 01342 719619
Fax: 01342 719617
E-mail: info@southdownpsv.co.uk
Web site: www.southdownpsv.co.uk
Man Dir: Steve Swain **Eng Dir:** Simon Stanford
Fin Dir: Peter Larking **Ops Dir:** Gary Wood.
Fleet: 25 - 4 double-deck bus, 21 single-deck bus.
Chassis: 5 Alexander Dennis, 2 DAF, 15 Dennis, 1 MAN, 2 Volvo.
Bodies: 5 Alexander Dennis, 4 East Lancs, 1 Ikarus, 15 Plaxton.
Ops incl: local bus services, school contracts, private hire.
Livery: Blue/White/Light Green.
Ticket System: Wayfarer TGX.

SOUTHERN TRANSIT

THE OLD CEMENT WORKS, SHOREHAM ROAD, BEEDING BN44 3TX
Tel: 01273 464754
Web site: www.southerntransit.co.uk
Prop: N Bird.
Ops incl: private hire, rail replacement.
Livery: Red/Cream

STAGECOACH SOUTH

BUS STATION, SOUTHGATE, CHICHESTER PO19 8DG
Tel: 0871 200 2233
Fax: 01243 755888
E-mail: south.enquiries@stagecoachbus.com
Web site: www.stagecoachbus.com/south
Fleet Names: Stagecoach in the South Downs, Stagecoach in Portsmouth.
Man Dir: Andrew Dyer **Eng Dir:** Richard Alexander **Ops Dir:** Tom Bridge **Comm Dir:** Mark Turner.
Fleet: 189 – 40 double-deck bus, 143 single-deck bus, 6 midibus.
Chassis: 84 Alexander Dennis, 36 Dennis, 6 Optare, 21 Scania, 35 Transbus, 7 Volvo.
Bodies: 25 Alexander, 105 Alexander Dennis, 6 Optare, 18 Plaxton, 35 Transbus.
Ops incl: local bus services, school contracts, private hire.
Livery: Stagecoach UK Bus
Ticket system: Wayfarer

SUSSEX COACHES

SAILORS CROSS, GREEN STREET, SHIPLEY, WEST SUSSEX RH13 8PB
Tel: 01403 741976
Fax: 01403 780605
E-mail: info@sussex-coaches.co.uk
Web site: www.sussex-coaches.co.uk
Dirs: S J Ayling, L Reading.
Fleet: 19, incl double-deck bus, single-deck bus, single-deck coach, double-deck coach, midicoach.
Chassis: BMC, DAF, Leyland, Mercedes, Scania, Volvo.

Bodies: Alexander Dennis, Duple, ECW, Irizar, Jonckheere, MCW, Neoplan, Plaxton, Van Hool.
Ops incl: local bus services, school contracts, excursions & tours, private hire.
Livery: Red & Gold

SUSSEX COUNTRY COACH HIRE
🚌♿
FARADAY CLOSE, WORTHING BN13 3RB
Tel: 01903 264077 **Fax:** 01903 690015
E-mail: admin@sussex-country.co.uk
Web site: www.sussex-country.co.uk
Ops incl: private hire, school contracts, excursions & tours.
Livery: Blue/Yellow/Green on White
A subsidiary of Compass Travel

TURBOSTYLE COACHES LTD
WALLAGE LANE, ROWFANT RH10 4NF
Tel: 01342 719900 **Fax:** 01342 719007
E-mail: info@turbostylecoaches.co.uk
Web site: www.turbostylecoaches.co.uk
Dirs: P James, Mrs L James.
Fleet: 12 – 11 single-deck coaches, 1 midicoach.
Chassis: 4 Dennis, 2 Mercedes, 3 Scania, 3 Volvo.
Bodies: 3 Irizar, 4 Plaxton, 1 Sitcar, 3 Sunsundegui.
Ops incl: school contracts, excursions & tours, private hire.
Livery: White with Red

W H MOTORS LTD
🚌♿⬛🅁24🆃🛠
KELVIN WAY, CRAWLEY RH10 9SF
Tel: 01293 510220 **Fax:** 01293 513263
Recovery: 01293 548111
E-mail: sales@wandhgroup.co.uk
Web site: www.wandhgroup.co.uk
Man Dir: G M Heron.
Fleet: 18 – 14 single-deck coach, 2 double-deck coach, 2 midicoach.
Chassis: 4 MAN, 2 Toyota, 12 Volvo.
Ops incl: excursions and tours, private hire, continental tours
Livery: White

WESTRINGS COACHES LTD
♿🚌
46 GRAYDON AVENUE, CHICHESTER PO19 8RG
Tel: 01243 672411
Web site: www.westringscoaches.co.uk
Dir: W J Buckland **Co Sec:** T S West
Ops incl: school contracts, excursions & tours, private hire.

WOODS TRAVEL LTD
🚌🍴⬛♿🛠
PARK ROAD, BOGNOR REGIS PO21 2PX
Tel: 01243 868080 **Fax:** 01243 871669

E-mail: info@woodstravel.co.uk
Web site: www.woodstravel.co.uk
Man Dir: R Elsmere
Transport Man: K Antonia
Excursions: L Glue **Tours:** K Elsmere
Co Sec: T Shaw-Morton.
Fleet: 14 - 13 single-deck coach, 1 midicoach.
Chassis: 13 DAF, 1 Mercedes.
Bodies: 13 Bova, 1 Sitcar.
Ops incl: school contracts, excursions & tours, private hire, continental tours.
Livery: Red/White/Blue.

WORTHING COACHES
🚌
117 GEORGE V AVENUE, WORTHING BN11 5SA.
Tel: 01903 505805
Fax: 01903 507285
E-mail: contact@worthing-coaches.co.uk
Web site: www.worthing-coaches.co.uk
Fleet: 12 – 11 single-deck coach, 1 double-deck coach.
Chassis: 12 Scania.
Bodies: 1 East Lancs, 11 Irizar.
Ops incl: excursions & tours, private hire, continental tours.
Livery: Red/White/Yellow
A subsidiary of Lucketts Travel - see Hampshire

ANDERSON'S COACHES
🚌♿⬛🛠
HOLMFIELD HOUSE, STRANGLANDS LANE, FERRYBRIDGE WF11 8SD
Tel: 01977 552980
Fax: 01977 557823
Partners: Paul Anderson, Gillian Anderson.
Fleet: 1 single-deck coach.
Chassis: 1 Setra.
Bodies: 1 Setra.
Ops incl: excursions & tours, private hire, continental tours.
Livery: Champagne.

ARRIVA YORKSHIRE LTD
♿
24 BARNSLEY ROAD, WAKEFIELD WF1 5JX
Tel: 01924 231300 **Fax:** 01924 200106
Regional Man Dir: Nigel Featham
Fin Dir: David Cocker
Eng Dir: Neil Craig
Head of Ops: Colin Newbury.
Fleet: 327 - 137 double-deck bus, 111 single-deck bus, 79 midibus.
Chassis: 31 Alexander Dennis, 99 DAF, 62 Dennis, 13 Optare, 35 VDL, 79 Volvo, 8 Wrightbus.
Bodies: 31 Alexander Dennis, 103 Alexander, 14 East Lancs, 6 Ikarus, 3 Northern Counties, 71 Optare, 50 Plaxton, 49 Wright.
Ops incl: local bus services.
Livery: Arriva UK Bus.

B L TRAVEL
🚌♿⬛
10 GRANGE VIEW, HEMSWORTH, NR PONTEFRACT WF9 4ER
Tel: 01977 610313 **Fax:** 01977 613999
E-mail: bltravelcoaches@aol.com
Proprietors: Brian Lockwood, Paul Lockwood.
Fleet: 17 - 8 single-deck bus, 3 single-deck coach, 6 minibus.

Chassis: 1 Ford, 3 Mercedes, 4 Optare, 2 VDL, 7 Volvo.
Bodies: 1 Ford, 4 Optare, 1 Plaxton, 2 Van Hool, 6 Wright, 3 Other.
Ops incl: local bus services, school contracts, excursions & tours, private hire, express.
Livery: Blue/Yellow.

BAILDON MOTORS LTD
♿🚌🛠
VICTORIA ROAD, GUISELEY, LEEDS LS20 8DG
Tel: 01943 873420
Fax: 01943 878227
E-mail: dalesmancoaches@btconnect.com
Web site: www.dalesmancoaches.co.uk
Fleet Name: Dalesman.
Dirs: K Hartshorne, Mrs P J Hartshorne.
Fleet: 6 – 4 single-deck coach, 2 midicoach.
Chassis: 3 DAF, 2 Mercedes, 1 VDL.
Bodies: 2 Unvi, 4 Van Hool.
Ops incl: school contracts, excursions & tours, private hire, continental tours.
Livery: White & Blue.
See also Dalesman.

BRITANNIA TRAVEL
🚌🍴♿⬛🛠
BRITANNIA HOUSE, 113 WESTON LANE, OTLEY LS21 2DX
Tel/Fax: 01943 465591
E-mail: Britannia-Travel@tinyworld.co.uk
Web site: www.britannia-travel.com
Props: Antony Broome, Mrs Susan Eastwood.
Fleet: 1 single-deck coach.
Chassis: Setra.
Body: Setra.
Ops incl: private hire.
Livery: Silver/Red.

BROWNS COACHES (SK) LTD
🚌♿⬛🛠
OLD FORGE GARAGE, WHITE APRON

STREET, SOUTH KIRKBY, PONTEFRACT WF9 3HQ
Tel: 01977 644777
Fax: 01977 643210
E-mail: sales@brownscoaches.com
Web site: www.brownscoaches.com
Fleet Name: Browns
Man Dir: Mrs J M Brown
Co Sec: Mrs M Stoppard
Gen Man: A Griffith
Eng Man: D Brown **Traffic Man:** S Covell.
Fleet: 13 - 5 single-deck coach, 4 midicoach, 4 minicoach.
Chassis: 1 Ford Transit, 4 Iveco, 4 Mercedes, 2 Scania, 2 Temsa.
Bodies: 1 Beulas, 1 Indcar, 1 Irizar, 1 Plaxton, 1 Scania, 2 Temsa, 4 Unvi, 2 Other.
Ops incl: private hire, school contracts, continental tours.
Livery: White.

CENTRAL GARAGE
STANSFIELD ROAD, TODMORDEN OL14 5DL
Tel/Fax: 01706 813909
E-mail: tonygled@hotmail.co.uk
Man Dir: David Paul Guest
Man: A J Gledhill.
Fleet: 3 - 1 midibus, 1 minibus, 1 minicoach.
Chassis/bodies: 3 Mercedes.
Ops incl: school contracts, private hire.

CITY TRAVEL YORKSHIRE LTD
UNIT 10A, MANYWELLS INDUSTRIAL ESTATE, CULLINGWORTH, BRADFORD BD13 5DX
Tel: 01535 275522
Fax: 01533 274400
E-mail: enquiries@citytraveluk.com
Web site: www.citytraveluk.com
Dir: Graham Town
Fleet: 13 - 6 single-deck bus, 5 single-deck coach, 1 midicoach, 1 minibus.
Chassis: 6 BMC, 1 DAF, 1 Ford Transit, 2 Irisbus, 1 Iveco, 1 Mercedes, 1 MAN.

Bodies: 1 Berkhof, 3 Beulas, 6 BMC, 1 Ford, 1 Noge, 1 Van Hool.
Ops incl: school contracts, private hire, excursions & tours.
Liveries: Coaches: Multicoloured; **School Buses:** Yellow.

CLARKSONS HOLIDAYS
See Wilfreda Beehive – South Yorkshire

CT PLUS (YORKSHIRE) CIC
GREENS INDUSTRIAL PARK, CALDER VALE ROAD, WAKEFIELD WF1 5PF
Tel: 01924 377084 **Fax:** 01924 365324
E-mail: info@hctgroup.org
Web site: www.hctgroup.org
Ch Exec: Dai Powell **Dep Ch Exec:** Jude Winter **Ch Fin Off:** Douglas Downie
Ch Ops Off: Jon McColl.
Fleet (East & West Yorkshire): 72 - 57 single-deck bus, 15 minibus.
Chassis: 57 BMC, 2 Mercedes, 13 Optare.
Bodies: 57 BMC, 2 Mercedes, 13 Optare.
Ops incl: local bus services, school contracts, park & ride (Hull).
Liveries: School Buses: Yellow;
Park & Ride: Black; **Local Buses:** WYPTE.
A subsidiary of the FCT Group – see CT Plus Ltd (London & Middlesex).

DALESMAN
VICTORIA ROAD, GUISELEY, LEEDS LS20 8DG
Tel: 01943 870228
Fax: 01943 878227
E-mail: dalesmancoaches@btconnect.com
Web site: www.dalesmancoaches.co.uk
Dirs: K Hartshorne, Mrs P J Hartshorne
Fleet: 6 – 4 single-deck coach, 2 midicoach.
Chassis: 3 DAF, 2 Mercedes, 1 VDL.
Bodies: 2 Unvi, 4 Van Hool.
Ops incl: excursions & tours, private hire, excursions & tours.
Livery: Blue/White.
See also Baildon Motors.

DEWHIRST COACHES LTD
TRAVEL TECH HOUSE, THORNCLIFFE ROAD, BRADFORD BD8 7DD
Tel/Fax: 01274 481208
E-mail: dewhirstcoaches@hotmail.co.uk
Web site: www.dewhirstcoaches.co.uk
Dirs: S R Dewhirst, M J Dewhirst, P A Dewhirst.
Fleet: 7 - 4 double-deck bus, 3 single-deck coach.
Chassis: 1 DAF, 1 EOS, 1 Scania, 2 VDL, 2 Volvo.
Bodies incl: 1 Alexander, 3 East Lancs, 1 EOS, 2 Van Hool.
Ops incl: school contracts, excursions & tours, private hire, continental tours.
Livery: Blue/White.

FIRST WEST YORKSHIRE
HUNSLET PARK, DONISTHORPE STREET, LEEDS LS10 1PL
Tel: 0845 604 5460
Fax: 0113 242 9721
E-mail: contact.us@firstgroup.com
Web site: www.firstgroup.com
Regional Man Dir: Dave Alexander **Service Delivery Dir:** Bob Hamilton **Strategic Devt Dir:** Richard Soper **Business Efficiency Man:** Ian Humphreys **Ops Dir:** Ben Gilligan.

Fleet: 924 – 484 double-deck bus, 397 single-deck bus, 20 midibus, 23 articulated bus.
Chassis: 95 BMC, 56 Dennis, 20 Optare, 45 Scania, 708 Volvo.
Bodies: Alexander, BMC, Marshall, Mercedes, Northern Counties, Optare, Plaxton, Wright.
Ops incl: local bus services, school contracts.
Livery: FirstGroup UK Bus
Ticket System: Wayfarer 3.

FOUR SQUARE COACH COMPANY
HOYLE MILL ROAD, KINSLEY, PONTEFRACT WF9 5JB
Tel: 01977 616398
E-mail: foursquarecoachco@btinternet.com
Web site: www.four-square.co.uk
Fleet: 6 – 5 single-deck coach, 1 minibus.
Chassis: 1 Renault, 2 Scania, 3 Volvo.
Bodies: 2 Irizar, 3 Sunsundegui, 1 Other.
Ops incl: private hire, excursion & tours.
Livery: White with Blue/Yellow.

FOURWAY COACHES
FOURWAY'S GARAGE, LOW MILLS, GHYLL ROYD, GUISELEY, LEEDS LS20 9LT
Tel: 0113 250 5800
E-mail: fourway@freezone.co.uk
Web site: www.fourwaycoaches.co.uk
Fleet: 34 – 15 single-deck coach, 8 midicoach, 10 minibus, 1 minicoach.
Chassis: 5 DAF, 1 Irisbus, 6 Iveco, 1 LDV, 9 Mercedes, 1 Transbus, 3 Volkswagen, 8 Volvo.
Ops incl: private hire, excursions & tours.
Livery: White/Multicoloured.

GAIN TRAVEL EXPERIENCE
6 FAIR ROAD, WIBSEY, BRADFORD BD6 1QN
Tel: 01274 603224
Fax: 01274 347298
E-mail: gail@gaintravel.co.uk
Web site: www.gaintravel.co.uk
Man Dir: Gail Bottomley **Dirs:** Ian Bottomley, Darren Bottomley **Man:** Beryl LeaRoyd.
Fleet: 3 single-deck coach.
Chassis: 1 VDL, 2 Van Hool.
Bodies: 3 Van Hool.
Ops incl: excursions & tours, private hire.
Livery: White with Blue/Green

STANLEY GATH (COACHES) LTD
WHALEY ROAD, BARUGH GREEN, BARNSLEY S75 1HT
Tel: 01226 205800
Fax: 01226 205830
E-mail: info@stanley-gath.co.uk
Web site: www.stanley-gath.co.uk
Ops incl: excursions & tours, private hire, school contracts.
Livery: Grey/Cream.
A subsidiary of Tate's Travel Group – see South Yorkshire.

GELDARD'S COACHES LTD
16B ASHFIELD WAY, WHITEHALL ESTATE, WHITEHALL ROAD, LEEDS LS12 5JB
Tel: 0113 263 9491
Fax: 0113 231 1447
E-mail: info@geldardscoaches.co.uk
Web site: www.geldardscoaches.co.uk
Fleet: 49 - 39 double-deck bus, 2 single-deck bus,

8 single-deck coach.
Chassis: AEC, DAF, Leyland, MCW, Scania, Volvo.
Ops incl: local bus services, school contracts, private hire.

J D GODSON
65 STATION ROAD, CROSSGATES LS15 8DT
Tel: 0113 264 6166
Fax: 0113 390 9669
E-mail: godsonscoaches@hotmail.com
Web site: www.godsonluxurycoachesleeds.co.uk
Man Dir: David Godson.
Fleet: 14 – 4 single-deck bus, 10 single-deck bus.
Chassis: 2 Bova, 2 DAF, 2 Irisbus, 4 Leyland, 2 Mercedes, 2 Volvo.
Bodies: 2 Alexander, 2 Bova, 2 Caetano, 1 Hispano, 2 Leyland, 1 Mercedes, 3 Plaxton, 1 Other.
Ops incl: local bus services, school contracts, private hire.
Livery: Red/Beige.

B & J GOULDING LTD
64 THE RIDGEWAY, KNOTTINGLEY WF11 0JS
Tel: 01977 672265
Fax: 01977 670276
E-mail: info@bjgoulding.co.uk
Web site: www.bjgoulding.co.uk
Prop: G.W. Goulding
Fleet: 3 - 1 minicoach, 2 minibus.
Chassis: 1 Ford, 2 Mercedes.
Ops incl: excursions & tours, private hire, continental tours.
Livery: White with Red/Yellow/Blue.

HALIFAX BUS COMPANY
18 STONECROFT MOUNT, SOWERBY BRIDGE HX6 2SB
Tel: 01422 363600
Fleet: 40 - midibus, minibus.
Chassis: Enterprise, Ford, Iveco, Mercedes, Optare.
Ops incl: local bus services
Livery: Red

HALIFAX JOINT COMMITTEE
1 VICAR PARK ROAD, NORTON TOWER, HALIFAX HX2 0NL
Tel: 01422 353330
Fleet: double-deck bus, single-deck bus, midibus.
Ops incl: local bus services, school contracts, private hire.
Liveries: Green/Orange, Metro School Bus (Mybus) Yellow.

HUDDERSFIELD BUS COMPANY
PENISTONE ROAD, WATERLOO, HUDDERSFIELD HD5 5QU
Tel: 0843 289 5134
E-mail: info@centrebus.com
Web site: www.centrebus.info
Fleet Names: Centrebus, Huddersfield Bus Company.
Man Dir: Peter Harvey **Area Man:** David Brooks
Fleet: 53 –3 double-deck bus, 27 single-deck bus, 23 minibus.
Chassis: 6 DAF, 1 Dennis, 28 Optare, 3 Scania, 7 VDL, 8 Volvo.

The Little Red Book 2012 - in association with Transport Benevolent Fund

Bodies: 16 East Lancs, 1 Marshall, 28 Optare, 7 Plaxton, 1 Wright.
Ops incl: local bus services.
Liveries: Blue/Orange, Green.
Part of Centrebus Holdings - Jointly owned by Centrebus and Arriva.

HUNTERS COACHES LTD

30 TYNWALD ROAD, MOORTOWN, LEEDS LS17 5ED
Tel: 0113 239 0034 **Fax:** 0113 239 0101
E-mail: sales@huntercoaches.co.uk
Web site: www.huntercoaches.co.uk
Fleet: 11 – 3 double-deck bus, 6 single-deck coach, 2 midicoach.
Chassis: 1 BMC, 4 King Long, 1 Mercedes, 4 Scania, 1 Volvo.
Bodies: 1 BMC, 3 East Lancs, 1 Irizar, 4 King Long, 1 Plaxton, 1 Other.
Ops incl: school contracts, private hire, excursions & tours.
Livery: White/Blue.

INDEPENDENT COACHWAYS LTD

LOW FOLD GARAGE, NEW ROAD SIDE, HORSFORTH, LEEDS LS18 4DR
Tel: 0113 258 6491 **Fax:** 01757 630666
E-mail: coaches@thornes.info
Man Dir: Philip Thornes **Co Sec:** L J Thornes
Ch Eng: D Hindle.
Fleet: 5 single-deck coach.
Chassis: 5 Volvo.
Bodies: 5 Plaxton.
Ops incl: private hire.
Livery: Blue/Grey.
Ticket System: Wayfarer.
A subsidiary of Thornes Independent – see North Yorkshire.

J & B TRAVEL LTD

PICKUP BUSINESS PARK, GRANGEFIELD ROAD, STANNINGLEY, LEEDS LS28 6JP
Tel: 0113 258 6870 **Fax:** 0113 239 0075
Web site: www.jandbtravel.co.uk
Fleet: 11 – 5 double-deck bus, 3 single-deck coach, 3 midicoach.
Chassis: 1 BMC, 1 DAF, 1 MCW, 2 Mercedes, 1 Solbus, 5 Volvo.
Bodies: 3 Alexander, 1 BMC, 1 Hispano, 1 MCW, 1 Northern Counties, 1 Plaxton, 1 Solbus, 1 Sunsundegui, 1 Van Hool.
Ops incl: school contracts, private hire.
Liveries: School Buses: Yellow; **Coaches:** White with Blue/Orange.

JACKSONS OF SILSDEN

UNIT 8, RYEFIELD WAY, BELTON ROAD, SILSDEN, KEIGHLEY BD20 0EF
Tel: 01535 652376 **Fax:** 01535 653300
E-mail: enquiries@jacksonsofsilsden.com
Web site: www.jacksonsofsilsden.com
Fleet: 11 – 3 midibus, 1 midicoach, 7 minibus.
Chassis: 5 LDV, 4 Mercedes, 2 Optare.
Ops incl: local bus services, excursions & tours, private hire.
Livery: White with Blue.

JAK TRAVEL LTD

368 BRADFORD ROAD, SANDBEDS, KEIGHLEY BD20 5LY

Tel: 01274 566200 **Fax:** 01274 566803
E-mail: office@jaktravel.co.uk
Web site: www.jaktravel.co.uk
Dirs: A Bonson, Mrs K Bonson.
Fleet: 5 – 4 single-deck coach, 1 midicoach.
Chassis: 1 Temsa, 4 Volvo.
Bodies: 4 Plaxton, 1 Temsa.
Ops incl: excursions & tours, private hire.
Livery: Blue with Red/White.

K-LINE TRAVEL

STATION YARD, STATION ROAD, HONLEY, HUDDERSFIELD HD9 6BF
Tel: 0843 289 5134
E-mail: info@centrebus.com
Web site: www.centrebus.info
Man Dir: Peter Harvey **Area Man:** David Brooks
Fleet: 31 – 1 double-deck bus, 15 single-deck bus, 15 midibus.
Chassis: 7 DAF, 1 Leyland, 15 Optare, 8 VDL.
Bodies: 1 Ikarus, 3 Northern Counties, 15 Optare, 1 Plaxton, 11 Wright.
Ops incl: local bus services, school contracts.
Livery: Blue/White.
Part of Centrebus Holdings - Jointly owned by Centrebus and Arriva.

J J LONGSTAFF & SONS LTD

EASTFIELD GARAGE, STONEY LANE, MIRFIELD WF14 0DX
Tel: 01924 463122
Web site: www.longstaffofmirfield.com
E-mail: jjlongstaff@btconnect.com
Fleet Name: Longstaff of Mirfield
Dirs: G Kaye, S Kaye
Fleet: 2 - 2 single-deck bus.
Chassis: 2 Volvo.
Bodies: 2 Wright.
Ops incl: local bus service, school contracts.
Livery: Blue/Grey/White.
Ticket System: Wayfarer Saver.

A. LYLES & SON

63 COMMONSIDE, BATLEY WF17 6LA
Tel: 01924 464771
Fax: 01924 469267
E-mail: alyles&son@aol.com
Web site: www.web-cell.co.uk/alyles
Senior Partner: Terence Lyles **Partner:** Howard Lyles.
Fleet: 8 - 2 single-deck bus, 6 single-deck coach.
Chassis: 2 Bova, 1 DAF, 1 Dennis, 1 Duple 425, 2 Van Hool, 1 VDL.
Bodies: 1 Berkhof, 2 Bova, 1 Duple, 1 Optare, 1 Northern Counties, 2 Van Hool.
Ops incl: local bus services, school contracts, excursions & tours, private hire, continental tours.
Livery: Beige/Brown/Red.

M TRAVEL LTD

52 EDWARD STREET, NORMANTON WF6 2QU
Tel: 07787 575956
Fleet: 30 – 25 double-deck bus, 5 single-deck bus.
Chassis: 9 DAF, 11 Dennis, 1 Irisbus, 6 MCW, 3 Optare.
Bodies: 5 Alexander, 5 East Lancs, 1 Irisbus, 6 ECW, 12 Optare, 1 Plaxton.
Ops incl: local bus services, school contracts.
Livery: Green/Yellow/Red/White.

DAVID PALMER COACHES LTD

THE TRAVEL OFFICE, WAKEFIELD ROAD, NORMANTON WF6 2BT
Tel: 01924 895849
Fax: 01924 897750
E-mail: info@davidpalmercoaches.co.uk
Web site: www.davidpalmercoaches.co.uk
Dirs: Andrew Palmer, Lisa Palmer.
Fleet: 10 – 1 double-deck bus, 4 single-deck coach, 4 minibus, 1 minicoach.
Chassis: 1 AEC, 1 LDV, 4 Mercedes, 2 Van Hool, 2 VDL.
Bodies: 2 Mercedes, 1 Park Royal, 4 Van Hool, 3 Other.
Ops incl: school contracts, excursions & tours, private hire, continental tours.
Livery: Silver.

PULLMAN DINER
Ceased operations since LRB 2011 went to press.

RED ARROW COACHES LTD

ASPLEY HOUSE, LINCOLN STREET, HUDDERSFIELD HD1 6RX
Tel: 01484 420993 **Fax:** 01484 540409
E-mail: info@redarrowcoaches.co.uk
Web site: www.redarrowcoaches.co.uk
Dirs: Steven R. Moore, Suichwant Singh.
Fleet: 10 - 9 single-deck coach, 1 midicoach.
Chassis: 1 Ayats, 2 Bova, 2 DAF, 1 Dennis, 2 MAN, 2 Scania.
Bodies: 1 Ayats, 2 Bova, 1 Caetano, 2 Plaxton, 4 Van Hool.
Ops incl: excursions & tours, private hire, continental tours, school contracts.

JOHN RIGBY TRAVEL

231 BRADFORD ROAD, BATLEY WF17 6JL
Tel: 01924 485151 **Fax:** 01924 485161
E-mail: rigbytransport@hotmail.co.uk
Web site: www.johnrigby.co.uk
Props: John Rigby.
Fleet: 7 - 5 single-deck coach, 1 midicoach, 1 minicoach.
Chassis: 1 DAF, 1 Dennis, 3 MAN, 1 Mercedes, 1 Volvo.
Bodies: 2 Caetano, 1 Marcopolo, 1 Mercedes, 1 Van Hool, 2 Other.
Ops incl: private hire, school contracts.
Livery: Red & White.

ROLLINSON SAFEWAY LTD

RSL HOUSE, 65 HALL LANE, LEEDS LS12 1PQ
Tel: 0113 231 1355 **Fax:** 0113 231 1344
Web site: www.rollinson.co.uk
Fleet Name: Air-Line Connections
Man Dir: Paul Rollinson **Dir:** Peter Rollinson
Contracts Man: M J Joyce.
Fleet: 82 – 3 single-deck bus, 72 minibus.
Chassis: 3 BMC, 2 Ford Transit, 20 Mercedes, 43 Renault, 5 Vauxhall, 9 Volkswagen.
Ops incl: private hire, school contracts.
Liveries: Brown/Gold, White with Blue/Red;
School Buses: Yellow.

ROSS TRAVEL

THE GARAGE, ALLISON STREET, FEATHERSTONE WF7 5BL
Tel: 01977 791738 **Fax:** 01977 690109
E-mail: info@rosstravelgroup.co.uk

Web Site: www.rosstravelgroup.co.uk
Props: Peter Ross, Mary Ross, Andrew Stirling, Stephen Ross.
Fleet: 18 - 1 single-deck bus, 6 single-deck coach, 9 midibus, 1 midicoach, 1 minibus.
Chassis: 2 DAF, 7 Mercedes, 5 Optare, 2 Scania, 2 Volvo.
Bodies: 1 Alexander, 2 Bova, 5 Optare, 4 Plaxton, 2 Sitcar, 1 UVG, 2 Van Hool, 1 Volvo.
Ops incl: local bus services, school contracts, private hire, continental tours.
Livery: Red/White.
Ticket System: Wayfarer.

SAFEWAY COACHES LTD
82 TALBOT STREET, BATLEY WF17 5AJ
Tel: 01924 472521
Web site: www.safewaycoaches.com
Fleet: 12 – 5 single-deck coach, 4 midicoach, 3 minibus.
Chassis: DAF, LDV, MAN, Mercedes, Setra, Volvo.
Ops incl: school contracts, excursions & tours, private hire.

SHEARINGS HOLIDAYS
MILL LANE, NORMANTON WF6 1RF
Tel: 01977 603088
Fax: 01977 603114
Ops Man: Martin Guy.
See Shearings Holidays, Greater Manchester.

STAR TRAVEL COACH HOLIDAYS
29 QUEEN STREET, HORBURY, WAKEFIELD WF4 6LP
Tel: 01924 261166
Fax: 01924 277194
E-mail: info@startravelcoachholidays.co.uk
Web site: www.startravelcoachholidays.co.uk
Fleet: 14 – 3 single-deck coach, 1 single-deck bus, 6 midibus, 2 midicoach, 2 minibus.
Chassis: LDV, Mercedes, Neoplan, Optare, Scania, Setra, Volvo.
Ops incl: local bus services, excursions & tours, private hire.
Liveries: Buses: Red & White; **Coaches:** Maroon.

STEELS LUXURY COACHES LTD
61 MAIN STREET, ADDINGHAM LS29 0PD
Tel: 01943 830206
Fax: 01943 831499
E-mail: info@steelscoaches.co.uk
Web site: www.steelscoaches.co.uk
Dir: T Steel **Co Sec:** Mrs J Steel.
Fleet: 7 - 3 single-deck coach, 4 midicoach.
Chassis: 2 Irisbus, 4 Mercedes, 1 Volvo.
Bodies: 4 Plaxton, 3 Other.
Ops incl: excursions & tours, private hire, school contracts, continental tours.
Livery: White/Red/Black.

STEVENSONS TRAVEL
THE WILLOWS, LIDGATE CRESCENT, SOUTH KIRKBY, PONTEFRACT WF9 3NR
Tel: 01977 645060.
E-mail: stevensonstravel@hotmail.co.uk
Partners: Ricky Stevenson, Michelle Mills.
Fleet: 9 minibus.
Chassis: 1 Fiat, 4 Ford Transit, 2 Iveco, 2 LDV.
Ops incl: school contracts, excursions & tours, private hire.

E STOTT & SONS LTD
COLNE VALE GARAGE, OFF SAVILE STREET, MILNSBRIDGE, HUDDERSFIELD HD3 4PG
Tel: 01484 460463
Fax: 01484 461463
E-mail: info@stottscoaches.co.uk
Web site: www.stottscoaches.co.uk
Dirs: Mark Stott, Carl Stott
Fleet: 35 - 4 single-deck bus, 12 single-deck coach, 3 midibus, 16 minibus.
Chassis: 5 Dennis, 9 Mercedes, 9 Optare, 12 Volvo.
Bodies: 2 Caetano, 9 Optare, 19 Plaxton, 2 Sunsundegui, 1 Van Hool, 2 Other.
Ops incl: local bus services, school contracts, excursions & tours, express, private hire.
Livery: White with Red/Black/Silver.
Ticket System: Wayfarer 3.

STRINGERS PONTEFRACT MOTORWAYS
102 SOUTHGATE, PONTEFRACT WF8 1PN
Tel: 01977 600205
Fax: 01977 704178
E-mail: enquires@stringerscoaches.co.uk
Web: www.stringerscoaches.co.uk
Prop: Mark G Stringer
Ops Man: Mark E Stringer
Sec: Sonia A Stringer **Ch Eng:** Chris Palmer.
Fleet: 10 - 3 single-deck coach, 6 midibus, 1 midicoach.
Chassis: 5 Alexander Dennis, 1 Mercedes, 1 Optare, 3 Volvo.
Bodies: 2 Jonckheere, 1 Optare, 3 Plaxton, 3 Transbus, 1 Van Hool.
Ops incl: local bus services, school contracts, excursions & tours, private hire.
Livery: Black/White/Red.
Ticket system: Wayfarer.

TETLEYS MOTOR SERVICES LTD
76 GOODMAN STREET, LEEDS LS10 1NY
Tel: 0113 276 2276
Fax: 0113 276 2277
E-mail: sales@tetleyscoaches.com
Web site: www.tetleyscoaches.com
Dir: Ian Tetley
Co Sec: Angela Tetley
Ch Eng: David Leach
Ops Man: Stephen Cunniff.
Fleet: 19 – 1 double-deck bus, 15 single-deck coach, 2 midicoach, 1 minibus.
Chassis: 1 DAF, 1 Dennis, 1 Irisbus, 2 Mercedes, 1 Renault, 13 Volvo.
Bodies: 1 Northern Counties, 13 Plaxton, 2 Van Hool, 1 Volvo, 2 Other.
Ops incl: school contracts, private hire, express.
Livery: Blue lettering on White.

TLC TRAVEL LTD
7 LINTON STREET, BRADFORD BD4 7EZ
Tel: 01274 727811
Fax: 01274 723640
E-mail: enquiries@tlctravelltd.co.uk
Web site: www.tlctravelltd.co.uk
Fleet: 23 - 5 midibus, 18 minibus.
Chassis: 1 Mercedes, 22 Optare.
Ops incl: local bus services.
Livery: Red/White.

TRANSDEV KEIGHLEY & DISTRICT
CAVENDISH HOUSE, 91-3 CAVENDISH STREET, KEIGHLEY BD21 3DG
Tel: 01535 603284 **Fax:** 01535 610065
E-mail: enquire@keighleyanddistrict.co.uk
Web site: www.keighleybus.co.uk
Fleet Name: The Zone.
Chief Exec: Martin Gilchrist
Marketing Dir: Nigel Eggleton.
Fleet: 116 - 22 double-deck bus, 79 single-deck bus, 15 midibus.
Chassis: 16 BMC, 15 Dennis, 10 Leyland, 75 Volvo.
Bodies: 16 BMC, 2 ECW, 16 Northern Counties, 19 Plaxton, 63 Wright.
Ops incl: local bus services, school contracts.
Liveries: Buses: Blue/White, Blue/Red;
School Buses: Yellow.
Part of the Blazefield group which is owned by Veolia Transdev.

TRAVEL EUROPE
19 PARKINSON CLOSE, EASTMOOR, WAKEFIELD WF1 4NR
Tel: 07901 914899
Fleet: 3 single-deck coach.
Chassis/Bodies: 3 Setra.

TWIN VALLEY COACHES
INDUSTRIAL ROAD, SOWERBY BRIDGE HX6 2RA
Tel/Fax: 01422 833358
E-mail: twinvalleycoaches@talktalk.net
Web site: www.twinvalley.co.uk
Dirs: D Pilling, E Pilling.
Fleet: 5 - 2 single-deck coach, 1 midicoach, 2 minibus.
Chassis: 2 LDV, 2 Mercedes, 1 Volvo.
Ops incl: private hire, school contracts.
Livery: Green/White.

WELSH'S COACHES LTD
FIELD LANE, UPTON, PONTEFRACT WF9 1BH
Tel: 01977 643873 **Fax:** 01977 648143
E-mail: info@welshscoaches.com
Web site: www.welshscoaches.com
Man Dir: John Welsh **Co Sec:** Judy Welsh.
Fleet: 8 - 5 single-deck coach, 3 minicoach.
Chassis: 3 Mercedes, 5 Setra.
Bodies: 3 Mercedes, 5 Setra.
Ops incl: school contracts, excursions & tours, private hire, continental tours.
Livery: Green/White/Red.

WHITE ROSE BUS COMPANY LTD
WASHINGTON STREET, LEEDS LS3 1JE
Tel: 0843 289 5135
E-mail: info@centrebus.com
Web site: www.centrebus.info
Man Dir: Peter Harvey **Area Man:** David Brooks.
Fleet: 43 – 3 double-deck bus, 39 single-deck bus, 1 midibus.
Chassis: 17 Dennis, 2 MAN, 1 Optare, 13 Scania, 10 VDL.
Bodies: 15 Alexander, 3 East Lancs, 12 MCV, 1 Optare, 11 Scania, 1 Wright.
Ops incl: local bus services.
Part of Centrebus Holdings - Jointly owned by Centrebus and Arriva.

AD-RAINS OF BRINKWORTH

THE COACH YARD, THE COMMON, BRINKWORTH SN15 5DX
Tel: 01666 510874
Recovery: 07831 303295
Prop: Adrian Griffiths **Ops Man:** Colin Minchin.
Fleet: 16 - 4 single-deck bus, 6 single-deck coach, 6 midibus, 1 midicoach, 1 minibus.
Chassis: 1 LDV, 5 Dennis, 6 Mercedes, 1 Optare, 3 Volvo.
Bodies: 1 Jonckheere, 1 Neoplan, 1 Optare, 11 Plaxton, 2 Other.
Ops incl: local bus services, school contracts, private hire.
Livery: White/Blue/Yellow.
Ticket system: Wayfarer.

ANDREW JAMES QUALITY TRAVEL (ANDYBUS AND COACH LTD)

UNIT 6, WHITEWALLS, EASTON GREY, MALMESBURY SN16 0RD
Tel: 01666 825655 **Fax:** 01666 825651
Recovery: 07740 88710
E-mail: ajcoaches@andrew-james.co.uk
Web site: www.andybus.co.uk
Dir: Andrew James.
Fleet: 20 - 4 single-deck coach, 8 single-deck bus, 6 midibus, 1 midicoach, 1 minibus.
Chassis: 1 Alexander Dennis, 2 Bova, 7 Dennis, 1 MAN, 2 Mercedes, 5 Optare, 1 Renault, 1 Toyota.
Bodies: 2 Bova, 1 Caetano, 1 Ikarus, 1 Marshall, 6 Optare, 7 Plaxton, 1 UVG, 1 Other.
Ops incl: local bus services, school contracts, private hire.
Liveries: Bus - Cream/Orange; **Coach** - Yellow/Black.
Ticket System: Wayfarer.

APL TRAVEL LTD

PEAR TREE COTTAGE, CRUDWELL SN16 9ES
Tel: 01666 577774 **Fax:** 01249 721402
E-mail: apltravel@btconnect.com
Web site: www.apltravel.co.uk
Dirs: Alan Legg, Shane Legg, Elizabeth Legg.
Fleet: 18 - 5 single-deck bus, 7 single-deck coach, 5 midibus, 1 midicoach.
Chassis: 1 Bova, 5 Dennis, 3 MAN, 4 Mercedes, 3 Optare, 2 Volvo.
Bodies: 2 Berkhof, 1 Bova, 2 Ikarus, 2 Jonckheere, 1 Noge, 3 Optare, 6 Plaxton, 1 Other.
Ops incl: local bus services, school contracts, excursions & tours, private hire.
Livery: White with logos.
Ticket System: Wayfarer.

ASSISI TRAVEL

1 OLD SARUM COTTAGES, THE PORTWAY, OLD SARUM, SALISBURY SP4 6BY
Tel/Fax: 01722 415181
E-mail: assisi@hotmail.co.uk
Web site: www.salisburycoaches.co.uk
Prop: Kevin Tedd.
Fleet: 8 - 4 single-deck coach, 3 midicoach, 1 minicoach.
Chassis: 1 Dennis, 4 Mercedes, 3 Volvo.
Bodies: 1 Autobus, 1 Jonckheere, 2 Mercedes, 1 Plaxton, 1 Sunsundegui, 1 Van Hool.
Livery: White with Red/Blue.

BARNES COACHES

UNIT E, WOODSIDE ROAD, SOUTH MARSTON BUSINESS PARK, SWINDON SN3 4AQ
Tel: 01793 821303 **Fax:** 01793 828486
E-mail: travel@barnescoaches.co.uk
Web site: www.barnescoaches.co.uk
Dirs: Lionel Barnes, Terry Barnes, Luke Barnes, Matt Barnes.
Fleet: 28 - 27 single-deck coaches, 1 double-deck coach.
Chassis: 9 Bova, 19 Volvo.
Bodies: 9 Bova, 1 East Lancs, 18 Van Hool.
Ops incl: local bus services, excursions & tours, school contracts, private hire, continental tours.
Livery: Green.

BEELINE (R & R) COACHES LTD

BISHOPSTROW ROAD, WARMINSTER BA12 9HQ
Tel: 01985 213503
Fax: 01985 213922
E-mail: markhayball@beelinecoaches.co.uk
Web site: www.beelinecoaches.co.uk
Dirs: Mark Hayball, Andrew Hayball
Gen Man: Noel Ennis.
Fleet: 32 - 20 single-deck coach, 8 midicoach, 4 minibus.
Chassis: 4 LDV, 14 Mercedes, 14 Volvo.
Bodies: 4 Jonckheere, 23 Plaxton, 5 Van Hool.
Ops incl: local bus services, school contracts, private hire.
Livery: White/Beige.
Ticket system: Setright

BETTER MOTORING SERVICES

104a SWINDON ROAD, STRATTON ST MARGARET, SWINDON SN3 4PT
Tel: 01793 823747
Fax: 01793 831898
E-mail: bmscoaches@btconnect.com
Fleet Name: BMS Coaches.
Prop: D G Miles **Fleet Eng:** M J Hopkins
Sec: Mrs M Mulhern.
Fleet: 11 - 9 midicoach, 2 minicoach.
Chassis: 2 Ford, 9 Mercedes.
Bodies: 2 Autobus, 2 Esker, 2 Mellor, 3 Optare, 2 Other.
Ops incl: school contracts, excursions & tours, private hire, continental tours.
Livery: Coffee/Cream.

BODMAN COACHES

88 HIGH STREET, WORTON, DEVIZES SN10 5RU
Tel: 01380 722393
Fax: 01380 721969
E-Mail: bodmancoaches@btinternet.com
Tran Man: Nigel Denny
Ops Man: Graham Carter.
Fleet: 43 - 12 single-deck bus, 17 single-deck coach, 14 midibus.
Chassis: 4 Alexander Dennis, 3 DAF, 13 Dennis, 2 Irisbus, 3 MAN, 7 Mercedes, 3 Optare, 7 Volvo.
Ops incl: local bus services, school contracts, excursions & tours, private hire.
Livery: White/Green.
Ticket System: Wayfarer.
Associated with Hatts Travel.

CALNE TRAVEL

11 WESSINGTON AVENUE, CALNE SN11 9RR
Tel: 01249 821821 **Fax:** 01249 821222
E-mail: customercare@calnetravel.co.uk
Web site: www.calnetravel.co.uk
Prop: K Witte.
Fleet: 11 single-deck coach.
Ops incl: local bus services, school contracts, private hire.
Livery: White with Red/Blue lettering.

CHANDLERS COACH TRAVEL

158 CHEMICAL ROAD, WEST WILTS TRADING ESTATE, WESTBURY BA13 4JN
Tel: 01373 824500 **Fax:** 01373 824300
E-mail: info@chandlerscoach.co.uk
Web site: www.chandlerscoach.co.uk
Prop: Margaret l'Anson **Operations:** Christopher l'Anson.
Fleet: 10 single-deck coach.
Chassis: 2 Alexander Dennis, 1 MAN, 7 Volvo.
Bodies: 1 Bova, 2 Caetano, 1 Jonckheere, 3 Plaxton, 3 Volvo.
Ops incl: school contracts, excursions & tours, private hire, continental tours.
Livery: White/Gold/Burgundy.

COACHSTYLE LTD

HORSDOWN GARAGE, NETTLETON, CHIPPENHAM SN14 7LN
Tel/Fax: 01249 782224
E-mail: mail@coachstyle.ltd.uk
Web site: www.coachstyle.ltd.uk
Owners: Andrew Jones, Mrs A L Jones.
Fleet: 12 - 1 single-deck bus, 10 single-deck coach, 1 midibus.
Chassis: 1 Dennis, 1 Mercedes, 10 Volvo.
Bodies: 1 Berkhof, 1 Caetano, 1 Marshall, 4 Jonckheere, 5 Plaxton.
Ops incl: local bus services, school contracts, excursions & tours, private hire, continental tours.
Livery: White with Purple.

DANGERFIELDS TRAVEL LTD

ELGIN INDUSTRIAL ESTATE, SWINDON SN2 8EJ
Tel: 01793 534445
Fax: 01793 531648
Web site: www.dangerfields.co.uk
Fleet: single-deck coach, midicoach, minibus.
Ops incl: private hire.
Livery: Gold/Black,

ELLISON'S COACHES

THE GARAGE, HIGH ROAD, ASHTON KEYNES, SWINDON SN6 6NX
Tel: 01285 861224
Fax: 01285 862115
E-mail: sales@ellisonscoaches.co.uk
Web site: www.ellisonscoaches.co.uk
Prop: Alan Ellison,
Fleet: 20 - 1 single-deck bus, 19 single-deck coach.
Chassis: 1 Autosan, 1 BMC, 6 Dennis, 4 Duple 425, 1 Mercedes, 7 Neoplan.
Ops incl: school contracts, excursions & tours, private hire, continental tours.
Livery: White/Green/Red.

FARESAVER BUSES

THE COACH YARD, VINCIENTS ROAD,
BUMPERS FARM INDUSTRIAL ESTATE,
CHIPPENHAM SN14 6QA
Tel: 01249 444444
Fax: 01249 448844
E-mail: sales@faresaver.co.uk
Web site: www.faresaver.co.uk
Prop: JV Pickford **Ops Man:** D J Pickford
Ops Man: D Beard **Ch Eng:** D Watts.
Fleet: 65 - 15 single-deck bus, 30 midibus,
20 midicoach.
Chassis: 15 Dennis, 49 Mercedes, 1 Optare.
Bodies: 1 Alexander Dennis, 3 Caetano,
5 Marshall/MCV, 1 Optare, 55 Plaxton.
Ops incl: local bus services, school contracts,
private hire.
Liveries: White/Mauve, Silver & Purple.
Ticket System: Wayfarer 3.

G-LINE MINICOACHES

Ceased trading since LRB 2011 went to press.

GO SOUTH COAST LTD

TOWNGATE HOUSE, 2-8 PARKSTONE ROAD,
POOLE BH15 2PR
Tel: 01202 680888 **Fax:** 01202 670244
E-mail: alex.carter@gosouthcoast.co.uk
Web site: www.touristcoaches.co.uk,
www.go-ahead.com
Fleet Names (Wiltshire): Bell's Coaches,
Kingston Coaches, Lever's Coaches, Tourist
Coaches, Wilts & Dorset.
Chairman: David Brown **Man Dir:** Alex Carter
Eng Dir: Steve Hamilton **Fin Dir:** Matt Dolphin
Divisional Dirs: Marc Morgan Huws, Ed Wills.
Fleet: 625 - 252 double-deck bus, 125 single-
deck bus, 91 single-deck coach, 1 articulated bus,
12 open top bus, 137 midibus, 7 minibus.
Chassis: 2 Bristol, 104 DAF, 49 Dennis, 2 Ford,
4 Iveco, 5 LDV, 33 Leyland, 1 MAN, 50 Mercedes,
99 Optare, 106 Scania, 2 Toyota, 168 Volvo.
Bodies: 10 Alexander Dennis, 2 Autobus,
4 Beulas, 1 Bova, 6 Caetano, 2 ECW, 56 East Lancs,
2 Ford, 12 Ikarus, 4 Irizar, 2 Jonckheere, 5 LDV,
25 Leyland, 47 Mercedes, 41 Northern Counties,
153 Optare, 76 Plaxton, 73 Scania, 27 Transbus,
22 Van Hool, 55 Wright.
Ops incl: local bus services, school contracts.
Liveries: Orange/Cream.
Ticket System: Wayfarer TGX.
Part of the Go-Ahead Group

HATTS TRAVEL

HAM VILLA, FOXHAM, CHIPPENHAM
SN15 4NB
Tel/Recovery: 01249 740444
Fax: 01249 740447
E-mail: info@hattstravel.co.uk
Web site: www.hattstravel.co.uk
Man Partner: Adrian Hillier **Ops Man:** Andy
Bridgeman **Traffic Man:** Phil Turner **Workshop
Man:** Mike Henderson **Bodyshop Man:** Ashley
Davis **Accts Man:** Lynne Pegler **Holidays:** Pat
Huston **Group Sales Man:** Marilyn Nelson.
Fleet: 71 – 14 single-deck bus, 18 single-deck
coach, 2 double-deck coach, 10 midibus,
10 midicoach, 17 minibus.
Chassis: 14 Alexander Dennis, 3 Ayats, 4 Bova,
7 Ford Transit, 2 Iveco, 3 MAN, 24 Mercedes, 4
Neoplan, 3 Optare, 2 Toyota, 1 Van Hool, 4 Volvo.
Bodies: 14 Alexander Dennis, 3 Ayats, 4 Bova,

2 Caetano, 2 Ferqui, 7 Ford, 1 Indcar, 1 Jonckheere,
1 Marcopolo, 5 Mellor, 1 Mercedes, 4 Neoplan,
1 Noge, 3 Optare, 5 Plaxton, 1 Unvi, 4 UVG,
3 Van Hool, 9 Other.
Ops incl: local bus services, Salisbury Park &
Ride, school contracts, excursions & tours, private
hire, continental tours.
Livery: Purple/White.
Ticket System: Wayfarer.
See also Bodman Coaches, Stones of Bath
(Somerset).

KINCH COACHES LTD

HORNBURY HILL FARM, MINETY,
MALMESBURY SN16 9QH
Tel: 01666 860339 **Fax:** 01666 860537
E-mail: info@kinchcoaches.co.uk
Web site: www.kinchcoaches.co.uk
Fleet incl: double-deck bus, single-deck coach,
double-deck coach, midicoach.
Ops incl: school contracts, private hire.
Livery: Two tone Blue & Cream.

MANSFIELD'S COACHES

27 FINCHDALE, COVINGHAM, SWINDON
SN3 5AL
Tel/Fax: 01793 525375
Prop: R E Mansfield **Man:** A Mansfield
Tran Man: P Mansfield **Sec:** Mrs M S Mansfield.
Fleet: 3 – 2 midicoach, 1 minibus.
Chassis: 3 Mercedes.
Ops incl: excursions & tours, private hire,
express, school contracts.
Livery: Yellow/Green/Red.
Ticket System: Setright.

PEWSEY VALE COACHES LTD

HOLLYBUSH LANE, PEWSEY SN9 5BB
Tel/Fax: 01672 562238
E-mail: pewseyvalecoaches@aol.com
Web site: www.pewseyvalecoaches.co.uk
Dirs: Andrew Thorne, Dawn Thorne, Anne
Thorne.
Fleet: 12 single-deck coach.
Chassis: 3 Bova, 1 Dennis, 1 Leyland, 2 Setra,
5 Volvo.
Bodies: 1 Berkhof, 3 Bova, 1 Plaxton, 2 Setra,
5 Van Hool.
Ops incl: local bus services, school contracts,

excursions & tours, private hire, continental tours.
Livery: White/Blue/Red.
Ticket system: Almex.

SEAGER'S COACHES LTD

Business acquired by Hatt's Travel.

STAGECOACH WEST

See Gloucestershire

TEST VALLEY TRAVEL LTD

BANNISTER BARN, NEWTON LANE,
WHITEPARISH SP5 2QQ
Tel/Fax: 01794 884555
Dirs: Mr J M Norman, Mrs A N Norman.
E-mail: falconlomax@hotmail.co.uk
Fleet: 3 minibus.
Chassis/Bodies: 3 LDV.
Ops incl: private hire, school contracts.
Livery: Green/Gold/White.

THAMESDOWN TRANSPORT

BARNFIELD ROAD, SWINDON SN2 2DJ
Tel: 01793 428400 **Fax:** 01793 428405
Recovery: 01793 428432
E-mail: customerservices@thamesdown-
transport.co.uk
Web site: www.thamesdownbus.com
Man Dir: Paul Jenkins **Eng Dir:** Nigel Mason
Fin Controller/Co Sec: Cliff Connor
Ops Dir: David Burch.
Fleet: 90 - 19 double-deck bus, 71 single-deck
bus.
Chassis incl: 1 Daimler, 29 Dennis, 1 Leyland,
8 Optare, 28 Scania, 8 Transbus, 15 Volvo
Bodies: 17 Alexander Dennis, 1 ECW,
1 Northern Counties, 8 Optare, 27 Plaxton,
8 Transbus, 28 Wright.
Ops incl: local bus services, school contracts.
Livery: Blue/Green.
Ticket System: Wayfarer TGX 200.

TOURIST COACHES LTD

**(Incorporating Bells Coaches Ltd, Kingston
Coaches, Levers Coaches Ltd)**
See Go South Coast Ltd.

WILTS & DORSET BUS COMPANY LTD

See Go South Coast Ltd.

ASTONS COACHES
VEOLIA TRANSPORT ENGLAND PLC

BROOMHALL, CLERKENLEAP, WORCESTER
WR5 3HR
Tel: 01905 820201
Fax: 01905 829249
Recovery: 07860 693712
E-mail: info@astons-coaches.co.uk
Web site: www.astons-coaches.co.uk
Gen Man: Richard Conway **Tran Man:**
Matthew Wells **Ops Man:** Jon Elsdon
New Bus Dev Man: Becki Muir
Sales & Mktg Man: Anna Woodward.
Fleet: 36 - 4 double-deck bus, 9 single-deck bus,
18 single-deck coach, 3 midibus, 2 minibus.
Chassis: 1 Alexander Dennis, 1 MAN,
6 Mercedes, 7 Optare, 12 Scania, 8 Volvo.
Bodies: 1 Berkhof, 1 Duple, 4 East Lancs, 3 Irizar,
1 Jonckheere, 7 Optare, 3 Sunsundegui,
6 Van Hool, 8 Other.
Ops incl: local bus services, school contracts,
private hire, express, continental tours.
Ticket system: ERG.
A subsidiary of Veolia Transport UK

N N CRESSWELL COACH HIRE

WORCESTER ROAD, EVESHAM WR11 4RA
Tel/Recovery: 01386 48655
Fax: 01386 48656
E-mail: nncresswell@btinternet.com
Props: Mrs Mary Shephard, Mrs Elizabeth
Everatt.
Fleet: 21 - 14 single-deck coach, 2 midicoach,
5 minibus.
Chassis: 2 Bedford, 12 Dennis, 7 Mercedes.
Bodies: 21 Plaxton.
Ops incl: local bus services, school contracts,
excursions & tours, private hire.
Livery: Blue/White.
Ticket System: Wayfarer.

DIAMOND BUS LTD
See West Midlands

DUDLEY'S COACHES

POPLAR GARAGE, ALCESTER ROAD,
RADFORD, WORCESTER WR7 4LS
Tel: 01386 792206
Fax: 01386 793373
E-mail: info@dudleys-coaches.co.uk
Web site: www.dudleys-coaches.co.uk
Fleet: 17 - 16 single-deck coach, 1 minibus.
Chassis: 1 Leyland, 1 Toyota, 15 Volvo.
Bodies: 1 Caetano, 1 Jonckheere, 10 Plaxton,
5 Van Hool.
Ops incl: local bus services, school contracts,
excursions & tours, private hire.
Livery: Green/Cream.

EUROLINERS

1631 BRISTOL ROAD SOUTH, REDNAL,
BIRMINGHAM BH45 9UA
Tel: 0121 453 5151
Fax: 0121 453 5504
E-mail: info@euroliners.co.uk
Web site: www.euroliners.co.uk
Prop: Anthony Armstrong
Fleet: 15 - 2 single-deck coach, 5 midicoach,
8 minicoach.

Chassis: 5 LDV, 10 Mercedes.
Bodies: 6 Mercedes, 4 Optare, 5 Plaxton.
Ops incl: local bus services, school contracts,
private hire.

FIRST MIDLANDS

HERON LODGE, LONDON ROAD,
WORCESTER WR5 2EU
Tel: 08450 100 111
Fax: 01905 351104
Regional Man Dir: Nigel Barrett **Regional
Eng Dir:** Mick Brannigan **Regional Comm
Dir:** Steve Wickers **Regional Fin Planning
Dir:** David Marshall.
Fleet Name: First Wyvern
Fleet (Worcestershire & Hereford):
160 – 9 double-deck bus, 127 single-deck bus,
2 single-deck coach, 22 midibus.
Chassis: 44 Alexander Dennis, 1 BMC,
69 Dennis, 1 Leyland, 23 Optare, 5 Transbus,
17 Volvo.
Bodies: 4 Alexander, 44 Alexander Dennis,
1 BMC, 5 Caetano, 23 Optare, 56 Plaxton,
5 Transbus, 22 Wright.
Ops incl: local bus services, school contracts.
Livery: FirstGroup UK Bus.
Ticket System: Wayfarer

HARDINGS INTERNATIONAL

*Ceased operations since LRB 2011 went to press; new
business in the process of formation.*

HARRIS EXECUTIVE TRAVEL

58 MEADOW ROAD, CATSHILL,
BROMSGROVE B61 0JL
Tel: 01527 872857
Fax: 01527 872708
E-mail: accountsharristravel@msn.com
Web site: www.harriscoaches.com
Joint Man Dirs: J G Harris, S W Harris.
Fleet: 7 - 6 single-deck coach, 1 minicoach.
Chassis: 7 Mercedes.
Bodies: 7 Neoplan.
Ops incl: excursions & tours, private hire,
continental tours.
Livery: White/Red/Yellow/Orange.

KESTREL COACHES

UNITS 1&2, BARRACKS ROAD, SANDY LANE,
STOURPORT-ON-SEVERN DY13 9QB
Tel/Fax: 01299 829689
Prop: M Wood.
Fleet: 10 - 4 single-deck coach, 3 midicoach,
3 minibus.
Chassis: 1 Bedford, 2 Bova, 1 Citroën, 1 DAF,
1 LDV, 2 Mercedes, 2 Toyota.
Bodies: 2 Bova, 3 Caetano, 1 Leyland,
2 Mercedes, 1 Relay, 1 Van Hool.
Ops incl: local bus services, school contracts,
private hire.
Livery: White.
Ticket System: Almex

WHITTLE COACH & BUS LTD

FOLEY BUSINESS PARK, STOURPORT ROAD,
KIDDERMINSTER DY11 7QL
Tel: 01562 820002
Fax: 01562 820027
E-mail: info@whittlecoach.co.uk

Web site: www.whittlecoach.co.uk
Fleet Name: Whittles.
Chairman: Peter Shipp **Fin Dir:** Peter Harrison
Gen Man: Andrew McKinnon
Ops Man: Paul McLellan.
Fleet: 32 – 6 single-deck bus, 19 single-deck
coach, 7 midibus.
Chassis: 17 Alexander Dennis, 15 Volvo.
Bodies: 1 Berkhof, 6 Caetano, 25 Plaxton.
Ops incl: local bus services, school contracts,
excursions & tours, private hire, express,
continental tours.
Livery: Bus: Green/White; **Coach:** White with
Blue/Green/Yellow Relief.
Ticket system: Wayfarer III.
A subsidiary of the EYMS Group.

WOODSTONES COACHES LTD

ARTHUR DRIVE, HOO FARM
INDUSTRIAL ESTATE, WORCESTER ROAD,
KIDDERMINSTER DY11 7RA
Tel: 01562 823073
Fax: 01562 827277
E-mail: enquiries@woodstones.org.uk
Web site: www.woodstones.org.uk
Man Dir: Ivan Meredith
Dir: Richard Meredith.
Fleet: 6 single-deck coach.
Chassis: 6 Volvo.
Bodies: 6 Plaxton.
Ops incl: school contracts, excursions & tours,
private hire.
Livery: White/Orange/Yellow/Red.

YARRANTON BROS LTD

EARDISTON GARAGE, TENBURY WELLS
WR15 8JL
Tel: 01584 881229
E-mail: info@yarrantons.co.uk
Web site: www.yarrantons.co.uk
Dirs: A L Yarranton (**Gen Man**), M L Yarranton,
D A Yarranton.
Fleet: 12 – 1 single-deck bus, 9 single-deck coach,
1 minibus, 1 minicoach.
Chassis: 5 Dennis, 1 Mercedes, 1 Scania, 1 Toyota,
1 Volkswagen, 3 Volvo.
Bodies: 2 Berkhof, 1 Caetano, 1 Jonckheere,
1 Mercedes, 2 Plaxton, 1 Scania, 1 Van Hool,
1 Volkswagen, 2 Wadham Stringer.
Ops incl: local bus services, school contracts,
excursions & tours, private hire, continental tours.
Livery: Green/White/Orange.

ALDERNEY

RIDUNA BUSES

ALLEE ES FEES, ALDERNEY GY9 3XD
Tel: 01481 823760
Fax: 01481 823030
Prop: A J Curtis.
Fleet: 5 - 2 single-deck bus, 2 single-deck coach, I minibus.
Chassis: 3 Bedford, I Freight Rover.
Bodies: 2 Duple, I Heaver, I Pennine.
Ops incl: local bus services, excursions & tours, private hire.

GUERNSEY

ISLAND COACHWAYS LTD

THE TRAMSHEDS, LES BANQUES,
ST PETER PORT GY1 2HZ
Tel: 01481 720210
Fax: 01481 710109
E-mail: admin@icw.gg
Web site: www.icw.gg
Man Dir: Hannah Beacom **Dir:** Ben Boucher
Ops Man: Tom Whyte
Strategic Planning Man: Rob Branigan
Fleet Man: Tom Wilson
Sales Man: Isabel de Menezes.
Fleet: 56 - 41 single-deck bus, 6 single-deck coach, 6 midicoach, I minibus, 2 minicoach.
Chassis: 41 Alexander Dennis, I Ford Transit, 3 Iveco, 6 Mercedes, 4 Renault, I Other.
Bodies: 8 Caetano, 33 East Lancs, I Leicester, 6 Plaxton, 8 Other.
Ops incl: local bus services, school contracts, excursions & tours, private hire.
Livery: Green/Cream, Green/Yellow.
Ticket System: Wayfarer TGX150.

JERSEY

CONNEX TRANSPORT (JERSEY) LTD

1A COLLETTE STREET, ST HELIER
JE2 3NX
Tel: 01534 877772 **Fax:** 01534 723999
Fleet Names: Connex, My Bus.
Fleet: 82 – 2 double-deck bus, 72 single-deck buses, 8 midibus.
Chassis: 7 Alexander Dennis, 67 Dennis, 8 Mercedes.
Ops incl: local bus services, school contracts.
Livery: Pale Blue.
A subsidiary of Veolia Transdev.

TANTIVY BLUE COACH TOURS

ALBERT QUAY, ST HELIER JE2 3NE
Tel: 01534 706706
Fax: 01534 706705

E-mail: info@jerseycoaches.com
Web site: www.tantivybluecoach.com
Man Dir: Chris Lewis
Gen Man: Carl Pickering
Eng Man: Tony Donahue
Fleet: 47 - 33 single-deck coach, 14 minibus.
Ops incl: excursions & tours, private hire.
Livery: Blue.

WAVERLEY COACHES LTD

UNIT 3, LA COLLETTE, ST HELIER
JE2 3NX
Tel: 01534 758360
Fax: 01534 732627
Web site:
www.norfolkhoteljersey.co.uk/waverley
Dir/Gen Man: S E Pedersen
Ch Eng: Peter Evans.
Fleet: 17 - 11 single-deck coach, I midicoach, 5 minibus.
Chassis: 3 Ford Transit, 6 Cannon, I Iveco, 5 Leyland, 2 LDV.
Bodies: I Bedwas, 3 Ford, 6 Leicester, 2 LDV, 5 Wadham Stringer.
Ops incl: excursions & tours, private hire.
Livery: Yellow/White.

ISLE OF MAN

DOUGLAS CORPORATION TRAMWAY

See Section 5 – Tram and Bus Rapid Transit Systems.

ISLE OF MAN TRANSPORT

TRANSPORT HEADQUARTERS,
BANKS CIRCUS, DOUGLAS
IM1 5PT
Tel: 01624 663366
Fax: 01624 663637
E-mail: info@busandrail.dtl.gov.im
Director of Public Transport: Ian Longworth.
Fleet Name: Bus Vannin
Fleet: 129 - 68 double-deck bus, 17 single-deck bus, 6 midibus, 38 trams.
Chassis: 8 Alexander Dennis, 25 DAF, 16 Dennis, 12 Mercedes, 6 Transbus, 7 VDL, 11 Volvo, 6 Wrightbus.
Bodies: 56 East Lancs, 5 Marshall, 12 Mercedes, 17 Wright.
Ops incl: local bus/tram services, private hire.
Livery: Red/Cream.
Ticket System: Wayfarer.

PROTOURS ISLE OF MAN LTD

AIRPORT GARAGE, BALLASALLA IM9 2AN
Tel: 01624 822611
Fax: 01624 822389
E-mail: info@protours.co.im

Chairman & Man Dir: W R Lightfoot
Dirs: J F Cairns, F G Kinnear
Ops Man: D Bennett
Ch Eng: A Lancaster.
Fleet: 28 - 3 single-deck bus, 13 single-deck coach, 2 midibus, 5 midicoach, 3 minibus, 2 vintage coach.
Chassis: 2 Bedford, 2 BMC, I Bova, 3 DAF, 4 Iveco, I LAG, 4 Leyland, I MAN, 2 Mercedes, I Optare, 5 Scania, I Toyota, 2 Volvo, I Other.
Bodies: 3 Berkhof, 2 BMC, I Bova, 4 Duple, 4 Irizar, 3 Leicester, I Optare, 3 Plaxton, 2 Van Hool, I Wadham Stringer, 4 Other.
Ops incl: school contracts, excursions & tours, private hire, express, continental tours.
Livery: White/Blue/Green/Yellow.

ISLES OF SCILLY

HERITAGE TOUR

SANTAMANA, 9 RAMS VALLEY,
ST MARY'S TR21 0JX
Tel: 01720 422387
Props: G Twynham, Mrs P Twynham.
Fleet: I single-deck bus (1948 vehicle).
Chassis: Austin K2.
Body: Barnard.
Ops incl: excursions & tours, private hire.
Livery: Blue/Cream.

ISLAND ROVER

THE NOOK, CHURCH STREET,
ST MARYS TR21 0JT
Tel/Fax: 01720 422131
E-mail: admin@islandrover.co.uk
Web site: www.islandrover.co.uk
Prop: Glynne Lucas.
Fleet: 2 single-deck coach, I open top bus.
Chassis: I Austin, I Bedford, I Leyland.
Bodies: I East Lancs, I Plaxton, I Other.

⚙	Vehicle suitable for disabled	⚙	Seat belt-fitted Vehicle	R24	24 hour recovery service
T	Toilet-drop facilities available	🍴	Coach(es) with galley facilities	⬛	Replacement vehicle available
R	Recovery service available	❄	Air-conditioned vehicle(s)	🚌	Vintage Coache(s) available
🚌	Open top vehicle(s)	🚻	Coaches with toilet facilities	⚡	Hybrid Buses

ABERDEEN, CITY OF

BLUEBIRD BUSES LTD
GUILD STREET, ABERDEEN AB11 6NA
Tel: 01224 597550
Fax: 01224 584202
E-mail: bluebird.enquiries@stagecoachbus.com
Web site: www.stagecoachbus.com/bluebird
Fleet Name: Stagecoach Bluebird.
Man Dir: Andrew Jarvis **Eng Dir:** Stevie Drain.
Fleet: 219 - 14 double-deck bus, 51 single-deck bus, 78 single-deck coach, 12 double-deck coach, 6 articulated coach, 31 midibus, 27 minibus.
Chassis: 25 Alexander Dennis, 17 Dennis, 36 MAN, 1 Mercedes, 6 Neoplan, 26 Optare, 6 Van Hool, 3 Volkswagen, 99 Volvo.
Bodies: 80 Alexander Dennis, 6 Neoplan, 11 Northern Counties, 26 Optare, 84 Plaxton, 6 Van Hool, 3 Wright, 3 Others.
Ops incl: local bus services, school contracts, express.
Livery: Stagecoach UK Bus/Megabus/Citylink.
Ticket System: ERG TP5000.

CENTRAL COACHES
DEREK SMITH HOUSE, HARENESS ROAD, ALTENS, ABERDEEN AB12 3LE
Tel: 01224 890089
Fax: 01224 897415
E-mail: central898989@yahoo.co.uk
Web site: www.centraltaxisaberdeen.co.uk
Ops incl: local bus services, school contracts, excursions & tours, continental tours.

FIRST IN ABERDEEN
395 KING STREET, ABERDEEN AB24 5RP
Tel: 01224 650000
Fax: 01224 650099
Web site: www.firstgroup.com
Man Dir: David Stewart
Ops Dir: Duncan Cameron
Eng Dir: Iain Ferguson.
Fleet: 163 - 16 double-deck bus, 117 single-deck bus, 26 articulated bus, 2 midibus.
Chassis: 1 Bluebird, 2 Optare, 160 Volvo.
Bodies: 36 Alexander, 1 Bluebird, 2 Optare, 124 Wright.
Ops incl: local bus services, school contracts, private hire.
Livery: FirstGroup UK Bus.

FIRST ABERDEEN LTD, COACHING UNIT
FIRST ABERDEEN LTD, 395 KING STREET, ABERDEEN AB24 5RP
Tel: 01224 650000
Fax: 01224 650123
Recovery: 01224 650151
E-mail: coachhire.aberdeen@firstgroup.com
Web site: www.firstgroup.com
Man Dir: David Stewart **Ops Dir:** Duncan Cameron **Eng Dir:** Iain Ferguson
Coaching Ops Man: Tom Gordon.
Fleet: 27 – 21 single-deck coach, 6 midicoach.
Chassis: 2 BMC, 2 Dennis, 6 Mercedes, 7 Scania, 10 Volvo.
Bodies: 2 BMC, 7 Irizar, 2 Jonckheere, 1 Optare, 15 Plaxton.
Ops incl: school contracts, excursions &

tours, private hire, continental tours.
Livery: First Group Magenta/Blue/Grey
A subsidiary of First Group.

FOUNTAIN EXECUTIVE
HILL OF GOVAL, DYCE, ABERDEEN AB21 7NX
Tel: 01224 729090   **Fax:** 01224 729898
E-mail: fountainexe@hotmail.com
Web site: www.fountainexecutive.co.uk
Prop: Michael Ewen.
Fleet: 10 - 5 single-deck coach, 1 midicoach, 2 minicoach, 2 minibus.
Chassis: 5 Mercedes, 5 Scania.
Bodies: 5 Irizar, 3 Unvi, 2 Other.
Ops incl: private hire, continental tours.
Livery: Gold.

WHYTES COACHES LTD
SCOTSTOWN ROAD, NEWMACHAR, ABERDEEN AB21 7PP
Tel: 01651 862211
Fax: 01651 862918
E-mail: sales@whytes.co.uk
Web Site: www.whytes.co.uk
Man Dir: Steven W Whyte.
Fleet: 25 – 10 single-deck coach, 10 midicoach, 5 minibus.
Chassis: 10 DAF, 1 Ford Transit, 13 Mercedes, 1 Volkswagen.
Bodies: 10 Bova, 1 Ford, 7 Plaxton, 2 Unvi, 5 Other.
Ops incl: school contracts, excursions & tours, private hire, express, continental tours.
Livery: Light Green.

ABERDEENSHIRE

ALLAN & BLACK
DRUMDUAN DEPOT, DESS, ABOYNE AB34 5BN
Tel: 01339 886326
Fax: 01339 886608
E-mail: info-enq@allanandblackcoaches.co.uk
Web site: www.allanandblackcoaches.co.uk
Props: Andrew C Brown, Murray W Brown, Jane W Brown, Cameron W Brown.
Fleet: 12 – 1 double-deck bus, 8 single-deck coach, 2 minibus, 1 minicoach.
Chassis: 1 Iveco, 5 Mercedes, 5 Scania, 1 Volvo.
Bodies: 2 Berkhof, 1 East Lancs, 2 Mercedes, 1 Neoplan, 2 Setra, 3 Van Hool, 1 Other.
Ops incl: local bus services, school contracts, private hire.
Livery: White & Purple.
Ticket System: Almex.

AMBER TRAVEL
Operations ceased since LRB 2011 went to press

BAIN'S COACHES
STATION GARAGE, STATION ROAD, OLDMELDRUM AB51 0EZ
Tel: 01651 872365
E-mail: enquiries@bainscoaches.co.uk
Web site: www.bainscoaches.co.uk
Fleet incl: single-deck bus, single-deck coach, midicoach, minibus, minicoach.
Ops incl: local bus services, school contracts, private hire.

J & M BURNS
DINNESWOOD, TARVES, ELLON AB41 7LR
Tel: 01651 851279
Fax: 01651 851844
E-mail: info@burnscoaches.co.uk
Web site: www.burnscoaches.co.uk
Fleet: 16 – 8 single-deck coach, 5 midicoach, 3 minicoach.
Ops incl: school contracts, private hire, excursions & tours.
Livery: Purple.

CHEYNES COACHES
ALLANDALE, DAVIOT, INVERURIE AB51 0EJ
Tel: 01467 671400
Fax: 01467 671479
E-mail: lesley@cheynescoaches.co.uk
Web site: www.cheynescoaches.co.uk
Partners: W A Cheyne, R Cheyne, L A Cheyne, M F Cheyne.
Fleet: 11 - 2 single-deck bus, 4 single-deck coach, 3 midicoach, 2 minibus.
Chassis: 1 DAF, 2 Ford Transit, 2 Leyland, 3 Mercedes, 3 Volvo.
Bodies: 1 Bova, 2 Ford, 3 Plaxton, 3 Van Hool, 2 Other.
Ops incl: school contracts, excursions & tours, private hire.
Livery: Silver/Pink/Purple.

DEVERON COACHES LTD
6 UNION ROAD, MACDUFF AB44 1UJ
Tel: 01261 833555
E-mail: gary@deveroncoaches.com
Web site: www.deveroncoaches.com
Fleet: 46 - 2 single-deck bus, 20 single-deck coach, 7 midibus, 8 midicoach, 9 minibus.
Ops incl: local bus services, school contracts, private hire, excursions & tours.
Livery: Red/White.

KINEIL COACHES LTD
ANDERSON PLACE, WEST SHORE INDUSTRIAL ESTATE, FRASERBURGH AB43 9LG
Tel: 01346 510200
Fax: 01346 514774
Man Dir: Ian Neilson.
Fleet: 41 - 25 single-deck coach, 5 midibus, 10 midicoach, 1 minibus.
Chassis: 1 Alexander Dennis, 1 DAF, 11 Mercedes, 5 Optare, 1 Scania, 22 Volvo.
Ops incl: local bus services, school contracts, excursions & tours, private hire, continental tours.
Livery: Blue/White/Red.

MAYNES COACHES LTD
CLUNY GARAGE, 4 MARCH ROAD WEST, BUCKIE AB56 4BU
Tel: 01542 831219   **Fax:** 01542 833572
E-mail: info@maynes.co.uk
Web site: www.maynes.co.uk
Dirs: Gordon Mayne, David Mayne, Kevin Mayne.
Fleet (Buckie): 14 –12 single-deck coach, 1 midicoach.
Chassis: 10 MAN, 2 Mercedes, 2 Volvo.
Bodies: 1 Jonckheere, 9 Neoplan, 3 Plaxton, 1 Van Hool.

Ops incl: local bus services, school contracts, excursions & tours, private hire, continental tours.
Livery: Blue/White/Gold.
Ticket System: Setright.
Additional operations at Elgin and St Margaret's Hope – see Moray, Orkney

ALEX MILNE COACHES
THE GARAGE, 4 MAIN STREET, NEW BYTH
AB53 5XD
Tel: 01888 544340
Fax: 01888 544154
E-mail: info@alexmilnecoaches.co.uk
Partners: Alex Milne Brian Milne.
Fleet: 10 - 2 single-deck coach, 4 midicoach, 4 minibus.
Ops incl: local bus services, school contracts, private hire, excursions & tours.
Livery: Blue/White.
Ticket system: Wayfarer

M W NICOLL'S COACH HIRE
THE BUSINESS PARK, ABERDEEN ROAD,
LAURENCEKIRK AB30 1EY
Tel: 01561 377262   **Fax:** 01561 378822
E-mail: malcolm.nicoll@lineone.net
Web site: www.nicoll-coaches.co.uk
Man Dir: M W Nicoll **Dir:** I J Nicoll
Service Man: A Gordon
Office Man: M Forrest.
Fleet: 38 - 12 single-deck coach, 4 midibus, 12 midicoach, 10 minibus.
Chassis: 2 Bova, 3 Ford Transit, 1 Leyland, 19 Mercedes, 2 Optare, 1 Toyota, 10 Volvo.
Ops incl: local bus services, school contracts, private hire.
Livery: White.
Ticket System: Almex.

J D PEACE CO ABDN LTD
FARE PARK, ECHT, WESTHILL AB32 7AL
Tel: 01330 860542   **Fax:** 01330 860543
E-mail: info@peacescoaches.co.uk
Web: www.peacescoches.co.uk
Dirs: David J Collie, Kathleen Collie.
Fleet: 14 - 7 single-deck coach, 3 midicoach, 4 minibus.
Chassis: 6 Bova, 2 Ford Transit, 5 Mercedes, 1 Volvo.
Ops incl: school contracts, private hire.

RS TAXIS & MINICOACH HIRE
BLACKSTOCK, SAUCHEN, INVERURIE
AB51 7RD
Tel: 01330 833314
Ops incl: local bus services, private hire.

REIDS OF RHYNIE
22 MAIN STREET, RHYNIE, BY HUNTLY
AB54 4HB

Tel/Fax: 01464 861212
Recovery: 07831 173681
Owner: Colin Reid.
Fleet: 6 minibus.
Chassis: 4 Ford Transit, 2 LDV.
Ops incl: local bus services, school contracts, private hire.
Livery: White/Blue/Water Green
Ticket system: Wayfarer 3

SHEARER OF HUNTLY LTD
OLD TOLL ROAD, HUNTLY AB54 6JA
Tel: 01466 792410   **Fax:** 01466 793926
E-mail: shearerofhuntly@btconnect.com
Dirs: James W Shearer, Irene E Shearer.
Fleet: 15 - 1 single-deck coach, 2 midicoach, 12 minibus.
Chassis: 1 Dennis, 9 Ford Transit, 3 LDV, 2 Mercedes.
Ops incl: school contracts, private hire.

SIMPSON'S COACHES
21 UNION STREET, ROSEHEARTY,
FRASERBURGH AB43 7JQ
Tel: 01346 571610   **Fax:** 01346 571070
E-mail: info@simpsonscoaches.co.uk
Web site: www.simpsonscoaches.co.uk
Prop: Ron Simpson, Pat Simpson.
Fleet: 11- 8 single-deck coach, 2 midicoach, 1 minibus.
Chassis: 2 Bova, 2 MAN, 3 Mercedes, 4 Volvo.
Ops incl: excursions & tours, private hire, continental tours.
Livery: Silver/Blue.

VICTORIA COACHES
LONGSIDE ROAD, PETERHEAD AB42 3LA
Tel: 01779 480480
Fax: 01779 474850
E-mail: info@victoriacoaches.co.uk
Web site: www.victoriacoaches.co.uk
Props: Mr & Mrs Ewan Mowat & Son.
Fleet: 19 – 5 single-deck coach, 8 minicoach, 6 minibus.
Chassis: 4 Ford Transit, 10 Mercedes, 1 Scania, 4 Volvo.
Ops incl: school contracts, excursions & tours, private hire.
Livery: White with Green.

WATERMILL COACHES LTD
88 COLLEGE BOUNDS, FRASERBURGH
AB43 9QS
Tel/Fax: 01346 513050
E-mail: info@watermillcoaches.co.uk
Web site: www.watermillcoachesltd.co.uk
Fleet: 49 – 2 double-deck bus, 12 single-deck bus, 12 single-deck coach, 3 midibus, 16 midicoach, 4 minibus.
Ops incl: school contracts, private hire, excursions & tours.

GLENESK TRAVEL CO LTD
5 MANSE ROAD, EDZELL DD9 7TJ
Tel: 01356 648666
Ops incl: local bus services, private hire.
Fleet: 12 - 5 midicoach, 7 minibus.
Livery: White with Blue.

JP COACHES
UNIT 3, ORCHARDBANK INDUSTRIAL
ESTATE, FORFAR DD8 1TD
Tel: 01307 461431
Fax: 01307 467028
E-mail: jpminicoaches@btconnect.com
Web site: www.jpcoaches.co.uk
Man Dir: J Petrie.
Fleet: 42 – single-deck coach, midibus, midicoach, minibus.
Chassis: Dennis, Ford Transit, LDV, Mercedes, Optare, Volvo.
Ops incl: local bus services, private hire.
Livery: White with Black/Orange.

RIDDLER'S COACHES LIMITED
CAIRNIE LOAN, ARBROATH
DD11 4DS
Tel: 01241 873464
Fax: 01241 873504
E-mail: charles_riddler@btconnect.com
Web site: www.riddlerscoaches.co.uk
Dirs: C W Riddler, Mrs G M Riddler.
Fleet: 5 single-deck coach.
Chassis: 5 Volvo.
Ops incl: excursions & tours, private hire
Livery: Blue/White

SIDLAW EXECUTIVE TRAVEL
(SCOTLAND) LTD
UNIT 5, ARDYLE INDUSTRIAL ESTATE,
PERRIE STREET, DUNDEE DD2 2RD
Tel: 01382 610410
Fax: 01382 624333
E-mail: travel@sidlaw.co.uk
Web site: www.sidlaw.co.uk
Dir: Bob Costello **Fleet Eng:** Jamie Costello.
Fleet: 12 - 3 single-deck coach, 3 midicoach, 6 minibus.
Chassis: 8 Mercedes, 1 Neoplan, 1 Scania, 1 Setra, 1 Volkswagen.
Ops incl: school contracts, excursions & tours, private hire.
Livery: White/Silver.

STRATHTAY SCOTTISH
OMNIBUSES LTD
See Dundee City

TEEJAY TRAVEL LTD
WEST NEWBIGGING BUSINESS PARK,
ARBROATH DD11 4RH

Tel: 01241 854717
E-mail: tomjordan@teejaytravel.co.uk
Web site: www.teejaytravel.co.uk
Ops incl: local bus services, private hire
Livery: White with Blue lettering

ARGYLL & BUTE

BOWMAN'S COACHES (MULL) LTD
SCALLCASTLE, CRAIGNURE,
ISLE OF MULL PA65 6BA
Tel: 01680 812313
E-mail: info@bowmanstours.co.uk
Web site: www.bowmanstours.co.uk
Props: A Bowman, S Bowman, I Bowman,
I Bowman **Gen Man:** A Bowman.
Fleet: 12 - single-deck bus, single-deck coach,
midibus.
Chassis: Bova, DAF, Dennis, Mercedes, Volvo.
Bodies: Bova, Jonckheere, Plaxton.
Ops incl: local bus services, excursions &
tours, private hire.
Livery: Cream/Red.
Ticket System: Setright, Almex.

CRAIG OF CAMPBELTOWN LTD
BENMHOR, CAMPBELTOWN PA28 6DN
Tel: 01586 552319   **Fax:** 01586 552344
E-mail: enquiries@westcoastmotors.co.uk
Web site: www.westcoastmotors.co.uk
Fleet Name: West Coast Motors.
Chairman/Man Dir: W G Craig
Dir: C R Craig
Co Sec: J M Craig
Tran Man: D M Halliday
Fleet Eng: D Martin.
Fleet: 71 - 6 double-deck bus, 28 single-deck
bus, 30 single-deck coach, 2 midibus,
3 midicoach, I minibus.
Chassis: Bedford, DAF/VDL, Dennis, Freight
Rover, Leyland, MAN, Mercedes, Optare,
Scania, Volvo.
Bodies: Alexander, Ikarus, Irizar, Jonckheere,
Mellor, Onyx, Optare, Park Royal, Plaxton,
Van Hool, Wright.
Ops incl: local bus services, school contracts,
excursions & tours, private hire, express.
Livery: Red/Blue/Honeysuckle.
Ticket System: Wayfarer.
See also Oban & District Buses, Glasgow
Citybus, Glasgow Sightseeing.

GARELOCHHEAD COACHES
WOODLEA GARAGE, MAIN ROAD,
GARELOCHHEAD PA65 6BA
Tel: 01436 810200
Fax: 01436 810050
Web site: www.garelochheadcoaches.co.uk
Prop: Stuart McQueen.
Ops incl: local bus services.

HIGHLAND HERITAGE COACH TOURS
CENTRAL ADMINISTRATION OFFICE,
DALMALLY PA33 1AY
Tel: 01838 200393
E-mail: info@highlandheritage.co.uk
Web site: www.highlandheritage.co.uk
Man Dir: Ian Cleaver
Fleet: 18 single-deck coach.
Chassis: 18 Volvo.
Bodies: 18 Van Hool.
Ops incl: excursions & tours.
Livery: Gold.

HIGHLAND ROVER COACHES
AWE SERVICE STATION, TAYNUILT
PA35 1HT
Tel/Fax: 01866 822612
E-mail: angus@crunachy.plus.com
Prop: Angus Douglas.
Fleet: 3 - I single-deck coach, I minibus,
I minicoach.
Chassis: 3 Mercedes.
Bodies: I Beulas, I Mercedes, I Onyx.
Ops incl: local bus services, school contracts,
excursions & tours, private hire.
Livery: Brown/Orange/White.
Ticket system: Almex.

ISLAY COACHES
BARDARAVINE, TARBERT PA29 6YF
Tel: 01496 840273
Prop: B Mundell Ltd
Ops incl: local bus services.
Fleet incl: single-deck coach, midibus.
Livery: Green/White.

McCOLLS OF ARGYLL LTD
*Ceased operations since LRB 2011
went to press*

OBAN & DISTRICT BUSES LTD
GLENGALLAN ROAD, OBAN
PA34 4HH
Tel: 01631 570500
Fax: 01631 567252
E-mail: enquiries@westcoastmotors.co.uk
Web site: www.westcoastmotors.co.uk
Fleet Name: Oban & District.
Man Dir: Colin Craig **Dir:** W G Craig
Depot Controllers: David Hannah, Donnie
McDougal **Workshop Supervisor:** Iain
McDonald.
Fleet: 23 - 16 single-deck bus, 2 single-deck
coach, 2 midicoach, 2 minibus, I midibus.
Chassis: 4 DAF, 3 Dennis, 2 LDV, 10 Leyland,
2 Mercedes, I Optare, I Volvo.
Bodies: 10 Alexander, 2 KL Conversions,
I Onyx, I Optare, 5 Plaxton, 4 Wright.
Ops incl: local bus services, school contracts,
private hire, express.
Livery: Red/Blue/Honeysuckle.
Ticket System: Wayfarer 3
A subsidiary of West Coast Motors.

WILSON'S OF RHU
RHU GARAGE, MANSE BRAE, RHU G84 8RE
Tel: 01436 820300
Fax: 01436 820337
E-mail: info@wilsonsofrhu.co.uk
Web site: www.wilsonsofrhu.co.uk
Ops incl: local bus services, private hire.
Livery: Grey/White/Red

BORDERS

AUSTIN TRAVEL
STATION ROAD, EARLSTON
TD4 6BZ
Tel: 01896 849360
Fax: 01896 849623
E-mail: austin@travel.gbtbroadband.co.uk
Web site: www.scotlnetours.co.uk
Partners: Douglas Austin, Barry Austin.
Fleet: 7 - 4 single-deck coach, 2 midicoach,
I minicoach.

Chassis: 2 Bova, 3 Mercedes, 2 Setra.
Bodies: 2 Bova, 2 Esker, 2 Setra, I Other.
Ops incl: school contracts, excursions &
tours, private hire, continental tours.
Livery: Pearlescent white

FIRST SCOTLAND EAST LTD
See Falkirk/Stirling

JAMES FRENCH & SON
THE GARAGE, COLDINGHAM,
EYEMOUTH TD14 5NS
Tel/Fax: 01890 771283
Man Dir: Peter Redden.
E-mail: frenchs.garage@virgin.net
Web site: www.jamesfrenchandson.com
Fleet incl: single-deck coach.
Ops incl: excursions & tours, private hire.

MUNRO'S OF JEDBURGH LTD
OAKVALE GARAGE, BONGATE,
JEDBURGH TD8 6DU
Tel: 01835 862253
Fax: 01835 864297
E-mail: info@munrosofjedburgh.co.uk
Web site: www.munrosofjedburgh.co.uk
Man Dir: Ewan Farish
Eng Dir: Bruce Campbell.
Fleet: 32 - 14 single-deck bus, 9 single-deck
coach, 5 midibus, 3 midicoach, I minicoach.
Chassis: 2 Alexander Dennis, 3 DAF,
4 Dennis, I Enterprise, 6 EOS, I Iveco,
7 MAN, 3 Mercedes, 4 Optare, I Transbus.
Bodies: 2 Alexander Dennis, I Crest, 2 Ikarus,
7 MCV, 4 Optare, 6 Plaxton, I Transbus,
7 Van Hool, I Wadham Stringer, I Other.
Ops incl: local bus services, school contracts,
private hire.
Livery: White with Red stripes.
Ticket System: Wayfarer TGX150.

PERRYMAN'S BUSES LTD
RAMPARTS BUSINESS PARK, NORTH ROAD,
BERWICK UPON TWEED
TD15 1TX
Tel: 01289 308719
Fax: 01289 309970
Web site: www.perrymansbuses.com
Dirs: R J Perryman L M Perryman.
Fleet: 30 - 15 single deck bus, 5 single-deck
coach, 6 midibus, 4 minibus.
Chassis: 2 Alexander Dennis, I Ford,
4 MAN, 11 Mercedes, 12 Optare.
Bodies: 2 Alexander Dennis, 4 MCV,
12 Optare, 10 Plaxton.
Ops incl: local bus services, school contracts,
private hire
Livery: White with Red/Blue.
Ticket System: Wayfarer TGX.

TELFORD'S COACHES LTD
I GEORGE STREET, NEWCASTLETON
TD9 0RA
Tel/Fax: 01387 375677
Recovery: 07711 280475
E-mail: alistair@telfordscoaches.com
Web site: www.telfordscoaches.com
Man Dir: Alistair S Telford **Co Sec:**
Doreen S Telford **Ch Eng:** Rod Swan
Ops Man: Sarah Little.
Fleet: 17 - 9 single-deck coach, 2 midicoach,
4 minibus, 2 minicoach.

Chassis: 1 DAF, 1 Ford, 1 Ford Transit,
6 Mercedes, 8 Volvo.
Bodies: 1 Bova, 2 Jonckheere, 4 Mercedes,
10 Plaxton.
Ops incl: local bus services, school contracts,
excursions & tours, private hire, express,
continental tours.
Livery: White with Blue vinyls.
Ticket System: Almex.

A WAIT & SON
WEST END GARAGE, CHIRNSIDE, DUNS
TD11 3UJ
Tel/Fax: 01890 818216
Ops incl: local bus services, school contracts,
private hire.

CLACKMANNANSHIRE

FIRST SCOTLAND EAST LTD
See Falkirk/Stirling.

HUNTER'S COACHES
THE GARAGE, LOCHIES ROAD,
CLACKMANNAN FK10 4ENH
Tel: 01259 215560
Fax: 01259 723638
E-mail: hunterscoaches@btconnect.com
Web site: www.huntersexecutivecoaches.
co.uk
Prop: John Hunter.
Fleet: 18 – 10 single-deck coach, 1 midibus,
5 midicoach, 2 minibus.
Chassis: Alexander Dennis, Bova, DAF,
Dennis, Ford Transit, Mercedes, Scania, Volvo.
Ops incl: local bus services, school contracts,
private hire, excursions & tours.
Livery: Blue.

M LINE
RIVERBANK INDUSTRIAL ESTATE, ALLOA
FK10 1NT
Tel: 01259 212802
E-mail: info@m-line.co.uk.
Web Site: www.m-line.co.uk.
Ops Man: Tom Matchett, Andy McLellan
Eng: Dave Craig.
Fleet: 18 - 8 double-deck bus, 1 double-deck
coach, 9 single-deck coach.
Chassis: 2 Iveco, 1 Leyland, 1 Neoplan,
4 Scania, 1 Setra, 9 Volvo.
Ops incl: local bus services, school contracts,
excursions & tours, private hire, continental
tours.
Livery: Cream/Beige.

MACKIE'S COACHES
32 GLASSHOUSE LOAN, ALLOA FK10 1PE
Tel: 01259 216180
Fax: 01259 217508
E-mail: enquiries@mackiescoaches.com
Web site: www.mackiescoaches.com
Fleet: 19 - 7 single-deck bus, 12 single-deck
coach
Chassis: 7 Bova, 1 DAF, 11 Volvo.
Bodies: 7 Bova, 1 Duple, 1 Ikarus,
1 Jonckheere, 4 Van Hool, 5 Wright.
Ops incl: local bus services, school contracts,
excursions & tours, private hire.
 Liveries: Buses: White/Red; **Coaches:**
White/Brown/Beige.
Ticket System: Wayfarer.

WOODS COACHES
R24
2 GOLF VIEW, TILLICOULTRY FK13 6DH
Tel: 01259 751753
Fax: 01259 751824
E-mail: jwcoaches@btinternet.com
Web site: www.woodscoaches.net
Owner: James Woods **Ops Man:** John
Woods.
Fleet: 15 – 2 single-deck coach, 10 midicoach,
3 minicoach
Chassis: 2 Bova, 12 Mercedes, 1 Volvo.
Bodies: 2 Bova, 1 Sunsundegui, 12 Unvi.
Ops incl: school contracts, excursions &
tours, private hire.
Livery: Silver with two tone Blue stripes.

DUMFRIES & GALLOWAY

ANDERSON'S COACHES
UNIT 1, WHITSHIELS INDUSTRIAL ESTATE,
LANGHOLM DG13 0HX
Tel: 01387 380553
Fax: 01387 380553
Partners: I R Anderson, K Irving
Ch Eng: C Anderson.
Fleet: 6 - 2 single-deck bus, 2 minibus,
2 minicoach.
Chassis: 1 AEC, 3 Ford Transit, 1 Freight
Rover, 1 Leyland.
Bodies: 2 Plaxton, 1 PMT, 1 Robin Hood,
1 Other.
Ops incl: local bus services, school contracts,
private hire.
Livery: Red/Orange/Yellow stripe.
Ticket System: Almex.

WILLIAM BROWNRIGG
THE GARAGE, THORNHILL DG3 5LZ
Tel/Fax: 01848 330203
Dir: William Brownrigg.
Fleet: 9 - 5 single-deck coach, 1 midicoach,
3 minibus.
Chassis: Bova, Mercedes, Volvo.
Bodies: Alexander Dennis, Bova, Reeve
Burgess, Van Hool.
Ops incl: local bus services, school contracts,
excursions & tours, private hire.
Livery: Orange/White.
Ticket System: Almex.

DGC BUSES
DUMFRIES & GALLOWAY COUNCIL,
COUNCIL OFFICES, ENGLISH STREET,
DUMFRIES DG1 2HR
Tel: 01387 260136
Prop: Dumfries & Galloway Council.
Fleet: 49 – 18 single-deck bus, 19 midibus,
12 minibus.
Chassis: 3 Alexander Dennis, 3 BMC, 3 DAF,
9 Dennis, 6 LDV, 1 Leyland, 21 Mercedes, 2
Optare, 1 Renault.
Bodies: 8 Alexander Dennis, 3 BMC, 1 Ikarus,
2 Marshall/MCV, 2 Mercedes, 4 Optare,
12 Plaxton, 5 Wright, 12 Other.
Ops incl: local bus services, school contracts.
Livery: Red/Yellow.
Ticket System: Almex.

HOUSTON'S MINICOACHES
13 STEVENSON AVENUE, LOCKERBIE
DG11 2PG

Tel: 01576 203874
Fleet incl: single-deck coach, single-deck bus,
midibus, midicoach, minibus.
Ops incl: local bus services, school contracts,
private hire, excursions & tours.
Livery: Blue/White.

A & F IRVINE & SON
99 MAIN STREET, GLENLUCE DG8 0PT
Tel: 01581 300345
Fleet: 5 – midibus, midicoach.
Ops incl: local bus services, private hire,
excursions & tours.
Livery: White with Red lettering.

JAMES KING COACHES/ABC TRAVEL
36 MAIN STREET, KIRKCOWAN, NEWTON
STEWART DG8 0HG
Tel: 01671 830284
Fax: 01671 830499
E-mail: enquiries@kingscoachhire.com
Web site: www.kingscoachhire.com
Prop: James King.
Fleet: 39 - 4 single-deck bus, 22 single-deck
coach, 7 midibus, 3 midicoach, 3 minibus.
Chassis: 2 Bova, 1 Dennis, 2 Ford Transit,
1 LDV, 1 MAN, 8 Mercedes, 8 Optare, 1 Scania,
1 Toyota, 22 Volvo.
Bodies: 2 Autobus, 2 Bova, 1 Caetano, 1 Irizar,
2 Jonckheere, 1 LDV, 8 Mercedes. 8 Optare,
3 Plaxton, 14 Van Hool, 3 Wright.
Ops incl: local bus services, school contracts,
excursions & tours, private hire, continental
tours.
Livery: White.
Ticket System: Almex

KIWI LUXURY TRAVEL
80 QUEEN STREET, NEWTON STEWART
DG8 6JL
Tel: 01671 404294
Fax: 01671 403310
E-mail: kiwitravel@btconnect.com
Web site: www.kiwitravelltd.co.uk
Dirs: Ian Allison, Janet Allison.
Fleet: 4 - 3 single-deck coach, 1 minicoach
Chassis incl: 3 Volvo.
Bodies incl: 1 Caetano.
Ops incl: local bus services, school contracts,
excursions & tours, private hire.

MacEWAN'S COACH SERVICES
JOHNFIELD, AMISFIELD, DUMFRIES DG1 3LS
Tel: 01387 256533
Fax: 01387 711123
Prop: John Mac Ewan **Ch Eng:** Peter
Maxwell.
Fleet: 65 - 5 double-deck, 22 single-deck bus,
9 single-deck coach, 1 double-deck coach,
12 midibus, 4 midicoach, 12 minibus.
Chassis: 1 AEC, 2 Bedford, 1 Bristol, 1 DAF,
3 Dennis, 3 Ford Transit, 1 Iveco, 4 LDV,
2 Leyland, 5 MAN, 5 MCW, 18 Mercedes,
3 Optare, 5 Scania, 2 Transbus, 9 Volvo.
Bodies: 10 Alexander, 2 Autobus, 3 Crystal,
1 DAB, 2 Drinkwater, 2 Duple, 1 ECW, 1 East
Lancs, 1 Irizar, 1 Jonckheere, 4 LDV, 4 Marshall/
MCV, 5 MCW, 2 Montano, 3 Optare,
17 Plaxton, 2 Transbus, 1 Van Hool, 3 Wright.
Ops incl: local bus services, school contracts.
Livery: White/Red/Blue.
Ticket system: ERG Transit 400.

Mc CULLOCH AND SON

MAIN ROAD, STONEYKIRK, STRANRAER
DG9 9DH
Tel/Fax: 01776 830236
E-mail: mcculloch.coaches@virgin.net
Fleet Name: McCulloch Coaches.
Partners: D F McCulloch, E A McCulloch.
Fleet: 8 - incl: 1 single-deck bus, 3 single-deck
coach, 1 midibus, 1 midicoach, 1 minicoach.
Chassis: 1 Bedford, 4 Mercedes, 2 Optare,
3 Volvo.
Bodies: 1 Caetano, 1 Duple, 2 Optare,
4 Plaxton.
Ops incl: local bus services, excursions &
tours, school contracts, private hire.
Livery: White/Blue lettering.
Ticket System: Ticket books.

OOR COACHES LTD

SWORDWELL COTTAGE, ANNAN
DG12 6QZ
Tel: 01461 202159
E-mail: info@oorcoaches.co.uk
Web site: www.oorcoaches.co.uk
Ops incl: local bus services, private hire.

STAGECOACH WEST SCOTLAND

See South Ayrshire

FISHERS TOURS

16 WEST PORT, DUNDEE DD1 5EP
Tel/Fax: 01382 227290, 461999
Recovery: 07974 180771
E-mail: fisherstours@btconnect.com
Web site: www.fisherstours.co.uk
Props: James Cosgrove, Catherine Cosgrove.
Fleet: 26 – 23 single-deck coach, 3 midibus.
Chassis: 2 DAF, 5 Dennis, 3 Iveco, 5 Leyland,
2 Mercedes, 9 Volvo.
Bodies: 1 Beulas, 1 Duple, 1 Hispano,
1 Leicester, 1 Marcopolo, 1 Marshall, 8 Plaxton,
9 Van Hool, 3 Wadham Stringer.
Ops incl: local bus services, school contracts,
excursions & tours, private hire, express,
continental tours.
Livery: White with Blue/Yellow.
Ticket System: Almex.

NATIONAL EXPRESS DUNDEE

44-48 EAST DOCK STREET,
DUNDEE DD1 3JS
Tel: 01382 201121
Fax: 01382 201997
Web site: www.nxbus.co.uk/dundee
Man Dir: Phil Smith
Traffic Man: William Murphy
Ch Eng: Frank Sheach
Business Man: Elsie Turbyne.
Fleet: 131 - 23 double-deck bus, 78 single-
deck bus, 9 single-deck coach, 15 midibus,
4 midicoach, 1 minibus, 1 minicoach
Chassis: 1 DAF, 2 Dennis, 1 Ford Transit,
5 Mercedes, 15 Optare, 15 Scania, 92 Volvo.
Bodies: 3 Alexander, 3 Berkhof, 1 Ferqui,
1 Ford, 1 Ikarus, 2 Northern Counties,
15 Optare, 13 Plaxton, 15 Scania, 77 Wright.
Ops incl: local bus services, school contracts,
excursions & tours, private hire.
Livery: Red/White.
Part of the National Express Group

SIDLAW EXECUTIVE TRAVEL (SCOTLAND) LTD

UNIT 5, ARDYLE INDUSTRIAL ESTATE,
PERRIE STREET, DUNDEE DD2 2RD
Tel: 01382 610410
Fax: 01382 624333
E-mail: travel@sidlaw.co.uk
Web site: www.sidlaw.co.uk
Dir: Bob Costello **Fleet Eng:** Jamie Costello.
Fleet: 12 - 3 single-deck coach, 3 midicoach,
6 minibus.
Chassis: 8 Mercedes, 1 Neoplan, 1 Scania,
1 Setra, 1 Volkswagen.
Ops incl: school contracts, excursions &
tours, private hire.
Livery: White/Silver.

STRATHTAY SCOTTISH OMNIBUSES LTD

OFFICES 47-51, EVANS BUSINESS CENTRE,
JOHN SMITH BUSINESS PARK,
KIRKCALDY KY2 6HD
Tel: 01382 313700
Fax: 01382 614552
Recovery: 01382 228345

E-mail: eastscotland.enquiries@
stagecoachbus.com
Web site: www.stagecoachbus.com
Fleet Name: Stagecoach Strathtay
Man Dir: Charlie Mullen
Eng Dir: Jim Penrose
Ops Man: Martin Hall
Depot Eng: Alan Hughes
Fleet: 109 - 48 double-deck bus, 32 single-
deck bus, 11 single deck coach, 17 midibus,
1 minibus.
Chassis: 32 Alexander Dennis, 3 Dennis,
1 Iveco, 12 MAN, 6 Mercedes, 11 Optare,
5 Transbus, 39 Volvo.
Bodies: 37 Alexander Dennis, 13 Alexander,
17 East Lancs, 4 Jonckheere, 11 Optare,
13 Plaxton, 7 Transbus, 4 Wright, 1 Other.
Ops incl: local bus services, school contracts,
excursions & tours, private hire, express.
Livery: Stagecoach UK Bus/Citylink/Megabus.
Ticket System: ERG.
Part of the Stagecoach Group.

LIDDELL'S COACHES

1 MAUCHLINE ROAD, AUCHINLECK
KA18 2BJ
Tel: 01290 424300/420717
Fax: 01290 425637
Prop: J Liddell
Ch Eng: J Quinn
Co Sec: Ms J Samson
Ops Man: Ms M Milroy.
Fleet: 24 - 8 double-deck bus, 10 single-deck
coach, 4 midicoach, 2 minibus.
Chassis: 3 DAF, 2 Dodge, 2 Freight
Rover, 10 Leyland, 6 Volvo.
Bodies: 8 Alexander, 1 Bova, 1 Caetano,
3 Duple, 1 ECW, 1 East Lancs, 2 Jonckheere,
4 Plaxton, 2 Reeve Burgess, 1 Wright.
Ops incl: local bus services, school contracts,
excursions & tours, private hire, express.
Livery: White with Brown/Orange/Lemon
stripes.
Ticket System: Setright.

MILLIGAN'S COACH TRAVEL LTD

LOAN GARAGE, 20 THE LOAN,
MAUCHLINE, KA5 6AN
Tel/Recovery: 01290 550365
Fax: 01290 553291
E-mail: enquiries@milliganscoachtravel.co.uk
Web site: www.milliganscoachtravel.co.uk
Dir: William J Milligan.
Fleet: 20 - 18 single -deck coach, 1 midicoach,
1 minibus.
Chassis: 5 Bova, 1 DAF, 1 Ford Transit,
2 Leyland, 2 MAN, 3 Scania, 6 Volvo.
Ops incl: school contracts, excursions &
tours, private hire.
Livery: Black and Silver.

ROWE & TUDHOPE COACHES

UNIT 2, PALMERMOUNT INDUSTRIAL
PARK, KILMARNOCK ROAD,
DUNDONALD KA2 9BL
Tel: 01563 851349
E-mail: info@roweandtudhope.com
Web site: www.roweandtudhope.com
Prop: George Rowe.
Fleet: 14 – 2 double-deck bus, 6 single-deck

Scottish Operators

coach, 2 midicoach, 4 minicoach.
Chassis: I DAF, 2 Dennis, I Ford Transit,
5 Mercedes, 5 Volvo.
Bodies: I Bova, I Crest, I Jonckheere,
2 Onyx, 2 Van Hool, 6 Other.
Ops incl: school contracts, private hire.
Livery: White with Blue vinyls.

STAGECOACH WEST SCOTLAND

See South Ayrshire

EAST LOTHIAN

EVE CARS & COACHES

SPOTT ROAD, DUNBAR EH42 IRR
Tel: 01368 865500 **Fax:** 01368 865400
E-mail: admin@eveinfo.co.uk
Web site: www.eveinfo.co.uk
Partners: Gary Scougall, Vona Scougall.
Ops incl: local bus services, school contracts,
private hire.

FIRST SCOTLAND EAST LTD

See Falkirk/Stirling.

PRENTICE COACHES LTD

STATION GARAGE, HOSPITAL ROAD,
HADDINGTON EH41 3BH
Tel: 01620 822620
Fax: 01620 823544
E-mail: mail@prentice.info
Web site: www.prenticeofhaddington.info
Fleet: 18 – 6 single-deck coach, 2 midibus,
10 midicoach.
Chassis: I Alexander Dennis, I Bedford,
I Dennis, I Irisbus, 12 Mercedes, I Scania,
2 Volvo.
Bodies: 15 Plaxton, 3 Other.
Ops incl: local bus services, school contracts,
excursions & tours, private hire.
Livery: Silver/Blue.
Ticket System: Wayfarer.

EAST RENFREWSHIRE

ARRIVA SCOTLAND WEST

See Renfrewshire

HENRY CRAWFORD COACHES LTD

SHILFORD MILL, NEILSTON
G78 3BA
Tel: 01505 850456
Fax: 01505 850479
E-mail: henrycrawford@talk21.com
Web site: www.henrycrawfordcoaches.co.uk
Dirs: James Crawford (Ops), John Crawford
(Eng), Isobel Crawford (Co Sec).
Fleet: 26 – 21 single-deck coach, 5 minicoach.
Chassis: I Bova, 2 Leyland, 5 Mercedes,
18 Volvo.
Bodies: I Bova, 2 Duple, I Indcar, I Optare,
3 Plaxton, 16 Van Hool, 2 Other.
Ops incl: private hire, school contracts.
Livery: White/Red.

RIVERSIDE TRANSPORT LTD

15 CARLIBAR ROAD, BARRHEAD G78 IAA
Tel: 0141 881 1104
Fax: 0141 881 1130
Web site: www.riversidetransport.co.uk
Dirs: Mrs A Cowden, M Cowden.
Ops incl: local bus services.

SOUTHERN COACHES (NM) LTD

LOCHIBO ROAD, BARRHEAD G78 ILF
Tel: 0141-881 1147
Fax: 0141 881 1148
E-mail: reservations@southerncoaches.
co.uk.
Web site: www.southerncoaches.co.uk
Dirs: R Wallace, D Wallace, Mary Wallace.
Fleet: 19 - 17 single-deck coach, 2 minicoach.
Chassis: 2 DAF, 2 Toyota, 15 Volvo.
Bodies: 2 Caetano, I Jonckheere, 8 Plaxton,
8 Van Hool.
Ops incl: school contracts, excursions &
tours, private hire, express.
Livery: Cream/Blue/Orange.

EDINBURGH, CITY OF

AAA COACHES

UNIT 7, RAW CAMPS INDUSTRIAL ESTATE,
KIRKNEWTON EH27 8DF
Tel: 01506 883000
Fax: 01506 884000
E-mail: info@aaacoaches.co.uk
Web site: www.aaacoaches.co.uk
Man Dir: Mr J T Renton.
Fleet: 17 - 13 single-deck coach, 3 midibus,
I minibus.
Chassis: I Bova, I Dennis, I LDV, 4 MAN,
3 Mercedes, 7 Volvo.
Bodies: 4 Jonckheere, 2 Leyland, 4 Marcopolo,
2 Plaxton, 2 Sunsundegui.
Livery: White.

ALLAN'S COACHES EDINBURGH

THE COACH YARD, NEWTONLOAN TOLL,
GOREBRIDGE EH23 4LZ
Tel/Recovery: 01875 820377
Fax: 01875 822468
E-mail: coaches@allanscoaches.co.uk
Web Site: www.allanscoaches.co.uk
Prop & Ops Man: David W Allan **Ch Eng:**
Neil Mitchell **Office Man:** Mrs Dawn Allan.
Fleet: 10 - 8 single-deck coach, I midicoach,
I minibus.
Chassis: 2 DAF, 4 Iveco, 3 Mercedes.
Bodies: 2 Bova, 2 Mercedes, 5 Plaxton.
Ops incl: school contracts, excursions &
tours, private hire, express.
Livery: Allan's Blue.

CITY CIRCLE UK LTD

BUTLERFIELD INDUSTRIAL ESTATE,
BONNYRIGG EH19 3JQ
Tel: 0131 220 1066 **Fax:** 01875 822762
E-mail: edi@citycircleuk.com
Web site: www.citycircleuk.com
Man Dir: Neil Pegg **Fin Dir:** Johnson
Mitchell **Ops Man:** John Blair **Asst Ops
Man:** Jennifer Gibson **Eng:** James Mellon.
Fleet: 15 single-deck coach.
Ops incl: excursions & tours, private hire,
continental tours.
Livery: White with Grey, Red.
Associated with City Circle UK Ltd, London.

EDINBURGH COACH LINES LTD

81 SALAMANDER STREET, LEITH,
EDINBURGH EH6 7JZ
Tel: 0131 554 5413 **Fax:** 0131 553 3721

E-mail: enquiries@edinburghcoachlines.com.
Web site: www.edinburghcoachlines.com.
Dir: Patrick Kavanagh **Gen Man:** Peter Fyvie
Traffic Man: Gary Forbes-Burns.
Fleet: 28 – 3 single-deck bus, 21 single-deck
coach, 3 midicoach, I minicoach.
Chassis: I Dennis, 3 MAN, 3 Mercedes,
17 Scania, 4 Volvo.
Bodies: 7 Irizar, 7 Plaxton, 10 Van Hool,
3 Other.
Ops incl: local bus services, school contracts,
excursions & tours, private hire, continental
tours.
Liveries: Pink/Purple/White, Megabus Blue/
Yellow.
Ticket System: Wayfarer TGX.
A subsidiary of Bernard Kavanagh & Sons –
see Republic of Ireland.

EDINBURGH TOURS LTD

ANNANDALE STREET, EDINBURGH EH7
4AZ
Tel: 0131 554 4494
Fax: 0131 554 3942
E-mail: info@edinburghtour.com
Web site: www.edinburghtour.com
Man Dir: W Ian G Craig
Fin Dir: Norman J Strachan
Ops Dir: William W Campbell
Eng Dir: William Devlin.
Fleet: 47 – 2 double-deck bus, 45 open-top
bus.
Chassis: 13 AEC, 32 Dennis, 2 Volvo.
Bodies: 7 Alexander Dennis, 27 Plaxton,
13 Park Royal.
Ops incl: local bus services, private hire.
Livery: Various.
Ticket system: Casio.
A subsidiary of Lothian Buses PLC.

FAIRWAY TRAVEL

6 BRIARBANK TERRACE, EDINBURGH
EH11 IST
Tel: 0131 467 6717
Fax: 0131 467 6717
E-mail: davy@fairwaytravel.freeserve
Web site: www.fairwaytravel.co.uk
Prop: D Innes.
Fleet: 4 - I single-deck coach, 2 midicoach,
I minibus.
Chassis: I DAF, I Setra, 2 Toyota.
Bodies: 2 Caetano, I Leyland, I Setra.
Ops incl: school contracts, excursions &
tours, private hire, continental tours.
Livery: Blue and Red on White.

FIRST SCOTLAND EAST LTD

See Falkirk/Stirling.

LIBERTON TRAVEL

17-29 ENGINE ROAD, LOANHEAD EH20
9RF
Tel: 0131 440 4400
Fax: 0131 448 0008
E-mail: sales@libertontravel.co.uk
Dirs: Iain Smith, Alan Boyd.
Fleet: 10 - 7 single-deck coach, 2 minibus,
I minicoach.
Chassis: I Dennis, I Ford Transit, I Freight
Rover, I Mercedes, 6 Volvo.
Bodies incl: I Caetano, I Marcopolo,
4 Plaxton.

The Little Red Book 2012 - in association with Transport Benevolent Fund

Ops incl: school contracts, excursions & tours, private hire.
Livery: White.

LOTHIAN BUSES PLC

♿🚌
ANNANDALE STREET, EDINBURGH
EH7 4AZ
Tel: 0131 554 4494
Fax: 0131 554 3942
E-mail: mail@lothianbuses.com
Web site: www.lothianbuses.com
Man Dir: W Ian G Craig **Fin Dir:** Norman J Strachan **Ops Dir:** William W Campbell
Eng Dir: William Devlin **Chairman:** Christopher J Walton **Non Exec Dirs:** Ron Hewitt, Ann Faulds, Donald Macleod, Marjory Rodger, Jane Gray, Ian McKay, John Martin.
Fleet: 643 - 500 double-deck bus, 143 single-deck bus.
Chassis: 218 Dennis, 6 Optare, 15 Scania, 404 Volvo.
Bodies: 6 Optare, 225 Plaxton, 15 Scania, 397 Wright.
Ops incl: local bus services.
Livery: Maroon/White.
Ticket system: Wayfarer TGX200.

FALKIRK

COLES COACHES
113 EASTBURN DRIVE, FALKIRK FK1 1TX
Tel: 01324 461721
Web site: www.colescoachesfalkirk.co.uk
Fleet: single-deck bus, single-deck coach.
Ops incl: school contracts, private hire.

DEWAR COACHES
24 PARKHEAD ROAD, GLEN VILLAGE, FALKIRK FK1 2AR
Tel: 01324 629275
Fax: 01324 613303
E-mail: info@dewarcoaches.co.uk
Web site: www.dewarcoaches.co.uk
Fleet: 6 – 5 single-deck coaches, 1 midicoach.
Chassis: 1 Mercedes, 5 Volvo.
Ops incl: private hire, excursions & tours, continental tours.
Livery: White.

FIRST SCOTLAND EAST LTD
♿🚌❄🚐
CARMUIRS HOUSE, 300 STIRLING ROAD, LARBERT FK5 3NJ
Tel: 01324 602200
Fax: 01324 611287
E-mail: contact.scotlandeast@firstgroup.com
Web site: www.firstgroup.com/scotlandeast
Fleet Names: First Scotland East, Midland Bluebird.
Man Dir: Paul A Thomas **Ops Dir:** John Gorman.
Fleet: 447 – 159 double-deck bus, 200 single-deck bus, 19 single-deck coach, 66 midibus, 3 minibus.

Chassis: 59 Alexander Dennis, 3 Leyland, 10 Mercedes, 7 Optare, 167 Scania, 199 Volvo.
Bodies: 85 Alexander Dennis, 21 East Lancs, 12 Marshall/MCV, 4 Mercedes, 15 Northern Counties, 10 Optare, 80 Plaxton, 218 Wright.
Ops incl: local bus services, school contracts, private hire, express.
Livery: FirstGroup UK Bus.
Ticket System: Almex.

P. WOODS MINICOACHES
20 CALDER PLACE, HALLGLEN FK1 2QQ.
Tel: 01324 613085.
Fax: 01324 717976.

FIFE

FIFE SCOTTISH OMNIBUSES LTD
♿🚌🚌❄🚽
OFFICES 47-51, EVANS BUSINESS CENTRE, JOHN SMITH BUSINESS PARK, KIRKCALDY KY2 6HD
Tel: 01592 642394
Fax: 01592 645677
Recovery: 01383 511911
E-mail: eastscotland.
enquiries@stagecoachbus.com
Web site: www.stagecoachbus.com
Fleet Name: Stagecoach in Fife.
Man Dir: Charlie Mullen
Chief Eng: Mike Williams.
Fleet: 343 - 149 double-deck bus, 115 single-deck bus, 49 single-deck coach, 27 midibus, 3 minibus.
Chassis: 56 Alexander Dennis, 20 Dennis, 3 Leyland, 56 MAN, 3 Mercedes, 27 Optare, 9 Scania, 22 Transbus, 147 Volvo.
Bodies: 104 Alexander, 77 Alexander Dennis, 7 East Lancs, 2 Leyland, 44 Northern Counties, 27 Optare, 51 Plaxton, 9 Scania, 22 Transbus.
Ops incl: local bus services, school contracts, excursions & tours, private hire, express.
Liveries: Stagecoach UK Bus, Citylink.
Ticket System: ERG

HAMISH GORDON COACHES
🚌🚌❄
BANK PLACE GARAGE, LESLIE KY6 3LD
Tel: 01592 620202
Web site: www.hamishgordoncoaches.co.uk
Prop: Hamish Gordon
Fleet: 11 – 8 single-deck coach, 2 midicoach, 1 minibus.
Chassis: 5 Bova, 1 Duple 425, 1 EOS, 4 Mercedes.
Ops incl: school contracts, private hire.

KINGDOM COACHES
Ceased trading since LRB 2011 went to press.

MOFFAT & WILLIAMSON LTD
♿🚌🚌🚌❄🚽🔧
OLD RAILWAY YARD, ST FORT, NEWPORT-ON-TAY DD6 8RG
Tel: 01382 541159 **Fax:** 01382 541169

E-mail: enquiries@moffat-williamson.co.uk
Web site: www.moffat-williamson.co.uk
Dirs: John Williamson, Iain Williamson
Accounts Asst: Sharon Smith.
Fleet: 62 - 2 single-deck bus, 45 single-deck coach, 10 midibus, 4 midicoach, 1 minibus.
Chassis: 4 Alexander Dennis, 13 Dennis, 1 Ford, 6 Mercedes, 8 Optare, 1 VDL, 29 Volvo.
Bodies: 1 Alexander Dennis, 1 East Lancs, 8 Optare, 47 Plaxton, 3 Wadham Stringer, 1 Other.
Ops incl: local bus services, school contracts, excursions & tours, private hire, express.
Livery: Brown/Cream/Orange.

RENNIES OF DUNFERMLINE LTD
🚌🚌❄🚫R🔧🚽
WELLWOOD, DUNFERMLINE KY12 0PY
Tel: 01383 620600
Fax: 01383 620624
E-mail: gordon@rennies.co.uk
Web site: www.rennies.co.uk
Gen Man: Gordon Menzies **Tran Man:** Iain Robertson **Ch Eng:** George Clark.
Fleet: 59 - 20 double-deck bus, 7 single-deck bus, 28 single-deck coach, 4 midicoach.
Chassis: 4 Autosan, 2 BMC, 1 Bova, 15 Dennis, 4 Mercedes, 42 Volvo.
Bodies: 4 Autosan, 13 Alexander, 1 Berkhof, 2 BMC, 1 Bova, 5 Caetano, 5 Jonckheere, 7 Northern Counties, 14 Plaxton, 1 Sunsundegui, 1 Van Hool, 1 Wadham Stringer, 4 Other.
Ops incl: local bus services, school contracts, excursions & tours, private hire, express, continental tours.
Liveries: Blue/White, Citylink.
Ticket system: Almex.
A subsidiary of the Stagecoach Group.

ST ANDREWS EXECUTIVE TRAVEL
🚌🚌🚽❄
BROWNHILLS GARAGE, ST ANDREWS KY16 8PL
Tel: 01334 470080
Fax: 01334 470081
E-mail: orders@saxtravel.co.uk
Web Site: www.saxtravel.co.uk
Dir: Gordon Donaldson.
Fleet: 17 - 9 midicoach, 8 minicoach.
Chassis: 17 Mercedes.
Ops incl: excursions & tours, private hire.
Livery: White and Green.

GLASGOW, CITY OF

ALLANDER COACHES LTD
🚌🚽🚌❄🔧🚽
UNIT 19, CLOBERFIELD, MILNGAVIE, GLASGOW G62 7LN
Tel: 0141 956 1234
Fax: 0141 956 6669
E-mail: gary@allandercoaches.co.uk
Web site: www.allandertravel.co.uk
Man Dir: James Fulton Wilson

♿ Vehicle suitable for disabled	🪑 Seat belt-fitted Vehicle	R24 24 hour recovery service
🚽 Toilet-drop facilities available	🍴 Coach(es) with galley facilities	🚐 Replacement vehicle available
R Recovery service available	❄ Air-conditioned vehicle(s)	🚌 Vintage Coach(s) available
🚌 Open top vehicle(s)	🚻 Coaches with toilet facilities	🔋 Hybrid Buses

Dir: Mrs Elizabeth Wilson **Tran Man:** Gary Wilson **Ch Eng:** Graham Wilson
Co Sec: Miss Margaret Brown.
Fleet: 26 - 3 double-deck bus, 3 single-deck bus, 14 single-deck coach, 3 midicoach, 1 minibus, 2 minicoach.
Chassis: 18 DAF, 3 Dennis, 3 Mercedes, 2 Volvo.
Bodies: 3 Alexander Dennis, 18 Bova, 3 Sitcar, 2 Wright.
Ops incl: local bus services, school contracts, excursions & tours, private hire.
Livery: Black/Orange/Gold.

ARRIVA SCOTLAND WEST
See Renfrewshire.

CITY SIGHTSEEING GLASGOW
ST GEORGE'S BUILDING, 153 QUEEN STREET, GLASGOW G1 3BJ
Tel: 0141 204 0444
Fax: 0141 248 6582
Web site: www.citysightseeingglasgow.co.uk
E-mail: info@citysightseeingglasgow.co.uk
Man Dir: Colin Craig **Ops Man:** Donald Booth.
Fleet: 10 open top bus.
Chassis: 4 Scania, 6 Volvo.
Bodies: 2 Alexander Dennis, 2 East Lancs, 2 Optare.
Ops incl: excursions & tours, private hire.
Livery: City Sightseeing Red.
Ticket system: Wayfarer 3
A subsidiary of West Coast Motors – see Argyll & Bute.

DOIGS OF GLASGOW LTD
TRANSPORT HOUSE, SUMMER STREET, GLASGOW G40 3TB
Tel: 0141 554 5555
Fax: 0141 551 9000
E-mail: andy@doigs.com
Web site: www.doigs.com
Chairman/Man Dir: Andrew Forsyth
Co Sec: Iain Forsyth.
Fleet: 15 - 1 double-deck bus, 1 single-deck bus, 1 articulated bus, 8 single-deck coach, 1 midicoach, 3 minicoach.
Chassis incl: DAF, Dennis, LDV, Mercedes, Scania, 3 Volvo.
Bodies: 1 Caetano, 1 East Lancs, 7 Irizar, 1 Marcopolo, 2 Mercedes, 1 Optare, 3 Sunsundegui, 1 Wright.
Ops incl: school contracts, excursions & tours, private hire, continental tours.
Livery: Silver/Red lettering.

FIRST GLASGOW
197 VICTORIA ROAD, GLASGOW G42 7AD
Tel: 0141 423 6600
Fax: 0141 636 3228
Web Site: www.firstgroup.com
Regional Man Dir: Mark Savelli
Man Dir: Ronnie Park
Fleet: 992 - 432 double-deck bus, 514 single-deck bus, 11 single-deck coach, 10 midibus, 5 minibus, 20 articulated bus.
Chassis: 39 Alexander Dennis, 4 Bluebird, 1 BMC, 209 Dennis, 14 Optare, 1 Renault, 122 Scania, 602 Volvo.
Ops incl: local bus services, express.
Livery: FirstGroup UK Bus.

GLASGOW CITYBUS LTD
729 SOUTH STREET, GLASGOW G14 0BX
Tel: 0141 954 2255
Email: mail@glasgowcitybus.co.uk
Web site: www.glasgowcitybus.co.uk
Man Dir: Colin Craig.
Fleet: 27 – 1 double-deck bus, 8 single-deck bus, 18 midibus.
Chassis: 7 Alexander Dennis, 6 DAF, 8 Dennis, 2 Optare, 1 Scania, 3 VDL
Bodies: 7 Alexander Dennis, 1 Alexander, 1 East Lancs, 2 Optare, 9 Plaxton, 1 UVG, 6 Wright.
Ops incl: local bus services.
Livery: Red/White/Blue/Yellow.
A subsidiary of West Coast Motors – see Argyll & Bute.

JOHN MORROW COACHES
18 ALBION INDUSTRIAL ESTATE, HALLEY STREET, YOKER, GLASGOW G13 4DJ
Tel: 0141 951 8888   **Fax:** 0141 952 6445
E-mail: info@clantours.com
Web site: www.clantours.com
Prop: John Morrow.
Fleet: 19 - 16 single-deck bus, 1 single-deck coach, 1 midicoach, 1 minicoach.
Chassis: 2 Alexander Dennis, 1 Leyland, 7 Mercedes, 5 Optare, 1 Toyota, 3 Volvo.
Ops incl: local bus services, school contracts, excursions & tours, private hire.
Livery: Brown/Cream.
Ticket system: Almex.

SCOTTISH CITYLINK COACHES LTD
BUCHANAN BUS STATION, KILLERMONT STREET, GLASGOW G2 3NP
Tel: 0141 352 4454
E-mail: info@citylink.co.uk.
Web site: www.citylink.co.uk.
Ops incl: private hire, express.
Livery: Blue/yellow.
Ticket system: Wayfarer.

SELVEY'S COACHES
HILLCREST HOUSE, 33 HOWIESHILL ROAD, CAMBUSLANG G72 8PW
Tel: 0141 641 1080
Fax: 0141 641 2065
Owner: A G Selvey.
Fleet: 8 - 5 single-deck coach, 2 midicoach, 1 minicoach.
Chassis: 3 Bedford, 2 Leyland, 1 Mercedes, 2 Volvo.
Bodies: 1 Duple, 1 Jonckheere, 1 Mercedes, 3 Plaxton.
Ops incl: excursions & tours, private hire, school contracts.
Livery: Maroon/Red/Yellow.

STAGECOACH GLASGOW
See Stagecoach West Scotland – South Ayrshire.

HIGHLAND

D&E COACHES LTD
39 HENDERSON DRIVE, INVERNESS IV1 1TR
Tel: 01463 222444   **Fax:** 01463 226700
Recovery: 07770 222612

E-mail: info@decoaches.co.uk
Web site: www.decoaches.co.uk
Man Dir: Donald Mathieson **Dir:** Elizabeth Mathieson **Co Acct:** Gayle Kennedy **Ops Man:** Willie Bell **Ch Eng:** Calum McGregor **Workshop Foreman:** Bryan Fiddy.
Fleet: 28 – 2 double-deck bus, 2 single-deck bus, 13 single-deck coach, 3 midicoach, 4 minibus, 4 minicoach.
Chassis: 8 Bova, 1 DAF, 2 Dennis, 9 Mercedes, 4 Volkswagen, 4 Volvo.
Bodies: 2 Alexander Dennis, 1 Berkhof, 8 Bova, 1 Duple, 2 Esker, 2 Optare, 4 Plaxton, 2 Unvi, 3 Van Hool, 4 Volkswagen.
Ops incl: local bus services, school contracts, private hire.
Livery: White.
Ticket system: Almex.

TIM DEARMAN COACHES
Ceased trading in April 2011.

FRASER'S COACHES
THE GARAGE, MUNLOCHY IV8 8NE
Tel: 01463 811219
E-mail: fraserscoaches@yahoo.co.uk
Web site: www.fraserscoaches.com
Prop: Charles Fraser.
Fleet: 9 – double-deck bus, single-deck coach, midicoach, minibus.
Ops incl: school contracts, private hire.

SCOTBUS LTD
5 DARNAWAY AVENUE, INVERNESS IV2 3HY
Tel: 01463 214410
E-mail: info@scotbus.co.uk
Web site: www.scotbus.co.uk
Fleet: 17 - 8 double-deck bus, 3 single-deck bus, 2 single-deck coach, 4 minibus.
Ops incl: local bus services, school contracts, private hire.
Livery: Blue/White.

SHIEL BUSES LTD
BLAIN GARAGE, ACHARACLE PH36 4JY
Tel/Fax: 01967 431272
E-mail: shiel.buses@btconnect.com
Web site: www.shielbuses.co.uk
Dir: Donnie MacGillivray.
Fleet: 21 - 7 single-deck coach, 2 midibus, 8 midicoach, 3 minibus, 1 minicoach.
Chassis: 1 Ford Transit, 10 Mercedes, 1 Optare, 2 Toyota, 7 Volvo.
Ops incl: local bus services, school contracts, private hire.
Livery: Blue/Silver.
Ticket system: Amex
Incorporates White Heather Travel

SPA COACHES
KINETTAS, STRATHPEFFER IV14 9BH
Tel: 01997 421311
Fax: 01997 421983
E-mail: info@spacoaches.co.uk
Web site: www.spacoaches.com
Prop: N MacArthur.
Fleet: 24 - 15 single-deck coach, 7 midicoach, 2 minibus.
Chassis: 1 Leyland, 7 Mercedes, 2 Toyota, 14 Volvo.
Ops incl: school contracts, excursions &

tours, private hire, continental tours.
Livery: Orange/White.

STAGECOACH HIGHLAND
6 BURNETT ROAD, LONGMAN
INDUSTRIAL ESTATE, INVERNESS IV1 1TF
Tel: 01463 239292 **Fax:** 01463 251360
Recovery: 01463 239292
E-mail:
highland.enquiries@stagecoachbus.com
Web site: www.stagecoachbus.com
Fleet Name: Stagecoach in the Highlands.
Man Dir: Steve Walker **Ops Dir:** Bob Hall
Eng Dir: Russell Henderson **Traffic Man:**
Scott Pearson **Eng Man:** Callum MacGregor
Comm Man: William Mainus
Ops Man: Ali Mac Donald.
Fleet: 174 - 22 double-deck bus, 76 single-
deck bus, 58 single-deck coach, 18 midibus
(excludes Orkney – see separate entry).
Chassis: 30 Alexander Dennis, 46 Dennis,
7 Mercedes, 11 Optare, 80 Volvo.
Ops incl: local bus services, school contracts,
excursions & tours, private hire, express.
Livery: Stagecoach UK Bus/Citylink/Megabus.
Ticket System: Wayfarer/ERG.

GRAHAM URQUHART TRAVEL LTD
28 MIDMILLS ROAD, INVERNESS IV2 3NY
Tel: 01463 222292 **Fax:** 01463 238880
E-mail: enquiries@grahamurquharttravel-
inverness.co.uk
Web site: www.grahamurquharttravel.co.uk
Dir: John G Urquhart **Sec:** John G Prant.
Fleet: 6 - 3 single-deck coach, 2 midicoach,
1 minicoach.
Chassis: 3 Mercedes, 1 Scania, 2 Volvo.
Bodies: 1 Irizar, 2 Unvi, 2 Volvo, 1 Other.
Ops incl: excursions & tours, private hire.

WESTERBUS
THE GARAGE, GAIRLOCH IV21 2BH
Tel: 01445 712255
Props: Messrs MacKenzie & MacLennan.
Fleet: 10 – 6 single-deck coach, 3 midicoach,
1 minibus.
Ops incl: local bus services, school contracts,
private hire.
Livery: White with Two Tone Blue.

INVERCLYDE

ARRIVA SCOTLAND WEST
See Renfrewshire.

GILLEN'S COACHES LTD
11 DELLINGBURN STREET,
GREENOCK PA15 4RN
Tel/Fax: 01475 744618
Recovery: 07785 873299
Dir: Samuel McPherson.
Fleet: 14 - single-deck bus, midicoach,
minibus, minicoach.
Ops incl: local bus services, excursions &
tours, private hire.
Livery: White.
Ticket system: Wayfarer.

HARTE BUSES
OCEAN TERMINAL, PATRICK STREET,
GREENOCK PA16 8UU
Tel/Fax: 01475 787781

E-mail: info@hartebuses.co.uk
Web site: www.hartebuses.co.uk
Dir: Peter Harte MBE.
Fleet: 3 single-deck bus, 1 single-deck coach
Chassis/Bodies: 1 Bova, 1 MAN, 2 Mercedes
Operations: local bus services.
Livery: Orange/Gold.

McGILLS BUS SERVICE LTD
99, EARNHILL ROAD, LARKFIELD
INDUSTRIAL ESTATE, GREENOCK
PA16 0EQ
Tel: 01475 711122 **Fax:** 01475 711133
Web Site: www.mcgillsbuses.co.uk
Chairman: J Easdale **Man Dir:** R Roberts
Fin Dir: G Davidson **Gen Man:** B Hendry
Eng Dir: B Smith.
Ops incl: local bus services.
Livery: Blue/White.
Also at Barrhead (see Renfrewshire).

PRIDE OF THE CLYDE COACHES LTD
11 DELLINGBURN STREET, GREENOCK
PA15 4RN
Tel: 01475 888000
Fax: 01475 888333
E-mail: info@prideoftheclyse.net
Web site: www.prideoftheclyde.net
Fleet incl: single-deck coach, midicoach,
minicoach, minibus.
Ops incl: private hire.
Livery: White with Blue.

MIDLOTHIAN

ALLAN'S COACHES EDINBURGH
THE COACH YARD, NEWTONLOAN TOLL,
GOREBRIDGE EH23 4LZ
Tel/Recovery: 01875 820377
Fax: 01875 822468
E-mail: coaches@allanscoaches.co.uk
Web Site: www.allanscoaches.co.uk
Prop & Ops Man: David W Allan **Ch Eng:**
Neil Mitchell **Office Man:** Mrs Dawn Allan.
Fleet: 10 - 8 single-deck coach, 1 midicoach,
1 minibus.
Chassis: 2 DAF, 4 Iveco, 3 Mercedes.
Bodies: 2 Bova, 2 Mercedes, 5 Plaxton.

Ops incl: school contracts, excursions &
tours, private hire, express.
Livery: Allan's Blue.

CITY CIRCLE UK LTD
BUTLERFIELD INDUSTRIAL ESTATE,
BONNYRIGG EH19 3JQ
Tel: 0131 220 1066
Fax: 01875 822762
E-mail: edi@citycircleuk.com
Web site: www.citycircleuk.com
Man Dir: Neil Pegg **Fin Dir:** Johnson
Mitchell **Ops Man:** John Blair **Asst Ops
Man:** Jennifer Gibson **Eng:** James Mellon.
Fleet: 15 single-deck coach.
Ops incl: excursions & tours, private hire,
continental tours.
Livery: White with Grey, Red,
A subsidiary of City Circle, London,

FIRST SCOTLAND EAST LTD
See Falkirk/Stirling.

WILLIAM HUNTER
OAKFIELD GARAGE, LOANHEAD
EH20 9AE
Tel: 0131 440 0704 **Fax:** 0131 448 2184
E-mail: sales@hunterscoaches.co.uk
Web Site: www.hunterscoaches.co.uk
Props: G I Hunter, W R Hunter.
Fleet: 14 - 12 single-deck coach, 2 minibus.
Chassis: 3 Toyota, 11 Volvo.
Bodies: 3 Caetano, 11 Van Hool.
Ops incl: school contracts, private hire.
Livery: Brown/Cream.

LIBERTON TRAVEL
See City of Edinburgh.

McKENDRY TRAVEL
100 STRAITON ROAD, LOANHEAD
EH20 9NP
Tel: 0131 440 1013
Fax: 0131 448 2160
E-mail: dmckendry@btconnect.com
Web site: www.mckendrycoaches.co.uk
Dir: Ann McKendry **Tran Man:** Stuart
McCaw.

Fleet: 15 - 1 double-deck bus, 12 single-deck coach, 2 minibus.
Chassis: 1 Dennis, 1 Ford Transit, 1 Freight Rover, 1 Leyland National, 4 Scania, 5 Volvo.
Bodies: 1 Caetano, 2 Jonckheere, 2 Plaxton, 5 Van Hool.
Ops incl: excursions & tours, private hire, school contracts.
Livery: White/Blue/Purple/Red vinyls.

MORAY

BLUEBIRD BUSES LTD
See Aberdeenshire.

CENTRAL COACHES
Ceased trading since LRB 2011 went to press.

MAYNES COACHES LTD
⬛⬛⬛⬛ R R24 ⬛ T
LINKWOOD WAY, ELGIN IV30 1XS
Tel: 01343 555227
Fax: 01542 833572
E-mail: info@maynes.co.uk
Web site: www.maynes.co.uk
Dirs: Gordon Mayne, David Mayne, Kevin Mayne.
Fleet (Elgin): 10 – 7 single-deck coach, 3 minicoach.
Chassis: 4 MAN, 2 Mercedes, 1 Renault, 2 Volvo.
Bodies: 2 Marcopolo, 1 Neoplan, 1 Optare, 2 Plaxton, 2 Van Hool, 2 Other.
Ops incl: local bus services, school contracts, excursions & tours, private hire.
Livery: Blue/White/Gold.
Ticket System: Setright.
Additional operations at Buckie and St Margaret's Hope – see Aberdeenshire, Orkney.

NORTH AYRSHIRE

CUMBRAE COACHES
⬛
14 MARINE PARADE, MILLPORT,
ISLE OF CUMBRAE KA28 0ED
Tel: 01475 530692
Web site: www.cumbraecoaches.co.uk
Prop: A G Wright.
Fleet: 3 single-deck bus.
Chassis: 3 Alexander Dennis.
Bodies: 3 Alexander Dennis.
Ops incl: local bus services, private hire.
Livery: Red/White.

MARBILL COACHES LTD
⬛⬛⬛⬛
HIGH MAINS GARAGE, MAINS ROAD,
BEITH KA15 2AP
Tel: 01505 503367
Fax: 01505 504736
E-mail: enquiries@marbillcoaches.com
Web site: www.marbillcoaches.com
Man Dir: Margaret Whiteman
Eng Dir: David Barr
Ops Dir: Connie Barr.
Fleet: 66 - 26 double-deck bus, 20 single-deck bus, 18 single-deck coach, 2 minicoach.
Chassis: 2 Bova, 34 Leyland, 2 Mercedes, 28 Volvo.
Bodies: 26 Alexander, 2 Bova, 25 Plaxton, 1 Sitcar, 12 Van Hool.
Ops incl: school contracts, excursions & tours, private hire.

MILLPORT MOTORS LTD
⬛
16 BUTE TERRACE, MILLPORT,
ISLE OF CUMBRAE KA28 0BA
Tel: 01475 530555
Fleet: 2 single-deck bus.
Chassis: 1 Dennis, 1 Volvo.
Bodies: 1 Caetano, 1 Wright.
Ops incl: local bus services, private hire.
Livery: Blue/White.
Ticket System: Almex.

SHUTTLE BUSES LTD
⬛⬛⬛
CALEDONIA HOUSE, LONGFORD
AVENUE, KILWINNING KA13 6EX
Tel: 01294 550757 **Fax:** 01294 558822
E-mail: enquiries@shuttlebuses.co.uk
Web site: www.shuttlebuses.co.uk
Man Dir: David Granger.
Fleet: 26 - 5 single-deck coach, 14 midibus, 4 midicoach, 3 minibus.
Chassis: 2 Dennis, 1 Ford Transit, 1 Leyland, 7 Mercedes, 5 Optare, 2 Renault, 6 Volkswagen, 2 Volvo.
Bodies: 1 Alexander Dennis, 1 Autobus, 4 Caetano, 2 Mercedes, 5 Optare, 3 Plaxton, 10 Other.
Ops incl: local bus services, school contracts, private hire.
Livery: Yellow/White.
Ticket System: Wayfarer TGX.

STAGECOACH WEST SCOTLAND
See South Ayrshire.

STEELE'S OF STEVENSTON
1 PORTLAND PLACE, STEVENSTON
KA20 3NN
Tel: 01294 463268 **Fax:** 01294 462007
E-mail: info@rbsteeles.co.uk
Web site: www.rbsteeles.co.uk
Fleet: single-deck coach, midicoach.
Ops incl: private hire, excursions & tours.
Liveries: Silver/Pink, White

NORTH LANARKSHIRE

A&C LUXURY COACHES
⬛⬛⬛⬛
4 HILLHEAD AVENUE, MOTHERWELL
ML1 4AQ
Tel: 01698 252652 **Fax:** 01698 259898
E-mail: enquiries@acluxurycoaches.co.uk
Web site: www.acluxurycoaches.co.uk
Prop: Alex Grenfell.
Fleet: 6 - 3 single-deck coach, 2 midicoach, 1 minicoach.
Chassis: 3 Mercedes, 1 Neoplan, 2 Volvo.
Bodies: 1 Neoplan, 1 Plaxton, 1 Van Hool.
Ops incl: school contracts, private hire, excursions & tours.

A TRIP IN TIME LTD
4 BRUCE STREET, COATBRIDGE ML5 2AL
Tel: 01236 622302
Prop: B Cutmore.
Ops incl: local bus services, school contracts.

BRUCE COACHES LTD
⬛⬛⬛⬛
40 MAIN STREET, SALSBURGH ML7 4LW
Tel: 01698 870909
Prop: J Bruce
Fleet: 14 single-deck coach

Chassis: Bova, Scania
Bodies: Bova, Caetano
Ops incl: express
Livery: National Express

CANAVAN'S COACHES
CEDAR LODGE, COACH ROAD, KILSYTH
G65 0DB
Tel: 01236 822414
Prop: M, G, H, & J Canavan.
Ops incl: local bus services.

DUNN'S COACHES LTD
⬛⬛⬛⬛⬛
560 STIRLING ROAD, AIRDRIE ML6 7SS
Tel: 01236 722385
Fax: 01236 722385
Prop: Craig Dunn.
Fleet: 11 - 4 single-deck bus, 7 single-deck coach.
Chassis: 2 Alexander Dennis, 2 Dennis, 1 Mercedes, 6 Volvo.
Bodies: 1 Jonckheere, 2 Plaxton, 1 Van Hool, 6 Volvo, 1 Wright.
Ops incl: local bus services, school contracts, excursions & tours, private hire, express.
Livery: White.
Ticket System: Wayfarer TGX.

ESSBEE COACHES (HIGHLANDS & ISLANDS) LTD
⬛⬛⬛⬛⬛
7 HOLLANDHURST ROAD, GARTSHERRIE
ML5 2EG
Tel: 01236 423621
Fax: 01236 433677
Man Dir: B Smith
Gen Man: J Kinnaird
Ops Man: S Stewart.
Fleet: single-deck bus, single-deck coach, double-deck coach, midicoach, minibus.
Ops incl: School contracts, excursions & tours, private hire.
Livery: Red/Silver.
Ticket System: Wayfarer.

FIRST GLASGOW
See Glasgow, City of

GOLDEN EAGLE COACHES
⬛⬛⬛⬛ T
MUIRHALL GARAGE, 197 MAIN STREET,
SALSBURGH, BY SHOTTS ML7 4LS
Tel: 01698 870207
Fax: 01698 870217
E-mail: info@goldeneaglecoaches.com
Web site: www.goldeneaglecoaches.com
Dirs: Peter Irvine, Robert Irvine, Ishbel Irvine.
Fleet: 22 - 8 double-deck bus, 14 single-deck coach.
Chassis: 1 Bova, 5 Dennis, 4 Leyland, 1 MCW, 11 Volvo.
Bodies: 2 Jonckheere, 1 MCW, 7 Van Hool, 12 Other.
Ops incl: school contracts, excursions & tours, private hire.
Livery: White, Gold & Maroon.

IRVINE'S OF LAW
⬛⬛⬛⬛ R24 ⬛
LAWMUIR ROAD, LAW ML8 5JB.
Tel: 01698 372452
Fax: 01698 376200
Web site: www.irvinescoaches.co.uk
Prop: Peter Irvine

Man: Gordon Graham
Ch Eng: Scott Fisher.
Fleet: 40 - 14 double-deck bus, 13coach, 13 midibus.
Chassis incl: DAF, Dennis, Optare, Scania, Volvo.
Bodies incl: Optare, Plaxton, Van Hool.
Ops incl: local bus services, excursions & tours, school contracts, private hire, express, continental tours.
Livery: Red/Cream.
Ticket System: Wayfarer.

LONG'S COACHES LTD
Ceased trading since LRB 2011 went to press.

MACKENZIE BUS & COACH SERVICES
149 WHITELEES ROAD, CUMBERNAULD G67 3JS
Tel: 01324 841878
Man Dir: Kirstine Mackenzie
Co Sec: Kenneth Mackenzie
Tran Man: Robert Mackenzie.
Fleet: 3 single-deck bus.
Chassis: 1 Dennis, 2 Mercedes.
Bodies: 2 Plaxton, 1 Wadham Stringer.
Ops incl: local bus services, school contracts.
Livery: Graphite Grey & Silver.
Ticket System: Wayfarer TGX 150.

MACPHAILS COACHES
40 MAIN STREET, SALSBURGH, BY SHOTTS ML7 4LW
Tel: 01698 870768
Fax: 01698 870826
E-mail: macphail7@aol.com
Web site: www.macphailscoaches.com
Dirs: Martin MacPhail, Henry MacPhail.
Fleet incl: single-deck coach, minibus.
Chassis incl: 8 Volvo.
Bodies incl: 1 Plaxton, 7 Van Hool.
Ops incl: excursions & tours, private hire, continental tours.

McCREADIE COACHES
53 MOTHERWELL STREET, AIRDRIE ML6 7HU
Tel: 01236 769666
Prop: L T McCreadie.
Ops incl: local bus services, school contracts, private hire.

McNAIRN'S COACHES
30 NORTHBURN ROAD, COATBRIDGE ML5 2HY
Tel: 01236 441188
Fax: 01236 422083
Prop: J McNairn.
Fleet: double-deck bus, single-deck coach, midibus.
Ops incl: local bus services, school contracts, private hire.
Livery: Cream.

M.C.T. GROUP TRAVEL LTD
NETHAN STREET DEPOT, NETHAN STREET, MOTHERWELL ML1 3TF
Tel: 01698 253091
Fax: 01698 259208
E-mail: enquiries@mctgrouptravel.com

Web site: www.mctgrouptravel.com
Man Dir: Desmond Heenan
Dir: Oswald Heenan.
Fleet: 14 - 4 single-deck bus, 6 single-deck coach, 4 midicoach.
Chassis: 1 Iveco, 3 MAN, 1 Mercedes, 4 Toyota, 5 Volvo.
Bodies: 1 Esker, 1 Indcar, 4 Jonckheere, 1 Optare, 7 Other.
Ops incl: school contracts, excursions & tours, private hire, continental tours.
Livery: Turquoise/Silver

MILLER'S COACHES
FASKINE BRAE, SIKESIDE ROAD, AIRDRIE ML6 9HR
Tel: 01236 763671
Owner: W Miller
Tran Man: T Miller.
Fleet: 12 - 8 single-deck coach, 4 minicoach
Chassis: 8 Leyland, 4 Mercedes.
Bodies: 2 Alexander, 1 Mellor, 8 Plaxton, 1 Reeve Burgess.
Ops incl: local bus services, school contracts, private hire.
Livery: Black/White/Grey.

SILVERDALE COACHES
FLOWERHILL INDUSTRIAL ESTATE, AIRDRIE ML6 6BH
Tel: 01236 765656
Prop: J Chapman.
Ops incl: local bus services, school contracts, private hire.
Livery: Red/White.

STEPEND COACHES
Ceased trading since LRB 2011 went to press.

WILLIAM STOKES & SONS LTD
Ceased trading since LRB 2011 went to press.

TRAMONTANA
CHAPELKNOWE ROAD, CARFIN, MOTHERWELL ML1 5LE
Tel: 01698 861790
Fax: 01698 860778
E-mail: wdt@tiscali.co.uk
Web site: www.brittnet.net/tramontanacoach
Prop: W D Telfer.
Fleet: 6 single-deck coach.
Chassis: 6 Volvo.
Bodies: 2 Berkhof, 2 Caetano, 2 Jonckheere.
Ops incl: private hire.
Livery: White.

WJC COACHES
26 BROWNSBURN INDUSTRIAL ESTATE, AIRDRIE ML6 9SE
Tel: 01236 268011
Web site: www.wjcbuses.co.uk
Prop: W J Carson
Fleet: double-deck bus, single-deck bus, single-deck coach.
Ops incl: local bus services, school contracts, private hire, express.

ORKNEY

M & J HARCUS
PIEROWALL, ISLE OF WESTRAY
Tel: 01857 677758
Ops incl: local bus service.

J & V COACHES
VART TUN, STROMNESS KW16 3LL
Tel: 01856 851425
Web site: www.jandvcoaches.co.uk
Ops incl: excursions & tours, private hire.

MAYNES COACHES LTD
ST MARGARETS HOPE KW17 2TG
Tel: 01856 831333
Fax: 01542 833572
Recovery: 07836 322200
E-mail: info@maynes.co.uk
Web site: www.maynes.co.uk
Dirs: Gordon Mayne, David Mayne, Kevin Mayne.
Fleet (Orkney): 7 – 5 single-deck coach, 2 minicoach.
Chassis: 2 MAN, 1 Mercedes, 1 Renault, 3 Volvo.
Bodies: 3 Berkhof, 2 Marcopolo, 1 Plaxton.
Ops incl: school contracts, excursions & tours, private hire.
Livery: Blue/White/Gold.
Ticket System: Setright.
Additional operations at Buckie and Elgin – see Aberdeenshire, Moray.

STAGECOACH IN ORKNEY
6 BURNETT ROAD, LONGMAN INDUSTRIAL ESTATE, INVERNESS IV1 1TF
Tel: 01463 233371
Fax: 01463 251360
E-mail: highland.enquiries@stagecoachbus.com
Web site: www.stagecoachbus.com
Gen Man: Monty Smillie.
Fleet (Orkney): 34 – 12 single-deck bus, 12 single-deck coach, 9 midibus, 1 minibus.
Chassis: 10 Optare, 24 Volvo.
Bodies: 11 Jonckheere, 10 Optare, 10 Plaxton, 3 Van Hool.
Ops incl: local bus services, school contracts, excursions & tours, private hire.
Livery: Stagecoach UK Bus.

PERTH & KINROSS

ABERFELDY MOTOR SERVICES
BURNSIDE GARAGE, ABERFELDY PH15 2DD
Tel: 01887 820433
Fax: 01887 829534
E-mail: aberfeldymotors@btconnect.com
Web site: www.aberfeldycoaches.co.uk
Prop: John Stewart **Co Sec:** Lynda Stewart
Ch Eng: David Matthew.
Fleet: 8 - 6 single-deck coach, 1 midicoach, 1 minicoach.
Chassis: 2 Bova, 2 Mercedes, 4 Volvo.
Bodies: 2 Bova, 1 Plaxton, 1 Sitcar, 3 Van Hool, 1 Other.
Ops incl: excursions & tours, private hire, continental tours, school contracts.
Livery: Blue.

CABER COACHES LTD
CHAPEL STREET GARAGE, ABERFELDY PH15 2AS
Tel: 01887 820090
Fax: 01887 829352
E-mail: cabercoaches@btinternet.com

Man Dir: Kenneth Carey **Sec:** Alexander Carey.
Fleet: 10 - 2 single-deck coach, 1 midibus, 2 midicoach, 5 minibus.
Chassis: 2 DAF, 3 Ford Transit, 2 LDV, 3 Mercedes.
Ops incl: local bus services, school contracts, private hire.
Livery: White.
Ticket system: Almex.

CRIEFF TRAVEL
Ceased operations since LRB 2011 went to press.

DOCHERTY'S MIDLAND COACHES
PRIORY PARK, AUCHTERARDER PH3 1GB
Tel: 01764 662218 **Fax:** 01764 664228
E-mail: info@dochertysmidlandcoaches.co.uk
Web site: www.dochertysmidlandcoaches.co.uk
Props: Jim & Edith Docherty, Colin Docherty, Neil Docherty, William Docherty.
Fleet: 31 - 6 single-deck bus, 10 single-deck coach, 8 midibus, 3 midicoach, 4 minicoach.
Chassis: 1 Bova, 1 Leyland, 11 Mercedes, 2 Optare, 1 Renault, 2 Scania, 13 Volvo.
Bodies: 3 Alexander Dennis, 1 Bova, 2 Irizar, 2 Jonckheere, 13 Plaxton, 2 UVG, 3 Van Hool, 2 Volvo, 3 Wright.
Ops incl: local bus services, school contracts, excursions & tours, private hire, express.
Livery: White/Black/Grey.
Ticket System: Almex.

EARNSIDE COACHES
GREENBANK ROAD, GLENFARG, PERTH PH2 9NW
Tel: 01577 830360 **Fax:** 01577 830599
E-mail: info@earnside.com.
Web site: www.earnside.com
Dirs: David Rutherford, Fiona Rutherford, Gary Rutherford.
Fleet: 10 - 8 single-deck coach, 1 minibus.
Chassis: 1 Ford Transit, 3 Neoplan, 6 Volvo.
Bodies: 1 Berkhof, 1 Ford, 1 Jonckheere, 3 Neoplan, 4 Plaxton.
Ops incl: local bus services, school contracts, excursions & tours, private hire, continental tours.
Livery: White.
Ticket system: Almex.

KINGSHOUSE TRAVEL
BALQUHIDDER, LOCHEARNHEAD FK19 8NY
Tel: 01877 384768
E-mail: travel@kingshouse-scotland.co.uk
Web site: www.kingshousetravel.co.uk
Fleet: single-deck coach, midibus, midicoach, minibus.
Chassis: Iveco, LDV, Mercedes, Renault, Volvo.
Ops incl: local bus services, school contracts, private hire, excursions & tours.
See also Aberfoyle Motors (Stirling).

MEGABUS
10 DUNKELD ROAD, PERTH PH1 5TW
Tel: 01738 522456
Web site: www.megabus.com
Ops incl: express.
Livery: Stagecoach UK Bus/Megabus Blue/Yellow.
Part of the Stagecoach Group.

SMITH & SONS COACHES
THE COACH DEPOT, WOODSIDE, COUPAR ANGUS, BLAIRGOWRIE PH13 9LW
Tel: 01828 626262
Fax: 01828 628518
Recovery: 01828 626262
E-mail: info@smithandsonscoaches.co.uk
Web site: www.smithandsonscoaches.co.uk
Partners: Ian F Smith, Gordon Smith, Kenneth F Smith.
Fleet: 28 – 7 single-deck bus, 13 single-deck coach, 4 midibus, 3 midicoach, 1 minibus.
Chassis: 3 Bova, 1 DAF, 2 Dennis, 1 LDV, 8 Mercedes, 4 Optare, 9 Volvo.
Bodies: 3 Bova, 4 Jonckheere, 5 Optare, 5 Plaxton, 2 Sitcar, 6 Van Hool, 3 Other.
Ops incl: local bus services, Perth Park & Ride, school contracts, private hire.
Liveries: Coaches: White with Orange; **Perth Park & Ride:** Blue.
Ticket System: Almex.

STAGECOACH SCOTLAND LTD
OFFICES 47-51, EVANS BUSINESS CENTRE, JOHN SMITH BUSINESS PARK, KIRKCALDY KY2 6HD
Tel: 01738 629339
Fax: 01738 643264
Recovery: 01738 629339
E-mail: eastscotland.enquiries@stagecoachbus.com
Web site: www.stagecoachbus.com
Fleet Name: Stagecoach in Perth.
Man Dir: Charlie Mullen **Ch Eng:** Jim Penrose **Ops Man:** Gus Beveridge **Depot Eng:** John Dick.
Fleet (Perth): 77 - 13 double-deck bus, 39 single-deck bus, 9 single-deck coach, 16 midibus.
Chassis: 13 Alexander Dennis, 4 Dennis, 19 MAN, 16 Optare, 25 Volvo.
Bodies: 24 Alexander Dennis, 18 Alexander, 7 East Lancs, 3 Northern Counties, 16 Optare, 9 Plaxton.
Ops incl: local bus services, tram services, school contracts, excursions & tours, private hire, express.
Livery: Stagecoach UK Bus/Megabus.
Ticket System: ERG.

ELIZABETH YULE
STATION GARAGE, STATION ROAD, PITLOCHRY PH16 5AN
Tel: 01796 472290 **Fax:** 01796 474214
E-mail: sandra.elizabeth-yule@btconnect.com
Web site: www.elizabethyulecoaches.co.uk
Partners: Elizabeth Yule, Sandra Bridges.
Fleet: 8 - 4 single-deck coach, 1 midibus, 2 midicoach, 1 minibus.
Chassis: 1 Ford, 3 Mercedes, 4 Volvo.
Ops incl: local bus services, school contracts, excursions & tours, private hire.
Livery: White.
Ticket System: Almex.

RENFREWSHIRE

ALAN ARNOTT
16 TURNHILL CRESCENT, WEST FREELANDS, ERSKINE PA8 7AX
Fleet Name: S & A Coaches, City Sprinter.

ARRIVA SCOTLAND WEST
GREENOCK ROAD, INCHINNAN, PAISLEY PA4 9PG
Tel: 08700 404343 **Fax:** 0141 561 4171
Web site: www.arrivabus.co.uk
Fleet Names: Arriva, SPT.
Regional Man Dir: Nigel Featham **Area Man Dir:** Richard Hall **Head of Ops:** Alistair McDougall.
Fleet: 185 - 8 double-deck bus, 169 single-deck bus, 2 single-deck coach, 3 midibus, 3 minibus.
Chassis: 5 DAF, 113 Dennis, 2 Leyland, 6 Mercedes, 1 Renault, 21 Scania, 21 VDL, 2 Volkswagen, 14 Volvo.
Bodies: 56 Alexander, 2 Bluebird, 15 East Lancs, 3 Mercedes, 1 Northern Counties, 69 Plaxton, 6 Scania, 2 Van Hool, 30 Wright, 1 Other.
Ops incl: local bus services, express.
Livery: Arriva UK Bus.

COLCHRI LTD
WESTWAYS BUSINESS PARK, PORTERFIELD ROAD, RENFREW PA4 8DJ
Tel: 0141 886 6093
Prop: Anthony Morrin.
Fleet: single-deck bus, midibus, minibus.
Ops incl: local bus services.

GIBSON DIRECT LTD
6 NEIL STREET, RENFREW PA4 8TA
Tel: 0141 886 7772
E-mail: enquiries@gibsondirectltd.com
Web site: www.gibsondirectltd.co.uk
Operations: local bus services, private hire, school contracts.
Livery: Blue/White.

VIOLET GRAHAM COACHES
Ceased operations since LRB 2011 went to press.

McGILLS BUS SERVICE LTD
3 MURIEL STREET, BARRHEAD G78 1QB
Tel: 01475 711122 **Fax:** 01475 711133
Web Site: www.mcgillsbuses.co.uk
Chairman: J Easdale **Man Dir:** R Roberts
Fin Dir: G Davidson **Gen Man:** B Hendry
Eng Dir: B Smith.
Ops incl: local bus services.
Livery: Blue/White.
See also Mc Gills Bus Service Ltd, Greenock (Inverclyde).

SHETLAND

ANDREW'S (SHETLAND) LTD
THE DYKES, WORMADALE, WHITENESS ZE2 9LJ
Tel: 01595 840292 **Fax:** 01595 840252
E-mail: andrews.adventures@virgin.net
Web site: www.andrewscoachhire.com
Man Dir: Morris H S Morrison
Dir: Andrew G S Morrison.
Fleet: 9 - 5 single-deck coach, 1 midibus, 1 midicoach, 1 minibus, 1 minicoach.
Chassis: 3 Mercedes, 1 Optare, 5 Volvo.
Ops incl: local bus services, school contracts, private hire, continental tours.
Livery: Red/White.
Ticket system: ERG.

The Little Red Book 2012 - in association with Transport Benevolent Fund

R G JAMIESON & SON

♿🚐❄

MOARFIELD GARAGE, CULLIVOE, YELL
ZE2 9DD
Tel: 01957 744214
Fax: 01957 744270
E-mail: rhjamieson@hotmail.com
Partner: Robert H Jamieson.
Fleet: 5 - 3 single-deck coach, 1 midicoach,
1 minibus.
Chassis: 1 Bedford, 1 Dennis, 1 Ford Transit,
2 Mercedes.
Bodies: 1 Beulas, 1 Duple, 1 Ford, 2 Plaxton.
Ops incl: local bus services, school contracts,
excursions & tours, private hire, continental
tours.
Livery: White/Blue (three shades).

JOHNSON TRANSPORT

WESTVALE, BRAE ZE2 9QG
Tel: 01806 522443
E-mail: enquiries@johnsontransport.co.uk
Web site: www.johnsontransport.co.uk
Prop: G Johnson.
Fleet: 9 - 2 single-deck coach, 2 midibus,
1 midicoach, 4 minibus.
Chassis: 1 Dennis, 2 Ford Transit, 2 Iveco,
3 Mercedes, 1 Volvo.
Ops incl: local bus services, school contracts.
Livery: Blue/White/Orange.

JOHN LEASK & SON

♿🚐❄

ESPLANADE, LERWICK ZE1 0LL
Tel: 01595 693162
Fax: 01595 693171
E-mail: info@leaskstravel.co.uk
Web site: www.leaskstravel.co.uk
Partners: Peter R Leask, Andrew J N Leask.
Fleet: 20 - 8 single-deck bus, 6 single-deck
coach, 1 midibus, 2 midicoach, 2 minibus,
1 minicoach.
Chassis: 1 Alexander Dennis, 8 DAF, 1 Iveco,
3 Mercedes, 1 Optare, 2 Temsa, 1 VDL,
1 Volkswagen, 2 Volvo.
Bodies: 1 Alexander Dennis, 3 Ikarus,
1 Mercedes, 1 Optare, 3 Plaxton, 1 Sitcar,
2 Temsa, 2 Van Hool, 4 Wright, 2 Other.
Ops incl: local bus services, school contracts,
private hire.
Livery: Ivory/Blue.
Ticket system: ERG.

WHITES COACHES

♿

ENGAMOOR, WEST BURRAFIRTH,
BRIDGE OF WALLS, ZE2 9NT
Tel: 01595 809433
E-mail: john@engamoo-shetland.co.uk
Partner: John White.
Fleet: 5 - 1 single-deck bus, 2 midibus,
1 midicoach, 1 minibus.
Chassis: 1 Ford Transit, 3 Mercedes, 1 Scania.
Ops incl: local bus services, school contracts,
private hire.
Livery: White/Yellow/Black.

DODDS OF TROON LTD

🚐📶❄T

4 EAST ROAD, AYR KA8 9BA
Tel: 01292 288100
Fax: 01292 287700
E-mail: info@doddsoftroon.com

Web site: www.doddsoftroon.com
Man Dir: James Dodds **Ops Dir:** Douglas
Dodds **Admin Dir:** Norma Dodds.
Fleet: 23 - 20 single-deck coach, 3 midicoach.
Chassis: 4 Leyland, 3 Toyota, 16 Volvo.
Bodies: 4 Alexander Dennis, 3 Caetano,
6 Jonckheere, 2 Plaxton, 6 Van Hool, 2 Volvo.
Ops incl: school contracts, excursions &
tours, private hire.
Livery: Green/Cream.

IBT TRAVEL GROUP

CAIRN HOUSE, 15 SKYE ROAD,
PRESTWICK KA9 2TA
Tel: 01292 477771
Fax: 01292 471770
E-mail: briant@ibtravel.com
Partner: Ian Black.
Fleet: 3 single-deck coach.
Chassis: 3 Volvo.
Bodies: 3 Van Hool.
Ops incl: continental tours, private hire.
Livery: Blue/Gold flash.

KEENAN OF AYR COACH TRAVEL

🚐📶📶📶

DARWIN GARAGE, COALHALL, BY AYR
KA6 6ND
Tel: 01292 591252
Fax: 01292 590980
Web site: www.keenancoaches.co.uk
Dirs: Tony Keenan, Jamie Keenan.
Fleet: 20 - 2 double-deck bus, 6 single-deck
bus, 10 single-deck coach, 1 midibus,
1 midicoach.
Chassis incl: 8 Leyland, 8 Volvo.
Bodies: 8 Alexander, 4 Duple, 2 Plaxton,
6 Van Hool.
Ops incl: school contracts, excursions &
tours, private hire.
Livery: Red/Yellow/Orange/White.

MILLIGAN'S COACH TRAVEL LTD

🚐📶📶❄R📶T

LOAN GARAGE, 20 THE LOAN,
MAUCHLINE, KA5 6AN
Tel/Recovery: 01290 550365.
Fax: 01290 553291.
E-mail: enquiries@milliganscoachtravel.co.uk
Web site: www.milliganscoachtravel.co.uk
Dir: William J Milligan.
Fleet: 20 - 18 single-deck coach, 1 midicoach,
1 minibus.
Chassis: 5 Bova, 1 DAF, 1 Ford Transit,
2 Leyland, 2 MAN, 3 Scania, 6 Volvo.
Ops incl: school contracts, excursions &
tours, private hire.
Livery: Black and Silver.

STAGECOACH WEST SCOTLAND

♿🚐📶📶📶❄T

SANDGATE, AYR KA7 1DD
Tel: 01292 613700
Fax: 01292 613501
Web site: www.stagecoachbus.com
Man Dir: Bryony Chamberlain
Ops Dir: Rob Jones **Eng Dir:** John Harper.
Fleet: 396 - 70 double-deck bus, 191 single-
deck bus, 18 double-deck coach, 63 single-
deck coach, 6 articulated bus, 43 midibus,
5 minibus.
Chassis: 30 Alexander Dennis, 49 Dennis,
15 Leyland, 84 MAN, 5 Mercedes, 18 Neoplan,
54 Optare, 27 Scania, 115 Volvo.
Ops incl: local bus services, school contracts,

private hire, express.
Livery: Stagecoach UK Bus.
Ticket System: ERG.

ALFRA COACH HIRE

26 MACHAN ROAD, LARKHALL ML9 1HG
Tel: 01698 887581
Prop: F Russell.
Fleet: 4 minibus.
Chassis: 2 Ford Transit, 1 Freight Rover,
1 Leyland.
Ops incl: private hire.
Livery: White.

R. & C. S. CRAIG

TOWNFOOT, ROBERTON, BY BIGGAR
ML12 6RS
Tel: 01899 850655
Dirs: R Craig, C S Craig **Traf Man/Ch Eng:**
J Harvie **Gen Man:** R Craig.
Fleet: 3 - 2 minibus, 1 minicoach.
Chassis: Freight Rover.
Ops incl: school contracts, private hire.
Livery: White.

FIRST GLASGOW

See City of Glasgow.

HENDERSON TRAVEL

♿🚐

UNIT 4, WHISTLEBERRY PARK,
HAMILTON ML3 0ED
Tel: 01698 710102
Fax: 01698 719110
E-mail: admin@htbuses.com
Web site: www.henderson-travel.co.uk
Ops incl: local bus services, school contracts.
Liveries: Blue/White, SPT.

PARK'S OF HAMILTON (COACH HIRERS) LTD

📶📶❄R24📶T

14 BOTHWELL ROAD, HAMILTON ML3 0AY
Tel: 01698 281222
Fax: 01698 303731
Web site: www.parksofhamilton.co.uk
Chairman: Douglas Park **Ch Eng:** Malcolm
Fisher **Co Sec/Dir:** Gerry Donnachie **Ops
Man:** Michael Andrews **Dir:** Hugh McAteer.
Fleet: 100 - incl: single-deck coach, double-
deck coach.
Chassis incl: Iveco, Neoplan, Volvo.
Bodies incl: Beulas, Jonckheere, Neoplan,
Plaxton, Van Hool.
Ops incl: local bus services, school contracts,
excursions & tours, private hire, express,
continental tours.
Livery: Black.
Ticket System: Wayfarer.

SILVER CHOICE

📶🚐❄R24📶T

1 MILTON ROAD, EAST KILBRIDE G74 5BU
Tel: 01355 249499
Fax: 01355 265111
Recovery: 07966 315360
E-mail: enquiries@silverchoicetravel.co.uk
Web site: www.silverchoice.co.uk
Dir: David W Gardiner **Ch Eng:** Jim Beaton.
Fleet: 12 - 10 single-deck coach, 1 double-
deck coach, 1 midicoach.
Chassis: 5 Bova, 1 Iveco, 1 Mercedes,
1 Scania, 4 Volvo.

Scottish Operators

Bodies: 1 Beulas, 5 Bova, 3 Plaxton, 3 Van Hool.
Ops incl: school contracts, excursions & tours, private hire, continental tours.
Livery: Silver.

WILLIAM STOKES & SONS LTD
Ceased operations since LRB 2011 went to press.

STONEHOUSE COACHES LTD
48 NEW STREET, STONEHOUSE ML9 3LT.
Tel: 01698 792145
Fax: 01698 793220
Fax: Prop: N Collison.
Ops incl: local bus services, school contracts, private hire.
Livery: White/Pink/Navy.

STUART'S COACHES LTD
CASTLEHILL GARAGE, AIRDRIE ROAD, CARLUKE ML8 5UF
Tel: 01555 773533   **Fax:** 01555 752220
E-mail: stuartscarluke@btconnect.com
Web site: www.stuarts-coaches.com.
Prop: Stuart A Shevill.
Fleet: 58 - 7 double-deck bus, 25 single-deck coach, 10 midibus, 15 midicoach, 1 minibus.
Ops incl: local bus services, school contracts, private hire, express.
Livery: Silver/Blue.
Ticket system: Almex.

THE RURAL DEVELOPMENT TRUST
1 POWELL STREET, DOUGLAS WATER ML11 9PP
Tel: 01555 880551
E-mail: mail@ruraldevtrust.co.uk.
Web site: www.ruraldevtrust.co.uk
Man Dir: Gordon Muir.
Fleet: 10 - 1 midibus, 3 midicoach, 6 minicoach.
Chassis: 7 Mercedes, 1 Optare, 1 Toyota, 1 Other.
Bodies: 1 Caetano, 6 Mercedes, 1 Optare, 1 Plaxton, 1 Other.
Ops incl: local bus services, school contracts, private hire.

WHITELAWS COACHES
LOCHPARK INDUSTRIAL ESTATE, STONEHOUSE ML9 3LR
Tel: 01698 792800
Fax: 01698 793309
E-mail: enquiries@whitelaws.co.uk
Web site: www.whitelaws.co.uk
Man Dir/Co Sec: Sandra Whitelaw Ginestri
Dir: George Whitelaw
Ops Man: Lindsay McGowan
Ch Eng: Donald McGowan.
Fleet: 38 - 16 single-deck bus, 11 single-deck coach, 11 midibus.
Chassis: 3 Alexander Dennis, 1 Iveco, 3 Leyland, 17 MAN, 14 Volvo.
Bodies: 6 Alexander Dennis, 9 Marshall/MCV, 2 Plaxton, 4 Van Hool, 5 Volvo, 12 Wright.
Ops incl: local bus services, school contracts, excursions & tours, private hire, continental tours.
Livery: Silver with Red/White/Blue.
Ticket System: Wayfarer TGX 150.

STIRLING

ABERFOYLE COACHES LTD
MAIN STREET, ABERFOYLE FK8 3UG
Tel: 0844 567 5670
Fax: 01877 382998
E-mail: sales@aberfoylecoaches.com
Web site: www.aberfoylecoaches.com
Fleet: 7 - 1 single-deck bus, 3 single-deck coach, 2 midicoach, 1 minibus.
Chassis: Alexander Dennis, Iveco, MAN, Mercedes, Volvo.
Ops incl: local bus services, excursions & tours, private hire.
Livery: White.
A subsidiary of Kingshouse Travel (see Perth & Kinross).

BILLY DAVIES EXECUTIVE COACHES
TRANSPORT HOUSE, PLEAN INDUSTRIAL ESTATE, PLEAN, STIRLING FK7 8BJ
Tel: 01786 816627
Fax: 01786 811433
Web site: www.daviescoaches.com

E-mail: billy@daviescoaches.com
Prop: Michelle Davies.
Fleet: 12 - 4 double-deck bus, 5 single-deck coach, 1 midicoach, 1 minibus, 1 minicoach.
Chassis: 1 Alexander Dennis, 1 Ayats, 2 Bova, 1 Iveco, 4 Leyland, 1 Mercedes.
Bodies incl: 1 Alexander Dennis, 1 Ayats, 1 Beulas, 2 Bova, 1 Mercedes, 1 Plaxton, 1 Van Hool.
Ops incl: local bus services, school contracts, private hire.
Livery: Blue.
Ticket system: Wayfarer.

BRYANS COACHES LTD
WHITEHILL FARM, DENNY FK6 5NA
Tel: 01324 824146
E-mail: info@bryanscoaches.com
Web site: www.bryanscoaches.com
Fleet: 13 – 3 single-deck bus, 6 single-deck coach, 1 midibus, 1 midicoach, 2 minibus.
Chassis: Alexander Dennis, Bova, DAF, Dennis, LDV, Mercedes, Volvo.
Ops incl: local bus services, school contracts, private hire, excursions & tours.

FERGUSON MINIBUS HIRE
33 SPEY COURT, BRAEHEAD, STIRLING FK7 7QZ
Tel/Fax: 01786 461538
E-mail: john.ferguson2@virgin.net
Ops incl: local bus services, private hire, excursions & tours.
Livery: White/Blue.

FIRST SCOTLAND EAST LTD
CARMUIRS HOUSE, 300 STIRLING ROAD, LARBERT FK5 3NJ
Tel: 01324 602200
Fax: 01324 611287
E-mail: contact.scotlandeast@firstgroup.com
Web site: www.firstgroup.com/scotlandeast
Fleet Names: First Scotland East, Midland Bluebird.
Man Dir: Paul A Thomas
Ops Dir: John Gorman .
Fleet: 447 – 159 double-deck bus, 200 single-deck bus, 19 single-deck coach, 66 midibus, 3 minibus.
Chassis: 59 Alexander Dennis, 3 Leyland, 10 Mercedes, 7 Optare, 167 Scania, 199 Volvo.
Bodies: 85 Alexander Dennis, 21 East Lancs, 12 Marshall/MCV, 4 Mercedes, 15 Northern Counties, 10 Optare, 80 Plaxton, 218 Wright.
Ops incl: local bus services, school contracts, private hire, express.
Livery: FirstGroup UK Bus.
Ticket System: Almex.

FITZCHARLES COACHES LTD
87 NEWHOUSE ROAD, GRANGEMOUTH FK3 8NJ
Tel: 01324 482093
Fax: 01324 665411
E-mail: info@fitzcharles.co.uk
Web site: www.fitzcharles.co.uk
Man Dir: Ronnie Fitzcharles
Dir/Sec: Olive King **Accts & Training:** David Fitzcharles
Transport Man: Allan Dick.
Fleet: 16 - 15 single-deck coach, 1 minibus.
Chassis: 2 DAF, 1 Mercedes, 13 Volvo.

Bodies: 2 Ayats, 4 Caetano, 6 Plaxton, 4 Sunsundegui.
Ops incl: local bus services, school contracts, excursions & tours, private hire, express, continental tours.
Livery: Red/Cream.
Ticket System: ERG TP5000.

HARLEQUIN COACHES LTD
Ceased operations since LRB 2011 went to press.

MACKENZIE BUS & COACH SERVICES
149 WHITELEES ROAD, CUMBERNAULD G67 3JS
Tel: 01324 841878
Man Dir: Kirstine Mackenzie
Co Sec: Kenneth Mackenzie
Tran Man: Robert Mackenzie.
Fleet: 3 single-deck bus.
Chassis: 1 Dennis, 2 Mercedes.
Bodies: 2 Plaxton, 1 Wadham Stringer.
Ops incl: local bus services, school contracts.
Livery: Graphite Grey & Silver.
Ticket System: Wayfarer TGX 150.

MITCHELL'S COACHES
PRESIDENT KENNEDY DRIVE, PLEAN FK7 8AY
Tel: 01786 814319
Fax: 01786 814165
E-mail: mitchellscoaches@btconnect.com
Fleet: 12 – 1 double-deck bus, 4 single-deck coach, 5 midibus, 1 midicoach, 1 minibus.
Chassis: Dennis, Ford Transit, Iveco, Mercedes, Scania, Volvo.
Ops incl: local bus services.
Livery: White.

MYLES COACHES
PLEAN INDUSTRIAL ESTATE, PLEAN FK7 8BJ
Tel: 01786 817128
E-mail: enquiries@mylescoaches.com
Web site: www.mylescoaches.com
Ops incl: local bus services, private hire.
Livery: White.

WEST DUNBARTONSHIRE

LOCHS AND GLENS HOLIDAYS
SCHOOL ROAD, GARTOCHARN G83 8RW
Tel: 01389 713713
E-mail: enquiries@lochsandglens.com
Web site: www.lochsandglens.com
Tran Man: Brian Nichols.
Fleet: 16 single-deck coach.
Chassis: 16 Volvo.
Bodies: 11 Jonckheere, 5 Van Hool.
Ops incl: excursions & tours,
Livery: White with blue letters,

McCOLL'S COACHES LTD
BALLAGAN DEPOT, STIRLING ROAD, BALLOCH G83 0IY
Tel: 01389 754321
Fax: 01389 755354
E-mail: mccolls@btconnect.com
Web site: www.mccolls.org.uk
Man Dir: William McColl

Dirs: Thomas McColl, Janet McColl
Co Sec: Ann McKinlay
Ops Man: Liam McColl
Head Mechanic: Eddie McKinley,
Fleet: double-deck bus, single-deck bus, coach, minibus.
Chassis: DAF, Dennis, Ford, Ford Transit, Leyland, MCW, Mercedes, Volvo.
Bodies: MCW, Mercedes, Other.
Ops incl: local bus services, school contracts, excursions & tours, private hire

WEST LOTHIAN

LES BROWN TRAVEL
UNIT 3, BLOCK 12, WHITESIDE INDUSTRIAL ESTATE, BATHGATE EH48 2RX
Tel: 01506 656129   **Fax:** 01506 656129
E-mail: les-brown@btconnect.com
Web site: www.lesbrowntravel.com
Props: Les Brown, Colin Brown,
Fleet: 8 - 2 midicoach, 6 minicoach.
Chassis: 5 Ford Transit, 3 Mercedes.
Ops incl: school contracts, excursions & tours, private hire.
Livery: White with Blue, Red.

BROWNINGS (WHITBURN) LTD
22 LONGRIDGE ROAD, WHITBURN EH47 0DE
Tel: 01501 740234   **Fax:** 01501 741265
E-mail:
george@browningscoaches.fsnet.co.uk
Web site: www.browningscoaches.co.uk
Dirs: George Browning, Eric Browning, Gary Knox.
Fleet: 15 - 3 double-deck bus, 12 single-deck coach.
Chassis: 3 Alexander Dennis, 3 Leyland, 9 Volvo.
Bodies: 2 Berkhof, 1 ECW, 2 Plaxton, 5 Van Hool, 3 Wadham Stringer.
Ops incl: private hire, school contracts.
Livery: Red/White/Blue.

DAVIDSON BUSES LTD
YARD 3, INCHCROSS INDUSTRIAL ESTATE, BATHGATE EH48 2HS
Tel: 01506 870226
Web Site: www.davidson-buses.com
Man Dir: Ian Davidson **Dir:** Francis Gartland.
Ops incl: local bus services.

FIRST SCOTLAND EAST LTD
See Falkirk/Stirling.

E & M HORSBURGH LTD
180 UPHALL STATION ROAD, PUMPHERSTON EH53 0PD
Tel: 01506 432251
Fax: 01506 438066
E-mail: horsburgh@btconnect.com
Web site: www.horsburghcoaches.com
Dirs: Eric Horsburgh, Mark Horsburgh **Gen Man:** Ronnie Nicol **Ch Eng:** Brian Martin.
Fleet: 76 - 26 double-deck bus, 8 single-deck bus, 4 single-deck coach, 34 midibus, 4 midicoach, 16 minibus, 4 minicoach.
Chassis: 16 Alexander Dennis, 10 LDV, 10 Leyland, 2 MAN, 12 Mercedes, 10 Optare, 4 Scania, 12 Volvo.

Bodies: 16 Alexander Dennis, 6 ECW, 2 Irizar, 10 LDV, 2 MCW, 1 Mellor, 12 Mercedes, 6 Northern Counties, 10 Optare, 3 Plaxton, 2 Van Hool.
Ops incl: local bus services, school contracts, excursions & tours, private hire.
Livery: White/Yellow.
Ticket System: Almex.

McKECHNIE OF BATHGATE LTD
2 EASTON ROAD, BATHGATE EH48 2QG
Tel: 01506 654337 **Fax:** 01506 654337
E-mail: pmkcoach@aol.com
Dir: Peter McKechnie **Co Sec:** Catherine McKechnie.
Fleet: 8 - 4 single-deck coach, 2 midicoach, 2 minicoach
Chassis: 1 Leyland, 4 Mercedes, 3 Volvo.
Ops incl: school contracts, private hire.

MARTIN'S COACH TRAVEL
1 SUMMERVILLE COURT, UPHALL STATION, LIVINGSTON EH54 5QG
Tel: 01506 435968. **Fax:** 01506 435968.
E-mail: martcoach@aol.com
Web site: www.martincoaches.co.uk
Prop: Tony Martin.
Fleet: 4 - 3 single-deck coach, 1 midicoach.
Chassis: 1 Iveco, 1 Scania, 1 Toyota, 1 Volvo.
Bodies: 1 Beulas, 1 Caetano, 1 Irizar, 1 Other.
Ops incl: school contracts, excursions & tours, private hire.
Livery: White.

PRENTICE WESTWOOD LTD
WESTWOOD, WEST CALDER EH55 8PW
Tel/Recovery: 01506 871231
Fax: 01506 871734
E-mail:
sales@prenticewestwoodcoaches.co.uk
Web site:
www.prenticewestwoodcoaches.co.uk
Dirs: Robbie Prentice, David Cowen
Ops Mans: Jock Johnston, David Reid.
Fleet: 51 - 9 double-deck bus, 30 single-deck coach, 4 double-deck coach, 5 midibus, 3 midicoach.
Chassis: 10 Bova, 2 DAF, 6 Leyland, 3 MAN, 4 Mercedes, 4 Optare, 1 Scania, 21 Volvo.
Bodies: 5 Alexander Dennis, 3 Berkhof, 1 Beulas, 10 Bova, 2 ECW, 1 East Lancs, 1 Ikarus, 5 Jonckheere, 1 Northern Counties, 4 Optare, 13 Plaxton, 1 Sitcar, 1 Unvi, 3 Van Hool.
Ops incl: local bus services, school contracts, excursions & tours, private hire, continental tours.
Livery: Red/White/Blue.
Ticket System: Almex.

WESTERN ISLES

COMHAIRLE NAN EILEAN SIAR
BUS COMHAIRLE, SANDWICK ROAD, STORNOWAY, ISLE OF LEWIS HS1 2BW
Tel: 01851 709728 **Fax:** 01851 709750
Head of Service: Donald Stuart
Fleet Man: Donald Stewart
Fleet Eng: Neil McLeod.
E-mail: bus@cne-siar.gov.uk

Web site: www.cne-siar.gov.uk
Fleet Name: bus na comhairle
Fleet: 19 – 1 single-deck bus, 8 single-deck coach, 9 midibus, 1 midicoach.
Chassis: 8 Dennis, 10 Mercedes, 1 VDL.
Ops incl: local bus services, school contracts, private hire.
Livery: White/Yellow stripe.

GALSON-STORNOWAY MOTOR SERVICES LTD

1 LOWER BARVAS, ISLE OF LEWIS
HS2 0QZ
Tel: 01851 840269 **Fax:** 01851 840445
E-mail: galson@sol.co.uk
Dir: I Morrison
Ops Man: I Morrison.
Fleet: 13 - 7 single-deck coach, 2 midibus, 1 midicoach, 3 minibus.
Chassis: 3 Ford Transit, 3 Mercedes, 7 Volvo.
Bodies: 7 Plaxton, 3 Van Hool, 3 Other.
Ops incl: local bus services, school contracts, excursions & tours, private hire.
Livery: White/Yellow/Brown.
Ticket System: ERG.

HEBRIDEAN COACHES

HOWMORE, SOUTH UIST HS8 5SH
Tel: 01870 620345 **Fax:** 01870 620301
Recovery: 01870 620345
E-mail: heboc@hebrides.net
Partner: D A MacDonald.
Fleet: 11 - 3 single-deck coach, 3 midicoach, 5 minibus.
Chassis: 3 Dennis, 3 Ford Transit, 2 LDV, 3 Mercedes.
Bodies: 2 Ford, 1 Mellor, 1 LDV, 4 Plaxton, 3 Other.
Ops incl: local bus services, school contracts, excursions & tours, private hire.
Livery: Cream/Green.
Ticket System: Almex.

LOCHS MOTOR TRANSPORT LTD

CAMERON TERRACE, LEURBOST, LOCHS, ISLE OF LEWIS HS2 9PE
Tel: 01851 860288 **Fax:** 01851 705857
Dirs: C MacDonald, R MacDonald, S MacDonald, A MacDonald
Ch Eng: I MacKinnon.
Fleet: 6 – 1 single-deck bus, 5 single-deck coach.
Chassis: 1 Alexander Dennis, 5 Volvo.
Bodies: 1 Alexander Dennis, 5 Plaxton.
Ops incl: local bus services, school contracts, private hire.
Livery: Blue/Cream.

NOTES

ANGLESEY

ARRIVA BUSES WALES
See Conwy

CARREGLEFN COACHES
CARREGLEFN GARAGE, AMLWCH LL68 0PR
Tel: 01407 710139
Fax: 01407 710217
Prop: Alun Lewis
Fleet: 11 - 1 single-deck bus, 7 single-deck coach, 3 minicoach.
Chassis: 1 MAN, 2 Toyota, 8 Volvo.
Bodies: 4 Caetano, 1 Duple, 5 Plaxton.
Ops incl: local bus services, school contracts, excursions & tours, private hire.
Livery: Blue/Cream

EIFION'S COACHES LTD
MONA INDUSTRIAL PARK, GWALCHMAI LL65 4RJ
Tel: 01407 721111
Fax: 01407 721122
E-mail: mail@eifionscoaches.co.uk
Web site: www.eifionscoaches.co.uk
Ops incl: local bus services, school contracts, private hire, excursions & tours.
Livery: White with Red/Green/Yellow logos.

W C GOODSIR
THE GARAGE, CROSS STREET, HOLYHEAD LL65 1EG
Tel: 01407 764340
Ops incl: local bus services, school contracts, private hire.
Livery: White/Black/Yellow/Orange.

GWYNFOR COACHES
Tel: 01248 722694
Prop: H Hughes.
Fleet: 8 – 5 single-deck coach, 2 midicoach, 1 minibus.
Chassis: 1 DAF, 2 Mercedes, 1 Toyota, 4 Volvo.
Ops incl: local bus services, school contracts, private hire.

HDA TRAVEL LTD
GILFACH, LON GOES, GAERWEN LL60 6DE
Tel: 01248 421476
Prop: H D Ashton.
Fleet: 2 midibus.
Chassis: 1 Mercedes, 1 Optare.
Ops incl: local bus services.

O R JONES & SONS LTD
THE BUS & COACH DEPOT, LLANFAETHLU, HOLYHEAD LL65 4NW
Tel: 01407 730204
Fax: 01407 730083
Recovery: 01407 730759
E-Mail: ioj.orj@hotmail.co.uk
Ops Man: Iolo O Jones **Tran Man:** Maldwyn O Jones.
Fleet: 22 - 2 double-deck bus, 6 single-deck bus, 6 single-deck coach, 3 midibus, 1 midicoach, 1 minibus, 2 minicoach, 1 vintage.
Chassis: 1 Bedford, 2 Bova, 2 Bristol, 9 DAF, 1 Enterprise, 1 Iveco, 1 MAN, 4 Mercedes, 1 Scania.

Bodies: 2 Bova, 1 Caetano, 1 Duple, 1 East Lancs, 2 ECW, 2 Ikarus, 1 Irizar, 4 Optare, 2 Plaxton, 1 Unvi, 2 Van Hool, 3 Other.
Ops incl: local bus services, school contracts, excursions & tours, private hire.
Livery: Silver.
Ticket system: Wayfarer.

W E JONES & SON
THE GARAGE, LLANERCHYMEDD LL71 8EB
Tel: 01248 470228
Fax: 01248 852893
Props: Gwilym Evans Jones, Wyn Evans Jones.
Fleet: 11 - 1 double-deck bus, 5 single-deck bus, 3 single-deck coach, 2 midibus.
Chassis: 2 DAF, 3 Dennis, 1 Iveco, 1 MCW, 2 Mercedes, 2 Volvo.
Bodies: 1 Alexander, 1 Carlyle, 1 Duple, 1 Marshall, 1 MCW, 2 Optare, 4 Plaxton.
Ops incl: local bus services, school contracts, private hire.
Livery: Red/White.

LEWIS-Y-LLAN
MADYN INDUSTRIAL ESTATE, AMLWCH LL68 9DL
Tel: 01407 832181
Fax: 01407 830112
Props: A H Lewis, R M Lewis.
Fleet: 12 - 3 double-deck bus, 1 single-deck coach, 8 midibus.
Chassis: 4 Dennis, 1 Leyland, 1 MCW, 3 Mercedes, 3 Optare.
Bodies: 1 East Lancs, 1 ECW, 1 Marshall, 1 MCW, 3 Optare, 5 Plaxton.
Livery: White/Blue.

BLAENAU GWENT

GARY'S COACHES OF TREDEGAR
42 COMMERCIAL STREET, TREDEGAR NP22 3DJ
Tel: 01495 726500
Fax: 01495 726400
Recovery: 01495 723264
E-mail: sales@garys-coaches.co.uk
Web site: www.garys-coaches.co.uk
Props: Mr & Mrs G A Lane
Ops Man: D Williams **Ch Eng:** G Cresswell.
Fleet: 14 - 12 single-deck coach, 1 midicoach, 1 midibus.
Chassis: 2 DAF, 1 Dennis, 1 Leyland, 2 Mercedes, 8 Volvo.
Bodies: 1 Bova, 4 Duple, 2 Mercedes, 5 Plaxton, 2 Van Hool.
Ops incl: excursions & tours, private hire, school contracts, continental tours.
Livery: White/Blue.

HENLEYS BUS SERVICES LTD
HENLEYS COACH GARAGE, VICTOR ROAD, CWMTILLERY, ABERTILLERY NP13 1HU
Tel: 01495 212288 **Fax:** 01495 320720
E-mail: admin@henleys.org.uk
Web site: www.henleysbusservicesltd.co.uk
Dir: Martin Henley **Head Mech:** Michael Henley **Sec:** Daphne Henley.
Fleet: 10 – 1 single-deck bus, 5 single-deck coach, 3 midibus, 1 minicoach.
Chassis: 2 Leyland, 4 Mercedes, 1 Optare, 1 Setra, 2 Volvo.

Bodies: 1 Duple, 2 Jonckheere, 1 Leicester, 1 Mercedes, 1 Optare, 3 Plaxton, 1 Setra.
Ops incl: local bus services, school contracts, excursions & tours, private hire.
Livery: White/Orange/Green.
Ticket system: Wayfarer.

STAGECOACH IN SOUTH WALES
See Torfaen

BRIDGEND

R & D BURROWS LTD
Ceased operations since LRB 2011 went to press.

CRESTA COACHES
UNIT 6, LITCHARD INDUSTRIAL ESTATE, BRIDGEND CF31 2AL
Tel: 01656 660366
Fax: 01656 660566
E-mail: bookings@crestacoaches.co.uk
Web site: www.crestacoaches.co.uk
Fleet: 13 – 8 single-deck coach, 4 midicoach, 1 minicoach.
Chassis: 1 Dennis, 1 MAN, 5 Mercedes, 6 Volvo.
Bodies: 1 Marcopolo, 1 Noge, 5 Plaxton, 1 Sitcar, 1 Van Hool, 4 Other.
Ops incl: school contracts, excursions & tours, private hire.
Livery: White with Red/Yellow/Blue.

EASYWAY MINI COACH HIRE LTD
KENT ROAD, BRIDGEND INDUSTRIAL ESTATE, BRIDGEND CF31 3TU
Tel: 01656 655655
Fax: 01656 647777
E-mail: easywayminibus@aol.com
Web site: www.easywayminicoachhire.co.uk
Dir: R A Morris.
Ops incl: local bus services.

EXPRESS MOTORS
37 COMMERCIAL STREET, KENFIG HILL CF33 6DH
Tel: 01656 740323
Prop: D V Evans.
Fleet: 10 single-deck coach.

FIRST CYMRU BUSES LTD
See City & County of Swansea

G M COACHES LTD
MOUNTAIN VIEW GARAGE, TY FRY ROAD, CEFN GRIBWR, BRIDGEND CF32 0BB
Tel: 01656 740262
A subsidiary of EST Bus - see Vale of Glamorgan.

GWYN JONES & SON LTD
WHITECROFT GARAGE, BRYNCETHIN CF32 9YR
Tel: 01656 720300 **Fax:** 01656 725632
Recovery: 01656 720182
Chair: John Gwyn Jones **Dir:** Miriam J Jones.
Fleet: 22 single-deck coach.
Chassis: 1 Dennis, 1 Leyland, 2 MAN, 3 Mercedes, 4 Scania, 2 Setra, 9 Volvo.
Bodies: 4 Berkhof, 1 Irizar, 4 Jonckheere, 2 Marcopolo, 1 Mercedes, 4 Plaxton, 2 Setra, 4 Van Hool.
Ops incl: excursions & tours, private hire, continental tours, school contracts.
Livery: White/Gold/Maroon.

LLYNFI COACHES
♿ 🧷 ♿♿ ❄ ⚒ T

UNIT 7-9, HEOL TY GWYN INDUSTRIAL ESTATE, MAESTEG CF34 0BQ
Tel: 01656 739928
Fax: 01656 727858
Props: David Stolzenberg, Liam Morgan.
Fleet: 11 – 1 single-deck bus, 7 single-deck coach, 1 midibus, 1 midicoach, 1 minibus.
Chassis: 4 Autosan, 1 DAF, 1 Iveco, 1 King Long, 1 MAN, 1 Mercedes, 1 Optare, 1 Scania, 1 Volvo.
Bodies: 4 BMC, 1 Irizar, 1 King Long, 1 Noge, 1 Optare, 2 Plaxton, 1 Other.
Ops incl: local bus services, school contracts, excursions & tours, private hire.
Livery: Yellow or White.

PENCOED TRAVEL LTD
♿♿ 🧷 ❄ ⚒

18 CAER BERLLAN, PENCOED CF35 6RR
Tel: 01656 860200 **Fax:** 01656 864793
E-mail: info@pencoedtravel.co.uk
Web site: www.pencoedtravel.co.uk
Man Dir: Denise Cook
Dir: Andrea Talbot
Ops: David Morris
Ch Eng: Neil Cook.
Fleet: 11 - 2 double-deck bus, 9 single-deck coach.
Chassis: 2 Bova, 7 DAF, 2 Leyland.
Bodies: 2 Bova, 1 Plaxton, 6 Van Hool.
Ops incl: school contracts, excursions & tours, private hire, continental tours.
Livery: White/Blue.

STAGECOACH IN SOUTH WALES
See Torfaen

TRAVEL FINAL
2 BRIDGE STREET, BLAENGARW CF32 8AY
Tel: 01656 871933

Prop: K Jones.
Ops incl: local bus services, school contracts.

CAERPHILLY

CASTELL COACHES LTD
♿♿ 🍴 🧷 ❄ R24 ⚒ T

UNIT 9, TRECENYDD INDUSTRIAL ESTATE, CAERPHILLY CF83 2RZ
Tel: 029 2086 1863
Fax: 029 2086 1864
Recovery: 07967 636659
E-mail: sales@castellcoaches.co.uk
Web site: www.castellcoaches.co.uk
Co Sec: Mrs S Kerslake (Tel: 07801 515119)
Dir: C Kerslake
Ops Man: B Kerslake (Tel: 07801 515117).
Fleet: 21 - 5 double-deck bus, 12 single-deck coach, 3 midicoach, 1 minibus.
Chassis: 2 Bova, 4 DAF, 6 Leyland, 4 Mercedes, 7 Volvo.
Bodies: 2 Bova, 1 Duple, 2 Jonckheere, 4 Leyland, 4 Mercedes, 6 Plaxton, 2 Van Hool.
Ops incl: excursions & tours, private hire, continental tours, school contracts.
Livery: White with multicolour.

HARRIS COACHES
BRYN GWYN STREET, FLEUR-DE-LIS NP2 1RZ
Tel: 01443 832290
Man Dir: John Harris.
Fleet Name: Shuttle.
Ops incl: local bus services.
Livery: Cream/Maroon/Red.

HOWELLS COACHES LTD
UNIT 4, PENALLTA INDUSTRIAL ESTATE, HENGOED CF82 7QZ
Tel: 01443 831554
Fleet incl: double-deck bus, single-deck coach, midibus, minibus.

STAGECOACH IN SOUTH WALES
See Torfaen

CARDIFF

CARDIFF BUS
♿ ♻

SLOPER ROAD, LECKWITH, CARDIFF CF11 8TB
Tel: 029 2078 7703
Fax: 029 2078 7742
E-mail: talktous@cardiffbus.com
Web site: www.cardiffbus.com
Chairman: Cllr Joseph Carter **Man Dir:** David Brown **Fin Dir/Co Sec:** Cynthia Ogbonna **Dir of Service Delivery:** Gareth Mole.
Fleet: 237 - 13 double-deck bus, 205 single-deck bus, 19 articulated bus.
Chassis: 24 Alexander Dennis, 118 Dennis, 63 Scania, 32 Transbus.
Bodies: 24 Alexander Dennis, 1 Alexander, 13 East Lancs, 117 Plaxton, 43 Scania, 32 Transbus, 7 Wright.
Ops incl: local bus services.
Livery: Blue-Green/Orange.
Ticket System: Wayfarer TGX 150.

CREIGIAU TRAVEL LTD
♿ ♿♿ 🍴 ❄

LLYSYWEN, STAR LANE, CAPEL LLANILLTERN, CARDIFF CF5 6JH
Tel: 02920 890220
E-mail: info@creigiautravel.co.uk
Web site: www.creigiautravel.co.uk
Fleet: 19 - 13 single-deck coach, 1 double-deck coach, 4 midicoach, 1 minibus.
Chassis: 5 Mercedes, 1 Neoplan, 13 Volvo.
Ops incl: school contracts, excursions & tours, private hire.

CROESO TOURS
Ceased operations since LRB 2011 went to press.

GREYHOUND COACHES CO
Ceased operations since LRB 2011 went to press.

HEART OF WALES BUS & COACH LTD
YNYSFACH YARD, HEOL YR YNYS, TAFFS WELL, TONGWYNLAIS, CARDIFF CF15 7NT
Man Dir: Clayton Jones.
Fleet Name: St David's Travel.
Ops incl: local bus services, school contracts.

NEW ADVENTURE TRAVEL LTD
UNIT 1, EXCELSIOR ROAD, EXCELSIOR INDUSTRIAL ESTATE, CARDIFF CF14 3AT
Tel: 02920 616589
Dir: Kevyn Jones.
Fleet: 55 - double-deck bus, single-deck bus, single-deck coach, midibus, midicoach.
Chassis: Alexander Dennis, Bluebird, Bova, DAF, Irisbus, Leyland. MAN, Mercedes, Optare, Scania, Setra, Toyota, Transbus, Volvo.
Ops incl: local bus services, private hire.
Also trades as Humphreys Coaches.

STAGECOACH IN SOUTH WALES
See Torfaen

WALTONS COACHES
VIKING PLACE, ROATH DOCK, CARDIFF
CF10 4TS
Tel: 02920 489955
E-mail: waltonscoaches@btconnect.com
Web site: www.waltonscoaches.com
Dirs: B J Walton, Mrs S F Walton, R J Walton,
D McCarthy.
Fleet: 4 - 1 single-deck coach, 3 midicoach.
Chassis: 1 DAF, 3 Mercedes.
Ops incl: private hire, school contracts.
Livery: Blue/White/Red.

WATTS COACHES LTD
OLD POST GARAGE, BONVILSTON
CF5 6TQ
Tel/Fax: 01446 781277
E-mail: enquiries@wattscoaches.co.uk
Web site: www.wattscoaches.co.uk
Dirs: Clive P Watts, Carol Watts, James Watts.
Fleet: 30 - 1 double-deck bus, 19 single-deck
coach, 2 double-deck coach, 7 midibus,
1 midicoach.
Chassis: 1 Ayats, 2 Bova, 2 DAF, 6 Dennis, 1 Iveco,
3 Leyland, 2 Mercedes, 1 Neoplan, 6 Scania,
1 Van Hool, 5 Volvo.
Bodies: 1 Alexander, 1 Ayats, 2 Beulas, 2 Berkhof,
1 Bova, 4 Irizar, 3 Jonckheere, 1 Neoplan,
12 Plaxton, 1 Unvi, 2 Van Hool.
Ops incl: school contracts, excursions & tours,
private hire, continental tours.
Livery: Cream/Red/Gold.

WHEADONS GROUP TRAVEL LTD
STATION TERRACE, ELY BRIDGE,
COWBRIDGE ROAD WEST, CARDIFF
CF5 4AA
Tel: 02 20 575333
Fax: 02920 575384
E-mail: admin@wheadons-group.co.uk
Web site: www.wheadons-group.co.uk
Chairman: E K Wheadon **Man:** R Tucker
Ch Eng: S Osling.
Fleet: 19 - 9 single-deck coach, 8 midicoach,
2 minibus.
Chassis: 2 LDV, 3 Mercedes, 5 Toyota, 9 Volvo.
Bodies: 5 Caetano, 1 Jonckheere, 2 LDV,
2 Mercedes, 5 Plaxton, 4 Van Hool.
Ops incl: private hire, school contracts,
excursions & tours.
Livery: Blue/Yellow/Silver over White.

CARMARTHENSHIRE

BRODYR WILLIAMS LTD
BRYNEGLUR GARAGE, UPPER TUMBLE
SA14 6BW
Tel: 01269 841338
Fleet: 12 – 11 single-deck coach, 1 midicoach.
Chassis: DAF, EOS, Mercedes, Van Hool, VDL,
Volvo
Ops incl: school contracts, private hire.

BYSIAU CWM TAF/TAF VALLEY COACHES
PENRHEOL, WHITLAND SA34 0NH
Tel: 01994 240908 **Fax:** 01994 241264
E-mail: info@tafvalleycoaches.co.uk

Web site: www.tafvalleycoaches.co.uk
Dirs: Clive Edwards, Heather Edwards.
Fleet Name: Taf Valley Coaches.
Fleet: 18 - 13 single-deck coach, 3 midibus,
1 midicoach, 1 minicoach.
Chassis: 1 Bova, 3 Dennis, 1 Enterprise, 2 Irisbus,
1 LDV, 1 Leyland, 2 Mercedes, 7 Volvo.
Bodies: 1 Alexander, 1 Berkhof, 1 Beulas, 1 Bova,
1 Jonckheere, 10 Plaxton, 1 Van Hool, 2 Other.
Ops incl: local bus services, excursions & tours,
school contracts, private hire, continental tours.
Livery: White/Silver/Blue.

CASTLE GARAGE LTD
BROAD STREET, LLANDOVERY SA20 0AA
Tel: 01550 720335
E-mail: enquiries@castle-garage.com
Web site: www.castle-garage.com
Man Dir: Derek Jones.
Fleet: 8 - 2 midibus, 1 midicoach, 5 minibus.
Chassis: 4 LDV, 4 Mercedes.
Ops incl: local bus services, school contracts,
private hire.

GARETH EVANS COACHES
80 GLYN ROAD, BRYNAMMAN
SA18 1SS
Tel: 01269 823127
Fax: 01269 824533
Props: K Davies, Mrs S Davies.
Fleet: 10 – 5 single-deck bus, 3 single-deck coach,
2 minibus.
Chassis: 2 Autosan, 1 Ford Transit, 3 Leyland,
1 Mercedes, 2 Scania, 1 Setra.
Ops incl: school contracts, private hire.

FFOSHELIG COACHES
MAES Y PRIOR, ST PETERS, CARMARTHEN
SA33 5OS
Tel: 01267 237584
Fax: 01267 236059
E-mail: ffoshelig@btconnect.com
Web site: www.ffoshelig.co.uk
Prop: Rhodri Evans.
Fleet incl: single-deck bus, single-deck coach,
midibus, midicoach.
Chassis: Autosan, Dennis, Mercedes,
Optare, Setra, Van Hool, Volvo.
Bodies: Jonckheere, Optare, Plaxton, Setra,
Van Hool, Volvo.
Ops incl: local bus services, school contracts,
private hire, excursions and tours.
Livery: Cream with Red vinyls.

FIRST CYMRU BUSES LTD
See City & County of Swansea

JONES INTERNATIONAL
STATION ROAD, LLANDEILO
SA19 6NG
Tel: 01558 822985
Fax: 01558 822984
Props: Meirion Jones, Myrddin Jones, Neil Jones
Office Man: Carole Thompson
Ch Eng: Andrew Vale.
Fleet: 3 - 1 double-deck bus, 2 single-deck coach.
Chassis: 1 DAF, 2 Leyland
Bodies: 1 Northern Counties, 1 Plaxton,
1 Van Hool.
Ops incl: excursions & tours, private hire,
express, continental tours, school contracts.
Livery: Yellow/Blue.

JONES LOGIN – TEITHIAU OSAFON/ QUALITY COACH TRAVEL
LOGIN, WHITLAND SA34 0UX
Tel: 01437 563277
Fax: 01437 563393
E-mail: info@joneslogin.co.uk
Web Site: www.joneslogin.co.uk
Dirs: Endaf Jones, Arwel Jones, Ann Jones
(Co Sec), Hannah Jones .
Fleet: 15 – 1 single-deck bus, 11 single-deck
coach, 1 midicoach, 2 minibus.
Chassis: 5 Alexander Dennis, 2 LDV, 1 Mercedes,
1 Optare, 1 Scania, 6 Volvo.
Bodies: 1 East Lancs, 1 Irizar, 2 LDV, 1 Optare,
11 Plaxton.
Ops incl: local bus services, school contracts,
excursions & tours, private hire, continental tours.
Livery: Turquoise/Midnight Blue/White.
Ticket System: ERG.

LEWIS COACHES WHITLAND
THE GARAGE, WHITLAND
SA34 0AA
Tel: 01944 240274
E-mail: enquiries@lewiscoacheswhitland.co.uk
Web Site: www.lewiscoacheswhitland.co.uk
Dir: E Lewis.
Fleet: 5 - 2 single-deck coach, 2 midicoach,
1 minibus.
Chassis: 1 LDV, 2 Mercedes, 2 Volvo.
Bodies: 1 LDV, 2 Plaxton, 2 Other.
Ops incl: local bus services, school contracts,
private hire.
Livery: White/Green with mink stripes.
Ticket System: Wayfarer.

MORRIS TRAVEL
ALLTYCNAP ROAD, JOHNSTOWN,
CARMARTHEN SA31 3QY
Tel: 01267 235090
Fax: 01267 238183
E-mail: morristravel2000@@yahoo.co.uk
Web site: www.morristravel.co.uk
Man Dir: T J Freeman
Ops Dir: C J Freeman
Co Sec: C M Freeman
Ch Eng: A Jones
Traffic Man: V R Shambrook
Traffic Controllers: D Rowe, L Davies.
Fleet: 30 - 13 single-deck bus, 12 single-deck
coach, 2 midibus, 3 minibus.
Chassis: 5 Alexander Dennis, 3 Autosan,
7 Dennis, 2 LDV, 2 Mercedes, 6 Optare, 2 Renault,
3 Volvo.
Bodies: 4 Alexander Dennis, 3 Jonckheere,
2 LDV, 2 Marshall/MCV, 6 Optare, 6 Plaxton,
3 UVG, 4 Wadham Stringer.
Ops incl: local bus services, school contracts,
private hire.
Livery: Blue/Navy/White.
Ticket System: Wayfarer.

GWYNNE PRICE COACHES
38 HEOL LLANELLI, TRIMSARAN SA17 4AA
Tel: 01554 810217
Fleet: 17 – 14 single-deck coach, 1 midibus,
2 minibus.
Chassis: Autosan, Bedford, DAF, Dennis, LDV,
Leyland, MAN, Mercedes.
Ops incl: school contracts, private hire.
Livery: White.

THOMAS BROS
TOWY GARAGE, LLANGADOG
SA19 9LU
Tel: 01550 777438
Fax: 01550 777807
Prop: Gareth Thomas.
Fleet: 18 – 11 single-deck coach, 4 midicoach, 2 minibus.
Ops incl: school contracts, excursions & tours, private hire.
Livery: Cream/Green.

GWYN WILLIAMS & SONS LTD
DERLWYN GARAGE, LOWER TUMBLE
SA14 6HS
Tel: 01269 841312
Fax: 01269 842256
E-mail: info@gwynwilliamscoaches.com
Web site: www.gwynwilliamscoaches.com
Fleet: 33 - 12 single-deck bus, 12 single-deck coach, 1 midibus, 1 midicoach, 7 minibus.
Chassis: 1 Alexander Dennis, 7 Dennis, 1 Ford Transit, 3 LDV, 10 Leyland, 1 MAN, 2 Mercedes, 1 Optare, 1 Renault, 1 Volkswagen, 4 Volvo.
Ops incl: local bus services, school contracts, private hire, excursions & tours.
Livery: Two tone Blue/Red.

WINDY CORNER COACHES
WINDY CORNER GARAGE, PENCADER
SA39 9HP
Tel: 01559 384779
E-mail: windycornercoaches@hotmail.co.uk
Web site: www.windycornercoachespencader.co.uk
Fleet: 18 - 13 single-deck coach, 2 midibus, 1 midicoach, 2 minibus
Ops incl: school contracts, private hire.

CEREDIGION

ARRIVA BUSES WALES
See Conwy

CERBYDAU CENARTH COACHES
FALLS GARAGE, CENARTH
SA38 9JP
Tel: 01239 710463
Fleet: 16 – 10 single-deck coach, 1 midibus, 5 minibus.
Ops incl: school contracts, private hire.

VINCENT DAVIES COACHES
VICTORIA TERRACE, LAMPETER
SA48 7DF
Tel: 01570 422493
Fax: 01570 422490
Prop: E D V Davies.
Fleet: 16 - 1 single-deck bus, 3 single-deck coach, 4 midicoach, 8 minibus.
Ops incl: school contracts, private hire.

EVANS COACHES TREGARON LTD
OLD STATION YARD, TREGARON
SY25 6HX
Tel: 01974 298546
Fleet: 12 - 1 single-deck bus, 5 single-deck coach, 3 midibus, 1 midicoach, 2 minibus.
Chassis: 2 Dennis, 5 Mercedes, 1 Optare, 4 Volvo.
Ops incl: local bus services, school contracts, private hire.

BRODYR JAMES
GLANYRAFON, LLANGEITHO, TREGARON SY25 6TT
Tel: 01974 821255 **Fax:** 01974 251618
Dirs: D E James, T M G James.
Fleet: 16 - 11 single-deck coach, 2 midibus, 2 midicoach, 1 minibus.
Chassis: 4 Dennis, 1 Ford Transit, 1 MAN, 3 Mercedes, 1 Toyota, 5 Volvo.
Bodies: 2 Caetano, 1 Jonckheere, 3 Mercedes, 10 Plaxton.
Ops incl: local bus services, school contracts, private hire.
Livery: White/Red/Gold.
Ticket System: ERG TP5000.

G & M COACHES
PONTFAEN GARAGE, PONTFAEN ROAD, LAMPETER SA48 7JL
Tel: 01570 422389
Fleet: 10 – 8 single-deck coach, 1 midibus, 1 minibus.
Ops incl: school contracts, private hire.

R J JONES TRAVEL
TYNYGRAIG, TY NANT, YSTRAD MEURIG, ABERYSTWYTH SY25 6AE
Tel: 01974 261474
Web site: www.rjjonestravelsy25.co.uk
Prop: R J Jones.
Fleet: 5 – 4 single-deck coach, 1 midicoach.
Chassis: 1 BMC, 1 Dennis, 3 Setra.
Ops incl: school contracts, private hire.
Livery: Red & White.

LEWIS COACHES
BRYNEITHIN YARD, LLANRHYSTUD SY23 5DN
Tel/Fax: 01974 202495
E-mail: lewisgarage@btconnect.com
Web site: www.lewis-coaches.com
Prop: Gwyn R Lewis.
Fleet: 19 - 14 single-deck coach, 3 midibus, 2 minibus.
Chassis: 4 Autosan, 4 DAF, 1 Dennis, 1 MAN, 2 Mercedes, 3 Optare, 1 VDL, 3 Volvo.
Bodies: 4 Autosan, 2 Berkhof, 1 Caetano, 1 Ikarus, 1 Jonckheere, 3 Optare, 1 Plaxton, 4 Van Hool, 2 Other.
Ops incl: local bus services, private hire, excursions & tours.
Livery: White/Blue.
Ticket System: Wayfarer.

LEWIS-RHYDLEWIS CYF
PENRHIW-PAL GARAGE, RHYDLEWIS, LLANDYSUL SA44 5QG
Tel: 01239 851386
E-mail: post@lewis-rhydlewis.co.uk
Web site: www.lewis-rhydlewis.co.uk
Dir/Co Sec: Maldwyn Lewis.
Fleet: 23 - 14 single-deck coach, 2 midicoach, 6 minibus, 1 minicoach.
Chassis: 2 Bedford, 1 BMC, 3 Dennis, 5 Ford Transit, 1 Irisbus, 1 Iveco, 3 Leyland, 1 Mercedes, 2 Setra, 4 Volvo.
Bodies: 1 BMC, 1 Duple, 12 Plaxton, 2 Setra, 7 Other.
Ops incl: local bus services, school contracts, private hire, excursions & tours.
Livery: Cream/Red/Orange/Maroon.

MID WALES TRAVEL
BRYNHYFRYD GARAGE, PENRHYNCOCH, ABERYSTWYTH SY23 3EH
Tel: 01970 828288
Fax: 01970 828940
E-mail: enquires@midwalestravel.co.uk
Web site: www.midwalestravel.co.uk
Dir: J M Evans
Co Sec: J H Morgan.
Fleet: 21 – 10 single-deck coach, 9 midibus, 2 midicoach.
Chassis: 6 Alexander Dennis, 3 Dennis, 1 Enterprise, 4 Mercedes, 4 VDL, 3 Volvo.
Bodies: 2 Alexander, 4 Alexander Dennis, 9 Plaxton, 1 UVG, 4 Van Hool, 1 Other.
Ops incl: local bus services, school contracts, excursions & tours, private hire.
Livery: White with Blue.

RICHARDS BROS
MOYLGROVE GARAGE, PENTOOD INDUSTRIAL ESTATE, CARDIGAN SA43 3AG
Tel: 01239 613756
Fax: 01239 615193
E-mail: enquiries@richardsbros.co.uk
Web site: www.richardsbros.co.uk
Gen Man: W J M Richards
Ch Eng: D N Richards
Traf Man: R M Richards
Ops Man: S M Richards.
Fleet: 68 - 24 single-deck bus, 22 single-deck coach, 4 midicoach, 4 minibus, 14 midibus.
Chassis: 6 Alexander Dennis, 31 DAF, 9 Dennis, 4 LDV, 8 Mercedes, 8 Optare, 2 Volvo.
Bodies: 5 Alexander Dennis, 2 Autobus, 1 Caetano, 3 Carlyle, 1 Duple, 2 Ikarus, 4 LDV, 4 Marshall/MCV, 2 Northern Counties, 10 Optare, 12 Plaxton, 4 Transbus, 13 Van Hool, 5 Wright.
Ops incl: local bus services, school contracts, excursions & tours, private hire, continental tours.
Livery: Blue/White/Maroon.
Ticket System: ERG.

CONWY

ALPINE TRAVEL
CENTRAL COACH GARAGE, BUILDER STREET WEST, LLANDUDNO LL30 1HH
Tel: 01492 879133
Fax: 01492 876055
E-mail: chris@alpine-travel.co.uk
Web site: www.alpine-travel.co.uk
Dirs: Bryan Owens, Patricia Owens, Christopher Owens, Christopher Bryan Owens.
Fleet: 72 - 40 double-deck bus, 2 single-deck bus, 27 single-deck coach, 2 midibus, 1 midicoach.
Chassis: 1 Autosan, 2 Bristol, 6 Dennis, 7 Duple 425, 3 Irisbus, 39 Leyland, 2 MAN, 5 Mercedes, 7 Volvo.
Bodies: 9 Alexander, 1 Autosan, 2 Beulas, 1 Caetano, 8 Duple, 27 ECW, 2 East Lancs, 5 Marcopolo, 2 Mercedes, 11 Plaxton, 2 Roe, 1 Sunsundegui, 1 Wadham Stringer.
Ops incl: local bus services, school contracts, excursions & tours, private hire, continental tours.
Livery: Red/White/Green.
Ticket System: Setright.

ARRIVA BUSES WALES

IMPERIAL BUILDINGS, GLAN-Y-MOR ROAD, LLANDUDNO JUNCTION LL31 9RU
Tel: 01492 564022
Fax: 01492 592968
Regional Man Dir: Phil Stone
Area Man Dir: Michael Morton
Head of Ops: Simon Finnie
Head of Eng: Nigel Cross
Business Analyst: Charys Green.
Fleet: 228 - 11 double-deck bus, 123 single-deck bus, 7 open-top bus, 87 midibus.
Chassis: 112 Dennis, 6 Leyland, 35 Optare, 1 Scania, 60 VDL, 14 Volvo.
Bodies: 10 Alexander Dennis, 4 ECW, 8 Northern Counties, 35 Optare, 104 Plaxton, 67 Wright.
Ops incl: local bus services, school contracts, private hire, express.
Livery: Arriva UK Bus.
Ticket System: Wayfarer TGX150.

LLEW JONES INTERNATIONAL

STATION YARD, LLANRWST LL26 0EH
Tel: 01492 640320
Fax: 01492 642040
Recovery: 07795 347476
E-mail: sales@llewjones.com
Web site: www.llewjones.com
Man Dir: Stephen Jones
Fin Dir: Eirlys Jones **Ops Man:** Kevin Williams
Workshop Man: Erfyl Roberts
HR & Compliance Man: Julie Jones.
Fleet: 33 - 22 single-deck coach, 8 midibus, 2 midicoach, 1 recovery low-loader.
Chassis: 4 DAF, 6 Dennis, 1 Iveco, 1 MAN, 7 Mercedes, 6 Optare, 3 Scania, 1 Setra, 1 VDL, 3 Volvo.
Bodies: 3 Ayats, 1 Beulas, 1 Caetano, 2 Duple, 1 Hispano, 3 Irizar, 3 Mercedes, 1 Noge, 7 Optare, 8 Plaxton, 1 Setra, 1 Unvi.
Ops incl: local bus services, school contracts, express, private hire.
Livery: White/Blue/Magenta Flashes.
Ticket system: Wayfarer TGX 1000.

ROBERTS MINI COACHES

RHANDIR GARAGE, RHANDIR LL22 8BW
Tel: 01492 650449
Fleet: 6 - 4 midicoach, 2 minibus.
Chassis: 1 Iveco, 4 Mercedes, 1 Renault.
Ops Inc: schools contracts, private hire.

DENBIGHSHIRE

ARRIVA BUSES WALES

See Conwy

GHA COACHES LTD

MILL GARAGE, BETWS GWERFIL GOCH, CORWEN LL21 9PU
See full entry under Wrexham.

M & H COACHES

UNIT 2, BRICKWORK GARAGE, TREFNANT, DENBIGH LL16 4UH
Tel: 01745 730700
Prop: Mrs M. Owen.
Fleet: 16 - 8 single-deck coach, 6 midibus, 1 midicoach, 1 minibus.

Chassis: 1 BMC, 2 Mercedes, 5 Optare, 1 Renault, 1 Scania, 1 Setra, 5 Volvo.
Livery: Blue/White.
Ops incl: local bus services, school contracts, private hire.

VOEL COACHES LTD

PENISA FILLING STATION, FFORD TALARGOCH, DYSERTH LL18 6BP
Tel: 01745 570309
Fax: 01745 570211
E-mail: sales@voelcoaches.com
Web site: www.voelcoaches.com
Man Dir: W M Kerfoot-Davies
Comm Man: Michelle Kerfoot Higginson.
Fleet: 32 - 8 double-deck bus, 18 single-deck coach, 2 midibus, 4 minibus.
Chassis: Bristol, DAF, Dennis, Leyland, Mercedes, MCW, Optare, Scania, Volkswagen, Volvo.
Bodies: Alexander, Caetano, ECW, Jonckheere, MCW, Mercedes, Optare, Plaxton, Van Hool, Volkswagen, Volvo.
Ops incl: local bus services, school contracts, excursions & tours, private hire, continental tours.
Livery: Orange.

FLINTSHIRE

A N ANDREW COACHES

RHEWL ROAD, MOSTYN, RUTHIN LL15 2YH
Tel: 01745 560853
Fleet: 5 - 4 single-deck coach, 1 midicoach.
Chassis: 1 Leyland, 1 Mercedes, 3 Volvo.
Ops incl: school contracts, private hire.

ARRIVA BUSES WALES

See Conwy

EAGLES AND CRAWFORD

RUTHIN ROAD, MOLD CH7 5LG
Tel: 01352 700217/8
Fax: 01352 750211
E-mail: eaglesandcrawford@supanet.com
Partners: J F, J K & W P Eagles.
Fleet: 9 - 6 single-deck coach, 3 minibus.
Chassis: 1 Autosan, 4 Dennis, 1 LDV, 1 MAN, 2 Volkswagen.
Bodies: 1 Autosan, 1 Marcopolo, 4 Plaxton, 3 Other.
Ops incl: local bus services, excursions & tours, private hire, continental tours.
Livery: White/Blue/Orange.
Ticket System: Almex.

FOUR GIRLS COACHES

THE OLD POST OFFICE YARD, CORWEN ROAD, PONTYBODKIN, MOLD CH7 4TG
Tel: 01352 770438
Fax: 01352 770253
E-mail: carolyn_fg@hotmail.com
Web site: www.fourgirlscoaches.co.uk
Partners: Mrs Carolyn Thomas, Mrs Elaine Williams, Gwyn Thomas, Peter Williams.
Fleet: 9 - 7 single-deck coach, 1 minibus, 1 minicoach.
Chassis: 1 Mercedes, 1 Toyota, / Volvo.
Bodies: 1 Caetano, 1 Onyx, 6 Plaxton, 1 Van Hool.
Ops incl: school contracts, private hire.
Livery: Turquoise/Red/Yellow.

H D HUTCHINSON & SON

NEWLYN, PADESWOOD ROAD, BUCKLEY CH7 2JW
Tel: 01244 543907
Ops incl: local bus services, school contracts, private hire.

JONES MOTOR SERVICES

CHESTER ROAD, FLINT CH6 5DZ
Tel: 01352 733292
Fax: 01352 763353
E-mail: tours@jonescoaches.co.uk
Web site: www.jonesholidays.co.uk
Partner: A Jones.
Fleet: 10 - 9 single-deck coach, 1 midicoach.
Chassis: DAF, Iveco, Leyland.
Bodies: Caetano, Duple, Plaxton, Van Hool.
Ops incl: excursions & tours, private hire, express, continental tours, school contracts.
Livery: Blue.

OARE'S COACHES

TY DRAW, BRYNFORD, HOLYWELL CH8 8LP
Tel: 01352 713339 **Fax:** 01352 714871
Prop: G A Oare
Fleet: 13 - 1 single-deck bus, 7 single-deck coach, 1 midibus, 1 midicoach, 3 minibus.
Chassis: 2 Ford Transit, 1 Leyland, 1 Mercedes, 1 Optare, 2 Scania, 1 Vauxhall, 5 Volvo.
Livery: White/Red/Silver.
Ops incl: local bus services, school contracts, private hire.

P. & O. LLOYD

RHYDWEN GARAGE, BAGILLT CH6 6JJ
Tel: 01352 710682
Man Dir: David Lloyd.
Fleet: 37 - 5 double-deck bus, 10 single-deck bus, 13 single-deck coach, 8 midibus, 1 minibus.
Chassis: 3 Autosan, 4 BMC, 5 Leyland, 3 MAN, 10 Optare, 2 Scania, 10 Volvo.
Bodies: 8 Alexander, 3 Autosan, 4 BMC, 1 Jonckheere, 2 Northern Counties, 10 Optare, 9 Plaxton.
Ops incl: local bus services, private hire, school contracts.
Liveries: Cream/Red or Cream/Maroon/Gold; Yellow (school buses).
Ticket System: Almex.

PHILLIPS COACHES

ABBEY BUS GARAGE, BAGILLT ROAD, GREENFIELD, HOLYWELL CH8 7EP
Tel: 01352 711993
Fleet: 7 - 3 single-deck bus, 1 single-deck coach, 2 midibus, 1 minibus.
Chassis: 1 Dennis, 3 Leyland, 3 Optare.
Ops incl: local bus services, school contracts.

TOWNLYNX

CAETIA LLWYD, NORTHOP ROAD, HOLYWELL CH8 8AE
Tel: 01352 710489
Prop: S A Lee.
Fleet: 18 - 5 double-deck bus, 6 single-deck bus, 7 midibus.
Chassis: 5 Alexander Dennis, 1 BMC, 1 Dennis, 4 Leyland, 2 Mercedes, 3 Optare, 2 Volvo.
Ops incl: local bus services, school contracts.
Livery: White/Yellow/Blue.

Welsh Operators

ARRIVA BUSES WALES
See Conwy

ARVONIA COACHES LTD
THE SQUARE, LLANRUG LL55 4AA
Tel: 01286 675175
Fax: 01286 676406
E-mail: info@arvonia.co.uk
Web site: www.arvonia.co.uk
Prop: R. Morris.
Fleet: 5 - 4 single-deck coach, 1 minibus.
Chassis: 3 Mercedes, 1 Neoplan, 1 Setra.
Bodies: 3 Mercedes, 1 Neoplan, 1 Setra.
Ops incl: excursions & tours, private hire,
continental tours.
Livery: White/Orange/Red.
Ticket System: Almex.

CERBYDAU BERWYN COACHES
UNIT 1, TREFOR WORKSHOPS, TREFOR,
CAERNARVON LL55 5LH
Tel: 01286 660315
Fax: 01286 660110
E-mail: berwyncoaches@aol.com
Props: Brian Japheth, Mrs Marwa Japheth.
Fleet: 27 – 3 double-deck bus, 1 single-deck bus,
12 single-deck coach, 8 midibus, 2 midicoach,
1 minibus.
Chassis: Dennis, Leyland, Mercedes, Optare,
Volvo.
Ops incl: local bus services, school contracts,
private hire.
Livery: White/Yellow/Brown.

CAELLOI MOTORS (T. H. JONES & SON)
UNIT 17, GLAN Y DON INDUSTRIAL ESTATE,
PWLLHELI LL53 5YT
Tel: 01758 612719
Fax: 01758 612335
E-mail: tours@caelloi.co.uk
Props: Eryl B Jones, Thomas H Jones.
Fleet: 8 – 1 double-deck bus, 2 single-deck bus,
5 single-deck coach.
Chassis: 1 DAF, 1 Optare, 1 Scania, 5 Volvo.
Bodies: 1 Alexander, 1 Optare, 1 Plaxton,
4 Van Hool, 1 Wright.
Ops incl: local bus services, school contracts,
excursions & tours, private hire, continental tours.
Livery: Multi.
Ticket System: Almex.

CLYNNOG & TREFOR
THE GARAGE, TREFOR, CAERNARFON
LL54 5HP
Tel: 01286 660208   **Fax:** 01286 660538
E-mail: info@clynnogandtrefor.com
Web site: www.clynnogandtrefor.com
Dirs: D C Jones, E W Griffiths **Co Sec:** I
Williams.
Fleet: 29 - 5 double-deck bus, 4 single-deck bus,
16 single-deck coach, 4 minibus.
Chassis: 5 Leyland, 4 LDV, 3 Mercedes,
1 Transbus, 16 Volvo.
Bodies: 4 Alexander Dennis, 6 Jonckheere, 4
LDV, 5 Northern Counties, 7 Plaxton, 3 Van Hool.
Ops incl: local bus services, school contracts,
private hire.
Livery: White.
Ticket system: Wayfarer TGX.

EMMAS COACHES
INTERNATIONAL LTD
GARTH YARD, PENMAENPOOL,
DOLGELLAU LL40 1YF
Tel/Recovery: 01341 423934
Fax: 01341 423321
E-mail: info@emmascoaches.co.uk
Web site: www.emmascoaches.co.uk
Dir: Barrie Thomas.
Fleet: 9 - 3 single-deck coach, 2 midibus,
1 midicoach, 2 minibus, 1 minicoach.
Ops incl: local bus services, school contracts,
excursions & tours, private hire.
Livery: White/Blue, Green/Gold.

EVANS LLANIESTYN
NANT BACH, LLANIESTYN LL53 8SW
Tel: 01758 730634
Fleet incl: single-deck coach, midicoach, minibus.
Ops incl: school contracts, private hire.

EXPRESS MOTORS
THE GARAGE, LLYNFI ROAD, PENYGROES,
CAERNARFON LL54 6ND
Tel: 01286 881108
Fax: 01286 882331
Web site: www.expressmotors.com
E-mail: jones14@btconnect.com
Props: Eric Wyn Jones, Jean A Jones
Ops Man: Kevin Wyn Jones
Ch Eng: Ian Wyn Jones
Service Man: Keith Jones.
Fleet: 38 - 1 double-deck bus, 10 single-deck bus,
7 single-deck coach, 1 double-deck coach,
1 open-top bus, 8 midibus, 4 midicoach,
2 minicoach, 2 vintage.
Chassis: 1 Bedford OB, 2 Bristol, 3 DAF,
3 Dennis, 12 MAN, 3 Mercedes, 12 Optare,
1 Scania, 1 Volvo.
Bodies: 4 Alexander Dennis, 1 Crest, 2 Duple,
1 ECW, 3 East Lancs, 1 Hispano, 2 Marcopolo,
2 Marshall, 3 Neoplan, 12 Optare, 1 Plaxton,
1 Scania, 3 Van Hool, 1 Wright.
Ops incl: local bus services, school contracts,
private hire.
Livery: Yellow/White.
Ticket System: Wayfarer 3.

GRIFFITHS COACHES
3 ELIM COTTAGES, Y FELINHELI LL56 4JR

Tel: 01248 670530 **Fax:** 01248 671111
Prop: Hefin Griffiths
Fleet: 9 - 1 double-deck bus, 2 single-deck bus,
5 single-deck coach, 1 midibus.
Chassis: 1 Leyland, 1 Mercedes, 7 Volvo.
Bodies: 1 Alexander, 1 Duple, 1 ECW,
1 Jonckheere, 1 Plaxton, 3 Van Hool.
Ops incl: private hire, school contracts.
Livery: White.

JOHN'S COACHES
81 MANOD ROAD, BLAENAU FFESTINIOG
LL41 4AF
Tel: 01766 831781   **Fax:** 01766 831781
Prop: J R Edwards.
Fleet: 6 – 1 single-deck coach, 2 midibus,
1 minibus.
Chassis: 1 DAF, 1 Ford Transit, 2 Mercedes.
Bodies: 1 Ford Transit, 2 Plaxton, 1 Van Hool.
Ops incl: local bus service, school contracts,
private hire.
Livery: White/Red.
Ticket System: Wayfarer

NEFYN COACHES LTD
WEST END GARAGE, ST DAVIDS ROAD,
NEFYN LL53 6HE
Tel: 01758 720904   **Fax:** 01758 720331
Dirs: B G Owen, M A Owen, A. G Owen.
Fleet: 17 - 2 single-deck coach, 14 midibus,
1 minibus.
Chassis: 1 Dennis, 12 Mercedes, 2 Optare,
1 Scania, 1 Volvo.
Bodies: 1 Alexander, 2 Optare, 9 Plaxton,
2 Van Hool, 2 Wright, 1 Other.
Ops incl: local bus services, school contracts,
excursions & tours, private hire.
Livery: Silver/Red/Yellow.

PADARN BUS LTD
Y GLYN INDUSTRIAL ESTATE, LLANBERIS,
LL55 4EN
Tel: 01286 870880   **Fax:** 01286 871191
E-mail: info@padarnbus.co.uk
Web site: www.padarnbus.co.uk
Fleet Name: Padarn Bus.
Man Dir: David Hulme
Ops Dir: Darren Price **Dir:** David Price.
Fleet: 48 –9 double-deck bus, 23 single-deck bus,
5 single-deck coach, 1 open top bus, 9 midibus,
1 midicoach.

The Little Red Book 2012 - in association with *tbf* Transport Benevolent Fund

Chassis: 4 Alexander Dennis, 16 Dennis, 4 Leyland, 2 MCW, 4 Mercedes, 1 Neoplan, 7 Optare, 10 Volvo.
Bodies: 9 Alexander, 4 Alexander Dennis, 1 Caetano, 3 East Lancs, 1 ECW, 1 Jonckheere, 1 Leyland, 2 MCW, 2 Mellor, 1 Neoplan, 7 Optare, 13 Plaxton, 1 Sitcar, 2 Wright.
Ops incl: local bus services, school contracts, private hire.
Livery: Red.
Ticket System: Wayfarer 3/TGX

SILVER STAR COACH HOLIDAYS LTD
13 CASTLE SQUARE, CAERNARFON LL55 2NF
Tel: 01286 672333 **Fax:** 01286 678118
E-mail: enquiries@silverstarholidays.com
Web site: www.silverstarholidays.com
Man Dir: Elfyn William Thomas
Co Sec: Helen Jones
Ch Eng: Barry Thomas
Ops Man: Eric Wyn Thomas.
Fleet: single-deck coach, vintage.
Chassis: AEC, DAF, Leyland, Neoplan, Setra, Volvo.
Bodies: Burlingham, Neoplan, Plaxton, Setra, Van Hool.
Ops incl: school contracts, excursions & tours, private hire, continental tours.
Livery: Green coaches/Blue buses.
Ticket System: Wayfarer 3.

WILLIAMS OF BALA
BODOLWYN GARAGE, ARENIG STREET, BALA LL23 7AH
Tel: 01678 520777
Web site: www.williamsofbala.co.uk
Props: G & A Williams.
Fleet: 4 – 3 single-deck coach, 1 midicoach.
Chassis: 1 Mercedes, 3 Volvo.
Bodies: 4 Plaxton.
Ops incl: local bus services, school contracts, private hire.

MERTHYR TYDFIL

SIXTY SIXTY COACHES
THE COACH DEPOT, MERTHYR INDUSTRIAL PARK, PENTREBACH CF48 4DR
Tel: 01443 692060 **Fax:** 01443 699061
E-mail: enquiries@sixsixty.co.uk
Web site: www.sixtysixty.co.uk
Props: G Handy, CT Handy.
Fleet: 18 - 3 single-deck bus, 9 single-deck coach, 2 double-deck coach, 3 midibus, 1 midicoach.
Chassis: 6 DAF, 3 Dennis, 1 Leyland, 3 Mercedes, 2 Scania, 3 Volvo.
Bodies: 3 Alexander, 2 Caetano, 1 Duple, 3 Plaxton, 3 Reeve Burgess, 5 Van Hool, 1 LAG.
Ops incl: local bus services, school contracts, excursions & tours, private hire.
Livery: Silver.
Ticket system: Wayfarer.

STAGECOACH IN SOUTH WALES
See Torfaen

MONMOUTHSHIRE

CHEPSTOW CLASSIC BUSES
UNIT 6, BULWARK INDUSTRIAL ESTATE, BULWARK, CHEPSTOW NP16 5QZ

Tel/Fax: 01291 625449
E-mail: chepstowclassic@btconnect.com
Web site: www.chepstow-classic-buses.co.uk
Fleet: 20 - 6 double-deck bus, 6 single-deck bus, 8 minibus, also heritage vehicles.
Chassis: Bristol, Dennis, Leyland, Mercedes, Scania.
Bodies: Alexander, East Lancs, ECW, Northern Counties, Plaxton.
Ops incl: local bus services, private hire.
Livery: Blue.

REES COACH TRAVEL & EUROPEAN TRAVEL
WAUNLAPRA, LLANELLY HILL, ABERGAVENNY NP7 0PW
Tel: 01873 830210
Fax: 01873 832167
Web site: reestravel@yahoo.co.uk
E-mail: info@reestravelorangehome.co.uk
Snr Partner: Neville A Rees
Partners: Nigel A Rees, Mrs Margo E Rees.
Fleet: 11 - 9 single-deck coach, 1 midicoach, 1 minibus.
Chassis: 2 Alexander Dennis, 3 DAF, 1 Ford, 1 Neoplan, 1 Scania, 2 Setra, 1 Toyota.
Ops incl: local bus services, school contracts, excursions & tours, private hire, continental tours.
Livery: Green/White.

STAGECOACH IN SOUTH WALES
See Torfaen

TOWN & COUNTRY BUS LTD
HAWTHORNE COTTAGE, THE CAUSEWAY, UNDY, CALDICOT NP26 3DP
Tel: 01633 861611
Dir: T R Ward.
Ops incl: local bus services.
Livery: Green/White/Blue.

NEATH & PORT TALBOT

BLUEBIRD OF NEATH/ PONTARDAWE
9-10 LONDON ROAD, NEATH SA11 1HB
Tel/Fax: 01639 643849
Fleet Name: Bluebird Coaches (Neath).
Prop: Ian S Warren
Ch Eng: George Warren **Co Sec:** Ms Melanie Evans.
Fleet: 13 - 11 single-deck coach, 1 midibus, 1 minibus.
Chassis: 1 Bova, 2 DAF, 1 Dennis, 2 Mercedes, 1 Temsa, 6 Volvo.
Bodies: 1 Alexander, 1 Berkhof, 1 Bova, 1 Caetano, 3 Jonckheere, 3 Plaxton, 1 Temsa, 1 Van Hool, 1 Other.
Ops incl: excursions & tours, private hire, continental tours, school contracts.
Livery: White/Blue/Red.

DANSA
CRYNANT BUSINESS CENTRE, CRYNANT BUSINESS PARK, CRYNANT, NEATH SA10 8PX
Tel: 01639 751067 **Fax:** 01639 750805
E-mail: mail@dansa.org.uk
Web site: www.dansa.org.uk
Fleet: 4 - 1 midibus, 3 minibus.
Chassis: Optare.
Bodies: Optare.
Ops incl: local bus services, community transport services.

FIRST CYMRU BUSES LTD
See City & County of Swansea

NELSON & SON (GLYNNEATH) LTD
74A HIGH STREET, GLYNNEATH SA11 5AW
Tel/Fax: 01639 720308
E-Mail: nelsoncoaches@aol.com
Fleet Name: Nelson's Coaches.
Man Dir: J L R Nelson **Co Sec:** Mrs J Nelson
Fleet Eng: P Watkins **Tran Man:** G Powell.
Fleet: 15 - 13 single-deck coach, 2 midicoach.
Chassis: 2 Bova, 3 DAF, 4 Dennis, 2 Irisbus, 2 Mercedes, 2 Volvo.
Bodies: 1 Berkhof, 2 Bova, 6 Plaxton, 1 UVG, 4 Van Hool, 1 Other.
Ops incl: school contracts, excursions & tours, private hire.
Livery: White with Orange reliefs.

RIDGWAYS COACHES
UNIT 22, ENDEAVOUR CLOSE, PURCELL AVENUE INDUSTRIAL ESTATE, PORT TALBOT SA12 7PT
Tel: 01639 883374
E-mail: info@ridgwayscoaches.co.uk
Web site: www.ridgwayscoaches.co.uk
Prop: D Ridgway.
Fleet: 8 – 1 double-deck bus, 2 single-deck bus, 4 single-deck coach, 1 midicoach.
Chassis: 4 DAF, 1 MAN, 1 Mercedes, 1 Setra, 1 Volvo.
Bodies: 1 Marshall, 1 Optare, 4 Plaxton, 1 Setra, 1 Wright.
Ops incl: local bus services, school contracts, private hire, excursions & tours.
Livery: Orange/White.

SOUTH WALES TRANSPORT (NEATH) LTD
UNIT 19, MILLAND ROAD INDUSTRIAL ESTATE, NEATH SA11 1NJ
Tel: 01639 643311
Fax: 01639 644963
E-mail: info@southwalestransport.com
Web site: www.southwalestransport.com
Fleet: 24 – 10 single-deck bus, 5 single-deck coach, 7 midibus, 1 midicoach, 1 minibus.
Chassis: 7 Alexander Dennis, 2 Dennis, 1 MAN, 2 Mercedes, 8 Optare, 4 Volvo.
Bodies: 1 Alexander Dennis, 1 Jonckheere, 6 MCV, 1 Marcopolo, 1 Noge, 8 Optare, 4 Plaxton, 2 Other.
Ops incl: local bus services, school contracts, private hire.
Livery: Green & White

D J THOMAS COACHES LTD
MILLAND ROAD INDUSTRIAL ESTATE, NEATH SA11 1NJ
Tel/Fax: 01639 635502
E-mail: contact@djthomascoaches.com
Web site: www.djthomascoaches.com
Man Dir/Co Sec: Mrs Andrea Gibson
Man Dir: Richard Thomas **Ch Eng:** Lee Gibson.
Fleet: 19 - 14 single-deck coach, 4 midicoach, 1 minibus.
Chassis: 2 Bova, 5 Mercedes, 1 Renault, 11 Volvo.
Bodies: 3 Berkhof, 2 Bova, 1 Mercedes, 7 Plaxton, 3 Van Hool, 1 Volvo, 2 Other.
Ops incl: local bus services, excursions & tours, private hire, school contracts.
Ticket system: Wayfarer.

TONNA LUXURY COACHES LTD

TENNIS VIEW GARAGE, HEOL-Y-GLO,
TONNA SA11 3NJ
Tel: 01639 636738 **Fax:** 01639 646052
Fleet Name: Ken Hopkins.
Dirs: K M Hopkins, A Hopkins.
Fleet: 11 - 7 single-deck coach, 4 midicoach.
Chassis: 4 Mercedes, 1 Setra, 6 Volvo.
Bodies: 1 Caetano, 9 Plaxton, 1 Setra.
Ops incl: school contracts, private hire.
Livery: White/Blue.

WILKINS BROS (CYMMER) LTD

UNIT 1, EASTERN AVENUE, CYMMER, PORT
TALBOT SA13 3PB
Tel/Fax: 01639 852710
Fleet: 15 – single-deck bus, single-deck coach,
midicoach.
Ops incl: school contracts, private hire.

NEWPORT

NEWPORT TRANSPORT LTD

160 CORPORATION ROAD, NEWPORT
NP19 0WF
Tel: 01633 670563 **Fax:** 01633 242589
Web site: www.newporttransport.co.uk
E-mail: enquiries@newporttransport.co.uk
Fleet Name: Newport Bus.
Chairman: W Routley **Man Dir:** S Pearson
Fin Dir: D Jenkins.
Fleet: 88 - 13 double-deck bus, 49 single-deck
bus, 7 single-deck coach, 1 open-top bus,
17 midibus, 1 heritage double-deck bus.
Chassis: 17 Dennis, 1 Leyland, 6 Optare,
57 Scania, 7 Volvo.
Bodies: 36 Alexander, 7 Irizar, 1 Longwell Green,
6 Optare, 30 Scania, 8 Wright.
Ops incl: local bus services, school contracts,
excursions & tours, private hire.
Livery: Green/Cream.
Ticket System: Wayfarer TGX150.

STAGECOACH IN SOUTH WALES

See Torfaen

WELSH DRAGON TRAVEL

21 BEAUFORT ROAD, NEWPORT NP19 7ND
Tel: 01633 761397
E-mail: alan.smith5@ntworld.com
Prop: Alan Barrington Smith.
Fleet: 4 - 1 double-deck bus, 2 single-deck coach,
1 open-top bus.
Chassis: 1 Bedford, 1 Bristol, 2 Leyland.
Ops incl: local bus services, school contracts,
private hire.
Livery: Red/Cream.
Ticket System: Almex.

PEMBROKESHIRE

ACORN TRAVEL LTD

SWANLEIGH, HIGH STREET, FISHGUARD
SA65 9AT
Tel: 01348 874728 **Fax:** 01348 872797
E-mail: acorntravel@aol.com
Web site: www.acorntravel.co.uk
Fleet: 2 single-deck coach, 1 midibus.
Chassis: 1 Mercedes, 1 Optare, 1 Volvo.
Ops incl: local bus services, private hire,
excursions & tours.
Livery: White.

W. H. COLLINS & CO LTD

CUFFERN GARAGE, ROCH,
HAVERFORDWEST SA62 6HB
Tel: 01437 710337
Fleet Name: Collins Coaches.
Props: P N & M Collins.
Fleet: 11 – 1 single-deck coach, 10 minibus.
Ops incl: local bus services, school contracts,
private hire.
Livery: Blue/Grey/White.

EDWARDS BROS

THE GARAGE, BROAD HAVEN ROAD, TIERS
CROSS, HAVERFORDWEST SA62 3BZ
Tel: 01437 890230
Fax: 01437 890337
E-mail: edwardsbros@tiscali.co.uk
Prop: Robert Edwards.
Fleet: 19 – 4 single-deck bus, 8 single-deck coach,
4 midicoach, 3 minibus.
Chassis: 2 Alexander Dennis, 1 Bova, 1 Fiat,
1 LDV, 6 Mercedes, 1 Optare, 7 Volvo.
Bodies: 2 Alexander Dennis, 1 Autobus, 1 Bova,
1 Jonckheere, 1 LDV, 1 Marshall/MCV, 3 Mercedes,
1 Optare, 4 Plaxton, 3 Van Hool, 1 Other.
Ops incl: local bus services, school contracts,
excursions & tours, private hire.
Livery: Coaches: Gold; **Buses:** White.
Ticket System: ERG.

FIRST CYMRU BUSES LTD

See City & County of Swansea

MIDWAY MOTORS (CRYMYCH) LTD

MIDWAY GARAGE, CRYMYCH SA41 3QU
Tel: 01239 831267
Fax: 01239 831279
E-mail: reesmidway@hotmail.com
Dirs: Elan Rees, Iwan Rees.
Fleet: 15 - 1 single-deck bus, 9 single-deck coach,
2 midibus, 2 midicoach, 1 minibus.
Chassis: 3 Alexander Dennis, 4 Mercedes,
1 Renault, 1 Setra, 1 Toyota, 4 Volvo.
Bodies: 1 Alexander Dennis, 4 Caetano,
4 Mercedes, 2 Plaxton, 1 Setra, 1 Van Hool.
Ops incl: local bus services, school contracts,
excursions & tours, private hire, continental tours.
Livery: Silver/Blue.
Ticket system: Electronic.

RICHARDS BROS

MOYLGROVE GARAGE, PENTOOD
INDUSTRIAL ESTATE, CARDIGAN SA43 3AG
Tel: 01239 613756 **Fax:** 01239 615193
E-mail: enquiries@richardsbros.co.uk
Web site: www.richardsbros.co.uk
Gen Man: W J M Richards
Ch Eng: D N Richards **Traf Man:** R M Richards
Ops Man: S M Richards.
Fleet: 68 - 24 single-deck bus, 22 single-deck
coach, 4 midicoach, 4 minibus, 14 midibus.
Chassis: 2 Alexander Dennis, 31 DAF, 9 Dennis,
4 LDV, 8 Mercedes, 8 Optare, 2 Volvo.
Bodies: 5 Alexander Dennis, 2 Autobus,
1 Caetano, 3 Carlyle, 1 Duple, 2 Ikarus, 4 LDV,
4 Marshall/MCV, 2 Northern Counties, 10 Optare,
12 Plaxton, 4 Transbus, 13 Van Hool, 5 Wright.
Ops incl: local bus services, school contracts,
excursions & tours, private hire, continental tours.
Livery: Blue/White/Maroon.
Ticket System: ERG .

SILCOX MOTOR COACH
COMPANY LTD

WATERLOO GARAGE, PEMBROKE DOCK
SA72 4RR
Tel: 01646 683143
Fax: 01646 621787
Web site: www.silcoxcoaches.co.uk
E-mail: travel@silcoxcoaches.co.uk
Man Dir: K.W. Silcox **Dir:** J Silcox
Traffic Man: H J Dix
Coach Hire Man: P Daley.
Fleet: 78 - 39 single-deck bus, 22 single-deck
coach, 14 midibus, 3 minibus.
Chassis: 2 Bova, 21 Dennis, 1 LDV, 26 Leyland,
1 MAN, 13 Mercedes, 7 Optare, 1 Transbus,
6 Volvo.
Bodies: 2 Berkhof, 1 Bova, 8 Caetano,
2 Marcopolo, 3 MCV, 3 Mellor, 2 Optare,
30 Plaxton, 1 Transbus, 1 Van Hool, 2 Wadham
Stringer, 23 Other.
Ops incl: local bus services, school contracts,
excursions & tours, private hire, continental tours.
Livery: Red/Cream.
Ticket System: ERG.

SUMMERDALE COACHES

SUMMERDALE GARAGE, LETTERSTON
SA62 5UB
Tel: 01348 840270
Props: D G Davies, G R Jones.
Fleet: 12 – 9 single-deck coach, 1 midibus,
1 midicoach, 1 minibus.
Livery: Yellow/Blue.

POWYS

A. & E. HIRE

PENYBRYN, LLANGYNIEW, WELSHPOOL
SY21 0JS
Tel: 01938 810518
Dir: Arwyn P Davies.
Fleet: 2 minibus.
Chassis/Bodies: 2 Ford Transit.
Ops incl: school contracts, private hire .

A W COACHES LTD

BODAWEL GARAGE, WESLEY STREET,
LLANFAIR CAEREINION SY21 0RX
Tel/Fax: 01938 810452
Dirs: A Watkins, Mrs S Watkins.
Fleet: 7 – 4 single-deck coach, 2 midicoach,
1 minibus.
Livery: Cream/Orange/Brown.

ROY BROWNS COACHES

15 HIGH STREET, BUILTH WELLS
LD2 3DN
Tel: 01982 552597
Fax: 01982 552286
E-mail: neil@rbci.fsnet.co.uk
Web site: www.roybrownscoaches.co.uk
Prop: N W Brown
Ops Man: P H Davies.
Fleet: 26 - 11 single-deck coach, 4 midibus,
3 midicoach, 8 minibus.
Chassis: 3 DAF, 5 Dennis, 6 LDV, 2 MAN,
3 Mercedes, 4 Optare, 2 Toyota, 1 Volvo.
Bodies: 1 Alexander, 6 Caetano, 4 LDV, 1 Noge,
1 Neoplan, 4 Optare, 6 Plaxton, 3 Other.
Ops incl: local bus services, school contracts,
excursions & tours, private hire.
Ticket System: Setright.

CELTIC TRAVEL
NEW STREET, LLANIDLOES SY18 6EH
Tel/Fax: 01686 412231
E-mail: info@celtictravel.co.uk
Web site: www.celtictravel.co.uk
Props: W P L Davies, Mrs J Davies
Ops Man: P Davies.
Fleet: 23 – 1 double-deck bus, 1 single-deck bus,
1 open top bus, 11 single-deck coach, 1 midicoach,
8 minibus.
Chassis: 3 Dennis, 6 Ford Transit, 1 LDV,
2 Leyland, 1 Mercedes, 1 Renault, 9 Volvo.
Bodies: 2 Alexander, 6 Ford Transit, 1 Mercedes,
1 Park Royal, 6 Plaxton, 3 Van Hool, 3 Wadham
Stringer, 1 Other.
Ops incl: local bus services, school contracts,
excursions & tours, private hire, continental tours.
Livery: Grey with green/red lettering.

CENTRAL TRAVEL
53 CHURCHILL DRIVE, NEWTOWN
SY16 2LH
Tel: 01686 627901
Prop: R W Bowen.
Fleet: 4 – 2 single-deck coach, 2 minibus.
Chassis: 1 LDV, 1 Mercedes, 1 Scania, 1 Volvo.
Livery: White.

COOKSONS COACHES & TRAVEL
HOPE LANE, HOPE, WELSHPOOL SY21 8HF
Tel: 01938 553465
Prop: M Cookson.
Fleet: 16 – 13 single-deck coach, 1 midicoach,
2 minibus.
Livery: Grey with Black Lettering.

R G GITTINS COACHES
THE GARAGE, DOLANOG, WELSHPOOL
SY21 0LQ
Tel/Fax: 01938 810439
E-mail: LandGGittins@aol.co.uk
Prop: R G Gittins.
Fleet: 2 – 1 single-deck coach, 1 midicoach.
Chassis: 1 MAN, 1 Mercedes.
Bodies: 1 Caetano, 1 Optare.
Ops incl: school contracts, private hire.
Livery: White.

GOLD STAR TRAVEL
71 CLEDAN, TREOWEN, NEWTOWN
SY16 1NB
Tel/Fax: 01686 628895
Web site: www.coachhirenewtown.com
Prop: H B Williams.
Fleet: 9 – 3 single-deck coach, 2 midicoach,
4 minibus
Livery: White with Gold & Blue Lettering.

HERDMAN COACHES
HOM GARAGE, CLYRO, HAY-ON-WYE
HR3 5JL
Tel: 01497 817100

Fleet: 14 - 5 single-deck coach, 1 midibus,
8 minibus.
Livery: Pale Blue & White.

GWYN JONES (MEIFORD)
THE GARAGE, MEIFOD
SY22 6DB
Tel: 01938 500249
Partners: Jean Jones, Martin Jones.
Fleet: 1 single-deck coach.
Chassis: Scania.
Body: Van Hool.
Ops incl: school contracts, excursions & tours,
private hire, continental tours.
Livery: Green/White.

LLOYDS COACHES
OLD CROSVILLE GARAGE, DOLL STREET,
MACHYNLLETH SY20 8BH
Tel: 01654 702100
Fax: 01654 703900
E-mail: info@lloydscoaches.com
Web site: www.lloydscoaches.com
Prop: D W Lloyd
Gen Man: R Jones.
Fleet: 29 – 5 single-deck bus, 8 single-deck coach,
11 midibus. 2 midicoach, 3 minibus.
Chassis: 5 Alexander Dennis, 2 Dennis, 2 Ford
Transit, 11 Mercedes, 2 Optare, 7 Volvo.
Bodies: 1 Alexander, 3 Alexander Dennis, 2 Ford
Transit, 1 Marshall, 2 Optare, 19 Plaxton, 1 Other.
Ops incl: local bus services, school contracts,
private hire.
Livery: Silver.
Ticket system: Wayfarer.

OWEN'S MOTORS LTD
TEMESIDE HOUSE, STATION ROAD,
KNIGHTON LD7 1DT
Tel: 01547 528303
Fax: 01547 520512
Ops Man: D Owen
Ch Eng: T Owen
Sec/Dir: J Owen.
Fleet: 8 - 7 single-deck coach, 1 minibus.
Chassis: 3 Dennis, 1 LDV, 4 Volvo.
Bodies: 1 Caetano, 1 LDV, 6 Plaxton.
Ops incl: local bus services, school contracts,
excursions & tours, private hire, continental tours.
Livery: Blue/Grey.

REYNOLDS COACHES
EBRAN-DDU, FELINDRE, KNIGHTON
LD7 1YN
Tel: 01547 510234
Props: J G Reynolds, S J Reynolds.
Fleet: 4 - 3 single-deck coach, 1 minibus.
Chassis: 1 Leyland, 1 LDV, 2 Volvo.
Ops incl: school contracts, private hire.
Livery: Pale Blue/Dark Blue.

RHIEW VALLEY MOTORS LTD
TRECYNON ROAD, BERRIEW, WELSHPOOL
SY21 8BG
Tel: 01686 640554
Dir: D G Haycock
Fleet: 9 – 5 single-deck coach, 4 minibus.
Livery: White with Gold & Blue Lettering.

STAGECOACH IN SOUTH WALES
See Torfaen

STOCKHAMS COACH & TAXIS
19 PLASDERWEN, LLANGATTOCK,
CRICKHOWELL NP8 1HY
Tel: 01873 810559
Fax: 01873 810343
Prop: Mrs Nancy Stockham.
Fleet: 9 - 3 single-deck coach, 2 minibus, 4 taxis.
Chassis incl: 1 Ford Transit, 1 Leyland, 2 Volvo.
Ops incl: school contracts, private hire.
Livery: Green/Cream.

STRATOS TRAVEL
A subsidiary of Owens Coaches Ltd – see
Shropshire

TANAT VALLEY COACHES
THE GARAGE, LLANRHAEDR YM
MOCHNANT, OSWESTRY SY10 0AD
Tel: 01691 780212   **Fax:** 01691 780634
E-mail: info@tanat.co.uk
Web site: www.tanat.co.uk
Dirs: Michael Morris, Peter Morris
Ops Man: Nick Culliford.
Fleet: 50 – 6 double-deck bus, 21 single-deck
bus, 17 single-deck coach, 2 midibus,
2 midicoach, 2 minibus.
Chassis: 6 Dennis, 4 LDV, 8 Leyland, 9 Mercedes,
2 Neoplan, 5 Optare, 16 Volvo.
Bodies: 3 Alexander Dennis, 3 Berkhof, 3 Carlyle,
1 Duple, 1 ECW, 1 East Lancs, 3 Jonckheere,
4 LDV, 3 Neoplan, 11 Northern Counties,
5 Optare, 10 Plaxton, 6 UVG, 1 Wright.
Ops incl: local bus services, school contracts,
excursions & tours, private hire.
Livery: White/Yellow/Orange.
Ticket System: ERG.

VEOLIA TRANSPORT CYMRU PLC
See Rhondda Cynon Taf,
City & County of Swansea

WEALES WHEELS
THE GRADING STATION, LLANDEWI,
LLANDRINDOD WELLS, POWYS
LD1 6SE
Tel: 01597 851141
Fax: 01597 850007
Prop: M J Weale.
Fleet: 10 – 4 single-deck coach, 1 midibus,
2 midicoach, 3 minibus.
Livery: White & Yellow.

♿	Vehicle suitable for disabled			Seat belt-fitted Vehicle		R24	24 hour recovery service
T	Toilet-drop facilities available		ⅲ	Coach(es) with galley facilities			Replacement vehicle available
R	Recovery service available		✳	Air-conditioned vehicle(s)			Vintage Coach(es) available
	Open top vehicle(s)			Coaches with toilet facilities			Hybrid Buses

WILLIAMS COACHES
♿ 🅿 Ⓜ ⌨ ▣ R24 ☎ T
CAMBRIAN WAY, BRECON LD3 7BE
Tel: 01874 622223
Fax: 01874 625218
Recovery: 01874 611534
E-mail: office@williams-coaches.co.uk
Web site: www.williams-coaches.co.uk
Fleet: 26 - 20 single-deck coach, 1 midicoach,
3 minibus, 2 minicoach.
Chassis: 1 DAF, 1 Dennis, 1 Fiat, 2 Ford Transit,
1 Irisbus, 1 Iveco, 1 LDV, 1 MAN, 3 Mercedes,
1 Neoplan, 6 Scania, 6 Setra, 1 Temsa.
Bodies: 1 Caetano, 2 Ford Transit, 6 Irizar,
1 Jonckheere, 1 LDV, 1 Neoplan, 1 Plaxton,
2 Sitcar, 6 Setra, 1 Temsa, 1 Van Hool, 3 Other.
Ops incl: school contracts, private hire,
excursions & tours, continental tours.
Livery: Cream with Orange & Brown Reliefs.

RHONDDA CYNON TAF

CAVENDISH COACHES
🅿 Ⓜ 🍴 ▣ R R24
UNIT 6, RIDGEWELL WAY, LLWYNYPIA
CF40 2JP
Tel: 01443 434153
Fax: 01443 381813
E-mail: sales@cavendishcoaches.co.uk
Web site: www.cavendishcoaches.co.uk
Dir: Stephen Hollister.
Fleet: 10 – 7 single-deck coach, 2 midibus,
1 minibus
Chassis: 1 DAF, 1 Iveco, 2 Mercedes, 1 Renault,
2 Scania, 3 Volvo.
Bodies: 1 Beulas, 1 Berkhof, 1 Bova, 2 Irizar,
2 Jonckheere, 2 Mercedes.
Ops incl: school contracts, excursions & tours,
private hire, continental tours.
Livery: White with multi-colours.

CHAPMANS TRAVEL LTD
🅿 Ⓜ 🍴 ▣
PADFIELD COURT BUSINESS PARK,
TONYREFAIL CF39 8HQ
Tel: 0800 849 7140
Web site: www.chapmanstravel.co.uk
Fleet: 16 – single-deck bus, single-deck coach,
midibus, midicoach, minibus.
Chassis: Bluebird, Bova, Dennis, Ford Transit,
Mercedes, Setra, Volvo.
Ops incl: school contracts, excursions & tours,
private hire.

EDWARDS COACHES LTD
♿ Ⓜ 🅿 ⌨ T ▣ R ☎
NEWTOWN INDUSTRIAL ESTATE,
LLANTWIT FADRE CF38 2EE
Tel: 01443 202048
Fax: 01443 217583
E-mail: admin@edwardscoaches.co.uk
Web site: www.edwardscoaches.co.uk
Man Dir: Mike Edwards **Dirs:** Shaun Edwards,
Jason Edwards, Kelly Edwards, Jessica Edwards.
Fleet: 163 – 13 double-deck bus, 14 single-deck
bus, 113 single-deck coach, 11 midibus,
4 midicoach, 8 minibus.
Chassis: 2 Bluebird, 18 Bova, 6 DAF, 17 Dennis,
6 Ford Transit, 1 LDV, 4 Leyland, 9 MAN, 4 MCW,
5 Mercedes, 1 Optare, 5 Scania, 14 Setra, 3 VDL,
65 Volvo, 1 Volkswagen.
Bodies: 3 Alexander, 1 Berkhof, 2 Bluebird,
18 Bova, 11 Caetano, 5 Duple, 6 Ford, 5 Irizar,
4 Jonckheere, 1 LDV, 4 MCW, 6 MCV,
6 Marcopolo, 1 Marshall, 1 Mercedes, 8 Northern

Counties, 1 Optare, 41 Plaxton, 14 Setra, 2 Sitcar,
8 Van Hool, 1 Volkswagen, 13 Wright.
Ops incl: local bus services, school contracts,
excursions & tours, private hire, express,
continental tours.
Livery: White/Blue, Blue, Yellow.

FERRIS COACH HOLIDAYS
🅿 Ⓜ 🍴 ▣
THE COACH HOUSE, CARDIFF ROAD,
NANTGARW CF15 7SR
Tel: 01443 844222
E-mail: sales@ferriscoachholidays.co.uk
Web site: www.ferriscoachholidays.co.uk
Dirs: J Ferris, L Ferris.
Fleet: 29 – 17 single-deck coach, 10 double-deck
coach, 1 midicoach, 1 minibus.
Chassis: Bova, Mercedes, Neoplan, Temsa,
VDL, Volkswagen, Volvo.
Ops incl: excursions & tours, continental tours.

GLAMORGAN BUS CO LTD
UNIT 4, ABERAMAN INDUSTRIAL ESTATE,
ABERAMAN, ABERDARE CF44 6DA
Tel: 01685 877722
Ops incl: local bus services, school contracts.
Livery: Blue/White

GLOBE COACHES
Ⓜ ⊠ 🅿 🍴 ▣ ☎
BROOKLANDS, FFORCHNEOL ROW,
GODREAMAN, ABERDARE CF44 6HD
Tel: 01685 873622
Fax: 01685 876526
E-mail: wayne@globecoaches.entadsl.com
Web site: www.globecoaches.co.uk
Prop: Wayne Jarvis.
Fleet: 17 - 13 single-deck coach, 4 midibus,
1 minibus, 1 minicoach.
Chassis: 6 Mercedes, 11 Volvo.
Bodies: 2 Berkhof, 2 Caetano, 1 Jonckheere,
9 Plaxton, 2 UVG, 1 Volvo.
Ops incl: local bus services, excursions & tours,
private hire, school contracts, continental tours.
Livery: White/Blue.

V G JARVIS COACHES
WAYNESFIELD, EAST AVENUE, ABERDARE
CF44 8AS
Tel: 01685 882222
Ops incl: school contracts, private hire

KEEPINGS COACHES
RHEOLA HOUSE, PENRHIWCEIBER,
MOUNTAIN ASH CF45 3TE
Tel: 01443 474849
Ops incl: school contracts, private hire.

LASER TRAVEL LTD
UNIT 4, FOUNDRY ROAD, TONYPANDY
CF40 2XD
Tel: 01443 431133
Fax: 01433 431433
E-mail: laser251@aol.com
Web site: www.lasertravel.co.uk
Ops incl: school contracts, excursions & tours,
private hire.

MAINLINE COACHES LTD
🅿 Ⓜ 🍴 ⊠
KINGS HEAD GARAGE, GLANNANT ROAD,
EVANSTOWN CF38 8RL
Tel: 02920 291030
Fax: 01443 676695
E-mail: sales@mainlinetravel.co.uk

Web site: www.mainlinetravel.co.uk
Fleet: 34 – 2 double-deck bus, 30 single-deck
coach, 2 minibus.
Chassis: 5 Bova, 2 Ford Transit, 3 MAN, 16 Scania,
8 Volvo.
Bodies: 2 Alexander, 6 Berkhof, 5 Bova, 2 Ford,
10 Irizar, 1 Marcopolo, 1 Noge, 7 Plaxton.
Ops incl: school contracts, excursions & tours,
private hire, continental tours.
Livery: Green/Yellow.

MAISEY MINICOACH HIRE
🅿
GELYNOG YARD, CASTELLAU ROAD,
BEDDAU, PONTYPRIDD CF38 2RA
Tel/Fax: 01443 205462
E-mail: info@maiseybus.co.uk
Web site: www.maiseybus.co.uk
Partners: Brian Evans, Graham Evans,
Colin Evans.
Fleet: 7 - 1 midibus, 6 minicoach.
Chassis: 1 Iveco, 6 Renault.
Bodies: 1 Mellor, 6 Other.
Ops incl: school contracts, private hire.
Livery: White.

STAGECOACH IN SOUTH WALES
See Torfaen

THOMAS OF RHONDDA
♿ 🅿 Ⓜ 🍴 ⊠ T
BUS DEPOT, ABERRHONDDA ROAD,
PORTH CF39 0AG
Tel: 01443 433714
Fax: 01443 436542
E-mail: enquiries@thomasofrhondda.co.uk
Web site: www.thomasofrhondda.co.uk
Props: W A Thomas, I G Thomas, J E Thomas,
D Thomas, T D Thomas, A A Thomas.
Fleet: 41 - 2 double-deck bus, 2 single-deck bus,
26 single-deck coach, 3 double-deck coach,
5 midibus, 3 minibus.
Chassis: 7 Bova, 5 Dennis, 2 Ford Transit, 1 LDV,
2 Leyland, 6 MAN, 5 Mercedes, 1 Optare, 4 Scania,
7 Volvo.
Bodies: 8 Berkhof, 7 Bova, 4 Caetano, 1 Duple,
2 Ford, 1 LDV, 5 Marcopolo, 1 Northern Counties,
2 Optare, 6 Plaxton, 2 Van Hool, 1 Wright.
Ops incl: local bus services, excursions & tours,
school contracts, private hire, continental tours.
Livery: Gold.
Ticket System: Almex.

BRENT THOMAS COACHES LTD
Ⓜ 🅿 ⊠
FOUNDRY ROAD INDUSTRIAL ESTATE,
TONYPANDY CF40 2XD
Tel: 01443 431240
Fax: 01443 441586
E-mail: info@brentthomascoaches.com
Web site: www.brentthomascoaches.com
Fleet: 11 – 7 single-deck coach, 2 midicoach,
2 minibus.
Chassis: 1 Ford Transit, 1 Iveco, 2 Mercedes,
7 Volvo.
Bodies: 1 Berkhof, 1 Ford, 6 Jonckheere,
1 Plaxton, 2 Other.
Ops incl: excursions & tours, private hire.
Livery: Green/Grey/Cream

VEOLIA TRANSPORT CYMRU PLC
BROOMHALL, CLERKENLEAP, WORCESTER
WR5 3HR
Tel: 01905 820201 **Fax:** 01905 829249
Web site: www.veolia-transport.co.uk

The Little Red Book 2012 - in association with *tbf* Transport Benevolent Fund

Chairman: John O'Brien **Man Dir:** Vacant **Ch Eng:** Dave Witte.
Ops incl: local bus services, school contracts, private hire, express.
Livery: Red/White.
Headquarters relocated to Worcester – operations in South Wales remain at Abercrave, Cross Gates, Newport at the time of going to press.

CITY & COUNTY OF SWANSEA

BRIGGS COACHES LTD

ELBA CRESCENT, SWANSEA SA1 8QQ
Tel: 01792 462979
Web site: www.briggscoaches.co.uk
Prop: W G Briggs.
Fleet: midibus, midicoach, minicoach.
Ops incl: school contracts, private hire, excursions & tours.
Livery: White with Blue/Yellow/Red.

DIAMOND HOLIDAYS
Operations ceased since LRB 2011 went to press. Some operations to Edwards Coaches Ltd (see Rhondda Cynon Taf).

FIRST CYMRU BUSES LIMITED

HEOL GWYROSYDD, PENLAN SA5 7BN
Tel: 01792 582233
Fax: 01792 561356
Web site: www.firstgroup.com
Regional Man Dir: Justin Davies
Gen Man: Kevin Hart.
Fleet: 348 - 4 double-deck bus, 249 single-deck bus, 12 articulated bus, 45 single-deck coach, 36 midibus.
Chassis: 29 Alexander Dennis, 8 BMC, 180 Dennis, 3 Mercedes, 8 Optare, 23 Scania, 39 Transbus, 54 Volvo.
Bodies: 16 Alexander, 29 Alexander Dennis, 8 BMC, 6 Caetano, 19 Irizar, 97 Marshall, 4 Northern Counties, 8 Optare, 84 Plaxton, 39 Transbus, 32 Wright.
Ops incl: local bus services, school contracts, excursions & tours, private hire, express.
Livery: FirstGroup UK Bus.
Ticket System: Wayfarer III.

LETS GO TRAVEL WALES

AZTEC CENTRE, QUEENSWAY, FFORESTFACH, SWANSEA SA5 4DJ
Tel: 01792 586605
Web site: www.letsgotravelwales.com
Fleet: 23 – 3 single-deck bus, 17 single-deck coach, 2 midibus, 1 minibus.
Chassis: DAF, Dennis, Ford Transit, Mercedes, Volvo.
Ops incl: school contracts, private hire, excursions & tours.

VEOLIA TRANSPORT CYMRU PLC
See entry above under Rhondda Cynon Taf.

TORFAEN

PHIL ANSLOW COACHES

UNIT 1, VARTEG INDUSTRIAL ESTATE, VARTEG, PONTYPOOL NP4 7PZ
Tel: 01495 775599
Fax: 01495 774000
E-mail: enquiries@philanslowcoaches.co.uk
Web site: www.phil-anslowcoaches.co.uk

Ops incl: local bus services, school contracts, private hire.
Livery: Purple/White.

B'S TRAVEL

13 EAST VIEW, GRIFFITHSTOWN NP4 5DW
Tel/Fax: 01495 756889
E-mail: kay@bstravel.fsnet.co.uk
Partners: James Benning, Kay Benning.
Fleet: 4 - 1 single-deck coach, 1 midicoach, 1 minibus, 1 minicoach.
Chassis: 1 LDV, 1 MAN, 2 Mercedes.
Bodies: 1 Autobus, 1 Jonckheere, 1 Gem, 1 LDV.
Ops incl: private hire, school contracts.
Livery: White.

JENSON TRAVEL

UNIT 10, PONTNEWYNYDD INDUSTRIAL ESTATE, PONTNEWYNYDD, PONTYPOOL NP4 6YW
Tel/Fax: 01495 760539
E-mail: jenson01@btconnect.com
Web site: www.jensontravel.co.uk
Props: Gwyn Jenkins, Miss Nicola Jenkins **Tran Man:** Nicola Jenkins **Ch Eng:** Peter Ryan **Eng:** Kyle Reynolds **Apprentice Eng:** Jack Robinson.
Fleet: 21 – 12 single-deck coach, 2 midicoach, 2 minibus, 5 minicoach.
Chassis: 5 Dennis, 1 Ford Transit, 8 Mercedes, 7 Volvo.
Bodies: 1 Autobus, 1 Crest, 3 Jonckheere, 1 Mellor, 2 Optare, 6 Plaxton, 1 Sunsundegui, 5 Wadham Stringer.
Ops incl: school contracts, excursions & tours, private hire.
Livery: Blue/White.

STAGECOACH IN SOUTH WALES

1 ST DAVID'S ROAD, CWMBRAN NP44 1PD
Tel: 01633 838856   **Fax:** 01633 865299
E-mail: south.wales@stagecoachbus.com
Web site: www.stagecoachbus.com
Man Dir: John Gould **Comm Dir:** Richard Davies **Eng Dir:** David Howe.
Fleet: 363 - 3 double-deck bus, 54 single-deck

bus, 28 single-deck coach, 184 midibus, 94 minibus.
Chassis: 177 Alexander Dennis, 23 MAN, 1 Mercedes, 110 Optare, 52 Volvo.
Bodies: 87 Alexander Dennis, 4 Caetano, 8 East Lancs, 4 Jonckheere, 4 Marshall/MCV, 5 Northern Counties, 111 Optare, 135 Plaxton, 5 UVG.
Ops incl: local bus services, school contracts, express.
Livery: Stagecoach UK Bus.
Ticket System: ERG.

VALE OF GLAMORGAN

CARING COACHES

UNIT 10, TY VERLON TRADING ESTATE, CARDIFF ROAD, BARRY CF63 2BE
Tel: 01446 421117
Web site: caringcoaches-barry.co.uk
Ops incl: school contracts, private hire.

EST BUS LTD

UNIT 2, CROSSWAYS IND ESTATE, LLANTWIT MAJOR ROAD, COWBRIDGE CF71 7LJ
Tel: 01446 773333
Web site: estcoachbus.com
Dir: C Hookings.
Fleet: 38 – 7 double-deck bus, 22 single-deck bus, 6 single-deck coach, 3 minibus.
Chassis: BMC, DAF, Dennis, Leyland, MAN, MCW, Mercedes, Optare, Volvo.
Ops incl: local bus services, school contracts.
Livery: Maroon/Cream.
Incorporating Cartel Travel, GM Coaches (see Bridgend).

WATTS COACHES LTD

OLD POST GARAGE, BONVILSTON CF5 6TQ
Tel/Fax: 01446 781277
E-mail: enquiries@wattscoaches.co.uk
Web site: www.wattscoaches.co.uk
Dirs: Clive P Watts, Carol Watts, James Watts.
Fleet: 30 - 1 double-deck bus, 19 single-deck coach, 2 double-deck coach, 7 midibus, 1 midicoach.
Chassis: 1 Ayats, 2 Bova, 2 DAF, 6 Dennis, 1 Iveco, 3 Leyland, 2 Mercedes, 1 Neoplan, 6 Scania, 1 Van Hool, 5 Volvo.

Bodies: 1 Alexander, 1 Ayats, 2 Beulas, 2 Berkhof, 1 Bova, 4 Irizar, 3 Jonckheere, 1 Neoplan, 12 Plaxton, 1 Unvi, 2 Van Hool.
Ops incl: school contracts, excursions & tours, private hire, continental tours.
Livery: Cream/Red/Gold.

WREXHAM

ACTON COACHES
109 HERBERT JENNING AVENUE, ACTON PARK LL12 7YA
Tel/Fax: 01978 352470
Prop: D B Evans.
Fleet: 1 midicoach.
Chassis: 1 Mercedes.
Bodies: 1 Plaxton.
Livery: Blue/White.
Ops incl: school contracts, private hire

ARRIVA BUSES WALES
See Conwy

GEORGE EDWARDS & SON
🔒♿♿🍴❄
BERWYN, BWLCHGWYN
LL11 5UE
Tel/Fax: 01978 757281
Web site: www.ukcoachbreaks.co.uk
Props: G F & G Edwards.
Fleet: 5 single-deck coaches.
Chassis: 1 Bova, 2 DAF, 2 VDL.
Bodies: 1 Bova, 4 Van Hool.
Ops incl: school contracts, private hire.
Livery: Red/Ivory/Maroon.

GHA COACHES LTD
UNIT 11, VAUXHALL INDUSTRIAL ESTATE, RUABON, WREXHAM LL14 6UY
Tel: 01978 820820
E-mail: info@ghacoaches.co.uk
Web site: www.ghacoaches.co.uk
Props: E G & A Lloyd Davies.
Fleet: 180 - double deck bus, single deck bus, single-deck coach, midibus, minibus, minicoach.
Chassis: BMC, Bova, DAF, Dennis, Iveco, Leyland, MAN, NCW, Mercedes, Optare, Scania, Volvo.

Bodies: Alexander, Autobus, Berkhof, BMC, Bova, Duple, ECW, East Lancs, Jonckheere, Marshall, MCW, Mellor, Northern Counties, Optare, Plaxton, Scania, UVG, Van Hool, Wright.
Ops incl: local bus services, private hire, school contracts.
Livery: Grey/Red/Maroon.
Includes Bryn Melyn Motor Services, Chaloner's, Hanmer's Coaches, Vale Travel.

HAYDN'S TOURS & TRAVEL
🔒◪
COLLIERY ROAD, CHIRK
LL14 5PB
Tel/Fax: 01691 773267
E-mail: christopherwilliams@virgin.net
Prop: Chris Williams.
Fleet: 1 single-deck coach.
Chassis: Duple 425.
Ops incl: excursions & tours, private hire, school contracts.
Livery: Red/White/Yellow/Orange.

D. JONES & SON
♿🔒
CENTRAL GARAGE, KING STREET, ACREFAIR LL14 3RH
Tel: 01978 824666
Mobile: 07739 206623
Dir: David Jones
Ops Man: Gary Jones.
Fleet: 10 - 5 single-deck bus, 5 midibus.
Chassis: 2 Alexander Dennis, 3 Dennis, 1 Mercedes, 4 Optare.
Bodies: 2 MCV, 4 Optare, 1 Plaxton, 3 UVG.
Ops incl: local bus services, school contracts.
Livery: Blue/White.
Ticket system: Wayfarer TGX.

E JONES & SONS
MOUNTAIN VIEW, BANK STREET, PONCIAU
LL14 1EN
Tel: 01978 841613
Props: J B & G Jones.
Fleet: 9 – 5 single-deck coach, 4 midicoach.
Chassis: 1 Bedford, 5 Mercedes, 2 Scania, 1 Volvo.
Livery: Blue/White/Orange.

PAT'S COACHES LTD
🔒♿♿🍴❄
DERWEN HOUSE, SOUTHSEA ROAD, SOUTHSEA, WREXHAM, LL11 6PP
Tel: 01978 720171 **Fax:** 01978 758459
E-mail: enquiry@patscoaches.co.uk
Web site: www.patscoaches.co.uk
Partners: P C Davies, J M Davies, D K Davies.
Fleet: 13 – 12 single-deck coach, 1 midicoach.
Chassis: 1 MAN, 1 Mercedes, 1 Neoplan, 4 Scania, 6 Volvo.
Bodies: 2 Berkhof, 2 Neoplan, 2 Plaxton, 6 Van Hool, 1 Other.
Ops incl: school contracts, excursions & tours, Private hire, continental tours.
Livery: White/Red/Yellow.

PRICES COACHES
THE HAVEN, BERSHAM ROAD, SOUTHSEA
LL11 6TF
Tel/Fax: 01978 756834
Props: David Price, Terence Price.
Fleet: 6 - 1 double-deck bus, 4 single-deck coach, 1 midicoach.
Chassis: 1 Dennis, 1 Mercedes, 4 Volvo.
Bodies: 1 Northern Counties, 2 Plaxton, 2 Van Hool, 1 Other.
Ops incl: school contracts, private hire.
Livery: Primrose/Green/Orange.

STRAFFORDS COACHES
🔒♿♿❄
UNITS 7/8, FIVE CROSSES INDUSTRIAL ESTATE, MINERA, WREXHAM LL11 3RD
Tel: 01978 756106
Fax: 01978 722705
E-mail: info@straffordscoaches.co.uk
Web site: www.straffordscoaches.co.uk
Props: Mr & Mrs G A Strafford.
Fleet: 13 - 9 single-deck coach, 4 midicoach.
Chassis: 1 DAF, 1 Dennis, 1 Iveco, 4 Mercedes, 4 Scania, 2 Van Hool.
Bodies: 1 Berkhof, 1 Indcar, 4 Irizar, 1 Optare, 1 Plaxton, 1 Unvi, 3 Van Hool, 1 Other.
Ops incl: school contracts, private hire, excursions & tours, continental tours.
Liveries: White, Silver.

Welsh Operators

A1 COACH TRAVEL

35 NORBURGH PARK, FOYLE SPRINGS,
LONDONDERRY BT48 0RG
Tel/Fax: 028 7130 9323
Prop: J Bradshaw.
Fleet: single-deck coach, midicoach.
Chassis: Mercedes, VDL.
Ops incl: private hire, continental tours, school contracts.

AGNEW TRAVEL

15 TANNAGHMORE NORTH ROAD,
LURGAN, Co ARMAGH BT67 9JA
Tel: 028 3832 6755
E-mail: info@agnewcoachhire.com
Web site: www.agnewcoachhire.com

AIRPORTER

QUAYSIDE SHOPPING CENTRE, STRAND
ROAD, LONDONDERRY BT48 7EP
Tel: 028 7126 9996
E-mail: info@airporter.co.uk
Web site: www.airporter.co.uk
Man Dir: Niall McKeever **Dirs:** Janet McKeever,
Norma Smyth.
Fleet: midicoach.
Chassis: Mercedes.
Ops incl: airport express.
Livery: White.

ALLEN'S TOURS

29 DONEGAL ROAD, BELFAST
BT12 5JJ
Tel: 028 9091 5613
E-mail: info@allenstours.co.uk
Web site: www.allensbelfastbustours.com
Prop: Benn Allen.
Fleet: open top bus, midicoach.
Ops incl: private hire, excursions & tours,
sightseeing tours.

BRITTONS COACH TOURS

21 COOLERMONEY ROAD, BALLYMAGORRY,
STRABANE, Co TYRONE BT82 0JX
Tel: 028 7184 1815
Web site: www.brittonscoaches.co.uk
Ops incl: excursions & tours, private hire, school
contracts, continental tours.

R G J BULLICK COACH HIRE

71 NEWRY STREET, RATHFRILAND,
Co DOWN BT34 5PZ
Tel: 028 4063 8006
E-mail: Ronnie@rjgbullick.co.uk
Web site: www.rjgbullick.co.uk
Fleet: single-deck coach, midicoach.
Ops incl: private hire.

CHAMBERS COACH HIRE

3A BALLYWEANEY ROAD, CLOUGHMILLS,
Co ANTRIM BT44 9JG
Tel: 028 2764 1880
Fax: 028 2764 1613
E-mail: mail@coachireland.com
Web site: www.coachireland.com
Chief Exec Officer: Liam Reed **Dir:** Shaun
Reid **Bus Dev Man:** Eugene Donnelly.
Fleet: 46 – 28 single-deck coach, 2 double-deck
coach, 8 midicoach, 8 minicoach.

Ops incl: local bus services, school contracts,
excursions & tours, private hire, continental tours.
Livery: Yellow/Black.

CROSS COUNTRY COACHES LTD

31 BALLYLINTAGH ROAD, COLERAINE
BT51 3SP
Tel: 028 7086 8989
Fax: 028 7086 9191
E-mail: sales@crosscountrycoaches.com
Web site: www.crosscountrycoaches.net
Dirs: J R Telford, B Telford.
Fleet: 5 - 4 single-deck coach, 1 vintage.
Chassis: 1 Bedford, 4 DAF.
Bodies: 1 Duple, 4 Van Hool.
Ops incl: school contracts, excursions & tours,
private hire, continental tours.
Livery: White with Yellow/Green/Blue/Red logo

DARRAGH COACHES

22 LISHEEGHAN ROAD, BALLYMONEY, CO
ANTRIM BT53 7JY
Tel: 028 2954 0684
Fax: 028 2954 0785
Recovery: 07736 485999
E-mail: rdarragh@hotmail.co.uk
Prop: Robert Darragh.
Fleet: 13 – 6 single-deck coach, 2 midibus,
1 midicoach, 4 minibus.
Chassis incl: 1 MAN, 1 Toyota, 4 Volvo.
Ops incl: school contracts, excursions & tours,
private hire.

EUROCOACH

47 MULLAGHTEIGE ROAD, BUSH,
DUNGANNON, Co TYRONE BT71 6QU
Tel: 028 8772 3031
Web site: www.eurocoachni.co.uk
Props: Sam Sinnamon, Lorna Sinnamon.
Fleet: 22 – single-deck coach, midicoach, minibus.
Ops incl: school contracts, private hire,
excursions & tours.
Livery: Red/Orange, White.

FIRST AIRCOACH/FIRST NORTHERN IRELAND LTD

AIRPORT BUSINESS PARK, DUBLIN AIRPORT,
Co DUBLIN
Tel (Dublin): 00 353 1 844 7118
Tel (Belfast): 028 9023 0655
Fax: 00 353 1 844 7119
E-mail: info@aircoach.ie
Web site: www.aircoach.ie
Customer Services Man: Brendan Gallagher.
Fleet: 58 – 3 single-deck bus, 44 single-deck
coach, 11 articulated bus.
Chassis: 11 Mercedes, 4 Scania, 21 Setra,
22 Volvo.
Bodies: 4 Irizar, 19 Jonckheere, 11 Mercedes,
21 Setra, 3 Wright.
Ops incl: airport operations, express.
Livery: Blue.
A subsidiary of First Group Plc.

GILES TOURS

63 ABBEYDALE AVENUE, NEWTOWNARDS
BT23 8RT
Tel/Fax: 028 9181 1099
E-mail: enquiries@gilestours.co.uk
Web site: www.gilestours.co.uk
Dirs: Neil Giles, Patricia Giles
Fleet: single-deck coach, midicoach.

Ops incl: excursions & tours, private hire,
continental tours.

LAKELAND TOURS

ENNISKILLEN AIRPORT, TRORY, ENNISKILLEN,
Co FERMANAGH BT94 2FP
Tel: 028 6632 9900
Fax: 028 6634 2979
Recovery: 07779 026597
E-mail: lakelandtours@btconnect.com
Web site: www.lakelandtours.co.uk
Prop: Ian McCutcheon.
Fleet: 4 - 2 single-deck coach, 2 midicoach.
Chassis: 2 Mercedes, 1 Setra, 1 Volvo.
Bodies: 1 Esker, 1 Plaxton, 1 Setra, 1 Unvi.
Ops incl: school contracts, excursions & tours,
private hire.

LOGANS EXECUTIVE TRAVEL

58 GALDANAGH ROAD, DUNLOY,
BALLYMENA BT44 9DB
Tel: 028 2765 7203 **Fax:** 028 2765 7559
E-mail: coaches@loganstravel.com
Web site: www.loganstravel.com
Prop: Sean Logan.
Fleet: 35 – 18 single-deck coach, 11 midicoach,
6 minibus.
Chassis incl: 3 LDV, 12 Mercedes, 18 Volvo.
Bodies incl: 3 LDV, 12 Mercedes, 18 Plaxton.
Ops incl: local bus services, school contracts,
excursions & tours, private hire.

LYNCH COACH HIRE

80 CASTLEFIN ROAD, CASTLEDERG,
Co TYRONE BT81 7EE
Tel: 028 8167 1344 **Fax:** 028 8167 1578
E-mail: info@lynchcoachhire.com
Web site: www.lynchcoachhire.com
Prop: Paul Lynch.
Fleet: 8 – 2 single-deck coach, 4 midicoach,
2 minibus.
Chassis: 2 Ford Transit, 4 Mercedes, 2 Volvo.
Bodies: 3 Alexander Dennis, 2 Euro, 2 Van Hool,
1 Other.
Ops incl: school contracts, excursions & tours,
private hire.

McGREAD OMAGH

110A TATTYREAGH ROAD, FINTONA,
Co ARMAGH BT78 2HU
Tel: 028 8284 1731
Fax: 028 8284 1916
E-mail: wjdunne@lineone.net
Web site: www.mcgreadomagh.com
Props: Bill Dunne, Isabella Dunne.
Fleet: 18 – single-deck coach, midibus, midicoach,
minicoach.
Chassis: 1 DAF, 3 Ford Transit, 1 Iveco, 1 LDV,
9 Mercedes, 1 Renault, 1 Volkswagen, 1 Volvo.
Ops incl: excursions & tours, private hire.

ORCHARD COUNTY TRAVEL

22 ALTATURK ROAD, RICHHILL, Co ARMAGH
BT61 9SG
Tel: 028 3887 9917
Fax: 028 3887 9919
Web site: www.orchardcountytravel.co.uk
Props: William Browne, Elizabeth Browne.
Ops incl: school contracts, private hire,
excursions & tours.

Northern Ireland

O. ROONEY COACH HIRE LTD

4 DANA PLACE, HILLTOWN, NEWRY,
Co DOWN BT34 5UE
Tel: 028 4063 0825
Fax: 028 4063 8028
Recovery: 077721 510955
E-mail: oliver@orcoachireland.com
Web site: www.orcoachireland.com
Man Dir: Oliver Rooney.
Fleet: 8 – 1 single-deck bus, 3 single-deck coach,
2 midibus, 1 midicoach, 1 minicoach.
Chassis incl: 2 Dennis, 1 Leyland, 4 Mercedes.
Bodies: 2 Alexander Dennis, 1 Mercedes,
4 Plaxton, 1 Other.
Ops incl: local bus services, excursions & tours,
school contracts, private hire.
Livery: White with Red/Yellow stripe.

SLANE'S COACH & TAXI HIRE

60 DUNDALK STREET,
NEWTOWNHAMILTON, Co ARMAGH
BT35 0PB
Tel: 028 8308 8715
Fleet: single-deck coach, midicoach, minibus.
Ops incl: private hire.

SLOAN TRAVEL (SLO-COACHES LTD)

51 KILLOWEN OLD ROAD, ROSTREVOR,
NEWRY, Co DOWN BT34 3AE
Tel: 028 4173 8568
Fax: 028 4173 8568
E-mail: brendanmsloan@hotmail.com
Web site: www.sloantravel.com
Dir/Ch Eng: B M Sloan **Sec:** Ms M Sloan.
Fleet: 2 - 1 single-deck coach, 1 minibus.
Chassis/Bodies: 1 Ford, 1 Setra
Ops incl: local bus services, school contracts,
excursions & tours, private hire.
Livery: Silver/Black/Red/Blue/Yellow.

SWILLY BUS SERVICE

SPRINGTOWN INDUSTRIAL ESTATE,
SPRINGTOWN ROAD, LONDONDERRY
BT48 0LY
Tel: 02871 262017
Fax: 02871 260582
Prop: Londonderry & Lough Swilly Railway
Co Ltd.
Fleet: 79 – 75 single-deck bus, 4 single-deck
coach.
Chassis: DAF, Dennis, Leyland, Scania, Van Hool.
Bodies: Alexander, Leyland, Plaxton, Van Hool,
Wright.
Ops incl: local bus services, school contracts.
Liveries: White (Buses); Yellow (School Buses).

TRANSLINK

MILEWATER ROAD, BELFAST BT3 9BG
Tel: 028 9089 9400
E-mail: feedback@translink.co.uk
Web site: www.translink.co.uk
Fleet Names: Ulsterbus, Citybus, Goldline,
Metro, Ulsterbus Tours, Northern Ireland Railways
Chairman: Veronica Palmer OBE **Group Chief
Exec:** Catherine Mason **Board Members:** John
Doran, Sean Hogan, Ruth Laird, Gary Lennon,
John Trethowen **Chief Op Officer:** Philip
O'Neill **HR & Organisational Development
Dir:** Gordon Milligan **Fin Dir:** Stephen
Armstrong **Comm & Services Dir:** David
Brown **Gen Man (Bus Services):** Frank Clegg
Marketing Exec: Ciaran Rogan **Infrastructure**

Exec: Clive Bradberry.
Fleet: 1,782 – 279 double-deck bus, 1,103 single-
deck bus, 220 single-deck coach, 26 double-deck
coach, 8 articulated bus, 102 midibus, 44 minibus.
Chassis: Ayats, Enterprise, Irisbus, Iveco, Leyland,
Mercedes, Optare, Scania, Volvo.
Bodies: Alexander, Alexander Dennis, Ayats,
Irizar, Mercedes, Nu-Track, Optare, Plaxton,
Sunsundegui, Transbus, Ulsterbus, Van Hool,
Wright.
Ops incl: local bus services, excursions & tours,
school contracts, private hire, express, continental
tours.
Liveries incl: Pale Blue/White (Ulsterbus),
Pink/White (Citybus, Metro), Blue/Gold/White
(Goldline).

TRAVELWISE COACHES

9A VICTORIA ROAD, LARNE Co ANTRIM
BT40 1RY
Tel: 028 2827 8600
Fleet: single-deck coach, midicoach.

ALLIED COACHES

113 GRANGE WAY, BALDOYLE INDUSTRIAL
ESTATE, BALDOYLE, DUBLIN D13
Tel: 00 353 1 832 8300
Fax: 00 353 1 832 8299
E-mail: info@alliedcoaches.ie
Web site: www.alliedcoaches.ie
Man Dir: Jim Nolan **Man:** Seamus Nolan.
Fleet: 7 - 3 single-deck coach, 2 minicoach,
2 minibus.
Chassis incl: DAF, Mercedes.
Bodies incl: Berkhof, Marcopolo.
Ops incl: excursions & tours, private hire
Livery: Silver

ARAN TOURS LTD

14 LOWER ALBERT ROAD, SANDYCOVE,
Co DUBLIN
Tel: 00 353 1 280 1899
Fax: 00 353 1 280 1799

ARDCAVAN COACH TOURS LTD

ARDCAVAN, Co WEXFORD
Tel: 00 353 53 912 2561
Fax: 00 353 53 912 3093
E-mail: info@ardcavan.com
Web site: www.ardcavan.com
Dirs: Philip O'Leary, George O'Leary.
Fleet: 15 – 12 single-deck coach, 2 midicoach,
1 minibus.
Chassis incl: Mercedes, Scania, Setra, Van Hool,
Volvo.
Bodies incl: Esker, Irizar, Jonckheere, Mercedes,
Plaxton, Setra, Van Hool.
Ops incl: private hire, express.
Livery: White.

BARRY'S COACHES LTD

THE GLEN, MAYFIELD, CORK CITY
Tel: 00 353 21 450 5390, 450 1669
(emergencies only)
Fax: 00 353 21 450 9628
E-mail: info@barryscoaches.com
Web site: www.barryscoaches.com
Fleet: 15 – 1 single-deck bus, 5 single-deck coach,
6 midicoach, 2 minibus.
Chassis: EOS, Ford Transit, MAN, Mercedes,
Scania, Volvo.

Bodies: EOS, Euro, Ford, Indcar, Van Hool.
Livery: White.
Ops incl: local bus services, private hire.
A subsidiary of Bernard Kavanagh & Sons,
Urlingford.

BARTON TRANSPORT

STRAFFAN ROAD, MAYNOOTH, Co KILDARE
Tel: 00 353 1 628 6338
Fax: 00 353 1 628 6722
E-mail: info@bartons.ie
Web site: www.bartons.ie
Man Dir: Patrick Barton **Man:** Feargal Barton
Chief Eng: Brendan Barton.
Fleet: 44 - 1 double-deck bus, 12 single-deck bus,
18 single-deck coach, 6 midibus, 7 midicoach.
Chassis: 1 Autosan, 2 BMC, 23 DAF/VDL,
3 Irisbus, 1 Leyland, 5 MAN, 7 Mercedes, 2 Temsa.
Bodies: Autosan, Ayats, Beulas, BMC, Berkhof,
Euro, Ikarus, Indcar, Marcopolo, Optare, Plaxton,
Temsa.
Ops incl: local bus services, private hire, school
contracts.
Livery: Cream with Red/Blue.

BLUEBIRD COACHES LTD

72 KILBARRON DRIVE, COOLOCK,
DUBLIN 5
Tel/Fax: 00 353 1 847 7896.
Dirs: Ronnie Bruen, Keith Bruen.
Fleet incl: double-deck bus, single-deck coach.
Chassis incl: Leyland, MAN, Scania.
Bodies incl: East Lancs, Irizar.
Ops incl: private hire, express, school contracts.
Livery: Cream/Red.

BUCKLEY'S TOURS LTD

WOODLANDS INDUSTRIAL ESTATE,
KILLARNEY, Co KERRY
Tel: 00 353 64 663 1945
Fax: 00 353 64 663 1903
E-mail: info@buckleystours.com
Web site: www.buckleystours.com
Fleet: 41- midicoach, minicoach, minibus.
Chassis incl: Iveco, Mercedes, Volkswagen.
Ops incl: excursions & tours, private hire.
Livery: White.
Associated with Kerry Coaches, Killarney.

BURKE BROS (COACHES) LTD

CLARETUAM, TUAM, Co GALWAY
Tel: 00 353 93 55416
Fax: 00 353 93 55356
E-mail: info@burkesbus.com
Web site: www.burkesbus.com
Dirs: P Burke, Ms M Burke **Ops Man:** P Steede.
Fleet: 11 - 9 single-deck coach, 2 midicoach.
Chassis: DAF, Mercedes, VDL, Volvo.
Bodies: 7 Plaxton, 4 Van Hool.
Ops incl: local bus services, private hire, express,
continental tours.
Livery: White.

BUS EIREANN

BROADSTONE, PHIBSBOROUGH, DUBLIN 7
Tel: 00 353 1 703 4111
Fax: 00 353 1 830 5377
E-mail: info@buseireann.ie
Web site: www.buseireann.ie
Chairman: Dr John Lynch **Ch Exec:** Tim
Hayes **Ch Op Officer:** Martin Nolan **Board**

Members: Bill McCamley, John Moloney, John Griffin, Susan Donohue, Tom Hussey, Micheal O'Faolain **Co Sec:** Martin Nolan **Ch Mech Eng:** Joe Neiland **Man HR:** Des Tallon **Man Sales & Marketing:** Barry Doyle.
Fleet: 1300 - double-deck bus, single-deck bus, single-deck coach, double deck coach.
Chassis: Alexander Dennis, BMC, DAF, Dennis, Irisbus, Leyland, Mercedes, Optare, Scania, VDL, Volvo.
Bodies: Alexander, Alexander Dennis, BMC, Berkhof, Caetano, East Lancs, Eurocoach, Hispano, Irizar, Leicester, Optare, Plaxton, Scania, Sunsundegui, Van Hool, Wright.
Ops incl: local bus services, school contracts, excursions & tours, private hire, express, continental tours.
Livery: Green/Orange/Red/White.
Ticket System: Wayfarer.

BUTLERS BUSES
17 BROOKVALE, COBH, Co CORK
Tel: 00 353 21 481 1660
Fax: 00 353 21 238 0242
E-mail: ian@butlers-buses.com
Web site: www.butlers-buses.com
Prop: Ian Butler.
Fleet incl: single-deck coach, midicoach, midicoach, minibus.
Chassis incl: Fiat, Mercedes, Volvo.
Ops incl: excursions & tours, private hire, continental tours.
Livery: White.

CAHALANE COACHES
UNIT 6, KILBARRY ENTERPRISE CENTRE, DUBLIN HILL, CORK
Tel: 00 353 21 430 4606
Fax: 00 353 21 430 1200
E-mail: info@cahalane-coaches.ie
Web site: www.cahalane-coaches.ie
Fleet incl: minicoach, midicoach, minibus.
Chassis incl: Ford Transit, Mercedes.
Ops incl: excursions & tours, private hire, continental tours.
Livery: White

CALLINAN COACHES LTD
KINISKA, GLAREGALWAY, Co GALWAY
Tel: 00 353 91 798324
Fax: 00 353 91 798962
Recovery: 00 353 87 241 3691
E-mail: info@callinancoaches.ie
Web site: www.callinancoaches.ie
Man Dir: T Callinan.
Fleet: 47 - 46 single-deck coach, 1 double-deck coach.
Chassis: Scania, VDL, Volvo.
Bodies: Berkhof, Irizar, Volvo
Ops incl: excursions & tours, private hire, continental tours.
Livery: White.

CAROLAN COACH HIRE
SPIDDAL LODGE, SPIDDAL, NOBBER, Co MEATH
Tel: 00 353 46 905 2336
Fax: 00 353 46 905 2552
E-mail: info@carolancoachhire.ie
Web site: www.carolancoachhire.ie
Fleet incl: single-deck coach, midicoach, minibus, minicoach.

Ops incl: excursions & tours, private hire, continental tours.

GERRY CARROLL COACH HIRE
BALLYMAKENNY ROAD, DROGHEDA, Co LOUTH
Tel: 00 353 41 98 36074
Prop: Gerry Carroll **Dir:** Patrick Carroll
Sec: Betty Carroll.
Fleet: 3 coach.
Chassis: Bedford.
Bodies: Plaxton
Ops incl: local bus services, excursions & tours, private hire.
Livery: White/Blue

CITYLINK
FORSTER STREET, GALWAY
Tel: 00 353 91 564163
E-mail: info@citylink.ie
Web site: www.citylink.ie
Man Dir: Cathy Cullen.
Livery: Blue/Yellow.
A division of Metroline, part of Comfort DelGro. Service operations and fleet outsourced to Callinan Coaches Ltd.

COLLINS COACHES
DRUMCONRATH ROAD, CARRICKMACROSS, Co MONAGHAN
Tel: 00 353 42 966 1631
Fax: 00 353 42 967 2013
E-mail: info@collinscoaches.ie
Web site: www.collinscoaches.ie
Man Dir: D Collins.
Fleet: 5 single-deck coach.
Ops incl: excursions & tours, private hire, Dublin commuter express.
Livery: White with Blue.

CONWAY COACH AND CHAUFFEUR DRIVE LTD
RAHEEN, LIMERICK
Tel: 00 353 61 303030
Fax: 00 353 61 303202
Props: R Conway (Gen Man), Val Conway
Prop/Ch Eng: Patrick Conway **Prop/Sec:** Audrey Hurley **Traf Man:** R Hurley.
Fleet incl: midicoach.
Livery: White/Red.

CORCORANS EXECUTIVE TRAVEL
8 COLLEGE STREET, KILLARNEY, Co KERRY
Tel: 00 353 64 663 6666
Fax: 00 353 64 663 5666
Web site: www.corcorantours.com
Fleet incl: single-deck coach, midicoach, minibus, minicoach.
Chassis incl: MAN, Volkswagen.
Ops incl: excursions & tours, private hire.
Livery: White

CORDUFF TRAVEL
ROSSPORT, BALLINA, Co MAYO
Tel: 00 353 97 88949 **Fax:** 00 353 97 88055
E-mail: info@cordufftravel.ie
Web site: www.cordufftravel.ie
Ops incl: excursions & tours, private hire, express.

Ops incl: excursions & tours, private hire, continental tours.

GERRY CARROLL COACH HIRE

Livery: White.
Incorporating Walsh's Coaches, Westport

COYLES COACHES
GWEEDORE, LETTERKENNY, Co DONEGAL
Tel: 00 353 74 953 1208
Fax: 00 353 74 953 1718

CREMIN COACHES
GEARAGH, KILKEEL, Co CORK
Tel: 00 353 86 238 5611 **Fax:** 00 353 27 66906
E-mail: info@cremincoaches.com
Web site: www.cremincoaches.com
Fleet incl: single-deck coach, midicoach, minibus, minicoach.
Chassis incl: DAF, Ford, Mercedes, Renault, Volvo
Ops incl: excursions & tours, private hire.
Livery: White

CRONIN'S COACHES LTD
SHANNON BUILDINGS, MALLOW ROAD, CORK
Tel: 00 353 21 430 9090
Fax: 00 353 21 430 5508
E-mail: cork@croninscoaches.com.
Web Site: www.croninscoaches.com.
Dirs: D. & Joan Cronin **Ch Eng:** Niall Cronin
Gen Man: Nora Cronin.
Fleet: 63 – 2 double-deck bus, 48 single-deck coach, 5 midicoach, 3 minibus, 5 open top bus.
Chassis: EOS, Leyland, MAN, Mercedes, Scania, Setra, Van Hool, VDL, Volvo.
Bodies: Alexander, Berkhof, Caetano, East Lancs, EOS, Indcar, Jonckheere, Noge, Plaxton, Setra, Van Hool.
Ops incl: school contracts, private hire, sightseeing tours.
Livery: Silver, White with red flash.

MARTIN CROWLEY
CLANCOOLBEG, BANDON, Co CORK
Tel/Fax: 00 353 23 42150
Fleet incl: minicoach, midicoach
Ops incl: private hire

DERO'S COACH TOURS LTD
22 MAIN STREET, KILLARNEY, Co KERRY
Tel: 00 353 64 6631251
Fax: 00 353 64 6634077
E-mail: info@derostours.com
Web site: www.derostours.com
Dirs: Ms E. O'Sullivan Quille, Ms C. O'Sullivan (Sales Dir), D O'Sullivan.
Fleet: 10 – 6 single-deck coach, 3 midicoach, 1 minicoach.
Ops incl: excursions & tours, private hire
Livery: White with multi Red/Silver/Orange. Also relief drivers and guide agency.

DOHERTY'S COACHES
14 MAIN STREET, DUNGLOE, Co DONEGAL
Tel: 00 353 74 952 1105
Fax: 00 353 74 952 1867
E-mail: enquiries@dohertyscoaches.com
Web site: www.dohertyscoaches.com
Prop: Seamus Doherty.
Fleet incl: single-deck coach, midicoach, minibus.
Chassis: Ford, Mercedes, Volkswagen.
Ops incl: local bus services, excursions & tours, private hire, express.
Livery: White

DONNELLY COACHES
46 IRISH STREET, ENNISCORTHY,
Co WEXFORD
Tel: 00 353 53 923 3956
Ptnrs: James Donnelly, Mary Donnelly,
Keith Donnelly.
Fleet: 5- 3 midicoach, 2 minibus.
Chassis/Bodies: 2 Ford Transit, 3 Mercedes.
Ops incl: school contracts, excursions & tours,
private hire.
Livery: White/Orange

DONOGHUES OF GALWAY
TARAMUID, CLARENBRIDGE, Co GALWAY
Tel: 00 353 91 776677
Fax: 00 353 91 776434
E-mail: info@donoghuesofgalway.com
Web site: www.donoghuesofgalway.com
Man Dir: Joe Donoghue.
Fleet incl: single-deck coach, midicoach,
minicoach.
Livery: White.

DONOVAN'S COACHES LTD
HEADFORD, KILLARNEY, Co KERRY
Tel: 00 353 64 775 4041
Fax: 00 353 64 775 4041
Dirs: Joe & Maureen Donovan
Ch Eng: Joseph Donovan.
Fleet: 7 - 4 single-deck coach, 1 midicoach,
2 minibus.
Chassis: 2 Ford Transit, 1 Mercedes, 4 Volvo.
Bodies: 1 Caetano, 3 Jonckheere, 1 Mercedes.
Ops incl: local bus services, school contracts,
excursions & tours, private hire.

P. DOYLE LTD
ROUNDWOOD, Co WICKLOW
Tel: 00 353 1 281 8119
E-mail: willrosa@eircom.net
Web site: www.glendaloughbus.com
Fleet Name: St Kevins Bus Service.
Prop/Traf Man: P Doyle
Gen Man/Ch Eng: J Doyle **Sec:** John Doyle.
Fleet: 5 single-deck coach.
Chassis: DAF, Leyland, Scania, VDL.
Bodies: Plaxton, Irizar, Van Hool.
Ops incl: local bus service.

Livery: Blue/Cream.
Ticket System: Setright.

TONY DOYLE COACHES LTD
BALLYORNEY, ENNISKERRY, Co WICKLOW
Tel: 00 353 1 286 7427
Fax: 00 353 1 274 8025
E-mail: info@tonydoyle.com
Web site: www.tonydoyle.com
Dir: Tony Doyle.
Fleet: 15 - incl single-deck bus, single-deck coach,
midibus, midicoach, minibus, minicoach.
Chassis: 6 Iveco, 5 MAN, 2 Mercedes, 2 Scania.
Bodies: 6 Beulas, 1 Esker, 3 Indcar, 2 Irizar,
3 Marcopolo.
Ops incl: local bus services, excursions & tours,
school contracts, private hire, continental tours.
Livery: White with Blue/Red logo.

THE DUALWAY GROUP
KEATINGS PARK, RATHCOOLE, Co DUBLIN
Tel: 00 353 1 458 0054
Fax: 00 353 1 458 0808
E-mail: info@dualwaycoaches.com
Web site: www.dualwaycoaches.com
Fleet Names: Dualway, City Sightseeing,
Gray Line.
Man Dir: Anthony McConn **Gen Man:** David
McConn **Fin Controller:** Trish McConn **Admin
Man:** Dawn Nolan.
Fleet: 62 - 17 double-deck bus, 3 single-deck bus,
6 single-deck coach, 30 open-top bus, 4 midicoach,
8 midibus, 1 minicoach.
Chassis: AEC, Ayats, Leyland, Mercedes, VDL,
Volvo.
Bodies incl: Alexander, East Lancs, Euro, Indcar,
Marcopolo, Optare, Park Royal, Plaxton, Wright.
Ops incl: local bus services, sightseeing buses,
excursions & tours, school contracts, private hire.
Livery: White, Red

DUBLIN BUS (BUS ÁTHA CLIATH)
59 UPPER O'CONNELL STREET, DUBLIN 1.
Tel: 00 353 1 872 0000
Fax: 00 353 1 873 1195
E-mail: info@dublinbus.ie
Web site: www.dublinbus.ie

Chairman: John Lynch **Ch Exec:** Joe Meagher
Dirs: Bill McCamley, William Mc Dermott, Marian
McGennis, Una McGrath, Arnold O'Byrne, Mary
Mooney, Grainne Tuke, Nuala Maher **Head of
Finance:** Paul O'Neill **Ch Eng:** Shane Doyle
Business Dev Man: Paddy Doherty **Human
Resources Man:** Gerry Maguire **Ops Man:**
Mick Matthews.
Fleet: 975 - 963 double-deck bus, 12 midibus.
Chassis: 10 Transbus, 964 Volvo, 1 Wrightbus
Hybrid.
Bodies: 95 Alexander, 370 Alexander Dennis,
447 Transbus, 63 Wright.
Ops incl: local bus services.
Livery: Blue/Yellow with Dublin Blue/White/
Darker Blue swoosh.

DUBLIN MINI COACHES
& CHAUFEUR HIRE
THE TRAVEL BANK LTD, WASDALE HOUSE,
14 CAMAC PARK, OLD NAAS ROAD,
DUBLIN 12
Tel: 00 353 86 178 0049
Fax: 00 353 1 696 1001
E-mail: info.dmc@o2.ie
Web site: www.dublinminicoaches.com
Man Dir: Stephen Millar.
Fleet: 12 – incl single-deck coach, midicoach,
minicoach.
Chassis incl: MAN, Mercedes.
Ops incl: excursions & tours, private hire.
Livery: Blue.

EIREBUS LTD
CORDUFF ROAD, BLANCHARDSTOWN,
DUBLIN 15
Tel: 00 353 1 824 2626
Fax: 00 353 1 824 2627
E-mail: info@eirebus.ie
Web site: www.eirebus.ie
Man Dir: Patrick Kavanagh
Tran Man: Derek Graham
Gen Man: Paul Curtis
Fleet Names: Budget Bus, Flybus, Urbus
Fleet: 48 - 32 single-deck coach, 9 midibus,
5 midicoach, 2 minicoach.
Chassis: Irisbus, MAN, Mercedes, Optare, Scania,
Toyota, Volvo.
Bodies incl: Beulas, Caetano, Euro, Indcar, Irizar,
Jonckheere, Optare, Plaxton, Van Hool.
Ops incl: local bus services, excursions & tours,
express, private hire.
Livery: White.
A division of Bernard Kavanagh & Sons,
Urlingford.

ENFIELD COACHES LTD
RATHCORE, ENFIELD, Co MEATH
Tel: 00 353 46 955 5666
Fax: 00 353 46 955 5777
E-mail: info@enfield coaches.ie
Web site: www.enfieldcoaches.ie
Man Dir: J Healy **Tran Man:** Ms L Healy.
Fleet incl: single-deck coach, midicoach, minibus.
Ops incl: excursions & tours, private hire.
Livery: Silver.

FAHERTY'S COACH HIRE
DRIMNEEN, MOYCULLEN, Co GALWAY
Tel: 00 353 91 85226
Fleet: 4 single-deck coach.
Ops incl: excursions & tours, private hire.

Legend

♿	Vehicle suitable for disabled	🔒	Seat belt-fitted Vehicle	R24	24 hour recovery service
T	Toilet-drop facilities available	🍴	Coach(es) with galley facilities	⬟	Replacement vehicle available
R	Recovery service available	❄	Air-conditioned vehicle(s)	⬚	Vintage Coach(es) available
⬚	Open top vehicle(s)	♿	Coaches with toilet facilities	🍃	Hybrid Buses

FINEGAN COACH HIRE
29 MAIN STREET, CARRICKMACROSS,
Co MONAGHAN
Tel: 00 353 42 966 1313
Fleet: 7 - 6 single-deck coach, 1 midicoach.
Ops incl: private hire.

FINLAY'S COACH HIRE
🔒♿❄
IRISH STREET, ARDEE, Co LOUTH
Tel: 00 353 41 685 6505
Fax: 00 353 41 685 7656
E-mail: finlaycoachhire@eircom.net
Web site: www.finlaybus.com
Ops incl: local bus services, school contracts,
excursions & tours, private hire.
Livery: White with Blue relief.

FINNEGAN – BRAY COACH & BUS
♿🔒
OLDCOURT INDUSTRIAL ESTATE,
BOGHALL ROAD, BRAY, Co WICKLOW
Tel: 00 353 1 286 0061
Fax: 00 353 1 286 8121
E-mail: finnegan-bray@oceanfree.net
Web site: www.finnegan-bray.ie
Dir: Eugene Finnegan.
Fleet: 22 - incl double-deck bus, single-deck
coach, midicoach, midibus, minibus.
Chassis incl: DAF, Dennis, MCW, Mercedes,
Optare, VDL, Volvo.
Bodies incl: 1 Alexander, Ikarus, Indcar, MCW,
Marcopolo, Optare, Plaxton, Van Hool.
Ops incl: local bus services, excursions & tours,
school contracts, private hire.
Livery: Red.

DECLAN FINNEGAN
KENMARE COACH & CAB, KENMARE,
Co KERRY
Tel: 00 353 64 41491
Fax: 00 353 64 42636
E-mail: info@kenmarecoachandcab.com
Web site: www.kenmarecoachandcab.com
Fleet incl: single-deck coach, midicoach, minibus.
Ops incl: excursions & tours, private hire.

FIRST AIRCOACH/FIRST NORTHERN
IRELAND LTD
AIRPORT BUSINESS PARK, DUBLIN AIRPORT,
Co DUBLIN
Tel (Dublin): 00 353 1 844 7118
Tel (Belfast): 028 9023 0655
Fax: 00 353 1 844 7119
E-mail: info@aircoach.ie
Web site: www.aircoach.ie
Customer Services Man: Brendan Gallagher.
Fleet: 58 – 3 single-deck bus, 44 single-deck
coach, 11 articulated bus.
Chassis: 11 Mercedes, 4 Scania, 21 Setra,
22 Volvo.
Bodies: 4 Irizar, 19 Jonckheere, 11 Mercedes,
21 Setra, 3 Wright.
Ops incl: airport operations, express.
Livery: Blue.
A subsidiary of First Group Plc.

FOXHOUND TRAVEL LTD
MONAGHAN ROAD, ROCKCORRY,
Co MONAGHAN
Tel: 00 353 42 974 2284
Fax: 00 353 42 974 2545
Fleet incl: single-deck coach, minibus.

MARTIN FUREY COACHES LTD
♿❄
MILLTOWN, DRUMCLIFFE, Co SLIGO
Tel: 00 353 71 916 3092
Fax: 00 353 71 916 3092
E-mail: info@fureysofsligo.com
Web site: www.fureysofsligo.com
Fleet incl: single-deck coach, midicoach, minibus.
Chassis incl: Mercedes, Volvo.
Ops incl: excursions & tours, private hire.
Livery: White

GALVINS COACHES
♿🔒⬚ R24 ⬟
MAIN STREET, DUNMANWAY,
Co CORK
Tel: 00 353 23 45125
Fax: 00 353 23 45407
E-mail: galvinscoaches@eircom.net
Dir: R E Galvin.
Fleet: 20 – 13 single-deck coach, 5 midicoach,
2 minibus.
Chassis incl: Mercedes, Scania, Setra, Volvo.
Bodies incl: Euro, Irizar, Jonckheere, Setra, Unvi,
Van Hool.
Livery: White

GALWAY CITY DIRECT LTD
♿♿❄
MINCLOON, RAHOON ROAD,
GALWAY CITY
Tel: 00 353 91 86 0814
Fax: 00 353 91 86 0815
E-mail: info@citydirect.ie
Web site: www.citydirectgalway.ie
Fleet Name: City Direct.
Fleet: 15 – 13 single-deck bus, 2 single-deck
coach.
Ops incl: local bus services, private hire.
Livery: Red.

GLYNNS COACHES.COM
♿🔒❄
KNOCKADERRY, TULLA ROAD, ENNIS,
Co CLARE
Tel: 00 353 65 682 8234
Fax: 00 353 65 684 0678
E-mail: info@glynnscoaches.com
Web site: www.glynnscoaches.com
Dirs: Niamh Cronin, Jackie Cronin.
Fleet: 16 – 1 single-deck bus, 6 single-deck coach,
1 midibus, 2 midicoach, 1 minibus, 5 minicoach.
Chassis: 1 BMC, 3 Iveco, 4 MAN, 7 Mercedes,
1 Setra.
Bodies: 4 Beulas, 1 BMC, 4 Esker, 3 Indcar,
3 Mercedes, 1 Setra.
Ops incl: school contracts, excursions & tours,
private hire.
Livery: White with Purple logo.

JAMES GLYNN
GRAIGUE NA SPIDOGUE (POST
GRAIGUECULLEN), NURNEY, Co CARLOW
Tel: 00 353 503 46616
Prop/Gen Man/Traf Man: J Glynn
Prop/Ch Eng: A Glynn **Prop/Sec:** Mrs J Glynn.
Fleet incl: single-deck bus, single-deck coach.
Livery: Cream/Blue.

HALPENNY TRANSPORT
♿🔒♿🍴❄
ASHVILLE, THE SQUARE, BLACKROCK,
DUNDALK, Co LOUTH
Tel: 00 353 42 932 2023
Fax: 00 353 42 932 3742
E-mail: info@halpennytravel.com
Web site: www.halpennytravel.com
Fleet Name: Halpenny Transport.
Man Dir: John Halpenny.
Fleet: 5 – 1 double-deck bus, 2 single-deck bus,
1 single-deck coach, 1 midicoach.
Chassis: 1 Dennis, 1 Mercedes, 3 Volvo.
Ops incl: local bus services, private hire,
continental tours.
Livery: Blue/Yellow/Red.

HEALY COACHES
⬚🔒❄
CASTLEGAR, GALWAY
Tel: 00 353 91 770066
Fax: 00 353 91 753335
E-mail: healybus@iol.ie
Web site: www.healytours.ie
Prop: Michael Healy, Paul Healy.
Fleet incl: single-deck bus, single-deck coach,
open-top bus, midicoach, midibus
Chassis incl: Dennis, Leyland, MAN, Mercedes,
Scania, Volvo.
Ops incl: local bus services, excursions & tours,
Galway sightseeing tours, private hire.
Livery: White with Blue lettering.

IRISH COACHES
🔒♿❄ R24 ⬟
ULSTER BANK CHAMBERS, 2-4 LOWER
O'CONNELL STREET, DUBLIN 1,
Tel: 00 353 1 878 8898
Fax: 00 353 1 878 8916
E-mail: dch@irishcoaches.ie
Web site: www.irishcoaches.ie
Chairman: Patrick Barton
Man Dir: D C Hughes
Dir: Dermot Cronin
Gen Man: Ms S Curtin.
Fleet incl: single-deck coach, midicoach.
Ops incl: excursions & tours, private hire,
continental tours.
Livery: Yellow.

BERNARD KAVANAGH & SONS LTD
🔒♿🍴❄⬟T
BRIDGE GARAGE, URLINGFORD, Co
KILKENNY
Tel: 00 353 56 883 1189
Fax: 00 353 56 883 1314
E-mail: info@bkavcoaches.com

Web site: www.bkavcoaches.com.
Fleet: 54 – 46 single-deck coach, 6 midicoach, 1 midibus, 1 minibus.
Chassis: MAN, Mercedes, Scania, Setra, Van Hool, Volvo.
Bodies: Alexander, Beulas, Euro, Hispano, Ikarus, Indcar, Irizar, Jonckheere, Setra, Sunsundegui, Van Hool.
Ops incl: local bus services, excursions & tours, private hire, express, continental tours.
Livery: White/Multi.
Associated with Barry's Coaches, Eirebus, Edinburgh Coach Lines (Scotland), Matt Kavanagh Coaches.

J J KAVANAGH & SONS
MAIN STREET, URLINGFORD, Co KILKENNY
Tel: 00 353 81 833 3222
Fax: 00 353 56 883 1172
E-mail: info@jjkavanagh.ie
Web site: www.jjkavanagh.ie
Joint Man Dir/Fin Cont: J J Kavanagh
Joint Man Dir/Ops Man: Paul Kavanagh
Maintenance Man: Edward Scully.
Fleet: 72 - 6 single-deck bus, 64 single-deck coach, 1 midibus, 1 midicoach.
Chassis: 1 MAN, 6 Mercedes, 1 Optare, 64 Setra.
Bodies: 1 Indcar, 6 Mercedes, 1 Optare, 64 Setra.
Ops incl: local bus services, private hire, excursions & tours, express, continental tours.
Livery: White with Blue/Green.
Incorporating Kenneally's Bus Service, Waterford.

MATT KAVANAGH COACHES
ROSANNA ROAD, TIPPERARY
Tel: 00 353 62 51563
Fax: 00 353 62 80808
E-mail: mattkavanagh3@aol.net
Web site: www.mattkavanagh.com
Fleet: 29 - single-deck coach, single-deck bus, midibus.
Ops incl: private hire, excursions & tours.
Livery: White with Blue/Yellow logo.
Associated with Bernard Kavanagh & Sons, Eirebus, Barry's Coaches.

PIERCE KAVANAGH COACHES
CHURCH VIEW, URLINGFORD, Co KILKENNY
Tel: 00 353 56 883 1213
Fax: 00 353 56 883 1599
E-mail: info@kavanaghcoaches.com
Web site: www.kavanaghcoaches.com
Dirs: Pierce Kavanagh Jnr, John Kavanagh.
Fleet: 38 – single-deck coach, single-deck bus, midicoach, minicoach, minibus, minicoach.
Chassis incl: BMC, Ford, MAN, Mercedes, Scania, Setra, Volvo.
Bodies incl: BMC, Beulas, Euro, Indcar, Irizar, Jonckheere, Plaxton, Sunsundegui, Van Hool.
Ops incl: private hire, excursions & tours.
Liveries: White, Red

KEARNEY COACHES
GLENFERRY COACHES LTD
FARRANASTIG, WHITECHURCH, CORK
Tel: 00 353 21 438 4351
Fax: 00 353 21 438 4353
E-mail: kearneysofcork@eircom.net
Web site: www.kearneysofcork.com
Fleet: 35 - double-deck bus, double-deck coach, single-deck bus, single-deck coach, midicoach, minibus.

Ops incl: school contracts, private hire.
Livery: White.

KEENAN COMMERCIALS LTD t/a ANCHOR TOURS
BELLURGAN, DUNDALK, Co LOUTH
Tel: 00 353 42 937 1405
Fax: 00 353 42 937 1893
E-mail: bookings@anchortoursireland.com
Web site: www.anchortoursireland.com
Fleet Name: Anchor Tours.
Man Dir: Seamus Keenan.
Fleet: 16 - single-deck coach, midicoach, minicoach.
Ops incl: private hire, excursions & tours, continental tours.
Livery: White.

KENNEDY COACHES LTD
ANNASCAUL, TRALEE, Co KERRY
Tel: 00 353 66 91 57106
Fax: 00 353 66 91 57427
E-mail: info@kennedycoaches.com
Web site: www.kennedycoaches.com
Dirs: Paddy Kennedy, Patrick Kennedy.
Fleet: single-deck coach, midicoach, minicoach.
Chassis incl: Mercedes, Scania, VDL.
Bodies incl: Esker, Irizar, Unvi.
Ops incl: private hire, excursions & tours, express.

P. J. KEOGH
PK SERVICES COMPLEX, SHANNON AIRPORT, Co CLARE
Tel: 00 353 61 471111 **Fax:** 00 353 61 471115
E-mail: info@pktravel.com
Web site: www.pktravel.com
Fleet Name: PK Travel.
Man Dir: P J Keogh **Tran Man:** Mike Lawlor.
Fleet: single-deck coach, midibus, midicoach, minicoach.
Ops incl: local bus services, private hire, excursions & tours, express.
Livery: White.

KERRY COACHES LTD
WOODLANDS INDUSTRIAL ESTATE, KILLARNEY, Co KERRY
Tel: 00 353 64 663 1945
Fax: 00 353 64 663 1903
E-mail: info@kerrycoaches.com
Web site: www.kerrycoaches.com
Man Dir: M Buckley **Ops Man:** Alan O'Connor.
Fleet Names: Buckley's Tours, Kerry Tours.
Fleet: 26 – single-deck coaches.
Chassis incl: MAN, Setra, Van Hool, Volvo.
Ops incl: excursions & tours, private hire, continental tours.
Livery: White.

KINGDOM COACHES
2 OAKPARK DRIVE, TRALEE, Co KERRY
Tel: 00 353 64 32496
Fax: 00 353 66 718 0123
E-mail: loch@eircom.net
Web site: www.kingdomcoaches.com
Fleet Names: Kingdom Coaches, O'Shea's of Kerry.
Fleet: single-deck coach, midicoach.
Chassis incl: Bova, Iveco, Mercedes.

Ops incl: excursions & tours, private hire.
Liveries: Gold, Silver.

LALLY COACHES
KINLAY HOUSE, MERCHANT'S ROAD, GALWAY
Tel: 00 353 91 562905
Fax: 00 353 91 564995
E-mail: info@lallytours.com
Web site: www.lallytours.com
Fleet: open top bus, single-deck coach, double-deck coach, midicoach.
Chassis incl: Leyland, MAN, Mercedes, Volvo.
Ops incl: local bus services, excursions & tours, private hire.
Livery: Metallic Green

DAVE LONG COACH TRAVEL LTD
CURRAGH, SKIBBEREEN, Co CORK
Tel: 00 353 28 21138

LUAS
See Section 5 – Tram and Bus Rapid Transit Systems.

McELLIGOTT COACHES
CLARINA CROSS, CLARINA, Co LIMERICK
Tel: 00 353 61 353477 **Fax:** 00 353 61 353035
E-mail: McElligotts@eircom.net
Web site: www.mcelligottcoaches.com
Prop: Kevin McElligott **Transport Man:** Maura Moore.
Fleet: 11 – 3 single-deck coach, 4 midicoach, 4 minicoach.
Chassis: 4 Mercedes, 7 Other.
Bodies: 5 Beulas, 6 Mercedes.
Ops incl: school contracts, excursions & tours, private hire.
Livery: Silver with Red logos.

JAMES McGEE BUS HIRE
BALLINA MAIN ROAD, FALCARRAGH, LETTERKENNY, Co DONEGAL
Tel: 00 353 74 913 5174
Fleet: minibus.
Livery: White

McGEEHAN COACHES
FINTOWN, Co DONEGAL
Tel: 00 353 74 954 6150
E-mail: coaches@iol.ie
Web site: www.mcgeehancoaches.com
Fleet: 5 - single-deck coach, minibus.
Chassis incl: Mercedes, Volvo.
Ops incl: local bus services, private hire, express.
Livery: White with Black logos.

JOHN McGINLEY COACH TRAVEL
MAGHEROARTY, GORTAHORK, LETTERKENNY, Co DONEGAL
Tel: 00 353 74 913 5201
Fax: 00 353 74 913 5960
E-mail: info@johnmcginley.com
Web site: www.johnmcginley.com
Prop: James McGinley.
Fleet: 21 – single-deck coach, minibus.
Chassis: Ford Transit, Mercedes, Volvo.
Bodies: Jonckheere, Plaxton, Van Hool.
Ops incl: local bus services, excursions & tours, continental tours, school contracts, private hire, express, continental tours.
Liveries: White with Blue/Orange; Black/Yellow.

The Little Red Book 2012 - in association with Transport Benevolent Fund

J J McGONAGLE
CLAR, REDCASTLE, Co DONEGAL
Tel: 00 353 74 938 2116
Fax: 00 353 74 938 2619
E-mail: foylecoaches@eircom.net
Web site: www.foylecoaches.com
Fleet Names: Foyle Coaches, North West Busways.
Fleet: single-deck coach, midibus, midicoach, minibus.
Ops incl: local bus services, private hire, excursions & tours.
Liveries: Coaches: White with Red/Orange/Yellow; **Buses:** Red.

MALAHIDE COACHES LTD
ST JOSEPHS, COAST ROAD, MALAHIDE, Co DUBLIN
Tel: 00 353 1 845 3809
Fax: 00 353 1 845 3099
E-mail: info@malahidecoaches.com
Web site: www.malahidecoaches.com
Fleet: 18 – double-deck bus, single-deck bus, single-deck coach, midibus, midicoach.
Ops incl: private hire, excursions & tours, school contracts.
Livery: Blue.

MANNING'S COACHES
CASTLE ROAD, CROOM, LIMERICK
Tel: 00 353 61 397311
Fax: 00 353 61 397931
E-mail: info@manningscoaches.com
Web site: www.manningscoaches.com
Fleet: 23 – single-deck coach, midibus, midicoach, minibus.
Ops incl: excursions & tours, private hire, continental tours.
Livery: White with logos.

ALAN MARTIN COACHES
13 ROSEMOUNT BUSINESS PARK, DUBLIN 11
Tel: 00 353 1 822 1122
Fax: 00 353 1 820 9364
E-mail: helpdesk@amconline.ie
Web site: www.amconline.ie
Dirs: A Martin, B C Martin **Ch Eng:** M Reilly
Traf Man: M Clarke.
Fleet Name: AMC Coaches.
Fleet: double-deck bus, single-deck bus, single-deck coach, midibus, minibus.
Ops incl: local bus services, school contracts, excursions & tours, private hire, express.
Livery: White with Red logos.

MARTIN'S COACHES (CAVAN) LTD
CORRATILLION, CORLOUGH, BELTURBET, Co CAVAN
Tel: 00 353 49 952 6222
Fax: 00 353 49 952 3116
E-mail: jimmartin@eircom.net
Dirs: James G Martin Snr, James G Martin Jnr, Derek Martin, Alan Martin.
Fleet: 16 - 4 single-deck bus, 6 midicoach, 6 minibus.
Chassis: 4 DAF, 6 Ford Transit, 6 Mercedes.
Bodies incl: 1 Caetano, 6 Ford Transit, 2 Marcopolo, 6 Mercedes, 1 Plaxton.
Ops incl: local bus services, school contracts, private hire.

DICK MARTIN COACHES
UNIT 7, ANNACOTTY BUSINESS PARK, ANNACOTTY, Co LIMERICK
Tel: 00 353 61 333102
E-mail: martinscoachhire@gmail.com
Web site: www.martinscoachhire.com
Fleet: 26 - single-deck coach, midicoach.
Ops incl: private hire.
Livery: White.

MICHAEL MEERE COACH HIRE
33 CHURCH DRIVE, CLARECASTLE, ENNIS, Co CLARE
Tel: 00 353 65 682 4833
Fax: 00 353 65 684 4544
E-mail: info@michaelmeere.com
Web site: www.michaelmeere.com
Fleet: 1 minibus.
Chassis: Mercedes.
Ops incl: private hire.
Livery: White with multi-coloured logos.

MATTHEWS COACH HIRE LTD
CALLENBERG, INNISKEEN, Co MONAGHAN
Tel: 00 353 42 937 8188
Fax: 00 353 42 937 8709
E-mail: info@matthewscoach.com
Web site: www.matthewscoach.com
Dirs: P Matthews, Mrs M Matthews.
Fleet: 28 – single-deck coach, midicoach.
Chassis: Mercedes, Scania, VDL, Volvo.
Bodies: Berkhof, Irizar, Marcopolo, Plaxton, Van Hool.
Ops incl: local bus services, private hire, excursions & tours, express, continental tours.
Livery: White

MIDLAND BUS CO LTD
BLYRY INDUSTRIAL ESTATE, ATHLONE, Co WESTMEATH
Tel: 00 353 90 647 2427
Fax: 00 353 90 647 8420
E-mail: info@midlandbus.com
Web site: www.midlandbus.com
Dirs: N. Henry, A Henry, B Henry.
Fleet: 10 - single-deck coach, midibus, midicoach.
Chassis: DAF, MAN, Volvo.
Ops incl: local bus services, private hire, school contracts, excursions & tours, express.

JOE MORONEY
OLD COURT INDUSTRIAL ESTATE, BRAY, Co WICKLOW
Tel: 00 353 1 276 1466
E-mail: info@joemoroney.com
Web site: www.joemoroney.com
Fleet: 4 - 3 single-deck coach, 1 midicoach
Chassis: 1 MAN, 3 Volvo.
Bodies: 1 Indcar, 3 Van Hool.
Ops incl: private hire, excursions & tours, express, continental tours.
Livery: White.

MORTON'S COACHES DUBLIN
TAYLOR'S LANE, BALLYBODEN, RATHFARNHAM, DUBLIN 16
Tel: 00 353 1 494 4927
Fax: 00 353 1 494 4694
E-mail: info@mortonscoaches.ie
Web site: www.mortonscoaches.ie
Prop: Paul Morton

Fleet: single-deck coach, double-deck coach, midicoach.
Chassis incl: BMC, DAF, Mercedes, Volvo.
Bodies incl: Ayats, BMC, East Lancs, Marcopolo, OVI, Wright.
Ops incl: school contracts, excursions & tours, private hire, continental tours.
Livery: White

NAUGHTON COACH TOURS LTD
SHANAGURRANE, SPIDDAL, Co GALWAY
Tel: 00 353 91 553188
Fax: 00 353 91 553302
E-mail: naugtour@iol.i.e
Web site: www.ontours.biz
Fleet Name: O'Neachtain Tours.
Dir: Steve Naughton **Dir/Sec:** Maureen Naughton.
Fleet: single-deck coach, open-top bus, midicoach.
Ops incl: excursions & tours, Galway sightseeing tours, private hire
Livery: Red

NOLAN COACHES
19 CLONSHAUGH LAWN, COOLOCK, DUBLIN 17
Tel: 00 353 1 847 3487
Fax: 00 353 1 867 8855
Mobile: 0862 592000
Prop: David Nolan.
Fleet: 2 single-deck coach.
Ops incl: school contracts, private hire.

O'CONNOR AUTOTOURS LTD
ROSS ROAD, KILLARNEY, Co KERRY
Tel: 00 353 64 663 1052
Fax: 00 353 64 663 1703
E-mail: oconnorautotours@eircom.net
Web site: www.oconnorautotours.ie
Dir/Gen Man: B O'Connor **Ch Eng:** R Downing **Sec:** C Enright **Traf Man:** D Fenton
Fleet: single-deck coach, midicoach, minicoach, minibus.
Ops incl: excursions & tours, private hire.
Livery: Maroon/Yellow.

FEDA O'DONNELL COACHES
RANAFAST, Co DONEGAL
Tel/Fax: 00 353 74 954 8114
E-mail: busfeda@eircom.net
Web site: www.fedaodonnell.com
Fleet: single-deck coach, minibus.
Chassis: Ford, Volvo.
Ops incl: express.

LARRY O'HARA MINI COACHES
13 SKIBBEREEN LAWN, WATERFORD CITY
Tel: 00 353 51 372232
Fax: 00 353 51 357566
E-mail: larryohara@eircom.net
Fleetname: O'Hara Autotours.
Props: Larry O'Hara, Helen O'Hara.
Fleet: 3 - 2 midicoach, 1 minibus.
Chassis/Bodies: 3 Mercedes.

O'MALLEY COACHES
FOILDARRIG, NEWPORT, Co TIPPERARY
Tel: 00 353 61 378119
Fax: 00 353 61 378002
E-mail: info@omalleycoaches.com
Web site: www.omalleycoaches.com

Republic of Ireland

Owner: E. O'Malley.
Ops incl: local bus services, school contracts, excursions & tours, private hire, express.
Livery: Blue/White.

O'SULLIVANS COACHES

FARRAHY ROAD, KILDORRERY, MALLOW, CO CORK
Tel: 00 353 22 25185
Fax: 00 353 22 25731
Prop: Gerard O'Sullivan
E-mail: gosull@indigo.ie
Web site: www.osullivanscoaches.com
Fleet: 15- 10 single-deck coach, 2 midicoach, 1 minibus, 2 minicoach.
Chassis: 1 Ford Transit, 4 Mercedes, 10 Volvo.
Bodies: 1 Berkhof, 2 Mercedes, 9 Van Hool, 3 Other.
Ops incl: school contracts, excursions & tours, private hire, continental tours.

JACKY POWER TOURS

2 LOWER ROCK STREET, TRALEE, Co KERRY
Tel: 00 353 66 713 6300
Fax: 00 353 66 712 9444
Fleet: 3 midicoach.

PROBUS & CAR

KENMARE, Co KERRY
Tel: 00 353 64 43500
Fax: 00 353 64 41903
E-mail: info@probusandcar.com
Web site: www.probusandcar.com
Ops incl: private hire.

ROVER COACHES

LYNN ROAD, MULLINGAR, Co WESTMEATH
Tel: 00 353 44 934 2449
Fax: 00 353 44 938 5020
E-mail: info@rovercoaches.ie
Web site: www.rovercoaches.ie
Prop: O'Brien Bros Coaches (Mullingar) Ltd.
Fleet incl: single-deck coach, midicoach.

Ops incl: private hire, excursions & tours.
Livery: White.

SEALANDAIR COACHING (IRELAND) LTD

53 MIDDLE ABBEY STREET, DUBLIN 1
Tel: 00 353 1 873 3411
Fax: 00 353 1 873 2639
E-mail: info@pabtours.com
Web site: www.pabtours.com
Fleet Name: PAB Tours.
Man Dir: Anthony Kelly.
Fleet: 7 single-deck coach.
Chassis: Volvo.
Bodies: Plaxton.

MATT SHANAHAN COACHES

ST MARTINS, LACKEN ROAD, KILBARRY, WATERFORD
Tel: 00 353 51 74192
Fleet: 2 - single-deck bus.
Ops incl: Waterford Crystal Tour.

SILLAN TOURS LTD

KINGSCOURT ROAD, SHERCOCK, Co CAVAN
Tel: 00 353 42 966 9130
Fax: 00 353 42 966 9666
E-mail: info@sillan.ie
Web site: www.sillantoursltd.ie
Fleet: 4 – 3 single-deck coach, 1 midicoach.
Chassis: 1 MAN, 3 VDL.
Bodies: 1 Indcar, 3 Marcopolo.
Ops incl: express, private hire.

ST KEVIN'S BUS SERVICE

See P Doyle Ltd, above.

SUIRWAY BUS & COACH SERVICES LTD

PASSAGE EAST, Co WATERFORD
Tel: 00 353 51 382209
Fax: 00 353 51 382676
E-mail: info@suirway.com
Web site: www.suirway.com
Fleet Name: www.suirway.com

Dir: Brian Lynch.
Fleet: 9 - 2 single-deck bus, 6 single-deck coach, 1 midicoach.
Chassis: 1 Alexander Dennis, 1 Mercedes, 7 Volvo.
Bodies: 1 Esker, 1 Plaxton, 5 Van Hool, 1 Volvo, 1 Wright.
Ops incl: local bus services, school contracts, excursions & tours, private hire.
Livery: White & Blue.

SWILLY BUS SERVICE

BALLYRAINE ROAD, LETTERKENNY, Co DONEGAL
Tel: 02871 262017
Fax: 02871 260582
Prop: Londonderry & Lough Swilly Railway Co Ltd.
Fleet: 79 – 75 single-deck bus, 4 single-deck coach.
Chassis: DAF, Dennis, Leyland, Scania, Van Hool.
Bodies: Alexander, Leyland, Plaxton, Van Hool, Wright.
Ops incl: local bus services, school contracts, excursions & tours, private hire.
Liveries: White (Buses); Yellow (School Buses).

TRAVEL DIRECT LTD

SEEFIN, CRAUGHWELL, Co GALWAY
Tel: 00 353 91 876876
Fax: 00 353 91 876555
E-mail: info@traveldirectireland.com
Web site: www.traveldirectireland.com
Man Dir: John Gavin.
Fleet incl: midicoach, minicoach.
Chassis: Mercedes.
Ops incl: excursions & tours.
Livery: White/Red

TREACY COACHES

ERRIGAL, KILLALA ROAD, BALLINA, Co MAYO
Tel: 00 353 96 22563
Fax: 00 353 96 70968
E-mail: treacycoaches@eircom.net
Dirs: A. Treacy (Gen Man), M. Treacy (Sec).
Fleet: single-deck coach, midicoach.
Ops incl: excursions & tours, private hire, express.
Livery: White/Blue.

WEXFORD BUS

RATHASPECK, WEXFORD
Tel: 00 353 914 2742
E-mail: info@wexfordbus.com
Web site: www.wexfordbus.com
Fleet: 9 – single-deck coach, midibus, midicoach.
Ops incl: local bus services, express, private hire.
Livery: White with Blue/Orange.

WHARTONS TRAVEL LTD

CROSSDONEY, Co CAVAN
Tel: 00 353 49 433 7000
Fax: 00 353 49 433 7634
E-mail: info@whartonstravel.com
Web site: www.whartonstravel.com
Fleet: 10 - single-deck coach, midicoach.
Chassis: 2 Mercedes, 8 Scania.
Bodies: Irizar, Plaxton, Van Hool.
Ops incl: private hire, excursions & tours, continental tours.
Livery: Red with multi-colours.

SECTION 5

Tram and Bus Rapid Transit Systems

This new section of LRB brings all of the tram systems together in one place, and also provides a brief profile of each of the principal Bus Rapid Transit systems

TRAM SYSTEMS

BLACKPOOL TRANSPORT SERVICES LTD

RIGBY ROAD, BLACKPOOL FY1 5DD
Tel: 01253 473001
Fax: 01253 473101
E-mail: debbie.vallance@blackpooltransport.com
Web site: www.blackpooltransport.com
Man Dir: Trevor Roberts
Eng Dir: Dave Hislop
Fin Dir: Sue Kennerley **Ops Man:** Guy Thornton.
Fleet: 35 trams.
Chassis/Bodies: Blackpool Transport, Brush, East Lancs, English Electric.
Livery: Green/Cream and special liveries.
Ticket System: Wayfarer/Almex A90.
15 new Bombardier Flexity trams are currently on order/in process of delivery.
See also main Blackpool Transport Services entry (Lancashire).

DOUGLAS CORPORATION TRAMWAY

STRATHALLAN CRESCENT, DOUGLAS, ISLE OF MAN IM2 4NR
Tel: 01624 696420
E-mail: pcannon@douglas.gov.im
Ops Supervisor: P Cannon.
Fleet: 20 horse drawn tramcars.
Builders: Metropolitan, Milnes, United Electric.

EDINBURGH TRAMS

EDINBURGH TRAMS, EDINBURGH EH12 5HD
Tel: 0800 328 3934

E-mail: info@edinburghtrams.com
Web site: www.edinburghtrams.com
Fleet: 27 trams, in course of construction/delivery.
Chassis/Bodies: CAF
Livery: Maroon/White
The system is currently in the process of construction

LONDON TRAMLINK

Part of TfL London Rail
COOMBER WAY, CROYDON CR0 4TQ
Tel: 020 8665 9695
Web site: www.tfl.gov.uk
Man Dir, London Rail: Mike Brown.
Fleet: 24 trams
Chassis/Bodies: Bombardier
Livery: Lime Green/Blue/White
6 new Stadler trams are currently on order.

LUAS

LUAS DEPOT, RED COW ROUNDABOUT, CLONDALKIN, DUBLIN 22
Tel: 00 353 1 461 4910
Fax: 00 353 1 461 4992
E-mail: info@luas.ie
Web site: www.luas.ie
Man Dir: Richard Dujardin
Gen Man: Brian Brennan.
Fleet: 40 trams.
Chassis/Bodies: Alstom Citadis.
Operated by Veolia Transdev Ireland for the Irish Railway Procurement Agency.

MANCHESTER METROLINK

METROLINK HOUSE, QUEENS ROAD, MANCHESTER M8 0RY
Tel: 0161 205 2000
Fax: 0161 205 8699
Web site: www.metrolink.co.uk
Gen Man: Carl Williams
Fleet: 94 trams.
Chassis/Bodies: 6 Ansaldo, 62 Bombardier, 26 Firema.
Liveries: White/Dark Grey/Blue or Silver/Yellow (Bombardier Cars).
Operated by RATP Dev UK Ltd for Transport for Greater Manchester.

MIDLAND METRO

METRO CENTRE, POTTERS LANE, WEDNESBURY WS10 0AR
Tel: 0121 502 2006
Fax: 0121 556 6299
Web site: www.nxbus.co.uk/the-metro
Fleet: 16 trams.
General Manager: Fred Roberts.
Chassis/Bodies: Ansaldo.
Liveries: Silver/Magenta (Network West Midlands) or Blue/Green/Grey/Red/Yellow.
Operated by National Express West Midlands for Centro.

NOTTINGHAM EXPRESS TRANSIT

NOTTINGHAM TRAM CONSORTIUM, NET DEPOT, WILKINSON STREET, NOTTINGHAM NG7 7NW
Tel: 0115 942 7777
E-mail: info@thetram.net
Web site: www.thetram.net
Commercial Manager: Colin Lea
Fleet: 15 trams.
Chassis/bodies: Bombardier.
Liveries: Green/White/Silver or advertising liveries.
Operated by Arrow Light Rail (Bombardier, Carillion, Veolia Transdev, Nottingham City Transport, Innisfree, Galaxy). The promoters are Nottingham City Council and Nottinghamshire County Council.

STAGECOACH SUPERTRAM

NUNNERY DEPOT, WOODBURN ROAD, SHEFFIELD S9 3LS
Tel: 0114 272 8282
Fax: 0114 279 8120
E-mail: enquiries@supertram.com
Web site: www.supertram.com
Gen Man: Glenn Stocks.
Fleet: 25 tramcars.
Chassis/Bodies: Duewag.
Livery: Blue/Orange/Red.
Operated by Stagecoach for South Yorkshire PTE.

NOTES

CAMBRIDGESHIRE BUSWAY

Route: Between St Ives and Cambridge, opened 2011.
Promoter: Cambridgeshire County Council, Busway Team, Shire Hall, Cambridge CB3 0AP.
Tel: 01223 716972
Fax: 01223 718188
E-mail: guidedbusway@cambridgeshire.gov.uk
Web sites: www.cambridgeshire.gov.uk and www.thebusway.info
Operators: Stagecoach East (see Cambridgeshire), Whippet Coaches (see Cambridgeshire).

CENTRELINK

Route: Between Gateshead and the Metro Centre Shopping Centre.
Promoter: Nexus (Tyne & Wear PTE).
Web site: www.nexus.org.uk
Operator: Go North East (Go-Ahead Group) (see Tyne & Wear).

EAST LONDON TRANSIT

Route: Between Ilford and Dagenham Dock, opened 2010.
Promoters Transport for London, London Boroughs of Barking and Dagenham, Redbridge.
Web site: www.tfl.gov.uk/corporate/projectsandschemes
Operator: Blue Triangle Buses (Go-Ahead Group) (see Essex, London & Middlesex).
The first bus only section, between Thames View and Dagenham, is now open. The second section will link Barking Town Centre with Barking Riverside.

FASTRACK

Route: Between Dartford and Gravesend, opened 2006.
Promoter: Kent Thameside Regeneration Partnership.
E-mail: info@go-fastrack.co.uk
Web site: www.go-fastrack.co.uk
Operator: Arriva Southern Counties (see Kent). Additional sections of route are planned.

FASTWAY

Route: Between Crawley, Gatwick Airport and Horley, opened 2003.
Promoters: Surrey and West Sussex County Councils; Crawley and Reigate & Banstead Borough Councils; BAA Gatwick; Go-Ahead Group.
Web site: www.fastway.info
Operator: Metrobus (Go-Ahead Group) (see West Sussex).

IPSWICH RAPID TRANSIT

Route: Between Kesgrave and Grange Farm, opened 1995.
Promoter: Suffolk County Council.
Operator: First East of England (see Suffolk).

LEEDS SUPERBUS

Route: Sections of the A61, A63 and A64 in Leeds, opened 1995.
Promoter: West Yorkshire PTE.
Operator: First West Yorkshire (see West Yorkshire).

LEIGH-SALFORD-MANCHESTER BRT

Route: Leigh to Manchester via Salford.
Promoter: Transport for Greater Manchester.
Web site: www.tfgm.com
The system is currently planned to open in 2013.

LUTON TO DUNSTABLE BUSWAY

Route: Houghton Regis to Luton via Dunstable.
Promoter: Luton Borough Council, Busway Team, Town Hall, George Street, Luton LU1 2BQ
Tel: 01582 547294
Fax: 01582 546453
E-mail: busway@luton.gov.uk
Web site: www.luton.gov.uk
The system is currently under construction.

RUNCORN BUSWAY

Route: Through Runcorn New Town (22 km), opened 1977.
Operators: Halton Borough Transport (see Cheshire), Arriva North West & Wales (see Merseyside).

SOUTH EAST HAMPSHIRE BUS RAPID TRANSIT

Route: Between Fareham and Gosport.
Promoter: Hampshire County Council, Environment Department.
Tel: 01962 846802
Fax: 01962 847055
Web site: www.hants.gov.uk
Operator: First Hampshire & Dorset (see Hampshire).
The first section of the system (3.4km) is currently under construction.

SWANSEA METRO

Route: Sections between Morriston, Swansea City Centre and Singleton Hospital, opened 2009.
Promoter: City & County of Swansea Council.
Web site: www.swansea.gov.uk
Operator: First Cymru (see City & County of Swansea).

Tram and Bus Rapid Transit Systems

SECTION 6

Indices

Several of the traders listed in this index will have more than one entry; only the first is shown here in each case.

Index - Trade

Index - Trade

Index - Trade

The Little Red Book 2012 - in association with *tbf* Transport Benevolent Fund

H

Index - Operator

T

The Little Red Book 2012 - in association with *tbf* Transport Benevolent Fund